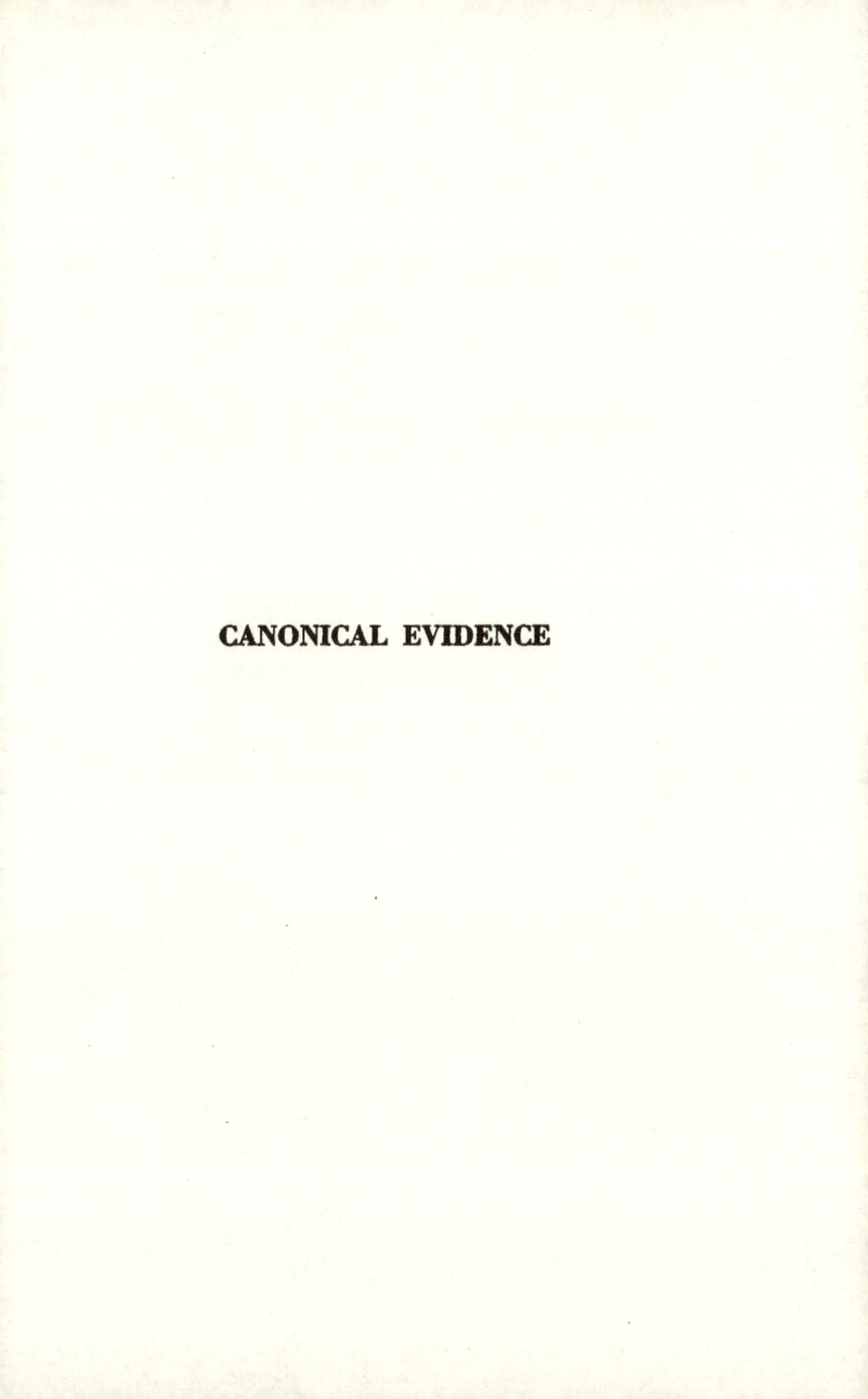

CANONICAL EVIDENCE

CANONICAL EVIDENCE
IN
MARRIAGE CASES

By

FRANCIS WANENMACHER

Doctor in Canon Law of the Catholic University of America
Pastor Consultor and Pro-Synodal Judge
of the Diocese of Buffalo

✝

DOLPHIN PRESS
PHILADELPHIA, PA.
1935

Nihil Obstat

LEO R. SMITH, D.D., J.C.D.
Censor Deputatus

15 OCTOBER, 1934

Imprimatur

✠ GUILLELMUS TURNER
Epus Buffalensis

THE DOLPHIN PRESS
PHILADELPHIA

To

BISHOP WILLIAM TURNER

FOREWORD

THE materials contained in these pages have accrued partly from research and consideration, partly from the practical experience that comes by having been engaged with marriage trials in the capacities of Substitute Defender of Marriage and Pro-Synodal Judge of the Diocese of Buffalo.

Nowadays there is hardly any class of canonical negotiations so common to both the clergy in care of souls and the curiae, as the unravelling of matrimonial tangles. And as the sanctity of marriage is more and more lost to sight by the World, such tangles become more and more frequent: a fact upon which the Supreme Pontiff Pius XI has lately dwelt in the Encyclical Letter *"Casti Connubii,"* 31 December 1930: "On Christian Marriage."

To aid in the settlement of marriage cases this book is published. It is not a textbook on the substantive law (ius substantivum) governing marriage; rather it presupposes that those who take it to hand are already somewhat versed in the fundamental norms and theory of the marriage law. It modestly seeks to be a guide in the processual law (ius processuale), that governs the evidence in marriage cases.

That it will not be an untrue guide seems to be assured by the author's friend Professor Doctor Louis Motry's having carefully read and corrected the text; and to him becoming and affectionate thanks are expressed.

BUFFALO, AT ST. BERNARD'S
20 AUGUST, 1935.

TABLE OF CONTENTS

INTRODUCTION

To Sources and Literature

In the scope of this work the matter of primary importance is the correct rendering of what is contained in the law, and the reader will not fail to discern from the parenthetical references to Canons, what is English version of the Code, and from the footnotes, what is of authentic source either published or unpublished, and what is commentatorial gloss.

§ 1. Sources

The sources quoted are not all of equal value, for some have the nature of present legislation and are of universal application, others are obsolete, others again are matters only of particular legislation, others still, notably the decisions of the Rota and of the Apostolic Signatura, are decisive only for the parties to the case (c. 17, § 3).[1] But even they lend us profitable aid by way of illustrating actual juridical practice and interpreting the mind of the Code, and their authority increases when several successive tribunals have given similar decisions in successive similar cases (auctoritas rerum similiter iudicatarum).[2]

The only universally authentic sources of present-day Canon law are the Codex Iuris Canonici and the legislation that supplements the Code. The work of codification was begun by Pius X, in 1904, and the completed Code was promulgated by Benedict XV, on 27 May 1917, as of universal validity in the Latin Church from 19 May 1918 (Romae, aas., ix).

The Code describes the law on evidence in marriage cases in two sections. Both of these are in the first part (Pars Prima,—De Iudiciis) of the fourth book (Liber Quartus,—De Processibus). The first section (Sectio I,—De iudiciis in genere) devotes the sixth (Titulus VI,—De causae introductione), seventh (Titulus VII,—De litis contestatione), and ninth title (Titulus IX,—De interroga-

[1] S. C. Consist., 11 feb. 1911 (aas., iii, p. 99).

[2] Aichner, § 13 (p. 38); Noval, n. 35; Seredi in jp., 1922, p. 64; cfr. also jp., 1927, pp. 99, 100.

tionibus partibus in iudicio faciendis) to the introductory evidence; then the tenth (Titulus X,—De probationibus) to the norms that govern proofs in any trial, and finally the twelfth (Titulus XII.—De processus publicatione, de conclusione in causa et de causae discussione) to the handling of the evidence after it is taken. The second section (Sectio II.—De peculiaribus normis in certis quibusdam iudiciis servandis), devotes chapters iv (Cap. iv.—De probationibus) and v (Cap. v.—De publicatione processus, conclusione in causa et sententia) of the twentieth title (Titulus XX.—De causis matrimonialibus) to describing specific norms for marriage trials. Besides this, valuable direction is gained from other parts of the Code, especially from the second (Pars Secunda.—De causis beatificationis Servorum Dei et canonizationis Beatorum, Titulus XXIII) and third (Pars Tertia.—De modo procedendi in nonnullis expediendis negotiis vel sanctionibus poenalibus applicandis) parts of the fourth book. Quotations from the Code are made by simply stating the Canon (c.) with the number of its paragraph or subdivision, *v. g.* (c. 1813, § 1, n. 1).

The supplementary legislation which forms an authentic source for this work consists first in the responses of the Pontificia Commissio ad Codicis Canones Authentice Interpretandos (abbr.: PC.), established by Benedict XV in his Motu Proprio of 15 September 1917 (aas., ix, p. 483). Pope Benedict accorded to this commission "uni ius . . . Codicis canones authentice interpretandi," and various responses and interpretations have emanated; contained, for the most part, in the Acta Apostolicae Sedis.

Besides this the Suprema Congregatio Sancti Officii (abbr.: SO.) issued a decree, which seems to be of extensive interpretation, De Competentia in Causis Matrimonialibus, under date of 27 January 1928 (aas., xx, p. 75). The abbreviation: SO, 1928.

Then the Sacra Congregatio de Disciplina Sacramentorum (abbr.: DS.) has issued an Instructio ad Rev.mos Ordinarios Locorum super Probatione Status Liberi ac Denuntiatione Initi Matrimonii, 4 jul. 1921 (aas., xiii, p. 348). The abbreviation: DS, 1921.

Then there has come from the same Congregation, the authentic Decretum, and Regulae Servandae in Processibus super Matrimonio Rato et non Consummato, 7 mai. 1923 (aas., xv, p. 389). The abbreviation: DS, Reg.

Lately too from the same Congregation the Normae Observandae in Processibus super Matrimonio Rato et non Consummato ad Praecavendam Dolosam Personarum Substitutionem, 27 mart. 1929 (aas., xxi, p. 490). The abbreviation: DS, Norm.

Even more recently from the same Congregation, the Instructio de Competentia Iudicis in Causis Matrimonialibus Ratione Quasi-Domicilii, 23 dec. 1929 (aas., xxii, p. 168). The abbreviation: DS,I.

Similarly this Congregation has issued Regulae Servandae in Processibus super Nullitate Sacrae Ordinationis vel Onerum Sacris Ordinibus Inhaerentium, 9 jun. 1931 (aas., xxiii, p. 457). The abbreviation: DS, Ordin.

Again the same Congregation: Litterae ad Excellentissimos Archiepiscopos, Episcopos atque Locorum Ordinarios: De Tractatione Causarum Matrimonialium, 1 jul. 1932 (aas., xxiv, p. 272). The abbreviation: DS, Lit.

Under date of 1 May 1934 the Congregation of the Holy Office has issued certain norms of proceeding in cases of dissolution of the marriage bond, by authority of the Supreme Pontiff, in favor of the Faith. (Not published).

With approval of Pope Pius XI there have lately been given by and for the Sacra Romana Rota: Normae S. Romanae Rotae Tribunali, 29 jun. 1934 (aas., xxvi, pp. 449 fol.) The abbreviation: R, Norm.

Some pre-Code constitutions of Supreme Pontiffs, and decrees of Councils or of the Roman Curia are hardly of less value, because by establishing the curial style and practice, they supply for gaps in the Code and otherwise aid the interpreting of the present law (cfr. cc. 6; 20; 23). These are noted as they occur in the text, and the place where they may be found is given in parentheses. Some however are especially noteworthy and, because they are more frequently quoted in the text, they are enumerated here in the order of time as they appeared, and there is set after each the abbreviation by which reference is made to it.

Corpus Iuris Canonici (Ed. Lipsiae, 1839; 1879-1881) of which the Decretales Gregorii IX (abbr.: X), the Liber Sextus Decretalium Bonifacii VIII (abbr.: VI) and the Clementis Papae V Constitutiones (abbr.: Clem.) contain the most pertinent chapters, though considerable light is likewise drawn from the Decretum Gratiani. Quotations from the Corpus are made in the traditional manner, *v. g.:* c. 1, X, De Probationibus, II, 19.[8]

Canones et Decreta Sacrosancti Oecumenici Concilii Tridentini (abbr: Conc. Trid.) (Ed. Ratisbonae, 1865) and especially the Sessio

[8] cfr. Cicognani, pp. 302, 311, 315, 317.

XXIV with its Decretum de Reformatione Matrimonii (abbr.: Tametsi).

Supremae Sacrae Congregationis Sancti Officii, Instructio, 21 aug. 1670 (cpf., i, n. 192; cicf., iv, n. 742). The abbreviation: SO, 1670.

Benedicti XIV Constitutio: "Dei Miseratione," 3 nov. 1741 (Bullarium Ben. XIV, i, n. 33; cicf., i, n. 318). The abbreviation: Dei Mis. This document gave the groundwork for the special modern procedure in marriage cases.

Supremae Sacrae Congregationis Sancti Officii, Instructio ad Episcopum Quebeccensem, 16 sept. 1824 (cpf., i, n. 784; cicf., iv, n. 866). The abbreviation: SO, 1824.

Sacrae Congregationis Concilii, (abbr.: SCC.) Instructio "Cum Moneat Glossa," 22 aug. 1840 (ass., i, p. 439; cpf., i, n. 911; cicf., vi, n. 4069). The abbreviation: SCC, 1840. This Instruction added certain special directions for cases involving the impediment of impotence and the dispensation from marriage ratified but not consummated.

Cardinalis Rauscher Instructio, known as the Instructio Austriaca, 4 mai. 1855 (coll. lac., v, n. 1302; analecta iuris pont., ser. ii, col. 2515 sq.). The abbreviation: IA. The provisions drawn up by the Cardinal Archbishop of Vienna were sent to Rome for approval and were examined, and approved "in forma ordinaria" as law for the Archdiocese of Vienna. Thence they came to have the force of law for all Austria, and a strong directive force for outside curiae. They were recommended to the American curiae by the Third Plenary Council of Baltimore (nn. 304, 307), and have been made use of by the Roman Rota.[4]

Supremae Sacrae Congregationis Sancti Officii, Instructio anni 1858 (cpf., i, n. 1153; cicf. iv, n. 946). The abbreviation: SO, 1858. This Instruction pointed out the manner of procedure to establish impotence or non-consummation, when the accurate observance of the legal forms was impossible.

Supremae Sacrae Congregationis Sancti Officii, Instructio anni 1868, "Ad Probandam Mortem Coniugis." (ass., vi, p. 436; aas. ii, p. 199; cpf., ii, n. 1321; cicf. iv, n. 1002). The abbreviation: SO, 1868.

Supremae Sacrae Congregationis Sancti Officii, Instructio ad Vicarium Apostolicum Oceaniae Centralis, 18 dec. 1872 (cpf., ii, n. 1392; cicf., iv, n. 1024). The abbreviation: SO, 1872.

[4] cfr. rd., iv, pp. 42, 243.

Supremae Sacrae Congregationis Sancti Officii, Instructio ad Ep. S. Alberti, 9 dec. 1874 (cpf., ii, n. 1427; cicf., iv, n. 1036). The abbreviation: SO, Alberti.

Supremae Sacrae Congregationis Sancti Officii, Instructio ad Ep. Nesquallien., 24 jun. 1887 (cpf., ii, n. 1465; cicf., iv, n. 1050). The abbreviation: SO, Nesquallien.

Supremae Sacrae Congregationis Sancti Officii, Instructio ad Episcopos Rituum Orientalium, 20 jun. 1883 (ass., xviii, p. 344; cicf., iv, n. 1076 cpf., ii, n. 1588). The abbreviation: SO, 1883. This Instruction modifies certain provisions of the Dei Mis. to meet peculiar conditions existing in the Orient.

Sacrae Congregationis Propagandae Fidei, (abbr.: PF.) Instructio, 1883 (ass., xviii, p. 369; cpf., ii, n. 1587; cicf., iv, n. 1076). The abbreviation: PF, 1883. This Instruction is addressed to the bishops of the United States, and is an almost verbal repetition of the preceding Instruction for the Orient, with the insertion however of §§ 95 and 96 of IA, with a change in § 24, and with the omission of §§ 34 and 46 fol.

Supremae Sacrae Congregationis Sancti Officii, Savannah, 1 aug. 1883 (cpf., ii, n. 1605; cicf., iv. n. 1083). The abbreviation: SO, Savannah.

Supremae Sacrae Congregationis Sancti Officii, Declaratio, 5 jun. 1889 (cpf., ii, n. 1706; cicf., iv, n. 1118). The abbreviation: SO, 1889. This declaration moderates the necessity of appeal and conformable sentences and is the forerunner of the important Canons 1990-1992.

Leonis XIII Constitutio "Consensus Mutuus," 15 feb. 1892 (cicf., iii, n. 613; cpf., ii, n. 1786). The abbreviation: Leo, 1892. In this the Pontiff abrogates the law of presumptive marriage by reason of betrothal and coition.

Pii X Constitutio " Provida," 18 jan. 1906 (cicf. iii, n. 670). The abbreviation: Prov. 1906. In this the Pontiff exempts certain mixed marriages in Germany from the observance of the Tametsi.

Sacrae Congregationis Concilii Decretum "Ne Temere," 2 aug. 1907 (cicf., vi, n. 4340). The abbreviation: Ne Temere. In this the canonical form of marriage, derived, with due changes, from Tametsi, was extended to the whole Latin Church, with effect from 19 April 1908.

Pii X Constitutio Apostolica "Sapienti Concilio" et Lex Propria Romanae Rotae et Signaturae Apostolicae, 29 jun. 1908 (aas., i, pp. 7; 20; cicf., iii, n. 682). The Abbreviations: Lex R., SA.

Sacrae Romanae Rotae Decretum "Constitutione" quoad Regulas Servandas in Iudiciis apud Sacram Romanam Rotam a Pio PP. X approbatas et confirmatas, die 4 aug. 1910 (aas., ii, p. 783). The abbreviation: R, Reg.

Signaturae Apostolicae Decretum "Regulae Servandae in Iudiciis apud Supremum Signaturae Apostolicae Tribunal approbatae et confirmatae a Pio Papa X," die 6 mart. 1912 (aas., iv, p. 187). The abbreviation: SA, Reg. In these and the above mentioned law and regulations for the Rota the procedure of the two tribunals is adduced in greater detail and with an elaborate scheme of judicial formulae. The present codified norms of procedure are derived from these regulations and law, with due changes.

Benedicti XV Chirographum "Attentis Expositis," 28 jun. 1915 (cicf., iii, n. 705; aas., vii, pp. 320, 325). The abbreviation: Chir. In this the Pontiff derogates from the accepted rules of procedure with respect to matrimonial cases, that they may have the same effect as though they were really unassailably adjudged (res iudicatae).

The decisions or definitive sentences of the Roman Rota (abbr.: R.), and of the Apostolic Signatura (abbr.: SA.), as well as those of special judiciary Commissions of Cardinals, the decisions of the Congregation of the Sacraments in cases of presumable death of a spouse or in cases of merely ratified and non-consummated marriage, rescripts of the Holy Office in cases of Pauline Privilege and similar cases (many of these being posterior to the Code) and, from remoter periods, the decisions of the Congregation of the Council in various marriage cases, valuable for the statement of juridical practice in use at the Roman Curia, are contained in various collections, but principally in:

Thesaurus Resolutionum S. Congregationis Concilii, Romae, 1739-1903 (abbr.: thes.).

Pallotini, Collectio Responsionum Propositis apud S. Congregationem Concilii, Romae, 1867-1893 (abbr.: pall.).

Collectanea S. Congregationis de Propaganda Fide, Romae, 1907 (abbr.: cpf.).

Acta Sanctae Sedis, Romae, 1865-1909 (abbr.: ass.).

Acta Apostolicae Sedis: Commentarium Officiale, Romae, 1909 fol. (abbr.: aas.).

S. R. Rotae Decisiones seu Sententiae, Romae, 1912 fol. (abbr.: rd.).

Codicis Iuris Canonici Documenta (apud Codicem), (abbr.: cicd.).

Codicis Iuris Canonici Fontes (ed. Gasparri) Romae, 1923 (abbr.: cicf.).

Some few sources are quoted as they appear in the works of such authors as Bassibey (abbr.: bass.), and Gasparri (abbr.: gasp.), or in the below mentioned periodicals.

Some unpublished marriage cases emanating from the Diocese of X. are likewise quoted.

The Corpus Iuris Civilis of Roman Law[5] can no longer be considered a subsidiary source of Canon law; but it is not entirely left unnoticed in this work because it likewise aids in giving the perspective of our Canons.

For similar purposes comparisons have been made, by way of footnote, with the law of New York State, as contained in the New York State Codified Laws (with supplements), (ed. McKinney, New York, 1924), and as expressed by authors who write on civil law and are mentioned under the heading of literature.

§ 2. Literature

The common and constant opinion of approved authors gives a norm for proceeding in matters about which the law is silent (cc. 6, n. 2; 20). Individual opinions of renowned writers may with some right claim attention when the position of the author is decidedly outstanding, or when the argument advanced is cogent. Hence the opinions of such authors have been as guides in laying down what is here contained, and generally the doctrine of authors is stated simply as it is proposed. But there are matters in which an opinion is expressed contrary to what another has written, and attention is called to the contrariety, lest the reader be confused by discovering elsewhere statements which do not seem to conform to what is here given.

The following works have been purused and are for the most part quoted in this work.

[5] cfr. Sohm, pp. 16-22; Cicognani, pp. 36-40.

I. WRITERS ON CANON LAW

Pre-Code Writers:

Aichner; Compendium Iuris Ecclesiastici, Brixinae, 1911.

Bassibey; Le Mariage devant les Tribuneaux Ecclesiastiques, Paris, 1899.

Boudinhon; Le Procés en Nullité de Mariage religieux, Lyons, 1892.

Bouix; De Iudiciis Ecclesiasticis, Parisiis, 1883.

Cosci; De Separatione Tori Coniugalis, Romae, 1773.

De Becker; De Sponsalibus et Matrimonio, Lovanii, 1903-1908.

Esmein; Le Mariage et le Droit Canonique, Paris, 1891.

Fanning; Vo. Presumption in Am. Cath. Encyclopedia, New York, 1913.

Feije; De Impedimentis et Dispensationibus Matrimonialibus, Lovanii, 1885.

Freisen; Geschichte des Canonischen Eherechts, Paderborn, 1893.

Gasparri; Tractatus Canonicus de Matrimonio, Parisiis, 1904 (2 vols.).

Hefele; Konziliengeschichte, Freiburg, 1873-1890.

Heiner; Grundriss des Katholischen Eherechts, Muenster in W., 1905.

De Processu Criminali Ecclesiastico, Romae, 1912.

Hilling; Der Kanonische Eheprozess, Bonn, 1916.

Kirsch; Vo. Ordeals in Am. Cath. Encyclopedia, New York, 1913.

Konings; Theologia Moralis S. Alphonsi, Bostoniae, 1876.

Lega; De Iudiciis Ecclesiasticis, Romae, 1905.

Praefatio ad S. R. R. Decisiones seu Sententiae, Romae, 1912 (rd., i).

Lehmkuhl; Theologia Moralis, Friburgi Brisgoviae, 1910.

Mansella; De Impedimentis Matrimonialibus Dirimentibus et de Processu Iudiciali, Romae, 1881.

Mascardus; De Probationibus, Venetiis, 1593.

Matharan; Casus de Matrimonio, Parisiis, 1893.

Meehan; Compendium Iuris Canonici, Roffae, 1899.

Menochius; De Praesumptionibus, Colon., 1686.

Noldin; De Principiis Theologiae Moralis, Oeniponte, 1908, 1914.

Periés; Code de la Procédure Canonique dans les Causes matrimoniales, Paris, 1894.

Pirhing; Synopsis Pirhingiana, Romae, 1849.

Reifenstuel; Ius Canonicum Universum, Romae, 1864-1870.

Sanchez; De Sancto Matrimonii Sacramento, Antverpiae, 1626.

Schmalzgrueber; Ius Ecclesiasticum Universum, Romae, 1843, 1845.
Schulte; Katholisches Eherecht, Giessen, 1855.
Smith; Elements of Ecclesiastical Law, vol. ii: Ecclesiastical Trials, New York, 1892.
The Marriage Process in the United States, New York, 1893.
Wernz; Ius Decretalium (vol. iv), Prati, 1908.

Post-Code Writers:

Antonelli; Medicina Pastoralis, Romae, 1920.
Ayrinhac-Lydon; Marriage Legislation in the New Code of Canon Law, New York, 1932.
Augustine; A Commentary on the New Code of Canon Law (vols. v, vii), St. Louis, 1921.
Blat; Commentarium Textus Codicis Iuris Canonici, (5 vols.), Romae, 1921—1924.
Capello; Tractatus Canonico-Moralis de Sacramentis iuxta C. I. C., Vol. iii, De Matrimonio, Taurinorum Augustae, 1923.
Cerato; Matrimonium a C. I. C. Integre Desumptum, Patavii, 1920.
Chelodi; Ius Matrimoniale iuxta Codicem Iuris Canonici, Tridenti, 1921.
Ius Poenale et Ordo Procedendi in Iudiciis Criminalibus, Tridenti, 1920.
Cicognani; Canon Law, Philadelphia, 1934 (ed. O'Hara-Brennan).
Creusen; see Vermeersch-Creusen.
De Becker; De Matrimonio Praelectiones Canonicae, ed. ix, Louvain, 1931.
De Smet; De Sponsalibus et Matrimonio, Brugis, 1923 (2 vols.).
Donohue; The Impediment of Crime, (diss. doct.) Washington, 1931.
Eichmann; Das Prozessrecht des Codex Iuris Canonici, Paderborn, 1921.
Farrugia; De Matrimonio et Causis Matrimonialibus, Taurini-Romae, 1924.
Gasparri; Tractatus Canonicus de Matrimonio, Civ. Vaticana, 1932 (2 vols.).
Gregory; The Pauline Privilege, (diss. doct.), Washington, 1931.
Haring; Grundzuege des Katholischen Kirchenrechts, Graz, 1924.
Der Kirchliche Eheprozess, Graz, 1929.
Hilling; Studien zum Eherecht, in akk., 1922.

Hohenlohe; Beitraege zum Einflusse des kanonischen Rechts auf Strafrecht und Prozessrecht, Innsbruck, 1918.

Das Prozessrecht des Kodex Iuris Canonici, Wien, 1921.

Jone; Die Unterlassung der Interpellation bei Anwendung des Privilegium Paulinum, in lqs., 1927.

Keller; De Usu Praesumptionis in Iure Canonico, in prm., 1934.

Knecht; Grundriss des Eherechts, Freiburg i. B., 1918.

Koestler; Woerterbuch zum Codex Iuris Canonici, Muenchen, 1927.

Kopler; Das kirchliche Prozessrecht nach dem neuen Codex Iuris Canonici, in lqs., 1918.

Krasa in lqs., 1934.

Labouré-Byrnes; Procedure in the Diocesan Matrimonial Courts of First Instance, New York, 1928.

Lanier; Guide Pratique de la Procédure Matrimoniale en Droit Canonique, Paris, 1927.

Linneborn; Grundriss des Eherechts nach dem C. I. C., Paderborn, 1922.

Manning, Presumptions of Law in Marriage Cases (diss. doct.) Washington, 1935.

Noldin-Schmitt; Summa Theologiae Moralis iuxta Codicem Iuris Canonici; Scholarum Usui accomodaverat H. Noldin, S.J., recognovit et emendavit A. Schmitt, S.J., Oeniponte, 1934 (vol. iii.).

Noval; De Processibus, Romae, 1920.

Oesterle; in lqs., 1929, 1933.

Peters: Die Ehe Nach der Lehre des hl. Augustinus, Paderborn, 1918.

Petrovitz; The New Church Law on Matrimony, Philadelphia, 1919.

Roberti; De Processibus, Romae, 1926 (2 vols.).

Sangmeister; Force and Fear (diss. doct.) Washington, 1932.

Schaefer; Das Eherecht nach dem Codex Iuris Canonici, Muenster i. W., 1924.

Schlenz: Wiederverehelichung auf Grund der Todeserklaerung des anderen Ehegatten infolge Verschollenheit, mit besonderer Beruecksichtigung der Kriegsverschollenheit, in akk., 1918, 1924.

Schmitt; see Noldin-Schmitt.

Timlin; Conditional Matrimonial Consent (diss. doct.) Washington, 1934.

Vermeersch-Creusen; Epitome Juris Canonici, Mechlinae-Romae, 1925-1933, 1934 (ed. v).

Vidal; see Wernz-Vidal.

Wernz-Vidal; Ius Canonicum auctore P. Francisco Xav. Wernz S. I. ad Codicis Normam Exactum opera P. Petri Vidal S. I. (vols. v, vi), Romae, 1928, 1927.

Woywod; A Practical Commentary on the Code of Canon Law, New York, 1929 (2 vols.).

Procedural Law of the Code, in hpr., 1931-1933.

Procedure in Cases of Matrimonium Ratum et Non Consummatum, New York, 1932.

II. WRITERS ON CIVIL LAW

1. On American Law

Abbott; Trial Evidence, New York, 1900.

American-English Encyclopedia of Law, ed. ii, Northport, L. I., N. Y., 1902.

Deutsch-Ballicer; How to Prove a Prima Facie Case, New York, 1928.

Lippman; The Sexual Aspect of Juridic Marriage, in U. S. Law Rev., 1931.

May; Marriage Laws and Decisions in the United States, New York, 1929.

McKelvey; The Law of Evidence, ed. ii, St. Paul, Minn., 1907.

Richmond-Hall; Marriage and the State, New York, 1929.

Tiffany; The Law of Persons and Domestic Relations, St. Paul, Minn., 1909.

2. On Roman Law

Morey; Outlines of Roman Law, New York, 1913.

Sohm; The Institutes (Engl. Trans. by Ledlie), Oxford, ed. iii, 1907 (1926).

III. PERIODICALS

Acta Apostolicae Sedis—Commentarium Officiale, Romae (abbr.; aas.).

Acta Sanctae Sedis, Romae (abbr.: ass.).

American Ecclesiastical Review, Philadelphia, (abbr.: aer.).

Apollinaris, Commentarium Iuridico Canonicum, Romae (abbr.: ap.).

Archiv fuer Katholisches Kirchenrecht, Mainz (abbr.: akk.).

Il Monitore Ecclesiastico, Romae (abbr.: ime.).

Jus Pontificium, Ephemeris Juridica, Romae (abbr.: jp.).

Periodica de Re Morali, Canonica, Liturgica, Romae (abbr.: prm.).

The Homiletic and Pastoral Review, New York (abbr.: hpr.).

Theologische-praktische Quartalschrift, Linz (abbr.: lqs.).

PART ONE

CHAPTER I

Preliminary Idea on Evidence

1. The word evidence (evidentia) is used in many meanings. In the science of logic it signifies the perspicuity of objective truth and hence the universal criterion of truth and the ultimate motive of certainty. In civil law it is commonly used as a synonym or refinement of the term "proof," for it is that by which an allegation in a cause is proved or disproved, or a fact is established or sought to be established. In the Canon law of the Decretals the term "evidence" (evidentia facti) had a technical meaning and indicated a specific means of proof corresponding to what is now called judicial notice (recognitio iudicialis). The Code neither retains the word in this meaning nor uses it at all as a substantive, though it speaks of facts that are evidently proved (evidentibus argumentis: cc. 1115,§1; 1814), or evidently plain (evidenter apparet; e. constet: cc. 1976;—2116,§2; cfr. also cc. 1625,§1; 1905).

Hence no confusion will result if the noun evidence is here used in a wide processual sense to denote whatever tends to make a matter clear. In such a sense canonical evidence in marriage cases pertains to all that body of allegation and denial, controversy and proof by which a marriage case is drawn to the attention and consideration of the ecclesiastical judge and to his certain persuasion of merit. This is brought about by proceedings undertaken partly by the litigants and partly by the court, so that the complete treatise on evidence includes also the matter of procedure in cognizance (de iudicii introductione et instructione).[1]

2. Of all this the most important part accrues to the proofs; but they are not the only necessary element of the procedure in cognizance of a case. For there is an introductory evidence that precedes the proofs, and there is a conclusive handling of the evidence that follows upon them and is meant to adjust them and prepare them in such a way that the judge can rightly decide on the merits of the case.

[1] Lega, i, Proemium, § 4 (p. 19).

Hence this treatise will have three parts: the first is on the introductory procedure that brings the case in its precisest form to the attention of the judge (terminus ad articulandum). This introduction consists in: 1) The making a plaint or petition,

2) The summoning of the respondent to answer the plaint,

3) The joining of issue, and

4) The questioning and hearing the parties to the suit. In this introductory stage of trial, the judge gains evidence of just what is wanted and contested, and of the preliminary circumstances surrounding the case, as well as of the allegations and denials of the litigants, but he has no evidence as yet that the merits of the case are as it is claimed they are. This is acquired by proof.

Accordingly the second part is on the proofs (terminus ad probandum). The Code first lays down general foundations touching the subject of proof, its object and effects, and then in seven chapters treats of the specific methods of proof by confession, by testimony, by expert inspection, by judicial notice, by document, by presumption and by the oath of the parties.

When the proofs have been duly offered the Canons require a definite handling of them: they must be published, they must be duly terminated, and they must be discussed. Hence the third part of this treatise consists of a concluding chapter on the publication of the proofs, the conclusion of the case, and the discussion of it (terminus ad discutiendum, concludendum, defendendum).

Upon evidence thus explored and discussed the court may pronounce its just sentence.

3. Not all marriage cases require the same procedure in cognizance. Cases to establish the freedom of a person to marry (status liberi) are primarily of an administrative nature, and are usually undertaken in administrative procedure (cfr. c. 1020), as *e. g.*, those cases in which it devolves upon a person of whom nothing is known to show that he is hitherto unmarried (cfr. n. **148**), and those cases where a Catholic plainly bound to observe the necessary canonical form of marriage, contracted informally and invalidly and now wishes to contract a new marriage in form. But when there are complications these cases may be tried in judicial procedure.[2]

[2] cfr. R., Impedimenti ad Matrimonium, 25 jan. 1911 (rd., iii, p. 30); Impedimenti, 26 aug. 1912 (rd., iv, p. 429); Impedimenti et Damnorum, 1 aug. 1913 (rd., v, p. 477); Vicariatus Apost. Ce-Li Central., 10 feb. 1917 (rd., ix, p. 23).

4. So too cases that have to do with proving the death of a spouse (mortis coniugis) rightly redound to a question of freedom to marry, and may be furthered in administrative procedure. But when such cases rest entirely upon indirect and artificial proofs (praesumpti mortis coniugis) they should, ordinarily at least, be heard in judicial proceeding.[3]

5. In cases of Pauline privilege (privilegii Paulini) the right to use that privilege is self-executory, but some summary and extra-judicial formalities of procedure are prescribed for purposes of just control and verification of the freedom to marry anew, and this must be observed likewise when there is question of dispensing from all interpellation.

6. Cases of separation from bed and board (separationis a toro et mensa; s. a toro et cohabitatione; s. corporum) may be tried either administratively or judicially,[4] and in fact, most such cases, if brought to the curia at all, are dealt with administratively; but if there is question of decreeing permanent separation the trial should be heard in strict judicial procedure.[5]

7. Cases introduced to establish the fact of non-consummation follow the judicial course, but the granting of the dispensation from non-consummated marriage (dispensationis matrimonii rati non consummati) is an act of administration and grace, rather than of justice.

8. The regular norm for nullity cases (nullitatis matrimonii) is that they be conducted in ordinary judicial proceeding, and this norm is followed whenever the nullity of the marriage is not at first sight plain from peremptory documentary evidence. But the cases most frequently appearing before the diocesan curiae have been of such peremptory and documentary nature and the Code has retained the purpose and, in part, the provisions of an earlier Declaration,[6] and provided an extraordinary procedure for them. When it is plain from an unimpeachably certain and authentic document that there exists an impediment of disparity of cult, order, solemn vow of chastity, marriage bond, consanguinity, affinity or spiritual relationship,

[3] cfr. Pii X, Constitutio Apostolica "Etsi Nos" 1 jan. 1912, n. 65 (aas., iv, p. 20); Lanier, p. 9; Haring, Grundzuege, p. 494.

[4] cfr. PC., 25 jun. 1932 (aas., xxiv, p. 284).

[5] cfr. R., Separationis, 20 apr. 1912 (rd., iv, p. 193)

[6] SO, 1889.

and at the same time it appears with equal certainty that no dispensation has been granted for these impediments, then, in these cases, the ordinary may omit the judicial solemnities recounted in the Code, and, with the intervention of the defender of the bond, declare the nullity of the marriage after having summoned (and heard) the parties (c. 1990; cfr. also cc. 1991; 1992).

9. The Declaration of 1889 had enumerated the impediment of non-age (impedimenti aetatis) among the cases which admit of this extraordinary procedure, and thus its omission from Canon 1990 gives rise to the question as to what procedure is necessary when a marriage appears to be invalid because of non-age. The omission of this impediment cannot be attributed to an oversight (cfr. c.6,n.3),[7] and hence it is plain that the Code did not mean cases of non-age to be settled by the extraordinary procedure; most likely this is because in many places where marriages occur under the prescribed age, vital statistics of birth are not kept by civil governments,[8] and, as is well known, the baptismal record does not offer peremptory proof of age (n. **369**).

Thus cases of non-age will usually be tried according to the ordinary judicial procedure. But it is not entirely clear whether they must always be so tried. For some cases of non-age are notorious, and when a fact is notorious, the notoriety supplies for proof (cfr. n. **145**). Whether the notoriety also relieves the case from undergoing all judicial procedure, such as the collegiate court, the plaint, summons, sentence and appeal is not clear from the Code.

Under the Decretals some informality of procedure was permitted in notorious cases,[9] and authors of the highest rank writing since the Code, seem to infer from this and from Canon 1747, n. 1, that when there is a case of nullity because of notorious non-age, judicial procedure is unnecessary (cfr. cc. 6n.4; 20; 22; 23).[10] But Noval maintains that although the Code accepts notoriety for proof, it makes no provision to relieve the case from the usual procedure in cognizance.[11] Even under the pre-Code law, notorious cases of nullity must

[7] cfr. Gasparri, nov. ii, n. 1283.

[8] V-Creusen, ii, n. 337.

[9] cfr. c. 21, X, De Iureiurando, II, 24; c. 13, X, De Desponsatione Impuberum, IV, 2; c. 9, X, De Accusationibus, Inquisitionibus et Denuntiationibus, V, 1; Lega, i, n. 454: "in notoriis vero nulla probatio, seu contentio iudicialis."

[10] W-Vidal, v, p. 842 (57); Lanier, p. 6.

[11] Noval, n. 445.

undergo some judicial procedure.[12] And in truth, every case of notoriety will require at least the summoning and hearing of the parties and defender (cfr. cc. 1587,§1; 1894,n.1; 1967) and nearly every case will require some further procedure so that the notoriety may be established, determined and applied (cfr. cc. 1892; 1894).[13]

10. In all judicial cases the proceedings as outlined in the Code should be carried out in detail whenever this can be done, but the omission of one or more items of procedure does not invalidate the acts, provided the procedure is observed in the essentials (cfr. cc. 1892; 1894). And in mission places where it is very inconvenient or impossible to carry out the details of the prescribed procedure, the ecclesiastical judge may conduct the trial with observance of the essentials only, and the Rota is instructed to accept the acts and define sentence on them.[14]

In all cases that are not strictly judicial some of the otherwise judicial procedure must be followed with due allowances or change, and some acts of procedure may be omitted. The proper omissions, allowances and changes are generally enumerated here, and where no mention is made of them, the reader will be able to perceive from what is laid down about the procedure in judicial cases, whether his case at hand requires or allows a special proceeding in some items because of the summary or administrative nature of the case.

Finally diocesan or national custom is not barred as a director in proceeding, so long as it remains within the purview of the Canons.[15] Thus in English-speaking countries the wise judge rightly seeks to avoid the "clamor et strepitus iudicii" by following the custom of hearing separation cases in quiet administrative procedure, and by issuing summons in the less imperative manner. These and similar customs are not entirely left unnoticed here.

[12] Feije, n. 586; Smith, Process, n. 617.

[13] cfr. SO., Africae, 18 mart. 1903 (cicf., iv, n. 1264; cpf., ii, n. 2165): "confecto processu."; Pondichery, 28 jun. 1865 (cicf., iv, n. 984; cpf., i, n. 1273): "fiant acta opportuna ad probandum."

[14] R, Reg., § 113; cfr. R., Vicariatus Apost. Chan-Si Sept., Null., 29 jun. 1923 (rd., xv, pp. 133, 134).

[15] Smith, Process, n. 448.

CHAPTER II

Introduction of the Suit by Plaint or Petition

"Epistola autem accusationis scripta erat syriace, et legebatur sermone syro."—I Esdrae, iv, 7.

11. Matrimonial matters that require the intervention of the curia are brought to its notice by denunciation and by plaint or petition. The Code recognizes both the denunciation of an impediment to a proposed marriage (c. 1027) and the denunciation of the invalidity of a marriage contracted (c. 1971,§2).

12. Before the celebration of a marriage all the faithful are required to spontaneously reveal impediments of which they have knowledge. The Code binds only the faithful; but the natural law of charity *per se* binds infidels as well, for it requires them to protect a neighbor against the spiritual harm that derives from marriage vitiated by impediments. This obligation is a grave one, and binds even those living in another diocese, and friends and relatives (cfr. n. **211**), in cases of impedient as well as of diriment impediments, whether the banns are dispensed or not, even when the denunciation would imply revelation of a crime, or when an oath of secrecy has been given (c. 1318) (cfr. n. **210**).[1]

The obligation may be fulfilled at any time before the marriage is contracted (c. 1027); the sooner the better, because increased inconvenience of the parties, and the probability of a marriage being contracted earlier than the denunciation are thereby avoided.

There is *per se* the same obligation of denouncing a marriage invalidly contracted (cfr. c. 1935,§2). When asked by a prelate of Hereford whether those must publicly contest a marriage who know that it has been invalidly contracted because of a diriment impediment arising from spiritual relationship, Innocent III declared they must denounce it to the Church.[2] But the obligation of denouncing a marriage already contracted does not extend to those which are valid but illicit by reason of an impedient impediment.

[1] Gasparri, nov., i, n. 169.

[2] c. 7, De Cognatione Spirituali, IV, 11.

13. The obligation of denouncing does not cease because of the temporal loss or inconvenience that accrues to the married parties, for these are not comparable with the spiritual loss that is avoided.[3] The obligation ceases: 1) When the denunciation would result in grave harm or danger to the person denouncing, or to his relatives, or to society at large, since neither the rule of charity nor the Canon law obliges under such difficulty. Hence persons excused from giving testimony in marriage cases according to the norm of Canons 1755, 1757,§3,n.2 are equally excused from spontaneously denouncing the impediment. Even when thus excused however, all, and especially priests, are obliged to hinder the celebration of an invalid marriage in as far as they can, *e. g.* by their admonition.

2) When the denunciation would be useless: thus in case it is known that a dispensation from the impediment has been obtained for the external forum, or for the internal forum alone, if the impediment is occult. If the impediment is publicly known and the dispensation applies only to the internal forum, Gasparri says the denunciation should be made,[4] to avoid scandal and in order that steps may be taken to procure dispensation in the external forum.

If a person has gained his knowledge of the impediment from one who is not worthy of belief (cfr. c. 1757), he is *per se* excused from denouncing it (cfr. c. 1942,§2); nevertheless if the marriage has not yet been contracted the denunciation may give rise to an investigation begetting other indications and proofs.[5]

In case of marriage about to be contracted the denunciation is not made useless by the fact that the denouncer alone knows of the impediment and cannot prove it (cfr. n. **40**). But in case of marriage invalidly contracted, the denunciation is useless unless the invalidity can be proved. Even when it can be proved the denunciation made by an outsider is usually useless, under the circumstances existing in English-speaking countries, especially when the impediment is already known to the parties; for the ecclesiastical court has no force with which to compel observation of its decision on the marriage, if the parties defy the spiritual authority. Hence in these countries a marriage contracted is not usually denounced unless a party to the marriage is himself prohibited from contesting it by

[3] Gasparri, nov., i, n. 172: "Plures AA. docent nec excusare damnum tertiae personae ex revelatione imminens."

[4] Gasparri, nov., i, n. 173.

[5] cfr. Gasparri, nov., i, n. 217.

judicial plaint (c. 1971,§1,n.1).[6] In that case he may denounce the invalid marriage. If the marriage is null because it was plainly in want of the necessary formality of contract, or if it is invalid by an impediment of disparty of cult, order, solemn vow, existing marriage bond, consanguinity, affinity or spiritual relationship, and the case is provable by peremptory document, so that it admits of the summary procedure of Canon 1990, the denunciation is sufficient, and the ordinary may declare the marriage null (cfr. n. **20**). If the case is not mentioned in Canon 1990, or is not devoid of complications, the only way open to the party is by denunciation to the promoter of justice (promotor iustitiae; formerly: procurator fiscalis) who is *ex officio* prosecutor for the Church.

14. The denunciation is made in writing signed by the denouncer, or it is orally made (cfr. c. 1936). If it is against a marriage not yet contracted it may be addressed to the ordinary of the place or the chancellor of the curia or the vicar forane, but it is best addressed to the pastor who will consider what is to be done and in more difficult cases, consult with the ordinary. If the denunciation is made against a marriage already contracted, it is addressed to the promoter, except for cases included in Canon 1990.

The promoter will consider whether he can take up the case as plaintiff *ex officio* (cfr. c. 1971,§1,n.2),[7] whether there is likelihood of proving invalidity, and whether the parties will be obedient to the decision of the court (cfr. n. **13**), and he will consult with the denouncer who must aid him in the matter of bringing proof (cfr. c. 1937). Nothing need be done about denunciations made by a manifest enemy, or a characterless person unworthy of belief, or anonymously made and wanting in circumstances that would make the statement of invalidity probable (cfr. c. 1942,§2). If it appears that there is no solid foundation to the denunciation, or that it would be useless for the promoter to proceed against the marriage, let this be written on the margin and the denunciation be placed in the archives (cfr. c. 1946,§2,n.1). If the promoter can rightly proceed

[6] cfr. Haring in lqs., lxxxiv (1931) p. 790; Močnik in lqs., lxxxvi (1933), p. 370.

[7] cfr. PC., 12 mart. 1929 (aas., xxi, p. 171); 17 feb. 1930 (aas., xxii, p. 196); 17 jul. 1933 (aas., xxv, p. 345); DS., 6 jun. 1933 (lqs., lxxxvii (1934), p. 149); cf. Haring in lqs., lxxxii (1929) p. 560; lxxxv (1932) p. 809; lxxxvi (1933) pp. 598, 820.

he should at once bring the case to the cognizance of the judge by his plaint.[8]

15. The judicial plaint or petition made by one or both of the parties to the marriage is the usual way of introducing a marriage case to court.

§ 1. Definition and Kinds of Plaint

16. The plaint, complaint, declaration, or petition is the act whereby the interested person calls upon the help of the judge to obtain executory decision in his favor. The plaint (accusatio) differs from the juridical petition (petitio, oratio) in that the plaintiff (actor) seeks executory decision in favor of a right claimed by him; the petitioner (orator) seeks by his petition to obtain a grant or favor to which he has no strict right. Hence we speak of plaint and plaintiff in suits to establish nullity of marriage or separation from bed and board, and the same terms may be applied with some degree of propriety, in cases of presumable death of a spouse and of Pauline privilege. In cases where a dispensation from ratified and non-consummated marriage is sought the proper terms are petition and petitioner.[9] But in fact, every judicial plaint contains also a petition, namely that the judge order the judicial execution of the right claimed (cfr. cc. 1706; 1707,§2; 1708,n.1; 1727; 1728; 1731,n.1). Hence the Code does not always strictly adhere to the terminology established for cases of non-consummation (cfr. however, cc. 1970; 1973), but uses the word petition in the sense of plaint made to claim a right (cfr. c. 1711,§1).

17. Both the plaint and the petition are distinguished from the denunciation; for the denouncer either has no standing whereby he may bring suit in court (cfr. n. **14**), or, if he has, does not petition the judicial execution of a right or favor, but merely notifies the pastor or curia of a fact.

18. Nothing in the nature of the thing prevents one from making a verbal plaint or petition, and the Code includes both verbal and written plaint under the Title (VI) "De libello litis introductorio."[10] Hence the verbal plaint introducing the case to court is sometimes, in

[8] PC., 17 jul. 1933 (aas., xxv, p. 345); cfr. c. 1955; Haring in lqs., lxxxvi (1933), p. 820.

[9] DS, Reg., n. 5, § 2.

[10] Decretals, X, II, 3 had the less comprehensive heading: "De Libelli Oblatione."

a wide sense, called a bill of plaint. In a strict sense the bill, writ or brief of controversy (libellum introductorium) is a short writing of the plaintiff clearly setting forth his plaint and petition to the judge.

19. According to whether the object of the suit is punishment for offense (actio criminalis) or decision and execution of a right (actio contentiosa; formerly: a. civilis) the criminal bill is distinguished from the contentious bill. With the former we have nothing to do here. The bill of plaint in marriage cases is a contentious bill touching on spiritual matters (res spiritualis; r. spirituali adnexum), and is distinguished from the contentious plaint in civil matters.

§ 2. Necessity of Plaint

20. The tendering a bill of plaint or petition is regularly necessary before procedure may begin. Whoever would convene another in a regularly judicial case must present a bill (c. 1706; cfr. c. 1955), and in marriage matters in particular, the collegiate tribunal of three judges cannot take cognizance of or define any case, unless the regular plaint or duly made petition shall have preceded (c. 1970). Innocent III had recognized the doctrine of the canonists that the bill of plaint was not necessary in notorious cases,[11] and Clement V declared it unnecessary in marriage and other summary cases which he ordered to procede without the din and solemnity of the courts.[12] The Code allows only the extraordinary procedure delineated in Canons 1990-1992 to be undertaken without the regular bill of plaint.[13]

21. The regular way of introducing one's case is by a written bill. A canon of Archbishop Hincmar coming down from the Council of Soissons (an. 853) states that the bill must be written and explicitly refers to the Roman (Justinian) law as its source.[14] But Clement III demanded that plaints in marriage cases be made in person and not by letter.[15] Later instructions mention both ways of entering plaint against the marriage.[16]

[11] c. 21, X, De Iureiurando, II, 24.

[12] c. 2, De Verborum Significatione, V, 11 in Clem.

[13] c. 1990: "praetermissis sollemnitatibus hucusque recensitis"; cpre. c. 1970; Noval, nn. 445; 849.

[14] c. 1, X, De Libelli Oblatione, II, 3.

[15] c. 2, X, Qui Matrimonium Accusare Possunt, etc., IV, 18; cfr. also, c. 2, X, De Verb. Signif., V, 11 in Clem.

[16] IA., §§ 126, 127, 215; PF, 1883, § 4.

The written bill is more conformable to the present principle of actuary procedure, and has the advantage of accuracy. But it is not always necessary. If one cannot write or is otherwise impeded from presenting a written bill he may make oral petition to the court (c. 1707,§1; cfr. c. 1936). Or, in cases of easier investigation and of lesser moment and hence to be rapidly negotiated, the admission of an oral petition made to him is left to the discretion of the judge (c. 1707,§2). Thus incidental questions may be proposed by oral petition (c. 1839). But the principal issue in marriage cases is never of lesser moment, nor usually of easier investigation, except those mentioned in Canon 1990. Hence the judge must usually insist on a written bill when the plaintiff is not impeded.

§ 3. Form and Procedure in Plaint

22. The bill is best if it is so short that there is nothing superfluous, so clear that uncertainty, obscurity, generality and contradiction are avoided, and orderly in arrangement. A commendable and orderly arrangement divides the bill into four parts:

1) The preamble will state the name of the court or judge to whom the plaint is addressed. It must be addressed to a judge competent to try the case (c. 1706; cfr. cc. 1560-1569; 1962; 1964). If a dispensation from ratified and non-consummated marriages is sought, the petition is to be addressed to the Holy Father and sent to the Congregation of the Sacraments.[17]

The full name of the plaintiff or petitioner together with residence or domicile, and his age, religion and station in life are next given. If the plaintiff appoint a proctor (procurator) (cfr. cc. 1655-1666) to carry on his suit, the name and address of the proctor may be added here.[18]

Then the full name of the respondent, together with residence or domicile, if either is known, and the age, religion and position in life of the respondent (c. 1708,n.1). In cases of nullity because of insanity, the name and address of the committee or guardian (curator) for the insane person must be added, not only that the judge may decide on his own competence, but that he may summon the insane person through committee of the latter (cfr. n. **46**).

[17] DS, Reg., n. 6, §1; The address: Palazzo della Cancelleria, Roma (Citta del Vaticano).

[18] Labouré-Byrnes, p. 69 certainly err in stating: "The plaintiff must... appoint a procurator . . . "

23. The main part of the bill should state the facts of the case and what the judge is petitioned to do with respect to the rights derived from them (c. 1708,n.1). The narration of facts (species facti, fundamentum f., quoad f.) may best follow the chronological order and must state the true story of pertinent events,[19] that occurred before, during and after the marriage, with dates and names of places and details that give point to the suit. The mention of civil divorce having been obtained, though not directly pertinent, is, under modern circumstances, useful (cfr. n. **345**).

It is not generally necessary to state the law (species iuris, fundamentum i., quoad i.), unless there be question of public law which the curia is not presumed to know (cfr. n. **146**), or of private law such as is derived from contract, or stipulation to the marriage.[20] But this pertains more properly to the narration of facts.

Much less is it now necessary to state the technical kind of action instituted.[21]

In order that the bill properly indicate that the plaintiff is rightfully making these allegations and assertions (c. 1708,§2), it will be useful to indicate the proofs for his contention, such as the names and addresses of witnesses or the text or names of documents.[22] Mention is made of these to indicate whence proof may be later derived, and to facilitate the preparation of interrogatories and the summoning of witnesses. The plaint may even be accompanied by the documentary proof of the case, but no bill of plaint need be accompanied by proofs.

24. 3) The conclusion of the bill gives the view of the plaintiff with reference to the case and must state exactly what is asked of the judge (petitio, conclusio). If the plaintiff seek the right to separate from bed and board he must state that, and petition that the term of separation be decreed. The judge will never give sentence

[19] cfr. c. 2361 on punishment for fraudulent or deceitful statement of untruth.

[20] W-Vidal, vi, n. 372: "Plerumque integer textus si est longior in separato scripto affertur, tali scripto in libello indicato."

[21] cfr. c. 6, X, De iudiciis, II, 1; W-Vidal, vi, nn. 369, 372.

[22] PF, 1883, § 5; IA., § 215; Noval, n. 386; Roberti, p. 423 (2), 424 (1) and some others have preferred to exclude mention of proofs from the bill and they interpret Canon 1708, § 2 as demanding, not indication of proofs, but evidence of a ground for petitioning. Contrary, Hohenlohe, p. 44 and others prefer that the sources of proof be indicated.

for permanent separation unless it is explicitly asked, even though the facts of the case would warrant it.[23] In case a judge, competent by proper authority, shall have conducted trial on nullity of marriage by reason of impotence, and proof of non-consummation but not of nullity is forthcoming, all the acts may be sent to the Congregation of the Sacraments, which may use them as the basis of a decision on the non-consummation of the marriage (c. 1963,§2), even without the dispensation from the marriage having been explicitly petitioned. Similarly in cases that come under Canon 1990 which need no bill of plaint, the decision of nullity may be given, even when no explicit petition has been made. But in other cases of nullity, if the bill does not state what is wanted of the judge, let it be amended.

25. The plaintiff may cumulate two or more actions, both possessory and petitory, in the same unit (c. 1670,§1), and hence the bill may ask for a decision in favor of more than one right with respect to the marriage. Thus it may ask immediate separation of the parties, and thereupon, a declaration of nullity of the marriage. Or the bill may contain an alternative petition. It is not infrequent in cases of impotence or lack of consent that plaint of nullity is made together with the alternative petition for dispensation from non-consummated marriage in case the court fails to declare the marriage invalid.[24]

The bill may state several grounds for separation, or contest the validity of a marriage on several impediments. The Rota receives many cases in which the marriage is contested on two or even three impediments, principally duress, lack of consent, stipulation against the essential qualities of marriage, and licit stipulations not fulfilled.[25] Let the plaintiff beware however lest too much zeal for freedom lead him to state contradictory grounds of nullity (cfr. c. 1669,§1). This was done by a lady in the diocese of X. who stated she had been married under duress inflicted by the husband and that she was constrained by her mother to demand that he marry her in order to rectify the illegitimacy of her offspring.

To the petition or plaint referring to the marriage, secondary petitions may be added such as the petition that a witness be at once

[23] Bouix, ii, nn. 148, 149.

[24] cfr. *e. g.*, R., Null., 16 mai. 1914 (rd., vi, p. 208).

[25] cfr. R., Ugentina, Null., 22 mart. 1910 (rd., ii, p. 124); Massilien., Null., 10 aug. 1912 (rd., iv, p. 401; aas., iv, p. 708); Null., 28 jan. 1914 (rd., vi, p. 26); Null., 2 mart. 1914 (rd., vi, pp. 88, 89); Nicien., Null., 31 jul. 1915 (rd. vii, p. 356; aas., viii, p. 109).

heard for future reference, or that the judge grant gratuitous advocacy or diminution of the customary judicial expenses (cfr. cc 1914-1916). If this be asked a testimonial of poverty from the plaintiff's pastor should be enclosed.

26. The bill must be signed by the plaintiff or his proctor (c. 1708,§3), for no one but the parties and the promoter, or, in rare instances, the defender [26] can tender a valid bill (cfr. c. 1971,§1).[27] If it is signed only by the proctor the power of proxy should be established by an enclosure signed by the plaintiff. In practice it is not unusual that the pastor of a party, or other priest engaged in the care of souls, negotiate in the plaintiff's name from the outset without written power of proxy. While this practice may be tolerated for cases coming under Canon 1990, it must be amended for cases tried in regular judicial procedure. In the well known case of G-C., the Rota rejected the bill of plaint as invalid for having been signed by the advocate rather than the party.[28] And the Congregation has lately directed that where possible, the petition for dispensation be both drawn up and signed by the petitioner himself.[29] But counsel, direction, and aid, on the part of an advocate, are not disapproved.

27. Either at the heading or at the signature the bill must state the day, month and year, and the address at which the plaintiff or his proctor dwell, or at which they claim residence to the effect of receiving legal papers (c. 1708, § 3). If a petition for dispensation from non-consummated marriage be sent directly to the Congregation, mention must be made of the diocese in which the petitioner lives.[30]

[26] The defender participates in marriage cases much more frequently than the promoter (cfr. cc. 1586-1590; 1967-1969; 1971,§1). Hence in describing the procedure, mention is generally made of the defender alone, but the norms pertaining to the defender are understood to apply, with proper restrictions, also to the promoter. When however, the promoter is mentioned alone in this book, it indicates that the pertinent act of procedure is his alone.

[27] Noval, n. 849; (cpre. c. 1955).

[28] R., Neo-Eboracen., Null., 29 dec. 1911 (rd., iii, p. 516); c. 14, De iudiciis, II, 1: "Statuimus praeterea ut principales personae non per advocatos sed per seipsas factum proponant..."

[29] DS, Reg., n. 6, § 2.

[30] DS, Reg., n. 6, § 1; Appendix I gives following exemplar: "Beatissime Pater,

"N. N. filia ...., e dioecesi ...., civitate ...., annos nata ....,

28. The bill may be composed in typewriting or in a legible hand. Black ink and white paper of decent proportions should be used. The pages should be numbered, and if folded letter-paper is used, the numbers should proceed from front to rear in consecutive order.[31] If single sheets of paper are used, only one side of each should be written on.

29. The plaintiff or his proctor may bring the bill in person to the judge or notary, or it may be sent through the mail. This is now approved by widespread custom although such bills were to be rejected under the law of the Decretals.[32] The bill sent by mail should

conditione ...., domicilium habens in civitate ...., via ...., sub parochia ...., ad pedes Sanctitatis Vestrae humiliter pervoluta, quae sequuntur exponit;

"Die ......, mense ......, anno ......, oratrix, tunc annum agens ......, praemissis denuntiationibus a iure statutis ac ritu civili, matrimonum, in paroechiali ecclesia ...., cum NN. filio ...., e dioecesi ...., et civitate ...., tunc annorum ...., professione ...., rite contraxit.

"Sed hoc matrimonium, contra oratricis ingenium, ad exitum perductum fuerat ab eius matre, quae omnem movit lapidem ut filiae animum sibi conciliaret; et cum nullum ab eiusmodi nuptiis daretur effugium, oratrix ad matrimonium celebrandum accessit, sperans fore, ut sensim sine sensu amor erga virum enasceretur.

"At spem fefellit eventus, nam coniugali consortio vix instituto, vir pravam indolem pandidit, ideoque defectus amoris in aversionem prorupit. Quapropter quindecim ab inito matrimonio diebus elapsis, vir oratrice relicta, ad paternam domum remeavit; postero autem die, ipsa, urgente matre, virum assequi debuit; cum quo tamen vix quinque diebus transactis, ad matrem reversa est, malens potius mori, quam cum eo intolerabilem vitam ducere.

"Tum ex hoc capite vir separationem a civili tribunali petiit atque obtinuit. Oratrix vero, apprime sibi conscia de non secuta matrimonii consummatione, tum ob perversam viri voluntatem, tum ob defectum amoris, imo aversionem ipsius oratricis, ad pedes Sanctitatis vestrae confugit, Apostolicam dispensationem super matrimonio rato et non consummato misericorditer implorans.

"Rationes autem ad petendam dispensationem sunt: 1. invincibilis oratricis aversio erga virum, absque ulla spe reconciliationis; 2. incontinentiae periculum, attenta eius iuvenili aetate; 3. desiderium transeundi ad alias nuptias, eidem nuper oblatas.

"Et Deus, etc.......

"Datum ...., die ...., mensis ...., anno ....,

"N. N. (Subscriptio, si fieri potest, manu ipsius oratricis)."; Various other formulae and exemplars may be found in DS, Appendix; R, Reg.; Labouré-Byrnes, Part III; Antonelli, vol. iii, of which some of the more important are given here in Latin or translation.

[31] PF., Litt. Encycl., 18 mai. 1896 (cpf., ii, n. 1929).

[32] Bouix, ii, n. 432.

be well sealed and full postage paid. Rome has complained of receiving many letters not stamped, upon which double postage must be paid.[33]

The bill is directed to the competent judge (c. 1706). Usually this is the diocesan ordinary or official (cfr. cc. 1560-1568; 1960-1964). In cases reserved to Rome anyone of the faithful is free to send a bill to the Holy See, but it is becoming and always advisable that this be done through one's own ordinary, who must add information of his own, (cfr. n. **609**).[34]

Usually the bill comes first into the hands of the diocesan chancellor or other notary designated for marriage cases. The notary will receive the bill and on the margin note the date of reception and his signature, and then further it to the ordinary or official for examination. The notary has no authority to examine the bill with a view to its acceptance or rejection, and must refrain from writing an opinion on the merits of the case or the competence of the court.

30. Meanwhile the judge or tribunal undertakes to examine the bill. In diocesan courts the tribunal of three is delegated by turn from among the synodal judges (c. 1576,§3) for each trial, after the acceptance of the bill, and hence there is, regularly at least, no tribunal appointed to examine the bill. The examination is undertaken by the ordinary or the official. But in difficult cases the tribunal may be appointed before the bill is definitely accepted, and then commissioned to examine it and decide on acceptance or rejection.

The judge will first see whether the court is competent in the case,[35] and whether the plaintiff has a right to bring suit to court (cc. 1609,§§1,2; 1709,§1). The examination may also entail an inquiry into the power of proxy, if the bill is signed by proctor, and other matters such as whether the canons allow the petitioned relief through court action (cfr. cc. 1017,§3; 1680; 1972), and whether the bill is properly made out. But especially and principally the judge must examine whether there is a *prima facie* foundation for the plaint or petition, and if the bill is found to be destitute of all foundation, he will reject it.[36] The examination of the bill proceeds without formality and no record need be made in the acts (c. 1609,§3).

[33] PF., Litt. Encycl., 18 mai. 1896 (cpf., ii, n. 1929).

[34] DS, Reg., nn. 7, 9, §2; cfr. SO., 27 jan. 1928, n. 1 (aas., xx, p. 75).

[35] cfr. DS, I.

[36] cfr. R., Romana, Reiectionis Libelli, 10 nov. 1923 (aas., xvi, p. 73); cpre. c. 1946, §2, n. 1.

31. This and the attempt to reconcile the parties and validate their marriage are the only preliminary inquests now directed for the judge. Under the pre-Code instructions there was an official preliminary inquest somewhat similar to that now prescribed for criminal cases (cc. 1939-1946), in which witnesses were summoned and parties sometimes underwent an extrajudicial physical inspection.[37] Sometimes this was found to defeat its own purpose, for it led to the refusal of parties or witnesses to submit to reëxamination when the trial proper was instituted. Hence no inquest, properly speaking, with questioning of parties or witnesses in judicial procedural form, is to be instituted.[38] Any necessary investigation must be entirely informal and usually will have been already undertaken by the pastor or other prudent priest before the plaint or petition was sent to the curia.[39]

32. If the judge observe that he is competent and that the plaintiff has the right to stand in court, he must as soon as possible admit or reject the bill, and in the latter case he must add the reasons for rejection (c. 1709,§1).

33. But it is directed that an attempt be first made to reconcile the parties provided their marriage is not so invalid that it cannot be validated. If the marriage is contested for want of consent, the judge will take care first of all to induce the party whose consent is said to be wanting, to renew consent; if because of defect of form or of an impediment that can be and is customarily dispensed, let him seek to induce the parties to renew their consent in legitimate form, or seek dispensation (c. 1965; cfr. cc. 1925; 1927). The judge himself may make the effort to reconcile the parties, or he may commission the pastor of a party or even a suitable layman to do this.[40]

[37] IA., §§ 140-142; Bassibey, n. 147.

[38] DS, Reg., n. 9, § 1; Noval, n. 849.

[39] DS, Reg., Appendix, II.

[40] DS, Reg., Appendix II (trans.): "The Most Reverend Ordinary N. directs the annexed bill of N. petitioner, to be transmitted to Rev. N. Pastor of N. and commissions him to provide, through himself or another, for the reconciliation of the spouses, in as far as he can and his pastoral prudence suggests. In so far as he cannot bring the aforesaid spouses to reconciliation let him inform the Curia of all that preceded, accompanied, followed the marriage ceremony, and of the causes for the petitioned dispensation of the marriage; and at the same time of the probity and credibility of the husband and wife; .... N. Vic. Gen.
N. Curiae Ep. Cancellarius."

But the effort at reconciliation need not be made if the known circumstances of fact and persons indicate that such an effort would be entirely useless.[41] And such uselessness may be presumed wherever the pastor has followed the Instruction of the Congregation, and already sought by prudent advice and exhortation to avoid separation and to reconcile the parties.[42]

34. If the judge accepts the case and decrees further procedure, the written bill and the signed decree of acceptance are returned to the notary for his signature (c. 1643,§2), who arranges, numbers and indexes them as well as all other documents of the case, that then or later come before the court. The portfolio of documents thus collected is entitled according to the nature of the case.[43]

If the plaint is verbally made the judge will direct the notary to reduce it to actuary form and the written bill is to be read to the plaintiff and approved by him (c. 1707,§3; cfr. c. 1643,§3), as expressive of his mind and intention.

Meanwhile, according to the necessities of the case, the ordinary or official appoints the members of the tribunal, nominates the defender, chooses an auditor, assigns a special notary for the case, and approves the advocate desired by the party. These ordinances may be decreed with the acceptance of the bill and in the same writing.

35. If the judge reject the bill he must state, in writing if demanded, the reasons for the rejection (c. 1709,§1). If the judge's

[41] DS, Reg., n. 10, § 1.

[42] DS, Reg., n. 10, § 2; Appendix III gives following (trans.): "N. (wife) with whom I spoke, has stated her matrimonial difficulties and points to the broken condition of her married life and the necessity of dissolving the marriage. Afterward I spoke to the husband who said he is willing to restore the cohabitation, but despairs of success because of the inflexibility of the wife.

"I did not think it well to insist further on the matter of reconciliation since the marriage seems to have been entered without love on the part of the wife, and seems not to have been consummated, and there is danger of incontinency on the part of the wife, which she adduces as ground for dispensation. From the investigation made, there is sufficient evidence of the uprightness and credibility of both spouses so that their assertions may be depended upon.

"Herewith is enclosed authentic certificate of the marriage of the said parties.

"Given at N. Parish (date)...... "

[43] Following exemplar after the style of Rota: "Case Number ....; Curia of X.; Nullity of Marriage: Smith-Jones; Presiding judge ....; Ponent ...."

decree reject the bill because of faults that can be amended, the plaintiff may introduce a new and properly composed bill to the same judge; if the judge reject the amended bill he must set forth the reasons for the new rejection (c. 1709,§2). In the interest of souls the curia should seek to aid in properly composing the bill.

Whatever be the reasons for rejection of the bill, the plaintiff is free to have recourse within ten days against the rejection to the superior tribunal (c. 1709,§3), presupposing, of course, that he is in good faith respecting his pretended right. The superior tribunal will be that metropolitan or suffragan court which constitutes the court of second instance in appeals from the other (cfr. c. 1594,§§1-3). The Rota also decides many cases of recourse against inferior courts that have rejected bills of plaint in marriage cases.[44]

The superior tribunal hears the party and the defender, and then defines the question of the bill's rejection as expeditiously as possible (c. 1709,§3). Then it notifies by signed decree, the appellant party as well as the inferior tribunal what decision it has made on acceptance or rejection of the bill. In case it decrees acceptance, the bill will be returned with the decree to the lower court, which must proceed with the case.[45]

The decision of the superior tribunal is final (c. 1709,§3 with 1880,n.7), but in case it declares the bill is to be rejected, it does not preclude the plaintiff or petitioner from offering another bill to another equally competent court (cfr. cc. 1560-1568; 1961; 1962; 1964).

36. If the judge neglects either to admit or reject the bill of plaint according to the norm of Canon 1709, and this neglect continues for the period of one month (cfr. c. 34,§3,n.3 with c. 1635), from the time of first presenting a properly formed bill, the interested party may insist, before the same judge, that he make a decision. This insistence may best be made in writing, but if it is orally made

[44] *e. g.*, R., Romana, Reiectionis Libelli, 10 nov., 1923 (aas., xvi, p. 73); Colonien., Reiectionis Libelli, 5 aug. 1924 (aas., xvii, pp. 84, 85); Scepusien., Null., seu Reiectionis Libelli, 10 jul. 1925 (aas., xviii, p. 108); Administrationis Apost. Silesiae Polonicae, Null., 4 aug. 1926 (aas., xix, p. 74); Romana, Null. Mat. (reiectionis libelli) 17 feb. 1931 (aas., xxiv, p. 97); Ravennaten., Null. Mat. (reiectionis libelli), 25 apr. 1931 (aas., xxiv, p. 98); Boianen., Campobassen., Null. Mat. (Reiectionis libelli), 23 dec. 1932 (aas., xxvi, p. 101).

[45] cfr. R., Colonien., Reiectionis libelli, 5 aug. 1924 (aas., xvi, pp. 84, 85); Osnabrugen., Reiectionis libelli, 27 oct. 1924 (aas., xvi, p. 85).

the notary must reduce it to writing and sign it in the acts. If the judge is still silent, the interested plaintiff may, after five days from the time of his insistence, have recourse to the ordinary of the place, against the recalcitrant official, vice-official or delegated judge, or, to a superior tribunal, in order that the judge be compelled to decide the case, or that another be appointed in his place (c. 1710).

In this case it does not seem certain whether recourse against the neglect of the ordinary may be made to the diocesan court of second instance, as in cases of recourse against rejection of the bill, or whether it must be directed to the Apostolic See (cfr. c. 1625,§1) and specifically to the Roman Pontiff (cfr. c. 1557,§1,n.3). Noval, n. 391 holds the latter view; Roberti, i, n. 286 and W-Vidal, vi, n. 377 hold the former, except for the case where the plaintiff would urge criminal action against the ordinary because of denial of justice.[46] It seems that even without criminal action the recourse may properly be made to either court: if it is made to the regular tribunal of second instance the superior judge may only appoint another judge in place of the neglectful ordinary (cfr. c. 1615,§3).[47] If the recourse is made to the Roman Pontiff the latter has also power to coerce the neglectful ordinary to perform his duty (cfr. c. 1625,§1 with c. 1710).

37. *Scholion:* The rules here given for the drawing up and tendering of the original plaint will be accomodated and applied with due allowances, to other plaints, motions and petitions, such as occur in incidental matters or in having recourse or making appeal to a higher tribunal on the principal issue.

§ 4. Effects of Plaint

38. The effects of a valid bill of plaint are:

1) It establishes a relationship between the plaintiff and the court, and this relationship is later completed, by issuance of summons, between the court and the respondent.

2) It furnishes direction and object matter for the proposed trial.

39. The bill of plaint is essentially the means of introducing one's controversy and litigation at court. Incidentally the bill may

[46] Similarly: Woywod in hpr., xxxi (1933), p. 1186.

[47] cfr. R., Clodien., Diffamationis, 5 mai. 1922 (rd., xv, p. 90).

touch on the proofs but it is not professedly a means of proof. Statements contained in it against the case of the plaintiff may however have the character of an unsworn written confession, and as such may serve as proof within the limits of extrajudicial confessions and private documents (cfr. nn. **183**, **379**, **380**), and if the telling statements are confirmed under oath at the joining of issue the confession may have the strength of a judicial confession (cfr. n. **179**).

40. A denunciation whether written or verbal, made against a proposed marriage before it is contracted, is not full proof of the impediment but may be sufficient to cause postponement of the marriage until further inquiry can be made, or a precautionary dispensation can be obtained, or even indefinitely, if the denouncer is an entirely reliable witness, and especially if he offers proof of repute of the impediment.[48]

[48] c. 27, X, De Sponsalibus et Matrimonio, IV, 1; c. 2, X, De Consanguinitate et Affinitate, IV, 14; c. 47, X, De Testibus et Attestationibus, II, 20.

CHAPTER III

Summons

"Et vocavit illum, et ait illi: quid hoc audio de te? Redde rationem."—Lc., xvi, 2.

41. When the bill of plaint or oral petition has been accepted the calling or summoning of the other party to court is in order (c. 1711,§1). The party called to answer the suit is termed defendant, respondent, party convened (reus, pars conventa), but in cases of non-consummation the term defendant (reus) is inappropriate.[1]

In cases of nullity and non-consummation, and otherwise too when the diocesan law requires his presence in the trial, the defender of the marriage bond (defensor vinculi, v. vindex, matrimonii adsertor) is a co-respondent with the married party, and holds a necessary and by law appointed proctorship (procurator natus) for the respondent in his absence.[2]

In neither ancient Roman nor ancient German law was there a summons issued by the judge: by the law of the twelve Tables the plaintiff brought the respondent to court, if necessary, by force inflicted before witnesses. Later this rude practice gave way to the authoritative summons of the magistrate. The early Canon law eagerly followed this change, and though the Decretals had no special Title under which the canons governing summons were ranged, such canons were to be found in the Decree and in the Decretals.[3]

§ 1. Definition and Kinds of Summons

42. In a wide sense the summons or citation (citatio) is any act of calling a person to court (vocatio in ius) who is required there, whether he be the plaintiff or respondent, the defender of the bond,

[1] DS, Reg., n. 5, § 2.

[2] In order to avoid confusion of the words "defender" and "defendant" the latter word is not further used in this book: in its place the word "respondent" is used.

[3] c. 6, C. XXIV, q. 3; c. 24, X, De Officio et Potestate Iudicis Delegati, I, 29; c. 19, X, De Foro Competenti, II, 2; c. 6, X, De Dolo et Contumacia, II, 14; c. 11, X, De Probationibus, II, 19; c. 1, De Iudiciis, II, 1 in Clem; c. 2, De Sententia et Re Iudicata, II, 11 in Clem.

a witness or an expert.[4] In a strict sense the summons is that act of the judge whereby the respondent is first called to undergo trial (conventio).

In this sense the summons is, in Canon law, an act of jurisdiction,[5] and constitutes a command of the judge (c. 1715,§1): it is more than an invitation to appear.

43. I. As distinguished from the summons of the judge (citatio ab homine) the Decretals of Clement III acknowledged also a summons by law (citatio a iure) whereby the law itself, under given circumstances, commanded the appearance of a respondent at court.[6] But the Code knows no such distinction.

II. There is likewise a distinction between real summons or arraignment by arrest,[7] and verbal summons. But again the Code does not provide for arrest, least of all in marriage cases.

III. The verbal summons of a judge is rightly divided a) according to its form, into the private or personal summons, which is personally intimated to the respondent, and the public or edictal summons, which is publicly announced by public edict.

b) According to its effect, the summons is either simple or peremptory: the latter sort of summons having the added quality that it is sufficient to pronounce the neglectful or disobedient recipient contumacious. The Decretals, following Roman law, required three summonses,[8] unless one were given peremptorily.[9] The Regulations for the Rota required a second summons or notice of concordance of doubts.[10] Every summons is now peremptory (c. 1714), *i. e.* final and urgent, so that it does not have to be repeated unless the judge intend to inflict punishment for contumacy as in Canon 1845,§2. But the judge may repeat the summons (cfr. c. 1843,§2).[11]

4 The Code uses the term in this wide sense in cc. 1570,§2; 1582, 1587; 1700; 1728; 1765; 1766,§1; 1849; 1967; 1990; 2010,§1.

5 Not so the serving of summons: cfr. Lega, i, n. 411; Roberti, i, nn. 288, 293.

6 cfr. c. 2, De Poenis, V, 8 in Clem.; c. 1, De Electione, I, 6 in VI.

7 cfr. c. 15, De Sententia Excommunicationis V, 11 in VI.

8 c. 2, X, De Dilationibus, II, 8.

9 c. 24, X, De Officio Iudicis Delegati, I, 29; cc. 6, 10, X, De Dolo et Contumacia, II, 14.

10 R, Reg., § 28, n. 1.

11 cfr. DS, Reg., n. 38, § 2.

§ 2. Necessity of Summons

44. The natural law requires that no injustice shall be inflicted, and hence suggests that a respondent be given opportunity to defend his rights, but it does not seem to demand this when the crime committed or the fact at issue is manifest and notorious.[12] Hence under the Decretals the summons was not necessary in notorious cases.[13] But although the Code relieves the plaintiff from proof in notorious cases (c. 1747,n.1), it does not seem to relieve the judge from the necessity of summoning the respondent. On the contrary it is plain from Canon 1555,§2 that only the cases pertaining to the Holy Office and the *ipso facto* dismissal of religious may be decided without summoning the respondent (cfr. c. 646). The summons is necessary even in notorious cases in order to be able to comply with Canon 1947 (cfr. c. 658,§1).[14]

If the litigant parties spontaneously present themselves to the judge to further their case, the summons is not necessary, but the notary or actuary must note in the acts that the parties were spontaneously present at the trial (c. 1711,§2; cfr. c. 162,§4).[15] In this case the respondent has a right to demand a delay in order to prepare his case.[16] Similarly if the respondent present himself in answer to an invalid summons even though reluctantly, his presence supplies for the invalidity of the summons,[17] unless it be shown that he did not know of the invalidity of the summons.[18]

[12] Noval, n. 392; cfr. I Cor., V, 3.

[13] c. 5, X, De Appellationibus, Recusationibus et Relationibus, II, 28; Bouix, ii, n. 160, q. 4; Bassibey, n. 247.

[14] Hence the statement of W-Vidal, vi, n. 384 (p. 330) that notoriety relieves the judge from the necessity of summons, seems to be incompatible with the Code.

[15] cfr. R., Heliopolitana, Iurispatronatus, 22 nov. 1913 (rd., v, p. 597; aas., v, p. 85): "Sacra Rota autem in hac materia secuta est has regulas nempe citationem non requiri ad validitatem iudicii si ista omittatur quando qui citari debuissent habent certam scientiam litis et hanc scientiam esse iudici perspectam ex probabilibus indiciis et coniecturis dubitari non possit"; Null., 8 jul. 1919 (rd., xi, pp. 119, 120).

[16] R., Muranen. seu Camberien., Null. Sententiae, 13 jul. 1918 (aas., xi, p. 395).

[17] R., Luganen., Iurium, 5 mart. 1915 (aas., viii, p. 240); Muranen. seu Camberien., Null. Sent., 13 jul. 1918 (aas., xi, p. 395).

[18] W-Vidal, vi, p. 337 (48).

§ 3. Procedure in Summons

45. Only the competent judge to whom the bill of plaint has been presented may summon the respondent. But in cases provided for in Canon 1990, and in cases of Pauline privilege the competent judge may summon even without presentation of the formal bill, either written or verbal. If the judge is not competent the summons is invalid and has no legal effects.

46. The Code does not prescribe the form in which the summons must be drawn up, but the essential elements of a valid summons are prescribed: first there is the act of writing a citation to appear and answer the matter of trial, and then there is the act of bringing this to the attention of the respondent.

I. The judge must call the respondent to trial. Hence the summons will bear 1) the name of the diocesan curia or other tribunal that requires the respondent's presence at court. The names of the judges who will hear the case need not be given, but the Rota generally states the name of the ponent. If the judge is to sit by delegated jurisdiction, he should state that he has been delegated and by whom: he need not send proof of his delegation.[19]

2) The full name and address of the respondent. If a wife has reassumed her maiden name, or taken a new name, and the judge is not able to ascertain under what name she is at present addressed, any summons that reaches her and makes it plain that precisely she is summoned will be valid (cfr. c. 47).[20] In case the respondent is insane it should be stated that the committee is being summoned, not in his own name but in the name of the insane person, and this name should be likewise given.

47. The second party to the marriage must be summoned as respondent to the plaint, even though there are ordinary indications that he will spurn the summons (cfr. n. **94**), and if the plaintiff seek relief from two marriages successively contracted, each respondent will be summoned (c. 1712,§2), but prudence will suggest that they

[19] Schmalzgrueber, lib. II, tit. iii, § 2, n. 27: "satis esse si delegatus dicat se delegatum quia exinde nascitur probabile dubium jurisdictionis."

[20] R., Treviren., Diffamationis, 15 mai, 1913 (rd., v, p. 122; aas., v, p. 285): "Notandum tamen est, ubi agitur de persona privata, contingere posse ut nomen eius iudici sit ignotum; tunc sufficit, in schedula citationis hanc personam designare huiusmodi qualitate aut officio, quae non possint convenire nisi illi soli, et ita personam citandam perfecte determinent. Quod iam vigebat iure Romano . . . et receptum est in iure canonico . . . ."

be not summoned to appear at the same time and place. If the respondent is insane the committee for the insane person must be summoned (cfr. cc. 93,§1; 1648,§1; 1713 iunct. c. 1651).[21] In cases of nullity or dispensation from non-consummated marriage, or in other cases, *v. g.* presumable death of spouse, for which the ordinary has directed that the defender have part, the official or delegated judge must, under pain of nullity of procedure, summon also the defender (c. 1587,§1). Likewise the plaintiff, respectively the promoter of justice must be notified to appear at the time and place of procedure (c. 1712,§3). Similarly witnesses and experts are called to court by the judge (c. 1765).

For cases of separation and for cases of nullity Innocent III had made it plain that the trial was invalid unless the respondent were summoned to defend his case.[22] But since cases of separation can now be decided in purely administrative procedure (cfr. n. **6**), it seems that the Canon law will not invalidate procedure undertaken without summons, provided no violence is done to the natural law of justice in the case. When in cases of evident nullity because of the informality of a Catholic's marriage, the administrative procedure is sufficient for declaration of nullity, the summons may be omitted without prejudice to the validity of procedure. In these cases however the judge must beware of the instances wherein a baptized Catholic is freed from the necessity of contracting in form (cfr. n. **150**), lest the failure to summon the respondent lead to a faulty decision.

In cases of nullity and of dispensation from non-consummated marriage, the respondent must likewise be summoned, even though it be an extraordinary and easily demonstrable case coming under the provisions of Canon 1990.[23] But since in these cases the defender is co-respondent (cfr. n. **41**) and is present to defend the case of the respondent, the procedure, it seems to me, is not invalid, even though the respondent is not himself summoned to trial.[24] This is intimated in the recent Instruction of the Congregation.[25]

[21] cfr. R., Marianopolitana, Null., 3 jul. 1922 (rd., xiv, p. 224).

[22] cc. 1, 4, X, Ut Lite non Contestata, II, 6.

[23] PC., 16 jun. 1931 (aas., xxiii, p. 354): "II. Utrum citatio partium, de qua in canone 1990, facienda sit ante declarationem nullitatis matrimonii.—R. ad II. Affirmative."

[24] Bassibey, n. 246.

[25] DS, Reg., n. 38, § 1: "Quoties . . . adhuc ignoretur ubi commoretur pars conventa aut etiam testis, *si rei gravitas postulet* locus est citationi per edictum."

Yet even in these cases the failure to summon the respondent himself certainly gives cause for integral reinstatement (restitutio in integrum) (cfr. c. 1905,§2,n.4).

In judicial cases where the defender has no part the failure to summon the respondent invalidates procedure and decision (cc. 1723; 1894,n.1).

48. 3) The command to appear (cfr. c. 1715,§1). However, since the judicial power of the Church is not generally appreciated by laymen of today, Bassibey rightly warns ecclesiastical judges to temper the categorical tone of the summons, lest the party summoned be contumacious,[26] and the regulations for cases of non-consummation speak of summoning in the manner of an invitation.[27] The judge may attach a letter explaining the Church's duty in the affair and politely urging the respondent to appear, or he may provide through the intervention of a friend of the respondent,[28] or through courier.

4) The place and time (year, month, day and hour) for appearance. The judge should fix the date at a reasonable advance of some days,[29] in order to give the respondent time for whatever preparation he desires to make.[30]

49. II. The matter of trial: This includes notice of who the plaintiff is, and what he asks of the court, and the basis of his plaint. 1) The full name of the plaintiff must be given. When the promoter initiates the action his name and office must be stated.[31] The address of the plaintiff or his proctor may be added, but this is not necessary, for the summons establishes a relationship between the court and the respondent: not between the plaintiff and the respondent.

2) What the plaintiff asks of the court (edictio actionis) and what is the basis of his plaint (causa petendi). It is not required that the technical name of the action sought,[32] nor that the most intimate crux of the case be mentioned in the summons, for this is often-

[26] Bassibey, n. 250.

[27] DS, Reg., n. 36: "Citatio parti et testi fit per litteras in modum invitationis, tamen praecepive."

[28] DS, Reg., n. 38, § 2.

[29] DS, Reg., n. 35.

[30] cfr. R., Mauranen. seu Camberien., Null. Sententiae, 13 jul. 1918 (aas., xi, p. 395).

[31] Roberti, i, n. 291.

[32] cfr. W-Vidal, vi, p. 334 (42).

times not yet known to the judge. It is therefore sufficient if the judge state in a general way (c. 1715,§1), whether the action purposes declaration of nullity, dispensation from non-consummated marriage, or separation, and it is expedient to add the ground for action. If nothing is stated about the matter of plaint, the summons is probably invalid (c. 1723). But since the introductory bill must state what is the matter of plaint, the judge provides sufficiently if he affixes to the command to appear a copy of the introductory bill of plaint (c. 1712,§1).

50. III. The written summons is concluded with the signature of the judge and the notary and is authenticated by the seal of the tribunal or curia (c. 1715,§2). In collegiate courts of three or more judges, the presiding judge alone, or his auditor, signs the summons with the notary.[33] The Code does not direct that the summons state the time and place of issuance, but these are usually added as in all public documents. Their omission would not invalidate the summons.

51. The summons will be written in duplicate, of which one copy, enclosed in an envelope,[34] will be sent to the respondent, the other retained among the acts (c. 1716) in the curial archive, for record.

52. If a summons that is strictly required (cfr. nn. **44, 47**) is so deficient in content that either the identity of the court summoning, or the identity of the person who is summoned, or the place to which he is summoned, or the time, or the matter of trial, or the identity of the plaintiff, or the authenticity of the summons is left in doubt, or if it is not canonically intimated to the respondent or the defender, the summons and the acts of procedure (acta processus)

[33] DS, Reg., Appendix, XXII suggests formula (trans.): "The V. Rev. N., Trial Judge, orders the respondent to convene at court on the ..... day of ..... A. D. ..... at ..... o'clock, in the ..... Bldg., at No. ....., ... St., to undergo examination under oath on the procedure introduced by N. his wife, and instituted in this Court by order of the S. C. of Discipline in the Sacraments, on the asserted non-consummation of the marriage of the said spouses, and on the reasons for petitioning dispensation. If the respondent does not appear at the time and place appointed, nor offers an excuse for his absence, he will be held to be in contempt of Court, and at the motion of the Defender of the Marriage Bond, the trial will proceed in his absence.

Given at .... this .... day ....

N. Trial Judge
N. Notary."

[34] DS, Reg., n. 37.

undertaken in the absence of the respondent and defender are of no moment (c. 1723; cfr. c. 1894,n.1). But the acts of proof on the merits of the case (acta causae) are valid for future canonical procedure between the same parties on the same issue (cfr. nn. 89, 229).

53. The act of summoning is completed by serving the summons. The Code mentions three methods of serving summons: by courier, by mail and by edict.

I. The regular and preferable[35] canonical method is by putting the written summons into the possession of the respondent (cc. 1712, §2; 1717,§1; 1721,§1), and calling his attention to the citation. But this verbal directing of his attention to the matter or reading of the summons to him, which is in some places customary, is not required for the validity of the summons. The serving is properly done by the messenger or courier (cursor) (cfr. cc. 1591-1593) of the curia, and he is admonished to deliver it quietly and privately, so as not to divulge the affair.[36] As a rule however our episcopal curiae have no regularly appointed couriers, and so the notary provides for serving the summons through the pastor or another clerical messenger, and this method is approved (cfr. cc. 1591,§1; 1592).

The summons may be served upon the respondent wherever he may be found (c. 1717,§1); hence not necessarily at his residence. To this end the courier may also enter the bounds of another diocese, if the judge think it advisable and so direct him (cc. 1717,§2; 1561, § 2).

It is not made entirely clear in the Code whether the summons may be sent into another diocese, to a respondent who is not, by reason of domicile or quasi-domicile, the subject of that ordinary whose court is issuing the summons. The pre-Code canonists held that in such cases the respondent may be invited by the judge to appear and take part in the trial, but that he could not be juridically summoned, and this has been lately restated by De Smet.[37] The summons would have to be served through the curia of that ordinary to whom the respondent is a subject (commissio rogatoria). On the other hand, while the Code foresees the regular proceeding in trial at the court of domicile or quasi-domicile of the respondent (c. 1561), it

[35] S. C. EE. RR., 11 jun. 1880, n. 14 (cicf., iv, n. 2005; cpf., ii, n. 1534); R, Reg., § 24, n. 1; SA, Reg., art. 16.

[36] DS, Reg., n. 37.

[37] De Smet, ii, p. 187(1); cfr. Lega, i, n. 411.

provides competence for the judge even when the respondent is not his proper subject, as in the case of vagrants (c. 1563), or in case the judge is ordinary of the place of contract (cc. 1565,§1; 1964), or finally, when the respondent is a non-Catholic (c. 1964). And it states no exceptions against the right of a competent judge to summon the respondent in any trial. Hence it seems to me that the respondent may be directly summoned by any competent judge, at least in matrimonial and other contentious cases. Regularly however, by reason of courtesy toward the respondent's proper curia, as well as of convenience, and even possibility of the respondent's appearance, the summons will be served by rogatory commission in such cases (cfr. c. 1570,§2), and generally the joining of issue and the questioning of the respondent will be undertaken by the curia of domicile or quasi-domicile (cfr. c. 1770,§2,n.3) (cfr. n. 228), unless the respondent prefers to appear at the principal seat of trial.

54. If the courier does not find the respondent at his dwelling, he may leave the summons with a member of the family or a servant, provided such person is willingly prepared to receive it and promises to give it to the respondent as soon as possible, and is not unfit to testify to his having received it (cfr. c. 1757,§1);[38] otherwise he will remit it to the judge, for service through the mails or by edict (c. 1717,§3) or by rogatory commission. He should, if possible, obtain approximate information of when the respondent will receive it. A husband and wife were separated in France and the wife emigrated to Buenos Aires. When the husband contested the validity of the marriage in Bordeaux, the curia of Buenos Aires was commissioned to question the wife, but could not find her nor did she respond to summons by edict. Then the judge and defender visited her mother in Bordeaux, who promised upon her expected arrival, to send her to the curia, but she did not appear. The Congregation of the Council gave permission to summon her by merely leaving the citation at the mother's house.[39] But citation through those who are not of the respondent's household is not provided in the Code.

55. When the courier conveys the summons to the respondent, he must write on its margin the day and hour,[40] at which it was served, and sign it (c. 1721,§1). And he does the same if he leaves it in

[38] Roberti, i, n. 294.

[39] SCC., In Burdigalen, Mat., 22 jun. 1895 (bass., p. 200 (4)).

[40] Roberti, i, n. 292: "et censemus a fortiori annum et mensem."

the hands of one of the household of the respondent, adding the name of the person to whom he tendered the summons (c. 1721,§2). But the omission of this formality does not invalidate the summons, though the curia cannot proceed unless it have notice of its delivery.

If the respondent refuse to receive the summons, the courier will remit it to the judge, with notice of the day and hour of refusal, and his signature (c. 1721,§4).

56. Proof that the summons has been served by courier is obtained by the courier's testimony of the fact (cfr. c. 1593). To this end the courier must write a report, stating that the summons was served and the name of the person to whom, and the place at which it was served, together with the date. To this he will append his signature (c. 1722,§1), and mention of his office.

The Instruction of 1923 directs that his report be made on the margin of that copy of the summons which is retained by the notary among the acts.[41] The custom at the Rota has been to write it on a separate paper.[42]

57. II. The second method of serving the summons is by mail. If it is difficult to serve the summons by courier, either because of distance or for some other reason, it may be sent, at the behest of the judge, by public mail, provided it be registered and a return receipt demanded (c. 1719). The receipt of registration and the return receipt will be preserved among the acts (c. 1722,§2). The latter constitutes full proof that the summons was received.[43]

58. A letter of summons should always be answered at once, and the readiness of the respondent to appear should be expressed in the answer. If the person summoned cannot come to court, he may state his reasons and ask to be heard by a delegated judge in the place where he resides. This holds especially when the party is ill or resides in another diocese (cfr. n. 228).

If a respondent is sure that the judge who summons him is incompetent in the case, *e. g.* because the case is already at issue before another judge (cfr. c. 1568), he should answer the citation and state the incompetence.

59. Canon 1719 allows the judge to use other means of transmitting the summons, providing such means may be considered very

[41] DS, Reg., n. 37; Appendix XVI suggests formula.

[42] Roberti, i, p. 441(1).

[43] R., Limburgen., Contumaciae, 13 feb. 1915 (aas., vii, p. 219).

safe in the conditions and under the laws of the country in which they are employed. This does not include use of the telegram: Rome has ordered that the telegram be not ordinarily used by bishops requesting grants *etc.*, because of the inconveniences experienced.[44] And since the identity of the addressee cannot well be established to the court, such notice does not constitute legal intimation of summons.

Similarly the telephone call cannot constitute a canonical summons, but if the respondent is thus called to court and appears, the trial will duly proceed (cfr. c. 1711,§2).[45]

60. III. When after diligent inquiry, the whereabouts of the respondent are still unknown, a summons by edict, long since known to the judicial practice of the Church,[46] is in order (c. 1720,§1), and this method is especially in place in cases of presumable death of a spouse.[47]

Pre-Code writers generally restricted the right to summon by edict to a judge delegated by the Holy See or at least to a bishop.[48] But the Code makes no distinction and permits any competent judge to summon by edict. It is another question however whether the curial judge acts wisely who summons by edict without consulting the ordinary, because of the many practical reasons which our times and circumstances advise against it.

61. The summons by edict must give notice of all the essentials required for personal summons (cfr. c. 1715), and in addition there is generally added a notice that ordinaries, pastors, and the faithful who may know of the whereabouts of the respondent should admonish him to appear personally or by proctor at the curia.[49]

It consists of two separate parts: 1) A copy of the summons is affixed by the courier at the doors of the chancery, and remains there as long as the prudent behest of the judge suggests (c. 1720,§2). The courier will write on it the date of posting, and the term during which it is to remain posted (c. 1721,§3). After this term the trial may properly begin in the absence or contumacy of the respondent.

[44] Litt. Encycl. Secret. Stat., 10 dec. 1891 (cpf., ii, n. 1775); cfr. SO, 24 aug. 1892 (cpf., ii, n. 1810; cicf., iv, n. 1159).

[45] cfr. PC., 12 nov. 1922 (aas., xiv, pp. 662, 663).

[46] cfr. c. 10, X, De Dolo et Contumacia, II, 14.

[47] SO, 1868; PF, 1883, § 43.

[48] cfr. Bassibey, n. 262.

[49] PF, 1883, § 43.

2) Notice of the summons is inserted in a public journal (c. 1720, § 2),[50] through which the party is most likely to be reached, and, other things being equal, the diocesan, or another Catholic journal is preferable. The Roman Rota publishes edictal summonses in the Acta Apostolicae Sedis.[51]

If either the press advertisement or the posted notice is impossible, even relatively, it may be omitted and then either announcement constitutes full edictal summons (c. 1720,§2). It may be that, under circumstances peculiar to modern times, both are rightly considered inadvisable. In that case the summoning of the defender is sufficient (cfr. n. **41**).

62. The summons by edict must be recorded and copies of the posted edict and of the press advertisement must be retained among the acts, and the courier must report on his having posted the edictal summons, and this secures proof of the fact.

63. *Scholion:* The rules just stated with respect to the summoning of the respondent are to be accomodated and applied to other

[50] According to Roberti, i, p. 444 (5), a public journal was first used to this purpose in SCC., Monacen., 23 feb. 1875.

[51] cfr. *e. g.*, aas., xxv, p. 102; Following form is suggested by DS, Reg., Appendix XXIII: "Rome; Dispensation of the Marriage of N. and N/

"Since the present place of dwelling of Mr. N., the respondent in this case, son of ...., by occupation a .... born in the city of ...., diocese of ....who in the year .... dwelt in the city of .... at no. ...., ... St., is not known, we by this edict peremptorily summon the said Mr. N. to appear personally at ...... o'clock on the ...... day of ...... in the year .... in the court room of this Tribunal (No. ...., ... St.), before the undersigned trial judge, to depose according to the questions proposed to him, on the case of the asserted non-consummation of his marriage, introduced to court by his wife N., to petition the Holy See for dispensation; which case will be tried by this Tribunal, by commission of the Sacred Congregation of the Sacraments, dated ....

"If he shall not appear at the time appointed, nor send excuse for his absence or mode of action, he will be held as contumacious, and the case will proceed in his absence, the very rev. defender of the bond upholding the interests of the marriage in the case.

"Local ordinaries, pastors, priests and all the faithful whosoever shall have knowledge of the domicile or place of dwelling of the aforesaid Mr. N. must see to it, if and in so far as they can, that this edictal citation comes to his knowledge.

"Given at ....., the ..... day of ..... in the year .....

N. Judge,
N. Notary."

acts of trial, such as the notification of decrees and decisions and the like, in so far as the nature of these acts allows (c. 1724). And similarly, these rules are to be accommodated and applied to the summoning or calling to court of the defender, plaintiff, witnesses, experts, *etc.* (c. 1765).

Some of the formalities proper to the summoning of a respondent are inapplicable to the summoning of others: 1) None but the respondent is ever summoned by edict.

2) No copy of the plaint need be attached when notifying the plaintiff, witnesses or experts to appear, but the defender must receive notice of what is contained in the plaint.

3) When several witnesses are living together in one family, a single notification may be used to call all of them to court, provided each is distinctly named. When several copies are sent to several witnesses, only one copy need be retained among the acts, but the notary must note how many exemplars were issued and to what witnesses.[52]

4) Summoning of others than the respondent by telephone is permissible as long as it brings the required persons to court. The Rota however makes all notifications to the plaintiff by formal writing,[53] and this practice may well be received in diocesan courts.[54]

§ 4. Effects of Summons

64. The first effect of a valid summons canonically served is the moral obligation in conscience on the part of the respondent to appear in answer to the summons (cc. 1842-1851) (cfr. nn. **100, 209**). However, except when an obligation accrues from the natural law, there is no canonical obligation to actively oppose the suit: the respondent may rest his case on the good judgment of the court.[55]

[52] R, Reg., § 19, n. 2.

[53] cfr. *e. g.*, R, Reg., § 18, n. 1.

[54] DS, Reg., Appendix XV suggests formula: "At the order of the V. Rev. N., trial judge in the procedure on the marriage which it is contended is ratified merely and not consummated, between N. and N., Madame N., dwelling at No. ......, ... St., the wife and petitioner in the case, is hereby notified to appear personally before the said judge in the court room of this tribunal at No. ......, ... St., on the .... day of .... in the year .... that she may undergo examination under oath in the case which she has introduced.

Given at .... this .... day of .... in the year ....,

N., Judge,
N., Notary."

[55] R, Norm., art. 66; 71.

The canonical effects of a valid summons pertain partly to the procedure (ius processuale) and partly to the litigated matter itself (ius substantivum).

65. When the summons has been canonically served on the respondent, or when, in lieu of a summons, the parties have spontaneously come to court, there accrue the following effects pertaining to procedure:

1) The disputed thing or right ceases to be intact (c. 1725,n.1), *i. e.* it is no longer a matter toward which the parties alone bear a relationship. For by summoning the respondent the judge enters upon a relationship toward him and toward the now litigated right.[56]

2) The trial belongs by preventive competence to that judge (court) alone, before whom the action was commenced (c. 1725, n. 2; cfr. c. 1568), and the plaintiff no longer has choice of competent judges. Nor does a party's change of domicile after service of summons affect the competence of the court.[57]

3) A judge delegated to try the case is confirmed in his jurisdiction so that it does not expire by expiration of the office or jurisdiction of the delegating judge (c. 1725,n.3; cfr. cc. 61; 207,§1).

66. 4) The case is pending; and hence by an old principle of law, the actual state of things must not be changed (by private authority) during litigation (c. 1725,n.5), and any attempt made against the actual state of things gives rise to action for redress (cfr. cc. 1854-1857). Thus with particular reference to marriage cases, although a former marriage be invalid or dissolved by any reason, it is not therewith allowed to contract another before the nullity or dissolution of the prior marriage be certainly and canonically established (c. 1069,§2). And if a person attempt a second marriage, before he is canonically pronounced free from the former marriage, the judge is canonically empowered to order that the parties be separated. But the wrongfully making an attempt does not *per se* invalidate the new marriage thus attempted: on the contrary, the newly attempted marriage may be valid, though illicit, if the former marriage was actually invalid or actually dissolved.

When the attempted marriage is invalid because of bigamy by reason of the first marriage still validly existing, the Code punishes

[56] Roberti, i, n. 297.

[57] Augustine, vii, p. 171 somewhat inaccurately states: "The judge or court before whom the action was brought *becomes competent,* and hence incompetency cannot be asserted afterwards"; (cfr. c. 1628, §§ 1, 2).

the perpetrator with canonical infamy (c. 2356), but this infamy does not prohibit the perpetrator from bringing action to establish his freedom from the former marriage.[58]

By public authority however, the judge may grant an injunction (c. 1672) ordering the separation, meanwhile, of the couple whose marriage is contested (inhibitio exercitii iuris). This is done especially on motion of the promoter or defender, or one of the parties, in order to avoid spiritual damage. And one of the parties may even of his own accord decline to permit the exercise of marital rights while the marriage is in doubt, and, if he is certain of its invalidity, a party must decline (cfr. n. **490**). It is easily seen however, that this is hardly an exception to the rule, but rather a confirmation of it.

67. 5) The trial is opened and litigation commences. Just when the proceeding or trial commences has been a subject of dispute among pre-Code canonists, and is not made very clear in the Code.[59] But when all the pertinent canons (cc. 1628,§1; 1629,§1; 1631; 1725; 1732; 1837) are considered it seems that the trial is commenced by summons, and fixed for dispute by the joining of issue.

68. Hence when the summons has been rightly made and canonically served the judge may proceed with the case, after waiting during the properly stated term, even when the respondent fails to appear at court. The respondent may fail to appear either because of his contempt for the command to appear, or because he is detained against his will, or because he does not actually know of the citation.

I. Contempt for the summons is shown: 1) When the respondent refuses to receive the summons upon delivery (cfr. cc. 1718; 1721,§4). The Countess C-G. instructed her servant to refuse all mail coming from the Curia, and later made plaint of nullity, for want of summons, against the procedure in Rotal court undertaken in her absence and contempt. But the Apostolic Signatura found that the Rota had summoned her, and declared that her failure to gain knowledge of the court's order to appear, must be attributed to her own contempt.[60]

[58] DS., 9 jun. 1932 (lqs., 1933, p. 373); cfr. *e. g.*, R, Null., 8 mart. 1913 (rd., v, p. 211); DS., Praesumptio Mortis Coniugis, 18 nov. 1920 (aas., xiv, p. 96).

[59] Roberti, i, n. 297: "...in Codice, qui ex uno capite dicit 'iudicium inceptum' per citationem (c. 1837), ex alio vero 'instantiae initium' fieri asserit litis contestatione (c. 1732); et in can. 1734 supponit interruptionem instantiae locum habere post litis contestationem (iuxta can. 1732), et simul eamdem interruptionem admittit post citationem, sc. 'lite pendente' (c. 1725, n. 5)."

[60] SA., Neo Eboracen., 10 jan. 1914 (aas., vi, p. 165).

2) When the respondent hides himself or otherwise prevents the summons from being delivered.[61]

3) When the respondent receives the summons but refuses to obey it (c. 1842).

If a party is detained against his will he is expected to send an excuse for his absence (cfr. cc. 1842; 1843,§1,n.2; 1849) and then procedure will generally be postponed until such time as he can come to court.[62] But if there is urgent reason to proceed at once, or if no excuse for absence is sent, the judge may proceed on the ground of the summons having been duly served.

69. II. The summons may have been canonically served (cfr. c. 1843,§1,n.1) without the respondent's ever becoming actually aware of it: 1) When relatives or servants have received the summons in the name of the respondent, but have never actually delivered it to him (cfr. n. **54**).

2) When the respondent is summoned by edict (cfr. n. **60**). In all these cases the respondent is considered as duly summoned, even when he has not been made actually aware that he is wanted at court, and in this case a fiction of the law supplies for the party's ignorance of the matter, lest the just procedure of the courts be impeded. Hence the judge proceeds with the trial in the contumacy or absence of the respondent (cfr. cc. 1842-1851).

70. Lastly the summons brings about an effect in substantive law, pertaining to the litigated matter itself; prescription is interrupted (c. 1725,n.4). This effect of the summons however, has no bearing on marriage cases (cfr. however, n. **413**), for prescription is excluded from matters touching the validity of marriage, since this matter comes under divine law (cfr. c. 1509,n.1), and even in cases of separation, there is no prescription against the right of a party to sue for separation, though there may be a presumption of condonation of offence which prevents action (cfr. c. 1129,§2) (cfr.n.**443**).

71. There is *per se* no proof on the merits of a case deriving from the contemptuous refusal of the respondent to appear.[63] But the judge is permitted to draw just conclusions from subsequent acts of disobedience (cfr. nn.**101, 102, 281, 283**).

[61] c. 5, X, Ut Lite non Contestata, II, 6; cfr. c. 2143, § 3.

[62] Contrary: Woywod in hpr., xxxi (1931) pp. 1187, 1188.

[63] IA., § 150.

CHAPTER IV

JOINDER OF ISSUE

"Circumsteterunt eum . . . multas et graves causas obiicientes . . . ; Paulo rationem reddente: quoniam neque in legem Judaeorum, neque in templum, neque in Caesarem quidquam peccavi."—Act., xxv, 7, 8.

72. The respondent answering the summons may agree with the plaintiff and be perfectly satisfied to have a separation awarded or the marriage declared void or he may rest the matter upon the good judgment of the court, or he may disagree and take exception either to the plaint and purpose of the plaintiff, and then his exception is a substantial one, covering the substance of his marriage rights (cfr. cc. 1667-1671), or to some incidental circumstance which, he contends, precludes the case from being tried as proposed. Such processual or incidental exceptions may be dilatory (exceptiones dilatoriae; cfr. c. 1628), or peremptive (exceptiones peremptoriae; cfr. c. 1629). Thus if the respondent propose an exception against the competence of the court or the person of the judge, claiming prejudice or interest, such an answer to the summons causes a delay in the trial but does not tend to extinguish it; if he contend *e. g.* that the fault for which separation is sought has been condoned (cfr. c. 1129) such an answer to the summons is peremptive and tends to extinguish the suit as having no place in court. In either case the exception, if valid, prejudices the suit as at present proposed.

Such processual and prejudicial exceptions do not often occur in marriage cases: when the respondent appears at court it is generally either in order to coincide with the plaintiff in his purpose, or to contest that purpose. The act of contesting is called the joining of the issue.

73. The joining of the issue or contesting of the suit (litis contestatio) is among the oldest, and was formerly one of the most important of the solemnities attaching to formal trial. In the early Roman law this solemnity was performed by the parties' solemn announcement of their intention to bring witnesses in favor of their contention ("testes estote"). Under Diocletian (Maximinian) the solemnity, retaining the same name, changed its nature, for thereafter it consisted in the plaintiff's renewing his contention aloud in court, and the respondent's contradiction announced aloud. In this form the solemnity passed over into the decretal law.[1]

But as the proceedings of courts became more and more documentary, so that finally everything was reduced to writing, the loud, open contestation was gradually abandoned, and as a consequence of this, the necessity of simultaneous presence of the parties. And so the Congregation of the Council arrived at a quiet concordance on the issue,[2] and the regulations for the Rota and the Apostolic Signatura provided for a written concordance to be signed by the ponent and the parties.[3]

§ 1. Definition and Kinds of Joinder

74. The Code describes the joining of the issue as the respondent's formal contradiction of the prayer of the plaintiff made before the judge for the purpose of litigating (c. 1726); it is the act whereby the plaintiff makes his claim and the respondent denies it in court with a view to litigation.

Under the same heading the Code speaks also of the concordance of doubts or issues (concordatio dubiorum; cc. 1728, 1729); the two expressions denote two phases of the same act: the contesting consists essentially in the judical contradiction on the part of the respondent; the concordance in the bringing the issue down to definite terms.[4]

75. According to the degree of solemnity observed, the joining of issue is either solemn and formal or it is simple and informal. Under the Decretals the solemn joining of issue was announced by a formula.[5] Under the Code there is no formula of joinder even when the issue is joined in the more solemn manner (cfr. n. 82). The "formal contradiction" mentioned in Canon 1726 refers rather to the formal end in view than to the use of a formula. For no solemn-

[1] c. un., X, De Litis Contestatione, II, 5: "per petitionem in iure propositam et responsionem secutam litis contestatio fiat."

[2] Bassibey, n. 565.

[3] R, Reg., § 12, n. 2; SA, Reg., art. 29, 30, 33; Lex Pr., Can. 23, § 1.

[4] The term "concordatio dubiorum" is of recent origin and came to use in the style of the Roman Congregations which settled contentious issues as well as others, by a response "ad dubia" (cfr. Bassibey, n. 565). The Lex R., can. 23, § 1 later used it as a synonym for "contestatio litis."

[5] Plaintiff: "Peto litem contestando quae in meo libello continentur."—R.: "Litem contestando nego in libello posita".

ity is necessary in joining issue, but it suffices that the parties appear before the judge or his delegated auditor, and the plaint or petition of the plaintiff and the contradiction of the respondent be written in the acts, so that it is plain what suit is being tried, *i. e.* what are the bounds of the controversy (c. 1727).

76. According to the manner in which several claims are contested, the joining of issue is either general, *i. e.* when all claims of plaintiff are denied in a general statement; or special, *i. e.* when the respondent contests each claim separately. Such separate contestation is not necessary.

§ 2. Necessity of Joinder

77. The formal and solemn joining of issue was not necessary for marriage cases even under the later Decretal procedure,[6] and is not now necessary in any trial (c. 1727),[7] but in the more implicated cases where the plaintiff's petition is neither clear nor simple, or where it is difficult for the respondent to know how to contest the plaint, the judge will summon the parties *ex officio* or at the motion of either, to rightly define the bounds of the controversy, *i. e.* for a concordance of doubts (c. 1728).[8] Thus frequently in judicial cases of separation from bed and board. In cases of nullity the issue is usually clear, and the formal concordance is but rarely required. But there are exceptions, as for instance when the parties are at variance upon the voiding impediment.[9]

78. In so far as the joining of issue is an accurate determination of the controversy, and an expression, at least implicit, of intent to oppose the suit, no trial, in the strict sense, can be conducted without it, and hence at least an informal joining of issue is necessary.[10] In

[6] cfr. c. 2, De Verborum Significatione, V, 11 in Clem. (an. 1306); cfr. however Innocent. III, in c. 4, X, Ut Lite non Contestata, II, 6 (ex an. 1205).

[7] R, Iurium, 5 mart. 1915 (rd., vii, p. 74).

[8] V-Creusen, iii, n. 149 call this concordance the "forma sollemnior" of the litis contestatio.

[9] cfr., *e. g.*, R., Null., 21 jan. 1911 (rd., iii, p. 16); Null. vel Dispen., 15 jul. 1911 (rd., iii, p. 341); Impedimenti ad Mat., et Damn., 31 aug. 1912 (rd., iv, p. 430): "... concordatis dubiis: 1) An constet de nullitate sententiarum primae et secundae instantiae. Et quatenus negative: 2) An sit locus restitutioni in integrum. Et quatenus affirmative ad alterutrum dubium: 3) An constet de existentia impedimenti in casu. 4) An sit locus refectioni damnorum in casu."

[10] Noval, n. 411; Eichmann, p. 125, alii apply the terms "fundamentum, basis iudicii, lapis angularis" to the joining of issue.

cases of nullity and dispensation from non-consummated marriage, and sometimes in cases of presumable death of spouse, the defender, by his presence at the trial, completes the joining of issue and contests the suit.[11] When the proper respondent is contumacious or is thought to be dead, or when both parties jointly bring plaint, the defender alone contests the suit.

In cases where the respondent is contumacious and there is no defender of the bond to contest the suit, *e. g.* in cases of separation, the Code provides for that part of the joining of issue which determines the exact bounds of controversy through the *ex officio* action of the judge (c. 1729,§1), guided by what is asked in the bill of plaint (c. 1844,§2); and the Code supplies for the respondent's will to contest (cc. 1730; 1844,§1), by placing the burden of proof upon the plaintiff (cfr. c. 1748,§2). In such cases the procedure is rather administrative than judicial.

The procedure of questioning required before the Pauline privilege may be used (cfr. nn. **94-99**) is not judicial, entails no suit in a proper sense, and hence there is no contesting of suit.

79. The issue is joined for the principal question in suit, and for such incidental questions as are defined by interlocutory sentence in formal trial (cfr. c. 1840,§2).

The proceeding in higher instance of appeal does not require a new joining of issue, for the intent to continue the controversy is implied in the appeal, and the bounds of the controversy are limited to what was at issue during the first instance (c. 1891,§1).

§ 3. Procedure in Joinder

80. The issue may be joined by any person who has a right to be a party to the suit. Hence not only the principals, such as the spouses, but likewise the promoter and defender (cfr. cc. 1844 iunct. 1850,§2), the proctors of the parties, and the committee of an insane person may join issue.

81. The judge presides at the joining of issue. In nullity cases requiring three judges for the definitive sentence, it is sufficient if one *v. g.* the official, vice-official or a delegated auditor preside, just as one

[11] R., Null., 28 jan. 1918 (rd., x, p. 14): "Nulla pariter quaestio esse potest quoad omissionem litis contestationis, praesertim quia in iudicio summario, quo causae matrimoniales pertractari debent, litis contestatio non requiritur; accusato enim impedimento et audita altera parte iam iudicii obiectum est determinatum."; cfr. also Lega, i, nn. 432 with footnote; 621, 3'.

alone may preside at the hearings. But when a difficult case requires an *ex officio* concordance of doubts, the tribunal of three should be consulted,[12] to avoid later judicial determination of unnecessary incidental questions.

82. The more solemn and formal present method of joining issue is as follows: On the day appointed (cc. 1715,§1; 1712,§3), usually at the first summons of the respondent, both parties make their simultaneous appearance at court. They may appear at this time by proxy, but must be later summoned for personal hearing (cfr. n. **109**).

Either party may propose processual or prejudicial exceptions (cfr. n. **72**), and the judge may then declare an adjournment until the entire court shall have considered and decided on the exceptions. If the exceptions are evidently without foundation the judge proceeds at once to the joining of issue.

The plaintiff repeats substantially what was stated in the bill, sometimes after hearing it reread to him, and the respondent is asked whether he contradicts the facts or contests the petition.

The claims of both parties are examined, and their intentions, as expressed in statement of articles or positions (cfr. n. **112**) are so harmonized that the suit can be clearly stated and clearly contested.[13]

If the parties appear and agree upon the statement of the issue or trial formula, the judge will see whether the issue as stated is presentable according to the law and whether it seems properly to arise from the *prima facie* facts of the case, and if so, will decree that the issue be formulated, as agreed (c. 1729,§2). If the parties do not agree upon the issue, or if the agreement does not seem proper to the judge he will, with the aid of the defender in cases where he is present, formulate the proper matter for trial if there be any, and state the trial formula in his written decree (c. 1729,§3). In nullity cases the trial formula is: "Is it certain that the marriage is null?" Formerly the Congregation used frequently to invert the trial formula and ask: "Is it certain that the marriage is valid?"[14] But this is now contrary to approved and established practice. In cases of im-

[12] cfr. R, Reg., § 32.

[13] cfr. R, Reg., § 32, 3'.

[14] cfr. *e. g.*, SCC., Nullius, Farfen., 15 jan., 26 mart. 1707 (cicf., v, n. 3045); cfr. n. **486**.

potence there is the implied formula: "Is it certain that the marriage is null, and, in so far as nullity is not certain, is there such *prima facie* evidence of non-consummation that the acts should be sent to the Congregation of the Sacraments (cfr. n. **156**).[15] In cases of separation the trial formula varies according to circumstances, *e. g.:* "Is it certain that there is canonical ground for separation? And in case the answer is affirmative: For how long? Whose fault is it?"

83. At this time, and generally before joinder is made, the precautionary sum to be deposited for judicial expense is determined and collected, and gratuitous advocacy is appointed if that has been petitioned and granted (c. 1631).[16]

The notary will write in the minutes whether and how the respondent contested the suit, and such details about this act of procedure as might have a bearing on the case. If the case is contested by a letter of the respondent, this letter will be preserved among the acts. The notary's record is signed by the parties or their proctors and by the judge and notary.

84. In practice, the joining of issue in most marriage cases is simple and informal and consists in the presence of the parties (not of necessity simultaneous) before the judge, and their contesting statements made in answer to his questions: first the plaintiff is questioned on what was contained in the bill, and then the respondent is questioned on the same issues and on whatever points arise from the answers of the plaintiff (cfr. nn. **117-120**). If the respondent neither appears nor gives a fair excuse for his absence he is declared contumacious (cc. 1842-1851) and the trial formula is drawn up *ex officio* with the aid of the defender in cases where he is present (cfr. n. **41**) on motion of the party who is present or of the promoter (cfr. n. **14**). But the judge may also proceed, without having first declared the party contumacious.[17] The contumacious party will be at once notified *ex officio* of what has been done, that he may propose exception, if he have any, against the trial formula or any article

[15] The Rota, but not the diocesan court, may formulate in impotence cases: "An constet de matrimonii nullitate in casu; et quatenus negative; An consilium praestandum sit SSmo pro dispensatione super matrimonio rato et non consummato in casu?" (cfr. R., Null., 16 jul. 1930 (aas., xxiii, p. 97); Null., 21 jul. 1930 (aas., xxiii, p. 98); Null., 25 jul. 1930 (aas., xxiii, p. 98).

[16] cfr. SA, Reg., art. 37.

[17] R, Norm., art. 70, § 1; 71.

of it, and clear himself of the contempt within a term that the judge shall see fit to appoint (c. 1729,§1).

85. When the issue has been joined the judge orders the trial to proceed, examines the parties and appoints a term for the bringing of witnesses and other proofs, and he notifies them of this term. He should first make some inquiries concerning the witnesses and documents, in order that he may know how difficult it will be to procure them and how long it will take. He may prorogue this term on motion of the parties, but must avoid protracting the trial too long (c. 1731,n.2).

§ 4. Effects of Joinder

86. Many of the effects formerly attributed to the joining of issue now derive from the summons, partly because the Code has transferred the greater importance to the summons, and especially in nullity cases because the basis of plaint and points at issue are, as a rule, accurately expressed in the summons. Nevertheless the joining of issue still has its effects both processual and substantive.

I. The processual effects are: 1) The matter and basis of plaint are determined, and the trial is fixed for dispute. Hence there is thereafter no change in the bill or in the trial formula, except for a grave reason, and then by a new decree of the judge at the motion of a party or the promoter or defender, and after hearing the other party and weighing his arguments (cc. 1729,§4; 1731,n.1).

Thus in cases of separation a party is not free to change at will the basis of plaint and separation.[18] In nullity cases the impediment alleged in the bill may be changed during the course of first instance, if there is *prima facie* evidence that another impediment is involved, and in practice it is not infrequent that the case is abandoned as far as the impediment contained in the bill is concerned, and is considered by reason of a new impediment that has shown itself during the course of trial.

It is the duty of the judge of first instance not only to allow the plaintiff to change the impediment mentioned in the bill or to add a new impediment, but even to suggest and direct the change if the welfare of souls can be thereby promoted, for the grave reason required by Canon 1729,§4 then becomes imperative. In a case that arose in Oregon City the plaintiff sought to have her marriage de-

[18] R., Separationis, 17 mart. 1913 (rd., v, p. 220).

clared void because of fictitious consent; the court rejected the plea on this ground, but examined into the further question whether a condition contrary to the obligation of marital fidelity had been affixed to the contract.[19] In a case that arose in Pekin the plaintiff sought only to prove duress, but the judges considered further whether the marriage was invalid by reason of non-consent and want of valid form.[20] However the judges may not consider an additional impediment that is not public by its nature, without at least implicit consent of the plaintiff.[21]

But the metropolitan court of second instance cannot permit that the bill be thus changed when the case is appealed to it. In the Rota such changes are frequently permitted, because the Rota may, by way of exception (cfr. c. 1599,§2), hear a marriage trial in first instance; but, when there is a change, a decision of nullity necessitates a new appeal, in order that two corroborative decisions pronounce for invalidity by reason of the new impediment.[22]

87. The bill is not considered changed: a) If the method of proof is retricted or changed;

b) If the petition or its accessories, such as judicial expense claims, are lessened. Thus a plaintiff is free to change suit of nullity to suit of separation merely, or to petition of dispensation from merely ratified non-consummated marriage, unless the promoter see fit to pursue the case of nullity on the ground of an impediment that is public by its nature.

c) If the circumstances of fact mentioned in the bill are illustrated or completed or bettered, as long as the object of the controversy remains the same (c. 1731,n.1; cfr. c. 1671).

[19] R., Oregonopolitana, Null., 6 jul. 1914 (aas., vi, p. 519).

[20] R., Vicariatus Apost., Ce-Li Central, Null., 10 feb. 1917 (aas., ix, p. 505); Florentina, Null., 28 jun. 1918 (aas., xi, p. 22).

[21] R., Trincomalien., Null., 1 feb. 1913 (rd., v, p. 84; aas., v, p. 202); Null., 21 apr. 1915 (rd., vii, p. 195); cfr. Bassibey, 525, 2.

[22] cfr. R., Null., 9 apr. 1915 (rd., vii, p. 152); Null., 15 dec. 1915, 3 apr. 1917 (rd., ix, pp. 68, 69); Vicariatus Apost., Ce-Li Central, Null., 10 feb. 1917 (rd., ix, p. 25); In R., Null., 9 apr. 1915 (rd., vii, p. 152) however the Rota did not consider the added impediment of clandestinity without obtaining consent of the Supreme Pontiff; Roberti i, p. 453 (2) remarks that the concordance formula used in the Rota: "an constet de nullitate matrimonii in casu", does not clearly express that the trial is restricted to those impediments mentioned in the bill.

The change of bill may be indicative of too great preoccupation in obtaining favorable decision. At Paderborn a case was introduced on the ground of duress. After being delayed during four years, the suit was heard anew with the added impediment of non-consent, but the Rota remarked upon the evident effort of the plaintiff to gain a decision of nullity at all costs.[23] In another case however, the plaintiff changed the basis of suit from disparity of cult to duress without prejudice to her interest.[24]

88. 2) The joining of issue certainly closes the introductory period of trial (cfr. n. **67**). Hence exceptions against the trial are thereafter precluded according to the norms of Canons 1628, 1629 (cfr. n. **84**).

89. 3) The joining of issue opens the period for further hearing of the parties (cfr. Ch. V), and for the bringing of proofs. The judge is not to proceed to receive testimony[25] or other proofs before the joining of issue, except in the case of contumacy (cfr. nn. **68, 69**), or when it is advisable to hear a witness who cannot surely or at least cannot easily be heard later, either because of probable death, or departure, or for some other just cause (c. 1730), or when the testimony is intended to establish a prejudicial exception against the trial (cfr. n. **229**).[26] Much of the questioning will be irrelevant unless the matter and basis of the suit are accurately determined beforehand. And thus in separation cases, nothing short of urgency will cause the witnesses to be heard before the issue is properly joined. In nullity cases the practice under pre-Code law was less restricted.[27] But under the Code there should ordinarily be no judicial hearing of witnesses or physical inspection before the joining of issue. Documents presented together with the plaint (cfr. n. **23**) may be received and reserved in the curial archives, but, strictly speaking, should not be considered and appraised beforehand.

[23] R., Paderbornen., Null., 27 jul. 1917 (aas., x, p. 217); cfr. also Null., 15 dec. 1915, 3 apr. 1917 (rd., ix, p. 74).

[24] R., Null., 21 dec. 1912 (rd., iv, p. 470).

[25] cfr. X, Lib. II, 6 Heading: "Ut Lite non Contestata, non Procedatur ad Testium Receptionem vel ad Sententiam Definitivam."

[26] W-Vidal, vi, p. 348 (17).

[27] Lega, i, n. 431.

90. 4) From the time of joining issue there begins the two year period during which the trial in first instance should be brought to an end (c 1620), and which, if no act of procedure is undertaken during the interim, causes the extinction of the proceeding (c. 1736).

91. II. Substantive effects: In civil contentious cases the joining of issue causes the possessor of another's goods to cease being in technical good faith (bona fides) for purposes of possession and prescription (c. 1731,n.3; cfr. c. 1512). But it does not affect the inner good faith of a party as to his right in the matter, and in marriage cases has nothing to do with the good faith of the parties respecting the validity of their marriage (cfr. nn. **489, 490**).

92. The statements made by the parties in joining issue (cfr. nn. **112, 113**) are accounted as proof of the case only when they are sworn to, and then only in so far as their answers under questioning of the judge, their confessions and their oaths (cfr. Ch. XIII, §5, n. **555** fol.), can be accounted as proof.

CHAPTER V

Questioning of the Parties

"Numquid lex nostra judicat hominem, nisi prius audierit ab ipso, et cognoverit quid faciat?"—Jo., vii, 51.

§ 1. Necessity of Questioning the Parties

93. The Roman law provided that the judge should, at his discretion, question the parties to a suit,[1] and canonical procedure customarily followed the civil usage in this matter, but the custom was not brought into written law until the Congregation of the Council issued the well known Instruction on marriage procedure "Cum Moneat Glossa."[2] Later on Pius X brought the questioning of the parties under more careful ruling in his delineation of the procedure for the Roman Rota.[3]

While in cases of a civil nature it was always left to the discretion of the judge whether or not to question the parties, the Instruction of Propaganda commanded that the parties be interrogated in marriage trials,[4] and Rome has remarked unfavorably upon the action of diocesan authorities who declared in favor of either nullity or validity without having heard the parties.[5] Now the Code ordains that the parties must be heard in marriage trials (cc. 1742,§1; 1990), and this must be observed also in judicial cases of separation from bed and board.[6] If one party cannot be questioned because of his contumacy, the trial may proceed without him.

94. In the procedure attending the use of the Pauline privilege, both the newly converted person and the other party who will not be converted nor live in peace with the convert must be questioned. The questioning of the party who remains infidel is called in canonical usage, the interpellation (interpellationes).[7]

[1] L. 21, D., De Part. Interrog., XI, 1, Ulpianus.

[2] SCC, 1840.

[3] R, Reg., §§ 137-146.

[4] PF, 1883, § 18.

[5] SCC., In Colonien., Mat., 29 mai. 1886, 19 jan., 3 aug. 1889; Mat., 24 sept. 1864 (bass., p. 241 (4)); R., Null., 11 apr. 1911 (rd., iii, p. 164).

[6] IA, § 217.

The interpellation must always be made except where the Apostolic See has otherwise declared (c. 1121, § 2). For since the Apostle gave a privilege to those whose conversion to the faith becomes a cause of oppression or undue hardship to them, it is necessary to ascertain whether, in a given case, the oppression or hardship has actually resulted: to this end the questioning of the infidel party is but a natural and proper means. Nor is one *ipso facto* relieved from the necessity of interpellating when it is evident that the interpellation can serve no purpose. It was asked by the Bishop of Portland (Me.) whether the interpellation is necessary when the infidel wife has obtained civil divorce from the now converted husband and remarried another, and when it is plain that both the infidel party and the new husband would resent the interpellation, possibly injure the interpellating messenger, and in any case, the former wife could not return to the first husband because the civil law prohibited. The Holy Office answered that all this was not sufficient of itself to simply drop the matter of interpellating the infidel party, but the bishop might in such cases use or obtain faculties wherewith to dispense from the making of the interpellation.[8] Canon 1125 seems to have simplified the matter even more (cf. n. **97**).

95. Whether the interpellation is necessary by divine or ecclesiastical law, cannot be ascertained from any uniform view of authors, for no such uniformity of opinion exists.[9] The Holy Office when giving response to a case sent from Cochin-China, has indeed declared that the interpellation is necessary in the case at issue, "ex divino praecepto"; but it is plain that the Congregation does not here answer *ex professo* the question of the origin of the law requiring interpellation.[10] When in 1816 the Congregation of Propaganda, at that time

[7] The Code uses the plural form (cfr. c. 1121, § 2), because the infidel person is asked about two things (cfr. n. **119**), not as though the interpellation were to be repeated: SO., 12 jun. 1850, Coccin. Occident. (cicf., iv, n. 910; cpf., i, n. 1044): "posse autem eam (interpellationem) facere pluries ex mera caritate."

[8] SO., 18 jun. 1884, Portland. (cicf., iv, n. 1088; cpf., ii, n. 1620); Hence when Capello, iii, n. 776 says that in such cases: "cessat *per se* necessitas interpellandi . . ." he refers to divine law, and does not state that ecclesiastical law permits omission of the interpellation without further ado.

[9] cfr. Jone, in lqs., 1927, pp. 345, 346.

[10] SO., 12 jun. 1850, Coccin. Occident. (cicf., iv, n. 910; cpf., i, n. 1044); cfr. also SO, 1824, resp. ad 3.

fully commissioned to negotiate in matters respecting the Pauline privilege, was directly asked "utrum . . . interpellatio partis . . . sit de iure divino . . .," the Congregation gave a practical answer entirely avoiding the question of the divine origin of the law.[11] A close examination of the Canons inclines one to conclude that the Church has continued in her Code the policy of avoiding the settlement of that question.

96. The question of the divine or ecclesiastical origin of the requirement of interpellation is quite apart from the question whether the interpellation is required for the validity of the ensuing marriage. Here again there is no unanimity among the recent, not to speak of the older authors.[12] But it seems that the interpellation is indeed required for the validity of a subsequent marriage. The Propaganda has declared that without the interpellation "non esse locum dissolutioni matrimonii,"[13] and in a very interesting case from India the Holy Office decided that a convert who had married a Catholic woman without interpellating his infidel wife, must, after three children were born of the recent marriage, leave the Catholic wife and return to the formerly infidel, but by now converted wife.[14] Now Canons 1121,§1 and 1122,§2 offer strong argument, even though it does not attain to certainty,[15] that the interpellation is required for the validity of a subsequent marriage.[16]

The invalidity of a subsequent marriage entered into without the interpellation of the infidel spouse having preceded, seems to derive from ecclesiastical, not divine law, whatever may be concluded about the obligation of interpellating deriving from divine law. This we see from the fact that the Church does not allow diocesan courts to declare such subsequent marriages invalid, but rather reserves such cases to the Holy Office,[17] where in fact, a *sanatio* is sometimes granted to supplant the neglected interpellation.[18]

[11] PF., 5 mart. 1816, Tunk. Occident. (cpf., i, n. 704, resp. ad 1).

[12] cfr. Jone, in lqs., 1927, pp. 345, 348 fol.

[13] PF., 5 mart. 1816, Tunk. Occident. (cpf., i, n. 704, resp. ad 1).

[14] SO., 20 jun. 1858, Pondicher. (cicf., iv, n. 947; cpf., i, n. 1162); cfr. also SO., 11 sept. 1878, Coreae (cicf., iv, n. 1057; cpf., ii, n. 1499).

[15] cfr. W-Vidal, v, p. 761 (68).

[16] cfr. De Smet, i, p. 326 (3); Nau, p. 178 (3); De Becker, nov., p. 245.

[17] PF, 1883, § 45; cfr. c. 1962.

[18] cfr. PF., 17 jan. 1836 (cpf., i, n. 845, resp. ad. 1).

97. Whatever be the origin or compelling force of the law, the Church can and does dispense from the interpellation.[19] In some cases this is done by means of a dispensation in the law (dispensatio a iure), in other cases there is granted a delegation in the law (delegatio a iure) in order that the proper persons may dispense, and in still other cases special faculties are given whereby the dispensation may be granted.

I. When, as in missionary lands, a convert has had several wives and it is ascertained, at least extrajudicially,[20] that he does not remember which was his first wife, or, though he remembers, it is extremely difficult to find her, a dispensation from the interpellation is granted by law, to the end that he may take as Christian wife whoever of his former wives (no other) will be baptized.[21] Hence an individual dispensation is not necessary in these cases.[22]

II. The Code grants a delegation whereby ordinaries, pastors and confessors may dispense even for the external forum from the interpellation. This delegation is derived from the Constitution of Gregory XIII,[23] which provides for cases where the husband or wife has been taken away captive into distant parts, and it is ascertained at least extrajudicially, that the interpellation cannot, because of distance, unknown whereabouts, or danger from hostile and barbarous persons, be duly made, or that, if it has been made, the answer has been awaited for a peremptory period and has not been forthcoming. Now, when the circumstances are the same,[24] the dispensation may be

[19] Canons 1121, § 2 and 1123 use the words "declarare, declaratio," but Const. Gregorii PP. XIII "Populis" 25 jan. 1585 (cicd., viii) and the PF. Formula facultatum tertia speak of the power of dispensing: "dispensandi."

[20] SO., 22 nov. 1871 (cicf., iv, n. 1019; cpf., ii, n. 1377); cfr. c. 39.

[21] c. 1125; Const., Pauli III, Pii V (cicd., vi, vii); cfr. Jone (lqs., 1927, p. 336 fol.).

[22] Although these Constitutions of Paul III and Pius V, speak only of dispensing men from making the interpellation, it seems that the dispensation in the law meant to hold equally when a woman has had several husbands. SO., 12 jun. 1850, Coccin. Occid. (cicf., iv, n. 910; cpf., i, n. 1044); 5 sept. 1855 (cicf., iv, n. 933; cpf., i, n. 1117).

[23] c. 1125; Const. Greg. XIII (cicd., viii); Quasi pastors (cfr. c. 451, § 2) and apparently all confessors are now included in the grant originally given to confessors of the Society of Jesus: cfr. Jone (lqs., 1927, pp. 336, 342); V-Creusen, ii, n. 435 doubting.

[24] c. 1125: "in eisdem adiunctis": there is no uniformity of opinion among authors as to what constitute the 'eadem adiuncta' under which the grant is made available. cfr. Jone (lqs., 1927, p. 340); c. 1127 inclines one not to be too punctilious in appraising the circumstances as similar.

granted in all regions, even though the original document of Gregory did not include them. In order to dispense by this delegation it is not necessary (as it is with the Constitutions of Paul III and Pius V) that the converted man or woman shall have had several spouses heretofore, or if he had, that he wishes to take one of them now as Christian spouse, for the convert dispensed according to the Constitution of Gregory may marry any other Christian.[25]

The Holy Office has further declared that bishops and vicars apostolic may dispense in other cases when necessity urges and there is no time to refer to the Holy See, and it is certain that the infidel party will neither be converted nor live in peace.[26] There arises the question whether this delegation by law for urgent cases still holds. The answer is affirmative: Canon 81 states the general principle that the ordinary may dispense in urgent cases (cfr. also cc. 15; 209). That this is applicable to dispensation from the interpellation derives from Canon 20, directing that, when the present law does not expressly delineate procedure, we are to follow the laws given for parallel cases, and the style and practice of the Roman Curia. Now Canons 1043 and 1045,§§1,2 give a good parallel law in a very similar matter, for they provide that the ordinary may dispense from impediments in urgent cases, just as the Holy Office provided for dispensation from interpellation. Besides this, the above mentioned decree of the Holy Office certainly gives us what was, at least, the manner and practice of the Curia in such cases. Some doubt arises whether this decree is expressive of the present practice of the Curia, as distinguished from pre-Code practice; but as long as no contrary practice is established, the raising of this doubt seems to be a begging of the question.[27]

III. Besides all this, some legates, bishops, vicars and prefects apostolic have special faculties whereby they may dispense from the

[25] A close examination of the concluding sentence of Gregory's constitution shows that we have here, not only a dispensation from interpellating, but by way of precaution, an act divorcing the legitimate marriage, which goes beyond the terms of the Pauline privilege. cfr. De Smet, i, n. 355; V-Vidal, v, nn. 636, 637.

[26] SO., 11 aug. 1859 (cicf., iv, n. 954; cpf., i, n. 1180): "Quoties coniugem infidelem nec Christi fidem amplecti, nec sine contumelia Creatoris cum converso velle cohabitare certo constet, Episcopi tamquam Apostolicae Sedis delegati, et Vicarii Apostolici, dispensare poterunt super interpellatione, dummodo urgeat necessitas, nec tempus suppetat recurrendi ad S. Sedem."

[27] cfr. Oesterle in lqs., 1929, p. 343.

interpellation,[28] and in places governed by the Congregation of Propaganda the concession is general.[29]

98. The delegated power wherewith ordinaries or other priests dispense from interpellating may be used only when there is sufficient cause at hand. Otherwise the dispensation is laid open to the danger of being invalidly granted. In various specific cases the Holy See has declared what may be considered a sufficient reason for dispensing from the interpellation. They are: 1. Impossibility of making the interpellation: In a case from China the Congregation of Propaganda declared the insanity of the heathen spouse to be sufficient cause.[30] Likewise if the whereabouts of the infidel party are unknown.[31]

2. Great risk or danger to life or liberty in making the interpellation.[32] The Holy Office has declared that in times of persecution the danger to the Christian spouse or to Christians generally which would result from the interpellation, is sufficient cause for dispensing from it.[33]

[28] cfr. *e. g.* Facultates sp., C. in akk., 1917, p. 433.

[29] PF., Formula Facultatum tertia (tum maior tum minor), 8 dec. 1919:

"24. Dispensandi cum gentilibus et infidelibus *plures uxores* habentibus ut post conversionem et baptismum, quam ex illis maluerint, si etiam ipsa fidelis fiat, retinere possint, nisi prima voluerit converti.

"25. Dispensandi super *interpellatione* coniugum in infidelitate relictorum pro omnibus *casibus ordinariis*, dummodo sc. adhibitis antea omnibus diligentiis, etiam per publicas ephemerides ad reperiendum locum ubi coniux infidelis habitat, iisque in irritum cessis, constet saltem summarie et extraiudicialiter coniugem absentem moneri legitime non posse aut monitum infra tempus in monitione praefixum suam voluntatem non significasse.

"26. Itemque dispensandi super *interpellatione* coniugis in infidelitate relicti, siquidem certo constiterit, saltem summarie et extraiudicialiter, interpellationem fieri non posse sine evidenti *gravis damni* aut coniugi iam ad fidem converso, aut christianis inferendi periculo.

"27. Permittendi ut accedente gravi causa, *interpellatio* coniugis infidelis *ante baptismum* partis quae ad fidem convertitur fieri possit; nec non, gravi pariter de causa, ab eadem interpellatione, ante baptismum partis quae convertitur, dispensandi, dummodo hoc in casu ex processu saltem summario et extraiudiciali constet interpellationem fieri non posse, vel fore inutilem." (apud Blat, De Sacramentis, p. 726; W-Vidal, v, p. 765 (79)). Cfr. commentary in Blat, pp. 678, 681; in prm., xi, p. (138), n. 119 fol.

[30] PF., 5 mart. 1787, Sutchuen. (cpf., i, n. 589).

[31] SO., 3 jun. 1874 ad Vic. Ap. Sutchuen Orient. (cpf., ii, n. 1415; cicf., iv, n. 1030).

[32] SO., 4 feb. 1891 ad Vic. Ap. Iapon. Merid. (cicf., iv, n. 1130; cpf., ii, n. 1746).

[33] SO., 11 sept. 1878, Coreae (cpf., ii, n. 1499 ad 2; cicf., iv, n. 1057).

3. Grave inconvenience in making the interpellation. The Holy See has declared that when the infidel party is so far away that the interpellation would be too uncertain and too difficult there is cause for dispensation.[34]

4. The morally certain knowledge that the infidel party will neither be converted nor live peaceably.[35]

The mere presumption of the existence of one of these reasons is not sufficient for the granting of the dispensation.[36] Much less can the dispensation be granted by the local ordinary when it is known that the infidel party would be converted if he or she were received again as spouse.[37]

99. When dispensation from the interpellation has been duly granted, the subsequent marriage of the converted party will be valid, even though it later become known that the other party wanted to live peaceably or to be converted or was converted at the time of the other's marriage.[38] But in order to escape the occurrence of such cases, the Congregation of Propaganda has decreed that it is not licit for the converted party to enter upon new nuptials without interpellation or a new dispensation if a year has passed since the dispensation from interpellation was last granted (cfr. n. **355**).[39] The

[34] Ben. XIV, 16 jan. 1745 (cpf., i, p. 442 (1)); SO., 11 jun. 1760 (cicf., iv, n. 811; cpf., i, n. 430); SO., 3 jun. 1874 ad Vic. Ap. Sutchuen. Orient. (cicf., iv, n. 1030; cpf., ii, n. 1415); SO., 29 nov. 1882, Mongoliae (cpf., ii, n. 1581; cicf., iv, n. 1075): "1. Qualis distantia in praedictis regionibus ubi viae sunt tam difficiles... An verbi gratia iter septem vel octo dierum... ?—R. Iuxta statuta Synodi Sutchuensis Cap. IX, n. viii, illam longitudinem sufficere, quae perpensis omnibus locorum et rerum adiunctis magnam affert difficultatem."

[35] SO., 11 aug. 1859 (cicf., iv, n. 954; cpf., i, n. 1180); SO., 4 feb. 1891, ad Vic. Ap. Iapon. Merid. (cicf., iv, n. 1130; cpf., ii, n. 1746).

[36] SO., 23 nov. 1769, Chensi et Chansi (cpf., i, n. 475; cicf., iv, n. 825).

[37] SO., 6 aug. 1856 (cpf., i, n. 1130; cicf., iv, n. 939).

[38] SO., 4 feb. 1891 ad Vic. Ap. Iapon. Merid. (cicf., iv, n. 1130; cpf., ii, n. 1746): "Matrimonium vero eius cum quo dispensatum fuerit, etiamsi postea innotuerit coniugem infidelem suam voluntatem iuste impeditum declarare non potuisse, et ad fidem etiam tempore initi matrimonii conversum fuisse, nihilominus numquam rescindi, sed validum esse debebit."; Here again the terms of the decree extend beyond what is contained in the Pauline privilege and indicate a positive act of divorce on the part of the Holy See. cfr. W-Vidal, v, p. 762 (68).

[39] PF., 26 jun. 1820, Sutchuen. (cpf., i, n. 743): "Utrum dilato ex parte fidelis per notabile tempus matrimonio post interpellationem factam, vel post obtentam ab ea dispensationem, nova interpellatio, aut dispensatio nova

silence of the Code does not seem to void this regulation (cfr. c. 1555, § 1).

§ 2. Parties' Obligation of Answering

100. The right to question the parties gives as a corollary the obligation by which parties are bound to answer the questions duly asked. Hence the Code says the parties are bound to acknowledge the truth (c. 1743,§1), and it is plain that, if the judge in a marriage trial ask a party whether he was baptized, whether he has consummated his marriage, the party must give a truthful answer.

Sometimes the decision in a marriage case hinges upon a wrongdoing of one of the parties which may amount to a delict: the party has been guilty of abduction,[40] he has inflicted intimidation and duress, or he has attempted marriage although bound by a solemn vow or by holy orders,[41] or he has been guilty of an adultery or concubinage which together with other circumstances go to invalidate the marriage.[42] He must confess the wrongdoing in the nullity trial. Canon 1743,§1 does indeed state that a party is not obliged to answer when a delict committed by him is at issue, for it means to relieve the accused in criminal trials from incurring punishment by his own confession. But in the marriage trial there is no question of punishment: it is the validity of the marriage that is really at issue; the delict is merely incidental though prejudicial to the main question, and the silence of a party would redound to the continuance of an invalid union. Hence a party is not excused from acknowledging his own wrongdoing in cases that affect the marriage bond.[43]

In cases of separation a guilty party may not, of course, make a false statement to the judge, but he is not obliged to acknowledge his guilt. For the separation sought amounts to a punishment, and he is not bound to acknowledge a crime so as to incur punishment. Hence the judge should in every case, examine whether a party's refusal to answer is justified or not (c. 1743, § 2).

necessaria sit.—R. Negative, quatenus fuerit facta interpellatio; affirmative, post annum, in casu dispensationis obtentae ab initio."

[40] On the exclusion from legal acts, and other punishments that await him, cfr. c. 2353.

[41] On the excommunication and degradation that await him, cfr. c. 2388, § 1.

[42] On the punishment, cfr. cc. 2357, 2359.

[43] The confession made in the course of a marriage trial cannot rightfully be used against the delinquent in a criminal trial (cfr. c. 1738 iunct. c. 20).

101. The wrongful refusal of a party to answer the questions of the judge does not carry with it any consequence predetermined by the Code; it is however left with the judge to determine what shall be made of the refusal, and whether it is to be estimated as the equivalent of a confession against his case (c. 1743,§2). In private contentious cases the judge may be more prone to account the disobedience as a confession; in marriage cases he will act with extreme caution. The Instruction of Cardinal Rauscher declared that the contumacy of a party was not to be construed as an argument against the validity of the marriage.[44] Nevertheless a case may arise where it is proper for the judge to view the party's refusal to answer, considered in all its circumstances, as the equivalent of a confession prejudicial to his case. Thus especially in cases of impotence or non-consummation, the silence of a husband regarding his sexual potentiality, especially when taken in conjunction with the physical inspection or his refusal to allow it, may be viewed as tantamount to an acknowledgment of physical weakness (cfr. n. **281**).

102. In cases of Pauline privilege the ordinary will grant a delay, if the infidel party requests it, during which he may consider his answer to the interpellation, with the admonition however, that after the expiration of the term, his failure to give answer will be presumed to constitute a negative and unsatisfactory response to the interpellation (c. 1122,§1).[45]

103. If a party to the marriage wrongfully refuse to answer the questions of the judge or if he be found to have lied in the answering, the judge may punish him by exclusion for a time, from participating in designated canonical rights (actus legitimi ecclesiastici) (cfr. c. 2256). And if he shall have answered falsely after taking oath to speak the truth, he may be punished by being placed under personal interdict (c. 1743,§3) (cfr. n. **107**).

§ 3. Form and Procedure in Questioning

104. In criminal cases the judge may not place the accused under oath to speak the truth; in ordinary contentious cases he may at his discretion; in cases involving the public good, he must question the parties under oath (iusiurandum de veritate dicenda) (c. 1744). Hence in cases that involve the validity or dissolution of the

[44] IA., § 150.

[45] cfr. Krasa: Keine Antwort auch eine Antwort (lqs., 1924, p. 140).

marriage bond, the oath is administered, whether the trial be by formal judicial procedure,[46] or by the simpler procedure delineated in Canon 1990 fol.[47] In cases of Pauline privilege the converted party generally makes a sworn deposition of his case; it is not the practice however, to require that the infidel party answer the interpellation under oath.

105. In some cases the respondent refuses to take oath on his answers and statements. The judge may then hear him without oath, but a note of the irregularity must be made in the acts.[48] In a prominent case that arose in New York, the respondent refused to swear to her testimony, but touched the bible and stated she would certainly tell the truth about the matter. The auditor caused a note of this to be made in the minutes of the trial.[49] In a more recent case from China the respondent refused to swear to his testimony, because as he stated later, he was intent on opposing the suit, and did not want his conscience burdened with a false oath.[50]

106. The Instruction "Cum Moneat Glossa" required that the party repeat his oath after the testimony is completed. The Code does not mention that the oath must be repeated after the questioning of the parties, but the subsequent Instruction for cases of non-consummation directly mentions and requires it,[51] as it also requires that the interrogated party sign the record of questions and answers.[52]

107. Before administering the oath to a party or witness, the judge should gravely admonish him of the sanctity of the oath, and the grievous crime committed by those who violate their oath; he should make mention of the peculiar gravity of the oath in the marriage matter and of the shameful effects of perjury; and if, in view of the religion and character of the person to be examined, he think it opportune, he may recall the penalty of personal interdict or sus-

[46] DS, Reg., nn. 39, 50, § 1.

[47] Bassibey, n. 44, note; Lega, i, n. 622, I.

[48] DS, Reg., n. 39.

[49] R., Neo-Eboracen., Null., 1 mart. 1913 (rd., v, p. 183; aas., v, p. 321).

[50] R., Ton-Kin Central., Null., 27 jun. 1916 (aas., ix, p. 246; rd., viii, p. 207).

[51] DS, Reg., n. 46; Appendix XX.

[52] DS, Reg., Appendix, XIX.

pension inflicted on perjurors (cfr. c. 1743,§3).[53] But prudence suggests that such methods be not usually employed.[54] It will usually be more effective to admonish a party or witness that a favorable decision from the court only then really clears the way to new nuptials, when it conforms with the objective truth respecting the question of validity, or non-consummation, or death of a former spouse, and consequently false testimony does not really assist the parties. This is not always otherwise understood. In a case at Amiens, a witness remarked that she had been told one might tell a small lie in testimony, in order to wrest a young person from such an embarrassing marriage.[55]

108. During the questioning the advocate may stand by the party. In cases of non-consummation the Congregation has directed that the parties may confer with or confront one another in court, if the judge think it well and there be no danger of quarrel or scandal.[56] In cases of nullity the tendency has been rather to exclude either from being present while the other party is being questioned (cfr. n. **231**).[57] But the Regulations for the Rota expressly allowed the confrontation.[58] The Code is silent on the matter and the judge is free to admit or exclude the adversary. When excluded, however, each party has the right to be informed about the questions asked the other, and the answers he has given (cfr. n. **571-573**), and these must be published together with the other acts of the case.

109. The parties must appear in person before the judge for the taking of oath and the answering of the questions (c. 1746), though in most other matters they may carry on the trial by the agency of their appointed advocates and proctors (c. 1647). The required oath cannot validly be taken by proxy (c. 1316, § 2).

110. Usually the parties must appear in person in the place where court is held. When the parties are persons of such distinction that they are exempted by their civil law from appearing in

[53] DS, Reg., n. 40; Appendix XVIII; Haring, Eheprozess, p. 52 rightly says the judge should not inflict the threatened punishments without the ordinary's concurrence; cfr. DS, Ordin., n. 31.

[54] cfr. DS, Ordin., n. 29, § 2.

[55] R., Ambianen., Null., 3 jan. 1917 (aas., x, p. 379; rd., ix, p. 2).

[56] DS, Reg., nn. 47, § 1; 55, § 3.

[57] Lega, i, n. 451, 5'.

[58] R, Reg., § 146, nn. 3, 4.

court, they may choose the place where they will be heard, but there are no such exemptions in our American civil law. Parties who are ill, infirm, or prevented by circumstances of their life from coming to court will be heard in their homes (c. 1746; cpre. c. 1770,§2,n.2); (cfr. n. 228). If one or both of the parties live outside the diocese, or at a very great distance from the place of court, the hearing may take place by rogatory commission in the court of the diocese where the party resides, or respectively, by delegated auditor at some suitable place within the diocese (cfr. c. 1770,§2,nn.3,4).[59]

111. The most fitting time for questioning the parties is immediately after the joining of the issue; in fact, the joinder of issue is usually so informal in marriage cases that it and the questioning seem to be but one act of procedure. The parties may be questioned at any stage of the trial before the conclusion of the case (c. 1742, § 3). After the conclusion the parties are not generally further questioned, but marriage cases are privileged in this respect, so that a party who has not yet been heard may even then be heard, or one who has been heard may even then be recalled for a second or third questioning (c. 1861).[60] In cases of Pauline privilege the interpellation must be made at a time when the converted party may validly and licitly remarry: *i. e.* after the convert's baptism and before the conversion and baptism of the other party.[61] In rare cases the Holy See grants the permission to interpellate the infidel party even before the baptism of the converted catechumen.[62]

112. The questionary or plan of questions is drawn up partly by the judge, partly by the defender and partly by the litigants. The judge sees to it that a direct examination precedes all cross examination, and to this end he may rightly introduce his own direct questionary before that of the defender or he may interrupt the order of

[59] cfr. PF, 1883, § 15; Smith, n. 522; Canon 1746 stops just short of mentioning this case for it enumerates those persons who are exempted from appearing at any court: the duty of the judge being, in the excepted cases, to visit the party.

[60] DS, Reg., n. 47, § 1; n. 55, §§ 2, 3.

[61] SO., 13 apr. 1859, Tchely Orient. (cpf., i, n. 1175; cicf., iv, n. 951).

[62] SO., 3 jun. 1874 ad Vic. Ap. Sutchuen. Orient. (cpf., ii, n. 1415; cicf., iv, n. 1030); V-Creusen, ii, n. 431: "Factae (interpellationes) ante baptismum, saltem ex dispensatione post baptismum data, renovari non debent, modo de permanente mala infidelis voluntate certo constet."

the defender's questions.[63] But generally the defender prepares the questions both for direct examination and for cross examination,[64] and then the judge has only to make such changes or additions during examination as the state of the case suggests.

The defender has a specially privileged character with respect to the questionary. It is his duty to prepare a questionary in all cases of nullity and non-consummation (c. 1968,n.1), and he will generally present one likewise in other cases, such as presumable death of a spouse, in which he is invited to have part. This questionary is presented closed and sealed, and is opened by the judge in court (c. 1968,n.1).

Besides the questions that are proposed *ex officio,* canonical procedure has long since accorded each party the right to prepare questions in writing (articuli) for the other party to answer, and to make spontaneous depositions (positiones) proposed for the other party to admit or deny.[65] This practice had the effect of rendering the case more readily definable because of the clearer exposition of the issues, narrowing down the field of inquiry and proof (concordance of issues: cfr. n. **74**), and sometimes of bringing about a confession from one party or the other. (cpre. c. 1747,n.3).

113. The practice of a party's stating his position or presenting his articles or questionary was gradually introduced and developed in the ecclesiastical courts from the more formal Roman method of *ex officio* questioning (interrogationes in iure). The Decretals nowhere establish the use of the positions and articles but speak of them as an accepted usage. Thus Clement V writes in the Council of Vienne that the usage should be retained even in trials conducted in simple procedure.[66] The glossators, notably Durantis, and commentators generally, completed the development of a system for the use of such spontaneous statements.[67] In the law of the Decretals

[63] SCC, 1840.

[64] This is presupposed by SCC, 1840 and DS, Reg., n. 50, § 1 stating that the defender's questions are first asked.

[65] R, Reg., § 147 gives formulas: "NN. moves that the judge admit statement of positions and questions, and summon the adversary to respond under oath .... ; (then for the judge) : "NN. has petitioned and obtained that NN. be summoned to the effect mentioned, to appear .... day, ... hour, ... place."

[66] c. 2, De Verborum Significatione, V, 11 in Clem.; cfr. c. 2, De Confessis, II, 9 in VI.

[67] cfr. W-Vidal, vi, n. 426; Hohenlohe, p. 53.

and lately too in the Regulations for the Rota a distinction was made between articles and positions. The articles were headings or questions upon which the opposing party should be interrogated; the positions were short statements of fact (pono quod) proposed that the opponent might agree with or deny the statement (credo vel non credo). But Lega was inclined to neglect the distinction between positions and articles, to identify them and view them as one and the same means of introducing evidence.[68] This idea has found favor in the Code.[69]

The parties may prepare their questionary themselves, or through proctors or advocates,[70] and the judge himself may aid a party in the proper preparing of the articles or questions.[71]

These positions, articles or questions must dwell on points of fact; not on points of law. If they are not conformable to correct procedure, or if they are not sufficient the judge may omit or change them, or supplement them as he sees fit.[72]

114. The plaintiff will be first heard, then the respondent.[73] If both parties unite to petition dispensation from non-consummated marriage, the wife will generally be examined first.[74]

115. The verbal statement of the parties' positions, and the questioning according to articles, as well as the questioning according to official questionary, is done by the judge or his delegated auditor, not by the parties, in accordance with Canons 1773-1781 (c. 1745,§2).[75] Hence in all hearings the adversary or the defender, if they desire to propose questions to the party, will mention them to the judge or auditor that he may ask the questions (c. 1773,§2).

It is not proper for the judge to acquiesce in the interested person's presenting a list of pertinent questions already answered by the plaintiff or respondent and sworn to before a notary public. Even in the less formal mode of procedure the Code requires that the

68 Lega, i, n. 422, 2'.

69 c. 1745, § 1: "articulos . . . quaeque vulgo positiones dicuntur."; SCC, 1840; IA, § 225; cfr. c. 1761, § 1.

70 cfr. R, Reg., § 146; R, Norm., art. 99.

71 PC., 12 mart. 1929 (aas., xxi, p. 170); cfr. R, Norm., art. 19, § 2, c.

72 cfr. R, Reg., § 140, n. 2; Noval, n. 437.

73 SO, 1858, § Primus; PF, 1883, § 17; DS, Reg., n. 50, § 1.

74 DS, Reg., n. 50, § 2.

75 DS, Reg., nn. 41, 50, § 1.

ordinary declare for invalidity only after the parties have been summoned for hearing.[76] If however the judge acquiesce in such extrajudicial questioning and answering this does not invalidate the procedure providing the necessary summons was not wanting; and in a case otherwise proved by document where the respondent will not appear before the court but has answered the pertinent questions extrajudicially and has sworn to them, the judge may, by way of exception, pronounce upon the case, even in the short procedure of Canons 1990-1992.

However in cases that do not require a judicial procedure of any kind it is proper for the ordinary to pass upon the matter in hand without requiring that the parties be judicially examined. Thus when an evidently and flagrantly aggrieved husband or wife seeks ecclesiastical approval of a separation from bed and board (cfr. cc. 1128-1131), the entire matter may be properly transacted through the agency of the parish priest, and without questioning the parties in court. Similarly when a Catholic or apostate who has attempted marriage without observing the form prescribed for validity (cfr. c. 1094) seeks to enter upon a new marriage with another person, the ordinary may rightly receive the party's statement, sworn to extrajudicially, *v. g.* before a notary public or Catholic pastor, that he has not validated the attempted marriage by later appearing before the proper priest and witnesses, and that he has not caused the marriage to be validated by correction at the root (sanatio in radice).[77]

In cases of Pauline privilege the interpellation should ordinarily be made with at least summary and extrajudicial formality, under the authority of the ordinary of the converted party (c. 1122,§1). This is frequently done by appointing the missionary priest as auditor for the bishop. But privately made interpellation is valid, and if the above mentioned formality cannot be observed, it is also licit (c. 1122,§2). Yet even when made by private authority, it is preferable that not the converted person, but another *v. g.* the missionary priest interpellate the infidel, lest the convert, inquiring for his own interest, incline to deceive himself.[78] The interpellation is valid however, even if the converted party alone interpellate the other, and it

[76] c. 1990: "citatis partibus"; cfr. PC., 16 jun. 1931 (aas., xxiii, p. 354).

[77] PC., 16 oct. 1919 (aas., xi, p. 479).

[78] SO, 1824; De Smet, i, n. 350.

is licit if the formal questioning cannot be done (c. 1122,§2). Interpellation by letter is not excluded.[79]

For the external forum it is required that there be proof of the interpellation having been made, and of the answer unfavorable to the Faith having been given (c. 1122,§2). When the interpellation is made by public authority, the written record of the procedure will constitute the usual proof (cfr. n. **355**);[80] when the interpellation is privately made the proof should consist in the testimony of two reliable witnesses, or of a letter proved to be genuine, but in an extreme case the oath of the converted person, when supported by the proper presumption, may be sufficient. The pastor or missionary must not admit the converted person to a new marriage without being certain of the interpellation and answers.[81] The validity of a subsequent marriage is not however dependent upon proving that the interpellation was made, but rather upon the actual state of the infidel's purposes as disclosed by the questioning and the answers.

116. The judge or auditor carefully asks and requires the answer to each separate question and the notary writes the questions and answers in the record. When a party has completed his depositions they are reread to him and an opportunity is given him of adding or suppressing, changing or correcting the record of his testimony (c. 1780,§1).[82] The questioning of the party is carried on, with due allowances, just as the questioning of witnesses (cfr. nn. **227** fol).

§ 4. Object of Questioning

117. The parties are first asked general questions: the party's full name and the names of the parents, the birthplace, age, religion, domicile (city, street and parish), and the place of present dwelling, situation or occupation. The plaintiff will then be asked on what score he brings his suit or petition, he will be asked to narrate all the pertinent events, to say whether he learned these from personal experience or from hearsay, and to state what witnesses or other proofs he may have for his contention.[83] Some of these matters will already

[79] Nau, n. 142.

[80] cfr. SO, 1824, Resp. ad 1.

[81] Gasp., ii, n. 1337.

[82] R, Reg., § 144; DS, Reg., Append. xix, n. 26.

[83] PF, 1883, § 17.

have been covered in the plaint, and this may be read to the party for reassertion or discussion, instead of asking each question over again. From the answers given it will be possible to know what more pertinent questions shall be asked, what form the specific questioning shall take, and how to go about the inquiry into other proofs.

118. There can be no ironclad list of specific questions: the party's role in the trial as plaintiff or respondent, the nature of the suit, the impediment or other ground which lies at the base of the plaint and the peculiar circumstances of each case will give the cue on the specific questions. However the judge may be guided by questions suggested in various instructions that come from the Roman Curia. In cases of impotence and non-consummation the following, or some of the following questions will be pertinent:

1. Does the party fulfil his religious obligations?

2. Does the party confirm or not, the plaint or petition in all its parts?

3. When and how did the petitioner learn that a non-consummated marriage might be dissolved by dispensation of the Roman Pontiff?

4. Did the petitioner have the counsel and aid of anyone in proposing this case and in drawing up the petition? Whose?

5. How long did the parties know one another before marriage?

6. When did they propose marriage, and how long was the engagement pending?

7. Did they marry with the consent of their parents and from mutual love?

8. Were the banns proclaimed?

9. Where was the marriage celebrated? Who was present? What celebration and ceremony was there?

10. An prima nocte eodem cubiculo et toro usi fuerint, officiisque coniugalibus ultro libenterque operam dederint? An matrimonium consummaverint?

11. Si non consummaverint, an postea ad consummandum conatus adhibuerint? Quoties? Quomodo? Et quonam exitu?

12. An oratrix coniugali operi navando dolorem aliquando experta fuerit?

13. An ei persuasum sit virum copulam perfecisse integre iuxta naturae legem?

14. An istius vestigia exterius, ut solitum est, reperta fuerint?

15. An ipse examinatus cognoscat vel suspicetur causas propter quas consummare nequiverint, licet iteratis vicibus etiam in sequentibut noctibus id conati fuerint? (Lack of consent? Duress? Aversion? Impotence?).

16. An id contigerit ob nimiam angustiam cunei mulieris? Vel ob immodicam sui penis crassitudinem? Aut propter debilitatem, ita ut nulla aut parvi momenti fuerit erectio?

17. (If the non-consummation is attributed to the infirmity of either party): Was either party ever infirm? And what was the nature of the infirmity?

18. What physicians did he consult? What remedies did he use? How long did he use them? And with what results?

19. Has the party any testimony of these physicians, or other documents pertaining to the matter?

20. How long did the parties live together? How long did they use the same sleeping chamber and bed?

21. Which party first deserted the other? What was the occasion or cause of it?

22. Was the marriage registered with or performed by civil authorities? When?

23. Did the parties institute civil proceedings? For separation or divorce? When?

24. Who was plaintiff?

25. On what basis was the suit instituted? With what results?

26. Did the parties relate their marriage difficulties either openly or secretly to their parents, relations, friends or neighbors?

27. To whom and when did they speak of the non-consummation or impotence? (names and residences)

28. What are the causes for petitioning dispensation? Are these causes still valid?

29. Does the petitioner know whether the other party consents to the present petition or not? Whence does he know that the other will consent or oppose?

30. What are the names, domiciles (city, street, diocese, parish), present residence of witnesses (seven) who can swear to the honesty of the petitioner, and especially to his truthfulness in the present matter?

31. (Especially if one party is contumacious or will surely spurn the case) What witnesses, related to that party, could testify in the matter?

32. Has the party any writings or documents, public or private, pertinent to the matter?

33. (If suit has been instituted in civil court) Can he furnish authentic copy of the procedure and decision of the civil judge?

34. Was there a physical inspection of either party in the civil trial? Has the party the written record of the expert's report? What matters pertaining to the inspection will illumine the case?

35. Does the party think the wife is still physically intact? Is she prepared to submit to corporal inspection by two woman obstetricians or two physicians?

36. (If she is not intact) By what means and when did the deflowering occur? Can the wife produce a physician who has already inspected her and who, absolved from the secrecy of his office, can testify to the condition of the wife after the definite separation from her husband? [84]

119. In cases of Pauline privilege the infidel spouse must be asked:

1. Whether he wants to be converted and receive baptism?

2. Whether he will peaceably live with the converted party and without contumely to the Creator (c. 1121,§1)?

The Congregation of Propaganda was asked whether the second question is necessary to the liceity and validity of the dissolution of the marriage, but, without referring to the question of validity, responded only that the second part of the interpellation must be observed.[85] In another case arising from the same vicariate it was asked whether the interpellation which omitted the first question but received a negative response to the second, was sufficient for the licit and valid contracting of a new marriage. The Congregation answered that the parties were not to be disquieted.[86]

[84] SO, 1858; PF, 1883, § 46; DS, Reg., nn. 42, 51, 52, 54, 56, § 1, 57, Append. xix, xxiv; cfr. DS, Norm, n. 4, §§ 3,4.

[85] PF., 5 mart. 1816, Tunkin Occident., ad 2 (cpf., i, n. 704); cfr. c. 1121, § 2.

[86] PF., 21 jul. 1841, Tunkin Occident. (cpf., i, n. 929): "Titia infidelis a suo marito infideli repudiata, et postea christiana facta, Paulo christiano nubere vult. Sacerdos illi praecipit interpellationem de iure suo marito infideli facere; sed illa sic tantum illum interpellavit: 'Visne ut ad te redeam ? seu visne me iterum ut tuam uxorem habere et recipere ?' Cui ille: 'Non, i quo volueris.' Statim Titia rediit ut cum Paulo nubat. Quaero an illud licite et valide possit sine nova interpellatione, et sine ulla ab ea dispensatione; an interpellatio a Titia facta modo supra relato valida et sufficiens sit ad matrimonium valide

In cases of dissolution of merely legitimate marriage in favor of the Faith, the petitioner must be asked at what time and with what attitude of mind (sincerity) he was induced to receive baptism.

120. In trials on the nullity of infidel marriages in which it is claimed that there was no consent to real marriage, but that the woman had been received merely as a concubine, the Holy Office has directed that the man be asked what proofs he has for his assertion; that he then be confronted with the conjectures which seem to establish the contrary, such as the nobility of the woman which makes it unlikely that she would be received as a mere concubine; or that in receiving her he had dismissed his concubines; or that he had even after his baptism consented to live peaceably with her, though he knew the Christian religion tolerates no concubines; or that he never contradicted her assertions that she was his true wife; or that she was received as his legitimate wife among his relatives and neighbors.[87]

121. Sometimes the parties' depositions are made according to a prearranged and fraudulent understanding between them:[88] this is called collusion. Evidently it is the part of the judge to scrutinize the testimony lest such collusion pass unnoticed.[89]

There is an indication of collusion: 1) When two parties of uncertain character jointly petition for declaration of nullity or dispensation from non-consummated marriage.[90] On the other hand when both parties stoutly uphold the validity of the marriage against action brought by the promoter of justice, their testimonies or confessions favoring nullity more easily escape the suspicion of collusion.[91]

2) When two parties who have hated each other for a long time, suddenly renew friendly relations at the prospect of a decision favorable to nullity.[92]

et licite contrahendum cum christiano.—R. Attentis locorum et temporum circumstantiis, non esse inquietandos, et rem arbitrio et prudentiae Vicarii Ap. remitti."

[87] SO, 1872.

[88] as Ben. XIV complained in Dei Mis., § 3.

[89] c. 5, X, De Eo Qui Cognovit, IV, 13; PF, 1883, §§ 19, 39.

[90] DS, Reg., n. 50, § 3.

[91] Smith, n. 483.

[92] cfr. R., Null., 7 feb. 1914 (rd., vi, p. 60).

3) When the parties attempt to keep members of their families from testifying in the case. In a case from France a certain Count R. testified that his son had upbraided him for "demanding to be heard and thus retarding the solution of the case," while the daughter-in-law had besought the father not to testify against the case. The Rota inferred thence that the parties had colluded.[93]

4) When one party has recently received a large sum of money from the other or his relatives, although the parties have been long separated. In a recent case the husband John M. had demanded and received 4,000 francs for abetting the civil divorce procedure, and the Rota inferred from this the likelihood of collusion in the trial on nullity that followed.[94]

5) When the depositions of the parties are in such perfect accord that the slightest details are spontaneously recounted alike by each party, or the identical language is used by both to express their testimonies (cfr. n. **270**).

122. Sometimes the depositions of the two parties are marked by discrepancies. If these are but slight and pertain to minor details rather than to the heart of the matter, it is an indication that there has been no collusion and the more pertinent testimony is rather strengthened than weakened (cfr. nn. **271-274**).

It is prescribed for cases of non-consummation that when numerous and notable discrepancies envelop the depositions of the parties, new questions be proposed *ex officio* or on the motion of the defender, with a view to composing the doubt or difficulty, and the parties, when reëxamined, may be told of each other's contradicting testimonies or not, according as the prudence of the judge shall dictate, under the circumstances present in the case.[95]

123. The Code provides for the questioning of the parties in a rubric (titulus IX) that just precedes the chapters on proofs. Evidently it is the mind of the Code that the questioning of the parties should clear the way for the proofs and aid the judge in discovering where the proper proofs may be found, and make it plain how he shall go about the questioning of the witnesses; for neither the introductory bill nor the joining of the issue which precede the ques-

[93] R., Null., 23 mai, 1912 (rd., iv, pp. 259, 260).

[94] R., Null., 10 dec. 1914 (rd., vi, pp. 342, 344).

[95] DS, Reg., n. 55, §§ 1, 3.

tioning, have necessarily exposed the circumstances of the suit in their entirety.[96]

The depositions of the parties however, are not testimonies in a strict sense, and the parties, though questioned, are not formally witnesses: at least not in criminal cases and civil contentious cases, for the parties are described as incapable of being witnesses (c. 1757, §3,n.1). At first sight the Code seems to make an exception for marriage cases and others that determine the civil or religious condition of a person for Canon 1757,§3,n.3 expressly admits the otherwise prohibited relatives as capable witnesses in such cases, if the facts cannot be otherwise evidenced; and taking this Canon in its grammatical sense alone, the exception might pertain as well to the spouses as to the relatives subsequently mentioned in the same Canon. But Canon 1757,§3,n.3 must be interpreted in unison with other parts of the Code: now Canon 1974 repeats that in marriage cases the other relatives mentioned in Canon 1757,§3,n.3 are habile witnesses, but is entirely silent about the husband and wife, and Canon 1757,§3,n.1 states that all those who are parties to the case are incapable of being witnesses. Hence the husband and wife are not formally witnesses in the suit on their marriage.[97]

Nevertheless the Rota uses the words "testis, testatur" in describing the statements of the parties,[98] and, in a case at Paris, quoted the husband's deposition along with the testimonies of other witnesses.[99] [100]

When the depositions of the parties are considered in the quality of a confession (cfr. Ch. VII) or when they are taken in conjunction with the oath which is generally obligatory in marriage cases (cfr. Ch. XIII) they may beget valid proof.

[96] W-Vidal, vi, n. 417.

[97] Eichmann, p. 215.

[98] R., Sueciae, Null., 19 aug. 1914 (rd., vi, p. 309; aas., vii, p. 53); Null., 9 apr., 1921 (rd., xiii, p. 74).

[99] R., Parisien., Null., 5 mai, 1914 (rd., vi, p. 200; aas., vi, p. 393).

[100] In civil law on divorce: Abbott, p. 951 (5): "A husband is forbidden to testify to material facts tending to establish the charge of adultery alleged by him in his complaint to have been committed by his wife."

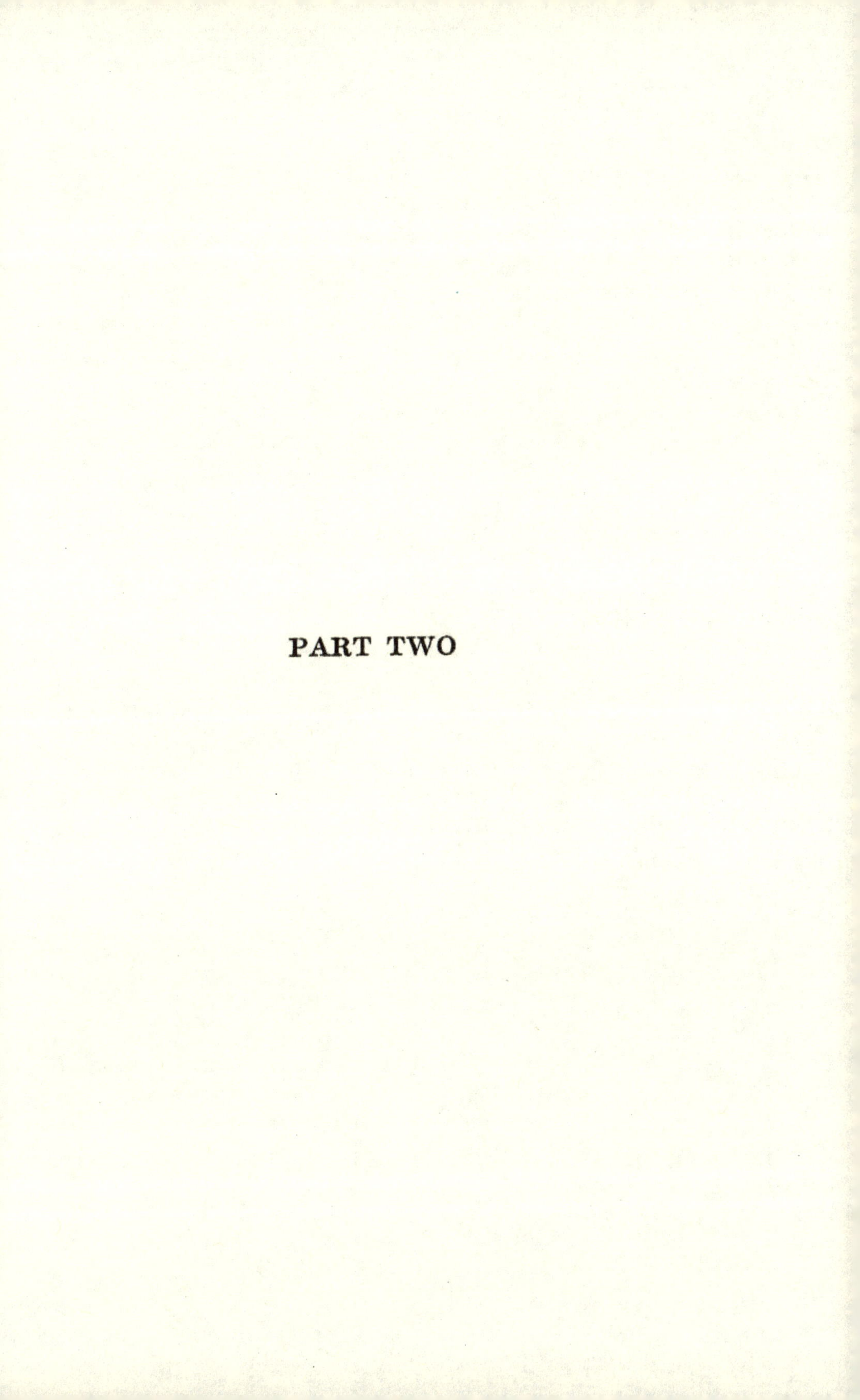

PART TWO

CHAPTER VI

Preliminary Idea on Proofs

"...multas et graves causas objicientes, quas non poterant probare."—Act., xxv, 7.

§ 1. Definition and Kinds and Theory of Proof

124. In a general way proof (probatio) is anything that serves to convince the mind, or collectively taken, proof is the sum total of the moment or argument by which a person is convinced of the truth. But Mascardus has given a definition more precisely suited to the judicial sense: Proof is a making plain to the judge by argument, of what has been until now doubtful or controverted, or: proof is a judicial act wherein a party to the suit, by arguments canonically proposed, begets moral certainty in the mind of the judge that the party's contention is true (probatio legitima; cfr. cc. 214,§1; 1069, § 2). This definition covers all the forms of proof unqualifiedly acknowledged as proof in the Decretals, and is even now pertinent to describe the judicial confessions and oaths of the parties. But judicial notice whereby the mind of the judge is won through the direct perspicuity of the truth, and presumptions which are a form of proof issuing from the law and the mind of the judge, manifestly cannot be described as judicial acts of the parties, and hence fall only under the more general definition. Sometimes proofs are considered in their effect, rather than in their cause, and then the word is used to describe the conviction, assurance or certainty that is begotten in the mind by the arguments proposed, and in this sense the judge is said to have proof of a case, and to be prepared to give his decision.

125. Proofs differ from one another in various respects:

I. By reason of the method of argument, proofs are ranged into the confession of parties, testimony of witnesses, inspection by experts, judicial notice, exhibition of documents, presumptions, and oaths of the parties. All these are discussed in detail in the following chapters.

126. What methods of proof were used in marriage cases during the earliest centuries we have no direct means of knowing, for there are but few early traces of ecclesiastical cognizance of marriage suits.[1]

[1] cfr. Noval, n. 833; Chelodi, n. 171.

It seems natural and proper to conclude that in the provinces where Roman law held sway, the early fathers judged of marriages according to the norms of evidence traditional in civil courts. Although these norms of Roman law were, as is well known, the most perfectly moulded in all the world at that time, they were not without their injustices, and the ecclesiastical courts did not at once escape the imperfections of their teacher. Thus Gratian still insisted on the terms of the law of Severus and Antonine, to the disparagement of a wife's right of action in cases of adultery,[2] and even Alexander III insisted on the traditional norm that the husband's testimony was preferable to that of the wife in cases of impotence.[3]

In the Germanic dominions, and in some others, local ecclesiastics followed, to an extent, the Germanic modes of proof, and in some places, cases of nullity of marriage were settled according to the artificial ordeals of the times. Thus Theutberga proved her innocence in her marriage dispute with King Lothar, by submitting, through one of her servants, to the test of hot water (cfr. also n. **570**). The influence of Roman law gradually introduced by the intercourse between the bishops and the Holy See, and the lustre of the Catholic Faith slowly ameliorated the barbarous customs and later abrogated what was inherently wrong. In 867 Pope Nicholas I prohibited the duell proferred by Lothar in his matrimonial tangle. The ordeals by fire and water were also discountenanced at a little later period,[4] and the purgation by oath and the cross-ordeal were urged, temporarily, in their place. Gradually even these gave way to more rational methods, while better institutions of the Germanic law, such as the use of character and opinion witnesses were refined and improved by the dictates of faith, reason and experience.[5] Thus the better elements of the Roman and Germanic processual law were slowly woven into a canonical texture, and the Church has, on her part, added new and distinctive methods of proof such as the physical inspection by experts.[6]

[2] c. 10, C. XXXII, q. 1.

[3] c. 6, X, De Desponsatione Impuberum, IV, 2; c. 3, C. XXXIII, q. 1; cfr. n. **570**.

[4] c. 8, X, De Purgatione Canonica, V, 34; c. 1-3, X, De Purgatione Vulgari. V, 35.

[5] c. 2, C. XXXIII, q. 1; c. 5, 7, X, De Frigidis et Meleficiatis et Impotentia Coeundi, IV, 15; c. 5, 7, 8, 9, 13, X, De Purgatione Canonica, V, 34; cfr. Kirsch.

[6] cfr. Eichmann, pp. 20, 21.

127. Even the surpassing norms of canonical procedure have had their vicissitudes however, and some methods of canonical proof formerly in use, have now been swept away. Thus the three year experiment (experiment triennale) is now abandoned as a formal means of proof. This procedure was formerly required in cases of impotence: the Emperor Justinian permitted by L. 10, De Repudiis, V, 17 that women might repudiate impotent husbands, without loss of dowry, if, during two years directly following upon the marriage, the unnatural impotence of the husband was made manifest by experiment; but later in 536 A. D. he extended the period of trial to three years in Novell. 22, cap. 6.[7]

During this three year term it was expected that the parties would ascertain whether the apparent frigidity and impotence could be overcome, and whether it was perpetual, and, in the Roman dominions at least, the plaintiff had to await the conclusion of this term. Celestine III prescribed the triennial experiment as of ancient standing in the Canon and civil law, and Honorius III again insisted on it.[8] The corporal inspection and expert testimony together with the character witnesses were rarely,[9] but not usually considered sufficient proof for pronouncement of nullity without the experiment.

The three year experiment was in usage until the beginning of the last century and has never been explicitly withdrawn. It gradually fell into desuetude however, and was insisted upon in the Roman Curia for the last time in a case of nullity of marriage at Forli, Italy, 20 Sept. 1817,[10] and is mentioned in another case of 23 Feb. 1850 as not requisite for the pronouncement of nullity.[11] More recent instructions on procedure in impotence cases leave it unnoticed,[12] and the Code makes no mention of it; thus it is clearly abrogated (cfr. c. 6,n.6).

128. Without ascribing to them special headings under Title X, De Probationibus, the Code makes passing mention of methods of

[7] W-Vidal, v, p. 248 (19).

[8] c. 5, 7, X, De Frig. et Mal. et Impot. Coeundi, IV, 15.

[9] cfr. c. 5, X, De Frig. et Mal. et Impot. Coeundi, IV, 15; cfr. cases recorded by Pallotini, xiii, § XIII, nn. 200-314.

[10] Gasparri, ii, n. 1499; Chelodi, n. 75.

[11] Pallotini, xiii, n. 80; Hence IA, § 175, still requiring it, was evidently prescribing an obsolete practice.

[12] cfr. W-Vidal, v, n. 223.

proof with which former jurisprudence has made us conversant: thus, conjecture (coniecturae: cc. 1023,§2; 1286; 1825,§1); accessory circumstances (adiuncta: cc. 1753, 1830,§§1,5; 1942,§2); indications (indicium: cc. 1757,§3; 1758; 1907,§2; 1946,§2,n.2); reason for belief (argumentum credibilitatis: c. 1975,§2; cfr. also cc. 973,§3; 1286; 1801,§3; 1804,§2; 1833,§2; 1942,§1; 2068,§2; 2106,n.2; 2148,§2); support to proof (adminicula: cc. 1758; 1790; 1975,§2) (adiumenta: c. 1829); repute (fama: cc. 1789,n.2; 1939,§1; 2020, §6; 2030; 2147,§§2,3).

129. II. By reason of their formality, proofs are either judicial (probatio judicialis), or extrajudicial (p. extrajudicialis). Judicial proof is that which is formally brought to the judge acting in his capacity as judge, *i. e.* during trial. Extrajudicial proof is that which is argued outside of trial. Only judicial proofs are valid for the purpose of judicial decision, but extrajudicial proofs may be reduced to judicial form by presenting them during trial according to the approved norms. Thus when a witness has given testimony before a notary, for future memorial of a thing, the record of such testimony becomes judicial proof through being received, examined, and approved by the judge.

130. III. By reason of the form of presentation, proofs are either written or oral, and the words are self-explanatory. There is no intrinsic reason why judicial decisions cannot be given on merely oral proof, without making any written record of them. Indeed, the early history of all peoples gives examples of trials thus held. But Innocent III decreed in the fourth Lateran Council, that all proofs and procedure must be written down by a notary, and from that time on, the courts have kept a written record of oral proofs, although they did not construe the rule of Innocent as forbidding the judge to be guided also by oral information privately imparted to him (cfr. n. **601**). Canon 1642,§1, has restated the rule that oral proofs must be reduced to writing.

131. IV. According to the time when the argument is wrought, proofs are ranged into preëstablished proofs (p. praeconstituta), which exist before trial begins, such as documents drawn up to certify an act, or testimony given for future memorial of a thing, and proofs that are to be established during litigation (p. constituenda), such as judicial confession, testimony, judicial notice.

132. V. By reason of their relationship with the matter at issue, proofs are either direct (p. directa), or indirect (p. indirecta). The direct proofs tend of themselves to establish or subvert the principal fact at issue, as *e. g.*, proof by witnesses that a person inflicted violence; the indirect proofs tend of themselves to establish or subvert some other fact, which forms the basis or ground of the principal issue, and thus indirectly prove the principal issue, as *e. g.*, when witnesses testify to a pagan upbringing as a proof of non-baptism (cfr. nn. **161-163**). In this sense too, the Code speaks of overcoming a presumption by indirect proof, *i. e.* through the subversion of a fact which is the basis of the presumption (c. 1826) (cfr. nn. **394, 395**). But the terms "direct proof" and "indirect proof" are also used in another sense:

133. VI. By reason of the directness or indirectness with which the argument tends to establish any specific fact, proofs are either natural and direct (p. naturalis, p. directa) or artificial and indirect (p. artificialis, p. indirecta). Natural proofs have a direct bearing upon the specific fact to be proved, whether it is the principal matter at issue or some other fact; artificial proofs establish the pertinent fact only by indirection or deduction. Authors are not unanimous in defining artificial and indirect proof, but there is general agreement that presumptions are of this category.[13] The Germanic ordeals were likewise artificial proofs. The natural proofs are usually presented by the parties to the suit, although judicial notice is a natural proof in which the judge seeks the argument for himself; artificial proofs are created by a disposition of the law, or by the discreet leanings of the judge's mind.

134. VII. By far the most important distinction is that which ranges proofs according to their cogency and effects, into complete, plenary or full proofs (p. plena, p. omnino plena, p. plenissima), and incomplete, semi-plenary or partial proofs (p. semiplena). As the words indicate, the full proofs fully evince the matter in question and completely win the mind of the judge, while partial proofs only partially evince the matter and, though they incline the mind of the judge, they do not fully win it to the truth of the contention.

135. The concept of full proof derives from the power of the arguments to overwhelmingly win the mind of the judge, under the given circumstances. It is possible that arguments be brought in

[13] W-Vidal, vi, n. 433; Roberti, ii, n. 324.

favor of both sides of a contention (probatio et reprobatio), which, if they could be separately considered without regard for each other, would be appraised on either side as bearing full proof. But when these are considered in view of the adversary's arguments, one or the other party fails to beget full proof, because his contention no longer wins the mind of the judge. It is not infrequent that witnesses are produced for both sides of a marriage suit, sufficient in number and apparently of such quality that, considered separately, they would constitute full proof for the contrary contentions. Thus witnesses swore on both sides of a consanguinity dispute, that the parties were and were not related within the diriment degree, but Clement III found one set of witnesses sufficiently cogent to be able to decide against the other.[14] Numerous cases of the Rota are marked with a similar contrariety in the parties' arguments. Precisely because of this experience, the Code provides for the contingency where conformative, unimpeachable, sworn witnesses may fail to beget full proof until their contention be augmented by more complete proofs (p. pleniores: c. 1791,§2). On the other hand it is not impossible that the argument which would ordinarily attain to only partial proof, may in a concrete instance, by virtue of peculiar circumstances and the presumptions arising from the characters of the persons concerned, convince the judge and thus amount to full proof.[15] This must be kept in mind when one reads in authentic decisions or the authors, that in some exceptional cases lighter or easier proofs (p. leviores) are sufficient.[16] For the exception stated for these cases, if it be not more apparent than real, pertains to the allowability of accepting in the prime quality of proof, such evidence as is usually admitted only as a support to other proofs, *e. g.* confession of a party, and it by no means indicates that these cases can be favorably decided short of full proof, *i. e.* proof that completely wins the mind of the judge to moral cer-

[14] c. 6, X, De Probationibus, II, 19.

[15] cfr. R., Null., 10 feb. 1912 (rd., iv, pp. 87, 88); Lega, i, n. 422: "Siquidem unum argumentum nihil vel parum probans in certa causa, in alia, ob mutata rerum adiuncta, plenissime aliquando probat.—Adest, ex adverso, periculum, ne iudicis animus retrahatur a vero, nempe a genuina factorum consideratione per has regulas nimis absolute a canonistis enunciatas, legum auctoritate et factorum enarratione firmatas. Quandoquidem iudex, in singula facti specie, debet peculiaria rerum adiuncta pensare ad sinceram rei notitiam hauriendam, quae sane non scatet ab examine et observatione alicuius regulae universalis."

[16] cfr. *e. g.* R., decis. 326 coram Ludovisio (gasp., nov., ii, n. 858; rd., xi, p. 97).

tainty (cfr. c. 1869,§2). And although by the Decretal of Pope Clement V,[17] and later instructions, marriage cases were accorded summary procedure, the abridgement pertained to the solemnities of trial only, and by no means to the proofs.[18]

136. The proper concept of incomplete or partial proof is not gained by setting up arithmetical computation, as though the partial or semi-plenary proof were one half (semiplena) of a complete proof, and the sum of two half proofs would make a full proof. Some few canonists have indeed been misled into such erroneous precision, but there is no text of the Decretals, nor any papal decree that ever speaks of an arithmetical precision in the proofs.[19] The Code follows its sources in avoiding a categorical gradation and arithmetical measurement of proofs. It speaks of that which is simply canonical proof (cc. 1122,§2; 1454; 1816) also of full proofs (cc. 1791,§1; 1835,n.3) and peremptory proof (c. 1905,§2,n.2), of proofs by all means complete (c. 2019) and proofs that are sufficient (cc. 658,§2; 1791,§2), but allows also that more adequate proofs may be demanded (cc. 1791,§2; 1810). It mentions proofs that relieve a party from further burden (cc. 1751; 1827), so as to require pronouncement in his favor. It makes mention also of partial or semi-plenary proof (c. 1829), and acknowledges some of these as more complete than others (c. 1830,§4). It speaks of a support or prop to the proofs (cc. 1758; 1790; 1829; 1975,§2), an indication of where the truth lies (cc. 1757,§3; 1758), and an argument derived from belief (c. 1975,§2).

There have been some jurists who denied the concept of partial proof and contended that if an argument does not completely prove it is no proof at all. But the canonists, have generally held to the distinction and rightly defended it.[20] The distinction is not only made in passing by the old and new texts of Canon law, but has been constantly urged for practice by implication; for the Decretals prescribe that a supplementary oath may be taken, but not when there is complete proof,[21] nor when there is no proof at all: evidently then,

[17] c. 2, De Iudiciis, II, 1 in Clem.

[18] Noval, n. 833.

[19] cfr. *v. g.*, c. 4, X, De in Integrum Restitutione, I, 41; c. 6, X, De Frig. et Mal. et Imp. Coeundi, IV, 15; c. 1, De Probationibus, II, 7 in Clem.; S. Pius V, const. "Intolerabilis," 1 jun. 1569, §§ 4, 6 (cicf., i, n. 130).

[20] W-Vidal, vi, p. 375 (5).

[21] c. 2, X, De Prob. II, 19.

when there is partial or incomplete proof, such as the Canons recognize in the deposition of one non-qualified witness, in private documents and in repute.

137. Because of their varying degrees of cogency, full and partial proofs are distinguished also in their effects. The chief effect of full proof is that it obliges the judge to give his decision according to it.[22] Thus when the plaintiff in a nullity case has fully proved that there is no true marriage, the decision must pronounce the marriage to be plainly invalid; if he fails to bring full proof, the presumption for validity proves the adversary's contention that nullity is not demonstrated and the decision must be given accordingly.

The effects of partial proof are: 1) That it opens the way, within the limits of c. 1830 (cfr. n. **543**), for supplementary oath; when thus supplemented the proof hitherto insufficient for a favorable judgement is made full proof.

2) That in cases which accrue to no one's prejudice, there is sufficient basis for granting what the petitioner asks. Thus the curia may properly permit the celebration of a marriage, when a party brings partial proof of free status, providing the marriage does not redound to the prejudice of another marriage known to have been already contracted (cfr. n. **544**).

3) That it is sufficient cause for insisting on official inquest. Thus if it is proved only partially that there is an impediment standing against a proposed marriage, especially when it is an impediment of divine origin, this is sufficient to stay the marriage, at least until further inquest shall have elucidated the matter, and in some cases permanently.[23]

138. VIII. Some proofs are peremptory (p. peremptoria, p. decretoria) *i. e.* they necessarily effect full proof in advance (p. probata), others do not necessarily effect full proof (p. probanda).

139. From the foregoing it is easily seen that a just and correct appraisal of proofs is of the utmost importance. Theoretically there are two distinct methods of proof appraisal: the purely legal method (systema legale; probatio per legem), and the method of free appraisal (systema morale, intimae persuasionis, liberae aestimationis). In

[22] W-Vidal, vi, n. 440 enumerate other effects which however are rather to be put down as further explanations of what is meant by full proof.

[23] cfr. c. 22, X, De Testibus et Attestationibus, II, 20; R., Null., 23 mart. 1915 (rd., vii, p. 124); cfr. cc. 1031,§1,n.3; 1039,§1; 1076,§3.

the purely legal system of appraisal the law establishes what efficacy the various arguments shall have, and allows no discretion to the judge. In the system of free appraisal, it is left entirely to the prudence or behest of the judge to make of the proofs what he will, and the law in no way limits the use of his discretion. Practically, the laws of civilized countries nowadays admit a mixed use of both legal valuation and judicial discretion, but the ordeals of ancient Germanic law afford a striking example of the purely legal system, while the early Roman law and the jury system of English and American law go far toward allowing the entirely free appraisal.

The pre-Code legislation in its leading sources of proof, inclined rather to the legal system than to the other.[24] The Decretals gave an efficacious and conclusive value to such proofs as the depositions of two witnesses,[25] and public documents.[26] The system of free appraisal was not however entirely lost to sight; Roberti, ii, n. 328 indeed asserts its preponderance over the other; especially in marriage cases was it incumbent upon the judge to evaluate for himself such proofs as the confession and the oath of parties, and the reports of experts. The Code has followed the same general trend, seeking on the one hand to free the judge from the strictures of a purely legal system, and on the other to avoid an unguided and faulty appraisal on his part. Hence the present canonical system of appraisal is a mixed system, which provides that the judge must give a proper estimation to arguments as *v. g.*, judicial confession (c. 1751), public documents (c. 1816) and legal presumptions (c. 1827), whose objective worth is beyond question, but on the other hand which also provides that he be generally free to appraise proofs according to his conscience and intimate sense of conviction. (c. 1869,§3; cfr. cc. 1824,§2; 1831,§2; 1836,§3).

§ 2. Burden of Proof

140. The business of bringing proof for one's contention has been looked upon in the old Germanic law from a different viewpoint than that taken by the Roman law. The Germanic law regarded the marriage state as a beneficial position, and when a doubt was cast upon one's position in marriage, especially when there was question

[24] cfr. S. C. EE. RR., 11 jun. 1880, § 16 (cpf., ii, n. 1534; cicf., iv, n. 2005); Noval., n. 441.

[25] c. 27, 28, X, De Test et Attest., II, 20.

[26] c. 1, 2, X, De Fide Instrumentorum, II, 22; c. 2, X, De Prob., II, 19.

of impotence, considered it a privilege for the accused party that he be allowed to prove the marriage valid, and thus the opportunity of bringing proof of validity was offered him and he was forced to accept it.[27] This view of the matter held in some early German ecclesiastical courts, but could not long withstand the logical force of the Roman view, which looked upon contracts as valid until the invalidity was proved, and thus placed the burden of proof upon him who would contest the marriage.

Following the Roman law [28] then, the Corpus generally held and now the Code constantly defines that the burden of proof lies with him who asserts (c. 1748,§1) ; to this effect, that if he does not prove his case, the one against whom he asserts is relieved of peril in the matter (c. 1748,§2). In nullity cases, the plaintiff must demonstrate that the marriage is invalid. If he does not win the judge to his view, the status of the marriage continues to be viewed as valid. In cases of non-consummation the petitioner must prove that things are intact; if he fails in this, the Holy See will not grant the divorcing dispensation. If a person give notice to the pastor or ordinary that a marriage about to be performed is obstructed by an impediment, the pastor or ordinary may order a reasonable delay in the marriage (cc. 1031,§1; 1039,§1) that such plaintiff may produce proofs, but cannot permanently hinder the marriage without any proof having been brought against it.[29]

141. Although he who denies need not, by the general norm, prove his negation, the plaintiff has the burden of proving his case in its entirety, and this includes the demonstration of positive facts and of negative facts that form an integral part of the ground of his contention. Thus if a person contest his marriage on the score of disparity of cult, he must prove not only the baptism or conversion of one spouse (cfr. c. 1070,§1), but also the non-baptism of the other. If he contest the marriage for want of proper form, claiming

[27] Freisen, pp. 355, 356.

[28] L. 2, ff. D. de Probat.: "semper onus probandi ei incumbit, qui dicit."

[29] SCC., In Signina, 23 feb. 1606 (pall., xiii, 465, n. 12); In Trivicana, 21 apr. 1708 (pall., xiii, 36, n. 68); R., Impedimenti ad Contrahendum, 11 mart. 1910 (rd., ii, p. 99): "Quare ut matrimonium Alfidii cum Petedia possit et debeat inhiberi, eos inhabiles esse ad contrahendum debet probari. Quod factum retinetur si, quod accusatur, impedimentum consanguinitatis in primo gradu lineae rectae, iuridice probetur saltem dubium existere."; Impedimenti ad Matrimonium et Damnorum, 31 aug. 1912 (rd., iv, p. 432).

that the properly registered witnesses were not really present at the celebration of the marriage, he must show that they were not. The burden of proof in no sense constrains the adversary to show that, besides being registered as present, they were actually present.[80]

142. In some cases the contention is based on a negation in law (negativum iuris), wherein it is denied that a thing has been done according to law. Thus in a case of nullity by reason of legal adoption, the interested person might prove that the adoption did not fulfil the legal standards which beget a diriment impediment before the civil and Canon law (cfr. c. 1080). But if the thing or act whose legality or validity is denied belongs to the class of things in general forbidden, *v. g.* clandestine marriage, the burden of proof devolves upon him who asserts legality or validity in a particular case (cfr. nn. **425, 509**).

In other cases the contention is based on a negation of quality (n. qualitatis),[81] wherein it is denied that a person possesses some quality. Thus if a plaintiff deny that his spouse is endowed with potency to fulfil the marital relations, he must prove the impotence. For the law presumes the presence of qualities generally bestowed by nature or commonly possessed (cfr. nn. **463, 466, 525**). If a plaintiff contest the marriage for want of proper form, claiming that the priest did not have the proper authority or delegation to perform the ceremony he must prove his denial.[82] For priests who perform weddings commonly possess the power, and are presumed to have secured the necessary delegation beforehand (cfr. nn. **376, 415**).

In other cases again the contention is based on a negation pregnant with fact (n. praegnans), wherein an affirmation is implicitly contained. Thus if a plaintiff contend that he did not contract his marriage with free will, he implicitly affirms duress and must prove it.

[80] R., Ugentina, Null., 22 mart. 1910 (rd., ii, p. 125): "Quare a recto tramite aberravit sententia Curiae Ugentinae declarans quod matrimonium praesens 'debba ritenersi nullo pel fatto che non si può provare la presenza dei testimonii Viva e Fracasso, segnati nel registro parrocchiale.' In praesenti enim causa minime probanda est praesentia duorum testium V. et F.; sed probandum potius est . . . vel duo testes non adfuisse . . . vel non rite adfuisse."

[81] This term must not be confounded with the similar term 'restricted' or 'qualified negative' (negativum qualificatum); cfr. n. **161**.

[82] R., Mediolanen., Null., 23 feb. 1910 (rd., ii, p. 62): "Sed placet concordia Mascardi, conclus. 984, ubi . . . n. 3 resolvit: 'si contra licentiam opponatur a tertio, ipsi incumbere probare: si vero a proprio parocho, transferri onus probandi in alienum sacerdotem et ipsos contrahentes."

143. Authors generally have stated the principle now given in Canons 1747 and 1827 that, when the plaintiff holds a position favored by law because of the legal presumption that militates for his contention, he is relieved of the burden of proof; for in this case the presumption speaks for him, and constitutes an advance proof of his contention. Evidently this is no exception to the general rule on the burden of proof, but a confirmation of it: if the presumption be urged in the plaintiff's favor, it is the respondent's part to refute the applicability of the presumption and prove his case, or sustain an adverse decision.[33] Thus when a Catholic has clandestinely contracted marriage without observing the ecclesiastical form, he need prove only that it was so contracted and was not afterward validated in form. If the adversary believe that the marriage was nevertheless valid, *v. g.* under the terms of Canon 1098, the burden of proof rests upon him.[34]

144. The burden of proof is shifted during trial when the respondent by his exception becomes plaintiff (quando reus excipiendo fit actor) (cfr. n. **72**). This occurs when the respondent's exception is not negative, but positive in character: chiefly in the action called reconvention (reconventio). Thus a plaintiff sues for separation because of his wife's adultery; she reconvenes and accuses him of adultery or of having caused or connived at or forgiven her adultery (cfr. cc. 1129,§1; 2218,§3): the burden of proof for this part of the suit rests upon the wife who has thus become plaintiff.[35]

Some marriage cases contain of themselves an implicit reconvention to the plaintiff's suit. Thus if a plaintiff seek to have his marriage declared void, on the ground that his spouse had been married before, and that the previous husband was still living at the time the plaintiff contracted the marriage in question, he need prove only that

[33] Lega, i, n. 444: "Proinde non videtur admittenda illorum sententia qui respondent quaestioni: cuinam onus probandi incumbat, per hoc principium; nempe illi inhaerere onus probandi, contra quem ius praesumit; ita cl. Santi, h. t., n. 8. Siquidem verum est hoc principium; sed aliud supponit altius; scilicet "semper onus probandi ei incumbit, qui dicit" L. 2 ff. De probat..."

[34] R., Null., 28 mai. 1909 (rd., i, pp. 51, 52); Lega, iv, n. 448: "Sed etiam quoad alia loca (i. e. ubi Caput Tametsi promulgatum non erat et nunc ubi forma Decreti "Ne Temere" non ad validitatem requiritur) impedimentum impediens clandestinitatis attenditur quoad effectum iuridicum stabiliendae posessionis"; cfr. Bassibey, n. 326.

[35] Eichmann, p. 137 gives an untenable example, because it involves a double reconvention. cfr. c. 1690, § 2.

the marriage was duly entered upon and that that previous husband was then still alive.[36] If the defender or respondent holds that the former marriage was invalid, the burden of proof is shifted to him: the present plaintiff need not prove the validity of that former marriage. Similarly if a marriage was contracted under duress, but the defender or respondent holds that the invalid marriage was afterward validated by coition undertaken with marital intent, he has the burden of proving the later validation.[37] But, if an impediment that is commonly dispensed is to be proved against a marriage contracted in Catholic form, the plaintiff must prove that no dispensation was granted.[38]

145. A party is relieved of the proving of such facts as are notorious according to the norm of Canon 2197,nn.2,3 (c. 1747).

Two kinds of notoriety are there given: juridical notoriety (notorium notorietate iuris) and factual notoriety (n. n. facti). An impediment or crime is marked by juridical notoriety: 1) When it has been declared by a competent judge, and the case has become unassailably adjudged (res iudicata; r. effectum habens iudicatae). Thus if the ecclesiastical courts have duly declared a marriage invalid, the invalidity need not again be proved, if the question of validity should arise prejudicially to a subsequent trial. For the acquirement of juridical notoriety it is not necessary that the judicial decision accrue from an ecclesiastical court: if the civil court give final decision on a matter in which it is competent, *v. g.* the adultery of a spouse in criminal procedure, there is at once juridical notoriety applicable to the ecclesiastical court.[39] Thus in cases of separation the ecclesiastical court may make use of the findings of the civil court.[40]

2) When it has been confessed by the delinquent party in court, according to the norm of Canon 1750. (cfr. nn. **175-181, 564**).

An impediment or crime is marked by factual notoriety if it is publicly known and has arisen under such circumstances, that it can

[36] cfr. PF, 1883, § 45 on exception in case of infidels later converted.

[37] R., Southwarcen., Null., 29 jul. 1926 (aas., xviii, p. 505); hence Cerato, p. 151 quoting Oietti, seems to have overstated the case when he says: "Passus metum debet metum probare; . . . Praeterea probari debet, metum per ratihabitionem non fuisse purgatum:"; similarly Linneborn, pp. 292, 293.

[38] cfr. c. 1990; PC, 16 jun. 1931 (aas., xxiii, pp. 353, 354); Bassibey, n. 459.

[39] cfr. c. 27, X, De Test. et Attest., II, 20; Chelodi, Ius Poenale, n. 4.

[40] Linneborn, p. 425.

be concealed by no artifice, and (in so far as criminal procedure is concerned) can be excused by no indulgence of the law. Factual notoriety is extremely rare and can hardly ever relieve one of the burden of proving facts that are of a transitory nature, *v. g.* a single act of adultery.[41] If the notorious fact is of a permanent nature, *v. g.* continuous cohabitation and concubinage, the party may be relieved of the burden of proof.[42]

Notoriety does not excuse one from proving a case unless the fact be notorious to the judge. In the case of juridical notoriety it is sufficient to show the judge the sentence of the court whereby a fact in question has achieved notoriety. In the case of factual notoriety the proof of notoriety is offered by witnesses (n. 188),[43] or judicial notice.[44] A Chinese priest testified in a nullity suit that it was notorious in Onang-Ting that the wife had never had any (sexual) relation with her spouse.[45]

When the impediment of age is notorious no further proof is required for dissolution of a marriage contracted with this impediment. But it is erroneous to suppose that non-age is usually notorious in these cases; on the contrary, there are numerous examples of child marriages where the precocious life and appearance of the party

[41] Reiffenstuel, lib. II, tit. xix, § 2, n. 37 sq: "istud notorium (facti) intelligendum est praecipue de notorio facti permanentis, nam satis est hoc allegari nec indiget alia probatione . . . Secus est dicendum de notorio facti transeuntis; nam, quia multa dicuntur notoria quae non sunt talia . . . " (ex c. 14, X, De Appellat, II, 28).

[42] cfr. c. 3, X, De Eo Qui Cognovit, IV, 13; R., Null. Mat., 31 mart. 1909 (rd., i, p. 25): "Licet difficilis probationis sit impedimentum affinitatis ex copula illicita, attamen docemur ex cap. 3, De eo qui cognovit consanguineam, illud sufficienter probatum haberi quando 'publicum et notorium fuerit, aut idoneis testibus comprobatum'"; R., Null., 23 mart. 1915 (rd., vii, p. 124); Hence Smith, n. 617 seems to overestimate the case when he says: "Consequently the law of the Church does not consider notoriety of itself a sufficiently full, complete and perfect proof of the invalidity of a marriage already contracted"; cfr. c. 1078; Hilling, Studien zum Eherecht (akk., 1922, p. 7); Wenz-Vidal, v, n. 580.

[43] Pallotini, xiii, 489, § XXVII, n. 92: "Unde ante omnia Iudex curare debet, ut sibi constet de notorio; non quia notorium probari oporteat, sed quod necessarium sit probare, illud notorie factum fuisse-. Quod ut probetur, ait, duo vel tres Testes requiruntur et sufficiunt."; compare c. 646, § 2.

[44] W.-Vidal, vi, n. 712.

[45] R., Vic. Apost. Ce-Li Central., Null., 10 feb. 1917 (rd., ix, p. 28; aas., ix, p. 507).

under canonical age deceived the civil authorities into unlawful issuance of a marriage license.[46]

§ 3. Object of Proof

146. The plaintiff proves his case by citing the law as contained in the Code or other authentic sources, particularly the Acta Apostolicae Sedis (cfr. cc. 9: 1819), and showing that the facts measure up to the terms of the law. He need not prove the law: at least not the general written law ("praetor enim novit iura"). When the law of custom comes into question, it may be necessary to prove that the custom amounts to law. Thus in decisions on cases of disparity of cult, arising before the Code came into force, the Rota has always been careful to show that what was originally a mere injunction against mixed marriages had been extended by long-standing custom to the measure of a diriment impediment.[47] But as impediments can no longer be established by custom (c. 1041), nullity cases need not now be thus proved, at least not in respect to the principal question.

Some marriage cases that come before the ecclesiastical judge, hinge upon the civil law and then it may be necessary for the plaintiff to cite and prove the civil law in question. For the ecclesiastical judge is not presumed to be acquainted with the civil laws. Thus in cases involving the diriment impediment of legal relationship from adoption, the law of that nation or state in which the marriage was contracted, will control the case (c. 1080).[48] Similarly too in cases where a marriage contracted in infidelity, seems to be invalid by an impediment established by the civil law.[49]

147. Facts are the proper object of proof: facts which are doubtful and controverted, and touch upon the issue. Hence evident, notorious, confessed, presumed facts are not generally proved, beyond the point of showing that they are evident, notorious, *etc.* Irrelevant facts protract the suit and distract from the true issue, and hence the judge must curb the party who would bring proof of them.

[46] Richmond-Hall, p. 128 fol.

[47] cfr. R., Parisien., Null., 13 jun. 1911 (rd., iii, p. 259). Similarly in pre-Code cases of dementia.

[48] cfr. Tiffany, pp. 48, 49.

[49] De Smet, i, n. 437: "Attamen, cum ex una parte sententia supra proposita non sit undequaque certa, cum etiam ex alia parte non facile constet de vi irritiva impedimentorum in variis legislationibus conditorum, non foret judicium proferendum absque praevio recursu ad S. Sedem."

What precise facts are relevant and require proof in a given case, must derive from the specific nature of the plaint or petition. Some practical points are subjoined respecting the specific objects of proof, in the more frequently occurring marriage suits.

148. Before a marriage is celebrated, it must be made plain that nothing stands in the way of celebrating it lawfully and validly (c. 1019,§1). Hence the parties must make clear that they are free to marry one another *i. e.* that there is no impediment. The proofs of freedom to marry were in former years much more stringently required than at present. Decrees of the Holy Office issued first for the universal Church by command of Clement X,[50] and later stressed for Oriental bishops,[51] demanded the hearing of witnesses in all cases, but this procedure had fallen into desuetude,[52] is not mentioned by the Code, and is not now required.[53] In its place there is a questioning of the parties by the pastor (c. 1020,§§1,2), a presentation of baptismal certificates (c. 1021,§1) which must be of recent issue [54] and must make reference to whatever marriage annotations are given in the record (c. 470,§2), and the announcement of the banns. (cc. 1022-1030; 1031,§3). In case a doubt arises whether there is an impediment, sworn witnesses will be called, unless there is question of an impediment which would redound to the loss of a party's reputation (c. 1031,§1,n.1), and if there be necessity for it the parties will be questioned under oath (c. 1031,§1,n.1.). But special local or diocesan regulations may require more formal procedure (cfr. c. 1023,§2).

149. After marriage the validity of the bond may be contested under various headings by reason of a diriment impediment (cfr. cc. 1067-1080) or of a defect of consent (cfr. cc. 1081-1093), or of a defect of form (cfr. cc. 1094-1103), and other actions or petitions may be instituted to secure separation from bed and board, dispensation from ratified non-consummated marriage, *etc.* In most of these cases the object of proof is almost coterminal with the suit or petition and is at first sight plain.

150. In cases of nullity by reason of defect of form the plaintiff must prove in addition to the informality of the marriage, that at

[50] SO, 1670.

[51] SO., 22 aug. 1890 (cicf., iv, n. 1128; cpf., ii, n. 1740).

[52] Gasparri, i, n. 172.

[53] R., Damnorum, 26 jul. 1913 (rd., v, p. 471, fol.); Chelodi, p. 19 (1).

[54] R., Damnorum, 26 jul. 1913 (rd., v, p. 471, fol.).

least one party to the marriage was bound to marry in canonical form (cfr. n. **426**). This is comparatively easy for a Catholic of Latin rite who was married between 19 April 1908 ("Ne Temere") and 18 May 1918. For he need only show that he had been baptized in the Catholic Church (cfr. nn. **371, 495**) or duly converted to it previous to his marriage. But for one married on or after 19 May 1918 (Code) it is not enough to show that he was baptized Catholic in infancy: he must further show that both his parents were Catholics, or in case at least one parent was not, that he himself had been brought up or instructed as a Catholic at some time after the age of reason was attained.[55]

151. The manifest consent of the parties constitutes marriage and no human power can supplant this consent (c. 1081, § 1). Among the oldest and most frequent headings under which parties have sought to contest their marriage is fictitious or simulated consent. A case of the kind was brought to Innocent III, wherein the plaintiff contended that he had given but fictitious consent to the clandestine marriage, for he had used the words "John hereby marries thee" whereas his name was not John, but he pretended it was John, in order, as he claimed, not to commit himself to a true marriage. Innocent answered that the fictitious name did not prove fictitious consent, which would have to be otherwise demonstrated, and he, the Pope, did not see how this could be demonstrated; if it were, the marriage was to be declared null.[56] Hence it is plain that non-consent is not proved by showing that one of the parties contracted under an assumed name (cfr. n. **470**).[57]

The proving of fictitious consent is among the most difficult nullity cases, because consent depends upon an act of the will which of itself is entirely internal, and because it is possible for the contractual parties to change their will at any moment without giving the least exterior sign of it. Hence the evidence of fictitious will must derive from circumstances, antecedent, concomitant and subsequent to the marriage contract, that cannot be reconciled with the giving of true consent, and from which there derives the logical and reasonable pre-

[55] cfr. c. 1099,§2; PC., 20 jul. 1929 (aas., xxi, p. 573); 17 feb. 1930 (aas., xxii, p. 195); 25 jul. 1931 (aas., xxiii, p. 388).

[56] c. 26, X, De Sponsalibus et Matrimonio, IV, 1.

[57] R., Null., 29 feb. 1916 (rd., viii, p. 56).

sumption of non-consent.[68] Such circumstances are *v. g.* reluctance to answer the questions of the officiating priest, flight after marriage, the refusal to enter upon marital relations, *etc.* (cfr. nn. **452, 561, 562**).

The circumstance of primary importance which must in every case be demonstrated, is the specific and sufficient reason (causa) for withholding the genuine and substituting the simulated consent.[59] Evidently the plaintiff does not allege a sufficiently specific reason by saying that he did not want to contract the marriage. The reason for simulating must be grave and proportionate, due attention being given to the natural character of the simulating person.[60] It need not however be shown that the reason for simulating be true, relevant or actual, providing it was thought so by the person simulating,[61] nor that the reason be honorable in purpose. The following reasons for simulation have been alleged in cases recently tried by the Rota: duress, even though it be insufficient of itself to cause invalidity under the terms of Canon 1087,§1,[62] the preservation of one's good reputation,[63] and social advantage derivable from fictitious marriage.[64]

The Rota warns against confounding the causes of simulation with the causes or motives of marriage, for the latter, even though they be less worthy motives, when accompanied by true marital consent, give occasion to valid marriage. Thus frequently brides seek marriage to gain independence from parental control, economic security, *etc.* This does not denote simulation.[65]

[58] Pellegrini, in jp., x (1930), p. 59: "Ceterum res est plane rationi consentanea. Ea quae ad veram intentionem internam pertinent, quae corde latent, quae mente concipiuntur, homines plerumque tuba non canunt; sunt ergo natura sua coniecturalia, quia nonnisi ex indiciis dignoscuntur quae per rerum circumstantias frequenter eveniunt. Sed novimus ex regula iuris quod probatio sequitur naturam actionis. Ex coniecturis igitur et adminiculis colligenda est probatio, si materia actionis sit coniecturalis. Alioquin perperam prorsus iudices adirentur..."; cfr. also ime., lxiii (1931), p. 76.

[59] R., Massilien., Null., 1 jul. 1911 (rd., iii, p. 326); Null., 9 jul. 1911 (rd., iii, p. 241); Null., 18 jul. 1911 (rd., iii, p. 349); Null., 13 dec. 1912 (rd., iv, p. 462); Parisien., 10 mart. 1920 (rd., xii, p. 48).

[60] R., Oregonop., Null., 6 jul. 1914 (rd., vi, p. 245; aas., vi, p. 517).

[61] R., Null., 9 jul. 1911 (rd., iii, p. 241); Null., 8 mart. 1913 (rd., v, p. 211).

[62] R., Null., 8 mart. 1913 (rd., v, p. 211); Null., 16 mart. 1920 (rd., xii, p. 70).

[63] R., Null., 18 jul. 1911 (rd., iii, p. 349).

[64] R., Vicariat. Apost. Sueciae, Null., 19 aug. 1914 (rd., vi, p. 311; aas., vii, p. 55).

[65] R., Null., 18 jul. 1923 (rd., xv, p. 167).

152. When it is claimed that the consent of a party was restricted to exclude the primary object and end (ipsum ius) or one or more of the essential properties (cfr. c. 1013), the three blessings or benefits of marriage (bona matrimonii), unity, indissolubility or progeny, it must be proved, not only that there was such a restricted consent, but that the restriction was an act of the will rather than an error of the intellect, that it excluded all right and obligation to these benefits of marriage, and not merely that it intended to violate the obligation assumed. These cases are among the most difficult to prove and will require from all persons concerned an intensive study on the substantive law on the question.

As with all cases of vitiated consent, it is doubly hard to establish nullity of the marriage, unless there is an acknowledgment or confession of non-consent on the part of the simulating party (cfr. n. 561).

153. Some marriages are contracted under a stipulation restricting the consent (conditio sine qua non; c. in pactum deducta). Such stipulations have respect either to a past or present fact or to a future event. A party can marry, though illicitly, with a stipulation respecting a past or present fact, *v. g.* that the other party have not had, or, be not suffering from a sexual disease. In that case the marriage is valid and effective from the beginning if the stipulation has been fulfilled or respectively, is being fulfilled, at the time of the marriage; otherwise it is invalid (c. 1092,n.4; cfr. c. 104). Stipulations pending future event can be affixed to the marriage in two ways: 1) publicly, *i. e.* when it is done with the permission of the ordinary, or when it is publicly affixed to the marriage contract in the act of entering upon that contract; 2) privately, as when no permission has been obtained to contract conditional marriage, and the stipulation is not mentioned in the act of entering upon the marriage contract, but the parties quietly and almost secretly attach a stipulation whose existence is known to, at most, only a few persons. Such a stipulation privately attached may be none the less public in the sense that it can be proved in the external forum (cfr. c. 1037). In both cases the stipulation pending future event holds off the effect of the marriage ceremony performed, until the stipulation is fulfilled, or the stipulating party or parties renounce its fulfillment (c. 1092, n. 3). But if the stipulation pending future event is directed against the substance of marriage or against an essential property of marriage, the fulfillment or non-fulfillment of the stipulation does not matter, for the marriage is then invalid by the mere affixing of the stipulation (c. 1092, n. 2).

In nullity cases where it is claimed that a restricted, conditional or stipulated consent was given, the invalidating intent must be demonstrated. This is more easily done when the restriction or stipulation is publicly made, which is very seldom. More often the parties or one of them claims after marriage that a stipulation had been privately, quietly, perhaps secretly appended to his marital consent. He must prove the fact and must further show that the consensual restriction was not merely an interpretative intention or representation (modus, causa, demonstratio) [66] but rather a true stipulation. Furthermore it must be proved that this stipulation was not withdrawn before marriage: this is governed by presumption unless contrary facts overthrow the presumption (cfr. nn. **474, 476**). Finally it must be proved that the stipulation remained unfulfilled,[67] except in the case of a stipulation against the substance or benefits of marriage, when the fulfillment or non-fulfillment does not matter. But it need not be shown that the other party consented to the stipulation, or even knew of it, provided one party's intent is shown to have been directed against the substance or benefits of marriage, thus precluding true marital consent.

154. A marriage is invalid when entered upon under grave duress, *i. e.* force or fear (vis vel metus) unjustly inflicted by another, under such circumstances that the person oppressed is obliged to choose marriage in order to free himself from the compulsion (c. 1087,§1). If it is claimed that the marital consent has been vitiated by such duress, the duress must be demonstrated; to this end sufficient proof is not offered when witnesses testify generically that the party was under duress; [68] the proofs must establish specific acts of duress inflicted upon the party.[69] These acts must be such as would gravely

[66] cfr. W-Vidal, v, n. 519.

[67] Gasparri, nov., ii, n. 917: "...partes de verificata conditione moneant parochum, qui id notare debet in libro matrimoniorum."

[68] R., Parisien., Null., 4 nov. 1915 (rd., vii, p. 446; aas., viii, p. 159); Lugdunen., Null., 5 jun. 1917 (rd., ix, p. 134; aas., x, p. 165); Paderbornen., Null., 27 jul. 1917 (rd., ix, p. 163; aas., x, p. 217).

[69] R., Colonien., Null., 1 jul. 1912 (rd., iv, p. 331; aas., iv, p. 672); Null., 4 jul. 1913 (rd., v, p. 425); Avenionen., Null., 6, 14, 24 jul. 1914 (rd., vi, p. 271; aas., vi, p. 677).

affect and oppress the person in question.[70] In case of absolute duress inflicted upon a man, such proportionate oppression consists in severe bodily maltreatment, threat of death or severe injury or imprisonment (cfr. n. **482**). In cases of the so-called qualified reverential fear and duress, confinement to quarters, blows, threats of banishment from home or disinheritance or suicide of the threatening mother or father, and insistence so importunate that it leaves no rest for the oppressed person, constitute the usual acts of compulsion.[71] It must be shown too that the oppressed person used whatever means were in his power to overcome the oppression.[72] But it need not be shown that the party under duress was constantly depressed in spirits.[73]

155. Marriage is rendered invalid by the impediment of existing marriage bond (ligamen). But converted infidels are not bound by this impediment when they use the Pauline privilege. In order that they be allowed to marry Catholics under this privilege, it must be evident that both parties to the former marriage had been unbaptized; secondly that the one who is about to marry has now been converted by valid baptism; thirdly that the other has not been thus converted, and fourthly that this other will not be converted now, nor live in peace with the converted party (cfr. nn. **94-99**).

Except for this case of Pauline privilege, an invalid attempt at marriage is made by him who is held by the bond of a former marriage, even though it was not consummated (c. 1069,§1). And although the former marriage be dissolved or void by any reason, it is not allowed to contract another, before the nullity or dissolution of the first is certainly and in the duly canonical way proved (c. 1069, §2).[74]

If a person make the claim that his former marriage is dissolved by the death of his spouse, he must prove that the death has occurred,

[70] R., Avenionen., Null., 6, 14, 24 jul. 1914 (rd., vi, p. 271; aas., vi, 677); Null., 7 mart. 1922 (rd., xiv, p. 52).

[71] cfr. R., Parisien., Null., 12 jun. 1919 (rd., xi, p. 100); Vicar. Apost. Insularum Gilbertin., Null., 1 jun. 1921 (rd., xiii, p. 129); Rheginen., Null., 27 oct. 1923 (rd., xv, p. 251).

[72] R., Parisien., Null., 21 mai. 1915 (rd., vii, p. 237; aas., viii, p. 46).

[73] R., Pitilianen., Null., 20 oct. 1916 (rd., viii, p. 332; aas., ix, p. 361): "Addendum deinde est in metus probatione non requiri ut in omnibus omnino actionibus sponsi se tristes et coactos ostendant."; Terraconen., Null., 15 feb. 1919 (aas., xi, p. 432; rd., xi, p. 14).

[74] On the irregularity, infamy, interdict, excommunication that await bigamists, cfr. cc. 985, n. 3; 2356.

and identify the person of the deceased with that of his spouse. The usual legal proof is by document, *i. e.* certificate of death issued by the proper ecclesiastical, civil, military or naval authorities, together with certificate of marriage (cfr. nn. **351**, **377**). When no such proof can be had, witnesses who saw the spouse die, or who saw him lying dead, are admitted (cfr. nn. **260**, **262**, **268**, **565**). In case there are not even witnesses of death, sufficient proof may be obtained by establishing a base of facts which give a legitimate personal presumption that death has overtaken the spouse (cfr. nn. **489-494**). To this end it is not sufficient to show that he has departed or absconded and has not been heard of for a great length of time.

The Church courts have always maintained the rule that a new marriage is not permissible until there is moral certainty of the dissolution of the first marriage. The texts of law which inculcate the carrying out of this rule are not however all of one tenor, and even in the Decretals we have the seemingly contradictory Canons of Clement III demanding a "certum nuntium de morte virorum",[75] and of Innocent III admitting the declaration of death on a presumptive basis.[76]

A more accurate regulation of these cases was given in the Instructions of the Holy Office of 1868, 1870, 1871, 1883.[77] But after the battle of Adua, the Holy Office on 20 July 1898 gave an even broader interpretation to the practice, and permitted ordinaries to allow the remarriage of war widows, on the general presumption of death, providing it were certainly established that their absconded husbands had taken part in that battle and had not been heard of since then.[78] The same response was given later in respect to those who were lost in the Russian-Japanese war.[79] These declarations, says W-Vidal, did not supply for want of certainty "quod iure divino requiritur" but rather indicate that moral certainty was already at hand.[80] And rightly, for the extent of catastrophe that accrued from

[75] c. 19, X, De Spons. et Mat., IV, 1.

[76] c. 5, X, Ut Lite non Contestata, II, 6: "§ 4. Si autem de carnali coniugio sit agendum, tamdiu alteruter coniugum expectetur, donec de ipsius obitu verisimiliter praesumatur... eo nequaquam obstante, quod de lapsu carnis possit opponi,..."; cfr. c. 2, X, De Secundis Nuptiis, IV, 21.

[77] cpf., i, nn. 192, 196; ii, nn. 1321, 1587, 1588. Concilii Balt. Plen. II Acta et Decreta gives the text of another Instructio SO., 12 jun. 1822.

[78] cfr. DS., Massanen. seu Rheginen., 12 mart. 1910 (aas., ii, p. 196 fol.).

[79] DS., Mohilovien., 16 dec. 1910 (aas., iii, p. 26).

[80] W-Vidal, v, p. 294 (52).

those battlefields gave the groundwork for a "valid presumption" even though, with respect to each individual, the case was not above all doubt. But it is remarkable that the Congregation explicitly states that the circumstances of these war-widows having entered upon new and illicit amours was to be taken into consideration.[81] This last appendage, says Schlenz, shows that the Roman Curia, in allowing remarriage, also takes cognizance of circumstances which are in themselves no proof of the death of the absconded person, but which in doubtful cases offer "causae impulsivae" of the desired permission, in view of the fact that the permission for remarriage occasions only material sin in case the absconded person is not really dead, while the refusal of permission occasions formal gave sin, namely the continuance of the concubinage in either case.[82] But diocesan curiae must beware lest they give decisions on this principle save after recourse to the Apostolic See. In fact, the cases arising out of the catastrophe of Messina were not settled on the same general presumption, in spite of the same widespread concubinage; for the absence of spouses could here be accounted for as well by the dispersion as by the death of families. The Congregation declared that cases were to be settled individually according to the norm of SO, 1868.[83]

156. For a just reason, and generally in favor of Catholics only, (cfr. however, n. **29**), the Apostolic See can and does grant a dispensation from the impediment of an already existing marriage bond, and at the same time dissolves the marriage, if it was merely ratified between baptized persons, but not consummated by marital coition (matrimonium ratum non-consummatum) (cfr. c. 1015,§1), or if, between infidels or between an infidel and a baptized non-Catholic, it remained merely valid and legitimate (matrimonium legitimum) (cfr.

[81] DS., Massanen., seu Rheginen., 12 mart. 1910 (aas., ii, p. 198): "'Dummodo agatur de viris, qui certo adstiterint pugnae de Adua et peractis opportunis investigationibus, indubitanter dignosci nequeat, an vir reapse mortuus ceciderit, attentis specialibus circumstantiis in casu exposito occurrentibus, et valida praesumptione obitus, Ordinarius permittere poterit transitum ad alias nuptias.' Ex quo apparet opportunas investigationes esse prius faciendas et quatenus hae evadunt sine effectu, perpendendae sunt speciales casus circumstantiae una simul cum valida mortis praesumptione. Et inter circumstantias perpensas in citata responsione S. O. erant accensendi illiciti amores viduarum ad nuptias convolare cupientium."

[82] Schlenz, in akk., 1924, p. 221; cfr. akk., 1924, p. 207 (1).

[83] DS., Massanen., seu Rheginen., 12 mart. 1910 (aas., ii, p. 199).

c. 1015,§3), even though consummated (c. 1119).[84] A marriage contracted between infidels, or between an infidel and a baptized non-Catholic can also be dissolved, even if both parties become converted and baptized, provided the marriage has not been consummated since it was sacramentally ratified by the subsequent baptism, or respectively, baptized condition of both parties.

Hence, if a marriage was ratified at the time of contract, the petitioner must prove that the marriage has never been consummated since it was contracted. The proof of non-consummation is effected by establishing a continuous alibi (casus coarctatus), or by expert inspection and testimony, or finally, by the depositions of the parties together with the character witnesses. The continuous alibi is intended to demonstrate that from the time of the marriage ceremony, the parties have never been together in such privacy that they could have consummated the marriage by coition. Proof of such alibi requires witnesses who can testify to the parties' whereabouts from the time of the marriage celebration down to the time of trial. In the diocese of X. a young man was induced to marry at her bedside, the child-bearing girl whom he had presumably impregnated. Immediately afterward he left the house never again to see his bride. The non-consummation of the marriage was established by witnesses proving the continuous alibi, and dispensation was granted.[85]

If the marriage was sacramentally ratified after being contracted, the petitioner must prove that the marriage was not consummated after it was thus ratified. The establishment of the continuous alibi of the parties since the time of ratification will be the ordinary proof; and in this case the alibi may be established either by witnesses, or by documentary evidence that a civil divorce had been granted previous to the sacramental ratification of the marriage, together with the supplementary oath of the petitioner or both parties, that they had not subsequently consummated the now ratified marriage, and together with the proper character witnesses (cfr. n. **189**).

[84] The Code does not expressly state that the legitimate marriage of an infidel and a baptized non-Catholic may be dissolved even though consummated (cfr. c. 1119; cfr. Const. Gregorii PP. XIII "Populis" 25 jan. 1585 (cicd., viii)), but this is a case where we rightly interpret the will of the Legislator (cfr. c. 18), from the actual practice of the Holy See (cfr. nn. **510, 511**).

[85] DS., 9 mai. 1923 (protocol. 1796/21) (unpublished); cfr. DeSmet, i, p. 305 (3) for other cases.

Usually the petitioner must prove that he has been baptized in the Catholic Church or converted to it from heresy or schism and is now a Catholic.

In cases where the marriage was never sacramentally ratified, even though one party has been baptized, proof of non-consummation is not required. But in these cases it must usually be proved that the petitioner has been baptized in the Catholic Church or converted to it from heresy or schism, and is now a Catholic. Secondly it must be proved that the other party was never baptized. Thirdly, that the marriage was not performed by reason of a dispensation granted from disparity of cult (cfr. c. 1120,§2).

In any of these above named cases the petitioner must also prove that there is a just reason for granting the dispensation. At one time the Holy See granted dispensation from non-consummated marriage for reasons of public interest only: the mere private interests of the parties were not accounted a sufficient reason.[86] But the present policy is to grant the dispensation by reason of the private interest of the parties and in special consideration of the present-day requirements for spiritual welfare. Hence in cases of impotence, non-consent, duress, the issue is now frequently joined at the Roman Rota in such a way that even though nullity cannot be proved, dispensation will be granted, provided the marriage was not consummated.[87] The Holy See granted the dispensation in a recent case at X., in which no other reason was alleged than the absolute incompatibility of the parties.[88] But the reason alleged must be true or the dispensation is invalid.[89] In cases of dispensation from merely legitimate marriage the incompatibility of the parties is likewise sufficient reason, and this

[86] cfr. Augustine, v, p. 346 (20).

[87] cfr. SCC., Romana seu Tibertina, Null. seu Disp. Mat., 12 mart. 1853 (pall., xiii, 117, § XIII, nn. 334, 335); R., Null., 16 mai. 1914 (rd., vi, p. 216); Null. vel Disp. Mat., 27 apr. 1915 (rd., vii, p. 213); Null., 25 mart. 1920 (rd., xii, p. 77); Null., 3 aug. 1921 (rd., xiii, p. 197): "Causam hanc adesse testatur Curia et recte. Primo enim licet dubitari de matrimonii validitate, attenta satis probabili viri impotentia, ... Sed insuper Susanna summopere desiderat fieri matrem ... Immo, quod peius est, expers non esset incontinentiae periculo.... Quibus accedit animorum aversio."

[88] De Smet, i, n. 330: "Caeterum eo ipso quod instantia in dissolutionem inducitur a conjugibus, vel alterutro eorum, passim merito jam supponitur causam adesse gravem, adeo ut practice non sit timenda precum repulsio ex solo capite deficientis causae proportionatae."

[89] DS., Reg., n. 103; cfr. cc. 40-42; 45.

is all the more taken into consideration, in view of the conversion of one or both parties to the true Faith (cfr. nn. **416**, **417**, **510-512**).

The just reason for granting the dissolution is not present if 1) the petitioner has, after his baptism, given the other party grave cause for separation; or if 2) the prospective new spouse of the petitioner has caused the separation of the parties; or if 3) grave scandal or amazement will ensue. These matters however, like other facts, are not presumed, and hence their negation need not be proved, unless evidence of them is offered (cfr. nn. **398**, **399**, **407**). Nevertheless parties and witnesses are to be interrogated on these points. Besides this, there must be moral impossibility of restoring conjugal life.

157. Antecedent and perpetual impotence makes a marriage nugatory by the natural law (c. 1068,§1). The proofs in cases of impotence must be of the fullest order and must cover all the elements of the case. Hence in cases of absolute impotence (impotentia absoluta) the plaintiff must prove that the party is actually impotent in the canonical sense, that the impotence preceded the marriage, that it is of its nature perpetual, and that there is no remedy for its cure, at least none short of a dangerous operation.[90] In cases of relative impotence (i. relativa; i. ad quam) the plaintiff must prove that the parties, although neither be absolutely impotent, cannot in fact consummate the marital coition with one another, and that this condition is similarly antecedent to the marriage, perpetual, and incurable.

158. Marriage is rendered invalid by the impediment of crime. Those who, while a legitimate, *i. e.* canonically valid marriage of either still subsisted, have committed adultery together, and have given each other a promise of future marriage, or have attempted marriage even by a merely civil ceremony, cannot validly contract marriage together (crimen neutro patrante) (c. 1075,n.1). If the parties claim their marriage is invalid by reason of this impediment, they must prove that they committed adultery together, and that they gave one another a promise of future marriage or actually attempted marriage, and that both the adultery and the promise or attempt took place while one and the same former marriage subsisted. These proofs are very difficult, as a rule, because of the secrecy with which the crime is usually perpetrated.

[90] R., Null., 25 mart. 1920 (rd., xii, p. 75).

Nevertheless there are sometimes witnesses: they testify to facts contiguous to the adultery and so cogent as to give a presumption of adultery. It is not required that the witnesses shall have seen the parties engaged in the very act of adultery itself (cfr. n. **520**). The same holds true in proving the pre-Code impediment of affinity by illicit coition,[91] or in proving adultery as a ground for separation from bed and board.[92]

In cases where the subsequent and now contested marriage had been permitted by the Holy See, either by grant of a dispensation from non-consummated marriage, or by establishment of the presumption of death of spouse, the question of an implicit dispensation from the impediment of crime must be considered (cfr. c. 1053). But if the presumption of death had been heard and the permission to marry anew had been granted by the diocesan ordinary, the dispensation from previous crime is not implicit, and must be proved, by him who upholds the subsequent marriage, to have been expressly granted.

159. Marriage is invalid if the necessary dispensation from a diriment impediment is invalid. In disparty of cult the dispensation may be invalid by reason of the failure of either party to make the required promises. A mixed marriage in X. was declared invalid by the Holy Office, because it was proved that the dispensation had been granted without the Catholic party's having made the required promises (cfr. cc. 1061,§1,n.2; 1071): the non-Catholic party alone had been asked to promise the Catholic upbringing of the progeny.[93] The dispensation may likewise be invalid by reason of the insincerity of the promise made by the infidel party respecting the religious liberty of the other, or by reason of the insincerity of either party respecting the promise to baptize and educate all the children as Catholics. Proof of this invalidity is derived from proof of prenuptial agreement between the parties to neglect fulfilling the promises after marriage, or from acts or words of either party before the marriage or immediately after it, which make it plain that he had no serious intention of fulfilling his promise.[94]

[91] R., Null., 11 apr. 1911 (rd., iii, p. 165).

[92] Pallotini, xiii, 393, § XXIII, n. 64; cfr. R., Null., 10 aug. 1923 (rd., xv, pp. 230, 231).

[93] SO., 18 mart. 1933 (num. Protoc. 2709/1929): unpublished.

[94] cfr. R., Parisien., Null., 11 aug. 1921 (rd., xiii, p. 210; aas., xiv, p. 512).

160. If the question of legitimacy arise, proof of legitimacy entails demonstration that the child derives from the named father and mother, and that the descent was legitimate. When there is no contrary proof, derivation from a husband is presumed (cfr. n. **535**), if the derivation from the wife is certain. Full or partial proof of this accrues from documents, witnesses, and from personal presumptions based on the sustentation and education of the child by the named husband and wife. Legitimate descent is shown by proof of valid or putative marriage (cfr. however c. 1114). Proof of legitimation subsequent to conception entails also proof that the parents were capable of marrying one another at the time of the conception or pregnation or birth (c. 1116).[95]

§ 4. Proof of Negation

161. In some cases the plaintiff is required to prove a negation, *i. e.* the denial that an event has taken place. Negations are either unrestricted (negativum purum, n. simplex, n. non-qualificatum), as in the statement that a person was never baptized; or they are restricted by time, place and circumstance (n. qualificatum), as in the denial that marital consent was expressed at the wedding ceremony.

Classical jurists seem to have somewhat misinterpreted texts in Roman law, so as to make them read that negations could not be proved (negativa non sunt probanda).[96] And this idea was taken into the Canon law with only slight modification.[97] This principle however, is not now adhered to, and the Code passes over it in silence, leaving the judge to determine from the nature of the case whether a negation is sufficiently proved or not.

Unrestricted negations or denials are by their nature so devoid of causes, effects and qualities from which direct proofs must be de-

[95] cfr. PC., 6 dec. 1930 (aas., xxiii, p. 25).

[96] Roberti, ii, n. 326, p. 28 (2): "Legebatur in aliquo textu Pauli, 2. D. XXII, 3: 'Ei incumbit probatio qui dicit, non qui negat'; et in Codice, 23 C. v. 19: 'Cum per rerum naturam factum negantis probatio nulla sit.' Sed hi duo textus alludunt ad casum in quo quis ex facto praetendit sibi exsurgere ius; in quo casu evidenter factum probare debet ipse, non adversarius qui factum negat; nam 'actore non probante, reus absolvitur.'"; Lega, i, n. 444.

[97] c. 23, X, De Electione, I, 6; c. 11, X, De Probationibus, II, 19: "... negantis factum per rerum naturam nulla est directa probatio"; Schmalzgrueber, lib. II, tit. cxix, n. 33; Bouix, i, n. 308.

rived, that there can be no direct proof of them.[98] Even unrestricted denials however, can be established by indirect proof,[99] and this is repeatedly done in cases of disparity of cult.

162. The law does not specify what indirect evidence is required to satisfactorily establish an unrestricted denial. The plaintiff must offer proof of such circumstances, events, beliefs and opinions as are incompatible with any other supposition than that the negation in question is morally certain. Usually in trials on disparity of cult it must be shown that one party was never baptized at all. Strict proof of this would require witnesses who could testify to every moment from the time of birth onward. In place of such an impossible alibi it is sufficient if the plaintiff show from the testimony of parents, sisters and brothers, and friends of long standing, that they never procured, witnessed, or heard of the party's being baptized, and that the religious, or respectively, irreligious condition of the party and his family has ever been such, as would make his baptism unlikely.[100] This should be supplemented by the testimony of a pastor, Catholic or Protestant, under whose care the party would have been, to the effect that the records of his Church give no evidence of the party's baptism. Finally there is required the oath of the party himself that he was never baptized since reaching the age of reason (cfr. c. 779). If all these elements of evidence cannot be had, it is for the judge to estimate whether the elements at hand sufficiently show that the party was not baptized.

163. Of a restricted denial more direct proof is possible because of the positive elements or qualifications attached to the denial. Thus if a person deny that he expressed consent at the wedding ceremony, witnesses may affirm his silence or remonstrance at that time. If a

[98] Hence the writer in aer., lxii (May, 1920), p. 563 inaccurately expresses the means of proving non-baptism: "When there is question of establishing the fact of non-baptism,... If possible direct certainty is to be furnished, that, namely, which is afforded by competent witnesses, or authentic documents. In default of such certainty, indirect certainty must be supplied by means of satisfactory presumption."

[99] This is indicated by the word "directa" inserted in the text of c. 23, De Elect., and c. 11, De Prob. above quoted; cfr. Pirhing, p. 275; W-Vidal, vi, p. 378 (22). Hence Smith, n. 470 seems to overestimate the matter when he says: "Such a denial cannot be proved, either directly or indirectly."; Noval, n. 440 idem.

[100] c. 10, X, De Praesumptionibus, II, 23: "Efficacior probatio requiritur ab eo, qui probare vult illud, quod non est verisimile" (tit. cap.).

person deny that he signed the contract of betrothal which bears his name, experts may determine that the signature is not his. If a person deny that he contracted a supposed marriage at a certain time and place, he may prove in various ways that he was not there at the stated time.

§ 5. Admissibility and Term of Proof

164. As a general norm, all proofs admissible in canonical procedure and proposed by the parties or their advocates or proctors are to be admitted as evidence in marriage cases. In addition the marriage case accepts some proofs, such as the testimony of near relatives, not admissible in civil contentious cases. On the other hand some proofs, such as confession and oath of parties are accepted in marriage cases only with restrictions.

165. Some facts or impediments are by the nature of the thing and by long-established canonical jurisprudence more securely and more properly proved by one sort of proof than by another. Thus events are proved by eye witnesses better than by hearsay witnesses; acts that are public by their nature, *v. g.* baptism, confirmation, are proved by document in preference to testimony, and impotence and insanity are preferably proved by expert inspection. As long as the more natural and canonically accustomed proof is obtainable, the judge may and should refuse to admit as conclusive, proofs that are not the best obtainable *ad rem.*[101] When it is plainly shown that the better form of proof cannot be had, *e. g.* when Church records have been destroyed, or when eye witnesses are dead, the judge may properly accept the proofs less preferred *ad rem,* and estimate them according to his conscience (cfr. nn. **192**, **261**, **351**).

166. The judge may also reject proofs which he sees are adduced in order to delay the trial, or will in fact delay it without being necessary or useful to it. Thus in contentious cases of a purely civil nature the judge should not ordinarily postpone trial for witnesses who live at a great distance or whose residence is unknown or for documents that cannot be had within a reasonable period of time. In cases affecting the marriage bond the judge may properly, and must postpone decision for nullity if the respondent claims that he has an overwhelming proof outstanding, and the judge believes in the claimant's sincerity and the probability that such proof will give a different turn to the case (cfr. cc. 1749, 1861). Even in such cases

[101] Gasparri, nov., i, n. 140.

however, it is not necessary to postpone beyond a reasonable time (which may be somewhat longer than in ordinary contentious cases), if the plaintiff has already offered proofs that are sufficient for establishing his suit.

167. The judge may properly decree a term within which the proofs are to be produced (cc. 1731,n.2; 1860,§2). This term may be protracted (prorogatio) at the behest of the judge, on motion of a party, and without restriction as to the number of such prorogations. The Code merely cautions that the judge should see to it lest the prorogation be unduly long (c. 1731,n.2), and the trial be too much protracted by prorogation (c. 1634,§3).

The time for alleging presumptions is by the nature of the thing, coterminal with the trial. Hence the judge may consider a proper presumption at any time before sentence is given, and a party may draw attention to one at any time before the discussion of the case is ended; but the facts on which the presumption is based must be proved within the term granted for other proofs (cfr. nn. **89**, **584**, **585**).

168. All proofs for the case should be furnished in the first instance, so that there will be no necessity of a supplementary procedure in succeeding instances. The Rota has complained of a lack of diligence on the part of curiae who neglect to exhaust the necessary witnesses in the first instance.[102] In an unpublished case from X. the Rotal ponent ordered the court of first instance to supplement its proofs by a series of fifteen new questions for the plaintiff and several new questions for the expert physician who had made the physical inspection of the respondent. Besides, he ordered that witnesses, relatives and friends of both parties, should supplement the formal responses of the character witnesses, by available testimony on the merits of the case. Evidently, the first instance had not exhausted the proofs at hand, before making its decision.[103]

When a supplementary procedure is necessary to exhaust the proofs, it should be promptly instituted.[104]

[102] R., Null., 16 mai. 1912 (rd., iv, p. 262).

[103] R., Null., 30 jul. 1928 (unpub.: prot. num. 902/23); cfr. also R., Null., 27 aug. 1912 (rd., iv, pp. 438, 439); Null., 18 feb. 1918 (rd., x, p. 27).

[104] cfr. R., Parisien., Null., 15 dec. 1920 (rd., xii, p. 274); R, Reg., § 14, n. 2 gives formula: "Let the party, or advocate or proctor be cited for hearing on ...... day ...... to the effect herewith expressed in writing"; cfr. R, Norm., art. 146, § 5.

CHAPTER VII

Confession of the Parties

"Veniebant, confitentes et annuntiantes actus suos."—Act., xix, 18.

169. The answers given by the parties to the questions of the judge, and other statements of the parties, made *v. g.* at the joining of the issue, constitute in some cases a confession, which generally has its own peculiar effects upon the proving of the case.

§ 1. Definition and Kinds of Confession

170. In the grammatical sense, a confession is any acknowledgment of fact. In the canonical sense the word 'confession' is used either sacramentally or processually. When used sacramentally as in the Fourth Title of Book Three of the Code and in Canon 1757, § 3, n. 2 confession designates a constituent part of the sacrament of penance. But with that sense of the word we have here nothing to do. The word is here used in its processual sense. The Code gives the definition of a confession: it is an acknowledgment or assertion of a fact, made by one of the contending parties against himself and in favor of his adversary, *i. e.* against his own case and in such a way as to aid the pretentions of the opposing party. Thus in cases of separation, when the respondent acknowledges the adultery or cruelty of which the plaintiff accuses him, and on which the suit for separation is based, this acknowledgment is a confession in the processual sense. But in a case respecting the legitimacy of a child, the mother's acknowledgment of adultery and illegitimacy is not a confession in the processual sense, because it militates to the prejudice of a third person, namely the child.[1]

In contentious procedure the essential element of the confession is not however, that a crime be acknowledged,[2] but that a fact militating against the party's contention be acknowledged. The word 'confessio' is sometimes used by the Rota in a broader sense signifying the party's deposition in behalf of his own suit.[3]

[1] cfr. Gasparri, nov., ii, n. 1113.

[2] This is the case only in criminal procedure, cfr. c. 1947.

[3] cfr. R., Parisien., Null. 11 aug. 1921 (rd., xiii, p. 216; aas., xiv, p. 518); Gravinen., Null., 2 jul. 1918 (rd., x, p. 62; aas., xi, p. 196).

The confession may be made in answer to the questioning of the judge or it may be spontaneously proferred (c. 1750). But it seems plain that in either case the prejudicial acknowledgment must be seriously and freely made, without threat, intimidation or duress, without collusion or subornation (cfr. c. 1751).[4]

171. I. According to the form in which they are made, confessions are variously divided: 1) The distinction of primary importance is that which ranges them in judicial and extrajudicial confessions. A judicial confession is one made before the judge acting in his capacity as judge, *i. e.* during trial. Generally, though not always, the judicial confession is made in the court-room. Hence an acknowledgment made before the judge outside of trial, or made before the notary of the court alone, is not a judicial confession. Neither is that to be accounted a judicial confession before the ecclesiastical court, which was confessed in a civil court upon a marriage case over which the Church has proper and exclusive competence.[5] Such confessions are rather extrajudicial. An extrajudicial confession is one made out of trial; hence the acknowledgment made to an absolutely incompetent judge (cfr. cc. 1557; 1558; 1960), or to the competent judge but outside of trial, or to the adversary, or to a disinterested person constitutes an extrajudicial confession. It is not however necessary that the acknowledgment be consciously made against one's case, or that the adversary accept it as a confession, but it is of course necessary that the interested party be able to prove in court that extrajudicial confession was really made.

2) A confession is written or verbal (cc. 1750; 1753) and the meaning of this distinction is self-evident. Thus an acknowledgment against the plaintiff's case contained in his written bill of plaint or petition is a written confession. But if the party makes an acknowledgment by word of mouth during the course of trial, and then at the court's behest signs the record of testimony, this is not viewed as a written, but rather as an oral confession.

172. II. According to the manner in which the acknowledgment of fact is signified, confessions are either expressly made, tacitly made, or presumptively made. And these terms are likewise mostly self-evident. The Decretals relate what was an example of presumptive confession: the flight of a party after the joining of issue was

[4] Roberti, ii, n. 332.

[5] W-Vidal, vi, n. 454.

presumed to constitute a confession.[6] The Code gives two legal presumptions of confession derived from disobedience in court: when a party refuses to give a specimen of his handwriting, the refusal is presumed to be a confession of the genuineness of a document whose authorship he would deny (c. 1800,§4); likewise when an infidel party answers the interpellation with contemptuous silence, this is presumptive confession of his bad will (c. 1122,§1). In other cases the Code leaves the judge free to derive a personal presumption of confession if the circumstances of the disobedience warrant it. (cc. 1743,§2; 1824,§2; 1831,§2; 1836,§3).

173. III. According to the extent of the acknowledgment made, confessions are either simple (c. simplex, c. pura), which plainly acknowledge a fact in its entirety, or qualified (c. qualificata, c. multiplex) which acknowledge in part, and in part contradict or excuse.

174. There has always been much discussion whether a confession is formally a means of proof. In the Decretals the Title on Confessions (Titulus xviii in X) was placed before that on proofs in general and the ensuing titles on specific proofs, and accordingly Innocent III mentions evidence by confession as distinct from evidence by proof.[7] On the other hand Innocent IV mentions confession as a means of proof,[8] and the Regulations for the Rota explicitly state that judicial confession is a proof.[9] Hence the Code now places the Chapter on Confessions as the first among the specific proofs (cfr. however c. 1747,n.3), and the authors in Roman and Canon law have long been accustomed to speak of confession as the "regina probationum et probatio probatissima."[10]

§ 2. Effects of Confession

175. The effects of a duly made judicial confession are chiefly two: that juridical notoriety is acquired by the confession (c. 2197, n. 2), and, that the adversary is relieved from the burden of all further proof (c. 1751; cpre. c. 1747,n.3).[11]

[6] c. 2, De Confessis, II, 9 in Sext.

[7] c. 24, X, De Verb. Signif., V, 40.

[8] c. 1, De Confessis, II, 9 in Sext.

[9] R, Reg., § 137.

[10] cfr. W-Vidal, vi, p. 385 (5).

[11] Other effects are given by W-Vidal, vi, n. 451, which are however contained in, or derive from these two.

Thus in cases of separation from bed and board the confession of the party against whom the suit is brought constitutes full proof,[12] except when the unnatural spontaneity of a confession indicates cause for suspecting it.[13] But the judge must distinguish between a confession of crime justifying separation and the expression of mutual consent of parties desiring separation, for mutual consent is not alone a sufficient ground to pronounce in favor of permanent separation of parties, except when it is made in favor of the religious and priestly vocation.[14]

176. Likewise if a party about to marry makes confession of a fact that renders the forthcoming marriage illicit, sufficient proof is at hand to hinder or postpone the marriage.[15][16]

177. If a convert would use the Pauline privilege, the confession of the infidel party that he will not be converted nor peacefully cohabit is accepted as full proof, even when such a confession is presumptively derived from the party's contemptuous silence (cfr. n. 172).[17]

178. In nullity and non-consummation suits the confession of a party is also a formal means of proof, even when it militates for the nullity or non-consummation of a marriage. The Regulations for the Rota explicitly state that just as the parties may derive proof from the confession of the adversary, so may the promoter of justice and the defender in cases involving the public good, and (explicitly) in marriage cases.[18]

But in cases of nullity the Church is an interested party and the principle of *ex officio* inquest is involved; hence the confession of a party does not always obtain the full effects that accrue from a confession in cases where the public good is not concerned. Hence if

[12] c. 12, X, De Praesumpt., II, 23; IA., § 232; Bassibey, n. 326; Eichmann, p. 215.

[13] Heiner, De Processu, p. 54.

[14] IA., §§ 206; 241.

[15] c. 13, X, De Praesumpt., II, 23.

[16] In civil law: May, p. 300: "A statement in an application for marriage license that this is to be the person's second marriage is admissible in proof of his first marriage."

[17] Thus the Code strengthens the assertion of Gasparri, ii, n. 1336, and it is no longer required that: "practice recurratur ad dispensationem ab interpellationibus."

[18] R, Reg., § 137; Eichmann, p. 140; cfr. DS, Ordin., n. 12.

the respondent makes a confession which favors the plea of nullity, this does not simply relieve the plaintiff from further burden of proof, nor is it rated as the "regina probationum."[19] In how far the confession settles the matter in these cases and to what extent the proof deriving from a sworn confession may be considered sufficient proof of nullity or non-consummation will be discussed in reviewing the appraisal of the oaths of the parties in Chapter XIII.

179. The value of a party's confession favoring the validity of a marriage depends upon whether the ecclesiastical court may and wishes to pursue the inquiry further or not. In those cases of nullity where the impediment is not of its nature public, and which consequently can be brought to court only by one or both of the parties themselves (cfr. cc. 1971,§1; 1973), the plaintiff's judicial confession favoring validity relieves the respondent from all further burden of proof.[20]

In cases which are of their nature public and may be brought to court by the promoter of justice, a confession in favor of the marriage does not necessarily relieve the respondent from the burden of proof, for the promoter may *ex officio* pursue the case. Nevertheless such a confession constitutes a presumption and argument in favor of validity.[21]

It lies with the court to reject the party's confession or statement favoring the marriage if it have just grounds to suspect such a confession (c. 1747,n.3).[22] Clement III rejected such a confession in a case of consanguinity, for the wife's statement favoring the

[19] c. 5, X, De Eo Qui Cognovit, IV, 13; R., Colonien., Null., 27 aug. 1910 (rd., ii, pp. 320, 321); Oregonop., Null., 6 jul. 1914 (rd., vi, p. 253; aas., vi, p. 524); W-Vidal, vi, n. 449 and Eichmann, p. 139 (2) must be understood in this sense: not in the sense that the judge must entirely disregard the confession of the parties.

[20] IA., §§ 149, 171; R, Reg., § 137, n. 3; R., Null., 6 dec. 1909 (rd., i, p. 156); Lugdunen., Null., 28 jun. 1912 (rd., iv, p. 310); Lugdunen., Null., 5 jun. 1917 (rd., ix, p. 131; aas., x, p. 162); Colonien., Null., 1 jul. 1912 (rd., iv, p. 332; aas., iv, p. 674).

[21] IA., § 149; R., Monterey. Angelorum, Null., 21 dec. 1917 (rd., ix, p. 317; aas., x, p. 421).

[22] R., Null., 6 dec. 1909 (rd., i, p. 157): "Unde relatis variis hac de re Doctorum opinionibus, De Luca ait: 'Verius tamen pro meo sensu videtur ut ista facti potius quaestio dicenda sit, quae proinde certam ac generalem regulam cuicumque casui applicabilem non recipiat, sed pro singulorum casuum circumstantiis prudenti ac recto beneque regulato iudicis arbitrio, non autem ex illo affectionis et voluntatis, quaestio decidi debeat' (De Luca, De Iudiciis, disc. 23, n. 26)."

marriage was not considered equal to the testimonies proving consanguinity.[23] In a case which arose in Paris the crux of the question of whether the "Tametsi" had been observed, depended on whether the respondent had had a domicile on the Rue Sarrazin, Paris, at the time of her marriage. She stated that she had, and this fact would have required pronouncement for validity. But the plaintiff brought proof that she had not a true domicile there, and the court neglected her assertion and pronounced for nullity.[24] In another case at Marseilles the Rota rejected the assertions which the respondent made in favor of validity, because it was plain that she acted from motives of hatred against the plaintiff.[25]

180. The joint confession of a man and woman not married to each other, that they are parents of a child, is proof of the parenthood, providing the mother was not married to another at the time of the child's conception or birth (cfr. nn. **535, 536**). When the child is born of a married mother however, neither the confession of the mother nor the joint confession of the mother and another who asserts he is the father, even though made on a death-bed and sworn to, is sufficient to overcome the presumption of legitimacy.[26]

181. When a party has made a judicial confession he cannot avoid its effects by a retraction or explanation, unless he retract or explain uninterruptedly upon making the confession or immediately after it. In that case the confession is taken as a misstatement, a slip of the tongue, and explanation but not proof will be asked. Thus the Rota allowed a party to interpret her words which seemed to be a confession against her suit for nullity.[27] If the retracting or explaining is not uninterruptedly joined with the confession, proof of the faultiness of the confession is necessary, or its effects cannot be avoided. The confessing party must prove that he made no judicial confession according to the terms of Canon 1750, or that the confession was not seriously, considerately, freely made, or that it was based on an erroneous apprehension of fact (cc. 1751; 1752).[28] A confession based on erroneous apprehension of law cannot be retracted

[23] c. 11, X, De Sententia et Re Iudicata, II, 27.

[24] R., Parisien., Null., 4 mart. 1916 (rd., viii, pp. 69, 70; aas., viii, p. 371).

[25] R., Massilien., Null., 10 aug. 1912 (rd., iv, p. 405; aas., iv, p. 711).

[26] cfr., c. 4, X, Qui Filii Sint Legitimi, IV, 17; Gasparri, ii, n. 1307; W-Vidal, v, n. 613.

[27] R., Null., 21 jan. 1911 (rd., iii, p. 25).

[28] R., Monetery. Angelorum, Null., 21 dec. 1917 (rd., ix, p. 318; aas., x, p. 422); Westmonasterien., Null., 11 apr., 1927 (aas., xix, p. 222).

even when the error can be proved, for confessions are directed by their nature to facts alone.[29]

On the disputed question whether a qualified confession can be divided, *i. e.* accepted in so far as it tells against the party confessing, and rejected in so far as it favors him, the Code is silent; hence, it seems, the matter is left to the prudence of the judge,[30] who must weigh the matter together with all other proofs and circumstances of the case. In this way the Rotal Auditors divided the confessions of parties in recent nullity cases.[31]

182. In order that an extrajudicial confession beget proof it must be duly brought into the acts of the trial (c. 1753). This is done by presenting to the court the document wherein the party has written such a confession, or the document authentically witnessing that such a confession was made, or by producing witnesses who can testify that the party made the confession to themselves, to the adversary, or to others.

183. The Code does not determine what value an extrajudicial confession shall have when duly brought into the acts, but leaves that to the discretion of the judge. It is his duty to estimate how far a confession shall be accepted as proof. In forming this estimate all the circumstances of the case must be considered (c. 1753). If the confession was made at a time and under circumstances which preclude the suspicion of fraud and self-deceit (tempore non suspecto), it may form part proof, and may even approximate full proof of a case. Thus if a fact concerning nullity or non-consummation was confessed before the marriage was contracted, or after the marriage but before there was any question of suing for declaration of nullity or dispensation, the confession will have great weight.[32] [33] In no case does an extrajudicial confession automatically relieve the adversary from the burden of proof.[34]

[29] Roberti, ii, n. 332; Lega, i, n. 453.

[30] Roberti, ii, n. 331; Contrary: Noval, n. 451.

[31] R., Null., 6 dec. 1909 (rd., i, pp. 156, 157); Cameracen., Null., 17 mai. 1922 (rd., xiv, p. 151).

[32] DS, Reg., n. 70; IA., § 148; cfr. R., Null., 29 feb. 1916 (rd., viii, pp. 50, 51); Lega, i, n. 458.

[33] In civil law: Abbott, pp. 105, 106: "Declarations of parties made while they were living together, are competent to characterize the nature of their cohabitation . . . Admissions and declarations made . . . after the cohabitation had ceased, are not competent except as against the declarant."

[34] W-Vidal, vi, p. 392 (43).

CHAPTER VIII

Witnesses and Testimony

"Non stabit testis unus contra aliquem,...sed in ore duorum aut trium testium stabit omne verbum."—Deut., xix, 15; Mat., xviii, 16.

§ 1. Definitions and Kinds of Witness and Testimony.

184. Events are most naturally proved by the word of reliable persons who have observed them. Such persons are in a large sense called witnesses (testes), and their assertion is called testimony (testimonium). In the legal and canonical sense those persons are also called witnesses whose presence at the solemnizing of a contract or other legal act is required for its validity or security. Such witnesses are required by the Canon law for valid betrothal and valid marriage (cc. 1017,§§1,2; 1094). With such witnesses we are here concerned only in so far as they may later serve to beget proof of what they witnessed. In the strictly probatory sense in which this chapter uses the word, witnesses are persons other than the plaintiff and respondent, who have observed something with their senses, and are then brought to prove by their assertion what they have observed. Their assertions offered in court as proof are called testimony.

185. Witnesses vary in kind according to their status before the court and according to the testimony they render.

I. Their status in court divides them into: 1) Simple witnesses (testes privati), expert witnesses (t. periti), and authorized witnesses (t. auctorizabiles, t. qualificati, t. publici, t. ex officio). Simple witnesses are those who testify to what has been casually observed; authorized witnesses are those who have been appointed to an office that they might observe or do, and then testify to acts observed or done in fulfillment of their office.[1] Such are ordinaries, pastors, notaries, court-messengers *etc.* in respect of the acts they are specially authorized to perform or witness (cfr. cc. 1593; 1800,§2). But the two witnesses required in conjunction with the pastor or ordinary for the solemnizing of marriage, do not participate in the special rank of

[1] On expert witnesses cfr. Ch. IX.

authorized witnesses in a subsequent trial on marriage; they bear testimony as simple witnesses.

The pastor testifies as an authorized witness regarding the form in which the marriage was solemnized, the external rendering of consent on the part of the parties, and regarding his having given to or withheld from another the delegation to solemnize a marriage under his competence.[2] But the pastor is not an authorized witness of events that took place other than in his official presence (cfr. c. 1791,§1), *e. g.* when he testifies to the hilarity of a bride at the wedding feast.[3]

2) Some are judicial witnesses (t. judiciales): those namely who testify before the judge or auditor, generally at court, and some are extrajudicial (t. extrajudiciales) who render their testimony before other persons and out of court.

3) Some are summoned witnesses (t. citati, t. inducti, t. acciti); those namely who have been called to testify, and some are spontaneous witnesses (t. spontanei, t. ultronei) who come of their own accord.

4) Some are documentary witnesses (t. documentarii, t. instrumentales) who have signed a document or are mentioned in it as witnesses, and some are extraneous witnesses (t. extranei) who are not written down in a document as having taken part in its making.

186. II. The sort of testimony rendered likewise creates distinctions: 1) Witnesses are conformative (contestes, t. concordati) when two or more testify alike to the same fact, or they are singular (t. singulares) when they are at variance. These latter vary with one another in several ways: first, they may contradict one another as when one witness testifies that a person was baptized, another that he was never baptized, and then the variance is called contradictory (singularitas contradictoria). Or, second, they may be contrary, as when one witness states that a man died in Europe, another that he died in America (s. obstativa, s. contraria, s. adversativa). Third, they may refer to various disconnected events, as when several witnesses testify to various occasions when each separately heard a person give a promise of marriage, but no two witnesses testify to the same event (s. diversativa). Fourth, they may complement one another and

[2] R., Null., 28 mai. 1909 (rd., i, p. 58); Null., 30 jun. 1910 (rd., ii, p. 235); Null., 28 jun. 1911 (rd., iii, p. 314).

[3] R., Pitilianen., Null., 16 aug. 1915 (aas., viii, p. 197; rd., vii, p. 434); Null., 21 dec. 1923 (rd., xv, pp. 315, 316); cfr. also Null., 25 feb. 1911 (rd., iii, p. 101).

weave together the threads of a complete story, as when one witness asserts that he heard a mother threaten her daughter, another that he saw her slap her, another that he saw her lock her up when she would not marry (s. adminiculativa, s. cumulativa).

187. 2) Some are witnesses of personal experience, others are hearsay witnesses, some are witnesses to notoriety, to current repute or to rumor, others again merely state an opinion of their own. It is the principal office of witnesses to report original, specific, individual, concrete events that they have themselves experienced, together with the circumstances of time, place *etc.* and such are witnesses of personal experience (t. de scientia). These are either eye witnesses (t. occulati, t. occulares, t. de visu), or ear witnesses (t. auriculares) according as they report what they have seen or what they have heard when the thing heard is an original event at issue, and not a version of the original event (cfr. c. 1789,n.2).[4] Those who testify that they learned from the parties or their relatives at an unsuspected time, that a marriage has remained unconsummated, are now known as quasi ear witnesses (quasi t. de scientia).[5] Witnesses who report a version of an event at issue are called hearsay witnesses (t. de auditu). These are direct hearsay witnesses (t. de auditu a videntibus) if they have heard of the event from those who saw it or otherwise experienced it; and they are indirect hearsay witnesses (t. de auditu auditus, t. de auditu alieno) if they heard of the event only from those who in turn merely heard of it.

188. Some witnesses report the notoriety (t. de notorietate); others the general current opinion or repute (t. de fama), others again the rumor (t. de rumore) of an event. Reiffenstuel, is careful to note the distinction between the general current repute and the mere rumor of an event, and the jurisprudence of the courts has followed the distinction.[6] If the opinion that an impediment exists is uniform, solid, constant and enduring, has been handed down from the not too recent past, or is common to the greater and more stable and reliable part of a community, and has a probable and proportionate cause or

[4] cfr. DS, Reg., n. 71, § 1; R., Colonien., Null., 1 jul. 1912 (rd., iv, p. 331); Null., 10 dec. 1914 (rd., vi, p. 349).

[5] DS, Reg., n. 60, § 2.

[6] Reiffenstuel, lib. II, tit. xx, n. 393 fol.; Canon 1939, § 1 is not so explicit, though it distinguishes between notoriety and repute.

origin it is considered to establish repute and sometimes notoriety;[7] if such opinion is restricted to a comparatively small part of the community or is simply the noisy chatter of people it is known as rumor.[8]

189. Witnesses who merely state an opinion of their own (t. de credulitate) are not witnesses in the truest probatory sense; nevertheless they are sometimes employed in cases of insanity, duress, and especially in cases of impotence and non-consummation, and they are then called "septimae manus" (character witnesses; G.: Eideshelfer; L. also: coniuratores, compurgatores, sacramentales). There is a diversity of view regarding the origin of the name: "septimae manus." The most probable explanation is that such witnesses are called "manus" because of the hands extended to take the oath on their opinion.[9]

The early history of these witnesses is likewise not too clear. De Smet notes that Augustus in his lex Julia required seven witnesses for divorce;[10] other authors find evidence that the "septimae manus" were derived from the ancient Germanic law.[11] This view seems to be correct. Freisen is of opinion that these witnesses were not generally employed in ecclesiastical marriage trials at the time of Gratian.[12] Nevertheless Gratian knew of the practice of calling the "septimae manus" and recounts the letter of Pope Gregory to Bishop John of Ravenna directing that a woman who complains of her husband's impotence may contract a new marriage if both parties, supported by the testimony of the "septimae manus," swear to the non-consummation.[13] Similar notices occur in the Decretals,[14] and

[7] cfr. SO, 1868, § 8; R., Null., 16 aug. 1920 (rd., xii, p. 231); Schlenz, in akk., xcviii (1918), p. 65.

[8] SCC., In Mileten. Null., 26 nov. 1768 (pall. xii, p. 556, n. 56: "inde exquirat, an criminis et illicitae copulae recens atque ad Causae opportunitatem excitatus fuerit rumor, vel constans fuerit, vigueritque etiam tempore prioris Matrimonii constantis inter R. et X. G."; Null., 4 jul. 1913 (rd., v, p. 426): "Publicum vero aut notorium non fit 'per rumorem viciniae'..."; Null., 8 jan. 1921 (rd., xiii, p. 7); Null., 12 nov. 1921 (rd., xiii, pp. 264, 265): "... Menochium dicentem toto tempore vitae suae, nunquam se vidisse processum, in quo fama legitime probata fuit."

[9] V-Creusen, n. 290; somewhat otherwise Gasparri, ii, n. 1486.

[10] De Smet, i, n. 371.

[11] Freisen, p. 342; Haring: Grundzuege, p. 899 (6).

[12] Freisen, p. 342.

[13] c. 2, C. XXXIII, q. 1.

[14] c. 5, 7, X, De Frig. et Malef. et Imp. Co., IV, 15.

all later instructions on cases of impotence and non-consummation, excepting only the Austrian Instruction, mention the "septimae manus."

In cases of impotence and non-consummation then, the parties must produce such witnesses who will testify for them (c. 1975,§1). The obligation of bringing such witnesses, has for sanction, not the invalidity of a procedure in which a party would not produce them, but rather a loss to the credibility of the party's assertions.[15]

The "septimae manus" are character witnesses who testify that they believe the party to be trustworthy in his depositions on the matter at issue (c. 1975,§1);[16] and they are opinion witnesses when they add that, in their opinion impotence or non-consummation is actually a fact in the case.[17] In addition to this, the "septimae manus" may also testify as eye witnesses if they have witnessed pertinent facts.[18]

There was some unclearness in the pre-Code law, as to whether such character witnesses were required in marriage cases other than those of impotence and non-consummation. The Instruction "Cum Moneat Glossa" was not clear on the question and the Congregation of the Council later insisted in individual instances on having these witnesses even in other marriage cases.[19] But a later Instruction of the Holy Office declared they were strictly necessary only in cases of non-consummation.[20] Such witnesses were however introduced in a recent case of pre-Code affinity from illicit coition.[21] The Code requires them only for cases of impotence and non-consummation, and does not insist on them then, if the impotence or non-consummation is otherwise made certain (c. 1975,§1). And the Rota has pronounced for non-consummation and recommended dispensation in cases where no character witnesses were heard.[22] But Haring remarks that when a diocesan court in Austria recently omitted them

[15] Noval, n. 855.

[16] DS, Reg., n. 58; R., Null., 5 jun. 1913 (rd., v, pp. 357-359).

[17] Noval, n. 853.

[18] SO, 1858, § Deinde.

[19] cfr. Bassibey, n. 356.

[20] SO., 16 feb. (jun.) 1894 (gasp., ii, n. 1486; bass., n. 356); SCC., Varsavien., 16 jun. 1894 (cicf., vi, n. 4291).

[21] R., Null., 23 mart. 1915 (rd., vii, p. 127).

[22] R., Null., vel. Disp., 15 jul. 1911 (rd., iii, p. 344); Null., 21 dec. 1923 (rd., xv, p. 318).

with the consent of the defender, because the case seemed to be clearly proved and the only character witnesses lived in far-off dioceses, the Congregation directed that they be heard notwithstanding.[23]

190. III. Finally according to their admissibility, witnesses are either entirely admissible and above all suspicion (t. habiles, t. admissibiles, t. omni suspicione maiores), or they are inadmissible (t. inadmissibiles). These are either unfit (t. non idonei) who lack sufficient discretion, or suspected (t. suspecti) whose bad will causes a presumption against them, or incapable (t. incapaces) who are excluded because of their office, or because of general spiritual welfare, or peace of families, or because of special danger of perjury.

§ 2. Admissibility of Witnesses

191. In the early Roman law the testimony of witnesses was almost the only means of proof before the law. Later on documentary evidence seemed to prevail and it became doubtful whether testimony was admissible against the word of documents, until under Constantine, testimony and documentary evidence were placed on a par. Gradual development of the proof by witnesses ensued, such as the questioning of the parties and their advocates, which led to abuses and cast suspicion upon the value of testimony, until the whole manner of bringing testimony to court was reformed under Justinian.

In the early middle ages the Church urged the use of witnesses among the Germanic peoples addicted to proof by ordeal, duel, *etc.*, and amid the almost universal decline of letters, testimony again became the surpassing proof. But in the fifteenth century the Law School of Bologna so extolled proof by document as to seek to proscribe proof by witnesses entirely.[24] This was followed in France under Charles IX, Louis XIV and the Code Napoleon.[25]

The Canon law neither holds the testimony of witnesses in general suspicion, nor recognizes in it a formal and rigid validity. Testimony is thus a pliable instrument of proof, hemmed in with safeguards which assure, as far as assurance can be obtained, that it shall lead to the truth. Such safeguards are: 1) that the testimony be sworn; 2) that it be not repeated on the same issue; 3) that the wit-

[23] Haring in lqs., 1932, pp. 154, 155.

[24] Noval, n. 457; W-Vidal, vi, n. 459.

[25] Roberti, ii, n. 334.

nesses may be called upon to confront one another; 4) that the party be present at the taking of oath by the witness, and 5) be allowed to take exception to the witnesses and to their testimonies; 6) that there be concordant witnesses; 7) that unfit, suspected and incapable witnesses be sufficiently excluded.

192. Hence in marriage cases as in all others proof by witnesses is admitted under the direction and moderation of the judge, according to the prescribed norms of law (c. 1754). The fact that a marriage was contracted may be proved by witnesses.[26] [27] So too before marriage, the freedom of the persons concerned, from other marriage bond, may be proved by testimony. In cases of non-consummation the grievances and the fact of non-consummation, in cases of presumable death of spouse the death or repute of death or the attendant circumstances, and in nullity cases all those facts that go to establish the impediment, especially when the impediment is not public by its nature, may be proved by witnesses. And even in those cases that are public by their nature and are generally to be proved by document, the proof may be by testimony if the usual documents have been destroyed or cannot be obtained.[28] But if documentary proof can be had in these cases, the testimony of witnesses is not admitted because it is not the best proof obtainable *ad rem* (cfr. n. 234).[29]

193. The value of testimony depends entirely upon the double supposition that the witness has not erred in perceiving, and correctly remembers what he testifies, and that he will not deceive the court in making his statement. Most people have the necessary truthfulness and right use of sense perception and memory, and so anyone may be a witness unless he is expressly repelled by law (c. 1756). If a person

[26] R., Null., 6 dec. 1909 (rd., i, p. 156).

[27] In civil law: Abbott, p. 102: "The contract or its solemnization before a clergyman or magistrate may be proved by the testimony of an eyewitness, and for this purpose a party is competent; . . . It is enough that the witness be able to testify that the marriage was celebrated according to the usual form, and he need not be able to state the words used."

[28] SO, 1868, § 3; Pallotini, xiii, p. 261, § XIV, n. 23; xiii, p. 457, § XXVI, n. 10; xiii, p. 468, § XXVII, n. 34; Gasparri, i, n. 168; DeSmet, i, n. 149; ii, n. 678; Chelodi, n. 142; W-Vidal, v, n. 357: "Imo iure antiquo cum libri parochiales nondum existerent, unice fere per huiusmodi testes de auditu causae nullitatis ex capite consanguinitatis fuerunt definiendae."

[29] Gasparri, nov., i, n. 140; Capello, iii, n. 148.

is introduced as a witness, the presumption is that he is admissible, and any asserted disqualification must be proved against him.[30]

The Canon law follows the law of nature in disqualifying some persons but it also goes beyond this in expressly repelling some who would be fitted to testify, if the natural qualifications were alone decisive. The Decretals knew many disqualifying circumstances: women, slaves, stage players, soldiers, the blind, the deaf and dumb were not generally received as witnesses,[31] although exception was frequently made to admit even such persons as witnesses in marriage cases.[32] Most of these disqualifications have long since fallen into desuetude and the Code makes no mention of them. Even the blind, deaf and dumb may be admitted as witnesses of those things which they are able to observe.

The wording of the Decretals did not distinguish between those who should be absolutely excluded from testifying, and those whose testimony might be admitted even though a suspicion attached; but in judicial practice this distinction has long since been made. The Code distinguishes the unfit and suspected who may be heard, from those who are simply incapable of bearing testimony in the case (c. 1758).

194. There are several classes of people excluded as unfit, suspected or even incapable in ordinary contentious cases, who are nevertheless admitted in cases touching the marriage bond.[33] On the other hand the Code does not attempt to exhaustively enumerate all the grounds of unfitness and suspicion (cfr. cc. 1760; 1764,§2), and, for proper reasons, the courts sometimes exclude persons not mentioned in the Code (cfr. n. **203**).

195. Children who have not attained the use of reason are excluded by nature as unfit to be witnesses. Because of the immaturity of their judgment, Canon law reasonably extends this exclusion, at least in ordinary contentious cases, to those who have the use of reason but have not attained the age of puberty (c. 1757,§1; cpre. c.

[30] R., Null., 11 apr., 1911 (rd., iii, p. 167).

[31] cfr. c. 17, C. XXXIII, q. 5; c. 10, X, De Verborum Signif., V, 40.

[32] c. 33, X, De Testibus et Attest., II, 20; c. 3, X, Qui Matrim. Accusare Possunt, IV, 18; c. 2, De Iudiciis, II, 1 in VI.

[33] SCC., In Florentina, Mat., 29 aug. 1857 (pall., xiii, p. 468, n. 28, § XXVII): "Ad favorem autem Matrimonii, vulgatissimi iuris est, admitti Testes etiam non omni exceptione maiores."; IA., §§ 157; 219.

88,§2 with c. 1648,§3). In marriage cases however the testimony is receivable, especially when sufficient other witnesses are not obtainable to bring out the truth of the matter.[34] [35]

In no case may an adult testify to events that took place before the adult reached the age of reason (cfr. cc. 779; 800), except that, for the case mentioned in Canon 1019,§2 the oath, based on hearsay, may be sufficient proof of baptism received in infancy. In cases where the brothers and sisters of a person seek to prove by their testimony that he was baptized in infancy, it is necessary that those brothers and sisters shall have been at least seven years old at the time of the asserted baptism (cfr. c. 88,§3). But when they seek to prove by their testimony that the parents of the party were not Christians, or were apostates, and that conditions existed in the family which were incompatible with the early baptism of the child, and thus establish a ground upon which the judge may draw the inference that the party was never baptized, even younger brothers and sisters may testify, since such facts could be ascertained even during the later infancy of the party.

In ordinary contentious cases the testimony of adults to what they observed after reaching the age of reason but before reaching the age of puberty is excluded as unfit,[36] but in marriage cases such testimony is admissible and may form full proof, if the judge is satisfied with the testimony, and especially if the facts were witnessed at an age that rather approached puberty.[37] In a marriage case tried by the Rota the defender objected to the testimony of such persons but the Rota did not sustain the objection.[38]

[34] Cerato, n. 6.

[35] In civil law: Abbott, p. 951: "A child, if of competent age and intelligence to be a witness, may testify against its parent ..."

[36] R., Nucerinae Paganorum, 27 jul. 1914 (rd., vi, p. 287).

[37] R., Null., 21 dec. 1912 (rd., iv, p. 472); Null., 9 aug. 1915 (rd., vii, pp. 392, 393): "Unus e praecipuis testibus qui nullitati matrimonii favent, est procul dubio Iustina, quae de vexationibus matris, eiusque minis testatur; atque haec, tempore dicti matrimonii, erat adhuc adolescentula, et proinde inidonea testis. Verum, ut recte animadvertit iudex primae instantiae, "agitur de auditis et visis uti sunt minae et arreptio cultri, ad quod memorandum non requiritur aetatis prudentia, sed satis est audiendi et videndi facultas et rerum praeteritarum memoria, quae in pueris et puellis est valde tenax."; Noval, n. 465; W-Vidal, vi, p. 403 (26).

[38] R., Null., 8 mart. 1913 (rd., v, p. 215); cfr. Vic. Apost. Chansi Sept., Null., 29 jun. 1923 (rd., xv, p. 131).

196. Persons who because of insanity have no use of reason whatever, are by nature's law entirely excluded from the office of witness (c. 1757,§1). Those who have some use of reason, such as monomaniacs and others who enjoy lucid intervals, may be heard although unfit, at the discretion of the judge, but their testimony can hardly amount to more than an indication of the truth or a prop to other arguments (c. 1758).

Persons who attempt to testify to a fact witnessed while they were drunk, are by the law of nature unfit to be witnesses.[39]

197. Persons who because of having the right use of reason are fit to be witnesses, are nevertheless open to suspicion if they cannot be depended upon to speak the truth. Those who have been condemned or declared by court as excommunicate (cfr. c. 1576,§1,n.1), are by that fact suspected (suspecti) (c. 1757,§2,n.1). When no judicial declaration or condemnation has been made the excommunicate are not *ipso facto* suspected (cfr. c. 1654,§2); but the judge may hold their testimony in suspicion if the facts warrant it.

198. Judicial condemnation for, or declaration of perjury renders one by that fact suspected (c. 1757,§2,n.1).[40] If no judicial condemnation or declaration has been made the judge may hear even those who have previously perjured themselves, but must carefully decide whether the testimony can be accounted of any value. In a well known case from New York, the court of third instance disagreed with the court of second instance and declared with some touch of humor that while the lady A. G. had understated her age in court during a previous examination, "it is a well known fact that a woman might give a wrong account of her age, and be a trustworthy witness in all other respects."[41]

199. Persons who have been declared or condemned by court as infamous (cfr. cc. 2293, 2314,§1, 2320; 2328; 2343,§§1,2; 2351, §2; 2356, 2357,§1; 2359,§2) are *ipso facto* suspected. Otherwise the judge may use his discretion with respect to the testimony of such, and he should be very cautious, especially in marriage cases,

[39] Noval, n. 464.

[40] On the interdict and other punishments that await perjurors cfr. cc. 1743, § 3; 2323.

[41] R., Neo Eborac., Null., 1 mart. 1913, 8 feb. 1915 (rd., v, p. 184; rd., vii, p. 29; aas., v, p. 322; aas., vii, pp. 300, 301).

with respect to the testimony of bigamists, even though they be infamous in fact only (cfr. c. 2356); for such persons cannot generally be depended upon for a conscientious and objective testimony regarding another's marriage.

200. Although the Decree of Gratian excluded apostates (cfr. c. 1325,§2) from the Faith as witnesses,[42] the Code does not mention them in this matter and they are not *ipso facto* excluded. Much less are Protestants and other non-Catholics *ipso facto* excluded: on the contrary they are explicitly allowed by Canon 2027,§1 for procedures on beatification, and are all the more admissible in marriage cases.[43] Protestants and other non-Catholics have been declared acceptable witnesses both in nullity cases and in cases where they testify to the freedom of a party to marry.[44] Nor is a witness to be excluded by reason of his being a 'liberal,' provided always of course that the character of the witness gives promise of truthful testimony.[45] But the judge may hold the testimony of non-Catholics suspected when there is sufficient reason.[46] In two recent cases the Rota withdrew practically all weight from the testimony of persons whose lives were not sustained by any principles of religion.[47] In an even more recent case the plaintiff contended that her atheist husband had not seriously made the promise to allow her the freedom of her religion, which promise was a stipulation *sine qua non* to the marriage. The Rota accepted the testimony of her equally irreligious father-in-law to the effect that his son had not seriously promised.[48]

[42] c. 24, C. II, q. 7.

[43] Eichmann, p. 143 deduces from c. 2027, § 1 that they should not ordinarily be admitted as witnesses; this inference does not seem to be well founded.

[44] R., Osnabrug. Null., 11 jan. 1912 (rd., iv, p. 22): SO., Constant., 2 apr. 1873 (cpf., ii, n. 1399, ad 1; cicf., iv, n. 1025); SO, Alberti., ad dubium 6 um.

[45] R., Null. 11 apr. 1911 (rd., iii, pp. 167, 168).

[46] R., Paderborn., Null., 27 jul. 1917 (rd., ix, p. 166).

[47] R., Parisien., Null., 4 mart. 1916 (rd., viii, p. 70; aas., viii, p. 371): ". . . neque mirandum eius depositionem esse mendacem, utpote quia emissam scripto tantum et absque iuramento et insuper a muliere perditis moribus et Deum non timente."; Impedimenti ad Contrahend., 11 mart. 1910 (rd., ii, pp. 100, 101).

[48] R., Parisien., Null., 11 aug. 1921 (aas., xiv, p. 519; rd., xiii, pp. 217, 218).

201. Persons who are of morals so abject,[49] as not to be worthy of belief, are suspected as witnesses (c. 1757,§2,n.2).[50] Although public concubinage does not necessarily render a witness suspected (cfr. cc. 2357,§2; 2256,n.2), such absolute depravity may be accounted by the judge as a sufficient cause of suspicion.[51] But the Rota does not always exclude those from bearing testimony who are acknowledged to be of loose morals.[52]

Although an accomplice is not a proper witness in a criminal case,[53] the crime of having inflicted duress upon a person in order to constrain him to marriage does not of itself render the guilty person's testimony suspected, unless he be the other party to the marriage.[54]

In cases of legitimacy of child, Gasparri seems to deny that the joint testimony of a wife and her adulterer constitute proof of adultery "quia non meretur fidem allegans turpitudinem suam." [55] But it is plain from what is written just above, that this principle of Roman law cannot be alleged as an absolute rule, and the judge may properly weigh the testimony of the adulterers according to his discretion. Whether the adultery, when proved, begets certainty of illegitimacy cfr. nn. **535**, **536**.

202. Public and grave enmity toward one or both of the parties renders witnesses by that fact suspected (c. 1757,§2,n.3). If the enmity is not public but comes to light in the course of trial the judge will use his discretion as to how far the testimony is suspectible.

[49] W-Vidal, vi, n. 466: "Qui ita abiectis sunt moribus . . . Qua in re abiectio morum praesertim sese refert ad morum pravitatem, non ad statum seu conditionem vitae, v. gr. pauperis."

[50] Haring: Eheprozess, p. 16 (2): "Eine etwas vage Bestimmung."; Such are also marked with infamy (c. 2293, § 3).

[51] R., Null., 23 mart. 1914 (rd., vi, p. 149): "Iulia enim, eiusque mater nullam prorsus merentur fidem: a) propter corruptos utriusque mores, nam illa Raphaelinae F. dicere non erubuit: 'Meglio concubina con questo Carlo M. che moglie del Nunzio'; hanc non puduit domi amasium filiae retinere, non obstante quod validum retineret matrimonium a sua filia cum Nuntio contractum." Null., 23 mart. 1915 (rd., vii, p. 128); Null., 6 jun. 1918 (rd., x, p. 45).

[52] R., Argentinen., Null., 23 feb. 1912 (rd., iv, p. 110; aas., iv, p. 392); Gravinen., Null., 2 jul. 1918 (rd., x, pp. 62, 63; aas., xi, p. 196).

[53] cfr. W-Vidal, vi, p. 405 (33).

[54] R., Lugdunen., Null., 2 apr. 1917 (rd., ix, p. 65; aas., x, p. 73); Lega, i, n. 264.

[55] L. 29, 1, Dig., De Probationibus et Praesumptionibus, XXII, 3; et alibi; cfr. Gasparri, ii, n. 1307; nov., ii, n. 1113.

Enmity gives rise to suspicion against a witness however high his character or however sure his veracity, for when occupied with enmity toward a person, the mind cannot engage itself with truthful conceptions, being impelled by a will to avenge one's injury.[56] Hence the judgement of a man is commonly disturbed and prejudiced in those things that affect his enemy.[57] This suspicion of an enemy's testimony holds also in cases of nullity and even in those cases that are difficult of proof.[58]

Witnesses are not rendered suspected because of an enmity that formerly existed and has been forgiven. Nor need the testimony of an enemy be suspected if he testify in favor of his enemy. In a case of non-consummation at X. two of the relatives of the respondent, while testifying in favor of non-consummation, nevertheless expressed the hope that the Church would not allow the petitioner to marry again and " treat another husband as badly as she had treated this one." [59]

203. Other persons too who seem to have a strong interest in the case at issue may be suspected in their testimony. Such interest may appear from various circumstances, and the Rota did not hesitate in a case from Marseilles to infer it from the fact that the testimony was rendered at a suspicious time.[60] The Decretals likewise deemed a witness suspected who knew of an impediment before the marriage was contracted, but culpably neglected to testify and impede the marriage at the proper time.[61] The testimony of a pastor, otherwise beyond exception, was deemed to be of no value, when he evidently strove to establish the validity of a marriage contracted under duress through his fault.[62]

Servants of the parties involved in the marriage suit are not *ipso facto* excluded from giving testimony, and even before the Code,

[56] R., Null., 8 jan. 1921 (rd., xiii, p. 10).

[57] c. 2, C. III, q. 5.

[58] R., Null., 25 feb. 1911 (rd., iii, p. 101); Null., 8 jan. 1921 (rd., xiii, p. 10).

[59] Archive X. (unpub.).

[60] R., Massilien., Null., 26 mai. 1913 (rd., v, p. 330); Nicien., Null., 15 mart. 1915 (rd., vii, p. 113; aas., vii, p. 351).

[61] c. 1, 2, X, Qui Matrimonium Accusare Possunt, etc. IV, 18.

[62] R., Pitilianen., Null., 20 oct. 1916 (rd., viii, p. 332; aas., ix, p. 362); cfr. Null., 27 aug. 1912 (rd., iv, p. 439); Null., 4 jul. 1913 (rd., v, p. 428); Null., 23 mart. 1914 (rd., vi, p. 150).

were admitted as valuable witnesses in marriage cases.[63] But the judge may hold their testimony in suspicion when there is an evident and peculiar devotion to, or dependence upon one of the parties (cfr. n. **194**).[64]

204. For reasons of public order some persons are entirely disqualified as incapable (incapaces). This incapacity is not absolute and refers only to those cases wherein the witness bears a determinate relationship to the litigants. All the headings but one, under which a person is rendered incapable of being witness, are derived also from the presumption that his relationship to the party will beget biased testimony. The one exception is based on the absolute seal of secrecy with which the Church guards the confessional.

The parties to the case are not capable witnesses (c. 1757,§3, n. 1) (cfr. nn. **66, 123**). Those who act in the name of the parties: the proctor in the suit, the advocates and defender, and others who assist and stand by, or have thus stood by the parties in the suit, are incapable witnesses (c. 1757,§3,n.1). Nevertheless the Rota has recently admitted the testimony of those who furthered the case in the capacity of advocates,[65] and in one case decided to overrule the objection of the defender against a former advocate's being witness in the case.[66] Physicians who have tended one or both of the parties are admitted as witnesses and are required in cases of insanity (cc. 1978; 1982; cfr. c. 2028,§1).

Under the law of the Decretals a judge who had previously tried the case, was rendered a suspectible but not incapable witness.[67] The

[63] SCC., In Mediolanen., Separationis, die 26 feb. 1859 (pall., xiii, 384, n. 31).

[64] R., Null., 19 jun. 1909 (rd., i, p. 70); Impedimenti ad Contrahendum, 11 mart. 1910 (rd., ii, p. 101).

[65] R., Null., 4 jul. 1918 (rd., x, p. 76): "Fides tamen deneganda non est... sac. Bartolo excusso in processu suppletorio. Hic quidem ad concubinatus scandala avertenda auctor fuit, ut causa introduceretur, verum iste zelus non debet ipsum a priori suspectum reddere . . . "; Parisien., Null., 11 aug. 1921 (aas., xiv, p. 519; rd., xiii, p. 218): "Neque hic testis tenore can.... repellendus est, quia ab eo tamquam advocato, ante causae introductionem actrix consilium petiit; nam nec in hoc iudicio neque in alio partibus assistit vel astitit, sed refert quae a partibus tempore non suspecto accepit."

[66] R., Null., 17 jan. 1912 (rd., iv, p. 46); Hence Haring: Grundzuege, p. 865 (8): "Ein Rechtsbeistand kann auch durch Aufgeben seiner Stellung gegenueber der Partei die Zeugenfaehigkeit nicht erlangen," cannot be unreservedly followed in marriage cases (cfr. c. 2027, § 2, n. 2).

[67] cfr. R., Diffamationis, 14 mai. 1913 (rd., v, p. 312).

Code disqualifies the judge and his assistants as incapable (c. 1757, § 3, n. 1). If the rare case should now occur that the judge of the trial has been witness to pertinent facts bearing on the marriage, and his testimony is absolutely necessary, he could be heard after he had severed all connection with the trial as its judge, just as former advocates or proctors are heard in similar circumstances.[68] He may certainly testify without restraint in higher instance, with regard to the procedure followed under his direction in lower instance.[69]

205. Priests are absolutely incapable of testifying to anything they may have learned from sacramental confession, or from a source in any way connected with the confessional. No passing of time, or death of the penitent, or release from the seal of confession on the part of the penitent removes the incapacity (c. 1757,§3,n.2).[70] Most civil courts acknowledge the inviolability of the confessional (cfr. cc. 889,§1; 890; 2369,§1), and the Church courts have long since refused to admit testimony learned in confession,[71] even when explicit permission has been given by the penitent. Thus the disqualifying extends beyond the usual limits of the seal of confession. In the Sforza-Cesarini legitimacy trial held in 1834-1837 a priest had testified by express permission of the mother of the child whose origin was in question, that at about the time of the child's conception the mother had confessed to him the sin of adultery. The Rota rejected the testimony on the ground that the very nature of the sacramental judgment seat prevented it from being mixed with contentions in the external forum.[72]

Confessors of the parties are not disqualified from testifying to events they know from other sources than the confessional,[73] even when they have similar knowledge derived from the confessional.[74] Nevertheless their testimony may be suspected because of the very restraint under which the confessor must testify in such cases.[75]

[68] cfr. Bassibey, n. 364.

[69] R., Diffamationis, 14 mai. 1913 (rd., v, p. 312).

[70] Note that in procedures on canonization and beatification the confessor is no longer an admissible witness (c. 2027, § 2, n. 1).

[71] c. 13, X, De Excessibus Praelatorum et Subditorum, V, 31.

[72] cfr. R., Null., 8 mart. 1913 (rd., v, p. 214); Lega, i, n. 459.

[73] SCC., In Parisien., seu Aurelien., 25 jul. 1896 (bass., p. 226 (1)).

[74] De Smet, i, n. 68.

[75] R., Null., 30 nov. 1910 (rd., ii, p. 341): "At ommisso quod hic testis non est omni exceptione maior utpote quia ratione sigilli sacramentalis non omnia revelare potest . . . "; cfr. Noval, n. 468.

It is moreover forbidden even to lay people, who may have acted as interpreter for sacramental confession or overheard a confession (cfr. cc. 889,§2; 903; 2369,§2) or otherwise gained knowledge by reason of the confession made, to testify to what they have thus learned, and if they do so, their testimony cannot even be taken as an indication of the truth (c. 1757,§3,n.2).

206. Relatives by blood or marriage in any degree of direct descent and in the first collateral degree are disqualified in ordinary contentious cases (c. 1757,§3,n.3). In the marriage suit the relatives of the parties are admitted and sought as witnesses (cc. 1757, §3,n.3; 1974; 1975,§1), because they are generally best able, and sometimes they alone are able to know the circumstances upon which the truthful issue depends, because it seems not unreasonable to expect that conscience will not generally be smothered in such spiritual cases and because in marriage cases, a biased testimony on the part of some relatives may easily be offset by the testimony of relatives of the other party.[76] This exception for the marriage suit is of very ancient usage and Clement III writing to the Bishop of Florence calls it then an ancient custom.[77] Thus in cases of nullity parents are permitted to bear testimony, *v. g.* regarding the duress inflicted upon their child.[78] Likewise in marriage cases which do not concern the validity of the sacrament the testimony of relatives is receivable.[79]

In some marriage cases the testimony of an outsider may be held as of no importance when it contradicts the testimony of the relatives of the parties concerned.[80] For when the relative is of such character as to be above all cause for suspicion his testimony is of great value.[81]

The peculiar admissibility of the relatives in marriage suits, does not however exclude the possibility of suspicion against them, if there are grounds for suspecting that they are not disinterested witnesses.

[76] R., Null., 6 jun. 1918 (rd., x, p. 44); Noval, n. 854.

[77] c. 3, X, Qui Mat. Acc. Possunt, IV, 18.

[78] R., Lugdunen., 2 apr. 1917 (rd., ix, p. 65; aas., x, p. 73); Gravinen., Null., 2 jul. 1918 (rd., x, p. 61; aas., xi, p. 195); Gasparri, ii, n. 954.

[79] c. 2, C. XXXV, q. 6; SO., 21 aug. 1670 (cpf., n. 192 ad 14); SCC., In Nullius, S. Martini, Obsequiorum Matrim., 28 jul. 1804 (pall., xiii, p. 384, § xiii, n. 30); In Theatina, Mat., 22 nov. 1856 (pall., xiii, p. 468, § xxvii, n. 29).

[80] cfr. R., Pitilianen., Null., 20 oct. 1916 (rd., viii, p. 331; aas., ix, p. 361).

[81] R., Null., 29 jul. 1920 (rd., xii, p. 225).

Thus Alexander III writing to Cardinal Matthew pronounces the testimony of a mother suspected when she testifies to the betrothal of her daughter to a wealthy nobleman.[82] And the courts incline to suspect the confession of illicit coition made by an affine in favor of nullity, even though such testimony may constitute valid proof (cfr. n. **564**).[83]

207. In some cases the testimony of relatives is prescribed. Thus if consanguinity, affinity or spiritual relationship be not sufficiently proved by document, it has been prescribed that the relatives of the parties be brought to testify to the relationship, if they can be had.[84] In cases of non-consummation the testimony of the relatives must not be purposely omitted.[85] A recent case from Paris was postponed by Rome (dilata) because certain intimates and relatives of the parties were not called to testify.[86] However relatives of the parties are not so necessary that sentence cannot be pronounced against the marriage without them.[87] If a party have no relatives, or if their testimony could not be pertinent in a case of impotence or non-consummation, he will produce character witnesses from among his reputable neighbors or other friends (c. 1975, § 1).[88]

§ 3. Production and Exclusion of Witnesses

208. The first step in effecting proof by testimony is the producing of the witnesses (inductio, productio testium). In the early Roman law the witnesses came to court at the friendly request of the contending party, but by the Justinian law the judge was empowered to command their presence. The Canon law has followed Justinian. The producing of witnesses consists, strictly speaking, in presenting the names and addresses of the desired witnesses to the

[82] c. 22, X, De Test. et Attest., II, 20; IA., § 155: "Consanguinei . . . tum tantum excludendi sunt, quando ex individua casus natura, peculiares oriantur rationes, eos de partium studio suspectos habere. § 156. In dijudicanda credibilitate consanguineorum . . . imprimis considerandum est an conjuges nullitatem matrimonii exoptent, necne."; cfr. Veszprimien., Null., 2 jun. 1911 (rd., iii, pp. 226, 227).

[83] cfr. R., Null., 6 apr., 1914 (rd., vi, p. 184); Paderbornen., Null., 27 jul. 1917 (rd., ix, p. 166).

[84] c. 1, C. XXXV, q. 6; c. 5, X, De Test. et Attest., II, 20; PF, 1883, § 32.

[85] DS, Reg., nn. 59; 62.

[86] R., Parisien., Null., 21 mai. 1915 (rd., vii, p. 238; aas., viii, p. 46).

[87] R., Veszprimien., Null., 2 jun. 1911 (rd., iii, p. 234).

[88] DS, Reg., n. 58.

judge, in order that he may then summon them to court (cc. 1761,§1; 1765). If these are not presented within a peremptory specified term, the party is presumed to renounce his demand to have the witness heard (c. 1761,§2).

In marriage cases witnesses are thus introduced by one or both of the parties or by the defender, or they may be summoned *ex officio* by the judge (c. 1759,§§1-3), even in cases that are not public by their nature.[89] It is prescribed for cases of non-consummation that the judge call witnesses *ex officio*, whenever a party does not procure the character witnesses, or procures only three or four, or if even the full quota of seven leaves the matter at hand uncertain, or if he prudently fears a collusion between the parties, or between a party and his character witnesses (c. 1975,§1).[90] But the circumstances of many places are such that a summoning by the ecclesiastical judge would be a useless act, and hence it is the custom that the interested persons generally persuade the witnesses to appear, and fetch them to court (cfr. c. 1711,§2).

209. Witnesses rightly summoned to court must obey the summons or make known the cause of their absence (c. 1766, § 1). As in summoning parties so in citing witnesses, the judge is sometimes answered by a peremptory refusal to appear, and the declaration that the witness cited does not know anything about the matter.[91] In a recent case the mother of a party when cited as witness wrote the judge a letter spurning the competence of the Catholic Church and expressed her displeasure at the conversion of her daughter to the Faith.[92] Such disobedience is not a product alone of the modern world, for Clement III mentions in a rescript of 1187-1191 that a witness who will not testify regarding a case of consanguinity is to be forced to his duty.[93]

Disobedient witnesses, who without legitimate reason fail to appear, or who after appearing refuse to answer, or take oath, or sign the record of their testimony, may be coerced by the competent judge with proper punishments (c. 1766,§2), but there should be great caution with regard to inflicting spiritual punishments (cfr. n. **107**).

[89] R., Null., 29 apr. 1922 (rd., xiv, p. 130).

[90] DS, Reg., nn. 61, 62, 72.

[91] cfr. R., Veszprimien., Null., 2 jun. 1911 (rd., iii, p. 226).

[92] R., Null., 21 dec. 1912 (rd., iv, p. 473); cfr. Null., 1 jul. 1912 (rd., iv, p. 327).

[93] c. 6, X, De Testibus Cogendis vel non, II, 21.

The disobedient witness loses all right to compensation for the expense he may have been subjected to in coming to court (cfr. n. **220**).

If a witness will render testimony only on condition that his name be withheld from the parties or their proctors, or one of them, the judge may receive the testimony under this condition (cfr. n. **576**).

210. There are two sources by which persons qualified to render testimony are excused from testifying: the having acquired their knowledge under the seal of secrecy and the danger of diffamation and harm to their relatives.

When a person has learned of a matter that naturally demands a discreet secrecy (secretum naturale), or has learned it under a promise of secrecy (s. promissum), even in the course of rendering advice of one friend to another (s. commissum simplex), he is not exempted by this from testifying even in ordinary contentious cases. For the authority of the law has a precedence over all such secrets, and if these were allowed to beget exemption from testifying no court could be effectively held. Decisions on this point covering even the case where the secrecy was sworn to, have been rendered from the time of the Decretals,[94] and the moralists have concurred in the matter.[95]

When a person has learned of a matter because his official or professional advice, aid, care were asked (s. commissum officiale, professionale), he is exempted from rendering testimony in ordinary contentious cases, and in cases of separation from bed and board. Thus pastors and other priests, officials of government, physicians, obstetricians, advocates, notaries and others held to official or professional secrecy are exempt (c. 1755,§2,n.1). And in the case of priests this pertains to professional secrets learned even apart from the confessional. In cases concerning dispensation and non-consummation, or the validity of a marriage most authors hold that the prudent judicial disclosure of the official secret does not impair the public trust, and the common spiritual good, particularly of the parties concerned, requires that the exemption shall not hold (cfr. c. 1318,§2).[96] And in fact, the Code prescribes the testimony of

[94] c. 18, X, De Test. et Attest. II, 20; c. 4, 11, X, De Test. Cog. vel non, II, 21; R., Diffamationis, 12 dec. 1913 (rd., v, pp. 633-635).

[95] Noldin, ii, p. 682 (1); Lehmkuhl, i, nn. 1442-1444.

[96] V-Creusen, ii, n. 292; De Smet, i, n. 68; W-Vidal, vi, p. 400 (22); Bassibey, n. 396.

professional men in some cases (cc. 1978; 1982).[97] Similarly when such professional or official persons are summoned to testify in a case regarding diriment impediments that stand against a marriage about to be contracted, they are obliged to testify.

If such persons have not been summoned, and there is question only of spontaneously disclosing professional secrets in answer to the publication of banns, some authors tend to excuse them from making the disclosure;[98] not however without contradiction.[99]

211. Relatives of a party in any degree of direct line, and in the first degree of collateral line, are not obliged to testify in ordinary contentious cases or in cases of separation, when their testimony would defame the related party, or cause dangerous vexations or other very grave evils such as judgment for separation. Neither is any witness in a separation case obliged to testify so as to defame himself (c. 1755,§2,n.2; cfr. c. 1823,§1). But when there is question of the dispensing of a supposedly non-consummated marriage or of the validity of a marriage contracted or about to be contracted, relatives are obliged to testify.[100] Thus if there is question of the impediment of crime or of the decretal impediment of affinity, the accomplice is obliged to testify regarding his sexual relations with the party in the suit.

212. If a witness appear without being invited, the judge may admit or repel him at his discretion (c. 1760,§1). The judge is cautioned to repel the witness however, if it is observed that his purpose is to delay the trial, or by other artifice, to obstruct the just and truthful issue (c. 1760,§2). Such purpose was formerly presumed by law to exist when spontaneous witnesses presented themselves in cases to establish the freedom of a person to marry,[101] but the legal presumption no longer exists; on the contrary, those who know of impediments to proposed marriages are obliged to denounce them (cfr. n. **12** fol.).

[97] However, R., Imolen., Null., 2 aug. 1913 (rd., v, p. 504): "Iam vero medicus Poggi qui ab Adelinde a secreto officii liberatus est, . . ."; R., Null., 23 nov. 1923 (rd., xv, p. 287).

[98] Lehmkuhl, ii, n. 868.

[99] Noldin, ii, n. 670, 3'; cfr. Lehmkuhl, i, n. 1444.

[100] Lega, i, n. 501.

[101] SO, 1670, § 4; PF, 1883, § 43.

213. The number of witnesses required or allowed in marriage cases is not stipulated. In cases of impotence and non-consummation mention is made that each party must bring seven character witnesses (c. 1975,§1). The exact number of seven is not required however for the validity of the case.[102] Nevertheless the Congregation prescribes seven, and if some are omitted the reason for the omission of them must be stated in the acts.[103] The judge may call for more than the customary seven character witnesses of each party.[104] In a case of duress at Milan, more than twenty witnesses were called upon for testimony.[105] Generally the judge should examine all witnesses introduced by the parties,[106] unless they are unfit, suspected, or incapable. The Rota remarked unfavorably upon a case in which two of the witnesses introduced, were not called for testimony.[107] On the other hand however, the judge has the right and obligation of seeing to it that a superfluity of witnesses is not admitted (c. 1762).

214. The exclusion of a witness for want of the proper qualities takes place either *ex officio* or at the instance of an interested person (reprobatio personae testis). If the judge sees that witnesses are clearly disqualified as incapable, he will at once and of his own accord, exclude them from bearing testimony, not however without hearing the defender on the matter.[108] But if he observes only that they are unfit or suspected, he may at his discretion, allow them to be heard (cc. 1764,§1; 1758). However the parties are usually in a better position than the judge to know the circumstances that stand against admitting a witness, and so they too are allowed to offer objection against the witness, who, they can show, should be excluded (c. 1764,§2). Yet it rarely happens in nullity cases that the parties seek to exclude witnesses, partly because they are not aware of their right in this matter, and partly because in many cases, both parties jointly petition the declaration of nullity, or at least, the respondent

102 DS, Reg., n. 59; R., Null., 15 nov. 1909 (rd., i, p. 138).

103 DS, Reg., n. 59.

104 DS, Reg., nn. 61, 62.

105 R., Mediolanen., Null., 1, 17 aug. 1916 (rd., viii, p. 289; aas., ix, p. 441).

106 SO, 1840.

107 R., Impedimenti ad Mat., et Damnorum, 31 aug. 1912 (rd., iv, p. 431): "Quamvis igitur non adprobandum sit duos testes inductos non fuisse auditos, defectus iste substantialis non est."

108 DS, Reg., n. 22, § 1.

does not actively oppose the suit. The defender however, is also allowed to take exception against a witness,[109] and is more likely to take advantage of his right.

215. The party who has introduced a witness may waive the opportunity of having been examined, but he cannot repudiate as unfit, suspected, or incapable the witness whom he himself has introduced, unless a hitherto unknown cause for such repudiation shall have newly occurred or become known (c. 1764,§3). Even when he desires to waive the questioning of his witness, the other party or the defender may in spite of this, demand that the witness be examined (c. 1759,§4).

216. The judge must carefully inquire into the grounds upon which the exclusion of the witness is sought. For neither the party nor the defender has a veto right against witnesses. If the judge at once perceive that the objection against the witness is frivolous, and based on futile reasons, or is urged in order to retard the trial, he will decree that the repudiation is not to be sustained (c. 1784).

If it appear that the exception is a just one, the judge will allow the objecting party a brief term in which to prove the reason for repudiating the witness, and the procedure of proof will be carried on as in other incidental matters (c. 1785). When there is a legal presumption against the witness, *v. g.* when he is plainly included among those incapable of testifying, the question will be settled on the spot. Similarly when the grounds for repudiating a witness as unfit or suspected are notorious, or can be easily and at once proved, or when they can be now proved, but cannot be proved later on, because a witness now obtainable will later on be absent, the incidental question of admitting or rejecting the witness will be at once settled (c. 1764,§5). But in many cases, where the witness is objected to because of an asserted unfitness or cause of suspicion, a detailed discussion will be necessary, and then the judge will reserve the discussion until the end of the trial. When the other witnesses have all been heard or when all proofs are completed the incidental question on the admission or exclusion of the witness will be settled, and if he is to be admitted, he will then be heard.[110] Against the decree admit-

[109] IA., § 158.

[110] Roberti, ii, p. 53(1); Noval, nn. 479, 480 believes that the question should be decided before publication of the other testimonies; V-Crusen, n. 176 *et al.* preferring that the question be decided only after the testimonies are

ting or repelling a witness the interested party may have recourse to the same judge (c. 1841), or in cases of non-consummation to the ordinary,[111] but may not appeal (c. 1880, n. 6).

217. In order that the parties and defender may be enabled to take exception against unfit, suspected or incapable witnesses,[112] the parties must make known to each other the names of the introduced witnesses before the questioning of them is begun; or, if the judge think that grave difficulty would arise from the publication of their names at that time, they must be made known at least before the publication of their testimonies (c. 1763). In cases of non-consummation however, it is left to the discretion of the judge whether the names of the character witnesses shall be published, and whether before or after the testimonies have been rendered.[113]

If the parties are to be admitted to the taking of testimony they should be warned that exception against the person of the witness should be made before the testimony is heard. If exceptions were indiscriminately allowed after the testimony is heard or published, parties would find reasons for repudiation whenever the testimony of a witness is unfavorable to their case.

In order to avoid frivolous exceptions against witnesses the Code directs that any repudiation must be made within three days after the names of the witnesses are made known to the party (c. 1764, § 4), and with double insistence, before the testimonies have been published (c.1783,n.1).[114] After these terms, the exception will not be admitted, unless the party show or at least affirm under oath, that the cause for repudiating the witness was not known to him before (c. 1764, § 4).[115]

218. There is an important difference between taking exception against the person of the witness and taking exception against

published. In non-consummation cases the incidental question must be settled before conclusion of trial (DS, Reg., n. 96) without reference to publication of testimonies.

[111] DS, Reg., n. 22, § 2.

[112] Bouix, i, p. 317.

[113] DS, Reg., n. 63, §§ 1, 2.

[114] R, Reg., § 115 allowed repudiation of the witness even after the testimony was published; but Roberti, ii, p. 52 (1) and W-Vidal, vi, p. 418 (66) rightly say this rule was "minus convenienter" given. R, Norm. omits it.

[115] c. 31, X, De Testibus et Attest., II, 20 permitted one to reserve the right of later repudiation.

his testimony (reprobatio testimoniorum). For a party may still object to the testimony when he cannot repudiate the witness. Thus nothing prevents a party from taking exception to the testimony of witnesses produced by himself (c. 1764,§3), or from taking exception against testimony even after the acts have been published (c. 1783, n. 2).

The testimony may be repudiated for various reasons: First, it may be pointed out that the manner of taking testimony was faulty. If the witness was examined without the party being cited to the taking of the oath, if the testimony was taken without oath, or taken out of court without sufficient reason, if the defender was not cited to the taking of testimony, if the witnesses were examined collectively, if the questions were misleading, obscure, *etc.* exception may be taken.

Second: the testimony itself may be excepted against for doubtful, wavering, obscure, contradictory, improbable, irrelevant, or evidently false statements. Sometimes it will be sufficient merely to point out the defect in the testimony; sometimes it will be necessary to prove the defect, as *e. g.* when the statement of a witness is branded as false.

219. Witnesses must not be paid for testifying even to what is true,[116] for the speaking the truth cannot be appraised in money, and besides, a paid witness is not perfectly free in his testimony. For this reason the Holy Office in 1670 required that in procedures to establish the unimpeded right of a person to marry, the witnesses be asked whether they had been paid for rendering testimony,[117] although it was later directed that the question is to be omitted whenever there were witnesses presumably of high character or known honesty, who would take offense at it.[118] If it is shown that any witness has been suborned by a party, there arises a presumption, not only that that witness's testimony is untrue, but likewise that other witnesses who favor that party have been suborned to false testimony.[119]

220. But there is a difference between suborning a witness and reimbursing him for the expenses necessarily incurred by travel, interruption of work *etc.*, in his coming to testify. Such expenses strictly measured are allowed by Canon 1787 and are awarded ac-

[116] c. 8, C. XXXV, q. 6; c. 1, X, De Test. et Attest., II, 20.

[117] SO, 1670, § 5; c. 1957 permits other precautions in criminal cases.

[118] SO., 2 apr. 1873, Constant. (cpf., ii, n. 1399, § 2; cicf., iv, n. 1025).

[119] R., Null., 1 aug. 1913 (rd., v, p. 497).

cording to the decree of the judge, after hearing the witness and party and, if necessary, experts on the question of amount. Canon 1909, § 2 permits that a deposit be demanded from the interested party, sufficient to cover expenses. If the deposit has not been made within the peremptory term stated by the judge, it may be taken to mean that the party has waived the opportunity of producing witnesses (c. 1788). In cases touching the marriage bond however, the judge must not let this technicality obscure the merits of the case.[120]

§ 4. Oath of Witnesses

221. Before giving testimony the witness swears to speak the truth (iusiurandum de veritate dicenda) (c. 1767,§1). It is mentioned in the Decretals that such an oath was required of witnesses in a case of consanguinity,[121] but of the later pre-Code instructions only the Regulations for the Rota make mention of this oath.[122]

The taking of the oath is required no matter how high the prestige or dignity of the witness may be. When, in other contentious cases, unfit or suspected persons are heard by decree of the judge, they are not generally required or permitted to swear to their testimony (c. 1758). But it seems to be the spirit of the Code to require the oath in marriage cases, even when it may be omitted in other cases (cfr. cc. 1744; 1830,§1), and the relatives of the parties as well as all other witnesses, whatever be the general suspicion that they are biased in the suit, are nevertheless required to take oath when testifying in non-consummation cases.[123]

However, the marriage of two natives was recently tried in New Pomerania, but the local judge did not think the parties of sufficiently cultured mind to realize the meaning of an oath. The mentality of the natives is indeed so low that the civil government does not admit them to take oath. Upon appeal, the Rota upheld the action of the Vicar Apostolic's court and pronounced sentence likewise upon un-

[120] Haring: Eheprozess, p. 25 raises the question of how to provide for the expenses of witnesses introduced by the defender or the judge, and says the parties' deposits must cover that; the answer can have but little practical value for us, since marriage trials in our diocesan courts are, in fact, nearly always conducted without demanding the advance deposit, and without awarding expense remuneration to the witnesses.

[121] c. 5, X, De Test. et Attest., II, 20.

[122] R, Reg., § 114, n. 2.

[123] DS, Reg., nn. 39; 58; 67; 69.

sworn evidence.[124] Another recent decision of the Rota remarks however, that the testimony of a pagan was given under oath.[125]

In purely contentious cases dealing with the mere private interests of the parties the oath of the witnesses may be omitted if both parties agree (c. 1767,§3). But not so in cases touching the marriage bond, for they are of public interest.[126]

Nevertheless it may happen that the oath cannot be administered. In England, ecclesiastical persons are forbidden by civil law to administer an oath.[127] Witnesses are accordingly heard under a promise to oblige themselves before God to speak the truth, and a declaration that they consider themselves as sworn witnesses, and would take formal oath if there were no hindrance.[128]

If a witness refuses to take oath, or is excused from it, his testimony may be heard, but mention of the excuse or refusal and the reason for it, must be made in the record (c. 1779).

222. The taking of oath must be mentioned in the record (c. 1779); [129] when this is forgotten the value of the testimony is obscured to the judge of higher instance.

223. The oath is tendered with mention of the name of God. In marriage cases a priest takes oath with his hand upon his breast (c. 1622,§1); [130] a lay Catholic places his hand upon the Holy Writ in its entirety or upon the book of Gospels. Jews may take oath upon the whole Writ or upon the Old Testament alone.[131]

[124] R., Vic. Ap. Nov. Pomeran., Null., 30 apr. 1913 (rd., v, p. 289; aas., v, p. 470).

[125] R., Vic. Apost., De Fianarantsoa, Null., 16 nov. 1920 (rd., xii, p. 262).

[126] Lega, i, n. 486; Noval, n. 484.

[127] Smith, Elements, Appendix IX.

[128] R., Null., 4 jul. 1913 (rd., v, p. 427) quoting Conc. Westmonast. I, Append. X, n. 10; SCC., In Parisien., Mat., 12 aug. 1882 (bass., n. 303).

[129] Noval, n. 498: "... saltem quandoque sufficit eas scripto redigere quoad substantiam; puto autem servandam esse regulam in superiore canone traditam, videlicet, mentionem esse faciendam quoad ipsa editi testimonii verba; nisi iudex, attenta causae exiguitate ..." refers, by these words, to the substance of the testimony rather than to the formality of the oath.

[130] In cases of sollicitation cfr. SO., 6 aug. 1897 (cicf., iv, n. 1190; cpf., ii, n. 1977); cpre. c. 1555, § 1.

[131] Bassibey, n. 304 quoting S. C. Inq., 24 mai., 13 jul., 17 aug. 1826.

Witnesses must swear that they will speak the whole truth, as far as they know it, and only what is true (c. 1767,§1). The formula is left to the determination of the judge (c. 1622,§3).[132]

224. The parties or their proctors may be present when the witnesses take oath (c. 1767,§2); this offers a safeguard against introducing and hearing witnesses without allowing the interested party to take the proper exceptions. Hence the parties should be cited to this solemnity, though the omitting to cite them does not invalidate procedure.[133] For the judge may properly decide, because of special difficulties that threaten, to keep the names and identity of the witnesses secret until just before the publication of their testimony (c. 1763).

225. If the judge think it necessary or helpful, witnesses may be called upon after their examination, to swear that they have spoken the truth, either in reference to all their statements or in reference to some only, even when they shall have sworn to speak the truth before rendering testimony (c. 1768).[134]

226. Witnesses may be called upon to observe secrecy regarding the questions asked and the answers given, until the acts or testimonies are published, or, in some cases, perpetually. And they may be required to take oath that they will observe the secrecy (cc. 1623, § 3; 1769). This oath should be given as one with the oath to speak the truth, or at least with the confirmatory oath after testimony is given.[135]

§ 5. Examination of Witnesses

227. When they ask to introduce their witnesses the parties may tender to the judge a statement of the points on which it is

[132] DS, Reg., Appendix, XVIII suggests formula: "I, N... swear that I shall speak the whole truth and nothing but the truth as well upon the separate articles as upon the question in its entirety, as I see the truth before God and my conscience, and I shall fully and faithfully make it known without adding, omitting or changing. So help me God, *etc.*"

[133] cfr. IA., § 163; Bassibey, n. 306.

[134] DS, Reg., n. 46; Haring: Eheprozess, p. 19 rightly says that too much oath-taking should be avoided and the repetition of oath after testifying should be demanded only when there are weighty reasons present.

[135] DS, Reg., Appendix XX: "I ...... swear that I have spoken the whole truth and only the truth and I shall never divulge the questions asked, nor the answers given, before the present trial is completed. So help me God, *etc.*"

desired that the several witnesses be examined (c. 1761,§1; cfr. c. 1745,§1). In order that both parties may properly draw up such questionaries, the judge may communicate to the adversary the various questions and points on which either one proposes that the witnesses be examined.[136] Neglect to present the questionaries begets a presumption that the party renounces his right to do so (cfr. c. 1761, § 2). While the parties to marriage cases sometimes neglect to present their questionaries (mostly because they do not know of their right to do so), the defender always presents his sealed up schedule of questions upon which the witnesses are to be examined (cc. 1745, §1; 1968,n.1). The judge too may prepare in advance his own list of questions, and he may have statements of the parties read to the witness in order to receive the latter's comment on the statements (cfr. nn. **112, 113**).[137]

228. The witnesses are examined in the place where court is held (c. 1770,§1). In cases where it is presumed by law that the usual safeguards are not required, or where it is impossible to examine the witnesses in the ordinary seat of the court, they may be examined elsewhere:

1. Cardinals, bishops and distinguished persons who are exempted by their civil law from the obligation of appearing before a judge for the purpose of testifying, may choose the place where they will render their testimony and must notify the judge of it (c. 1770,§2, n. 1).

2. Those who are ill or otherwise impeded by bodily or mental hindrance, or by the circumstances of their life from coming to court, will be heard in their homes (c. 1770,§2,n.2). The Code exemplifies this by mentioning nuns, but there seems to be no prohibition against sisters who are not cloistered coming to court.[138] In a case at Malines, the husband was interrogated in prison.[139] In a case at Amiens one Henri C. a paralytic, could not come to court, but answered the summons by a letter of testimony on the marriage, and this testimony received some consideration from the judges.[140]

[136] PC., 12 mart. 1929 (aas. xxi, p. 170).

[137] Haring, Eheprozess, p. 20.

[138] c. 2, De Iudiciis, II, 1 in VI; W-Vidal, vi, p. 400 (20).

[139] SCC., in Mechlinen., 28 mart. 1896 (ass., xxix, p. 163).

[140] R., Ambianen., Null., 3 jan. 1917 (rd., ix, p. 8; aas., x, p. 384).

3. Those residing outside the diocese and for whom it would be a great inconvenience to come to court, will be heard by rogatory commission, in the diocese where they reside, according to questions and instructions sent by the trial judge (c. 1770,§2,n.3; cfr. c. 1570,§2). But he may also see fit to let the defender of that diocese draw up his own questionary, on the basis of the articles proposed by the parties.[141]

Those who live within the diocese but at such a distance that, without great inconvenience or expense, neither they can come to court, nor can the judge go to them, will be heard by a nearby priest who is fit and worthy to be designated as auditor, and he will be assisted by some person who will act as notary. The trial judge designates the auditor *ad rem;* by way of exception (cfr. c. 1585, § 2), the notary *ad rem* will be appointed, it seems, by either the trial judge or the designated auditor. The Congregation even allows that, when no one can be had to act as defender or notary *ad rem*, the witness may be heard without either defender or notary.[142] Previous instructions had not so well provided for conditions in missionary lands. In all these cases the trial judge will send a list of questions to be asked, and such instructions as are opportune (c. 1770,§2,n.4).

5. When the judge undertakes judicial notice of a person or other object, he may examine witnesses on the spot, where the inspection is made (cfr. 1810).

The Code does not exhaust all the instances in which the examination of a witness outside the court room is permissible: there are other cases where the prudent judge may permit it.

229. The proper time for hearing witnesses is after the joining of issue. The Decretals insisted on the nullity of the procedure (cfr. n. 52), as well in marriage cases as in others, when the witnesses were heard before the respondent could contest the suit.[143] The Code too states that the judge shall not proceed to the hearing of witnesses or the receiving of other proofs, before the issue is joined; but, as in the Decretal, so in the Code exception is made for cases where the party is contumacious, or where there is pending the impossibility or difficulty of later obtaining the testimony because of probable death or departure of the witness, or for other such just reason (c. 1730).

141 R, Norm., art. 93, § 2; cfr. Haring in Iqs., 1930, p. 140.

142 DS, Reg., n. 24, § 4.

143 c. 1, 4, X, Ut Lite non Contestata *etc.*, II, 6.

In these cases the testimony should be taken in advance for future reference (ad futuram rei memoriam) (cfr. c. 2087,§3).[144]

Apart from this it is proper to hear witnesses beforehand, when an incidental question is to be settled; *v. g.* whether the plaintiff is qualified to contest the marriage (cfr. c. 1971).[145]

230. The character witnesses are the first witnesses heard: they are examined immediately after the parties.[146] Those produced by the plaintiff or petitioner are first heard, beginning with the nearest relatives, who are presumed to be best informed, and after them outsiders, such as servants and neighbors. But the judge is free to invert this order of testimony.[147]

231. It is plain from the Decretals that the Canon law of the middle ages required that the witnesses be not heard unless the parties were invited to be present at the hearing.[148] The introduction of a written procedure which could be afterward reviewed by the parties, and the danger lest some human respect incline the witnesses to favor the parties caused a change in this policy, and later instructions rather demanded that the parties be absent during the hearing of witnesses.[149] Both methods of proceeding have their advantages and disadvantages.[150] Lega however had suggested anew that if the parties were present they could suggest useful questions on the spur of the testimony given by the witnesses.[151] And Smith is authority for the statement that the custom in America has long favored a personal confronting of witness and parties, except when grave inconvenience would result.[152] But no evidence of such a custom, in ecclesiastical

[144] Meehan, p. 228: "Et in hoc reus melioris est conditionis quam actor ..." But now, the Code knows no preference.

[145] cfr. SO, 1928; Bassibey, n. 341; W-Vidal, vi, n. 487.

[146] SCC, 1840, § Deinde.

[147] DS, Reg., n. 66.

[148] c. 2, 41, X, De Test. et Attest., II, 20.

[149] IA., § 164; SCC., In Algaren, Mat., 17 dec. 1887 (bass., p. 227 (3)): "Coniux Gavinus... examini interfuit omnium testium a se introductorum. Quocirca magna suspicio habetur testes praesente et audiente actore interrogatos, sive ex humano respectu, sive ex urbanitate, sive alia ex causa vera reticuisse vel etiam falsa oggessisse."

[150] cfr. Roberti, ii, n. 346.

[151] Lega, i, n. 489.

[152] Smith, n. 450. That a similar custom exists in Spain, cfr. W-Vidal, vi, p. 410 (52) cit. Muniz, n. 316.

trials, has come to my notice. Following Rotal procedure,[153] the Code now chooses a middle path, leaving it to the discretion of the judge to permit the parties to be present at the hearing of the witnesses, or to exclude them (c. 1771). Or, if the judge see fit, he may exclude the principals but permit their advocates to be present.[154] Canon 1985 however offers reason to conclude that in cases of non-consummation the parties should not, ordinarily at least, be invited by the judge to be present, though they may be admitted if they ask it.[155]

232. The witnesses are to be examined singly and alone (c. 1772, § 1). A witness must not be examined in the presence of other witnesses who have testified or will testify in the case; much less should several witnesses be interrogated together and give answer in consort.[156]

It is left to the prudent decision of the judge whether the witnesses may confer with or confront one another or the parties in court, after the rendering of the testimonies (c. 1772,§2). This confrontation should take place only if all the following circumstances occur: 1) If witnesses dissent from one another or a party, in a grave matter touching the substance of the issue,

2) If there be no other easier method of being made certain of the truth,

3) If there be no fear of scandal or quarrels from the conference (c. 1772,§3).

233. The examination of witnesses is carried on by the judge or his delegated auditor (c. 1773,§1). The Code says nothing about the right of the associate judges in a tribunal of three. Although the presiding judge will do most of the questioning, the associate judges may, without doubt, directly question the witnesses, and if they do so, the questions and answers must certainly be written in

153 R, Reg., § 114, n. 6.

154 Smith, n. 450.

155 cfr. DS, Reg., n. 97, § 2.

156 PF, 1883, § 13; R., Colonien., Null., 1 jul. 1912 (rd., iv, p. 330; aas., iv, p. 672): "Iste defectus, quo invalidae redduntur eorum depositiones, per rescriptum Summi Pontificis sanatus est. At nec auctoritas pontificia sanare potest defectus naturales depositionum, quibus omnis earumdem vis probandi tollitur. . . . Imprimis notandum est eos simul, non seorsim, interrogatos fuisse, et unum simul responsum quaestionibus dedisse, et eandem depositionem subscripsisse, ita ut impossibile sit discernere quamnam partem mater, . . ."

the acts.[157] If the parties, advocates, promoter, defender are present at the questioning and have questions to propose to the witness, they will propose them to the judge or auditor, in writing or by verbal mention, that he may ask the questions of the witness (c. 1773, § 2). For the questioning, in Canon law, is properly the act of the judge or auditor alone, and neither the advocate of the party nor the defender should directly propose the questions. In some diocesan courts however, a custom has developed whereby, after his questioning of the witness, the judge calls upon the defender to propose verbal questions. Such a practice, if tolerated, does not invalidate procedure.[158]

234. The practice of obtaining testimony for marriage cases by sending witnesses to notaries public, there to make their sworn depositions, is not generally nor *per se* to be approved. In a recent case from Philadelphia the Rota pronounced the marriage invalid, and remarked that the witnesses who stood for validity had not deposed in judicial form, but rather before a notary public, and their written testimonies thus brought to court were not accorded consideration as good proof.[159] It would be too much to say that the judge cannot under any circumstances admit proof of that kind, *e. g.* in case a witness will not appear before the curial auditor. But if testimony is to be thus received by way of necessary exception, the judge should make note of reasons in the acts, and prescribe the questionary to be answered, and take necessary precautions against false testimony being given.[160] There is a danger of falsity in the testimony of such extrajudicial witnesses.[161] In the diocese of X., a case of disparity was decided favorably to the plaintiff who had introduced extra-

[157] cfr. R, Reg., § 71, n. 2; Haring: Eheprozess, p. 20 (3).

[158] SCC., Panormitana, Mat., 27 feb. 1886, 20 aug. 1887 (ass., xx, pp. 435, 436); cfr. Woywod in hpr., xxxii (1931), p. 166.

[159] R., Philadelphien., Null., 9 feb. 1920; 16 jul. 1921 (rd., xii, p. 42; xiii, p. 180).

[160] cfr. Nau, pp. 229, 230.

[161] Roberti, ii, p. 79 (1): "Testes extraiudiciales in Codice can. non recensentur. Nec generatim eos admittunt codices civiles. Habebantur in lege Gregorii XVI (§ 629, 630, 631, 632) et consistebant in voluntariis attestationibus a notariis receptis, quae dein in iudicium afferebantur ad probationem vel exceptionem, et substituebantur articulis facti, de quibus examen iudiciale erat peragendum. Cum saepius hi testes essent suspecti in desuetudinem abierunt."

judicial testimonies sworn to before a notary public, as evidence of her non-baptism. After she was married anew, an interested observer mailed to the Chancery an authentic and incontestible document certifying her baptism. If the case had been heard in due procedure before a curial auditor and defender, the falsity of the testimony might have been easily detected, and an erroneous decision of nullity avoided. For this reason it is directed for cases of dissolution of merely legitimate marriage in favor of the Faith, that character witnesses be introduced to testify to the veracity of such a witness, and that the trial judge refer to the Holy Office his view on the worth and credibility of such recorded testimony.

Much less is it allowed to send witnesses of disparity of cult, consanguinity, affinity, marriage bond or other impediments public by their nature to make depositions as to the fact of baptism, relationship, marriage, *etc.*, before a notary public, and on the basis of the testimony thus documentated, settle the marriage case in short procedure according to the norm of Canons 1990-1992 (cfr. nn. **192**, **350**). If the documentary evidence cannot be obtained, *e. g.* because Church records have been destroyed, the case must be tried in regular procedure, and this offers a safeguard against erroneous decision, while it does not deter a plain case from speedy settlement. In these cases the negative element of the impediment, *i. e.* the fact that baptism was not conferred, or that no dispensation had been granted may indeed be proved by testimony properly received, for the nature of the thing makes proof by public document impossible (cfr. n. **376**). Hence the Pontifical Commission on Interpretation of the Code declared other legitimate proofs admissible for this negative element of the case.[162]

235. When properly interrogated by the judge, witnesses must answer and speak the truth (c. 1755,§1). This duty binds in conscience under pain of grave sin.[163]

Witnesses who knowingly answer falsely to the questions of the judge or hide the truthful issue, are punishable by interdict, suspension *etc.*, according to the norms of Canon 1743,§3, and lose their

[162] PC., 16 jan. 1931 (aas., xxiii, pp. 353, 354); Hence Nau, p. 223 seems to have erred in viewing the Commission's interpretation of Canon 1990 as permitting that the fact of baptism be established by testimony: for the interpretation explains obscure passages but does not contradict plain words of the Code.

[163] Lehmkuhl, i, nn. 980, 981.

right to compensation for expenses (cfr. n. **220**); and all who suborn witnesses with gifts, promises or any such means, to the end that they testify falsely or hide the truth, are subject to the same punishments (c. 1755,§3) (cfr. n. **107**).

236. Great care must be taken that the subject matter of depositions strike at the heart of the case and cover the telling points. Hence eye witnesses in some cases and hearsay witnesses in all cases must be asked to give the source or ground of their information (c. 1774).[164] Thus it is not enough to testify that a marriage was entered upon under some named stipulation. If a witness knows of a stipulation having been appended to the marriage contract, he must state how he knows it and from whom, and with what words it was expressed.[165]

In cases of marriage voided by duress witnesses must testify to specific threats, scoldings, confinements, acts of violence, *etc.*, together with attendant circumstances, which constitute the duress inflicted (cfr. n. **154**).

Witnesses on consanguinity and affinity must testify not only that a diriment relationship exists between the parties, *v. g.* that they are second cousins, but must show the computation by which such relationship is derived from a common ancestor, or, in the case of affinity, from a brother or sister. Otherwise the testimony does not prove.[166]

In procedure to establish the liberty of a person to marry, the witnesses must likewise show the grounds for their testimony that the person in question is free from existing marriage bond.[167]

237. When hearsay witnesses testify, it is important that they be asked from whom they received their version of an event. For such witnesses will not be further heard, if it appear that the persons from whom they received their knowledge are absolutely incapable or entirely unfit to depose.[168] If the authors of the hearsay testimony

[164] cfr. DS, Reg., nn. 42, 70; Character witnesses are not usually asked the reason for their testimony: W-Vidal, vi, p. 411 (54).

[165] R., Null., 6 aug. 1915 (rd., vii, p. 381).

[166] c. 1, 7, X, De Consanguinitate et Affinitate, IV, 14.

[167] SO, 1670, §§ 9, 10; SO., 13 jan. 1869, Instr. ad Deleg. Ap. Aegypt. (cpf., ii, n. 1342; çicf., iv, n. 1008).

[168] c. 47, X, De Test. et Attest., II, 20: "cum satis videretur absurdum illos admitti, quorum repellerentur auctores"; SCC., In Mileten., Null., 26 nov. 1768 (pall., xii, 554).

are suspected witnesses, the hearsay testimony itself is open to suspicion. Hearsay witnesses must therefore be asked when they received their version of the event: was it before the marriage, or on the wedding day, or after it; was it at a time that leaves it free from suspicion, or was it at a time when the parties had already cherished the hope of having the marriage declared void, or had perhaps already begun the procedure? [169]

238. It is permissible to ask witnesses to testify to the repute or general current opinion of an event (cfr. n. **188**). In cases of impotence or of dispensation from ratified marriage, it is prescribed that witnesses be asked what the repute is, regarding the impotence or non-consummation.[170] Witnesses who testify to repute must be asked to give the causes from which the repute arose, and to name the persons by whom they know that such and such repute is abroad.[171]

239. In cases of impotence and non-consummation the physicians who have tended the parties are asked for their opinion whether the marriage cannot be or has not been consummated.[172] The character witnesses are also asked their opinion on the impotence or non-consummation.[173] In cases involving the sanity of a party it does not seem to be against the spirit of the Canon law if the intimates and associates of the party are called upon for an opinion on the matter.[174] In some cases of duress too, the opinion of witnesses has been asked, accepted and credited.[175] But as a rule the witnesses must be asked about facts and not about opinions. In the well known case between Countess A. and her husband Count S. the Rota, in the fourth instance, remarked unfavorably upon the fact that a judge of lower

[169] DS, Reg., n. 70.

[170] SO, 1858: "quaenam sit fama tam apud se, quam apud alios de hac praetensa non consummatione"; DS, Reg., Append. XXVII, q. 13.

[171] R., Null., 8 jan. 1921 (rd., xiii, p. 7).

[172] SO, 1883, Pars II, tit. vi, art. 5.

[173] SO, 1858, § Deinde; DS, Reg., Appendix XXVII, q. 13; cfr. R., Null., 10 feb. 1912 (rd., iv, pp. 91, 92).

[174] New York State law sets its face generally against allowing an opinion from other than experts, yet it allows expression of opinion from witnesses in cases of insanity: McKelvey, pp. 246, 247.

[175] R., Gravinen., Null., 2 jul. 1918 (rd., x, p. 67; aas., xi, p. 201); Cameracen., Null., 23 jun. 1911 (rd., iii, p. 301).

instance had asked a witness her opinion whether the plaintiff had married under duress.[176]

240. The judge must question witnesses in such a manner as to arrive most securely at the true issue. Hence the questions must have certain characteristics (c. 1775). They must be 1) Short: Several short questions are preferable to one that is very long, for simple folk cannot always grasp the meaning of a question that is modified by numerous and involved clauses.[177]

2) Simple: No more than one idea should be expected in the answer, lest a confused witness apply to one part of the question words intended as the answer to another part. If a compound question be asked and the witness does not clearly answer to each part, the question itself should be resolved into several simple questions.[178]

3) Plain: The question should have only one meaning, and hence must be neither captious, ambiguous nor misleading.

4) Impartial: The appearance of the questions should be colorless, such as: " Tell us what happened . . .; what did you observe on the day. . . ." Leading questions that indicate the subject matter, such as qualities of persons and circumstances of time and place, or suggest the answer that is expected or desired by a party, must be avoided (cfr. c. 2012,§1).[179] A judge of the Curia of Milan was rebuked by the Congregation of the Council for suggesting in his question that the answer to it was already known to the court and wanted confirmation. He began the question with: " It is known to this court that . . . *etc.*" [180] More recently the Rota denied all value to the confession of a husband because the local curia had opened several questions with the words: "Is it true that . . .," so that all the husband had to do was to answer "Yes" to their questions.[181] If however, suggestive questions be asked, this fault does not render

[176] R., Veszprimien., Null., 2 jun. 1911 (rd., iii, p. 228); Parisien., seu Nicien., 30 dec. 1915 (rd., vii, p. 469; aas., viii, p. 328); Null., 27 aug. 1912 (rd., iv, p. 444); Null., 10 dec. 1914 (rd., vi, p. 349).

[177] DS, Reg., n. 43, § 1.

[178] DS, Reg., n. 31.

[179] R., Null., 17 jan. 1912 (rd., iv, p. 39).

[180] SCC., In Mediolanen., 20 dec. 1884 (bass., p. 230 (1)).

[181] R., Null., 10 dec. 1914 (rd., vi, p. 345); cfr. Romana, Null., 27 mai. 1911 (rd., iii, p. 175); Null., 6 aug. 1915 (rd., vii, p. 381).

the procedure invalid in strictly judicial cases.[182] In cases of Pauline privilege, the Holy Office insists especially on colorless, impartial interpellation.[183]

In two recent cases the Rota rightly drew the suspicion that someone had suggested answers to witnesses. In one case the suspicion arose from the fact that the judge twice asked the same question in almost the same words, and the witness gave a negative response the first time but an affirmative response the second time.[184] In the other case a witness not trained in law, gave an important answer couched in precise legal terms, and the Rota held to the suspicion that the answer had been suggested to the witness by the advocate of the party.[185]

5) Relevant to the case on trial: Answers calculated only to satisfy curiosity must not be sought, and as this is a fault into which one may naturally and easily fall, the diocesan curiae avoid it only when special pains are taken to avoid it. Some questions however, pertain to a case only by laying the ground for more pertinent questions to follow: such questioning need not be excluded. It is admitted in repeated decisions of the Rota that, when direct proof cannot be had, the judge may select testimony of facts that point to the impediment at issue, even though the answers do not directly touch the heart of the matter (cfr. n. **520**).

6) Not unnecessarily offensive: The questioning of a parent who has disgracefully maltreated his daughter in order to coerce her to marry is inevitably offensive in its subject matter, but such ques-

182 R., Remotionis, 11 mart. 1909 (rd., i, n. 40); Null., 31 oct. 1919 (rd., xi, p. 149).

183 SO., Mongoliae, 29 nov. 1882 (cicf., iv, n. 1075; cpf., ii, n. 1581): "4. Quid censendum de responso negativo a parte infideli obtento, scilicet non velle converti aut pacifice cohabitare cum sua parte conversa, si istud responsum non quidem cordate sed quasi oblique obtentum fuerit? Verbi gratia si ille qui ad interpellationem missus fuit, infideli dicat: 'scisne? ista uxor a te antea dimissa, aut fugiens, nunc intravit in istam novam religionem europaeorum, et quaerit alium virum; an, si ad te rediret, adhuc reciperes pro uxore tua, et cum ea pacifice cohabitares, et quam nunc habes uxorem dimitteres?' Pars infidelis tali modo interrogata saepissime respondet negative, sed missionarius de eo non raro angitur." "Resp. ad 4. Quoad praeteritum acquiescat, facto verbo cum SSmo: sed in posterum interpellationes esse omnino faciendas iuxta formas ab Ecclesia praescriptas."

184 R., Philadelphien., Null., 9 feb. 1920 (rd., xii, p. 41).

185 R., Null., 19 mai. 1920 (rd., xii, p. 110).

tioning is not improper. But the manner of the questioning must be cautious, for it is the business of the examining judge to arrive at the truth, not to chide or disgrace the guilty.

241. As a rule, the judge should avoid questions that are argumentative: *i. e.* that call for an operation of the witness's mind, except in the case of character witnesses or of expert testimony (cfr. n. **313**). Thus it is best to avoid such questions as: "Why did you answer the questions of the priest at the altar?" However, in cases of dissolution of merely legitimate marriage to favor the Faith, the converted party is to be asked about the attitude of mind (sincerity) he had in receiving baptism. The judge must generally avoid questions that call for testimony on the operation of another's mind. In a recent case at X. several such questions were faultily and uselessly asked: *e. g.* "Do you think that your daughter took your threats seriously?" However, there are cases where such questions may be tolerated.[186] In cases of dissolution of merely legitimate marriage it is directed that pastors and other priests who shall have instructed the convert and prepared his way to conversion, be asked about the reasons that induced him to receive baptism.

242. A logical or chronological order should generally be observed in presenting the questions. Cross questioning is not entirely excluded,[187] but extremes should be avoided and the meaner artifices of cross examination should never have any place in the marriage trial.

243. A witness should be first asked general questions that lay the way for others more pertinent to the marriage case. The full name, birthplace, age, religion, situation or occupation, place of residence of the witness and particulars about his acquaintance or relationship with the parties, such as whether he be relative, friend, enemy, servant, business associate, will be asked, and later those questions that remotely refer to the events at issue. On the basis of the answers given, more specific questions may then be asked (c. 1774). Unless the testimony is thus introduced by more general questions, the specific questions of a judge will almost inevitably contain a suggestion leading to the answer.[188] But even in the general questioning clearness must not be lost sight of. In a case of non-con-

[186] cfr. *e. g.*, R., Null., 31 oct. 1919 (rd., xi, pp. 147, 148).

[187] Bassibey, n. 308.

[188] Noval, n. 494: "Hinc in iure romano praescriptum erat: 'qui quaestionem habiturus est non debet specialiter interrogare, quia hoc magis

summation at X. several witnesses were asked: "Do you know what the present case is about?" and all gave confused and fumbling answers, until the trial judge perceived that the question was not clear enough and discontinued asking the question.

244. The specific questions to be asked cannot be set down to rule but must spring from the heart of the matter. They will differ according to the impediment involved and the circumstances surrounding it.[189] However the judge may be guided by the questions suggested in various instructions that have been issued by the Roman congregations. In cases of duress:

I. As to the duress inflicted: 1. In what did the intimidation or duress consist? 2. Were there words of scolding; 3. Were there threats? 4. What threats? 5. Were there threats of disinheritance? 6. Were there threats of ejection from home? 7. Were there deeds of violence? 8. What deeds? 9. Were blows added? 10. Could such acts as were committed against a girl render cohabitation with her parents unbearable?

II. As to the persons who inflicted the violence: 11. Who were they? 12. Were they parents of the party or persons taking the place of parents? Was the party at all subject to them? 14. What was the character of the persons who inflicted duress? 15. Economic condition? 16. Mode of life? 17. How did they usually govern the family? 18. Were they used to inflicting violence? 19. Were they so prone to anger and violence that they easily carried out their threats? 20. Were they so obstinate as to suffer no contradiction or opposition? 21. What purpose prompted the duress? 22. Had those who inflicted the duress some advantage to be gained from the marriage? 23. Were they seeking to safeguard the family reputation by urging this marriage?

III. As to the character of the person who suffered under duress: 24. What is the sex of the intimidated party? 25. Age? 26. Education? 27. Character? 28. Was she (he) used to the infliction of violence? 29. From the person here accused of it? 30. Was she meek and timid? 31. Or strong and brave? 32. Was she subject to her parents in everything or was she usually free in the ordinary

suggerentis quam requirentis videtur'; hoc autem intellegendum est si quis 'non interrogaretur in genere; sed quando praecesserunt interrogatoria generalia, utique interrogari potest in specie.'"

[189] IA., § 161; R., Parisien., Null., 10 mai. 1916 (rd., viii, p. 146; aas., ix, p. 38); Mansella, p. 198.

affairs of life? 33. Did her parents keep her so confined that she could seek advice from no one? 34. Did they admit only those to speak with her who would persuade her to the projected marriage?

IV. As to the influence of the duress: 35. Had there existed a friendship between the parties? 36. Had the intimidated party at one time freely accepted the marriage project? 37. Why had she (he) changed her (his) mind? 38. Was it before or after the parents expressed their desire? 39. What was done to overcome the parents' wishes? 40. Were they asked to desist from the project? 41. Were others asked to intercede? 42. Did the intimidated party show an aversion to the marriage? 43. Was any sign of this aversion given at the wedding ceremony? 44. Did the intimidated party seem to consent willingly? 45. Did she seem to enjoy the festivities? 46. How did she act toward the other party? 47. Toward his family? 48. Did the parties freely and willingly enter upon marital relations? 49. Did they quarrel? 50. When did these quarrels begin? 51. What was their cause? 52. Was anyone taken into their confidence on the matter? 53. Who? 54. With what effect? [190]

245. In cases of impotence and non-consummation: 1. Are you a relative by blood or marriage to either party? In what degree and how? 2. How long have you known the party? 3. On what occasion did you come to know them? 4. Do you know anything of their piety and trustworthiness? 5. Do you think the parties have spoken the truth? 6. Do you think them incapable of perjury even in their own favor, in a matter so grave as this? 7. Do you know whether the parties married each other with free will and mutual love? 8. What signs of mutual love did they give before the marriage? 9. On the day of the marriage? 10. Afterwards? 11. Do you know whether they used the same bed? 12. Consummated the marriage? 13. Are you informed of the reason of the non-consummation? 14. Was it from want of consent in the marriage? 15. Or because of duress in entering it? 16. Or from abomination of each other dating from the marriage? 17. Or from absolute or relative impotence? 18. Or from any other cause? 19. Did the parties apply any remedies against their impotence? 20. What remedies? 21. Did the parties quarrel? 22. Did one injure the other? 23. What was the reason and occasion of their change of attitude toward each other? 24. How long did they live together? 25. Who first deserted the other?

[190] SO, 1883; PF, 1883, §§ 37, 38.

26. What do you think of the asserted non-consummation or impotence? 27. What do others say? 28. Do you know others, relatives or friends of either party, who are informed about this case and can testify in this suit? 29. Do you know when the petitioner thought of asking the Supreme Pontiff for a dispensation from this non-consummated marriage? 30. From whom did he learn of this power of the Supreme Pontiff? 31. What cause or reason is there for granting the dispensation? 32. Is there a possibility of reconciling the parties?[191]

If medical aid has been sought to remedy the physical defect, the physicians who tended the party will be asked: 1. What is the nature and quality of the disease under which you found the party laboring? 2. From what symptom do you conclude that the disease has this nature? 3. What is the physical constitution of the party? 4. What medicine or remedy did you prescribe? 5. What is the nature of this medicine or remedy? 6. What effects were produced? 7. Did the party tell you the marriage could not or had not been consummated? 8. Did any other person tell you that? What do you think of this asserted impotence or non-consummation?[192]

246. In cases where it is sought to establish the fact of death of a spouse: I. For a witness who saw the spouse dead: 1. Did you know the party well? 2. Did you see him die? 3. Where? 4. When? 5. Did you see him lying dead? 6. What caused his death? 7. Where is he buried? 8. Do you know others who saw him die or lying dead?

II. For a witness who heard of his death: 1. Who told you of the party's death? 2. Are the persons who told you of his death reliable? 3. Could they have had reason for starting an untrue rumor of his death? 4. When did you receive the news of his death? 5. When is he said to have died? 6. Where? 7. Under what circumstances?

III. If the case has to be decided on presumptions arising from the party's departure and failure to return: As to the hazard of death: 1. What was the party's age? 2. Religion? 3. Morality? 4. What was the condition of his health at the time of his departure? 5. Why did he leave his home? 6. When did he leave home? 7.

[191] DS, Reg., nn. 56, §2; 68; Appendix XXVII; SO, 1883, Pars II, tit. vi, art. 5; SO, 1858, § Deinde.

[192] SO, 1883, Pars II, tit. vi, art. 5.

Where did he set out for? If he left for sea, 8. Who were his companions? 9. From what port did he sail? 10. What was the name of his ship? 11. Who was its master? 12. Did the ship arrive at port of destination? 13. Was it shipwrecked? 14. Was shipwreck insurance paid on the ship? If he left on a journey, 15. Were there grave dangers in this journey? 16. Was there revolution in the land to which he went? 17. War? 18. Famine? 19. Epidemic? 20. Did he take part in the war or revolution? If he left for army service, 21. Was he engaged in battle? 22. Was he captured by the enemy? 23. Did he desert the army? 24. Was he sent on any dangerous exploit? As to the likelihood of fraudulent abscondence: 25. Did he depart with the consent of his wife and family? 26. What degree of devotion had he toward them? 27. Did he send back letters? 28. From what places? 29. Were they regularly received? 30. During how long a time were they received? 31. Did he state his purpose to return home? 32. When did the letters stop coming? 33. Was there repute of his death at home or at those foreign parts? 34. Had he any real estate? 35. Had he any expectation of a legacy from his parents or another person? 36. Had he a reason for fraudulently absconding himself? [193]

247. The questions to be proposed must not be communicated to the witness beforehand (c. 1776,§1). But the judge may inform the witness of the subject matter on which he is going to be examined, if the events in question are so remote or so likely to be out of memory that the witness will not otherwise be able to answer with certainty, and provided that the case is not endangered by the disclosure (c. 1776,§2).[194] Thus a witness may well be admonished to be prepared to answer on the events of the wedding day, or to look over letters, diaries, reports, *etc.* which refer to a certain period of time.

248. The witness answers the questions orally.[195] He is not permitted to read from a prepared paper unless there is question of numbers and accounts (c. 1777), and this, says Noval, is the only exception made.[196] However the Congregation allows for procedure

[193] SO, 1868, n. 7.

[194] DS, Reg., n. 43, § 2; R, Reg., § 114, n. 8.

[195] Haring: Eheprozess, p. 21 says the judge may "propter decentiam" write a question and allow a woman witness to write the answer;—all this of course, in the court-room; cfr. R., Null., 6 dec. 1921 (rd., xiii, p. 283).

[196] Noval, n. 496.

on non-consummation, that the judge may in a particular case, permit the reading of an important document, calculated to corroborate testimony or assist the memory of a witness.[197] And in the C.-G. case a witness was permitted to offer as his testimony a written paper covering the events witnessed. He was afterward questioned on the written testimony and asserted he had taken notes of the event at the time of their happening.[198]

249. The questions and answers are written down by the notary (c. 1773,§1). If they cannot be written word for word, either because of speed or impropriety or incongruity, the judge will dictate the answer as it should be written in the acts.[199] When the testimony is completed, and before the witness leaves the room, the questions and answers as recorded must be read, not simply shown,[200] to the witness by the notary. The witness is then permitted to add or withdraw, correct or change the record of his testimony (c. 1780,§ 1), and should be asked whether the written account fully responds to the sense of his answers.[201]

250. The testimony is then signed by the witness, judge or auditor, and notary (c. 1780,§2). If the witness cannot write he will make a cross on the paper and the judge or auditor and notary will sign.[202] The witness's failure to sign does not however invalidate the testimony.[203] The signature of the defender was formerly prescribed,[204] but the Code has omitted to mention the defender in this respect (c. 1780,§2) although his signature is still required in cases of non-consummation.[205]

251. The entire testimony should be taken at one session whenever possible, for collusion between the parties and witnesses is not then so likely to creep in. If all the witnesses cannot be had at one

[197] DS, Reg., n. 43, § 2; cfr. DS, Ordin., n. 34, § 2.

[198] R., Neo Eboracen., Null., 1 mart. 1913 (rd., v, pp. 175, 176; aas., v, p. 314).

[199] DS, Ordin., n. 35, § 2.

[200] Noval, n. 499.

[201] DS, Reg., nn. 46, 69, Appendix XXVII, q. 19.

[202] SCC, 1840, § Si examen; PF, 1883, § 14.

[203] R., Buffalen., Null., 30 jul. 1928 (unpub. Prot. N. 902-23).

[204] SCC, 1840, § Si examen; PF, 1883, § 14.

[205] DS, Reg., Appendix XXVII.

session the judge fixes an adjournment and the examination will be resumed at another sitting.[206]

252. The hearing of new witnesses and the rehearing of those already examined is permitted in ordinary contentious cases at the instance of a party or *ex officio,* but only before the testimonies are published (c. 1781). After the testimonies are made known, new witnesses may be admitted only for the gravest reasons (c. 1786). Clement III refused to admit new witnesses to prove that there was no impediment standing against a marriage about to be contracted, after the witnesses already produced had proved the impediment and their testimonies were published.[207] After the conclusion of trial is decreed, only such witnesses may be heard as were legitimately impeded before (c. 1861,§1).

However in cases that involve the marriage bond new witnesses may, for a grave reason, be heard at any time, even after the publication of the proofs, and the conclusion of the trial (cc. 1786; 1861, §1; 1983,§1), because of the gravity of these cases. The Code reads that new witnesses may be heard "super diversis articulis" but makes no mention of hearing new witnesses on the same points. But it has been customary in the past to hear new witnesses on the same points in marriage cases, even after the acts have been published,[208] and such hearing thus seems to be proper now. Naturally the practice of hearing all witnesses before the acts are published is to be encouraged.

Similarly witnesses who have already been heard may be again examined in marriage cases, even after the testimonies have been made known, provided the points on which they are questioned be different from those on which they were before examined (cfr. c. 1786; 1983,§2). If they are to be reëxamined on the same points, this should be done before the testimonies are published.

The Code is not too clear in expressing whether or not witnesses may, for a grave reason, be reëxamined on the same points after their testimonies have been published (cpre. cc. 1781; 1786; 1983,§2). It is of course plain that this must not be done except for a grave reason, and with precaution against the danger of collusion and falsehood.

[206] SCC, 1840, §§ Si examen, Peracta relatione; DS, Reg., n. 33, § 1.

[207] c. 6, X, De Prob., II, 19.

[208] c. 35, X, De Test. et Attest., II, 20; R., Nicien., Null., 15 mart. 1915 (rd., vii, p. 113; aas., vii, p. 351).

For experience has shown that in a losing suit parties resort to extreme and unfair measures which were never thought of as long as the unfavorable evidence had not been made known. However on the question whether such reëxamination may be allowed with precaution and for a grave reason, the recent pre-Code doctrine and practice may rightly guide the judge now (cfr. cc. 6,n.4; 23). The Congregation had denied a second hearing meant to clarify previous obscure testimony.[209] Lately however marriage cases have admitted of special favor even in this matter, and in a case of stipulation against the interests of progeny, the Apostolic Signatura ordered witnesses to be reëxamined on the same points after their earlier testimonies had been already published. Naturally though, the reformed testimonies did not escape the stigma of suspicion.[210]

Even before the testimonies have been published, and especially afterward, the judge must not recall witnesses unless he considers it necessary or useful, and he must be especially on his guard against the danger of collusion and subornation (cc. 1781; 1786).[211] For this reason when there is to be a rehearing after publication of testimonies, the other interested party and the defender will be heard on the matter (cc. 1786; 1983,§2).[212]

253. When the parties or their proctors were not present during the examination of the witnesses, the judge may decree that the testimony be communicated to them as soon as all the witnesses have been examined (c. 1782,§1). But the judge may put off making the testimonies known until such time as the other proofs shall have been exhausted if he deem it advisable (c. 1782,§2) (cfr. Ch. XIV).

§ 6. Appraisal of Testimony

254. Canons 1789-1791 give some norms for the appraisal of testimony, but they are not hidebound rules and the judge is free to set whatever value his prudence shall dictate, upon the various testi-

209 SCC., In Florentina, Mat., 29 jul. 1854 (pall., xiii, 466, § Ad).

210 R., Null., 17 jan. 1912 (rd., iv, p. 37 fol.); cpre. c. 1786: "nisi caute"; cfr. R., Baltimoren., Null., Causa Incident., 29 nov. 1911 (rd., iii, p. 504); Lega, i, n. 496, 4°; (cfr. n. **264**).

211 cfr. R., Nicien., Null., 11 jun. 1920 (rd., xii, p. 140); Parisien., Null., 23 jun. 1921 (rd., xiii, p. 149).

212 DS, Reg., n. 47, §§ 1-3; Canon 1786 mentions also the promoter; canon 1983 does not.

monies. Experience has shown that nervous and visual deception, lapse of years, forgetfulness, lack of calm judgment and especially sympathy with the interests of the parties play a large part in the truth or falsity of testimony.[213] Hence the judge is directed to have consideration for the personality of the witness, the source of his knowledge, the number of witnesses *etc.*, and he may find further direction in reviewing the Rota's appraisal of various testimonies, received, for the most part, from diocesan courts.

255. The Austrian Instruction declared that only sworn depositions were to have the force of legitimate proof,[214] and subsequent decisions of the Rota have rightly denied to unsworn testimony the same degree of proof-bearing value that sworn testimony has.[215] The Code requires that the oath be usually taken (cfr. nn. 221-226) and thus supports the previous legislation, but it does not stipulate any restriction upon the proof-bearing value of unsworn testimony. In some cases where the oath was not taken the Rota has confirmed the diocesan court's pronouncement of nullity.[216]

256. In estimating the worth of testimony the judge will have in mind the character and reputation of the witness (c. 1789,n.1). It has been the practice of the Roman Curia to ask a testimonial on the character of unknown witnesses in marriage cases.[217] This practice has been followed by the Rota to some extent, and is mentioned in the recent Instruction for cases of non-consummation.[218] It is desirable that the testimonial come from the pastor of the witness.

In a secret case of nullity tried in 1912 a certain priest Charles had testified in favor of the suit. The diocesan curia scored his testimony as precipitous and not disinterested. Thereupon the Rota

[213] cfr. Bouix, i, pp. 310, 316.

[214] IA., § 162.

[215] R., Null., 4 jul. 1913 (rd., v, p. 427); Ambianen., Null., 3 jan. 1917 (rd., ix, p. 8; aas., x, p. 384); Parisien., Null., 10 mart. 1920 (rd., xii, p. 53).

[216] R., Vic. Ap. Nov. Pomeran., Null., 30 apr. 1913 (rd., v, p. 289; aas., v, p. 470); Null., 4 jul. 1913 (rd., v, p. 427; Vic. Ap. Chan-Si Sept., Null., 29 jun. 1923 (rd., xv, p. 133). Hence one cannot agree with W-Vidal, vi, n. 471 in the full meaning of the statement that "depositio testis iudicialis qualiscunque non est valida, nisi sit iurata, saltem in ordine ad probationem efficiendam".

[217] SO, 1670; SO., 24 feb. 1847 (cicf., iv, n. 900; cpf., i, n. 1011); SO, 1858, § Praetereunda; PF, 1883, § 16.

[218] DS, Reg., n. 60, § 2.

called upon three other priests, neighbors of Charles, to testify to his reliability.[219]

But the testimonial of character admits of exception, and even when the pastor certifies to the character of witnesses the judge may make his own appraisal on the truthfulness of their testimony. Certain witnesses were recommended by the Curia of Nice and by their pastor for " uprightness, virtue and truthfulness," but in spite of this the Rota held the witnesses suspected, for it was found that the pastor mentioned had an interest in the suit, and it was not known to the court from what source the Curia had its information.[220] Again in a case of separation the wife was commended for her honesty and truthfulness, by the pastor and a high member of the Roman Curia, but the Bishop of Sandomierz gave a less favorable testimonial.[221] In a case of 1913 the vicar general gave an unfavorable testimony of the witness, and her testimony was then held to be of little value.[222]

257. The judge will appraise testimony likewise by the rank and position of the witness (c. 1789,n.1). The testimony of a pastor, even when he does not testify in his capacity as an authorized witness, should generally have great weight.[223] The Rota held the testimony of an old man in especially high esteem because he belonged to the French Academy.[224] [225] The testimony of a girl's father was highly valued because it was given on his death-bed.[226] Again, a presumption in favor of certain Protestant witnesses was derived from the fact that they testified in favor of a woman who had deserted their religion to become a Catholic.[227]

258. In ordinary contentious cases the testimony of the unfit and suspected, if at all heard, is taken only as an indication of the

219 R., Null., 27 aug. 1912 (rd., iv, p. 439); Parisien., Null., 17 mart. 1914 (rd., vi, p. 118; aas., vi, p. 411).

220 R., Parisien., seu Nicien., Null., 30 dec. 1915 (rd., vii, pp. 473, 474; aas., viii, p. 332); cfr. Colonien., Null., 27 aug. 1910 (rd., ii, p. 321); Null., 26 mart. 1920 (rd., xii, pp. 90, 91).

221 R., Separationis, 17 mart. 1913 (rd., v, p. 224).

222 R., Null., 4 jul. 1913 (rd., v, p. 428).

223 R., Null., 28 aug. 1911 (rd., iii, pp. 439, 442).

224 R., Parisien., Null., 17 apr. 1915 (rd., vii, p. 166; aas., vii, p. 448).

225 In civil law too, rank and position beget a presumption in the witness's favor; cfr. McKelvey, p. 204.

226 R., Null., 24 jun. 1912 (rd., iv, p. 303).

227 R., Osnabrugen., Null., 11 jan. 1912 (rd., iv, p. 23).

truth and a prop to other arguments (c. 1758), but in cases concerning the marriage status such testimony, especially that of the relatives to the parties, may possibly form full proof of the case.[228]

259. The value of testimony is determined by making comparisons at the source of the witness's knowledge (c. 1789,n.2). In the C.-G. case from New York, the testimony of Prince D. was held to be of no great moment because it was at variance with other testimony springing from the same source. He testified that A. G. had in his presence and in the presence of two others stipulated divorce as a condition to the marriage. Yet neither of these seemed to know anything about the stipulation.[229] Again, when witnesses said they had received their information from letters, these were asked for, and upon being answered that they were all lost, the Rota rated the testimony of less value.[230]

260. It is plain at first sight that hearsay testimony is to be appraised by the source from which it originates. Sometimes such testimony originates from another witness to the same suit; sometimes it takes its origin from the mouth of one of the parties; sometimes the hearsay was received at an unsuspected time; sometimes at a suspected time. Alexander III was precise in these distinctions,[231] and Innocent III declared that the testimony of hearsay witnesses was to be subjected to severe scrutiny or else it could not effect the dissolution of a marriage.[232] Direct hearsay testimony may be of great value and weight.

[228] R., Null., 29 jul. 1911 (rd., iii, p. 408): "Et 1. c. n. 37 idem auctor (Coscius) scribit: 'Quapropter viles etiam et minus honestae personae in huiusmodi causis probationem faciunt circa actus difficillimae probationis . . ."; V-Creusen, iii, n. 172.

[229] R., Neo Eboracen., Null., 8 feb. 1915 (rd., vii, p. 40; aas., vii, p. 311); cfr. Parisien., Null., 4 nov. 1915 (rd., vii, p. 451; aas., viii, p. 163).

[230] R., Null., 18 feb. 1918 (rd., x, pp. 33, 34); cpre. Null., 21 jan. 1911 (rd., iii, p. 22): "Et eo magis adhibenda est fides testibus deponentibus de exclusione vinculi perpetui a viro volita, quod verisimilia omnino testantur, ea scilicet quae optime quadrant cum nota viri indole, cum principiis ab eo propalatis, cum pecuniariis eiusdem angustiis, cum duobus finibus quos sibi in matrimonio contrahendo sibi proposuit iuxta concordem fere omnium testium depositionem."

[231] c. 1, X, De Consang. et Affinitate, IV, 14.

[232] c. 47, X, De Test. et Attest., II, 20; cfr. R., Null., 8 jan. 1921 (rd., xiii, p. 7).

The Instruction on the procedure to establish the presumable death of a spouse demands eye witnesses of the death if they can be had, but admits also the sworn testimony of reliable hearsay witnesses as full proof of the case.[233]

The Holy Office has also recorded the admissibility of hearsay witnesses in order to establish the freedom from previous marriage of a person about to marry, if they are necessary to establish the case.[234]

Similarly, cases of non-consummation are greatly aided by the report of what the parties said at a time when there was no thought of bringing suit, and when there were no other reasons for hiding the truth or venting what is false.[235]

A case came from Versailles under the heading of want of consent, and rested entirely upon the testimony of witnesses whose information was derived from the plaintiff in the suit. She had married under the explicit stipulation that her intended spouse had never had sexual coition with any other woman, and she had expressed the stipulation to her intended before the marriage. But there were no witnesses to the making of this stipulation, except those to whom she had afterward related it at a time when no suspicion could attach. After meeting with repeated unfavorable decisions in the diocesan courts and in the Rota, her plea was finally upheld by a special commission of Cardinals appointed by the Pope to reinstate the case in its entirety.[236]

Cases of duress have frequently been determined favorably to the plaintiff on the testimony of those who had heard the intimidated woman's account of events given before she was married, or on the wedding day, or right after it.[237] Full proof of duress was estab-

233 SO, 1868, § 5; cfr. DS., Praesumptio Mortis Coniugis, 18 dec. 1914 (aas., vii, p. 42).

234 SO., 13 jan. 1869, Instr. ad Deleg. Ap. Aegypt. (cpf., ii, n. 1342; cicf., iv, n. 1008).

235 DS, Reg., n. 70; R., Null., 15 nov. 1909 (rd., i, pp. 138, 139).

236 Commissio Specialis RR. PP. Cardinalium, Versalien., Null. (sine dato), (aas., x, pp. 388, 389).

237 R., Transylvanien., Null., 1 mai. 1912 (rd., iv, p. 222; aas., iv, p. 482); Parisien., Null., 17 apr. 1915 (rd., vii, p. 169; aas., vii, p. 451): "Testes omnes de auditu sunt, sed,... quattuor ex ipso ore Michaelae ante eius matrimonium, et ideo tempore non adhuc suspecto, rem didicerunt."; Parisien., Null., 11 dec. 1916 (rd., viii, p. 370; aas., ix, p. 469): "Neque dicatur praefatum metum reverentialem eiusque adiuncta iuridice non esse demonstrata, deficientibus

lished by witnesses who testified they had heard the girl's mother lament her having forced her daughter to marry.[238]

On the other hand the testimony of a priest V. was considered worthless in a case where the plaintiff wife herself was the sole source of his knowledge, and he had received her account of the events just at the time she presented her case.[239]

And in a case of pre-Code affinity by illicit coition, the Rota in 1914 refused to accept the testimony of two or three witnesses, who had heard the husband assert even before marriage that he had had coition with his future sister-in-law, as proof that fornication had actually taken place.[240]

261. When a witness offers indirect hearsay testimony (cfr. n. 187), it gives the judge occasion to inquire the names and addresses of those persons who are the sources of the hearsay and are themselves at least direct hearsay witnesses. If these direct hearsay witnesses are alive and can be heard, the indirect hearsay testimony is inadmissible proof, because it is not the best obtainable *ad rem* in its kind. If these direct hearsay witnesses are not alive or cannot be heard, the indirect hearsay may be accepted as a more or less weighty support to other proof, at the discretion of the judge (cfr. c. 2020,§5).[241]

262. When witnesses testify that an event is reputed to have taken place, the value of this testimony will increase according as the persons named as authors of this repute are grave and reliable, and as the causes are probable and proportionate, through which the

testibus ocularibus. Nam in causis quae sunt difficilis probationis, et praesertim in metu probando, admittuntur testes de auditu.... Porro in praesenti causa, quinque sunt testes de auditu ... qui rem audierunt ab ipsa Marcellina in tempore minime suspecto, scilicet ante ipsum matrimonium."

[238] R., Lugdunen., Null., 2 apr. 1917 (rd., ix, p. 65; aas., x, pp. 73, 74); cfr. Massilien., Null., 1 jul. 1911 (rd., iii, p 327); Massilien., Null., 30 apr. 1917 (rd., ix, p. 108; aas., ix, p. 578); Parisien., Null., 26 feb. 1910 (rd., ii, p. 68; aas., ii, p. 348); Catalanisiaden., Null., 28 jul. 1916 (rd., viii, pp. 231, 232; aas., viii, p. 488); Gravinen., Null., 2 jul. 1918 (rd., x, p. 62; aas., xi, p. 196).

[239] R., Lugdunen., Null., 5 jun. 1917 (rd., ix, p. 136; aas., x, pp. 166, 167); cfr. Parisien., Null., 4 nov. 1915 (rd., vii, p. 451; aas., viii, p. 163); Paderbornen., Null., 27 jul. 1917 (rd., ix, p. 166; aas., x, p. 220).

[240] R., Null., 6 apr. 1914 (rd., vi, p. 187).

[241] Schmalzgrueber, Pars III, tit. xx, nn. 111, 112 in accordance with a policy of favoring action in nullity cases, says: "nihil probat, . . . except. . . . in probanda consanguinitate ad effectum dirimendi matrimonium . . ." To which general rule Roberti, ii, pp. 72, 73 (2) rightly takes exception.

people have come by the repute.[242] When the repute is thus well substantiated, the testimony may form part proof or even full proof of the case.[243] Alexander III declared that the repute of the neighborhood was to be decisive in a case where a strictly clandestine union was upheld by the husband but contested by the wife on the ground of want of intention to contract marriage.[244] [245]

The Instruction of the Holy Office states that the testimony of two witnesses to the repute of the death of a spouse may be taken as full proof of the death, if other proofs cannot be had.[246] In questions of consanguinity too, repute is explicitly named as a source of proof.[247] In a case of affinity the decision for nullity was largely based on the testimony that there was a general repute that the impediment had been incurred by illicit coition.[248] Similarly for non-consummation,[249] and duress.[250]

When it is not established that the authors of a public repute are grave and reliable persons or that the causes of it are probable and proportionate the judge will consider the current talk rather as a rumor than as genuine repute (cfr. n. **188**). Pope Celestine III refused to admit such rumor as proof of a case of affinity by illicit coition.[251] Such rumor does not form full proof even when the validity of a marriage is not in question,[252] and usually it will hardly amount to a presumption or aid to proof.[253]

242 R., Null., 6 jun. 1918 (rd., x, p. 48).

243 R., Null., 8 jan. 1921 (rd., xiii, p. 7); Null., 12 nov. 1921 (rd., xiii, pp. 264, 265).

244 c. 11, X, De Praesumpt., II, 23.

245 In civil law, Abbott, p. 104: "The fact that the parties were reputed among friends and acquaintances to be man and wife will suffice, with evidence of cohabitation, if the reputation be a general or at least a consistent reputation. A divided repute is of no avail. A mere local repute, if residence is brief and frequently changed, is of little account alone, . . ."

246 SO, 1868, § 8; cfr. DS., Praes. Mort. Conj., 18 dec. 1914 (aas., vii, p. 44).

247 PF, 1883, § 32.

248 R., Null., 20 mai. 1910 (rd., ii, p. 164); Impedimenti ad Contrahend., 11 mart. 1910 (rd., ii, p. 100).

249 R., Null., vel Disp., 15 jul. 1911 (rd., iii, p. 344); Vic. Ap. Nov. Pomeraniae, Null., 30 apr. 1913 (rd., v, p. 288; aas., v, p. 468).

250 R., Parisien., Null., 11 dec. 1916 (rd., viii, p. 371; aas., ix, p. 470).

251 c. 5, X, De Eo qui Cognovit, IV, 13.

252 cfr. Gasparri, i, n. 152.

253 R., Trincomalien., Null., 1 feb. 1913 (rd., v, pp. 87, 88; aas., v, p. 205); Null., 6 apr., 1914 (rd., vi, pp. 187, 188); Ambianen., Null., 3 jan. 1917 (rd., ix, p. 9; aas., x, p. 385); Null., 6 jun. 1918 (rd., x, p. 48).

263. Witnesses who state their opinion of an event do not by this beget full proof of the fact, but rather an indication of and aid to proof, and this indication and aid is stronger or weaker according as the opinion is more or less directly derived from what the witnesses have perceived with their senses. Thus in cases which hinge on insanity, the opinion of people who have lived with a person may have some weight in establishing the question of that person's sanity or insanity. Similarly when a witness testifies to having seen a man and woman "solus cum sola, nudus cum nuda," the witness's opinion on the question of their having had sexual relations may have great weight (cfr. n. **520**).[254] The "septimae manus," in their capacity as opinion-witnesses do not beget full proof of non-consummation, much less of impotence, unless their opinion has other arguments in support of it. (c. 1975,§2).[255] In their capacity as character witnesses the "septimae manus" furnish an argument which gives strength to and establishes belief in the depositions of the parties. Their testimony sometimes furnishes just that measure of evidence which is necessary to give the whole deposition the value or effect of full proof; sometimes on the other hand, these witnesses line up on either side of a controversy to establish the trustworthiness of both petitioner and respondent, when the former stoutly denies the consummation of the marriage, and the latter as firmly asserts it. In such cases the testimony of these character witnesses, as is evident, hardly establishes the trustworthiness of either party in regard to the matter at hand.

264. The judge will be guided in his estimation of testimony by the constancy or inconstancy, the coherence or contradiction, the certainty or incertainty of the witness and his answers. A consistent, logical witness furnishes better proof than another who is uncertain, vaccillating and at variance with himself (c. 1789,n.3).[256] Hence when testimony has been altered upon reëxamination and no solid reason for the alteration is forthcoming, the witness does not easily escape the suspicion that naturally attaches, especially if the testi-

[254] W-Vidal, vi, n. 484; cfr. R., Null., 12 nov. 1921 (rd., xiii, p. 264).

[255] DS, Reg., n. 60, § 1.

[256] R., Osnabrugen., Null., 11 jan. 1912 (rd., iv, p. 23): "Praeterea cauta circumspectio qua singuli testes in deponendo utuntur, diligentia et subtilitas qua affirmant, se alias minas et offensiones audivisse et vidisse, alias nonnisi fando compertas habere, alias prorsus ignorare, omnino comprobant testium credibilitatem."

monies have previously been published.[257] In a case of duress from Los Angeles the Rota remarked upon the facility with which the mother of the plaintiff changed her testimony in the supplementary procedure, so as to make it more favorable to her daughter, without assigning any reason for her changed testimony.[258] However a witness who frankly and spontaneously corrects one or another of his statements just after the testimony has been rendered (cfr. n. 181) need not, by this, be considered untrustworthy.

265. One authorized witness (cfr. n. 185) deposing on things done *ex officio* is sufficient for plenary proof (c. 1791,§1), if he is above all exception,[259] but generally speaking, one simple witness is not sufficient *per se*.

The well known principle "unus testis, nullus testis" is derived from both Mosaic and Roman law,[260] and is found in the Decree of Gratian, applied to a marriage case hinging on consanguinity.[261] The recent jurisprudence of the Rota has repeated the same principle [262] and the Code says that the testimony of one witness does not of itself constitute full proof (c. 1791,§1; cfr. however c. 239,§1,n. 17).[263]

266. A single testimony does not even then constitute full proof of itself, when it is a confession of crime. There are some impediments of which a criminal action, perpetrated by a person not a party to the suit, is a constituent element, such as the act of coercion in the impediment of duress, and the act of illicit coition with the party in the pre-Code impediment of affinity. When a person admits having committed such an act, it does not relieve the plaintiff of the burden of further proof, for it is not a confession in prejudice to the

257 R., Null., 30 aug. 1911 (rd., iii, p. 466); Null., 17 jan. 1912 (rd., iv, p. 39, fol.); Parisien., seu Nicien., Null., 15 mart., 30 dec. 1915 (rd., vii, pp. 113, 469, 470; aas., vii, p. 351 and viii, pp. 328, 329).

258 R., Montereyen. Angelorum, Null., 21 dec. 1917 (rd., ix, pp. 318, 322; aas., x, pp. 422, 425, 426).

259 cfr. W-Vidal, vi, p. 423 (74).

260 Deut., xix, 15; Constantinus M., L. 9, § 1, C. de test., IV, 20.

261 c. 11, C. XXXV, q. 6; cfr. c. 22, X, De Test. et Attest., II, 20.

262 R., Null., 28 aug. 1911 (rd., iii, p. 442); Null., 17 jan. 1912 (rd., iv, p. 49); Null., 10 feb. 1912 (rd., iv, pp. 86, 87).

263 R., Null., 6 jun. 1918 (rd., x, p. 45), following Pirhing lib. II, tit. xx, sect. 2, § 1 (p. 288), states that there can be no valid custom of not requiring more than one witness.

person confessing, but rather in prejudice to the marriage and those who uphold it.[264] If it is proved that a witness had confessed to his crime at an unsuspected time, the judge may take this circumstance into consideration and allow the testimony greater proof-bearing value (cfr. n. **183**).

267. The testimony of one witness who is above all suspicion however, forms partial proof of what he testifies.[265] This partial proof, when attended by other partial proofs such as the oath of the parties, and justifiable presumption, may amount to sufficient evidence so that the case may be favorably decided, especially when the nature of the case is such that more witnesses cannot be had.[266] Thus when a parent confesses that he has coerced his daughter into marriage and there are other props of proof accruing from the testimony of the daughter herself or other sources, it may amount to full proof.[267] Similarly in the matter of proving the illicit coition to establish the pre-Code impediment of affinity, the confession of the person with whom the act was perpetrated, when aided by other supporting proofs in the case, may form full proof of the impediment.[268]

268. Some few cases however admit of one witness above all exception as sufficient proof. Thus when there is question of postponing or hindering a marriage about to be contracted, one witness, even though spontaneous, constitutes sufficient proof (cfr. n. **40**).[269]

In cases on the presumable death of a spouse the Instruction of the Holy Office makes explicit exception in allowing one eye witness to constitute plenary proof of the death.[270] But if a second marriage

[264] R., Null., 23 mart. 1915 (rd., vii, p. 126).

[265] R., Massilien., Null., 1 jul. 1911 (rd. iii, p. 327): "At dato etiam quod unicus sit testis, certissima doctrina est, unum testem, etsi plenam probationem non exhibeat, inducere tamen iuridicam veritatis praesumptionem, si omni exceptione testis maior sit."

[266] SCC., In Florentina, Mat., 29 jul. 1854 (pall, xiii, 428).

[267] R., Parisien., Null., 26 apr. 1916 (rd., viii, p. 136; aas., ix, p. 147); Lugdunen., Null., 2 apr. 1917 (rd., ix, p. 65; aas., x, p. 73); Montereyen. Angelorum, Null., 21 dec. 1917 (rd., ix, p. 319; aas., x, p. 423).

[268] R., Null., 20 mai. 1910 (rd., ii, p. 164); Null., 11 apr. 1911 (rd., iii, p. 166); Null., 29 jul. 1911 (rd., iii, p. 408).

[269] c. 22, X, De Test. et Attest. II, 20; IA., § 106; Feije n. 585; Bouix, i, n. 311; W-Vidal, vi, p. 423 (75).

[270] SO, 1868: "4. Interdum unus tantum testis examinandus reperitur, et licet ab omni iure testimonium unius ad plene probandum non admittatur,

is contested on the score of bigamy, and the impediment hinges on the question of the death of a former spouse, the testimony of one witness is not, of itself, sufficient evidence of nullity.[271]

When there is a question of proving that baptism has been conferred it has long been held that the testimony of one witness above all suspicion is sufficient, providing the testimony does not redound to the prejudice of another (c. 779).[272] This has generally been interpreted to mean that when baptism would constitute an impediment, *v. g.* disparity of cult, and thus lay the ground for the dissolution of a marriage already contracted, the testimony of one witness is not sufficient.[273] But in 1922 the Holy Office decided a case that came from China, on the testimony of only one witness. A man named Thac was born in 1898 of pagan parents, and married a pagan girl named Nam in 1918. The marriage was disrupted by the adulteries of the woman, and in 1921 the neighborhood missionary learned from a Catholic physician that he had baptized Thac in infancy without the knowledge of his parents. On this sole testimony the marriage was declared invalid by reason of disparity of cult.[274] Note however, that the Holy Office in making this decision, may have implicitly provided for dissolution of the marriage (c. 1119) in case it was not already invalid by disparity of cult.

In another case the plaintiff sought to establish the nullity of her marriage on the grounds of spiritual relationship. The relationship was proved to have arisen from her baptism, but a doctor testified that he had previously baptized the plaintiff when she was an infant. This testimony if admitted, would have destroyed the relationship ostensibly arising from the subsequent baptism, but the Rota refused to accept the single testimony as sufficient to prove the early

attamen ne coniux alias nuptias inire peroptans vitam coelibem agere cogatur, etiam unius testimonium absolute non respuit Suprema Congr. in dirimendis huiusmodi casibus, dummodo ille testis, recensitis conditionibus sit praeditus, nulli exceptioni obnoxius, ac praeterea eius depositio aliis gravibusque adminiculis fulciatur; sique alia extrinseca adminicula colligi omnino nequeant, hoc tamen certum sit, nihil in eius testimonio reperiri quod non sit congruum atque omnino verisimile."

[271] Bassibey, n. 375.

[272] cfr. can. 110, 112, Dist. IV, De Consecratione; Ben. XIV, De Synodo Dioeces., lib. VII, c. 6, n. 4 (Opera, vol. xi, Prati, 1844).

[273] cfr. Cerato, p. 33.

[274] SO. (PF.), 1 apr. 1922 (akk., cvii, 1927, p. 179).

baptism, and thus prejudice the suit of the plaintiff, and pronounced the marriage invalid.[275]

269. Testimony is properly appraised according to the concordance among several witnesses. But there must not be too much insistence on a mathematical counting of the number of witnesses.[276] During the middle ages there was at times and in some places too much insistence on a specific number of witnesses, often to the detriment of justice in both secular and ecclesiastical courts.[277] In practice, no strict mathematical rule of proof has flourished for very many years. Nevertheless the Code repeats the classical rule that when two or three witnesses, above all suspicion and firmly coherent in their testimony, depose in court under oath from personal experience upon a matter or event, their testimony constitutes sufficient proof (c. 1791,§2; cfr. c. 1122,§2).[278] Thus in a recent case the Rota received the coherent testimony of both parents that they had coerced their daughter, as full proof of such meagre coertion as they had exerted.[279] Two witnesses are also sufficient to prove the existence of public repute.[280]

270. In order that witnesses alone give full proof their testimonies must be conformative, *i. e.* corroborated by the testimony of other witnesses (cc. 1789,n.4; 1791,§2). However even corroboration may be overdone, and when the judge perceives that several witnesses render testimony in the same identical words, the judge may have reason to suspect collusion with or coaching of the witnesses.[281] If the testimony of the various witnesses is different in the respective assertions made, the judge will consider whether their testimonies are

[275] R., Null., 25 feb. 1911 (rd., iii, p. 93 fol.).

[276] Innocent III to the Bishops of London and Ely, in c. 22, X, De Test. et Attest., II, 20: "...ad multitudinem tantum respicere non oportet, sed ad testium qualitatem, et ad ipsorum deposita, quibus potius lux veritatis assistit . . . "

[277] W-Vidal, vi, n. 482.

[278] This rule is retained in its general outlines, in spite of the tendency of modern civil procedure to suppress all norms on the number of witnesses: cfr. Hohenlohe, p. 58.

[279] R., Null., 27 aug. 1912 (rd., iv, p. 442).

[280] SO, 1868, §8; R., Null., 8 jan. 1921 (rd., xiii, p. 7); Null., 12 nov. 1921 (rd., xiii, p. 265).

[281] cfr. R., Nicien., Null., 15 mart. 1915 (rd., vii, p. 113; aas., vii, p. 351); Mansella, pp. 159, 194.

contradictory or contrary, or whether they are simply diversative or complementary (c. 1790) (cfr. n. **186**).

271. Contrary and contradictory testimonies destroy rather than furnish proof. Nevertheless it is for the judge to seek to effect a concordance between the apparently discrepant testimonies,[282] or to decide, from the rank, character and certainty of the witnesses, whether one group must be believed rather than the other.[283]

If two groups of witnesses contradict one another, an internal discrepancy among the witnesses of one group discredits their testimony in favor of the other coherent group.[284] Witnesses cannot be expected to agree so perfectly however that no discrepancy can be detected in their testimonies. Hence minor discrepancies are not usually attended to.[285] The date of betrothals or marriage, time and circumstances of the marriage ceremony, *etc.* are oftentimes such unimportant details upon which a discrepancy among witnesses will not disparage the value of the testimony.[286] Such discrepancies are in fact rather a sign that there was no collusion among the varying witnesses.[287]

[282] R., Neo Eboracen., Null., 9 dec. 1911 (rd., iii, pp. 517, 518; aas., iv, p. 155).

[283] cfr. R., Nicien., Null., 30 dec. 1915 (rd., vii, p. 470) for splendid example of discerning true testimony from false.

[284] cfr. R., Null., 28 mai. 1909 (rd., i, p. 55).

[285] R., Neo Eboracen., Null., 1 mart. 1913 (rd., v, p. 189; aas., v, p. 327): "Ceterum meminisse iuvat, quae, circa accidentales testimoniorum circumstantias, habet divus Thomas: 'Si vero sit discordia testimoniis in aliquibus circumstantiis non pertinentibus ad substantiam facti . . . , talis discordia non praeiudicat testimonio . . . quin immo aliqua discordia in talibus facit testimonium credibilius, ut Chrysostomus dicit super Matthaeum' (IIa IIae quaest. 79, art. 9). Cui plene adhaeret Benedictus XIV, qui ita scribit: 'Expedit enim aliquando, ut aliqua adsit discordia inter testes, non in substantialibus, sed in accidentalibus; concordia siquidem in omnibus, hoc est tum in substantialibus tum in accidentalibus, tantum abest ut fidem conciliet, ut eam potius testibus minuat' (De Can. et Beat. Sanct., lib III, cap. 7, n. 10). Et hoc magis verum est, quando testes de his quae tempore remoto evenerunt, reddere debent testimonium, . . ."; Milevitan., Null., 23 dec. 1910 (rd., ii, p. 365); Parisien., Null., 17 apr. 1915 (rd., vii, p. 169; aas., vii, p. 450).

[286] R., Null., 23 mart. 1914 (rd., vi, p. 147); Ton Kin Central., Null., 27 jun. 1916 (rd., viii, p. 211; aas., ix, p. 250); Parisien., Null., 5 mai. 1914 (rd., vi, p. 205; aas., vi, p. 398).

[287] R., Null., 21 dec. 1912 (rd., iv, p. 474); Neo Eboracen., Null., 1 mart. 1913 (rd., v, p. 189; aas., v, p. 327).

272. Diversative testimonies can generally be reconciled, and then each witness furnishes partial proof of what is asserted, and together the testimonies may be so conclusive as to approach, even though they alone do not attain to full proof.[288] When however the testimony of a single witness is diversative from that of a party and favors nullity, it is not usually given much value.[289]

273. Complementary testimonies taken separately, generally furnish partial proof of the various assertions, and taken together have an added cumulative value, which may amount to full proof of the case (cpre. cc. 1790; 1791,§2).[290] This is especially so in cases of nullity by reason of the insanity of a party.[291]

274. Although the Code, in retaining the principle of proof by two or three witnesses, furnishes a guiding norm for the appraisal of testimony, the judge is bound by no ironclad rule; he may require further proof when there is a case of great importance or when there is some indication that the assertions of the witnesses are not true (c. 1791,§2).[292] In marriage cases it is especially important that the testimonies of two or three shall not be considered conclusive, as long as others remain unheard who are likely to bear offsetting testimony against the case.[293]

[288] cfr. Bouix, i, n. 315; contrary Cosci, lib. I, cap. iv, nn. 34, 35.

[289] R., Lugdunensis, Null., 5 jun. 1917 (rd., ix, p. 136; aas., x, p. 166): "Assertio vero alterius testis, Josephi Chappuis, de minis eiectionis filiae e domo paterna, reiicienda est, non solum quia unius testis est, sed etiam quia plane contradicit testimonio reae conventae, quae de aliis minis, praeter illas exhaereditationis, se nihil scire declarat."

[290] R., Null., 11 apr. 1911 (rd., iii, p. 169): "Hi testes videntur prima fronte singulares, sed non sunt stricte singulares sed potius contestes, quia referunt facta relativa ad eundem finem, seu referunt adminicula tendentia ad probandum factum secutae copulae. Iamvero hi testes singulares non singularitate obstativa sed tantum adminiculativa plene probant in iudicio."

[291] SCC., Corduben., Null., 26 feb. 1763 (pall., xii, n. 469); R., Vic. Apost. Chan-Si Sept., Null., 29 jun. 1923 (rd., xv, p. 129).

[292] IA., § 165: "Verum quando de circumstantia agitur, a qua valor matrimonii dependet, minime sufficit, relationem vel factum, quo testium veracitas in dubium vocetur, evictum haud esse, sed oportet probatum sit, eos intemeratae probitatis et suppositioni, quasi perjurio conscientiam gravare possint, locum haud esse."

[293] Bassibey, n. 376; c. 2020, § 2 requires eight witnesses "ad probandam famam virtutum" in cases of beatification.

One witness to the contrary may cause the judge to consider the case weakened and to require more proof.[294] On the other hand it may happen that a great number of witnesses to the contrary will not finally offset the proof accruing from the testimony of two witnesses above suspicion and in agreement on the facts witnessed. Especially in cases of duress it is laid down that two such witnesses testifying for duress are weightier than any number testifying generically for the liberty of the contract.[295] But when the contradicting witnesses do not testify generically but support their statement by specific facts proving freedom from duress, it is for the judge to estimate whether the party acted under duress or not (cfr. nn. **162**, **163**).

[294] cfr. R., Neo Eboracen., Null., 9 dec. 1911 (rd., iii, p. 517).

[295] R., Null., 26 mart. 1920 (rd., xii, pp. 93, 94): "ait Mascardus: 'Metus probatio magis conficitur ex testibus affirmantibus quam negantibus, quapropter doctores illam constituunt conclusionem, quod magis sit credendum duobus testibus deponentibus de metu, quam mille negantibus vel asserentibus de libera voluntate. Ratio autem a doctoribus ea redditur: nam deponentes super spontanea (ut sic loquar) voluntate, deponunt de actu mentali et invisibili, qui soli Deo notus est; alii vero deponentes de metu, attestantur de minis et tormentis vel similibus, quae sensu corporis percipiuntur' (Conclusio 1053, nn. 1, 2). Unde hic auctor concludit: 'Si unus testis deponeret de metu, et cum ipso alii testes de auditu concordent . . . talis probatio sufficit' (ibi n. 7)."; cfr. also R., Veszprimien., Null., 2 jun. 1911 (rd., iii, p. 235); Tarvisina, Null., 11 mart. 1912 (rd., iv, p. 141; aas., iv, p. 518); Montereyen. Angelorum, Null., 21 dec. 1917 (aas., x, p. 423); Parisien., Null., 15 dec. 1920 (rd., xii, p. 274); Cosci, lib. I, cap. viii, nn. 33; 36-81.

CHAPTER IX

Experts and Physical Inspection

"Ferunt secum signa virginitatis eius ad seniores urbis . . . , expandent vestimentum coram senioribus civitatis."—Deut., xxii, 15, 17.

275. The testimony of experts (periti, peritia) is an approved means of proof frequently used in marriage cases. Expert inspection and testimony were recognized in the Mosaic and in the Roman law,[1] though no legal systematic method of expert procedure was adhered to.[2] Some vestiges of the use of experts in the early Canon law, show that this means of proof was applied to cases involving the physical marital relations, at an early date. The Decree of Gratian cites a letter of Cyprian to Pomponian, de virginibus, written in A. D. 249, in which both the bodily inspection of women as a means of proving virginity and the expert obstetricians who were to make the inspection are mentioned.[3] Later we find Honorius III requiring the same means of proof for similar cases.[4] Hence the older Roman Rota made use of it, and the Congregation of the Council in 1840 likewise prescribed it. But it was not until the reëstablishment of the Rota on 4 Aug. 1910 that experts were viewed as a means of proof quite distinct from that by witnesses.[5] And the Code has carefully followed this distinction.

§ 1. Definition and Kinds of Expert

276. Experts in the grammatical sense are persons of special training, experience and ability in some craft or science. In the canonical and probatory sense they are persons thus endowed, acting in the capacity of witnesses who testify to the existence of a fact, such as whether a wife is physically intact, and reasoning thence, give an

[1] Noval, n. 514.

[2] W-Vidal, vi, n. 491.

[3] c. 4, 5, C. XXVII, q. 1; Freisen, p. 343.

[4] c. 7, X, De Frig. et Malef. et Imp. Coeundi, IV, 15.

[5] R, Reg., § 120 fol.

opinion or conclusion, such as whether the wife's marriage has been consummated, whether the party is impotent, whether the impotence is perpetual and incurable. Experts differ from both simple and authorized witnesses: these testify to what may be perceived by the senses of any normal person, whereas experts testify to facts that escape the notice of those not equipped by special training; neither simple nor authorized witnesses are generally allowed to render opinions but experts render weighty opinions according to their special science and craft, derived from the special facts observed. Thus the expert's office is somewhat analogous to that of a judge in so far as he forms and expresses his judgment or conclusion on the nature, concomitants, cause or effect of that to which his examination has made him a witness (cfr. however, n. **327**).

277. Experts are either judicial and formal (p. iudicialis, p. formalis) or extrajudicial and informal (p. extrajudicialis). Judicial experts are appointed by the judge and make formal inspection during trial; or beforehand, for later reference (cfr. c. 1730). Extrajudicial experts are those who make informal inspection on private authority.

§ 2. Necessity of Experts

278. The services of experts are now used whenever they are needed to establish some fact or to discover the true nature of some thing (c. 1792), *i. e.* whenever matters that lie beyond the capabilities of those who are not experts must be illustrated. Most marriage cases do not require the services of experts. In some cases it is left with the judge to decide whether or not to call for them, and in some cases experts are required by the Code.

In cases of impotence and non-consummation Canon 1976 requires that experts be employed and that they make an inspection or examination of the body. In some such cases it is necessary to examine the bodies of both the man and the woman, in other cases an examination of the man or of the woman only will be required. Such corporal examinations are made with a view to substantiating, if they are true, the claims and assertions of the parties regarding their physical condition, and to detect the falsity, if their claims be false.

There was no text of the Decretals that required the physical inspection of a man, but only of the woman; yet the courts had introduced this custom in cases of impotence, and it was considered mandatory by the Congregation of the Council in a case of 1794.[6] The genital organs of the man must be examined when the marriage is contested on the ground that he is impotent, or when dispensation is sought from marriage that is claimed to be not consummated because of the frigidity of the man. But if in the latter case, full proof of the integrity of the wife has been offered, the inspection of the man may be omitted.[7]

279. The Decretals and later legislation frequently mention the requirement of making a physical inspection of the woman. The inspection of the woman is necessary when the marriage is contested on the ground that she is impotent or when dispensation from ratified marriage is sought,[8] and canonical expert inspection is more frequently made in these than in all other cases.[9]

There are exceptions to the rule requiring the inspection of the woman. It will be omitted when it evidently can serve no purpose (c. 1976).[10] In trials on non-consummation the inspection is omitted if the two spouses have never been together and alone since the time of their marriage.[11] This case is not so very rare. In the diocese of X., the threat of arrest had been made, unless a man married the girl he had deflowered and impregnated. The young couple were quietly married and left the house of the pastor together, but as soon as the door was closed upon them the husband bade adieu and was not heard from again. Bassibey gives another case in which after the wedding night spent in dancing, the husband leaves never to return.[12]

The inspection may likewise be omitted in cases of non-consummation, if the woman claims the marriage has been consummated and the man claims it has not, and the reasons for the omission in this case are, as Gasparri says, patent to everyone.[13] Third, if the woman has had sexual relations at any time with another man, either by

[6] SCC., In Camerinen., Mat., die 20 sept. 1794 (pall., xiii, n. 52).

[7] DS, Reg., n. 84, § 2.

[8] DS, Reg., nn. 64, § 1; 84, § 1.

[9] Bassibey, n. 422.

[10] DS, Reg., n. 84, § 1.

[11] DS, Reg., nn. 64, § 1; 86.

[12] SCC., In Strigonien., Dispensat. Matrim., 12 sept. 1896 (bass., n. 425); For means of proof in such cases cfr. n. **156**.

[13] Gasparri, ii, n. 1500.

way of extra-marital coition or in that she was a widow at the time of her present marriage.[14] Fourth, if it is known that the husband and wife in question had had sexual relations before their marriage (cfr. n. **551**). Fifth, if the woman has undergone a surgical operation which destroyed her physical integrity.[15]

When the marriage is contested because of the impotence of the woman however, the circumstances just mentioned do not generally excuse from making the physical inspection, for it is not useless but may avail to disclose whether a condition exists which does not allow the rendering of the marriage debt.[16]

Moreover to determine virginity and non-consummation, it may be profitable in some circumstances to make an examination of other parts than the genital organs proper, such as the breasts, abdomen *etc.* even when the hymen is not intact. This was strongly urged by the defender in a case from Toulouse.[17] In another case that arose in France conclusions favoring non-consummation were drawn from the physical evidences that the parties had been in the habit of perpetrating practices against nature.[18] And recently dispensation from non-consummated marriage was granted, when the hymen was found slightly lacerated, but the experts based their opinion of non-consummation on other signs: there were no star-shaped points, no relaxation of the labia minora, there was tension at the orifice, and the expert could not introduce two fingers.[19]

In case of doubt whether the corporal inspection should be made or omitted, the decision lies with the judge; but the defender has a right to oppose the order of the court, and must be heard on the matter.[20]

280. When the examination of the woman is useless the testimony of doctors who examined her before, if there were any, or especially of those doctors who operated upon her, in case her physical integrity has been destroyed by an operation, will be received to prove the question of non-consummation.

[14] SO, 1883, Pars II, tit. vi, art. 5; DS, Reg., n. 64, § 1.

[15] Bassibey, n. 429.

[16] Bassibey, n. 429.

[17] SCC., In Tolosana., Disp. Mat., 25 mai. 1895 (bass., n. 435 (4)).

[18] SCC., In Burdigalen., 12 dec. 1896.

[19] DS. in Causa B. (num. prot. 3691/31); cfr. R., Null., 15 nov. 1909 (rd., i, p. 140).

[20] DS, Reg., n. 85.

Similarly when the examination cannot be made because of the refusal of a party to submit to it, the testimony of physicians who have examined the person in question will be received. It is of no uncommon occurrence that a party refuses to undergo the examination of his or her body. Bassibey recites an interesting example: in 1873 Cajetan B. and Marie V. had tried in vain for four months to consummate their marriage, and a surgeon examined the woman and declared there was constriction at the orifice and the uterus and vagina were wanting. The parties separated and the husband brought suit for nullity. Two other surgeons came likewise to the conclusion that the woman was impotent, after making extrajudicial examinations. When, later on, the judicial experts were appointed to make the official examination, the woman, tired of all this, refused to submit herself anew. The Archbishop sought to have the Congregation consent to his rendering decision of nullity on the basis of the three extrajudicial examinations, but this consent was twice refused, until, much later, the Congregation finally gave in, in the face of the woman's obstinate refusal.[21]

281. If in a case of non-consummation a party absolutely refuses to obey the decree of the judge and submit to physical inspection, the judge will decide from the circumstances of the case to what cause this disobedience is to be attributed,[22] and of what conclusions it is inferential, as well as whether the defect need be supplied by other arguments and proofs. In nullity cases, both the Congregation and the Rota have taken the refusal as a sign of impotence.[23]

282. The inspection of both parties must be made if the marriage is contested because of relative impotence. In such cases the physical inspection of both parties is necessary even though the physical integrity of the hymen is beyond doubt. For it is the comparison of the relative parts of the man and woman, in respect to size and conformation, that begets proof in these cases.[24]

283. In nullity cases where it is contended that a party could not have given consent to the marriage because of insanity, the opinion of experts is required (c. 1982). This is an innovation of the Code,

[21] Bassibey, n. 394; cfr. R., Null., 29 apr. 1922 (rd., xiv, p. 116).

[22] DS, Reg., n. 64, § 2.

[23] SCC., Neapolitana, 18 mart. 1826 (cicf., vi, n. 4002); R., Null., 8 jan. 1913 (rd., v, p. 37); Null., 11 nov. 1930 (aas., xxiii, p. 108).

[24] SCC., In Aquen., Disp. Mat., 28 jan. 1893 (bass., p. 329 (2)).

for as late as 1916 the Rota declared a marriage invalid, without asking the opinion of experts, and the judges were able to write into the decision, that no law required the services of experts in cases of insanity.[25]

In some cases the experts will be required by the judge to make a scientific examination of the insane person or of his actions that give rise to the suspicion of insanity. And this avails generally for greater certainty. In some cases the examination is impossible because of the absence of the person in question or his refusal to submit to such an examination, or it is useless because of the nature of the disease.[26] Thus the inspection may be omitted in the rare case where it is claimed that the party was insane at the time the marriage was contracted, though it is admitted that he may be no longer insane.

284. In cases of impotence or non-consummation it is allowed to hear as witnesses, those who have beforehand in their professional capacity, nevertheless by private, not public authority, made an inspection of the persons in question (c. 1978).[27] But in cases of insanity it is required that such medical testimony be heard in addition to the experts specially appointed by the court (c. 1982). The reason for requiring this seems to be that the Code foresees there will be numerous cases where the expert inspection is either impossible or useless.[28] [29]

285. The judge may properly call for medical experts and require an examination with a view to determining the existence or nature of some fact, disease, or disorder other than impotence and insanity. In a case of nullity tried in four instances the expert testimony of physicians was called upon to ascertain whether the woman in question was afflicted with the disease called ozena. The husband having suspected the presence of this disease had given his marital consent under the express stipulation that the woman did not have this disease. The first, third and fourth instances of trial gave sentence for nullity based on expert testimony.[30]

25 R., Ton Kin Central., Null., 27 jun. 1916 (aas., ix, p. 250; rd., viii, p. 211).

26 cfr. R., Vic. Apost. Chan-Si Sept., Null., 29 jun. 1923 (rd., xv, pp. 133, 134).

27 DS, Reg., n. 88.

28 Noval, n. 863.

29 In civil law Abbott, p. 947: "Defendant's physician is not competent as to facts derived from him in professional confidence."

30 R., Cameracen., Null., 19 jun. 1909, 11 aug. 1910, 23 jun. 1911 (rd., i, p. 68; rd., ii, p. 299; rd., iii, p. 292).

In a case established to impede the marriage of a man with the woman who was said to be his illegitimate daughter, it was claimed that she looked like his other children and hence was to be numbered with them. Expert testimony was called to testify on the similarity of appearance, voice, personality *etc.*[31]

Similarly the judge may call upon expert testimony in cases of separation from bed and board.[32] [33]

286. In cases where the genuineness or authorship of a document is in doubt it is directed that an inspection be made by experts (c. 1800,§1). But this behest of the Code is not binding under pain of nullity of the decision, and in the more simple cases the matter may be settled by judicial notice or by witnesses.

287. In marriage cases in which a point touching theology is not clear, one or more expert consultors on theology may be named *ex officio.*[34] It is plain of course that such expert consultors share only in that part of the expert's office which is analogous to that of judge, not in the part analogous to that of witness.

288. Whenever expert opinion is duly given without making the special expert examination usually required, the opinion is based upon testimony rendered in court by proper witnesses, or is confined to an abstract or hypothetical statement pertaining to the expert's special science.

289. If the judge does not decree that an expert inspection be made or that expert testimony be sought in a case where such inspection and testimony would lead to the solution of the case, either party or the defender may petition the judge to call upon experts for inspection or testimony.[35]

[31] R., Impedimenti ad Contrahendum, 11 mart. 1910 (rd., ii, p. 102); cfr. contra: Antonelli, ii, n. 698; Smith, n. 549 speaks of expert examination in cases of duress to determine "force of mind to resist threats; to see whether he or she is nervous and timid and easily frightened or not"; no case has come to my notice of experts having been employed for this purpose, and they would not, in fact, be of much avail.

[32] IA., § 227.

[33] In civil law Abbott, p. 947: "A husband's having the venereal disease, long after marriage, is *prima facie* evidence of his adultery."

[34] R, Reg., § 123, n. 1; R., Norm., art. 97.

[35] R, Reg., § 127, formula: "A decree is petitioned, appointing a sworn expert and instructing him to proceed..." The judge will decree: "Granted and to the purpose mentioned . . . day is named, and the place . . . "

290. In cases of impotence or non-consummation two experts are prescribed (c. 1979,§§1,2).[36] The Congregations have allowed however, that when under the circumstances prevailing in missionary countries two experts cannot conveniently be had, one is sufficient for the examination of the body of either man or woman. But the findings of this one are to be referred to two other experts, even though they live in a distant place, who shall under oath examine the findings and declare their agreement or disagreement with the conclusions reported.[37] Lately the Rota upheld this practice and declared for nullity even though the defender took exception to the impotent woman's having been examined by only one expert.[38]

Canon 1982 insinuates that at least two experts shall examine those who are said to have married in an insane condition. The judge is free to have the services of more. In a case on insanity recently tried in Holland ten experts were heard.[39]

In other cases the judge is free to have one or more experts according to his own discretion (c. 1793,§3). Reasonable petitions of the parties regarding the number of experts to be chosen should receive his consideration.[40]

291. The inspection of the genital organs of a man must be made by male physicians (c. 1979,§1).[41]

The Decretals directed always that the examination of the genital organs of a woman be undertaken by women,[42] and the Congregation of the Council has remarked upon the inappropriatness of medical men engaging in a matter "pudoris plenae."[43] Canon 1979,§2 still seems to prefer that women experts be employed, and with the constant increase of women physicians this behest should not be lightly disregarded. However the Congregation has never raised objection to the custom of long standing in French curiae, whereby men experts examine the bodies of women,[44] and the Code takes into consideration

36 DS, Reg., n. 89, § 1.

37 SO, 1883, Pars II, tit. vi, art. 5; PF, 1883, § 46; DS, Reg., n. 89, § 2.

38 R., Null., 28 mai. 1921 (rd., xiii, p. 126); 29 apr. 1922 (rd., xiv, p. 117).

39 R., Buscoducen., Null., 7 jan. 1918 (rd., x, p. 1; aas., x, p. 517).

40 R, Reg., § 122.

41 DS, Reg., n. 95.

42 c. 14, X, De Prob., II, 19; c. 6, 7, X, De Frig. et Malef. et Impot. Coeundi, IV, 15.

43 SCC., In Ianuen., Mat., 16 apr. 1791 (pall., xiii, n. 45).

44 Bassibey, n. 432; cfr. PF, 1883, § 46.

that in many countries nowadays women are not offended by this, and it allows male physicians as experts, if the woman to be examined prefers them or if the ordinary thinks an examination by men experts necessary (c. 1979,§2). Thus examination by male physicians is preferable to that of women who are merely practical obstetricians, in the more difficult cases, as for instance, when there is a suspicion lest some artificial means have been employed to effect the reädhesion of a deflowered membrane.[45]

If the examination is made with a view to determining a question of relative impotence, the same men experts who perform the physical examination of the man in question must always make the examination of the woman. For the whole value of the inspection in these cases rests upon the comparison between the genital organs of the parties in respect to size, conformation *etc.*[46]

§ 3. Qualities and Appointment of Experts

292. The chief qualifications of experts are ability, honesty and religion. The required ability is derived from training, knowledge, experience and skill in those matters in which the expert opinion is asked. In most cases of non-consummation, where generally only the fact of physical integrity is to be established by examination, the knowledge and experience generally possessed by accredited obstetricians is sufficient. If the judge doubts however whether such women are sufficiently instructed in some technical point to be discerned, a skilled medical man may be appointed to instruct them more accurately.[47] In cases involving impotence a much greater technical ability is frequently required. In cases involving the sanity of a party the usual experience and training of an ordinary practitioner are hardly sufficient: the expert should have had special training and experience with mind diseases.[48] The Code prefers that those persons

[45] DS, Reg., n. 89, § 1.

[46] SCC., In Varsovien., Mat., 27 jul. 1850 (pall., xiii, n. 204).

[47] DS, Reg., Appendix XXIX.

[48] R., Null., 10 jul. 1909 (rd., i, pp. 87, 88): "Cautissime certe in huiusmodi peritis seligendis hac nostra praesertim aetate procedendum est, cum inter scientiae medicae cultores non desint, et ipsi quandoque magni nominis, qui, limites propriae artis transgressi, de morbis psychicis tractantes, partes facultatum animae spiritualium nimis attenuant, et aliquando ad nihilum redigunt."

be designated as experts, who posess the qualifying diploma of the competent authorities (c. 1795,§1).[49]

293. The expert must moreover be a person whom the judge can implicitly trust for his honesty and piety. He should preferably though not necessarily be a Catholic.[50] Even with but mediocre ability, a soundly religious physician is preferable to a greater scientist in whom there is no religious conscience to direct his actions and opinions.[51] Those who have been condemned or declared as excommunicated, perjurors, infamous, and those who are of such abject morals that they cannot be held worthy of belief must not be appointed as experts (cc. 1795,§2; 1757,§2).

Any one who presumes to suborn an expert with gifts, promises or any such means, to the end that he render a false report or hide the truth, is punishable by interdict, suspension *etc.* according to the norms of Canon 1743,§3 (c. 1755,§3).

294. Moreover experts must not be appointed for the case at hand if any quality attaches which renders them incapable of being simple witnesses in the trial (c. 1795,§2; with c. 1757,§3). Thus a medical man may not be appointed for expert examination and testimony regarding his wife. Nor may those be appointed as experts who are related by consanguinity or affinity in any degree of the direct line or in the first degree of the collateral line to one of the parties.[52] Such relatives are indeed admitted as witnesses in marriage cases whenever in these cases the proper and necessary testimony cannot be had from other sources (c. 1757,§3,n.3). But the reasons for making this exception in favor of simple witnesses do not pertain to the appointment of experts.

For the same reason that relatives are excluded, those too are excluded who are connected with the parties by ties of love, or separated by great enmity, or who have some interest in the outcome of the suit (c. 1757,§2,n.3).[53]

295. Finally, because they are suspected of having formed convictions on the issue, those are not to be appointed as experts in cases

[49] DS, Reg., n. 87; Noval, n. 860.

[50] PF, 1883, § 46; SO, 1883, Pars II, tit. vi, a. 5.

[51] DS, Reg., n. 87; R., Null., 10 jul. 1909 (rd., i, p. 87); Null., 19 jul. 1913 (rd., v, p. 468).

[52] DS, Reg., n. 87.

[53] DS, Reg., n. 87.

requiring a bodily examination of the parties, who have examined them privately with respect to that matter upon which the petition for a declaration of nullity or of non-consummation is made (c. 1978).[54] It hardly makes any difference whether the previous examination was undertaken by a physician acting as the household practitioner with a view to curing the patient, or whether it was made expressly for the purpose of preparing an extrajudicial report on the party's physical condition as a means of introducing the suit.[55] The physician who has thus privately examined one party is not however excluded from making the expert examination of the other. Nor is the physician who has examined a party with respect to another disease, *v. g.* insanity, disqualified as expert in a case where the same party is to be examined with regard to impotence or non-consummation. Finally the physician who has previously made an examination excluding him from the office of expert in the case, may be introduced in order to give simple testimony regarding his earlier care and examination of the party and the observations he has made and the conclusions he has drawn, or he may be introduced as one of the character witnesses (c. 1978; cfr. c. 2028,§1).

296. In contentious cases of a merely private nature the judge may ask the parties, or one of them, with the consent of the other, which experts they desire to have chosen. The parties may properly report the names of such experts as they prefer, and the judge may appoint a term for the preparation of the list of names to be presented.[56] In cases touching the marriage bond the opinion of the defender should be heard as to which experts shall be appointed (c. 1793,§2).[57] But neither the defender nor the parties appoint or produce the experts as one produces witnesses: they are chosen *ex officio* by the judge or auditor (cc. 1793,§1; 1979,§§1,2).[58] For it is pre-

[54] DS, Reg., n. 88.

[55] Noval, n. 859.

[56] R, Reg., §§ 120, 121, n. 2.

[57] cfr. R., Null., 11 aug. 1913 (rd., v, p. 568).

[58] DS, Reg., n. 87: Following formula from DS, Reg., Appendix XXVIII: "The... day of... 19.. in procedure on the marriage of N. and N. claimed to be ratified and not consummated.

"The Rt. Rev. N. Judge Instructor, having heard the Defender of the Bond has decreed:

"That the legal inspection of the body of the lady N. the wife (and petitioner) be begun; and to this N. and N. are chosen by this decree as experts,

sumed that the judge rather than the parties will know those upon whom he may rely for honest scientific opinion.

297. Honorius III granted that the interested husband might take exception to the obstetrician appointed to make an examination of his wife,[59] and the right to take exception to the person appointed as expert, just as with witnesses, has always been upheld. Hence when any of the reasons obtain for which an expert should be excluded, either party or the defender may object to him (c. 1796,§1).

The reasons for the objection must be made plain to the judge. No attention need be paid to an objection that is not well founded,[60] and generally no attention need be paid to an objection raised by the party or defender against an expert whom the party or defender has himself proposed, unless he show that the reason for his objection lies in a fact just recently come to light (cfr. c. 1764,§3).

The judge determines by decree whether the objection is admissible or not (c. 1796,§2). It is well to accede as far as possible to the wishes of the interested party. When the exception against an expert is sustained the judge will replace him by another against whom there is no cause for objection (cc. 1796,§2; 1803,§2).

298. The interested party or the defender may also make known that he takes exception to the manner in which an examination was made, as for instance, when the directions of the law or of the judge are neglected.[61] In an unpublished case of non-consummation at X., the wife who had been examined by two physicians, both of whom rendered their certain conclusion that the hymen was intact, brought a letter to the Curia in which she pointed out that one of the physicians had very carefully and at great length examined her, while the other had completed the inspection in a moment. She did

and N. as matron. These are hereby notified and admonished to appear on the .... day of ....19.. at No. .... St. to perform the aforesaid inspection according to the Code of Canon Law and the Rules of the S.C.D.S. of 7 May, 1923.

"And of this, the aforesaid N. petitioner and the Defender of the Bond are likewise notified.

N. Judge,
N. Notary."

[59] c. 14, De Prob., II, 19.

[60] R., Null., 10 jul. 1909 (rd., i, p. 87): "Locus exceptioni non datur respectu medicorum peritorum quando liquet ipsos morum honestate et doctrina sana pollere, nec non de statu infirmi plene vel sufficienter esse informatos."

[61] W-Vidal, vi, n. 494.

not know that both physicians had pronounced in her favor, but suspected the one of having concluded contrarily. She was within her right when she thus objected to the method of examination, but she did not promote her case by it. The Congregation however decided favorably on this case.

Against the findings of the experts however no other exception is admissible than proof to the contrary.

299. There is no conscientious obligation to accept the designated office of expert, save in the rare and hardly practical instance in which a case on the nullity or non-consummation of a marriage could not otherwise be settled and no other capable expert could be found. If the expert accepts the designation he enters upon a quasi-contract to fulfil the office.[62]

300. The engagement to assume the duties of the office is implied by the expert's taking oath that he will faithfully fulfil his office (c. 1797,§1).[63] The Congregation of the Council disapproved cases when the expert's oath was omitted.[64] But the later regulations for the Rota permitted the judge to omit the oath, especially if the expert be called to give an opinion on theory rather than in a definite question of fact.[65] Now, the Code plainly expects that the experts take oath (c. 1797,§1).

The parties may be present when the experts take oath (c. 1797,§2).

301. The judge will admonish the expert to fulfil his duties faithfully, to keep secret the findings of the inspection, to employ only decent and licit means.[66] and to report upon the findings.[67] He may also set a time in which the report is to be returned.

[62] W-Vidal, vi, n. 496; Haring: Eheprozess, p. 22.

[63] DS, Reg., n. 95; DS, Reg., Appendix XXIX directs following oath: "I, N..... officially deputed as obstetrician (or physician) for canonical expert inspection of Mrs. N....., swear that I shall faithfully fulfil my office, and shall inquire into every point established by scientific experiment, which I believe contributes to evidence the consummation or non-consummation of the marriage; and that I shall observe especially the prescriptions of Chapter XIII of the Rules of the S. C. D. S. of May 7, 1923; and that I shall truthfully expose everything in written report and oral examination; and that I shall keep all secret. So help me God......*etc.*"

[64] SCC., In Nancien. et Tullen., Disp. Mat., 25 mai. 1895; In Matriten., Disp. Mat., 2 mai. 1895 (bass., p. 316 (2)).

[65] R, Reg., § 129, n. 1.

[66] cfr. SO., 2 aug. 1929 (aas., xxi, p. 490).

[67] DS, Reg., nn. 90, 95.

The expert who has taken oath must undertake his duties within the appointed term. If he seek to escape his duty without just cause, he is to be held for whatever pecuniary damages may have thus accrued to the parties (c. 1798). It will not easily occur that such damages are brought about by the neglect of the expert in marriage cases.

The judge may for a necessary or opportune reason shorten or extend the period in the course of which the inspection is to be made or the report rendered. If the time is to be extended, the parties and defender must be heard on the matter (c. 1799,§2).

When an expert dies after appointment, or becomes unable or unfit to carry out the commission, or is released from it, or is suspected, another will be substituted by the judge (c. 1803,§2), after hearing the parties and defender on the matter.[68]

The experts are bound in duty to fulfil their office with a view only to truth and justice. If an expert be found guilty of fraud the judge of the case may discharge him; and the competent judge may inflict other punishments upon him (cc. 1794; 1743,§3) (cfr. nn. **103**, **107**, **209**).

§ 4. Expert Inspection and Report

302. The parties will generally be permitted to be present while the expert is making his inspection in cases of insanity and in some other marriage cases where expert inspection is required (c. 1797, §2). However the judge may exclude the parties and their advocates for prudent reasons, such as the likelihood of quarrels and disturbances (c. 1797,§2; cfr. c. 1809).

In cases of impotence or non-consummation however, the spirit of decency has made it customary not to allow the other party to be present while the body of one party is being inspected. At the inspection of the man's body no one other than the expert is present; at the inspection of the woman's body no one other than the expert and the matron appointed by the judge (c. 1797,§2).

303. The "Cum Moneat Glossa" directed the judge, defender and notary to accompany the person to be examined to the house of the expert and there await the outcome of the inspection.[69] The in-

[68] R, Reg., § 133.

[69] SCC, 1840, § Iudex, defensor.

convenience of such procedure was pointed out by the Curia at Paris in a case sent to Rome,[70] and the practice of having the court officers thus accompany the person and wait during the inspection has long since been abandoned, without adverse comment by the Roman Curia,[71] if indeed it was ever extensively observed.[72]

304. Whenever a woman's body is inspected in cases of impotence or non-consummation it is ordered that a matron, designated by the judge, be present at the inspection (c. 1979,§3).[73] The matron should be of good reputation, above all suspicion, of advanced age and, if possible, a married woman.[74] The Congregation remarked unfavorably upon a nun having been delegated for this office.[75]

The matron takes oath and swears to keep secrecy about the proceedings.[76]

The chief purpose of the matron's presence is to insure Christian decorum at the inspection, and her presence is not required for the validity of the inspection. Hence where practical difficulties are encountered, some curiae simply send the women who are to be inspected to the offices of the designated trustworthy physicians, without designating a matron.[77] In a case from X., the defender objected to the absence of a matron at the inspection, but the Congregation of the Sacraments approved the grant of dispensation, without remark on the matron's absence.

305. The physical inspection of a woman must be safeguarded against fraud. By artificial means the lacerated hymen may be made to take on the appearance of being intact (coarctatio vasis) (cfr. n.

[70] SCC., In Parisien., 18 feb. 1888 (bass., p. 337 (7)).

[71] Gasparri, ii, p. 414 (1); Smith, n. 192.

[72] cfr. R, Reg., § 131, n. 2.

[73] DS, Reg., n. 90.

[74] DS, Reg., nn. 89, § 2; 91.

[75] SCC., In Parisien., Disp. Mat., 3 aug. 1889 (bass., p. 337 (2)).

[76] DS, Reg., n. 91; Appendix XXIX gives the following formula: "I, N...., officially designated to be present at the corporal inspection of Mrs. N., swear that I shall faithfully fulfil my office, by observing the prescriptions of Chapter XIII of the Rules of the S.C.D.S. of May 7, 1923 and by seeing to it that no fraud is committed, and that the norms of modesty are safely observed; and that I shall truthfully recount the proceedings in oral examination, and otherwise keep them secret. So help me God........ *etc.*"

[77] cfr. W-Vidal, v, n. 222.

320). As a precaution against this fraud there arose about two hundred years ago the practice of requiring the woman who is to be examined to submerge in a warm bath for one-half or three-quarters of an hour before the inspection of the genital parts takes place. At one time this bath was regarded as essential to the procedure, if not indeed necessary for its validity.[78] The "Cum Moneat Glossa" and several subsequent instructions have prescribed it,[79] but the language of the later instructions is somewhat mitigated and the warm bath has not been lately insisted on in practice.[80] Hence it is not now required if the judge and experts think it harmful, useless, or unnecessary.[81] The Code makes no mention of it and it is now usually omitted. It is certainly not required for the validity of the procedure.

306. Another fraud that seems to have been detected only in recent times, is the substitution of one person for another at the physical examination. The interested party fears the experts will report unfavorably upon the virginal condition of the wife: so when the judge has stipulated to which physicians or obstetricians the wife shall go in order to be examined, another woman who is supposedly intact, is sent to take her place, and give her name, and thus assure a report of non-consummation. The same fraud may be practiced by men in impotence or insanity cases. To obviate this the Congregation of the Sacraments has recently issued a supplementary Instruction providing that documents, or photographs, sealed by the curia, be sent to the experts, so that they may be sure of the identity of the person who comes for examination, and that the person who has been examined shall be personally identified by the experts at the time when they are questioned upon their report. If the person to be examined is already known to the experts, the identification procedure may be omitted but mention of the circumstance must be made in the acts. If the person cannot or will not appear for identification, the judge will question the experts on the identity of the person examined with the one described in the above mentioned documents (cfr. n. **356**).[82]

78 SCC., In Neapolitana, 14 apr. 1761 (pall., xiii, n. 48).

79 SO, 1840, § Procedendum.

80 W-Vidal, v, p. 839 (49).

81 SO, 1858; DS, Reg., n. 92.

82 DS, Norm., n. 4.

307. In impotence or non-consummation cases each expert makes a separate inspection of the woman's body: the experts do not examine the case together, nor aid one another in the inspection (c. 1980,§1). But when they have rendered dissonant reports upon their inspections the judge may permit that a joint inspection be made and a joint report be tendered. Even then however the experts must be separately examined by the judge on their report.[83]

It has been heretofore required too, that the physical inspections of the man be separately made, and the Congregation has pronounced unfavorably upon cases in which the examination was jointly made.[84] In a more recent case however the Rota accepted the proceedings of lower courts, although the physical inspection of the husband had been made by two physicians acting together.[85] The Code does not explicitly forbid that the physicians examine the man jointly. Nevertheless a separate inspection is desirable, since even unintentional collusion among experts is thus avoided, and the separate inspection is more conformable to past practice.

In cases of nullity by reason of insanity or of a stipulation regarding disease, or where experts must be called to examine documents, handwriting *etc.*, the rule of separate inspection does not obtain, and the experts are cautioned only that the examination must be scientifically carried on (c. 1982). The judge may however direct that separate, not joint, examinations be made.

308. When the experts are designated the judge will outline for them the matter for examination. This is of ancient practice, for the Decretals give us a letter of Innocent III directing a bishop to call to himself the women designated to make the physical examination and explain to them how they must examine the wife whose impotence was asserted.[86]

It is very important that the experts should be properly instructed beforehand. They are not expected to be experts in Canon law, and it is always possible that the real point at issue may escape their notice, if the judge does not make clear the state of the question and the objects of the examination. There is special need for this explanation in cases of impotence and non-consummation, for the

[83] DS, Reg., n. 93, § 2; cfr. c. 2031, n. 5.

[84] SCC., Parisien., 25 jan. 1890 (ass., xxii, p. 617, 618).

[85] R., Null., 8 jan. 1913 (rd., v, pp. 23, 24).

[86] c. 6, X, De Frig. et Mal. et Impot. Coeundi, IV, 15; cfr. c. 7, ibid.

words "impotence" and "consummation" are accepted with various meanings among different circles of men. The essence of potency or of consummation as the Church understands them will have to be carefully explained.[87] [88]

Hence the judge will prepare a list of the several points upon which the examination is to be made. In preparing these he will pay attention to the allegations which the parties and especially the defender make upon the matter, and to the headings upon which they express a wish that the examination be made (c. 1799,§1).

309. The following questions, taken mostly from instructions of the Holy Office,[89] will serve to guide the expert inspection and report in cases of impotence and non-consummation. The expert will seek to determine: I. Whether there are signs of impotence that attain to physical certainty, by reason of the conformation of parts or of some abnormality, and II. Whether there are signs begetting moral certainty of impotence.

With regard to the man: 1. "Utrum illius virilia sint iuxta naturae leges accurate conformata?

2. An penis naturalem habeat dimensionem, promptamque erectionem ad coeundum necessario duraturam?

3. An aliquo morbo fuerit affectus? A quanto tempore? Et cuiusnam characteris?

4. An fibrae compactae et consistentes, seu potius flaccidae lassaeque sint?

5. An testes sani, naturalisque magnitudinis, et utrum aliquo vitio laboraverint vel adhuc laborent? "

[87] R., Null., 8 jan. 1913 (rd., v, pp. 31, 32): "Praeprimis notandum venit, potentiam coeundi alio sensu sumi a medicis peritis et alio a iuris canonici interpretibus. Iuxta peritos . . . potentia coeundi ex parte viri idem est ac potentia ad copulam imperfectam, quae per se non sit apta ad generationem ex defectu veri seminis; et ideo eam distinguunt a potentia generandi, quae est potentia ad copulam perfectam, seu de se aptam ad prolis generationem; e contra, sacri iuris interpretes potentiam coeundi non distinguunt a potentia generandi. Et ideo utraque impotentia, sive coeundi, sive generandi, eo sensu quo sumitur a medicis peritis, constituit impedimentum, quod iure naturae dirimit matrimonium; at eo sensu quo ea definitur a canonistis, hoc impedimentum constituitur tantum ab impotentia coeundi, quia pro istis impotentia generandi est mera sterilitas, quae nec dirimit nec impedit matrimonium."; cfr. Null., 10 aug. 1922 (rd., xiv, p. 281).

[88] For notion of impotence in civil law cfr. Tiffany, p. 26 and cases cited.

[89] SO, 1840; SO, 1858; PF, 1883, § 46; SO, 1883, Pars II, tit. vi, art. 5.

Regarding the woman: 1. "An hymen sit integrum, vel confractum in totum vel in parte?

2. Hoc in casu an et qua naturali causa, seu potius e congressu extranei corporis contigerit?

3. An myrtiformes carunculae (star shaped points) inveniantur, eorumque magnitudo, numerus, conformatio qualis sit?

4. Quaenam sit conformatio partium, iunctura, durities, rugositas, color?

5. An constet hymen fuisse fractum et postea arte resarcitum?

6. An constet elasticitas qua coitio fieret quin hymen defloraretur?

7. An vagina talis sit conformationis et magnitudinis ut coitioni cum viro coaptetur?

When the expert gives his opinion that there is impotence, (especially if the opinion is based on moral rather than physical certainty): 1. What is the cause of the impotence?

2. Is it natural or acquired by sickness, excess *etc.*?

3. Is it perpetual?

4. Is it incurable?

5. If curable, is a dangerous operation necessary to cure it?

6. Does the impotence antedate the marriage? [90]

7. Are the signs of impotence doubtful or equivocal or certain?

310. When handwriting experts are employed, they will examine the writing in question, and compare it with other writings of which the authorship is known (c. 1800,§1).[91] The parties and the defender (cfr. c. 1968,n.1) are asked to propose and agree upon writings to be used for the comparison.

If the parties do not agree upon the writings to be used for comparison the judge will use for that purpose, such writings as the party has at another time or in some other way acknowledged to be his: or such as the person said to be the author of the writing has written in a public capacity and are kept in public archives or other public repositories, or such signatures *etc.*, as are warranted by the testi-

[90] R., Null., 22 dec. 1913 (rd., v, p. 674): "Ubi enim omnino desunt testiculi, vel atrophici sunt, vel, quod idem est, ubi deest unus, et alter atrophia omnimode affectus est, characteres corporis, uti monet supra citatus Antonelli, generatim iidem sunt ac in Eunuchis: "Vox stridula nempe et acuta, absentia barbae et pilorum in partibus ubi abundare solent, habitus femineus, forma rotunda corporis, etc.'".

[91] cfr. R., Alexandrina, Iurispatronatus et Praesent., 14 jan. 1914 (rd., vi, p. 5).

mony of a notary or other public authority to have been written in his presence (c. 1800,§2).

Even when there is an agreement regarding the writing with which the comparison is to be made, the judge should not admit for the purpose handwritings specially written for the comparison, or written at a time that admits of suspicion. There is always the possibility of collusion and dissimulation of handwriting, and although the dissimulation may not deceive an expert, the comparison of unsuspected lines is more easy and satisfactory. When such older papers cannot be had, or in the opinion of experts do not suffice for the purpose given, the judge, at the instance of a party or even *ex officio,* looks to it that new lines are written, without letting the author know their purpose, provided the required person is still alive. To this end he may cite the party and require him to write at dictation, if there is no better way to obtain the desired handwriting (c. 1800, §3). The dictation must be given in the presence of the judge or his delegate, notary and defender. Paper, ink and seal may also be examined in conjunction with the handwriting.[92]

311. If a party refuse to furnish a specimen of his handwriting, the refusal is, in cases not affecting the marriage bond, a confession of the genuineness of the document in question, to the prejudice of the party, unless he demonstrate a legitimate cause for the refusal (c. 1800,§4). In cases touching the marriage bond the refusal can have only such weight to the prejudice of the marriage bond, as may be accorded a judicial confession of the parties (cfr. nn. **101, 281**).

312. When the expert inspection is completed the experts will render report (relatio, renuntiatio) of the findings on the points raised by the judge and the defender (c. 1980,§2).

The expert's report must be made in writing for cases of impotence and non-consummation (c. 1980,§§2,3).[93] The law formerly required the report to be written out at the examination and handed at once to the waiting judge, but this is no longer done (cfr. n. **303**).

In other cases, both medical and otherwise, the report may be made in writing or it may be orally made before the judge; in the latter event the notary must write it down as given and the experts will sign it in the record (c. 1801,§1).

[92] For civil law on expert testimony and comparison of handwriting cfr. McKelvey, pp. 249-252; Abbott, p. 482 fol.

[93] DS, Reg., n. 93, § 1.

313. The expert's report should be couched in language that is clear, concise, simple and as far as possible devoid of the more rare technical phrases. It is self understood that the report must never assert what is false or conceal pertinent facts discovered (cfr. c. 1794). To secure a complete report experts must clearly state the answers to the questions proposed, the method in which the inspection was made, and the basic arguments upon which the expert opinion has been drawn from the plain facts (c. 1801,§3).[94]

The report may thus be divided as follows: I. An introduction containing 1. the full name of the expert; 2. degrees received in his branch of science; 3. offices that enhance his authority; 4. the name of the curia and judge requiring the report; 5. the full name of the person examined; 6. the proper reference to identification, by photograph or document or otherwise, of the person examined; 7. the points to be determined by the inspection; and 8. the date and place of the inspection;

II. The body of the report containing 1. answers to the questions proposed by the judge and the defender together with the discussion on the method of inspection, and arguments that pertain; 2. observations on the matter, spontaneously made by the expert;

III. Conclusion drawn as to 1. the certain, probable, doubtful existence of impotence, and its nature, absolute or relative, or 2. the fact of non-consummation, or 3. the insanity of the party, *etc.*

IV. Signature of the expert, and date and place of report.

314. Each expert must write his own separate report in cases of impotence and non-consummation (c. 1980,§2). The Rota recently drew attention to the irregularity of a case in which two physicians had tendered a joint report on the impotence of a man.[95] Nevertheless the procedure was accepted as valid.

In cases other than those on impotence and non-consummation the judge may direct that a joint report be made, in which the majority opinion is adopted for the leading report. But dissenting opinions must be noted,[96] and all designated experts sign the report jointly made (c. 1802).

[94] DS, Reg., n. 93, § 1; R., Null., 10 mai 1921 (rd., xiii, p. 96): "Officium enim periti est non solum insaniae determinare existentiam, sed etiam naturam et gradum statuere, ut inde appareat an qui ea laborat, sit capax actus humani vel secus, dum operatur."

[95] R., Null., 8 jan. 1913 (rd., v, p. 30).

[96] R, Reg., § 125, n. 1 adds: "at reticitis ipsorum nominibus," a provision not obligatory on diocesan curiae.

315. The first expert inspection is not always conclusive or final. In a case where a young woman, claiming her marriage was not consummated, had entered a monastery, Honorius III decided that the husband's objections to the procedure were reasonable, and ordered the young wife to be inspected anew by newly designated matrons.[97] Such repeated inspections were sometimes demanded by the Congregation of the Council, before the Code.[98] So too now, the judge may reject the reports, if the experts disagree either as to facts or conclusions, or if there is other solid ground for so doing, and call for new inspections by other experts (c. 1803,§1).

Or without requiring a new inspection the judge may subject the reports to further expert review. When practical obstetricians, even though they are in agreement, have made the inspection, the judge may give their reports, if he think fit, to some expert physician to examine and remark upon (c. 1980,§3). Similarly if experts are of contradictory, opposite, or varying opinions so that their reports leave the object of the inspection unascertained, the judge may give the report of each expert to the other for perusal and explanation of the contradictory statements.[99] Or he may give the reports of both to another expert of greater eminence and obtain his opinion. This was the practice of the Congregation of the Council and is adhered to by the Rota.[100]

In cases where experts, after they have rendered their reports, are suspected or found unfit for the office, the judge may likewise give their reports to another for his examination and opinion, or he may call upon new experts to make another inspection and render other reports (c. 1803,§2).

97 c. 14, X, De Prob., II, 19.

98 SCC., *In Ferentina, Mat.*, 18 aug. 1888 (gasp., i, n. 612): " ..... affirmans illius sexum incertum esse. Jussu Curiae episcopalis, Faustina medicorum examini submissa fuit, quorum tres dixerunt esse foeminam, duo esse virum. S. C. C., ad quam causa delata fuerat, rescripsit, die *24 Mart. eiusdem anni*: 'Dilata et fiat nova inspectio a tribus chirurgis a S. C. designandis, quem in finem Faustina Romam adveniet'. Jam vero ii chirurgi declaraverunt Faustinam pertinere potius ad sexum masculinum, certe esse ineptam ad matrimonii consummationem in sexu foeminino, et hoc vitium praecedere conjugium. Hinc S. C. die 8 aug. 1888, posito dubio: '*An constet de nullitate matrimonii in casu*' reposuit *affirmative*."

99 DS, Reg., n. 93, § 2.

100 R., Null., 5 jun. 1913 (rd., v, p. 360); cfr. SA., Sancti Miniati, Null., 20 mai. 1915 (aas., vii, p. 356).

316. In cases where the expert's inspection touches questions of insanity or the genuineness of documents the judge may, if he think it necessary, examine the experts orally, to obtain, for instance, an explanation of their written statement, or he may omit further questioning (c. 1801,§2).

Under the Instruction of 1858 the judge was free to omit the verbal examination of the experts in impotence and non-consummation cases, unless the issues remained doubtful.[101] The Congregation of the Council subsequently insisted more on examining the experts.[102] Now the judge must examine each expert upon the report he has made in these cases. Each expert must be separately questioned, even when a joint inspection and report has finally been allowed.[103] The questions are proposed by the judge who will also examine the experts upon whatever points the defender shall have brought forth in his questionary (cfr. n. **112**); the experts then respond under oath (c. 1981),[104] and the notary writes down the testimony.

This subsequent examination is especially important when there is question of declaring a marriage invalid by reason of impotence. It makes for the completeness of the procedure in any case where only the question of non-consummation is at issue, although it is probably not strictly necessary for validity of the procedure. Sometimes such a questioning of the experts becomes very inconvenient or impossible or entirely redundant, namely when a complete and exhaustive advance questionary has been meticulously answered in the written report, and then it is sufficient that all precautions were taken in the inspection and report. Rome has admitted those cases that were done without the subsequent examination, provided the procedure was "servata in substantialibus".[105]

[101] SO, 1858.

[102] Bassibey, n. 395.

[103] cfr. DS, Reg., n. 93, § 2.

[104] Haring: Eheprozess, p. 23 calls attention to the three times repeated oath of experts (cfr. *e. g.*, DS, Reg., Appendix XXIX, XXX, XXXII) and rightly thinks this burdensome, and that the judge need not insist on more than one oath contained in Formula XXIX of DS, Reg. (cfr. R, Reg., § 129, n. 2).

[105] SCC., In Molinen., Mat., 29 mart. 1890; cfr. R, Reg., § 131; cfr. Gasparri, ii, p. 414 (1).

317. The following questions or some of them are suggested when experts have performed the physical inspection of a woman in cases of non-consummation: After the general questions touching Name, Residence, Profession, *etc.:* 1. Has the expert examined NN. as identified by photograph or document? 2. Is there any relationship between the expert and the woman inspected or her husband? 3. How long and in what way has the expert known them? 4. Does he now confirm under oath, all parts of his written report? 5. Is there anything to add or correct or change in the expert's report? 6. Has he made the physical inspection and the report independently of the other experts? 7. Had the women been immersed in a warm bath, and how long a time? 8. In what method did the expert proceed in making the inspection? 9. Did he discover signs, known to his profession, of integrity or deflowerment of the woman? 10. Upon what principal arguments does the reported opinion rest? 11. Is there any suspicion of fraud, especially of artificial means having been employed to simulate integrity of the membrane? 12. Is the woman afflicted with any disease, defect, or anomaly which might have had an influence on the marital relations, especially during the time of cohabitation with her husband, and is this curable or incurable? 13. In case of contrariety among experts: How is the opinion of the expert to be reconciled with the contrary opinion of the other expert or physician, or with the contrary assertion of one or both parties? 14. What has the expert observed of the general constitution of the petitioner? 15. Does he know anything pertinent to this from the woman, and what? 16. Does he know anything pertinent to the physical condition of the other spouse, the petitioner's husband; and is his opinion corroborated or weakened by what has been brought out in the procedure, about the husband's condition? 17. To what cause does he ascribe the asserted non-consummation? 18. Are there any other experiments or means to be employed in order to find out the truth, and what means? 19. After the reading of these depositions, has the expert anything to add, detract, correct or change?[106]

When experts have inspected the husband similar questions, especially nos. 7, 8 and 11 may be asked.[107]

106 DS, Reg., Appendix XXX.

107 DS, Reg., Appendix XXXII.

318. If a matron was present at the inspection, she will also be examined under oath (c. 1981). The following questions are directed by the Congregation: 1. Was the matron continuously present during the inspection of the woman? 2. Was the bath prepared and taken, and how prepared and taken? How long did the woman remain immersed? 3. Did the physicians or obstetricians carefully fulfil their offices according to the norms set out for them, and with regard for Christian modesty? 4. Could there have been any fraud or deception in the inspection? 5. Has the matron any pertinent remarks to offer? 6. After the reading of these depositions, has she anything to add, detract, correct or change in the answers just given? [108]

319. The report and opinion of the experts may at once be intimated to the parties either at the behest of the judge or at the instance of one of the parties.[109] But they may also be kept secret at the discretion of the judge, until the publication of all the proofs (cfr. n. **253**).

§ 5. Appraisal of Expert Testimony

320. In order to evaluate the reports of experts in impotence and non-consummation cases, the judge must know how to account the physiological phenomena themselves. To this end the study of pastoral medicine is necessary.

The original and virginal appearance of the hymen is not always uniform, but may have an appearance very similar to a lacerated membrane.[110] When the marital coition is first engaged in the hymen is ordinarily lacerated, leaving a somewhat star-shaped appearance which is ordinarily the sign of the sexual relation having been con-

[108] DS, Reg., n. 94; Appendix XXXI.

[109] R, Reg., § 135, n. 2.

[110] Antonelli, i, n. 199: "Ex formis differentibus, quas hymen praebere potest, speciali nota dignus est hymen plus minus *dentatus* vel *fimbriatus*, cuius dentes vel fimbriae aliquando carunculas myrtiformes simulare possunt. Quod quidem maxime prae oculis ab advocatis ecclesiasticis et medicis in causis matrimonialibus habendum est, ne mulier deflorata iudicetur, cum e contra indicia haec hymenis a natura proveniant; quae vero damna sequi possint, hac notione neglecta, a decisionibus sequuturis, neminem latet; cum possint declarari consummata matrimonia, quae nullo modo consummata sunt.

"Absentia perfecta hymenis a nativitate aliquando observata fuit."; R., Null., 15 nov. 1909 (rd., i, p. 140).

summated.[111] But the delicate membrane is lacerated also through many other causes.[112]

When the hymen has been lacerated there are medical and even natural means, by which it may be made to seem entirely intact.[113] But Vermeersch-Creusen state that, according to the statement of a most expert physician, the vestiges of the operation that has brought this virginal appearance about, can hardly escape an expert physician, if he be instructed to look out for this, and if he perform an ocular inspection and be not content with his sense of touch.[114]

On the other hand, it is entirely possible and of not so very rare occurrence that the marital relations have been repeatedly consummated, without disturbing a pliable and elastic membrane. A professor at the Medical School at Paris relates that, in the maternity clinic there, out of seventy-five examined at random, thirteen were found to be intact, although all were pregnant.[115]

321. When the corporal inspection of a woman proved that the virginal membrane was still intact, the Church courts accepted this,

111 Antonelli, i, n. 199: "Cum virgo primum patitur coitum, ordinarie membrum virile lacerat hymenem cum dolore et plerumque cum parva effusione sanguinis (aliquando cum vera haemorrhagia), et virgo tunc dicitur virginitatem amisisse; fragmenta dein hymenis partim gangraena afficiuntur et decidunt, partim vero permanent, cicatricibus obducta et constituunt carunculas myrtiformes, quae sunt ordinaria signa pro consummatione matrimonii."

112 Antonelli, i, n. 199: "Ceterum notatu dignum est multas causas, praeter copulam et corpora mechanica, posse lacerationem hymenis inducere, quin mulier id advertat, uti sunt saltus, equitare more virorum, casus, repentina divaricatio crurum, conatus primi menstrui, sanguis coagulatus, ulcera, fluores albi, prolapsus uteri et vaginae et plures aliae. Ex his facile deduces hymenis lacerationem non posse *semper* et *tuto* testari mulierem non esse virginem, eo modo quo hymen mollis et elasticus non valet *certo* testari copulam locum non habuisse et proinde mulierem esse virginem."; cfr. also, ime., xliii (1931), p. 272.

113 SCC., In Neapolitana, Mat., 31 mart. 1770; In Bononien., Mat., 29 aug. 1857 (pall., xiii, nn. 48, 49); R., Null., 3 aug. 1921 (rd., xiii, p. 192): "Ad probationem vero physicam quod attinet,.... recolenda sunt quae habet Eschbach, nempe, ... c) crescentibus annis, cresci difficultatem dignoscendi verum ex physica inspectione (*Discept. Physiolog. Theol.*, discept. II).

114 V-Creusen, iii, n. 292.

115 Bassibey, n. 444 (1) quoting Pierre Budin, Obstetr. Gynec., Paris, 1886; Antonelli, i, n. 199: ". . . alias vero adeo mollis et elastica est ut permittat introductionem penis, quin laceretur."

with some misgivings,[116] as full proof of virginity.[117] But later on, as it became more widely known that this is no strict physiological proof, the jurisprudence of the courts changed slightly; yet the constant voice of canonists and the practice of the Roman Curia has admitted and still admits it as valuable partial proof,[118] which, with other indications, is generally considered conclusive.[119]

322. On the other hand, evidence that a woman is not intact is not physiologically conclusive proof that she has had sexual coition. Hence the judge must generally consider what other arguments or proofs may be required (cfr. n. **279**).[120] In a secret case, the Rota pronounced the marriage void because of impotence, after both parties asserted the impossibility of having marital relations together, and witnesses testified they had heard the husband assert his wife's impotence at an unsuspected time. Yet the experts disagreed as to potency and the hymen of the woman was not intact.[121] Slight lacerations are certainly not conclusive proof of coition.[122]

Pregnancy itself is possible without sexual coition. For the spermatozoa may be placed within the womb by artificial means and this is known as artificial fecundation,[123] or by a natural attraction, whenever the virile semen is emitted at the labia of the vagina. The Rota has recently declared for invalidity by reason of impotence, although it was admitted that the woman had conceived and that the husband had impregnated her; but he had not been able to effect the invasion which constitutes the marital coition.[124]

Nevertheless favorable decisions of nullity are much more difficult of attainment when it is certain that the woman is not intact, and no extenuating reason is offered.

[116] cfr. c. 4, 5, C. XXVII, q. 1; c. 14, X, De Prob. II, 19.

[117] De Becker, p. 419; Gasparri, i, nn. 604, 777; ii, n. 1304.

[118] SCC., Anconitana, Mat., 16 mart. 1793 (cicf., vi, n. 3884); In Bononien., Mat., 23 mai. 1857 (pall., xiii, nn. 48, 49).

[119] R., Null., 16 mai. 1914 (rd., vi, pp. 214, 215); Null., 17 aug. 1920 (rd., xii, p. 245); Pallotini, xiii, 48, § XIII, n. 58; cfr. Gasparri, ii, n. 1304.

[120] DS, Reg., n. 73.

[121] R., Null., 15 nov. 1909 (rd., i, p. 140).

[122] SCC., Versalien., 22 aug. 1908 (cicf., vi, n. 4352).

[123] Bassibey, n. 444, 3.; cfr. SCC., In Varsovien., Mat., 27 jul. 1850 (pall., xiii, nn. 203-205).

[124] R., Null., 17 aug. 1920 (rd., xii, p. 234); cfr. nn. **533**, **560**.

323. The direct findings of experts have a greater value of proof than the conclusions drawn from their findings. When the report of an expert contains merely the recountal of what he has observed in the course of his inspection, his testimony to these facts has at least the same value of conclusiveness as the testimony of a simple witness. Thus an expert's report on the condition in which he has found the hymen, *v. g.* that it is entirely intact,[125] or on the condition in which he has found the genital organs of the man, *v. g.* that they are small and undeveloped,[126] or on the condition in which he has found the mentality of a person, must not be easily set aside.[127] When the expert's report goes on to draw inferences from the observations made, these inferences must be accorded such deference as the ability and logic of the expert rightly demand from the judge,[128] but they are not necessarily conclusive, for the expert is not the arbiter of the case.[129] The same holds true with regard to expert inspection of documents.[130]

When the reports contain inductions and inferences not immediately and directly, but remotely and loosely construed from the known facts, they have but little value.[131] Frequently it is difficult to determine whether the statements made in the report contain the testimony of facts directly observed, or inferences and opinions of the expert.[132] The subsequent questioning of the expert should help to clear up this matter, so that the judge may go on to examine the inferences and accord them the proof-bearing value they deserve.

324. Concordant reports and testimony of experts are of stronger proof-bearing value than single testimony. When two or more ex-

[125] cfr. contra V-Creusen, iii, n. 292.

[126] cfr. contra SCC., In Ianuen., Mat., 16 apr. 1791 (pall., xiii, 69, n. 164).

[127] SCC., In Melevitana, Obsequiorum Matrim., 18 jun. 1831 (pall., xiii, p. 396, nn. 76, 77); R., Null., 10 jul. 1909 (rd., i, p. 87); Buscoducen., Null., 15 mai. 1915 (rd., vii, p. 219; aas., vii, p. 575).

[128] IA., § 174; Feije, n. 543.

[129] SCC., In Romana seu Tibertina, Null., 29 mai. 1852 (pall., xiii, 47); R., Null., 27 jul. 1920 (rd., xii, p. 209); Buscoducen., Null., 7 jan. 1918 (rd., x, p. 3; aas., x, pp. 517, 518); Noval, nn. 512, 530.

[130] Bassibey, n. 473.

[131] In civil law, McKelvey, p. 246: "expert opinion . . . is the most common, though, in the refinements of expert testimony which have developed, not always the most satisfactory method of proof."

[132] cfr. McKelvey, pp. 230-235.

perts agree upon facts witnessed during their expert inspection, their testimony, like that of other witnesses, is generally conclusive.[133]

The testimony of one expert may be conclusive when added to the depositions of parties or other personal presumptions, but does not of itself, constitute full proof, for experts are not authorized or *ex officio* witnesses. In a recent case the Rota declared that the testimony of one expert declaring the hymen of a woman to be intact, was not sufficient to prove that fact as an element to the proof of impotence in her husband.[134]

When two or more experts are in agreement on an inference immediately and legitimately derived from the known facts, there arises a strong argument in favor of their conclusions, and in some cases this argument is tantamount to conclusive proof. Thus the Instruction for Austria held that when two experts above all suspicion testified to the absolute impotence of a man or woman, such impotence was to be considered proved, unless the party concerned petitioned that another expert be added to make similar inspection. In the case of relative impotence the Instruction required the concurrent opinions of three experts above all suspicion.[135]

An added weight is given to expert testimony and opinion purporting to establish impotence, if it is learned from the testimony of parties or witnesses that the parties have unsuccessfully essayed, during a considerable period of time, to consummate the marriage.

325. The conclusions, inferences and opinions of experts should be based upon facts judicially proved, *i. e.* documentated, properly witnessed in court, or discovered by experts appointed by the judge in the course of official inspection. If they are founded on facts not judicially proved, they are not, strictly speaking, classified as expert's proofs.[136] Thus the Rota in a case of impotence has rejected expert opinion founded on the extraneous medical history of a case.[137] There

[133] IA., § 174.

[134] R., Null., 16 jul. 1910 (rd., ii, p. 285); Lega, i, n. 509. It is seen from this that Augustine, vii, p. 239 has inaccurately included experts among those qualified witnesses whose single testimony establishes full proof.

[135] IA., § 174.

[136] Smith, n. 544.

[137] R., Null., 22 dec. 1913 (rd., v, p. 673): "Primo notandum est iudicium Medicorum fundari non solum in repertis ex peracta inspectione corporis, sed etiam in factis ab aliis extraiudicialiter et sine iuramento relatis, quae iuxta peritos constituit 'criterium historicum'. . . . Iamvero excedit competentiam medici iudicare in causa matrimoniali de veritate vel secus huiusmodi factorum extraiudicialiter relatorum, unde cadit fundamentum 'historici critici.'"

is however a greater leniency observable in cases on lack of consent because of insanity.[138]

Informal inspections made by experts not appointed by the judge, but rather consulted by the parties, do not, strictly speaking, beget expert's proof in the canonical sense. Nevertheless, it has been the practice of the Roman Curia to ratify such informal inspections when a new inspection cannot at all or can only with considerable difficulty be undertaken, as is often the case in missionary countries.[139]

326. When the inspection has been formally made and the judicial report given, this constitutes legal proof available in another court as well as in the first instance of trial, provided the case at issue be centered upon the same persons (c. 1738).[140]

327. The judge must therefore weigh well the reports and testimony of experts and consider all the circumstances of the case (c. 1804,§1). When there is disagreement among the experts the judge must accurately inquire whether all the experts are in possession of all the facts of the case, as well as whether there is any suspicion of their ability or integrity.[141] In a recent case the Rota followed the opinion of women obstetricians holding for impotence and nullity, against the opinion of a physician holding for the potency of the party.[142] The judge is not obliged to follow the opinion of experts against his own conviction, least of all if that opinion is based upon facts not judicially proved, or is outside the realm of the expert's science.[143] Experience has shown how carefully the judge must weigh an expert's opinion that marks a man as perpetually impotent. For some men have been considered incurably impotent who later attained to potency.

[138] R., Ton Kin Central., Null., 27 jun. 1916 (rd., viii, p. 211; aas., ix, p. 250): "Ceterum in praesenti specie, peritia non omnino defuit; medici quidem sententiam suam de morbo Mariae ore proprio coram iudice non expresserunt, sed eorum dicta a pluribus testibus relata sunt."; Null., 16 aug. 1913 (rd., v, pp. 577, 578); Buscoducen., Null., 15 mai. 1915 (rd., vii, p. 215 fol.; aas., vii, pp. 572-583); Vic. Ap. Chan-Si Sept., Null., 29 jun. 1923 (rd., xv, pp. 133, 134).

[139] R., Null., 25 mart. 1920 (rd., xii, p. 75); Null., 8 jan. 1913 (rd., v, pp. 23, 24); Null., 5 jun. 1913 (rd., v, p. 359).

[140] W-Vidal, vi, n. 499.

[141] R., Null., 16 jul. 1910 (rd., ii, p. 281).

[142] R., Null., 15 nov. 1909 (rd., i, p. 140).

[143] R., Null., 28 aug. 1911 (rd., iii, p. 453 fol.); cfr. Buscoducen., Null., 7 jan. 1918 (rd., x, p. 3; aas., x, p. 518); Null., 16 jul. 1910 (rd., ii, p. 286); R, Reg., § 136; Lega, i, n. 509.

On the other hand the judge may infer from the reports of experts more than is contained directly in them, if concordant circumstances of the case warrant the inference; *e. g.*, that a husband is impotent, in a case where the experts cannot examine him, but find the hymen of the wife intact, and other proved circumstances concur.

328. *Scholion:* The Code states that the judge shall equitably estimate, according to local customary charges, the amount to be paid to experts as stipends and expenses, and charge these costs to the parties (c. 1805). He should state in the decree appointing the experts, which party shall pay these costs, and generally it will be that party at whose petition and in whose interest the examination is made (cfr. c. 1913,§1).[144] Such costs are subtracted from the money that is deposited with the court at the beginning of the trial (cfr. cc. 1626; 1631; 1909,§2). But some diocesan curiae do not require such deposits before trial: it is customary to state in the letter of appointment that the experts shall charge the customary costs to, and collect them from the person who is examined (cfr. n. **293**).

[144] R, Reg., § 130.

CHAPTER X

Judicial Notice

"Descendam et videbo, utrum clamorem qui venit ad me, opere compleverint, an non est ita, ut sciam.—Gen., xviii, 21.

329. An inspection of the object of controversy may sometimes be made by the judge himself, and this form of proof is called judicial notice (recognitio judicialis), formerly called self-evidence (evidentia facti).[1] There is an example of this form of proof in the Decretals, where Alexander III directs a bishop to personally review the territory whose boundary is in dispute, and decide the matter on the spot.[2] Ecclesiastical judges have availed themselves of this text to come to a clear view of cases by means of ocular inspection. Nevertheless such judicial notice was not recognized as a distinct means of proof until the Regulations for the Rota were published,[3] and the Code proposes it apart from expert testimony under its own rubric: "De Accessu et Recognitione Judiciali." It seems from this heading and from Canon 1806 that the Code anticipates a use for this proof chiefly in cases where property or fixed objects that cannot be brought to court are to be inspected. But of course there may be judicial notice of objects, such as documents, that are brought to the court (cfr. c. 1808,§1), or of persons. Thus in cases of insanity nothing prevents the judge from confirming with his own senses, the reports of experts as to the present mental condition of a party.[4] Similarly in suits for separation from bed and board because of alleged cruelty, the judge may take notice of personal injuries inflicted, and base his decision upon such judicial notice.

It is not becoming for reasons which are at once evident, that ecclesiastical judges should undertake judicial inspection in cases of non-consummation or impotence, even when the person to be inspected is the husband. In some missionary countries it is sometimes im-

[1] cfr. *v. g.* c. 15, X, De Restitutione Spoliatorum, II, 13.

[2] c. 9, X, De Praescriptionibus, II, 26.

[3] R, Reg., Tit. IV, Cap. VI.

[4] W-Vidal, vi, n. 501.

possible to have the services of competent experts, and for such cases provision has been made whereby the clergy provide for the physical inspection in whatever manner is most suitable to the circumstances of person and place.[5] But this is never to be interpreted as calling for judicial notice in non-consummation or impotence cases.

330. If the judge can undertake an inspection of the controverted matter, and deems such inspection necessary to the correct understanding or proof of the case, he will issue a decree to that effect, and state the points upon which the judicial notice is to be taken (c. 1806). The parties and the defender are heard in this matter. They may also propose that the judge take judicial notice of a mooted point,[6] but the compliance with or rejection of their demand lies with the judge, who will consider the best interests of the trial.[7]

The judge may undertake the judicial inspection in person or he may commission an auditor or delegated judge for that duty (c. 1807).[8]

331. The judge may take whatever right measures are necessary to make the judicial notice effective: I. He may be assisted by the services of experts if he deem their assistance necessary or useful to the case (c. 1808,§1). Hence it is not uncommon that expert inspection and judicial notice are made together in cases where a person's sanity is at issue. In impotence and non-consummation cases however, there is no judicial notice, even in conjunction with experts.

If experts assist at the judicial notice the same norms will be observed, as far as possible, in their regard, as are prescribed for experts appointed to make an inspection independently (c. 1808,§2).

II. If it seem to the judge that there is danger of quarrels or disturbances, he may exclude the parties and their advocates from the judicial inspection (c. 1809).

III. In the act of taking judicial notice the judge may examine witnesses, cited by himself or duly introduced by the parties before the judicial notice began, if he thinks this will be helpful to a fuller proof of the case, or to the clarifying of doubts for the removal of which the judicial notice was needed (c. 1810).

[5] SO., 6 aug. 1890 (cpf. ii, n. 1737; cicf., iv, n. 1127).

[6] R, Reg., § 166.

[7] W-Vidal, vi, n. 502.

[8] Roberti, ii, n. 365: "Iudex delegatus potest nimirum esse unus ex iudicibus collegii; secus non intelligitur quomodo ab auditore distinguatur"; Noval, n. 536 otherwise.

332. The notary must be present at the judicial notice. The presence of the notary is essential, for it is only by his writing the judicial notice into the record that it becomes a part of the actuary proofs (cfr. c. 1869,§2).

In cases affecting the marriage bond, the presence of the defender, or at least the summoning him to be present is also required (cfr. cc. 1587,§1; 1968, n. 1).

The notary will carefully see to it that the acts contain a record of the day and hour in which the judicial notice took place, what persons were present, and what was said or done or decreed by the judge during the course of the inspection (c. 1811,§1). Because an object may be subject to change according to the various hours of the day, the Code prescribes mention of the hour at which the judicial notice took place: a precaution that is not demanded for other documents that pertain to the proof of a thing (cfr. cc. 777,§1; 798; 1010, §1; 1103,§1; 1238; 1894,n.4) (otherwise *e. g.* cc. 1715,§1; 1866,§3).

The judge and the notary sign the record of judicial notice (c. 1811,§2).

333. As may be seen from the wording of Canon 1810, judicial notice is intended to be a subsidiary means of proof, and one can hardly imagine a marriage case the proof of which hinges entirely on judicial notice. In cases where such notice is taken, it renders proof that is full or partial or only an indication of the truth, according as the findings, in view of the method and thoroughness of the inspection, bring forth complete evidence of a fact or only some lesser light that does not attain to evidence.

CHAPTER XI

DOCUMENTS

"Scribe hoc ob monumentum in libro."—Ex., xvii, 14.

334. The Church did not make universal provision from the earliest times, that acts of public importance be made demonstrable for future contingencies; nevertheless she has antedated the civil governments by centuries in the keeping of vital statistics.[1] Ecclesiastical notaries, diocesan archives and parish records have provided cogent proofs in judicial procedures, and the present Code has established a renewed control whereby baptisms, weddings, deaths and similar acts that may have an effect upon the marriage case shall be demonstrable (actus ad futuram rei memoriam) (cfr. cc. 372-384; 576,§2; 1010,§1; 1103; 1238; 1523, n. 6).[2] As people are by nature inclined to put faith in what has been written, the demonstration of these acts is principally offered in the form of written documents.

§ 1. DEFINITION AND KINDS OF DOCUMENT

335. Documents may pertain to the substance of an act or they may pertain only to the proving of it. In the matter of engagements to marry (sponsalia de futuro) the written document pertains to the substance of the act: so that if there be no written engagement, or if it be not authenticated by the required signatures *etc.*, there is no valid engagement (c. 1017; cfr. cc. 1089,§1; 1529; 1874,§5 iunct. 1894, n. 4). We are not concerned here with this substantiating quality of documents. Generally documents pertain only to the proving of an act; and the law may prescribe that an act can be proved only by document (cfr. c. 1990), though this is very rare, or the law may allow that an act is demonstrable either by document or by other proofs. Documents are, then, writings or records by which facts may be proved.

[1] cfr. c. 1, X, De Libelli Oblatione, II, 3; On the history of parish baptismal, marriage and death records cfr. W-Vidal, v, n. 562.

[2] On the punishment for not keeping parish registers cfr. c. 2383.

336. The chapter heading of the Code (Lib. IV, Tit. x, Cap. v), speaks of proof by instruments and thus follows the usage of the Decretal (X, de Fide Instrumentorum, II, 22). The Roman,[3] and the early Canon law,[4] used the term "instrument" in so wide a sense that it designated the testimony of witnesses, as well as written evidence. Later however, the classical canonists strictly defined an instrument as a writing drawn up in order to prove a fact at some future time.[5] This sense of the word is retained in the Code, which somewhat distinguishes instruments (c. 1813,§1, n. 2) from other documents (documenta, acta, monumenta, scripturae) (cc. 1523, n. 6; 1813, §1, n. 3; 1822; 2020,§3), though in chapter v, the Code uses the words "instrumentum" and "documentum" without explicitly calling attention to the distinction (cfr. also cc. 374, 375).[6]

337. Documents appear in original (d. originale, archetypus, protocollum), or in exemplar form (exemplar, transumptum, copia). Original documents are those which the original authors first drew up; exemplars or copies are those which are copied from the originals. When documents are originally drawn up in more than one reproduction under corresponding date, and with the original writer's signature and seal, they are known as duplicates. When duplicates have been made out either has the force of an original document.

338. Either originals or exemplars may be authentic or non-authentic (cfr. cc. 1091; 1299,§3; 1813,§1, nn. 1,4; 1890).[7] An authentic original is one that has authoritativeness, as having been executed by the proper public officer (cfr. cc. 1089,§§1,2); an authentic copy is one whose conformity with the original is attested by a proper public officer, and generally a public seal is required for either as a necessary solemnity (cfr. cc. 470,§4; 2036,§2; 2055), except in chancery and parish registers where neither signature nor seal is required for authenticity (cfr. n. **344**).[8] In other cases, if no seal is

[3] L. 1, ff., De Fide Instrumentorum.

[4] c. 4, X, De Testibus Cogendis vel Non, II, 21.

[5] Reiffenstuel, II, tit. 22, n. 4; Pirhing, p. 299.

[6] W-Vidal, vi, p. 449 (6): "Difficile admodum est in concordiam reducere auctores antiquos inter se et multo magis cum modernis tum in explicatione illarum trium vocum (instrumentum, documentum, scriptura) tum in praecipua hac prima divisione et in notione documenti authentici et conditionibus requisitis ad illam appellationem."

[7] Noval, n. 541 seems to admit the distinction only for copies.

[8] R., Null., 30 jun. 1910 (rd., ii, p. 221); W-Vidal, vi, n. 511.

used the document is called certified but not authentic. The strictly legal sense of the word "authentic" as here used, is somewhat different from the sense in which older canonists sometimes used it synonymously with "public document" or "original document," and differs likewise from the character of genuineness, truthfulness and credibility in which sense it is also used in Canons 1284 and 1285,§1.[9]

339. Copies of parish registers should be exactly as the originals; nowadays however the parish records are commonly inscribed upon blank-form registers and excerpts from them are given on printed blank-forms. The complete filling out of such forms, when attested by signature and seal, constitutes an authentic copy even though it be not a word for word transcript from the register.[10]

340. Documents emanating from Rome are authenticated in the original by the signature of the Supreme Pontiff or of the officials at the head of the various congregations, tribunals and offices, together with the signatures of the proper protonotaries and the respective seals. Copies of such documents are authenticated only by the respective notaries of the congregation, tribunal, office from which the original issues (cc. 374,§1; 1813,§1,n.1). The signature of the bishop, vicar general, official, diocesan chancellor or notary coupled with the proper seal makes those documents authentic which issue from the diocesan curia within the respective spheres of the above named persons (cfr. c. 1283,§1). Authentic copies of such documents are issued by the chancellor or other proper notary. The signature of the pastor coupled with the seal of the parish authenticates documents of parochial origin in the original or in copy (c. 1813,§1, n. 4; cpre. cc. 470,§§3,4; 1089,§1; 1659,§2).[11] Assistant pastors or curates have no power *per se,* to authenticate parish documents, but it seems probable that such power can be either explicitly or implicitly delegated to them (cfr. c. 1089,§1) ;[12] hence the practice whereby assistant

[9] cfr. Blat, in lib. III pars iii, n. 153; cfr. c. 2034; W-Vidal, vi, n. 513; —Eichmann, p. 156, Woywod in hpr, xxxii (1932), p. 729, and Ayrinhac, n. 326, likewise confound the two ideas.

[10] Capello, iii, n. 149, 3°; DeSmet, ii, n. 678, iunct. c. 1021, § 1; Gasparri, nov., i, n. 142: But in nov. ii, n. 1080, Gasparri copies what he had written in his ed. 1904, ii, n. 1283 to the contrary.

[11] SCC., Platien., 3 jul. 1909 (aas., i, p. 658): "Quo in casu parochus, consuetudine universali ita rem interpretante, habetur ut notarius publicus ecclesiasticus . . . "

[12] Augustine, vii, p. 257.

pastors issue and sign baptismal certificates in order to authorize a person to receive one of the subsequent sacraments is not, of itself, to be condemned.

Civil documents are authenticated by the appointed civil officers or notaries. But these have no power to authenticate a document that is constitutive of an act which lies strictly within the ecclesiastical province (cfr. c. 374,§2).

341. A document is rendered non-authentic by having been drawn up by a person not properly constituted to issue such a document (cfr. cc. 374,§2; 1283,§2), or by the omission of the proper solemnities such as signature and seal. The classical canonists prescribed other solemnities, such as the invocation of God's name, the mention of the name of the reigning sovereign, accurate place and date.[13] Some of these are not essential now. Documents must however be properly dated and the place must be given (cfr. cc. 777,§1; 798; 1010,§1; 1103,§1; 1238; 1874,§5; 1894, n. 4). If mention of the place is omitted the required authenticity is at least uncertain (cfr. c. 1894, n. 4).[14] Mention of the date of document is even more clearly necessary for authenticity, and documents that are necessary to the substance of an act (cfr. n. **335**) are vitiated if not dated (cfr. c. 1894, n. 4). The Congregation of the Council declared betrothals invalid if the substantiating document did not make mention of the day, month and year.[15] In some such documents at least, full authenticity may be later acquired by correction of the defect (cfr. *e. g.* c. 1894). Documents that pertain only to the proving of an act have not the full quality of authenticity unless the correct date and place are affixed; nevertheless their probatory value is left to the discretion of the judge (cfr. n. **367**).

342. Documents may be either public or private. A document is public if it issues from a properly appointed public person acting precisely in his official capacity. That he acts precisely in the cap-

[13] Pirhing, p. 300.

[14] Hilling in akk, 1928, p. 100; cfr. DeSmet, i, p. 11 (5).

[15] SCC., Romana et aliarum, 27 jul. 1908 (cicf., vi, n. 4350). This response is to be considered with Canons 6, nn. 2, 4; and 23, requiring our interpretation of the Code to be, with due allowances, conformable to the old legislation: the more so in this matter, since the betrothal without date of betrothal is inconceivable: thus De Smet, i, n. 10; Capello, iii, n. 89; V-Creusen, ii, n. 281 and Hilling in akk., 1925, p. 98 fol. whose arguments seem to overcome the opposite view of N-Schmitt, iii, p. 536 (1), alii, relying on Canon 15.

acity of his office is seen 1) when the nature of the business written is not personal but official, 2) when the document is countersigned by another official, 3) when it contains an express statement that it is issued in the writer's official capacity, 4) when use is made of the public seal of office, and this latter is the commonest means of determining the writer's official capacity.

Thus the solemnities of authenticating a document as public are simpler now than under the law of the Decretals.[16] For formerly testimonials taken from the parish registers and signed and sealed by the pastor needed to be viséd by the bishop's curia (d. vidimata) to have authentication as public documents.[17] And the writings of ordinaries, even when signed and sealed by them, were not looked upon as public documents properly speaking, unless they were attested by a notary.[18] Custom had somewhat modified this rigor even before the Code,[19] and Canon 1813,§1 now places all such writings among the public ecclesiastical documents.

343. Documents that are not public are private documents. These are papers written or signed by private persons, or by public persons acting in a private capacity. The chief private documents used in marriage cases are pre-nuptial promises and contracts, letters and diaries, and written testimonies tendered in favor of or against the marriage suit (c. 1813,§3).[20] These are sometimes said to be authenticated, when they are attested by a public officer, *e. g.* pastor or notary, with signature and seal.

344. Public documents may issue from the ecclesiastical authorities, and then they are known as public ecclesiastical documents; or they may issue from the civil authorities, and are then known as public civil documents.

The following are the chief public ecclesiastical documents now met with in the marriage trial; 1) Dispensations of the Supreme

[16] cfr. Augustine, vii, p. 254 (1); Bouix, i, n. 321; W-Vidal, vi, p. 449 (8).

[17] SO., 24 feb. 1847 (cicf., iv, n. 900; cpf., i, n. 1011); PF, 1883, § 31; SCC., Platien., 3 jul. 1909 (aas., i, p. 658); Gasparri, i, n. 169; Schlenz in akk., 1918, p. 59.

[18] R., Placentina, Iurium, 31 mai. 1917 (rd., ix, p. 123; aas., ix, p. 585); Pirhing, p. 300.

[19] R., Heliopolitana, Iurispatronatus, 22 nov. 1913 (rd., v, p. 595; aas., vi, p. 83); Smith, n. 563.

[20] DS, Reg., n. 75.

Pontiff dissolving marriages that were not consummated since ratification.

2) Dispensations of the Holy Office, from the necessity of interpellating the infidel party in Pauline privilege cases, and dispensations of the Holy Office, the Congregation of the Sacraments, the Congregation for Orientals from diriment impediments;

3) Rescripts validating marriages at root (sanatio in radice);

4) Similar dispensations and rescripts granted by local ordinaries, or others empowered to grant dispensation (cfr. n. **97**).

5) Copies of the foregoing;

6) Instruments attested by ecclesiastical notaries (cfr. *e. g.*, c. 1089,§1);

7) Judicial decisions and acts of procedure (acta processus) or of proof (acta causae) (cfr. c. 1738), such as the sworn reports of designated experts;

8) Records of baptism, confirmation, first communion, ordination, religious profession, marriage,[21] betrothals,[22] and death contained in the registers of the parish, religious order, or diocese.

If such record is contained in one of the public books of the parish, religious order, or diocese the absence of the proper signature does not invalidate the entry as a credible public record.[23] If the record appears on a loose paper rather than in the properly bound public book, it may still be said to be in the registers and does not thereby lose its value as a public document, provided it bear the proper solemnities of authentication and the marks of genuineness.[24]

9) Exemplars and testimonials taken from such archives and authenticated by the pastor, ordinary, or an ecclesiastical notary (c. 1813,§1).

345. The Canon law receives as public civil documents all those which are rightly received as such according to the civil laws of the place (c. 1813,§2) in which they are drawn up or used. The chief public civil documents used in marriage cases are the records and certificates of birth, marriage, and death, marriage licenses, judicial

[21] DS, Reg., n. 75.

[22] R., Null., 28 aug. 1911 (rd., iii, p. 441).

[23] R., Null., 30 jun. 1910 (rd., ii, p. 221): "Sollemne est in H. S. O. ut libri, non subscripti, qui detinentur in archiviis, plenam fidem faciant de actis inibi relatis. . . . "

[24] R., Null., 6 dec. 1909 (rd., i, p. 158); cfr. Noval, n. 545.

records and decrees of divorce and separation,[25] decrees constituting a guardian, trustee, or proctor, or remanding persons to insane asylums, papers of legal adoption, and affidavits sworn to before notaries public.

Judicial papers emanating from the civil courts are public civil documents and may be urged as proof in ecclesiastical trials. But they are admitted only as proof of facts that lie within civil competence, *v. g.* proof of insanity, or of guilt as a cause of divorce. Hence, to the end that the petitioner be exonerated or charged with guilt as a cause of the disruption of his marriage, an authentic exemplar of the divorce decree must be sent on with the acts, in cases of dissolution of merely legitimate marriage in favor of the Faith.

In matters where the civil courts are not competent, such as when they declare marriage between Christians invalid, the dispositive part of such a decision has no value.[26] Yet in nearly every case of nullity, Pauline privilege, or dispensation from ratified marriage, tried in diocesan court, it is necessary to present the papers of civil divorce. This is the common practice and is prescribed in some dioceses.[27] The purpose of introducing such otherwise incompetent documents is to avoid conflict with the civil law. When such cases are heard before the Roman Rota the civil divorce papers need not always be shown.

Parties to marriage cases frequently present as evidence the written testimony of their friends sworn to before a civil notary, and attested, subscribed and sealed by him. Such documents have the value of public civil documents only in respect to the fact that they were thus attested by the notary, but the content of such documents by no means obtains the value of the content of a public document; it is nothing more than the testimony of a private person (cfr. nn. **234, 350, 373, 379**).

In cases where a former marriage between non-Catholics has been adjudged invalid by a church court of some non-Catholic denomination, the acts drawn up in such a court have the value of private documents, before the Catholic court, but they are not viewed

[25] DS, Reg., n. 75.

[26] PF, 1883, § 44; Chelodi, n. 78.

[27] The questions asked PC., 16 oct. 1919 (aas., xi, p. 479) regarding declaration of nullity by administrative action, mention only cases where civil divorce has been obtained, and the answers are given for such cases, but need not be restricted to these when no civil divorce is required to safeguard the ordinary's action: Haring: Ungueltigkeitserklaerung (lqs., 1926, p. 347).

as public documents (cfr. n. **378**),[28] and much less are the decisions of such a court acceptable, even though the marriage is invalidated upon grounds that render a marriage void in the Catholic Church.[29]

The records and certificates issued by ship companies, military headquarters, hospitals *etc.* are not in a strict sense public civil documents; but in the matter of proving the death of an absconded spouse they are accredited with great value (cfr. nn. **155, 351, 377**).

346. A document is genuine (d. genuinum) if it was written or signed by the person whose name is affixed; a non-genuine document is forged or apocryphal (d. apocryphum). Public documents whether ecclesiastical or civil are presumed to be genuine until the contrary is proved to evidence (c. 1814).[30] Private documents are not presumed to be genuine.

347. A document is either true and entire (d. integrum) or it is falsified, erased, interpolated (d. vitiatum, d. falsificatum). Public documents bear the presumption of integrity, as long as no suspicion arises from evident interstices, erasures, tampering *etc.*[31]

348. A document is a matter of public law (d. iuris publici) if it pertain to the general regime and welfare, *v. g.* duly promulgated laws (c. 1819), dispensations promulgated for an entire community; or it is of private law (d. iuris privati) if it pertain to the affair of individuals only, *v. g.* a marriage certificate. Sometimes the word "iuris publici" is used in another sense, to denote that which is published.

§ 2. Admissibility and Necessity of Documentary Proof

349. Proof by documents both public and private is admitted in any marriage trial (cc. 1812; 1990).[32] In their probative force

[28] PF, 1883, § 44.

[29] Although ministers of all religions are commissioned by civil law to perform marriages in New York State, the entry of a marriage in the parish register is evidence only "if the register is required by law to be kept" (May, p. 300); *i. e.* it is only then recognized as a public civil document, though it may otherwise be received as proof "both of the fact of marriage and of the date of solemnization" (Abbott, p. 103; cfr. p. 92).

[30] Smith, n. 591 inaccurately to the contrary.

[31] For the privation of office and other punishments that await falsifiers cfr. cc. 2362; 2406, § 1.

[32] DS, Reg., nn. 75, 76; PF, 1883, § 18.

documents are not limited by territorial boundaries: they are to be received when presented in courts even outside the territory in which they were drawn up. Parish and curial records supply documentary proof in most nullity cases where a defect of marriage form, or the impediments of age, marriage bond, spiritual parentage, affinity, public decency, consanguinity, order and solemn vow are in question, and in some other cases. Many marriage cases are settled entirely or nearly entirely by document.

350. In cases proposed for settlement according to the extraordinary procedure given in Canons 1990-1992, there is a question whether the proof of the existence of the impediment must be strictly documentary and peremptory (probatio praeconstituta et probata), or whether other proofs that might beget equal certainty, such as testimony sworn to before a notary (cfr. nn. **192, 234**), are sufficient for this procedure. It is certain that when the impediment is proved, the proof of no dispensation's having been granted need not be documentary, but may derive from any legitimate source (cfr. nn. **372, 375**). It is equally certain that in the impediment of disparity, proof of the negative part of the impediment, *i. e.* that one party never received baptism, cannot be strictly documentary (cfr. nn. **161, 162**). But some writers incline to hold that proof of the impediment in its positive part, *i. e.* proof of baptism, marriage bond, consanguinity, *etc.*, may also derive from a source other than documentary, without prejudice to the correct use of the summary procedure described in Canons 1990-1992.[33] Other writers have more properly held that in these cases strict documentary evidence is required.[34] The Declaration of the year 1889 from which Canon 1990 springs, required only that the impediment be evidenced by certain proofs (ex certis argumentis), if proof by document could not be presented.[35] But Canon 1990 omits the clause pertaining to other proofs and speaks only of an authentic document that cannot be contested (certo

[33] Nau, Appendix, n. 11 (pp. 223, 224); Gasparri, nov., ii, n. 1283 writes of this matter without the precision necessary to know whether or not he holds that the necessary certainty of the impediment, as well as of the lack of dispensation, may be derived from other than strict documentary evidence; Woywod in hpr., xxxiv (1933), p. 161 rightly remarks that the response of PC., 16 jun. 1931 (aas., xxiii, pp. 353, 354) is not satisfactorily clear on this point.

[34] Noval, n. 873; V-Creusen, iii, n. 296; Capello, iii, pp. 934, 936; Lanier, p. 3.

[35] SO, 1889.

et authentico documento), and no exception is made for equally certain proofs deriving from other sources, except in the matters of lack of dispensation and non-baptism, where the nature of the thing prevents the negative from being proved by document. Evidently the legislator's omission from the text of Canon 1990 of that clause of the Declaration of 1889 which allowed proof in summary procedure by other certain means, was purposeful. And so here we have the case described in Canon 6, n. 3, according to which Canon 1990, which concurs with the old law only in part, must be interpreted as the old law in that part, but in so far as it does not concur, must be interpreted by the native sense of the words of the Canon, and must, in our case, be read to require a peremptory document. This seems to be all the more plain if one considers that Canon 1990 enumerates only impediments that are public by their nature, *i. e.* can by the nature of the case, be peremptorily proved by public document, and that precisely these are usually most implicated cases when, because of some irregularity, they must be proved by other than strict documentary evidence. Hence even before the Code such cases were frequently heard by the Rota in strict judicial procedure whenever the proof was other than documentary.[36] And it is precisely in order that the truth may be better safeguarded that the Code requires three judges to decide on cases where the proof is principally derived from witnesses (cfr. c. 1576,§1, n. 1).

351. Cases to establish the death of a spouse must be proved by document whenever such proof can be had, and proof by testimony, repute and presumption is not to be admitted until it is shown that no proof by document can be had in the case. In the Instruction of 1868 the Holy Office prescribed that, when a certificate of death could not be had from the parish or curial archives, a document issuing from "some source or other" must be sought. If the absconded spouse went away with an army, the army records are to be searched for evidence that he was in battle; that he was captured; missing; that he deserted; that he exposed himself to risks; that he died. If he made a sea journey, the records of the ship company should be sought to inquire whether the ship arrived; whether anyone was lost,

[36] *e. g.*: R., Null., 28 mai. 1909 (rd., i, p. 50); Null., 30 jun. 1910 (rd., ii, p. 219); Melevitana, Null., 23 dec. 1910 (rd., ii, p. 358); Null., 25 feb. 1911 (rd., iii, p. 93); Parisien., Null., 13 jun. 1911 (rd., iii, p. 258); Baltimoren., Null., 29 nov. 1911 (rd., iii, p. 501); Trincomalien., Null., 1 feb. 1913 (rd., v, p. 83); cfr. Kauen., Null., 23 feb. 1929 (aas., xxii, p. 192).

etc. Certificates of death issuing from hospitals are likewise to be sought.[37]

352. If a marriage is attacked because of an asserted impediment of marriage bond already existing, the plaintiff must produce the document proving the first marriage, and if the respondent then claim that the first marriage was rightfully dissolved before the second marriage was contracted, he must exhibit the death certificate of the first spouse, or the sentence of nullity or dispensation from the first marriage, together with the certificate of the second marriage, and diligent comparison must be made especially as to the dates set forth in these documents.[38]

353. If a marriage is thought to be invalid for want of form and it is necessary to prove that a party to it had been brought up as a Catholic after the age of infancy (cfr. n. **150**), such proof will be forthcoming when a document of reception of first communion or confirmation is presented. In the absence of such documentary proof, other proofs are also admissible, such as the record of attendance at a Catholic school, or testimony.

354. Persons who are about to marry must show to the satisfaction of the pastor and sometimes of the curia, that they are free to marry, and for this reason the proper necessary investigations are to be undertaken (c. 1019 fol.).[39] When the ordinary has special reasons for doubt he may require a certificate of freedom to marry from the curia or pastor of the place from which strangers who intend to be married have come.[40] But the document now officially required to establish the freedom of a person from the bond of holy orders, religious profession and marriage already contracted, is a recently dated[41] baptismal certificate (c. 1021,§1).[42] Any such bond contracted in the bosom of the Church, even though it be by the mere validation or correction at the root of a heretofore invalidly attempted marriage, except it be contracted according to Canons 1104-

[37] SO, 1670, § 11; SO, 1868, §§ 2, 6; cfr. SO., 28 feb. 1866 (cicf., iv, n. 991; cpf., i, n. 1283); IA., § 246.

[38] PF, 1883, § 42.

[39] cfr. Hilling, Reformen Pius X in der kirchlichen Gesetzgebung (akk., 1917, p. 73 (2)).

[40] De Smet, ii, n. 686; V-Creusen, ii, n. 287.

[41] R., Damnorum, 26 jul. 1913 (rd., v, p. 474).

[42] DS., 4 jul. 1921 (aas., xiii, p. 348).

1107, must be noted in writing upon the baptismal registers of the persons who have contracted marriage or have been ordained or taken solemn vow (cfr. cc. 572,§2; 1011; 1103,§2),[43] and must be mentioned in any baptismal certificate subsequently issued from these registers (c. 470,§2).[44] If a previously married non-catholic asserts that his former marriage was invalid because attempted with a Catholic person outside the Church, the certificate of marriage will be required to prove that the marriage was really attempted invalidly, and the baptismal certificate of the Catholic party will be required to show that this attempt was never validated by the Church (cfr. n. 371).

355. In order that the validity of a marriage contracted after dispensation from the interpellation cannot be later contested, the granting of the dispensation should be noted in the parish book of marriages and in the curial register, together with the reason for the dispensation, *v. g.* that it had been extrajudicially ascertained that the infidel party could not be found; that he had been taken captive, *etc.*

356. In cases of non-consummated marriage a special document is called for to establish the identity of the husband or wife with that of the person who undergoes the physical inspection. At the opening of the case the petitioner must procure a document in original form or in authentic copy, duly drawn up by ecclesiastical or civil authority, which will identify the person concerned. To this end an authenticated photograph or description is sufficient. If such a document cannot be obtained, the trial judge may content himself with unauthentic documents such as photographs not authenticated, or with such certainty as may be obtained from witnesses. Or, in case the person in question is well known to those concerned, the proof of identity may be omitted and mention of this circumstance must be made in the acts.[45]

Similar precautions may properly be observed respecting the identity of unknown witnesses or experts, especially when they are heard by rogatory commission before another curia.[46]

[43] Ne Temere, IX, §2; DS, Reg., Formula III B: Facultates.

[44] cfr. DS., 4 jul. 1921 (aas., xiii, p. 348).

[45] DS, Norm, n. 1, §§ 1-4.

[46] DS, Norm, nn. 2, 3.

These documents, or exemplars of them will be given to the expert before he undertakes the physical inspection, in order that he may be sure of the identity of the person he later examines, unless he or the matron personally knows that person, and then mention of this is made in the acts (cfr. n. **306**).[47]

§ 3. Producing of Documentary Proof

357. Documents furnish proof when they are exhibited. To the Abbot of St. Augustine's appealing against the Archbishop of Canterbury, on the ground that his monastery was endowed with a certain privilege, Alexander III answered that the document containing the privilege should be exhibited for inspection.[48]

Documents may be brought before the notice of the judge quite informally and without any previous notice to produce.

358. The person who desires to bring forth documentary proof generally has the burden of furnishing the documents.[49] Nevertheless it is sometimes incumbent upon the judge to inquire, and examine parties and witnesses, with a view to bringing forth valuable documentary proof.[50] In the Roman law there was no constraint upon a party to produce documents which militated against his case, and this has been constantly retained by the Canon law for criminal cases,[51] and for contentious cases when the document in question is not the common affair of both parties.[52] Thus in suits for separation the accused party need not generally exhibit documents which would tend to bring the sentence of separation against him, unless he offers a defence which rests on such a document.[53] If a document belongs equally to both parties or treats of a matter pertaining to their common interest, either party may demand that it be exhibited by the other in whose keeping it is said to be, whatever be the nature of the contentious suit (c. 1822). In trials affecting the marriage bond

[47] DS, Norm, n. 4, §§ 1, 2.

[48] c. 4, X, De Fide Instrumentorum, II, 22.

[49] On the suspension or privation of office and fine that threaten those who refuse documents when rightly requested, cfr. c. 2406, § 2.

[50] DS, Reg., n. 76; R, Reg., § 14.

[51] cfr. Noval, n. 556.

[52] c. 1, X, De Probat., II, 19.

[53] W-Vidal, vi, n. 512.

the public documents involved usually pertain to both parties. Moreover the interests of religion represented by the defender are involved in these cases. And thus in these cases the judge may decree at the instance of either party or of the defender, that the plaintiff or respondent or any one else shall exhibit a document that seems to be necessary.[54]

359. The Code takes cognizance of the desire of a person to shield himself or his relatives by the withholding of even necessary documents. In cases of separation and others not affecting the marriage bond no one is held to exhibit documents, even though they be common to both parties, which cannot be exposed without loss of reputation, dangerous vexations, or other very grave evils liable to come upon himself or his relatives by blood or marriage in any degree of the direct line and in the first degree of the collateral line, or without violating a secret which one is bound to keep (cc. 1823,§1; 1755,§2, n. 2).

In cases concerning the marriage bond the danger of evil effects upon those mentioned in Canon 1755,§2 does not relieve one from obeying the order of the judge to produce documents which are necessary.[55] For first, the exposal of defamatory documents before the ecclesiastical court, bound as it is to secrecy, cannot ordinarily be said to threaten the reputation or peace of anyone. Secondly, the entire spirit of the Canon law, as expressed in the similar question on the exemption of witnesses (cfr. nn. **210, 211**), forbids the withholding of such documents as would prove *e. g.* the impediment of crime or affinity, just because the producing them in court might threaten, to an extent, one's reputation.

However, if some pertinent parts of a document can be copied and exhibited in authentic copy without the inconveniences described, the judge may decree that such parts be thus exhibited, even if the trial does not affect the marriage bond. This was ordained by Celestine II,[56] and has been retained in the Code (c. 1823,§2).

360. If a party refuse to produce a document rightfully ordered produced, which he is said to possess, the judge may, at the instance of the other party and after having heard the defender, discern by

[54] Lega, i, n. 535; Noval, n. 556; Smith, n. 588; W-Vidal, vi, n. 512; R, Reg., § 14, n. 1.

[55] cfr. Lehmkuhl, i, nn. 1442-1444.

[56] c. 5, X, De Fide Instrument., II, 22.

interlocutory sentence whether and how such document shall be exhibited (c. 1824,§1).[57]

If the party refuse to obey, it is for the judge to decide what shall be made of such refusal (c. 1824,§2). Judges should refrain however from establishing a presumption and jumping at the conclusion that a marriage is invalid because of such disobedience on the party's part.[58] However such refusal may be taken into proper consideration even in cases of validity of marriage (cfr. nn. **101**, **281**).

If the party deny that he has possession of the document, the judge may examine him and oblige him to take oath on the matter (c. 1824,§3). A marriage was recently contested on the claim that a stipulation contrary to the substance of the sacrament had been attached, and there was some suspicion that the parties were in collusion. They had received civil divorce and arranged their temporalities in civil process. The judge asked to see the civil documents by which these arrangements were drawn up, but was told that the transaction had been completed verbally and without any documents. The Rota did not acquiesce in this but concluded rather that such a document existed, but that it was not exhibited because it contained indications of collusion between the parties, at least in regard to their civil divorce.[59]

361. Persons desiring to offer proof by document in the diocesan court must deposit the documents with the chancery or notary of the court, in order that they may be examined by the judge, defender and the other party or his proctor or advocate (cc. 1819, 1820). After the trial the documents deposited will be returned to the parties (c. 1645,§1).[60] Documents deposited with the Roman Rota are placed in the Rotal archives; any examination of these documents must be made by the persons concerned, in the court room when the documents are presented, or later at the Rotal chancery, from which no one is allowed to remove them.[61] In some dioceses the chancellor or notary of the court mails or sends the documents to the defender in order that he may examine them and later send them back, together with

[57] DS, Reg., n. 76.

[58] W-Vidal, vi, p. 463 (41).

[59] R., Null., 10 dec. 1914 (rd., vi, p. 344).

[60] R. Norm., art. 61 says: "restitui eisdem poterunt, accedente Decani consensu."

[61] R, Reg., § 44, b; cfr. SA, Reg., art. 41-44.

his animadversions. Such practice does not offend against the reasonable security of documents and is not condemned by the Code (cfr. c. 1645,§§2,3).

362. In ordinary contentious cases and in cases of separation, documents must be presented before the conclusion of the case is decreed, unless they could not be had before, and in that case they may be offered later (c. 1861,§1; cfr. c. 1905,§2, n. 2).[62] The judge may decree the rejection of documents which are plainly called for or brought forth only to delay the case (cc. 1749; 1861,§2). If the document is admitted, the judge decrees its admission.[63] In marriage cases that affect the marriage bond, documents bearing on the issue may be presented at any time (c. 1861,§1), even after the conclusion of trial. Evidently documents then presented must be really important and contain new proofs capable of affecting the decision.[64] Similarly, they may at any time be contested (cc. 1861,§2; 1905,§2, n. 1).

In trials heard by the Rota documents must be presented at least thirty days before the discussion of the case so that those concerned may have time to examine them.[65] In recourses had to the Apostolic Signatura a term of at least forty days must intervene between the presenting of documents and the decision.[66] Diocesan courts are not so meticulously restricted.

§ 4. Contesting of Documentary Proof

363. When a document has been exhibited in proof of a case, it must be shown to the interested party, and a proper term must be granted for him to acquaint himself with it, and refute it if he can:

[62] R, Lex, can. 27, § 3; R, Reg., § 53, n. 1 gives formula (trans.): "(Statement of date and case heading as it appears in plaint):—NN., as appears from concordant allegation and testimony, offers new documents, just now come to hand: hence he urges that they be received ....(Signature)."

[63] R, Reg., § 53, n. 2 gives formula (trans.): " Statement of date and case heading): In view of the petition of NN., and of the circumstances and proof that the documents just now offered, only now came to hand, the Ponent permits the said documents to be admitted in trial, and grants a term of .... days for the adversary to respond to them. So ordered that the parties be notified. ....NN., Ponent."

[64] Bassibey, n. 474.

[65] R, Lex, can. 25, § 2.

[66] SA, Reg., art. 40.

otherwise the trial is invalid (cc. 1815; 1861,§2). He may take exception to it if he have reason to doubt: 1) Its authenticity, as for instance, when the notary or other officer who authenticated it was not legally constituted, or was infamous (infamia iuris), or was publicly excommunicated, or when it has not the proper and necessary solemnities such as seal and signature.

2) Its genuineness: as when the document has been forged, or when it is a copy of a forged original.

3) Its integrity: as when a document has been erased, interpolated, torn, or is irrecognizable in seal or signature.

4) Its accuracy; as when a pastor gives a certificate of marriage, without copying in detail the record contained in the register.

5) Its form: as when the prescribed witnesses, date, statement of place are wanting (cfr. c. 1017,§1).

6) Its credibility: when it states what is not true.

The question of its value may be proposed either incidentally or after the fashion of a leading issue, and the judge decides whether the document shall be recognized or whether the exception shall be sustained (c. 1815). Generally in marriage cases, such questions are merely incidental.

If a document be of some moment but wanting merely in solemnities such as statement of date and place, it is the judge's duty to see to it, either *ex officio* or at the instance of the defender or of the parties, that the necessary solemnities are added, lest the case be deprived of such a help.[67]

364. When documents are contested, proof for or against them is derivable from witnesses or the oath of a party, or from other documents, expert inspection, or judicial notice of the documents themselves. The best witnesses for or against a public document are documentary witnesses (cfr. n. **185**).[68] If such witnesses deny having signed or witnessed or taken the part ascribed to them, or state the facts otherwise than the document gives them, their concordant testimony may overcome the force of the document itself and prove it to be forged or false.[69] In 1203 a question arose whether the elected candidate for the bishopric of Lucana was irregular by reason of an attempted marriage. Among the documents purporting to prove the

[67] DS, Reg., n. 78.

[68] c. 10, X, De Fide Instr., II, 22.

[69] R., In Santandrien. seu Cubana, Mat., 16 apr. 1788 (pall., xii, p. 493).

marriage was one sent by the Archpriest of Lucana and the Sacristan and apparently signed in the name of by far the greater part of the Chapter. Innocent III rejected the document on the testimony of these men that they knew nothing of such document.[70] The Rota pronounced a marriage invalid from want of consent in a case where there was not sufficient evidence that consent had been expressed in the first place. For although the priest had made seemingly correct entries in the marriage register, it was proved by the testimony of those written down as the witnesses to the marriage, that one of them had been far off in the country and not at all present at the ceremony, and the other who was present had not witnessed any sign of consent on the part of the plaintiff.[71]

The testimony of extraneous witnesses may form proof of the worth of documents. In order however to prove the falsity of a public document by such testimony, the certainty and number and reliability of the witnesses must be conclusive.[72]

Document may be opposed to document, and if they are contrary to or contradictory of one another they mutually destroy proof,[73] unless one is shown to be unauthentic or forged.

Public documents cannot generally be contested or sustained by the oath of a party,[74] but private documents may be proved by the oath or confession of a party made at an unsuspected time.[75]

365. If a doubt arise whether or not a copy has been faithfully transcribed from the original the judge may decree at the instance of a party or of his own accord, that the original from which the copy was made be exhibited (c. 1821,§1) for the purpose of judicial notice. If this cannot be done or only with considerable difficulty, the judge may delegate an auditor or request the ordinary of the place (cfr. c. 1570,§2) where the original document is, to inspect and compare the papers, and may prescribe on what points and how the comparison shall be made. But the parties may assist at this comparison (c. 1821,§2). The regulations for the Rota provided that the notary

[70] c. 33, X, De Test. et Attest., II, 20.

[71] R., Null., 23 mart. 1914 (rd., vi, pp. 150, 151).

[72] Pirhing, p. 306; Mansella, p. 188; Bassibey, n. 472.

[73] cfr. c. 13, X, De Fide Instr., II, 22.

[74] c. 2, X, De Prob., II, 19.

[75] W-Vidal, vi, p. 457 (26).

might make the comparison of documents.[76] Under the Code the notary may likewise make the comparison in cases where plain comparison (nudum ministerium; merum executionis m.: *verb. ex* c. 54, §1) is required (c. 374,§1, n. 3). In each case the notary will report on the comparison made, and the findings will be communicated to the party concerned.[77] If however, there is a question involving a judgment on the document, *e. g.* whether it has been erased or interpolated; whether the handwriting is forged *etc.*, the notary is not competent; and such judicial action is to be undertaken by the judge or his auditor (cc. 1582; 1817; 1821), with or without the help of experts (cfr. nn. **286, 310**).

§ 5. Interpretation and Appraisal of Documents

366. In cases where the favor to the Faith holds sway (cfr. nn. **416-418**), the documents concerned admit, within proper limits, of broad interpretation. In other marriage cases the proof value of documents is not to be extended beyond what they contain in strict interpretation (cfr. cc. 50; 1321),[78] and this interpretation is to be made first of all according to the proper sense of the words considered in text and context. If any words then still remain doubtful or obscure, the purpose and circumstances of the document and the intention of the author will be considered (cfr. c. 18). Thus documents are to be so construed as to give effect if possible, to every word, phrase, and sentence, and an interpretation which requires a sentence, phrase, or word to be entirely rejected, is not to be received, unless the context, or purpose, circumstances *etc.* of the document, make it plain that such word *etc.* is not intended by the writer to restrict the sense. If a word is of doubtful or obscure meaning it may be clarified by the evident context. In a case of duress the Rota interpreted later words of the plaintiff in accordance with previous words in such a way as to favor nullity of the marriage.[79] Similarly general and

[76] R, Reg., § 63, n. 2 gives formula (trans.): "It is ordered that, on the motion of NN., a comparison of documents be made by the Notary."

[77] R, Reg., § 63, n. 2 (trans.): "Comparison having been made between the document presented and the original, the undersigned testifies that the two are plainly alike.—NN., Notary."

[78] Pirhing, p. 307.

[79] R., Vicariatus Apost. Nyanzae Septentrional., 13 mai. 1919 (rd., xi, p. 89): "Nam 'maiorem vim habent praecedentia verba ad determinationem sequen-

generic terms following or even preceding particular and specific terms are interpreted according to the limitations which the proper understanding of the particular and specific term imposes (cfr. nn. **397, 503**).

In general, public documents are to be interpreted in such sense that any act, *v. g.* betrothal, constituted by the instrument, is made valid. Thus when the language of a public document admits equally of two interpretations, one of which would invalidate, the other validate the act, the validating interpretation is to be received (cfr. n. **408**). Even when the act thus interpreted as valid, *e. g.* act of legal adoption, religious profession, stands to nullify a marriage later contracted, it is to be interpreted as valid (cfr. nn. **411, 412, 485, 486, 508, 524**), for the probatory value of public documents is available equally for or against the validity of a marriage.[80] In the case of doubtful disparity of cult because of doubtful baptism however, there is a legal presumption which stands for validity of the marriage (cfr. nn. **503-507**).

Private documents, such as letters, diaries *etc.* are to be interpreted according to the proper sense of the words used, but when they admit equally of two interpretations, one of which would prove the marriage invalid, this interpretation is not to be received (cfr. n. **414**). However, if the two interpretations are not equally inherent in the document; if rather, the text, context, purpose, circumstances *etc.* make it plain, according to proper rules of interpretation properly applied, that the invalidating construction of the document is alone true and possible, this must be adopted.

367. In appraising the worth and credibility of documents (fides d.), the judge must consider whether they are entire and true, genuine and authentic, in original form or in copy, and whether they are public or private documents. No document, whether public or private, has probatory force unless it is an original or an authentic copy, and the only exception to this is for documents of public law (cc. 1819; 1820).

If documents are shown to have been erased, corrected, interpolated or otherwise vitiated, the judge must consider whether to

tium, quam sequentia ad determinationem antecedentium . . . et antecedens non sapit naturam sequentis, sed sequens antecedentis ' uti ex Bartolo et Baldo tenuit in dec. 346.........."

[80] Pirhing, p. 301.

accept them as proof-bearing at all, and in case they are still of value, what degree of credibility may be allowed them (c. 1818). The law does not limit the value of such documents except by the conscience of the judge. In a case of spiritual relationship, nullity was declared on the ground of an interpolated but otherwise true and authentic document.[81]

The judge will beware lightly to discard valuable documents because of an erasure or correction, when the proper and original sense of the document is not to be misunderstood.[82] For he must seek to determine the truth in the matter. If a document has been subjected to such erasure or interpolation or correction that its meaning or genuineness or authenticity is left open to doubt, the judge will, of course, hold it to be of no value for the case.[83]

The giving of a false date, even through error, to documents necessary to the substance of an act, such as betrothal (c. 1017,§1), seems to invalidate the act.[84] Falsity of date may or may not destroy the proof-bearing value of any document. In a much disputed case it was found that the record of marriage was falsely dated. The parties had secretly married before a priest after two children had been born from their illicit relations with one another. To give the children a character of absolute legitimacy the priest, with the connivance of the parties, falsely dated the marriage record. In the trial on nullity it was contended that since the date was proved false the entire content of the document was to be considered false and unavailable as evidence. But the Rota did not sustain this contention: it held that while there was a motive for falsifying the date, it would be absurd to suppose that the priest had drawn up the entire document without having performed any marriage ceremony at all.[85]

368. Public documents endowed with the proper qualities give full proof of what is directly and primarily affirmed in them (c. 1816), because of the presumption of reliability that is accorded the public

[81] SCC., Leopolien., 30 jun. 1759 (cicf., v, n. 3686).

[82] c. 9, X, De Crimine Falsi, V, 20: "Verum nos literas ipsas, quae redargutae fuerant falsitatis, diligentius intuentes, nullum in eis falsitatis signum vel suspicionis invenimus, nisi paucarum literarum rasuras, quae nequaquam sapientis animum in dubitationem vertere debuerunt."; cfr. c. 3, X, De Fide Instr., II, 28; R., Null., 19 jan. 1910 (rd., ii, p. 29).

[83] c. 6, X, De Fide Instr., II, 22; Pirhing, p. 305.

[84] Hilling in akk., 1928, p. 101.

[85] R., Null., 6 dec. 1909 (rd., i, p. 158).

persons who wrote them. This evidence leads the judge to that moral certainty required by Canon 1869,§1 with such conclusiveness that no further discretion is left him,[86] and no supplementary proof is to be sought.[87] It is for this reason that proof by public document is called peremptory. This does not of course detract from the duty of the judge to scrutinize the authenticity and genuineness of such documents,[88] or the right of the parties to contest their certainty and integrity (c. 1815). For documents that are not authentic and genuine do not prove.[89] And even if authentic and genuine, witnesses are admitted to prove that the content is false. Moreover in cases proposed for settlement according to the norm of Canon 1990 the ordinary may reject the documents, if they seem to him to give only uncertain evidence, and cause the case to be decided in the ordinary judicial procedure.[90]

369. Only that is fully proved by public documents which is directly and primarily affirmed in them.[91] The baptismal record gives full evidence of the baptism performed upon the person named, and of the date of baptism, and of the God-parents; and the marriage record is proof of the marriage between the persons named, and of the date, and of the witnesses. But accessory information such as a statement of the date of birth, or of the qualities of the persons or of their domiciles, is not fully proved by its appearance in the public record of these sacraments.[92] [93]

[86] PF, 1883, § 32.

[87] cfr. c. 2, X, De Prob., II, 19; Reg. iur. xxxi in VI: "Eum, qui certus est, certiorari ulterius non oportet"; V-Creusen, ii, n. 287.

[88] DS, Reg., n. 77, § 1.

[89] c. 1, 2, X, De Fide Instr., II, 22.

[90] Noval, n. 873: "Queritur autem utrum ab Ordinario reputandum sit uti certum, authenticum et nulli contradictioni obnoxium illud documentum quod natura sua, sensu nunc explicato, sit dubium, sed declaratum fuerit authenticum et certum ab aliqua publica auctoritate aut ab aliquo tribunali. Arbitramur respondendum esse *affirmative* si declaratio facta fuit a) a iudice ecclesiastico, b) duplici sententia, c) ad normas trium canonum huius capitis, et proinde cum interventu defensoris vinculi in utraque instanta; alias *negative*, nam Ordinarius et defensor vinculi possunt et debent applicare illam regulam iuris: *res inter alios acta aliis nocere non potest.*"

[91] R., Parisien., Null., 9 jul. 1918 (rd., x, p. 83; aas., xi, p. 158).

[92] R., Parisien, Null., 4 mart. 1916 (rd., viii, p. 71; aas., viii, p. 372); Woywod, in hpr., xxxii (1932), p. 733.

[93] In civil law Abbott, p. 111: "The fact of birth may be proved . . . by a registry of baptism . . . but a mere registry of baptism is not, as an official

For this reason the impediment of age is not, strictly speaking, an impediment public by its nature, and is omitted from Canon 1990 (cfr. nn. **9, 350**). However, the mention of accessory facts gives a presumption of their truth, which may properly be considered with other proofs.[94] On the ground of non-age as shown by the date of birth set forth in the baptismal register, the Congregation declared the nullity of religious profession.[95]

370. In cases of legitimacy the names of the parents entered in the baptismal register are not, indeed, the primary statement of the record and full proof of this parentage is not thereby given. But in that case the presumption is so strong that it is only rebutted by strict proof to the contrary. On the other hand a baptismal entry that mentions illegitimacy is not of itself sufficient to overcome the contrary presumption (cfr. n. **535**), if the child's mother was married, or if the person in question has been in quasi possession of a legitimate name. The Congregation has ordered the correction of baptismal records which stated the person baptized was of a certain mother but of uncertain paternity, while he was commonly held by all to be the legitimate son of the woman mentioned and her husband.[96] When baptism is bestowed upon a child born out of wedlock, the name of the mother is to be inscribed in the baptismal record if the maternity is publicly evident, or if the mother spontaneously asks in writing or before two witnesses to have her name inscribed; similarly the name of the father is to be written down, provided he spontaneously asks it of the pastor in writing or before two witnesses, or if he be known as the father by some authentic public document; otherwise the child is to be written down as of an unknown father or of unknown parents (c. 777,§2). Care must be taken that the entry is so made as to avoid defaming anyone, and in particular cases where adultery, sacri-

registry of birth may be, evidence of the date of birth, though stated in it, further than to show that it must have been prior to the date recorded as that of baptism, . . . unless the statement of the time of birth is shown to have been made by direction of a member of the family since deceased, so as to bring it within the rule admitting declarations as to facts of pedigree."; Similarly in proof of death: Abbott, p. 92.

[94] R., Null., 28 aug. 1911 (rd., iii, p. 441); Parisien., Null., 9 jul. 1918 (rd., x, p. 83).

[95] SCC., Pisauren., 28 apr., 16 jun. 1781 (cicf., vi, n. 3815).

[96] SCC., In Tudertina, Legitimitatis, 16 jan. 1717 (pall., xiii, p. 443); Verulana, 9 aug., 1884 (cicf., vi, n. 4264).

lege *etc.* are concerned, one should report to the Congregation of the Council.[97]

371. The statement annexed to the record of baptism that non-Catholic parents have requested or consented to the Catholic baptism of their child, and have given guarantee of the Catholic rearing of the child, is not primary content of the baptismal entry, but it is the best proof that can be had of their intention (cfr. n. **165**), and is decisive of the fact that the child was aggregated to the Catholic Church, *v. g.* to the effect mentioned in Canon 1070,§1 (cfr. n. **495**).

When a baptismal register or certificate issued from it has the annotation of a marriage subsequently entered upon by the person baptized, this annotation is not to be considered a direct and primary content of the baptismal register, and does not beget full proof. Hence no marriage may be declared invalid because of bigamy or affinity, on the ground of such an annotation. The original marriage entry must be sought in such cases. But the annotation gives so strong a presumption of subsequent marriage, that no further marriage is permitted the party until it is shown that the marriage recorded has been dissolved, or that the entry was erroneously made.

372. In cases touching the Pauline privilege the interpellation made or the dispensation granted from making it, will be proved from the original document of dispensation, or from the parish marriage register, or the books of the curia.[98]

Similarly the curial register of secret marriages has the same force of proof for the external forum as has the parish register of public marriages. And the curial register of dispensations gives conclusive proof of dispensations granted, but does not give full proof that the impediment actually existed. In the diocese of X. a runaway husband who had posed as a Catholic at his first wedding, attempted a second marriage with a Catholic girl, posing this time as a non-baptized person. When the first marriage was later contested on the ground of disparity of cult, the entry in the curial marriage register of the husband's profession of no religion and of the granting of a dispensation for the second wedding were brought into evidence. But such an entry does not give full proof of the impediment; in the case mentioned it gave a presumption that the man had not been

[97] PC., 14 jul. 1922 (aas., xiv, p. 528).

[98] PF, 1883, § 45.

baptized, which together with other evidence was accepted by the Holy Office as proof of non-baptism.[99]

373. Any statement contained in the record of judicial acts written and authenticated (cfr. c. 1643,§1) by the chancellor or other notary of the court (cfr. cc. 372; 374; 1585) is considered as part of the direct and primary content of that document. As with affidavits attested by a notary out of court however (cfr. n. **345**), so here too one must discriminate between what the notary attests and what a witness testifies: the acts beget full proof that the witness spoke as the notary has attested, but they do not by his attest beget full proof that the testimony of the witness is true.

374. The impediments of consanguinity, affinity and public decency are to be proved by genealogical trees or charts of relationship arranged from the records of the proper parish or curial registers.[100] Such charts are not public documents however, even when composed from the parish registers and signed and sealed by the pastor, for they are not thus drawn up in the original registers; rather, they are arguments composed from public documents. For this reason the correctness of the chart must be made clear by diligent inspection and comparison of the series of authentic baptismal and marriage records which cover the relationships asserted.[101] Much more must the genealogical chart be diligently inspected if it is not drawn up from official registers but from the testimony of persons.[102]

375. From the absence of all mention in the proper public document there arises a presumption, more or less grave according to the circumstances, of the non-existence of some fact which must be recorded in these documents if it has taken place. If the baptismal certificate presented as evidence of freedom to marry contains

[99] SO, 18 mart. 1933 (Num. Protoc. 2709/1929) unpublished.

[100] Alexander II in c. 2, C. XXXV, q. 5; c. 3, X, Qui Matrimonium Accusare Possunt, IV, 18; PF, 1883, § 31.

[101] SCC., In Milevitana, 3 dec. 1842 (pall., xii, p. 565); In Apuana, Mat., 15 jun. 1899 (bass., n. 353 (1)).

[102] R., Trincomalien., Null., 1 feb. 1913 (rd., v, p. 88; aas., v, p. 206): "Pater Rouvellac certe omni fide est dignus; at non apparet ex actis num testes ex quibus hausit arborem genealogicam propinqui et affines fuissent alicuius ex sponsis, et quod maximum est, non apparet an isti, iuramento praestito, Patrem Rouvellac de consanguinitate edocuerint." For case of stipulation appended, and proved by comparison of parish registers, cfr. R., Null., 7 jun. 1920, 30 nov. 1921 (rd., xii, p. 128; rd., xiii, p. 277).

no mention of a marriage contracted, there arises a presumption that the person recorded has not contracted such a bond in the Church since the 19th of April 1908 when the "Ne Temere" went into effect. The fact that some pastors neglect to remit for notification in the baptismal register, a notice of marriage performed, or fail to copy such notice on the baptismal certificates issued by them, does not entirely destroy the presumption.

When no mention of a dispensation is made in the marriage register there arises a presumption that no dispensation was given.[103] If the curial registers are equally silent, the presumption amounts to a moral certainty,[104] which is sufficient for the ordinary to proceed with a declaration of nullity even in the extraordinary procedure delineated in Canon 1990 (cfr. n. **350**).[105] But of course natural proof that the dispensation was granted, such as the testimony of competent witnesses, overcomes such a presumption and destroys the certainty. Much more insistent proof to the contrary is required to overcome this presumption when mention is made in the records of a dispensation from one impediment, as *e. g.* consanguinity, but no mention is made of another known also to have existed, such as *e. g.* affinity (cfr. c. 1077);[106] or when mention is made of dispensation from one bond of consanguinity, when in fact, the bond of blood relationship is multiple.[107]

Similarly in cases touching on the use of the Pauline privilege the absence of all mention of the proper interpellation or dispensation therefrom, in both curial and parish registers, is a legal presumption that no such interpellation has taken place and that no dispensation has been granted.[108]

376. The matter is different however with respect to a mention in the marriage register of the proper delegation accorded a priest not having ordinary power to assist at marriages in the parish. When

[103] R., Null., 31 mart. 1909 (rd., i, p. 27); Imolen., Null., 2 aug. 1913 (rd., v, p. 506).

[104] R., Null., 20 mai. 1910 (rd., ii, p. 166).

[105] V-Creusen, iii, n. 296. However, the judge must have in mind the possibility of an implicit dispensation from marriage bond not consummated since ratification, or from consanguinity, affinity or crime, as noted in cicd., vi, and c. 1053 (cfr. nn. **97, 99, 158**).

[106] R., Null., 31 mart. 1909 (rd., i, p. 27).

[107] R., Parisien., Null., 12 jan. 1921 (rd., xiii, p. 12; aas., xiv, p. 472).

[108] cfr. PF, 1883, § 45.

it was necessary under the provisions of the "Tametsi" to be married in the presence of one's own pastor without regard to the pastor of the place in which the marriage was celebrated, there was far more opportunity of a priest's assisting at marriages invalidly for want of the proper delegation, than there is under the "Ne Temere" and the Code. Hence when cases of clandestinity were tried the judge sometimes derived a grave presumption of want of delegation, from the absence of mention in the marriage registers.[109] Even then however the presumption was not always so applied.[110]

While it is now safer to make mention of the accorded delegation, the absence of all mention of it in the marriage register does not afford strict proof or even a grave presumption that the priest performed the marriage without the necessary delegation. For both the Congregation of the Council and the Rota have in such cases rather ascribed the absence of mention of delegation to the inadvertence, forgetfulness, or neglect of the pastor of the place than pronounced the marriage invalid for want of delegation.[111] Whatever slight presumption may even now arise from the absence of mention of delegation is elided by favorable circumstances of person, custom and so on.[112] The want of mention of delegation is especially meaningless when it is observable from other entries in the parish register that an assistant priest, permanently stationed at the parish, frequently performed marriages.[113]

But if a marriage has been performed by a priest who has neither ordinary jurisdiction nor permanent delegation within the parish, and this marriage has thereafter either not been registered in any parish book at all, or has been registered only in the marriage register of a parish other than that in which the ceremony was performed, the delegation to perform the marriage is not to be presumed. Thus if an extraneous pastor visit his parishioner in a hospital and there perform the marriage, and cause no entry to be made in the marriage register of that parish in which the hospital is situated, he is not presumed to have obtained the proper delegation (cfr. n. **415**).

[109] R., Parisien., Null., 27 jan. 1912 (rd., iv, pp. 62, 63; aas., iv, p. 282).

[110] SCC., In Theatina, Mat., 16 mart. 1771 (pall., xiii, p. 261).

[111] SCC., In Theatina, Mat., 16 mart. 1771 (pall., xiii, p. 261); R., Parisien., Null., 9 jul. 1918 (rd., x, p. 83; aas., xi, p. 158).

[112] R., Parisien., Null., 9 jul. 1918 (rd., x, p. 84; aas., xi, p. 159).

[113] cfr. PC., 14 jul. 1922, dub. v. (aas., xiv, p. 527).

377. The value accorded to public civil documents has not always been defined with uniform accuracy in the pre-Code legislation. In a case arising in Scotland, Innocent III wrote that documents issuing from the Scottish King might be securely relied upon in the diocesan court, if the custom of that country held such papers as authentic for ecclesiastical courts.[114] In 1868 the Holy Office prescribed that, when a certificate of death could not be had from the parish or curial archives, the records of military headquarters, ship companies and hospitals might form proof of death.[115] The Instruction of 1883 allowed only extrajudicial value to public civil documents.[116] In some particular instances dispensation has been granted to the end that full faith might be placed in public civil documents.[117]

The Code now awards public civil documents full consideration, and they beget full proof of what they directly and primarily state (c. 1816; cfr. c. 1814).[118] The proof thus begotten is however always rebuttable. There are circumstances in which even now civil public documents must be scrutinized with respect even to their plain primary content. The Congregation of the Sacraments warned against the unqualified acceptance at their face value of testimonials of death issued by the Italian Government after the Massina disaster. Civil governments sometimes issue certificates of death basing the affirmation upon a presumption, and such certificates do not beget full proof before the ecclesiastical court.[119]

378. Documents issued by non-Catholic churches may also be brought into court but they constitute proof only in the quality and with the limitations of private documents (cfr. n. **345**).[120] Yet frequently they furnish the only proof to be had of a death, marriage or baptism. Baptismal records of heretical churches are frequently

[114] c. 9, X, De Fide Instr., II, 22.

[115] SO, 1868, §§ 2, 7; cfr. SO., 28 feb. 1866 (cicf., iv, n. 991; cpf., i, n. 1283); IA., § 246.

[116] PF, 1883, § 33.

[117] SCC., Leopolien., 15 dec. 1877, 23 mart. 1878 (cicf., vi, n. 4239); In Engolismen., Disp. Mat., 12 dec. 1891 (bass., n. 466).

[118] Hence W-Vidal, v, n. 385 seems now inaccurately to state that besides a public civil document of (civil) marriage, witnesses must be called to prove the marriage was (civilly) celebrated.

[119] DS., Massanen. seu Rheginen., 12 mart. 1910 (aas., ii, p. 196); cfr. Schlenz (akk., 1924, p. 222).

[120] PF, 1883, § 33.

required and accepted in the quality of full proof of the baptism bestowed, namely, when the judge may properly believe that they are genuine and credible. In a recent case involving the marriage of a French Catholic with an American Protestant lady, the testimony of the parish registers of an Episcopalian church was accepted by the Rota as full proof of the baptism of the lady, for it was supported by other circumstances that pointed to the likelihood of her having been baptized.[121]

379. Private documents when properly authenticated with the seal and signature of a public officer or notary or extracted from the files of public archives have, through the influence of custom, come to have the consideration of public documents, and may effect full proof, for they are presumed to have been recognized as genuine and credible before being accepted for the archives.[122] Thus the agreements signed by the parties as a condition to the dispensation from the impediment of disparity of cult or mixed religion, and retained in the curial or parochial archives, bear full proof that the signers externally, at least, agreed to the stipulations, although they do not preclude proof that the promises were not seriously made.[123]

Similarly there is full proof if a private document is attested by two documentary witnesses, who now acknowledge their signatures in court,[124] for this is equivalent to testimony on the subject matter of the document (cfr. n. **364**).

Private documents that are not publicly authenticated or retained in the public archives, even though they have a private seal affixed,[125] have only so much proof-bearing value as is demonstrated for them in a particular case, and for this reason they are known as "probationes probandae." This principle was derived from the Roman law,[126] and has always been retained in the Canon law. But the tendency of modern courts has been to relinquish the principle of purely legal appraisal and to admit private documents as proof whenever it

[121] R., Parisien., Null., 13 jun. 1911 (rd., iii, pp. 262, 263).

[122] Lega, i, n. 524; Smith, n. 563; Bouix, i, n. 322; Noval, n. 551; Somewhat otherwise Roberti, ii, p. 101 (1); cfr. R., Null., 30 jun. 1910 (rd., ii, p. 219, n. 3).

[123] R., Parisien., Null., 11 aug. 1921 (rd., xiii, p. 219; aas., xiv, p. 520); cfr. Pellegrini, in jp., x, (1930), p. 58.

[124] cfr. c. 2, X, De Fide Instr. II, 22.

[125] cfr. Pirhing, p. 303.

[126] L. 5, 7, Cod. de probationibus: "Instrumenta domestica . . . si non quoque adminiculis adiuventur, ad probationem sola non sufficiunt."

appears that they are plainly of value. In this progress the Canon law has also had a part.

380. The party who produces a private document must show that it is genuine. An acknowledgment of authorship made after the opening of a case on nullity, is proof of the genuineness of private documents only when they assert against the case of the producer and in favor of the validity of the marriage. When they tell against the validity of the marriage neither the acknowledgment of authorship on the part of the plaintiff, nor of the respondent, can form full proof of genuineness.[127]

If the authorship was acknowledged by the writer or signer at a time when there was no thought of a suit on the validity of the marriage, it does not even then, *per se,* give full proof of genuineness available against the validity of the marriage. Nevertheless the judge may take judicial notice of its genuineness and accept it as genuine even against the other party and the validity of the marriage (c. 1817).

But even when genuineness is established, this does not necessarily beget full proof that the content of the document is true. Hence the producer must show that the document is credible. Credibility is presumed when the content is acknowledged by a party to the suit and militates against that party and in favor of the validity of the marriage, just as in the similar case of extrajudicial confession (cfr. c. 1817), and thus the document may amount to full proof, or part proof, or nothing, according to the discretion of the judge and all other circumstances of the case (cfr. c. 1753).[128] But there is no legal presumption of the truth of what has been thus written, available against others. If the writing has been done or the signature given after the case of nullity is opened or when it is about to be opened, it has the same value as an extrajudicial confession made at such a time.

If the writing has been done or the signature given under circumstances that admit of no suspicion and particularly at an unsuspected time, *i. e.* before the marriage was performed or before there

127 IA., § 168.

128 Noval, n. 551.

129 R., Trincomalien., Null., 1 feb. 1913 (rd., v, p. 86; aas., v, p. 204); Null., 23 mart. 1915 (rd., vii, p. 126); Parisien., Null., 17 apr. 1915 (rd., vii, p. 168; aas., vii, p. 450); Parisien. seu Nicien., Null., 30 dec. 1915 (rd., vii, p. 476; aas., viii, p. 335).

was any thought of a suit against it, the judge may, according to his discretion, find in this a presumption of credibility and avail himself of such a document as part proof.[130] Thus in a case from Ravenna the Rota accepted private letters as full proof of the nullity of the marriage.[131] In a case tried at Paris, bearing on the question of domicile and clandestinity, the diocesan curia in first instance and later the Rota sustained the assertion of the plaintiff against that of the respondent, and against the entry made in the parochial marriage record, regarding the domicile of the spouse at the time of the marriage (cfr. n. **369**). For the plaintiff produced certain bakery bills, checks drawn for the payment of furniture, and a lease of property dated from the time just preceeding the marriage, on which the party's domicile was written as the plaintiff had stated it.[132] In other cases the Rota accepted the content of private letters as proof that there was no duress or other impediment.[133]

381. As long as the authorship of a document has not been duly established there is no legal proof forthcoming.[134] Anonymous letters cannot be brought as evidence in the trial. They generally receive but little attention, even before the contracting of a marriage and should be destroyed (cc. 1645,§4; 1942,§2; cfr. c. 1936). Yet they may be used at the prudent decision of the judge to give a hint as to the way of enquiry into the truth.[135]

[130] DS, Reg., n. 77, § 2; DS, Ordin., n. 60, § 2; Haring: Eheprozess, p. 26.

[131] R., Ravennaten., Null. Mat., 29 dec. 1911 (rd., iii, p. 524): "Etenim epistolae ab auctore scriptae, ex quibus directius quinam fuerit ipsius animus eruitur, certo certius plene probant.... Etsi enim agatur de scripturis privatis, tamen sunt optimum medium probandi illud quod est in votis actoris."

[132] R., Parisien., Null., 4 mart. 1916 (rd., viii, p. 71; aas., viii, p. 372); cfr. Null., 21 jan. 1911 (rd., iii, p. 23); Parisien., Null., 24 mart. 1911 (rd., iii, p. 158); Null., 1 aug. 1913 (rd., v, p. 491); Philadelphien., Null., 9 feb. 1920 (rd., xii, p. 39); Exercitiorum Spiritualium et Suspensionis, 16 jun. 1910 (rd., ii, p. 214); Pirhing, p. 303.

[133] R., Avenionen., Null., 6 (14) jul. 1914 (aas., vi, p. 681; rd., vi, p. 275); Null., 9 mart. 1915 (rd., vii, p. 88); Mediolanen., Null., 1 (17) aug. 1916 (rd., viii, p. 300; aas., ix, p. 451); Nicien., Null., 11 jun. 1920 (rd., xii, p. 135); Parisien., Null., 1 jul. 1920 (rd., xii, p. 185).

[134] DS, Reg., n. 77, § 1.

[135] Cfr. R., Diffamationis, 19 jun. 1911; 24 feb. 1912 (rd., iii, p. 274; iv, p. 112).

CHAPTER XII

Presumptions

"Et ipse Jesus erat incipiens quasi annorum triginta, ut putabatur, filius Joseph."—Luc., iii, 23.

382. Besides the natural proofs there are other means that aid the judge in arriving at moral certainty on the status of a marriage, and these means are artificial and indirect: *i. e.*, they tend to bring certainty upon the particular case at issue, not by directly proving the specific fact at issue in this individual case, but by drawing upon the experience of men and courts in similar cases (cfr. n. **133**). This experience of the past gives an indication of the present, leads to a conjecture, and in some cases brings such power to bear upon the mind of the judge that a norm is given from which a practically available certainty is derived with regard to the case at issue.[1] In all human negotiations men are constantly observing what indications they may draw from past experiences, conjecturing upon the constancy of their experience for the future, and acting on the reasonable presumptions which they themselves or society have established. Just so the ecclesiastical judge who is brought to face a question for the solution of which the natural proofs are either not at all cogent or are not sufficiently so to effect full proof and moral certainty, turns to the experience of the past and relies upon the norm which the jurisprudence of the Church has allowed or established as a rule of law, for the solution of just such doubts. Such rulings we call presumptions (praesumptiones).[2]

Scholion: As we are here treating of canonical proofs before the ecclesiastical court (forum externum), we do not generally refer to presumptions in the court of conscience (forum internum). Nevertheless, the presumptions applicable in the external forum have their effects in the internal forum, whether it be a matter of the confessor sitting as judge in the confessional, or a matter of the individual's

[1] S. Thomas, II-2, q. 47, a. 9, n. 2: "Certitudo non est similiter quaerenda in omnibus, sed in unaquaque materia secundum proprium modum . . ."

[2] Reg. iur. xlv in VI: "Inspicimus in obscuris quod est verisimilius et quod plerumque fieri solet."; cfr. Noval, n. 559.

judgment of his own conscience. Thus *e. g.* a marriage that is rightly presumed valid, and against which the certain truth does not clamor, prevents the interested party from conscientiously entering upon another marriage (cfr. n. 490). Even more: some presumptions have their own proper application in the forum of conscience alone; *e. g.* the personal presumption of a dutiful Catholic that illicit sexual thoughts and desires were not wilful. But in this wider sense of the word presumption, the matter redounds rather to a question of moral theology.[3]

§ 1. Definition and Kinds of Presumption

383. In the theological sense the word presumption denotes a vice opposed to the virtue of hope. In a wide canonical sense a presumption is sometimes spoken of as the basis of a law, and the law is made because of the presumption (cfr. c. 21): thus the law forbidding mixed marriages (c. 1060) is based on the presumption or conjecture that spiritual harm will overtake Catholic persons thus married, and the impediment of abduction (raptus) (c. 1074) is said to be based on the presumption or suspicion of non-consent.[4] In a stricter canonical sense the word presumption denotes the assumed liberty of proceeding to an act without real previous permission, and in this sense Canons 143; 337,§1; 600,n.4; 738,§1; 830; 845,§2; 848, §2; 874,§1 and 938,§2 speak of an interpretative or presumed permission (licentia praesumpta, consensus p.), and in this sense too, canonists speak of that presumed permission or delegation to assist at marriages, which is opposed to expressly given delegation (cfr. cc. 1095, §2; 1096), and which is not sufficient for valid assistance; or it denotes the arrogance of acting contrary to law with full knowledge and deliberation, and in this sense the Code uses the words "praesumpserit, praesumentes, praesumant" in Canons 98,§2; 1625,§2; 2229,§2; 2347; and 2388,§1. But we are not here concerned with presumptions as the word is used in these senses; rather we are concerned only with presumptions considered as proof of facts involved in marriage cases, and in this probative sense the Code defines a presumption as a probable conjecture on an uncertain issue (c. 1825,§1).

[3] cfr. Keller, in prm., 1934, pp. 39*-45*.

[4] SO., ad Ep. Albaniae, 15 feb. 1901 (cicf., iv, n. 1250; cpf., ii, n. 2101); other examples apud Keller in prm., 1934, p. 38*.

384. The value of the presumption as a substitute for natural proof depends upon whether the probable conjecture rises in effect above probability and attains to moral certainty in the case, while the allowableness of introducing presumptions into the case depends upon the uncertainty of the issue. For not every doubt, or fear of error, is sufficient to throw the case upon presumptions for its solution: there must be serious, reasonable, substantial doubt.[5] Every case demands a thorough and serious investigation of its immediate merits, before any presumption may be applied.[6] For every issue is uncertain when it is brought to court, and it is the part of the judge to investigate. In many cases this investigation will bring forth natural proofs that will of themselves dispel the doubt; if such natural proofs fail to dispel the uncertainty, the judge may apply the proper presumptions to the case. In some cases however, the doubt is of such a kind that natural proof can hardly be brought to bear upon it, as when, in the impediment of crime, it is doubted whether the coition was complete and perfect. In such cases too, the proper presumptions may be applied.[7] But in any case the artificial proof is admissible only when the doubt cannot be solved by natural proof.[8] Hence whenever there is mention of presumptions, their application is contingent upon the supposition that after thorough and serious investigation, wherein the possible natural proofs have been exhausted, there remains a serious and reasonable doubt on the issue. To this rule inevitable presumptions alone may form some exception.

385. In a strict sense the presumption differs from the conjecture, indication, and adjunct, somewhat as the whole differs from its parts. The Instruction of the Holy Office on the procedure in establishing the death of an absent spouse, under date of 1868, distinguishes among these four, and the Instruction of the Congregation of the Sacraments of 7 May 1923 again recently draws a distinction between presumptions and indications. The adjuncts are any special coincidences that accompany the facts on which the presumption is based; the indications, in a narrowed sense, are facts that stand in such

[5] SO, 1872.

[6] SO, Savannah, ad I.

[7] Pellegrini in jp., 1930, x, p. 58.

[8] Only in this sense can Eichmann, p. 135, be sustained when he says it is immaterial whether the judge derive moral certainty from direct or indirect proof, *i. e.* presumption.

relation to the presumption that reason and experience lead from them to the presumption, as from cause to effect; conjectures are conclusions drawn from such indications,[9] and amount to personal presumptions.

386. There is a greater distinction between presumptions and legal fictions. A legal fiction is a disposition contrary to truth, given in the law for a just cause and in a matter that admits of possibility,[10] but a presumption is used as a means of arriving at the truth, and deals with probability and moral certainty. When the presumption is employed the facts are uncertain; when the legal fiction is used the facts are certain. The presumption is a mode of proof; not so the legal fiction. The legal fiction does not admit proof to the contrary, for the contrary is already known to be a fact. But the presumption generally admits proof to the contrary, and when such proof is established the presumption gives way to the truth. Fictions are legal only, whereas the law admits personal as well as legal presumptions. In practice however, it is not always easy to distinguish between the fiction and the presumption. Canon, 1092,n.1 states that a stipulation affixed to the marriage contract respecting a necessary, impossible, or shameful future event is considered as though it had not been affixed. The wording of the Canon seems to denote that there is legal fiction here, but in fact, it is a rebuttable presumption of law (cfr. n. **475**).[11] However, marriage matters admit not only of presumptions but also of legal fictions: in respect of the canonical effects of marriage, the Code considers a marriage to which correction at the root has been accorded as though it had been valid from the beginning (c. **1138**,§1), and it considers a child born out of wedlock as legitimately born, if it is legitimized through the subsequent marriage of the parents (cc. **1114**; **1116**; **1117**).[12]

387. Finally a presumption differs from the favor of law. The latter is wider in its extent. The legal presumption has to do only with the proving of a case while the law's favor extends in marriage cases to other matters of procedure, whereby *e. g.* witnesses are heard

[9] Schlenz in akk., 1918, pp. 63-65; W-Vidal, vi, nn. 516, 517.

[10] V-Creusen, iii, n. 204.

[11] De Becker, nov., p. 122; cfr. Gasparri, nov., ii, nn. 886-889; Hence Cerato, n. 141 (p. 241) seems to have somewhat inaccurately stated this simply as a legal fiction.

[12] Other examples: Bouix, i, p. 326; V-Creusen, iii, n. 204; Cerato, p. 241; Gasparri, nov. ii, n. 917.

who would not be admitted in other cases, or are heard a second time even after their testimonies have been published, or a marriage case is reintroduced allowably, even after two conformable decisions have been rendered, *etc.* The favor of law which marriage cases enjoy is a consequence of the indissoluble sacramental character of marriage,[13] while the presumption of the validity of marriage is a consequence of this favor of law (c. 1014), as well as a logical deduction from the presumption of the validity of acts done (cfr. n. **408**). But the law may also favor the person contesting the marriage (cfr. nn. **418, 518**).[14]

388. Presumptions are, by reason of their source, divided in two great classes: personal presumptions and legal presumptions.

Personal presumptions (praesumptiones hominis) are conjectures of the individual judge (c. 1825,§1) drawn according to his judgment and experience, from the known facts of the case (cfr. n. **393**).[15] They are very nearly identical with those indications and conjectures just mentioned in n. **385**.

389. According then to the degree of directness[16] with which they are drawn from certain and determinate facts connected with the case, and consequently also, according to the degree of force with which they compel the mind, personal presumptions are known as light, grave, or vehement presumptions (p. levia, gravia, gravissima).[17]

Hence if the judge indulge personal presumptions which are light, weak, rash, which do not spring from certain and definite facts directly connected with the matter of controversy, or which are unduly extended in their scope, such presumptions do not take the place of natural proof and are not allowable (c. 1828). Thus it is not allowed

[13] Linneborn, p. 21; Cerato, n. 120 (p. 220).

[14] Note Roberti, ii, n. 450: "Quin immo ipsi favores . . . si bene considerentur, deprehenduntur potius apparentes quam reales: plerumque enim agitur de praesumptionibus, quae nisi destruantur, evidenter sententiam secumferunt."

[15] Schmalzgrueber, tit. 23, n. 1: "Praesumptio est conjectura seu judicium ex aliquo signo vel indicio orta, et probationis loco allegata, aut a judice assumpta ad adstruendam rei dubiae fidem."

[16] The directness of relationship required by c. 1828 does not cause the presumption to become a direct proof in the sense of nn. **132, 133.**

[17] DS, Reg., n. 81; cfr. Bouix, i, p. 326; Augustine, vii, p. 272; This distinction has also been applied to legal presumptions: cfr. V-Creusen, iii, n. 205.

to presume the nullity of a marriage from the contempt of court on the part of the respondent (cfr. n. **101**). Neither is it allowed to draw up presumptions for whole classes of marriages. There were some missionaries in America and Oceania who, dismayed at the frivolous view of marriage held by certain Methodists, and by pagans, and at the ease with which they divorced one another, set up the presumption that such marriages were generally to be looked upon as invalid, and attempted to settle marriage cases on this presumption. But the Holy Office forbade the undue inference.[18] The Rota points out another instance of undue proclivity to personal presumptions in a case in which the court of lower instance had formed a proverb into a presumption.[19]

390. Grave, reasonable, serious personal presumptions have not the value of full proof, and cannot alone be sufficient to offset the effect of the legal presumption for the validity of a marriage;[20] but they may have the value of part proof, and even against the validity of a marriage the personal presumptions of the judge may so corroborate the otherwise insufficient natural proofs, that the two together beget the required moral certainty of nullity.[21] Thus in a case from Strassburg the Rota gave sentence of nullity in favor of one Anna K. who asserted that in entering upon the civil marriage she had not the intention of contracting a true marriage but rather of performing a merely civil ceremony. Apart from her statement there were only the opinions of others or statements of witnesses not fully proving the case. But the Rota justified the personal presumption that the statement of intention given by the plaintiff was true.[22]

In cases of dispensation from ratified marriage a personal presumption of non-consummation is sometimes drawn from the circum-

[18] SO, 1872; SO, Nesquallien., § 3; cfr. Eichmann, p. 159.

[19] R., Null., 6 dec. 1909 (rd., i, p. 158): "Nec dicas: Semel mendax, semper mendax; nam haec est mera praesumptio."; cfr. however, reg. iuris viii, in VI: "Semel malus semper praesumitur esse malus."

[20] V-Creusen, iii, n. 206 (pp. 80, 81).

[21] R., Null., 10 feb. 1912 (rd., iv, p. 87); Null., 20 mai. 1912 (rd., iv, p. 240); Null., 12 nov. 1921 (rd., xiii, p 265); cfr. Pellegrini, in jp., 1930, x, p. 58.

[22] R., Argentinen., Null., 18 nov. 1918 (rd., x, p. 134; aas., xi, p. 362); Null., 10 feb. 1912 (rd., iv, p. 88): "Ideoque idem Reiff. habet: 'Praesumptio hominis, quae coeteroquin est rationabilis seu probabilis, ex se sola probat tantum semiplene; si vero adiuvetur publica fama vel aliis adminiculis, potest etiam plenam probationem facere."; Michoacan., Crediti, 7 jan. 1913 (rd., v, p. 18; aas., v, p. 197).

stances of the case. The Congregation of the Sacraments draws the attention of the trial judge to the causes from which non-consummation of the marriage commonly springs, and says that when there are facts or circumstances which indicate the presence of one of these causes, they give rise to a presumption in favor of non-consummation.[23]

391. Vehement, violent, very grave personal presumptions are recognized by Smith as giving "full proof in civil cases which are not of too great importance." [24] Schlenz, in treating of the procedure to be observed in cases of presumable death, comes to the statement that these indications may by their compelling force and number, 'lead to moral certainty which is sufficient for the judge to give his decision or sentence.' [25] And in fact the documents which have issued from the Holy Office in respect to proving the death of an absconded spouse, clearly support this doctrine.[26] The Code relates nothing of the probative value of personal presumptions, though it says that legal presumptions impose the burden of proof upon the party who has not the presumption in his favor (c. 1827). But commentators of the Code do not hesitate to imply that a vehement or violent personal presumption in the mind of the judge transfers the burden of proof to him against whom the presumption militates.[27] And this doctrine seems to be correct. But in any case all personal presumptions admit either direct or indirect proof to the contrary.[28]

It is the part of the judge alone to determine whether the personal presumption be light, grave, or vehement, what force of proof it possesses, and what degree of certainty is derivable from it (cfr. *e. g.*, c. 2251).[29] The Rota makes constant use of justified personal presumptions and employs them as well against, as in favor of the

[23] DS, Reg., nn. 80, 82.

[24] Smith, n. 602: a very inexact norm by which to be guided.

[25] Schlenz. in akk., 1918, p. 63; Similarly: Keller in prm., 1934, pp. 17*, 18*.

[26] SO., 8 mai. 1891 (cicf., iv, n. 1135; akk., 1918, p. 64): "De morte prioris coniugis certo constare posse etiam ex praesumptionibus, indiciis et adminiculis aliisque probationibus, quae de iure communi admittuntur, dummodo legitimae sint ac sufficientes, iuxta ea, quae habentur in n. 6 Instructionis . . . Ad probandum obitum coniugis (cicf., iv, n. 1002)."

[27] W-Vidal, vi, n. 520; V-Creusen, iii, n. 206.

[28] Smith, n. 602; V-Creusen, iii, n. 206.

[29] R., Michoacan., Crediti, 7 jan. 1913 (rd., v, p. 18; aas., v, p. 197); Null., 23 mart. 1915 (rd., vii, p. 125).

validity of a marriage.[30] With the same reason therefore, may they be employed in cases not affecting the marriage bond.

392. Legal presumptions (p. iuris) are probable conjectures stated in law as constituting artificial proof when the issue remains otherwise uncertain. They acquire the special character of legality through being established by the law itself (c. 1825,§1). When a presumption is stated in the Code, or in a subsequent authentic source of law it is a legal presumption in the proper and primary sense. The Code however mentions only a few legal presumptions with reference to marriage cases: on the validity of marriage (c. 1014), on the consummation of marriage (c. 1015,§2), on the validity of baptism in reference to marriage (c. 1070,§2), on the use of reason necessary to contract marriage (c. 1082,§2), on the conformity between external signs and internal consent (c. 1086,§1), on the continuance of matrimonial consent (c. 1093), on paternity and the legitimacy of a child born in wedlock (c. 1115,§§1,2), on the negative response in cases of Pauline privilege (c. 1122,§1), on the favor accorded to this privilege (c. 1127), on the condonement of adultery (c. 1129,§2), and on the inevitability of considering a marriage valid when one spouse is dead and the marriage remains heretofore uncontested (c. 1972).[31] Since the appearance of the Code the Congregation of the Sacraments has explicitly established further legal presumptions.[32]

But in a wider sense a presumption may be established by law, without being explicitely mentioned in the Code or subsequent authentic sources.[33] The past policy of canonical jurisprudence by which

[30] R., Parisien., Null., 17 mart. 1914 (rd., vi, p. 119; aas., vi, p. 412); Null., 19 jun. 1909 (rd., i, p. 71); Null., 29 jul. 1909 (rd., i, p. 124); Mileviten., Null., 23 dec. 1910 (rd., ii, p. 362); Null., 25 feb. 1911 (rd., iii, p. 101); Parisien., Null., 13 jun. 1911 (rd., iii, p. 261); Neo-Eboracen., Null., 9 dec. 1911 (rd., iii, pp. 517, 518); Null., 16 mai. 1912 (rd., iv, p. 264); Neo-Eboracen., Null., 8 feb. 1915 (rd., vii, p. 29; aas., vii, p. 300); Calatanisiaden., Null., 28 jul. 1916 (rd., viii, p. 231; aas., viii, p. 488); Montereyen. Angelorum, Null., 21 dec. 1917 (rd., ix, pp. 323, 324); Parisien., Null., 10 dec. 1918 (rd., x, p. 140; aas., xi, p. 426); Null., 24 mart. 1922 (rd., xiv, pp. 73, 75).

[31] Other legal presumptions not referring to marriage are contained in cc. 8,§2; 16,§2; 23; 63; 70; 88,§3; 133,§4; 200,§2; 205; 644,§2; 1299,§3; 1411,§2; 1432,§1; 1536,§1; 1814; 1904,§1; 2200; 2208; 2315.

[32] DS, Reg., cap. xii; DS, Ordin., cap. xiii, xiv.

[33] SA., De Manilla, Nullitatis et Restitutionis in Integrum, 6 apr. 1920 (aas., xii, p. 257): ". . . 'beneficium istud legis potius quam litigantium favore inductum est' ut constans tenuit Ordinis Nostri disciplina. Nec nomine *legis*

the courts have arrived at the more probable and morally certain solution in unclear cases, has been expressly stated by the Rota to be the governing norm under the Code,[34] and the Rota itself continues to make use of the presumptions established by the jurisprudence of the past, even though no mention is made of them in the Code.[35] Nor does Canon 1828 forbid this; on the contrary, such procedure is entirely consonant with the intention of Canon 20 directing that, in the absence of explicit guidance by the Code, the general principles of jurisprudence, the accustomed practice of the Roman Curia, and the common and constant doctrine of authors shall prevail. The post-Code commentators on Marriage have almost invariably treated of the presumptions established in past jurisprudence and not explicitly repealed, as though it is self-evident that they continue in force under the codified law, even though they are not mentioned in the Code.[36] Thus we have presumptions that are legal in a wider and secondary sense, and they are sometimes called factual presumptions.[37]

Legal presumptions beget proof by law (cfr. n. **139**): the law presumes; and hence the judge is not entirely free to use or neglect either the strictly legal presumptions nor those that are legal in a wider sense, but he must rather be guided by them. Nevertheless,

solummodo generale praescriptum Codicis heic intelligendum; verum etiam peculiaria praescripta et statuta, quibus a partibus contra venire non liceat—ut sunt fundationis tabulae, ultimae voluntates, pacta conventa, ceteraque id genus—ad effectum restitutionis in integrum ex hoc capite neglecti praescripti legis concedendae comprehendi, id innumeris Signaturae decisionibus firmatum est."

[34] R., Buscoducen., Null., 7 jan. 1918 (rd., x, p. 2; aas., x, p. 518): "Et nihil refert, si ius positivum in novo Codice sileat de amentia et Decretales Gregorii IX loquantur tantum de furioso a nuptiis arcendo . . . Cum enim consensus sit id, quod dat esse matrimonio, non uni furioso prohibendum est matrimonium, sed iis omnibus, quorum mens in actu contractus ita impedita est . . . . "

[35] R., Paderbornen., Null., 27 jul. 1917 (rd., ix, p. 162; aas., x, p. 216); Null., 23 dec. 1918 (rd., x, p. 143); Null., 29 apr. 1922 (rd., xiv, p. 124); Null., 3 jul. 1923 (rd., xv, p. 141); cfr. Null., 10 aug. 1923 (rd., xv, p. 232).

[36] cfr. *e. g.*, Schaefer, p. 194.

[37] Chelodi, n. 10: "In C. matrimonii praesumpti expresse mentio non fit, quod non impedit quominus, in iudiciis matrimonialibus . . . multiplices dari possint praesumptiones facti . . . "; Roberti, ii, p. 107(1): "Aliae praesumptiones consueverunt adduci ex naturali aequitate . . . "; Capello, iii, n. 640; Hilling, Studium zum Eherecht (akk., 1922, p. 7).

those that are legal only in the wider sense have not, *per se*, the same mandatory force that accrues to the others.[38]

393. To apply a legal presumption to any case, there must be a concrete basis in fact; that is, it must be shown that some definite fact or number of facts, upon which the presumption rests, is at hand. Thus to make use rightly of the presumption for the validity of a dispensation,[39] it must first be shown that the dispensation was actually granted, and granted to the persons in question. The burden of proving this factual basis of the presumption naturally devolves upon him who offers the presumption as proof.[40]

In proving the basis of a legal presumption only natural proofs are generally admissible. For a presumption arises from facts actually proved by natural evidence: one presumption cannot generally be the basis of a second presumption.[41] Thus if a marriage is contracted under an explicit stipulation pending a future event, and the parties who have made the stipulation willingly enter upon the exercise of marital relations without awaiting its fulfillment, they are presumed to renounce the stipulation (cfr. nn. **437-441**). But it must be shown by natural evidence that such marital relations were willingly entered upon by the parties. A suspected or presumed cohabitation and concubinage (cfr. c. 133,§4) is not a basis sufficient for the presumption of marriage.[42]

Nevertheless in cases of affinity by illicit coition the Rota has accepted the presumption established by Alexander III as proof of the fornication,[43] and having thus established the fact of coition, has in the same case further presumed that the coition was perfect and complete.[44]

394. There are two kinds of legal presumption: those which are merely legal, disputable, rebuttable (p. iuris simpliciter) and those which are legal and adjudged, conclusive, inevitable (p. iuris et de

[38] cfr. *e. g.*, R., Null., 10 aug. 1923 (rd., xv, p. 232).

[39] cfr. R., Colonien., Null., 27 aug. 1910 (rd., ii, p. 320); cfr. c. 84, § 2.

[40] Smith, n. 600.

[41] Noval, n. 564; American-English Encyclopedia of Law: word Presumption.

[42] cfr. Schaefer, p. 217; Smith, n. 462 seems to have inaccurately stated: "Once the existence of a clandestine marriage is proved or presumed, its validity is *eo ipso* presumed."

[43] cfr. c. 12, X, De Praesumptionibus, II, 23.

[44] R., Null., 31 mart. 1909 (rd., i, p. 26); Null., 10 feb. 1912 (rd., iv, p. 85).

iure) (c. 1825,§2). The law does not generally state more than that, from the establishment of certain primary facts, there arises vehement circumstantial evidence of further consequential facts.[45] It does not generally inhibit a person from offering proof that this peculiar circumstantial evidence is not convincing: that the case as it stands is really different from the legal inference drawn from the facts. In a word, the law does not generally give such strength to a presumption that a party is deterred from adducing either direct or indirect proof in favor of his case and against the presumption (c. 1826). Thus if a man would avoid the presumption of paternity (c. 1115,§1) with regard to a certain child, he may prove that he is not the husband of its mother, upon which fact the presumption is founded, or he may prove that he could not have had marital relations with the mother his wife, during the pertinent period of more than ten months, in which latter case he contests the validity of the presumption itself (cfr. n. **132**). And thus these merely legal presumptions are also called rebuttable.[46] Against rebuttable presumptions, one may urge in direct proof not only arguments arising from testimony, documents and other natural proofs,[47] but likewise other contrary presumptions either legal or personal.[48] If such presumptions are really rebutted they must give way to the truth (p. cedere debet veritati).

395. Sometimes the law so insists on a presumption that when once the basis for it has been established, the presumption is definitely accepted as truth. Such presumptions are called inevitable.

During the course of the twelfth and thirteen centuries several Popes: Alexander III, Clement III, Innocent III, Gregory IX established presumptions of this kind with respect to marital consent. When, for instance, it was proved that a man and woman were betrothed and subsequently had carnal relations, the Church presumed that this was done with marital consent, and that they were thereafter married (cfr. nn. **427**, **428**). And she insisted on this presumption

[45] cfr. Noval, n. 561.

[46] American-English Encyclopedia of Law distinguishes, as does Chelodi, n. 10, "rebuttable presumptions which are classed as rebuttable presumptions of law or presumptions of fact . . ."

[47] R., Parisien., Null., 17 mart. 1914 (rd., vi, p. 118; aas., vi, p. 410).

[48] R., Annecien., Finium Parochialium, 5 feb. 1918 (rd., x, p. 24; aas., xi, p. 151): "At praesumptio, nedum veritati, sed et alteri fortiori praesumptioni cedere debet."; Parisien., Null., 9 jul. 1918 (rd., x, p. 84; aas., xi, p. 159): "Imo in casu, haec praesumptio aliis in contrarium praesumptionibus eliditur."

so vehemently that it was considered in the external forum as a truth established beyond rebuttal. Thus the parties to such a union were not permitted by the judge to show that the presumption was false: that they had no mind to give marital consent when they indulged the coition: that they had acted merely from temporary passion. It was this denial of proof to the contrary that made such presumptions inevitable.

But the inevitability never extended to the factual basis of the presumption: one might always prove that the facts upon which the presumption rested were not true. Thus in case of the presumption of marriage by reason of betrothal and coition, it was permitted that the parties bring in witnesses or other proof to show that there was no sexual intercourse, or that it was not complete or natural, or that there was no betrothal, or that the betrothal was not valid or was dissolved, or that a diriment impediment existed.[49] Thus even inevitable presumptions were made to admit indirect proof against them (cfr. n. **132**).[50]

Later on, some canonists began to view even these presumptions as a little less inexorable, and admitted even direct proof against them in extraordinary cases. Such direct proofs were admissible when there was notoriety, confession, public document or an extraordinary number of witnesses.[51] That these exceptions were at least in part applicable to the inevitable presumptions on marriage is stated by Gasparri, who observes that canonists generally admitted evident proof against the presumption derived from betrothal and coition.[52]

There are now hardly more than two inevitable presumptions (cc. 1904,§1; 1972), (cfr. n. **412**).[53] One of these is expressly said to lose its quality of inevitability when it is introduced as an incidental question (c. 1972); for the other (c. 1904,§1), the exceptions recorded by Schmalzgrueber and Bouix are embodied in the extraordinary reasons which the Code allows for integral reinstatement (c. 1905,§2) against the otherwise unassailably adjudged case and the inevitable presumption deriving from it.[54]

[49] Gasparri, i, n. 90.

[50] cfr. R., Parisien., Null., 17 mart. 1914 (rd., vi, p. 120; aas., vi, p. 412).

[51] Schmalzgrueber, in lib. II, tit. 23, n. 12; Bouix, i, n. 328.

[52] Gasparri, i, n. 90.

[53] Noval, n. 561 views Canon 175 as likewise expressive of an inevitable presumption. For inevitable presumptions in civil law, cfr. McKelvey, p. 84.

[54] Noval, n. 677; W-Vidal, vi, p. 468 (16), and V-Creusen, iii, n. 205 hold that judicial confession, notoriety and public document are still admissible

396. When a legal presumption is established it supplies the necessary evidence and moral certainty of the fact thus presumed, and takes the place of natural proof, so that no natural proof is needed to establish that fact (c. 1747, n. 2).[55]

The party who has the legal presumption in his favor is thus freed from the burden of proof, which then falls upon the other party (c. 1827). This holds true whether the party adducing the legal presumption is he who asserts in the case or not (cfr. c. 1748,§1). For even he who asserts has proved his case, so far, by adducing and establishing the legal presumption in his favor.[56]

A legal presumption however relieves a party from the burden of proof only with respect to that fact which is properly covered by the presumption. Thus the litigant seeking to uphold a marriage has not the burden of proving its validity, for he has a favored position by reason of the general presumption for validity (cfr. n. 408); but if he raise the question of the court's competence he must prove his contention respecting the competence or incompetence.

Moreover, even though the presumption supplies the place of natural proof and decides where the burden of proof lies, it does not disturb the strict right of both parties to an impartial hearing of evidence contrary to the presumption.

397. When particular legal presumptions have been established with reference to a particular impediment, they may be brought to overcome the more general presumption in favor of validity of the marriage. The axiom of Boniface VIII: "generi per speciem derogatur" [57] applies as well to the matter of presumptions as to other

proof against an inevitable presumption. But as Canon 1826 plainly states that direct proof against inevitable presumptions is excluded, these authors are evidently speaking of the proofs which give rise to integral reinstatement and thus indirectly overcome the inevitable presumption of Canon 1904, § 1, by destroying the factual basis of the presumption, namely, the seeming justice of the sentence. Cfr. R., Null., 8 apr. 1919 (rd., xi, pp. 80, 81). But such proofs cannot be appealed to as a ground for declaring nullity of marriage contrary to the provisions of Canon 1972.

[55] Smith, nn. 438, 439, denies that merely legal presumptions induce moral certainty of the fact presumed; he would reserve such moral certainty to presumptions that are inevitable. But this doctrine is contrary to the constant jurisprudence of the Roman Curia; cfr. Bouix, i, n. 327.

[56] Thus Noval, n. 446 calls attention that this provision of Canon 1827 is not an exception to Canon 1748, § 1, but is entirely consonant with it.

[57] Reg. iur. xxxiv in VI.

matters.[58] And it is the repeated assertion of the Rota that marriages may be declared invalid on the strength of legal presumptions properly established. This will be seen in detail in the following paragraphs. Hence it is incumbent upon the judge to have a just consideration as well for specific presumptions which hold against validity in particular cases as for the general presumption in favor of validity of marriage.[59]

§ 2. Presumption of Fact.

398. In the field of legal presumptions the most general norm is that facts must be proved and are not to be presumed.[60] There are however some facts concerned in marriage cases, which are rightly presumable, when the proper basis is established. These will be discussed in the ensuing paragraphs.

399. The existence of an impediment is not generally to be presumed against persons who are about to contract marriage. Various hypotheses however at once present themselves: the impediment and the consequent illicitness of contracting marriage may be doubtful by reason of a doubt of law (dubium iuris) or a doubt of fact (dubium facti), and either doubt may pertain to an impediment of natural, divine, or ecclesiastical law. It is the first duty of the parties and their pastor to seek to solve the doubt, especially if it be one of fact, and to this end the marriage may be impeded for a time in all cases. But if the doubt cannot be solved the ordinary will render decision on whether the marriage is permissible with the existing doubt.

[58] cfr. Augustine, vii, p. 273, b).

[59] R., Null., 21 dec. 1912 (rd., iv, pp. 472, 473). Hence the restriction hinted at by Bouix, i, n. 327 saying that legal presumptions require the court's decisions to be conformable to them "in civilibus saltem" is not meant to impede the judge from pronouncing in marriage cases according to legal presumptions; Bouix seems to doubt the force of presumptions in criminal cases (cfr. however, c. 133, § 4).—Hence likewise the rule given in Augustine vii, p. 273, d) that "presumptions in favor of the validity of an act already posted are weightier than those in favor of its invalidity" must be understood only of two presumptions of which that favoring validity is not more general, but is as specific and pertinent as the other favoring invalidity.

[60] Commissio Specialis RR. PP. Cardinalium, Versalien., Null., (sine dato) (aas., x, p. 389): "In primis dici nequit conditionem fuisse a muliere positive revocatum. Nam haec revocatio est factum et facta non praesumuntur sed probantur."; Gasparri, ii, n. 903.

400. When there is a doubt of law pertaining to natural or divine law the authors have commonly applied the reflex principles of judgment on the licitness of acts, and held that the marriage is to be interdicted, lest it be needlessly exposed to the danger of nullity.[61] Canon 15 declaring that doubtful laws do not bind in doubt of law, cannot be introduced in contradiction to the received doctrine, for it evidently offers a norm only for ecclesiastical laws, as is seen from the heading: "De legibus ecclesiasticis" of Title I of the Code, and cannot be extended to divine laws. But in questions of potency another norm is applied, namely that no condition of the body is to be interpreted as an invalidating impotence, until it is proved that the natural (or ecclesiastical) law invalidates (cfr. nn. **142, 525** fol).

401. When there is a positive doubt of fact pertaining to certain natural or divine law the marriage must be interdicted, for the parties would, by marrying, expose themselves to the risk of an invalid marriage, to which the Church cannot supply the defect.[62] The Church has been constant in her refusal to dispense, or permit marriage, whenever there was a doubt whether the parties were related by blood in any degree of the direct line, or in the first degree of the collateral line.[63] The Holy Office refused on 6 April 1906 to permit the marriage of two persons who were living in concubinage and had begotten progeny, on the ground that there was a doubt lest they might be related in the first degree of the collateral line.[64] The Code has brought this policy into canonical form: marriage may never be permitted if there exists a doubt whether the parties are related by blood in any degree of the direct line or in the first degre of the collateral line (c. 1076,§3).[65] And since the issuance of the Code, the Pontifical Commission for its interpretation was asked what is to be done, if an illicit and occult coition had taken place before the birth of a girl, under circumstances that make it now doubtful whether the girl is not the daughter or sister of the person she desires to marry, to which the Commission answered that this is provided for in Canon

[61] DeBecker, pp. 265, 286; DeSmet, ii, n. 718; Cerato, p. 46; Haring, Grundzuege, p. 472.

[62] DeBecker, p. 286.

[63] SCC., Leodien., 14 dec. 1793 (cicf., vi, n. 3888); Aesina, 23 nov. 1805 (cicf., vi, n. 3926).

[64] Cerato, p. 123.

[65] DeBecker, p. 286 (1): "Et eadem prorsus solutio tenenda est quando impedimentum dubium iuris divini est simul dubium de facto; v. g. dubitatur utrum Titius et Caia sint frater et soror."

1076,§3.[66] However if there is not sufficient proof to establish a reasonable positive doubt, the marriage need not be prohibited.[67]

Similarly, in doubt whether a former marriage of one of the parties has been dissolved by death of the former spouse, the marriage is not permissible. But if there be not only doubt of death, but likewise doubt whether the former marriage was ever really contracted, the marriage may be interdicted until further inquiry can be made, but not permanently, for the former marriage is a fact to be proved but not presumed.[68]

In respect to cases of doubtful potency too, persons are presumed to be endowed with natural potency until impotence is proved in them (cfr. nn. **142, 525** fol.).

402. If there is a merely negative doubt of fact, the marriage may be prudently deferred for a reasonable time in order to make inquiries, but if no positive reason for doubting appears, the presumption favors the parties in their desire to marry (cfr. c. 1023,§§2,3). This applies also to the negative doubt of fact in regard to the freedom of a party from other marriage bonds: for when a person desires to contract marriage, and, after diligent inquiry, there is neither positive reason to believe him *de facto* already married, nor positive proof that he is free, the freedom of the person has the favor of law and the marriage is not to be obstructed.[69]

403. In a doubt of law with reference to an impediment of ecclesiastical origin, the Instruction for Austria made no distinction, but ordered the marriage deferred until the doubt was elucidated.[70] But it has been the opinion of grave authors that, whenever it is really probable that an impediment does not exist, the marriage is not to be impeded, and the Church removes the impediment if there really be one.[71] The Code has improved upon this doctrine and states that no invalidating and inhabilitating law, such as diriment marriage laws are, is binding if there be a doubt of law in the case (c. 15).[72]

[66] PC., 2-3 jun. 1918, IV, 5 (aas., x, p. 346).

[67] R., Impedimenti ad Contrahendum, 11 mart. 1910 (rd., ii, p. 96 fol.).

[68] Gasparri, nov., i, n. 221, who thus explains the seemingly contrary ruling of c. 12, X, De Spons. et Mat., IV, 1.

[69] cfr. SO, Alberti, § 18.

[70] IA., § 106.

[71] DeBecker, p. 269.

[72] Hence Innocent XI's condemnation of Proposition I (Const. "Sanctissimus Dominus Noster," 2 mart. 1679) does not apply, in its entirety, to marriage cases; cfr. Capello, iii, n. 38.

404. When there is a doubt of fact with respect to an impediment of ecclesiastical law it has been the doctrine of authors that the ordinary can dispense, provided the impediment in question is one in which the Church is used to dispense, and provided there is sufficient reason to dispense.[73] This is now confirmed by the Code (c. 15) which does not however require any other reason for dispensing than the doubt itself. Without the dispensation the marriage must not be permitted (cfr. c. 1031,§1).

405. When there is a positive doubt of fact with reference to an ecclesiastical law from which the Church grants no dispensation, it is not allowed to contract the marriage, for the parties thereby expose themselves to imminent risk of an invalid marriage which the Church will not validate.

406. Negative doubts of fact with respect to impediments of ecclesiastical law, are to be treated as those pertaining to natural or divine law (cfr. n. **402**).[74]

407. Facts are not to be presumed, and thus no one is presumed to have gone through the marriage ceremony with another; on the contrary this fact must be proved by the records, witnesses, or other natural proof.[75] When there is a known impediment to a proposed marriage, it may never be presumed that dispensation has been granted, and the fact of its granting must be proved before the marriage is contracted. Similarly, a marriage that has been invalidly entered upon is not presumed to have been validated by correction at the root; on the contrary, such validation must be proved.

§ 3. Presumption of Validity

408. When it is shown that an act or contract has actually been entered upon, there is a general presumption of law, known as the

[73] SO, Alberti, § 18; DeBecker, p. 286; Haring, Grundzuege, p. 472.

[74] Gasparri, nov., i, n. 216: "In hoc casu matrimonium permittat sine ulla dispensatione . . . e. g. si vir coivit cum muliere coniugata, seminavit prope vas et postea dubitat, num semen intra vas receptum sit . . . "

[75] Pallotini, xii, p. 477, nn. 31, 33, 36, 40: ". . . aliter tamen se res habet, cum dubium circa probationem seu existentiam ipsius Matrimonii versatur: hoc enim in casu favor obtinet libertatis, uti ad rem tradit Ursaya . . . "; SCC., Florentina, 10 sept. 1853, 28 ian., 18 mart. 1854 (cicf., vi; n. 4134) places the burden of proof on those asserting marriage: "An constet de matrimonio in casu ? R. .... negative."; R., In Ausculanum in Picina, Null., 28 mai. 1909 (rd., i, p. 58; aas., i, p. 532); Gasparri, i, n. 18; V-Creusen, ii, nn. 277, 279.

queen of presumptions, which holds the act or contract as valid, until invalidity is proved.[76] Thus when a dispensation is shown to have been granted, its validity is presumed.[77]

409. Betrothals of future marriage are presumed to be valid whenever they have been formally entered upon according to the customary or required solemnity (cfr. c. 1017,§§1,2).[78] In questions of nullity of marriage because of the pre-Code impediment of public decency (publica honestas) arising from previous betrothals, the Congregation of Propaganda directed that the matter of the validity of those previous betrothals be taken up, but explicitely stated that if those betrothals were formally entered upon in the special solemnity customary in the place, they were to be presumed valid, even to the effect of invalidating the marriage that followed with a first degree relative of the betrothed.[79] This form of the impediment is now obsolete and the presumption of validity of betrothals no longer has the effect of invalidating a subsequent marriage. But in the rare case that a suit for damages because of broken betrothals be brought before the ecclesiastical court, the betrothals entered upon in due form will have the presumption of validity.

410. In the Roman law the presumption of validity was applied to that highest type of legalized union between the sexes called "connubium," and thus the Church found a presumption for the validity of marriage at hand (cfr. n. **444**). Gradually she improved upon

[76] R., Colonien., Null., 27 aug. 1910 (rd., ii, p. 320); Parisien., seu Nicien., Null., 30 dec. 1915 (rd., viii, pp. 468, 469; aas., viii, p. 327).

[77] R., Baltimoren., Null., 30 jun. 1910 (rd., ii, pp. 222, 223; aas., ii, pp. 586, 587); Gasparri, nov., i, p. 133 (2) cit. S. Alphonsus vi, n. 901 affirming, and Rosset, n. 2430 doubting the application of the principle to this case.

[78] Aichner states (p. 587) that the invalidity of betrothals is to be presumed as long as the validity is not conclusively proved, because the presumption must stand for the freedom of the party to marry whom he will. But he wrote before the "Ne Temere" at a time when informal betrothals could be valid, and when the ecclesiastical courts admitted suit to enforce the promised marriage. But such suit is no longer admitted (c. 1017, § 2), and the question of liberty of choice can have nothing to do now with the presumption of validity of betrothals. Hence it is strange that Capello, iii, n. 106 now repeats the same presumption of invalidity.

[79] PF, 1883, § 34: "Itaque inquirendum erit, utrum istae formae fuerint, nec ne, servatae; si primum, praesumptio pro sponsalium valore aderit, contra quam nunquam erit iudicandum, nisi ex certis et evidentibus argumentis sponsalia nulliter contracta fuisse constiterit; si secundum . . ."

the Roman presumption in point of precision and universality of application. Pope Calixtus (an. 217-222) recognized the union between a noble or better class freeman on the one hand and a poor person or slave on the other as a true marriage, while the Roman law conceded to such unions only the lower legal status of "concubinatus" or "contubernium." St. Augustine wrote in his work "De Bono Coniugii" that when persons entered upon that legal union described by Roman law as "solius concubitus causa" this union was to be considered as a true marriage, if only the parties intended their union to be permanent and exclusive, and took no means to prevent childbirth. And he considered this "concubitus" a true marriage even when the parties to it were qualified by Roman law to enter upon the "connubium" which the law described as a union entered upon "liberorum quaerendorum causa."[80] This is an extension of the Roman presumption on the validity of marriage and a foreshadowing of the presumption as the Church law later came to know it. Later on, Gratian indicated a similar presumption in commenting on Pope Eleutherius,[81] and the more recent jurisprudence has explicitly and constantly adhered to the presumption of validity of marriage.

411. Under the Code marriage has the favor of law: hence when there is a doubt, we must hold to the validity of the marriage until the contrary is proved (c. 1014). This legal presumption has as its primary, proper, and immediate effect that the validity of a marriage is meanwhile and conditionally held certain. From the theological point of view and first of all, this effect is directed to the spouses, and thence to all the world, in so far as it directs all to respect in the parties to the marriage, the duties and rights that flow from valid marriage (cfr. n. **382**). In a canonical way this effect concerns the matrimonial court. For when the marriage is attacked, it devolves upon the judge to uphold its validity until nullity is proved. Hence it is stated above that the validity is meanwhile and conditionally held certain, *i. e.* on condition that and until the contrary is proved. Thus the presumption for validity must be construed as a support in both forums, to the marriage that is in possession and perhaps on trial. But it must not be so construed that it will uphold such a present union in which the parties are living, and destroy the presumptive validity of a former bond duly entered upon but since disrupted by factual separation or civil divorce (cfr. n. **486**).

[80] Peters, p. 32; cfr. c. 6, 7, C. XXXII, q. 2.

[81] c. 11, C. XXX, q. 5.

412. The presumption of validity is applied in the first place to the marriages of Catholics canonically contracted (cfr. n. **426**).

It is likewise applicable to the marriages of others, and holds with respect to the marriages of heretics (Protestants) and schismatics, when these marriages have been contracted according to civil or denominational custom,[82] or with other external ceremony signifying consent. Thus if there is question of a present marriage being invalid by reason of the impediment of crime, the presumption of validity adheres to the first marriage against which the crime was committed, even though it be the marriage of heretics or schismatics, when it is shown that the first marriage had been duly entered upon. In a case tried in the archdiocese of X., one John J., a Protestant, had married Mary M., a Protestant, before a Protestant minister or civil official, and certificate of this marriage was produced. There was likewise evidence of the baptisms of the parties. During this marriage Mary had sexual coition with Daniel D., a Catholic, and exchanged with him the promise of future marriage. Two years after the death of John, Mary, recently converted to the Catholic Church, married Daniel. But this marriage, presaged by marital infidelity, proved to be unhappy, whereupon Daniel denounced his marriage, and the promoter of the diocese brought action against it. In order to establish nullity by reason of the impediment of crime, there was no need of proving that the first marriage, between John and Mary, was valid; for validity is rightly presumed when the fact of the marriage having been duly contracted is proved.[83]

The marriages of infidels are likewise presumed to be valid, whenever it is shown, in a specific case, that the marriage was really entered upon with some external ceremony or other action signifying marital consent.[84] For although infidels are not bound by laws merely ecclesiastical (c. 12), the Church, when called upon to judge their marriages (cfr. c. 1038,§1), applies the presumptions which nature and correct jurisprudence unite in establishing.

413. A marriage that was not contested while both spouses lived, is, after the death of one or both spouses, so presumed to have

[82] SO, Nesquallien., §2; R. Argentinen., Null., 23 feb. 1912 (rd., iv, p. 107; aas., iv, p. 388); Moguntina, Null., 14 jul. 1921 (rd., xiii, pp. 166, 167).

[83] Metropolitan Curia of X, 29 oct. 1932 (unpub.).

[84] SO, 1872; SO, Alberti; SO, Nesquallien., §2; SO., 10 dec. 1885 (cicf., iv, n. 1097; cpf., ii, n. 1645); R., Ugentina, Null., 22 mart. 1910 (rd., ii, p. 125; aas., ii, p. 526); Smith, n. 459; DeSmet, i, p. 141 (7); Schaefer, p. 17.

been valid, that no proof is admitted against this presumption, unless the question arises incidentally (c. 1972) to another suit.[85] Hence after one of the spouses is dead, no one may seek declaration of nullity of such a marriage, as the principal object of suit.[86]

A person is however permitted to contest the validity of a former marriage to which one spouse is now dead, if the question of invalidity arises incidentally to another marriage suit, *e. g.* if a party had contracted a second marriage during the lifetime of the former spouse, he may now contest the former marriage in order to uphold the validity of the marriage in which he is now involved (cfr. c. 1733).

It appears from the wording of Canon 1972 that the marriage may also be impugned if the question of validity arises incidentally to a suit on legitimacy of children, even when the legitimate inheritance is made the principal end of the suit. John B. had contracted by proxy with Genevieve N., and several years after her death brought suit against the marriage in order to establish the legitimacy of the children he had begotten from a subsequent marriage contracted before her death. The Congregation received the plaint and gave decision of nullity of the former marriage.[87] Similarly the marriage

[85] Canon 1972 speaks of a presumption, and most authors, *v. g.* C. I. C. Index, Vo.: Praesumptio (ed. gasp.); Chelodi, n. 176; Capello, iii, n. 879; Gasparri, nov., ii, n. 1262; Salsmans in jp., viii (1928), p. 163 refer to this as an inevitable presumption. V-Creusen, iii, n. 287 state contrary, that there is no inevitable presumption contained in c. 1972, because the marriage can be directly impugned in incidental cases. But this fact detracts merely from the scope of influence, not from the force of the presumption (inevitable) within the given scope. Hence it seems that there is an inevitable presumption which, in effect, amounts to a peremptory exception against introducing the case, except under given conditions.

[86] V-Creusen, iii, n. 287 infer from the decision given in SCC., Barcinonen., 6 mai., 16 dec. 1893 (aas., xxvi, p. 407) that even after the death of a spouse, the marriage may be contested as a principal suit, if it was entirely impossible to contest it while both parties were living. But this seems to be untenable, since it is opposed by the wording of c. 1972 (cfr. cc. 6,n.1; 18).

[87] SCC., In Neapolitana, Mat., 7 jul. 1736 (gasp., ii, n. 970); SCC., 21 apr. 1842 (gasp., ii, n. 1482); cfr. also SCC., In Caesaraugustana, Mat., 10 mart. 1770; Gasparri, nov., ii, n. 1262. But not all decisions are uniform in tenor: SCC. in Januensi, Mat., 17 sept. 1842 (gasp., ii, n. 1482) denied the right of suit in such a case. Likewise SCC., Mediolanen., Null., 22 aug. 1908 (ass., xli, p. 781), where in footnote (1) the distinction is made between those cases from which some spiritual benefit may accrue by declaration of nullity, and those where temporalities alone are concerned; in these latter cases, the footnote says, the suit against validity is discountenanced. Hence some authors *v. g.*

may be contested after the death of a party if, as in a recent case that arose in Egypt, a civil court is about to base its decision whether the widow has a right to inheritance and to bear the deceased husband's name, on the decision of the ecclesiastical court respecting the validity of the marriage.[88]

In matters that admit of it, prescription may apply against the right of suit even though the question be introduced only incidentally.[89]

414. The simple legal presumption in favor of the validity of a marriage has as its chief canonical effects: 1) that it inclines the judge to pronounce in favor of the marriage contracted as long as moral certainty of nullity is not established by natural proofs and other particular presumptions (c. 1014). Even if there is not conclusive proof of validity, but on the other hand there is only a probable reason in favor of the nullity of the marriage, the judge must pronounce in favor of validity.[90]

2) When it is seen in the course of trial that a deed or word of the parties or another can be explained in two ways: one way favoring validity and the other way favoring nullity, the deed or word will be understood by the judge as entailing the validity of the marriage.[91] In the case of the woman who immediately before contracting marriage has undergone a surgical operation just in order to avoid the possibility of conceiving progeny after marriage, there is a question, entirely apart from the question of impotence, whether her marriage is invalid for want of true consent, or in other words, whether she has married with an intent on her part opposed to the essentials of marriage. Some authors claim the marriage is invalid for want of true consent. Gasparri holds their opinion is not *per se*

Chelodi, n. 176; Farrugia, n. 368 deny the right of suit "praesertim ad effectus patrimoniales." Gasparri, nov., ii, n. 1262 on the contrary, explicitly admits suit to this end.

[88] R., Aegypti, Null., Quaestio Incident., 20 jun. 1922 (rd., xiv, p. 190; aas., xiv, p. 600); cfr. c. 7, X, Qui Filii Sint Legitimi, IV, 17.

[89] Schmalzgrueber, lib. IV, tit. xviii, n. 27: "excipitur (ab accusando) si mortui iam sint coniuges et post 30 vel 40 annos moveatur lis a filiis super legitimitate quod matrimonium nullum fuerit, nam hac in casu cum cesset periculum peccandi ob quod perpetua est actio contra matrimonium nihil obstat quominus dispositio iuris communis locum habeat . . . "; cpre. c. 1508.

[90] R., Null., 30 jun. 1910 (rd., ii, p. 221).

[91] R., Vercellen., Null., 20 mart. 1911 (rd., iii, p. 130); cfr. Gasparri, ii, n. 922.

correct. For even after such a deed she may very well give marital consent without then restricting the act of her will with respect to future issue, which is the more probable, since she is convinced that actual pregnancy will not occur. And in such cases the favor accorded to marriage obliges the judge to presume that true consent was given,[92] as long as the perverse intention is not otherwise proved. Similarly when it is claimed that a marriage is invalid because of a stipulation attached and not fulfilled, but it is doubtful whether the attached intention was really a stipulation or just a representation attached to the contract without suspending the effects of it (cfr. n. **153**), the court will adjudge it a representation rather than a true stipulation.[93] However, this principle of interpretation in favor of validity, must not be urged to the exclusion of other proper rules of interpretation (cfr. n. **366**).

415. When it has been shown that the marriage was entered upon in due form before the priest, the presumption of validity bears with it the further presumption that the solemnities essential to the validity of the form were observed.[94] For when the outward form has been observed, the accessories are presumed to have been observed.[95] [96]

There is a question whether a priest who has performed a marriage ceremony, though not empowered by reason of the office of pastor *etc.* to assist at marriages, is presumed to have been vested with the necessary delegation from the authorized pastor *etc.* To this question the jurisprudence of the courts has not always given the same answer (cfr. n. **376**). A cathedral canon in Peru, having performed a marriage ceremony at the house of the bride, the plaintiff contested the validity of the marriage on the ground that this priest had not received the necessary delegation from either the pastor of the bride or the pastor of the groom or the archbishop or vicar gen-

[92] Gasparri, ii, n. 923: "At ultro admittimus in casu esse grave indicium contra debitam mulieris intentionem; quod ex circumstantiis augeri vel minui aut destrui potest."; Schaefer, p. 231.

[93] R., Null., 13 feb. 1915 (rd., vii, p. 46).

[94] R., Null., 6 dec. 1909 (rd., i, n. 160).

[95] R., Londonen., Incardinationis, 9 jan. 1912 (rd., iv, p. 16; aas., iv, p. 254).

[96] In civil law, Abbott, p. 101; p. 103: "Where solemnization was necessary by the law under which the marriage was contracted, if it is proved, and matrimonial cohabitation under it, the law presumes that all the necessary formalities were had, unless the contrary is shown; . . . ."

eral. There were no parish records of the marriage by which to prove or disprove the delegation, and the witnesses most necessary, namely the canon himself who had performed the marriage as well as the pastor and assistant pastor, were dead. The Congregation of the Council denied the case the legal presumption that delegation had been granted, but admitted there were personal presumptions in the case to prove that delegation had been accorded.[97] In a more recent case that arose in Paris however, the Rota placed the burden of proof upon the plaintiff, and required him to show that tacit delegation had not been granted.[98]

416. The presumption of validity gives way before that favor of law which the Church has customarily allowed to promote the true Faith.

That some doubts are to be settled in favor of the Christian Faith was asserted by Gregory IX,[99] and again by Benedict XIV who thus interpreted the Fourth Council of Toledo held in 633 under St. Isidore.[100] These all speak of the matter of baptizing the child of Jewish parents, of whom one has been converted to the Faith, while the other remains in infidelity, and does not wish the child baptized. And they conclude that in favor of the Faith, the right of a mother or father who does not wish the child baptized, succumbs to the intention of the other parent or even grandparent to have the child or grandchild baptized.[101]

[97] SCC., Mat., 1 feb. 1868 (ass., iii, p. 401): "I. Generatim solemnitates, quae pro forma actus sunt praescriptae, supponi non posse observatas, sed eas observatas fuisse ab eo ostendi debere, qui validitatem actus sustinet.

"II. Quare in matrimonio contracto coram extraneo Sacerdote supponi non posse facultatem eidem delegata fuisse, sed ostendi debere ab eo qui matrimonium sustinet.

"III. Eiusdem tamen demonstrationem ea ratione faciendam esse qua facta demonstrari possunt. . . . .

"IV. Militantibus autem validis praesumptionibus pro existentia delegationis non esse proferendam nullitatis Matrimonii sententiam, quamvis eius validitas undequaque non pateat."

[98] R., Parisien., Null., 9 jul. 1918 (rd., x, p. 82); cfr. aer., lv (1916), p. 432; Chelodi, n. 7; cfr. R., Divionen., Null., 20 jan. 1911 (rd., iii, p. 4; aas., iii, p. 284).

[99] c. 2, X, De Conversione Infidelium, III, 33.

[100] Ben. XIV, "Probe," 15 (17) dec. 1751 (cicf., ii, n. 418).

[101] cfr. Freisen, p. 639.

417. This favor to the Faith is applied to those marriage cases in which it is proposed to make use of the Pauline privilege (c. 1127).[102] When there is doubt whether the conditions requisite to the use of the privilege of the Apostle (cfr. cc. 1121-1123) have been sufficiently fulfilled, the Pauline privilege enjoys the favor of the law, and the converted party may divorce his infidel consort and be married anew to a Christian (cfr. c. 1120). Thus it is allowed to use the Pauline privilege even when the infidel party has responded that he will abide with the converted party without contemning the Creator, but there is solid reason to believe that he will not, and the matter is thus doubtful.[103] If he assert his desire to be converted but answer that he will not cohabit with the already converted spouse, his assertion that he will be converted may generally be considered insincere and the answers to both interpellations are presumed to be negative.[104] Similarly when it is doubtful whether the Christian party after his conversion gave the other a just cause for abandonment.[105] Again when there is doubt whether the interpellation in a given case may be properly omitted or not;[106] however Clement XIV has warned against indulging frivolous presumptions to the end that the interpellation be omitted.[107] Finally too when there is a doubt of the baptism of one party (cfr. nn. **510-512**).

Similarly the interests of the Faith are favored in those cases involving the marriage of infidels where there is opportunity to implore the Supreme Pontiff's dispensation from the marriage. For if there be a doubt about the requisites for such a dispensation, *e. g.* if it be doubted who was the true infidel wife among several infidel concubines, the Church favors conversion to the Faith, by dispensing

[102] cfr. SO., 5 aug. 1759, Coccin. (cpf., i, n. 421; cicf., iv, n. 810).

[103] SO., 7 aug. 1891 (cicf., iv, n. 1142; cpf., ii, n. 1762): "Licet infidelis, facta interpellatione, sine Creatoris contumelia se cohabitaturum polliceatur, pertinere ad Episcopum, ipsius onerata conscientia, ut omni adhibita diligentia, et perpensis singulorum casuum circumstantiis et moribus regionum, iudicet utrum parti ad fidem conversae permittenda sit cohabitatio iuxta ea quae traduntur a sa. me. Bened. XIV De Syn. Dioec. lib. XIII, cap. xxi, n. 1."

[104] Gasparri, ii, n. 1336.

[105] SO., 19 apr. 1899 (cicf., iv, n. 1220; cpf., ii, n. 2043); SO., 26 apr. 1899 (cicf., iv, n. 1222; cpf., ii, n. 2044); Cerato, p. 224.

[106] Linneborn, p. 377 (6); p. 379.

[107] SO., 23 nov. 1769, Chensi et Chansi (cpf., i, n. 475; cicf., iv, n. 825).

and divorcing the infidel marriage, and allowing remarriage of the converted person with a Catholic (cfr. n. **488**).[108]

418. But sometimes the existence or validity of the former infidel marriage is in open doubt, and in these cases there is no need to explicitly implore the papal dispensation. When the curia considers the question of validity in these cases, the favor of law rests rather upon the conversion of the infidels with the allowability of a new marriage than upon the supposed former marriage.[109] Hence the presumption for validity of the marriage gives way in these cases, if there is any true probability of nullity. The Holy Office has explicitely stated that there is a presumption of nullity in such cases.[110] Hence the same presumption of nullity was held by writers who preceded the Code,[111] and by writers who have commentated the Code.[112] De Smet rightly calls attention that in these cases the presumption may stand for the nullity of the infidel marriage, but that it need not be so applied, for the parties are to be permitted to continue their wedded life, unless scandal would arise from their cohabitation or danger to the Faith of the baptized party.[113] For the presumption militates against the validity of the infidel marriage only when it promotes the true Faith.[114]

[108] Thus in matters respecting the favor to the Faith, the word "res dubia" (c. 1127) need not always be understood as that "dubium positivum et probabile" spoken of in Canon 209. It may sometimes stand for negative doubt or ignorance.

[109] SO, Alberti, § 13; Urbanus VIII responsum P. de Lugo: "Pontifex, indicto consulto, dixit, quod ubi DD. sententiae utrinque probabiles intercederent, sequeretur opiniones, pro conditione locorum ac hominum, barbaris favorabiliores." (gasp., i, n. 21).

[110] SO., 18 mai. 1892 (cpf., ii, n. 1797; cicf., iv, n. 1156): "Si . . . examinato casu particulari supersit dubium, stet pro nullitate matrimonii, in favorem fidei."; SO., 26 apr. 1899 (cicf., iv, n. 1222; cpf., ii, n. 2044).

[111] Gasparri, i, n. 21: "Hoc principium: in dubio standum est pro valore matrimonii, fallit: 1) Si pro nullitate matrimonii sit favor fidei:"; DeBecker, pp. 150 (1), 192, 193 (1); McCarthy in aer., liv (1916), p. 336.

[112] DeSmet, i, p. 319 (5); Linneborn, p. 379 (5); Haring: Grundzuege, p. 559 (5); Gasparri, nov., i, n. 21; Vermeersch in prm., 1934, p. 203*.

[113] De Smet, i, p. 319 (5); V-Creusen, ii, n. 354.

[114] SO, Alberti, § 13. To explain the theological basis of the presumption in such cases, Lehmkuhl, ii, n. 991 and W-Vidal, v, n. 44 have recourse to the dispensing and divorcing power of the Supreme Pontiff whereby he, in cases that are not *de facto* invalid, and that do not come under the Pauline privilege, may dissolve the marriages of infidels if they were not consummated after the

419. Diriment impediments of ecclesiastical origin do not hold when there is a doubt of law (c. 15) and so the presumption in favor of validity holds as firmly when there is doubt of law as when there is doubt of fact.[115] Thus in the impediment of crime (uno patrante) it is disputed whether the perpetrator who murders with a view to future marriage, must acquaint the other party to the future marriage with his intent to marry, in order to incur the impediment. In the ensuing doubt of law a marriage entered into after such crime, will not be pronounced invalid unless the perpetrator shall have thus made known his intent, for the presumption favors validity (cfr. nn. **423**, **523**).[116]

Similarly if there is a doubt of the civil law regarding diriment legal relationship, the marriage contracted under such doubtful impediment is presumed valid.[117]

Similarly in another doubt of law on duress: before the Code there was controversy and doubt among authors whether duress must be inflicted precisely to extort consent, in order to constitute a diriment impediment (cfr. n. **483**). Faced with this doubt the Rota declared that no marriage could be pronounced invalid by reason of duress, unless the duress was inflicted precisely to that end, for the judge must "in doubt, whether of fact or of law, adhere to the validity of the marriage." [118]

420. In regard to the celebration of marriage there has been a doubt of law whether Catholics could take advantage of Canon 1098, n.1, and contract validly before witnesses only, in case the properly authorized priest is indeed materially present in the place, but is absent in the sense that he cannot be had to the purpose desired; *i. e.* he

conversion of the parties; otherwise: "sententiae humani iudicis tribueretur vis immutandi obiectivam rei veritatem pro casu quo dubium subiectivum de valore matrimonii coniungeretur cum obiectivo ipsius valore."

[115] R., Ugentina, Null., 22 mart. 1910 (rd., ii, p. 125): "Quare minime in iudiciis de matrimonii nullitate vigere potest distinctio inter dubium iuris et dubium facti, eo sensu quod in dubio circa aliquod punctum iuris aliquam nempe legem in se, matrimonium favore iuris gaudeat, in dubio vero circa aliquod factum, seu aliquod punctum, quod ex parte facti se teneat, matrimonium non gaudeat favore iuris."; Null., 30 jun. 1910 (rd., ii, p. 234); Cerato, p. 9.

[116] Schaefer, p. 201 (202).

[117] W-Vidal, v, p. 215 (61).

[118] R., Null., 29 nov. 1913 (rd., v, p. 613).

cannot perform the ceremony of their marriage because he is hindered by the state law, *e. g.* because the parties have not the documents required for legal marriage. Three decisions given just after the issuance of the "Ne Temere" pronounced marriage contracted under these circumstances before witnesses only, as valid and licit.[119] Later the Congregation of the Sacraments declared that such cases were to be referred individually, except in danger of death when any priest could dispense from the impediment of clandestinity.[120] Finally a decision of March 9, 1916 declared that marriages which had been entered upon before witnesses only, were to be accorded correction at the root.[121] Nevertheless some authors held that in spite of this decision, cases arising subsequent to the Code, must be settled in accordance with Canon 15, by a presumption of validity in favor of marriages thus contracted.[122]

Meanwhile two authentic interpretations of Canon 1098 have since made it plain that only physical absence of the pastor and ordinary is included in the scope of Canon 1098, n. 1, and in cases where there is in no sense a physical absence, the marriage cannot be validly contracted before witnesses alone. On the other hand however, the case where a pastor or ordinary, although materially present, cannot because of grave inconvenience or danger assist at the celebration of the marriage and ask and receive the expression of marital consent, is to be considered as physical absence to the end that parties may take advantage of Canon 1098, n.1, and contract before witnesses alone.[123]

It appears from this that when a pastor refuses his presence because he will not assist at the marriage, *e. g.* because he is not convinced that the parties are free to marry, or even because he is incensed at a party, this mere moral absence is not in any sense physical absence, and in this case marriage cannot be validly contracted without the presence of the proper priest. But if a particular case arise

[119] PF., 24 mart. 1909; DS., 24 (26?) nov. 1909; DS., 13 mart. 1910 (apud Capello, iii, p. 732 (11)): "Matrimonium potest valide et licite contrahi coram solis testibus sine praesentia sacerdotis competentis ad assistendum, *semper* ac, elapso mense, sacerdos competens haberi vel adiri nequit."

[120] DS., 31 jan. 1916 (aas., viii, p. 36).

[121] DS., n. 792/16 apud Linneborn, p. 331 (3).

[122] Capello, iii, n. 694; Schaefer, p. 278 (13).

[123] PC., 10 mart. 1928 (aas., xx, p. 120); PC., 25 jul. 1931 (aas., xxiii, p. 388); cfr. Oesterle, Staatliche Ehegesetz verbieten die kirchliche Trauung, in (lqs., 1933, p. 335).

in which marriage has been contracted before witnesses only, and there is a doubt of law whether the absence of the pastor and ordinary was a physical absence at least to the effect above stated, or rather a mere moral absence, the presumption stands in favor of physical absence and the validity of the marriage. If there is merely a doubt of fact whether there was physical absence of the pastor and ordinary, the presumption of validity holds only in case the marriage has been registered in accordance with Canon 1103,§3 (cfr. n. **426**.)

421. In how far the ecclesiastical judge can hold to the validity of a marriage in which there is question of a doubtful law of divine origin, is not entirely clear from the Code or the authors. In respect to cases of doubtful impotence, the Code makes specific application of the principle just given, and states that even when there is doubt of law a proposed marriage is not to be hindered (c. 1068,§2); hence, much less, dissolved.

Then there is the disputed question whether the affixing of a stipulation to observe perfect chastity after marriage, is against the substance of matrimony and invalidates the marriage, even when the "ius radicale in corpus" is conceded. Authors differ entirely and this constitutes a doubt of law. But it is agreed that if a marriage has been contracted with such a stipulation affixed, the presumption favors the validity of the marriage.[124]

422. Some authors have applied the principle of validity in doubt of law, just given, to the marriages of infidels related to one another in the first degree of collateral line, and stated that the brother and sister who have been previously married need not be separated when converted, unless the state has established an invalidating impediment of consanguinity.[125] Gasparri claims that it is the practice of the Holy Office to allow such couples to remain together, of which practice he gives a recent example.[126] Others contend the principle cannot be applied in this case, and the parties must, upon conversion,

[124] Cerato, p. 157; Schaefer, p. 243. Similarly in case of marriage after vow of chastity: Gasparri, i, n. 664.

[125] V-Creusen, ii, n. 354; De Smet, i, p. 319 (5); Gasparri, nov., i, nn. 220, 222, 708.

[126] SO., in Araucania, 13 dec. 1916 (gasp., nov., i, p. 433 (1)). But De Becker, nov, p. 76 (1): "utrum reapse praxis Sedis Apostolicae huic faveat opinioni dubitare licet."

be separated and allowed to marry anew.[127] This contention is in some measure supported by a letter and formula of the Holy Office.[128] In a practical case where such related parties will not or cannot be separated and marry others under pontifical dispensation from non-consummated ratified marriage, the curial judge will have to consult the Holy Office.

423. As however with doubts of fact there must be a prudent[129] and grave doubt,[130] in order to enjoin a judge against pronouncing nullity in a case otherwise clear, so also with doubts of law, the presumption favors the validity of the marriage only in case the opinion favoring the validity is truly and solidly probable.[131]

Such true and solid probability is not derived from the mere fact that one or another commendable author has defended the opinion, but rather from internal probability, or at least some community of adherence to such opinion on the part of a respectable number of authors. This is well illustrated by a recent case from Cambrai, in the second instance of which the Rota held for the validity of the marriage, applying the presumption for validity in doubt of law: for since Pitonius holds that stipulations privately appended to the marital consent, even when proved to have existed, are elided by the public marriage ceremony, and must be presumed with inevitable presumption, to have been retracted, the Rota in second instance held

[127] Lehmkuhl, ii, n. 991; Capello, iii, n. 522 who state without documentation that this is certainly the mind and practice of SO. and PF.; however cfr. Capello, iii, n. 202. Lehmkuhl, ii, n. 991 solves the difficulty arising to the future Christian marriage of the parties from the doubtful bond of the previous marriage contracted by the related persons.

[128] SO., 13 mart. 1736 (cicf., iv, n. 789, and p. 70 (1); cpf., i, n. 317).

[129] PF, 1883, § 40; R., Paderbornen., Null., 27 jul. 1917 (rd., ix, p. 163; aas., x, p. 217).

[130] R., Null., 22 apr. 1913 (rd., v, p. 268; aas., v, p. 445): "Domini auditores admiserunt quidem aliquod dubium, an Ernestus ante matrimonium domicilium paternum dereliquerit, minime deesse; existimarunt tamen agi de dubio levi ideoque non posse applicari principium in iure notum: 'In dubio standum est pro valore matrimonii.' Hoc sane valet, quando agitur de dubio probabili in favorem matrimonii, minime vero, quando agitur de dubio levi, imo levissimo, ut in casu; tale enim dubium spernendum est . . . "; Null., 19 jul. 1913 (rd., v, pp. 469, 470).

[131] R., S. Christophori de Habana, Null., 15 jul. 1910 (rd., ii, p. 270); Null., 10 dec. 1914 (rd., vi, pp. 347, 348); Mohilovien., Null., 18 apr. 1916 (rd., viii, pp. 125, 126; aas., viii, p. 420).

such opinion of Pitonius to constitute a doubt of law in favor of the marriage which had evidently been contracted with an explicit and unfulfilled stipulation, and applying the general presumption in favor of validity to the case, pronounced the marriage valid.[132] But when the case was appealed, the Rotal courts in third and fourth instances rejected the presumption on the ground that the opinion of Pitonius did not constitute a solid doubt of law, and declared the marriage invalid.[133]

Similarly in the question of disparity of cult, the Rota decided that the external probability attaching to the opinion of Santi-Leitner (and Gasparri), that a marriage entered into with a presumption of valid baptism is valid even if it is afterward found that baptism was not conferred or that it was invalidly conferred, should not beget a decision for validity by reason of the probable doubt arising in the case from this opinion.[134]

Similarly, there is no presumption of validity derivable in court from the fact that authors have held that ignorance of the impediment excuses from the impediment of crime.[135] In order therefore that the presumption in favor of validity be rightly applied in doubt of law, the opinion on the law causing such doubt must be, in the present state of canonical opinion and practice, truly and solidly probable.

424. In the doubt of law whether the marriages of infidels contracted under duress are by natural law valid or invalid, some authors have held that an exception is to be made against the presumption of validity If there is a doubt of fact whether the marriage was contracted under duress all admit that the presumption stands for validity. But when it is certain that duress was unjustly inflicted upon an unbaptized person, and this duress was the means of extorting marital consent, some of the gravest authors held the presumption to

132 R., Null., 19 jun. 1909 (rd., i, pp. 71, 72), quoting Pitonius, Disceptat. Eccl., pars I, discep. lii, n. 33, contra Pignatelli; cfr. W-Vidal, v, n. 470.

133 R., Cameracen., Null., 11 aug. 1910; 23 jun. 1911 (rd., ii, p. 299; iii, p. 292); cfr. also Null., 18 aug. 1916 (rd., viii, pp. 315, 316).

134 R., Parisien., Null., 13 jun. 1911 (rd., iii, pp. 260, 261); cfr. Ravennaten., Null., 29 dec. 1911 (rd., iii, p. 522); c. 1070, §2 now makes it abundantly clear that the marriage of a Catholic must be declared invalid, when it is proved that there actually was disparity of cult, by reason of the non-baptism of the other party.

135 Feije, n. 456.

be in favor of freedom and against validity. Thus Schmalzgrueber;[136] and Gasparri, who himself held theoretically that the canonical impediment of duress does not invalidate the marriages of unbaptized persons, contends nevertheless in his pre-Code edition, that, practically, the presumption must stand against validity and in favor of freedom in this case, because of the ruling of Urban VIII that that opinion is to be followed which is more favorable to barbarous peoples, *i. e.* to their conversion.[137] Thus too the Rota in 1918.[138]

Since the Code, some authors have believed that the presumption in favor of freedom has become strengthened, and they point out that duress and fear are not enumerated in the Code among the impediments binding only upon Christians, but rather among the defects of consent (Cod., Lib. III, tit. vii, cap. v, De consensu matrimoniali, c. 1087). Hence they believe the doubt of law regarding the applicability of the impediment of duress to the marriages of infidels, has all but vanished, and that the presumption for freedom in such cases is accordingly strengthened.[139] Others allow no valid argument derivable from this.[140] And in fact, Canons 1083,§2, n. 2 and 1089 are contained in the same chapter of the Code and under the same heading, yet both enumerate causes of invalidity which are not *per se* derivable from the notion of true consent, and do not invalidate the marriages of infidels.

In his post-Code edition Gasparri says the jurisprudence of the Roman Curia is against this presumption of liberty, for it acknowledges a marriage as invalid by duress only when it is proved that the duress is such that it renders marriage invalid.[141] But he does not cite any example of jurisprudence that denied the principle of liberty

136 Schmalzgrueber, lib. IV, tit. i, n. 401: "Quod in dubio pro matrimonio pronuntiandum sit, verum est regulariter, non tamen semper, praesertim quando dubius valor propter metum est; tunc enim melius pronuntiatur contra matrimonium, tum quia coacta matrimonia difficiles habent exitus, tum . . ."

137 Gasparri, i, n. 22; also Linneborn, pp. 291, 292.

138 R., Vicariatus Apost. Nyanzae Sept., Null., 10 mai. 1918 (rd., x, pp. 36-38; aas., xi, pp. 89-91). This case however does not give over much support; for, although the presumption in favor of freedom is explicitly stated, it does not clearly appear that the marriage contracted in infidelity was actually declared invalid by reason of duress rather than by reason of entire lack of consent.

139 Cerato, p. 149; Farrugia, n. 31.

140 Capello, iii, p. 650 (23).

141 Gasparri, nov., i, n. 22.

precisely to a marriage contracted in infidelity. Against the presumption for freedom it is also urged that Canon 1014 makes no distinction of cases and must be applied alike to the marriages of Christians and infidels.[142] The presumption in favor of validity of infidel marriages derives further from the natural principle which accepts an act done as validly done (cfr. n. **408**).[143] On this principle then, it seems the marriages of infidels are to be presumed valid even when entered upon under duress; unless there is a question of conversion to the Faith.

For then the presumption in favor of freedom is supported by another principle: in favor of the Faith the Church accords special consideration to the marriages of infidels, whether these are about to use the Pauline privilege or to petition a dispensation from the Supreme Pontiff from marriage contracted and not consummated since ratification by baptism, or finally even when the situation demands the juridical presumption of the invalidity of a doubtful infidel marriage (cfr. nn. **417, 418**). Hence in nearly all practical cases of infidel marriage contracted under duress, the ecclesiastical judge will be able to apply the presumption (of nullity) in favor of the Faith.[144] But some authors would require that cases of this kind be referred to the Holy See, rather than that the presumption of nullity be applied;[145] this precaution seems to be unnecessary.

§ 4. Presumption of Fact or Validity and Informal Marriage

425. In coming to the question whether the presumption of validity also covers informal and clandestine marriages, various situations or separate questions must be clearly distinguished. There is I. the question whether the marriage of a Catholic, entered upon with some ceremony or other, but without the form prescribed in Canon 1094, is to be accorded the presumption of validity; II. the question whether the sexual coition of betrothed persons is to be considered an expression of marital consent and constitutes presumptive marriage; III. whether a marriage invalidly performed for want of consent, or

142 Chelodi, n. 7.

143 Capello, iii, n. 610; Schaefer, p. 240; V-Creusen, ii, n. 279.

144 cfr. Vermeersch, in prm., 1934, p. 203*. Thus the seemingly conflicting statements of Gasparri i, n. 22 and Gasparri, nov., i, n. 22 are brought into unison.

145 Matharan, n. 225; Sangmeister, p. 165.

in which the consent is suspended pending the fulfillment of a stipulation, can be presumed to be validated by the marital consent as expressed by sexual coition and cohabitation; IV. whether a concubinage protracted for a longer or shorter time, but not entered upon in marriage form with the attendance of a priest, is to be considered a marriage as far as the marital consent and entering upon a marriage contract is concerned; V. whether informal clandestine marriages, which have certainly been contracted with marital consent, and are not voided by want of form, bear the presumption of validity against other impediments that stand to make the marriage doubtful. In three of these questions (II, III, IV) the question of validity resolves itself into a question of consent, and where a presumption of marital consent is established it is tantamount to a presumption of marriage. Sexual coition does not necessarily denote marital consent, but there are circumstances that lend a natural fitness to the presumption of marital consent, when the sexual coition is proved.

426. I. The presumption of validity as applied to Catholics, covers all public canonical marriages, *i. e.* marriages of which there is *prima facie* evidence that they were celebrated in accordance with the form prescribed by the "Tametsi" in its time, or as subsequently amended by the "Ne Temere," or now prescribed by the Code: that is, it covers all marriages contracted in the usual manner before a Catholic priest (cfr. nn. **376, 415**) and witnesses (species, figura matrimonii).

Marriages of Catholics and mixed marriages, entered upon without the assistance of a priest, under the clauses of Article VII or VIII of the "Ne Temere," or of Canon 1098,n.1, are also public canonical marriages whenever they are registered in accordance with the norm of Article IX of the "Ne Temere" or of Canon 1103,§3. Accordingly marriages thus contracted and registered enjoy the same presumption of validity.

Marriages thus contracted without a priest and not registered do not seem to have the presumption in favor of validity. Those marriages contracted in Hungary without the assistance of a priest, between 19 April 1908 and 23 February 1909, during which time there was a doubt of law on the validity of such marriages, were not later declared to be presumably valid because of this doubt, but were later provided with correction at the root.[146] For the presumption of valid-

[146] Chelodi, n. 128; p. 153 (1).

ity is not extensively interpreted to cover marriages of Catholics contracted without a priest (cfr. nn. **415, 449, 509**).

This restriction of the presumption has a very practical bearing; it is just in cases of marriage entered upon before a minister or magistrate in districts where there is not likely to be a priest for a month or more, that the ecclesiastical court must often decide upon the validity of the marriage. A Catholic girl has gone from her eastern home to an obscure place in the West, and there she meets a man apparently baptized, whom she marries before a minister or civil magistrate. Later she returns, seeks civil divorce and applies to her diocesan curia for declaration of nullity of her marriage on the ground that it was not contracted in form. But the curia, having inquired about the place where her marriage was performed, finds that a missionary sometimes visited, but there was no resident pastor in the district at the time of the marriage, and cannot ascertain whether the continued absence of an authorized priest was prudently foreseen at the time, or not. So the curia is in doubt whether the marriage is invalid for want of form or valid because of the prescription of Canon 1098,n.1. The criterion must rest with the registration of the marriage. If that marriage was afterward reported by the interested parties and registered in the proper parish books,[147] the doubtful marriage is to be presumed valid. If it was never reported and never registered, the presumption is against the validity, until it is shown that the specifications of Canon 1098 were fulfilled in the case.

For, although the registration of such a marriage is not theoretically required for validity, it may very well be required for the presumption of validity in a concrete and doubtful case. Chelodi gives another example of a merely prescriptive law, newly introduced into the Code, being made the basis of the presumption of invalidity. It is well known that under pre-Code law the silence of a party might be viewed as a presumptive sign of consent.[148] The Code now requires that the consent be expressed by words (c. 1088,§2), though these are not an absolute requirement for validity (c. 11). Yet even from this merely prescriptive and by no means invalidating requirement, Chelodi deduces the presumption that if a party to the marriage keeps silence instead of expressing the consent with words, there is,

[147] PF., 23 jun. 1830 ad Vic. Ap. Sinen. (cpf., i, n. 816): "ut ipsi de matrimonio rite inito legitime constet."

[148] Reg. iur. xliii in VI; Gasparri, ii, n. 964.

in case of doubt, presumable dissent, rather than consent,[149] and the marriage is presumably invalid. So it seems too that there is in a doubtful case, a presumption of invalidity when the marriage, entered upon without a priest, has not been registered according to Canon 1103,§3.

Much more does the presumption stand against validity if it is shown that the continued absence of a priest with jurisdiction for the marriage, or the danger of death said to have existed (cfr. c. 1098,n.1) were mere fictions.[150]

427. II. In case valid betrothals (sponsalia de futuro) are followed by sexual intercourse between the betrothed: The Roman law, Novella 74, provided that a betrothal followed by sexual intercourse between the betrothed thereby achieved the status of a marriage (sponsalia de praesenti).[151]

Perhaps it was the influence of this Roman law, just commencing again to lift its head at the first beginnings of the Renaissance, that influenced some glossarians to insist upon a similar presumption. The very early glossarians make no mention of a "matrimonium praesumptum," but Tancred writes that if a person betrothed to another, afterward betrothes himself to a second spouse "per verba de praesenti vel per verba de futuro" and carnal coition follows with this second betrothed, he must be held to have married this person, and he must remain with her. And Robert of St. Victor in repeating the same doctrine adds that this is true if the coition was effected with "maritali affectu." Otherwise, he thinks it is not a marriage, but there is a presumption of marriage.[152] Alexander III declared that a betrothal "de futuro" followed by coition may not be dissolved by a succeeding marriage.[153] This expresses a presumption that the first betrothal and coition constituted marriage. But Gregory IX writing to the Bishop of Cenomani went further and declared that if, after bethrothal for future marriage and succeeding coition, a man were to marry another woman even "in facie ecclesiae," he must return to the first betrothed, for although the marriage with this

[149] Chelodi, p. 131, n. 121.

[150] cpre. R., Colonien., Null., 27 aug. 1910 (rd., ii, p. 320).

[151] De Smet, i, p. 16 (3).

[152] Freisen, p. 209.

[153] c. 15, X, De Spon. et Mat., IV, 1; cfr. c. 8, X, De Restitutione Spoliatorum, II, 13.

first woman is but a presumed marriage, one may not bring proof against this presumption.[154] Here we have an inevitable presumption of marriage contracted.

The canonists from Robert of St. Victor on, have constantly insisted that we must not understand this inevitable presumption actually to constitute a marriage in case the parties, contrary to the presumption, engaged in the coition without marital consent.[155] Neither presumption nor decree of the Holy See could make the marriage valid if the consent were actually lacking (c. 1081,§1).[156] But it is admitted that the Holy See could derive this presumption from the frequent instances of clandestine marriage thus contracted in those times, and strengthen it by establishing a diriment impediment to any succeeding marriage of the parties against whom the presumption stands. This, says Freisen, was done by Alexander III and Gregory IX in the Decretals above mentioned.[157] It is very likely that the presumption arose and continued as a measure tending toward moral reform,[158] and rests on the assumption that if, in such circumstances, marital consent is not presumed, fornication must be presumed, and to this presumption of crime the Church is not easily inclined (cfr. however, n. **447**).[159]

428. The Council of Trent caused this presumptive marriage to disappear from canonical practice in all those places where the decree "Tametsi" was in force. For as soon as the Tridentine form became a requisite of the exchange of valid consent, there could be no longer any question of that consent being equivalently given by the sexual coition.[160] But there was always a very large part of the world where

[154] c. 30, X, De Spon. et Mat., IV, 1.

[155] Feije, n. 198.

[156] cfr. Freisen, p. 211; Linneborn, p. 265 (6).

[157] Freisen, pp. 209; 211. This inference is not however certain: Freisen seems even to contradict it himself on p. 29: "Auch die Entscheidung Gregor IX in c. 30, X (IV, 1), wonach die auf *sponsalia de futuro* folgende *copula* das Verhaeltnis zur Ehe mache, mit Ausschluss jedes Gegenbeweises, beruht auf einer zu starken Betonung der Ehe nach ihrer juristischen Seite."

[158] Knecht, p. 25.

[159] Feije, n. 197: That however "ecclesia praesumere **debebat** sponsos non fornicario, sed conjugali affectu se cognovisse," does not seem to be strictly correct; for the Constitution "Consensus Mutuus," Leo, 1892 shows how little the Church feels constrained to interpret the coition in that way. cfr. Gasparri, i, n. 89.

[160] cfr. De Smet, i, p. 17 (2).

the "Tametsi" was not in force, and there the presumption continued with all the effects of inevitability down to our own times.[161] It was abrogated by the Constitution of Leo XIII "Consensus Mutuus"; this Constitution not only did away with the inevitability of the presumption of consent, but no longer allowed it even as a simple legal presumption.[162]

No instance of any ecclesiastical court having derived even a personal presumption of marriage from betrothal and coition, in the interval between the "Consensus Mutuus" and the Code, has come to my notice, and the Code makes no mention of any such presumption. Nevertheless, De Smet, in writing that in the discipline of the new Code there seems to be no allowance made for presumed marriages, significantly explains in parentheses, that he means marriages presumable by inevitable presumption.[163] Evidently he supposes that the ecclesiastical court may presume the marital affection and consent to have been expressed by the sexual intercourse of betrothed persons, if there are sufficient indications to warrant this personal presumption. In practice, it will most frequently be found that mere fornication took place, without any marital consent. In no case can such a presumption be of any assistance to the judge unless neither party is held to contract marriage in form. Such is the case with non-Catholics, and in trials on the marriages of some non-Catholics the presumption may be the more readily established, if it favors the Faith (cfr. nn. **416-418**).[164]

[161] De Smet, i, n. 20.

[162] Leo, 1892: "...memoratos canones et alias quascunque iuris canonici ea de re dispositiones, etiam speciali mentione dignas, per hoc decretum nostrum abrogamus et abolemus . . . ". A superficial reading of Gasparri, i, n. 93 might lead one to believe that Gasparri held for the continuance of the simple legality of the presumption; but careful reading and comparison with the "Consensus Mutuus" will show that his assertion: "unice abrogata praesumptione juris et de jure, idest prohibitione recipiendi directam probationem contra matrimonium" is not meant to distinguish between the inevitable presumption and the simple legal presumption, but rather, between the abrogation of the presumption and the abrogation of clandestine marriages; cfr. Smith, n. 351.

[163] De Smet, i, p. 145 (2).

[164] De Smet, i, pp. 16, 17 (3) quotes Lafoucade, Etude historique des fiancailles, Bordeaux, 1902, to the effect that in Scotland and Sweden, the civil law still retains the inevitable presumption of marriage by reason of betrothal and coition.

429. *Scholion:* Under the jurisprudence of the Decretals, sexual coition following upon betrothals contracted by parents in the name of their children, and coition following upon a unilateral promise of marriage, and marriage attempted by children before puberty, were presumed to constitute an exchange of consent to "sponsalia de futuro" and thus constituted presumptive betrothal.[165] This presumption has, of course, entirely vanished since the "Ne Temere."

430. III. We next come to the question whether a marriage invalidly or not effectively entered upon, whether from want of consent, or from want of the fulfilment of a stipulation attached to the marriage contract, or by reason of some impediment which afterwards ceases, can be presumed to be validated or confirmed, when the parties have lived in marital cohabitation or have willingly entered upon sexual intercourse. Canon law has indeed established such legal presumptions of consent in this matter.

About the year 1200 Innocent III decided a case in which a soldier, derived from noble family, had been separated from the woman he married, on the ground that she was in servitude at the time of their marriage. The Pope acknowledged the justice of the decree of nullity, provided the plaintiff had not known of the servile condition of the woman at the time of the marriage, or had not, by word or deed, ratified the marriage after learning of her servitude.[166] He intimates here, that an invalid marriage may be validated, when the impediment has ceased, by the consent of the parties, expressed not alone by words but also by deeds, such as marital coition. But he does not here explicitly state that such validation is to be presumed, when the coition has taken place.

Such a presumption was stated more explicitly in 1203 by the same Innocent III in deciding a case of marriage entered upon with a stipulation pending future event. A woman had married with the explicit stipulation, imposed by her, that the marriage would hold only if her father and uncle consented. Later on, after having entered upon marital relations, the husband desired to have the marriage acknowledged void because the stipulation had not been fulfilled, and wished to prove that the relatives of the bride had not consented. But Innocent decided that since the parties had willingly entered upon

[165] cfr. c. 14, X, De Desponsat. Impub. IV, 2; c. 1, De Desponsat. Impub. IV, 2 in VI.

[166] c. 4, X, De Coniugio Servorum, IV, 9.

the marital coition after the stipulation was made, this wilful coition was tantamount to a renunciation of the stipulation, and constituted a vehement (inevitable) presumption of absolute consent and valid marriage.[167]

Again in respect to persons who were married while one of them was as yet under age, Clement III laid it down that as long as the impediment of age continued, the parties might properly be separated; but when both had attained the canonical age, and had willingly entered upon sexual intercourse together, this was to be considered a presumption that the parties had now given their maturer consent to the marriage which was until then invalid for want of age. And this presumption was inevitable, so that the parties were not to be permitted to bring proof that the coition was not accompanied by marital consent.[168] [169]

In the case of a woman who had been coerced by her foster father to marry a man she did not want, Clement III decreed that peaceful cohabitation of the parties during a year and a half constituted such evidence of the subsequent consent of the woman, that it was not to be permitted her to bring witnesses to prove that she had not consented.[170] Here likewise we have an inevitable presumption of consent given.

431. The groundwork of these presumptions is to be sought in the then acknowledged validity of clandestine marriages. A marriage which was invalid in the beginning, even by an impediment that was in fact public and by its nature public,[171] could in those times be privately validated by the mere renewal of consent, after the impediment had ceased. And so too, after the impediment had ceased, the words and conduct of the parties could give rise to a presumption that the consent of the parties had been thus privately expressed.

The inevitability of such presumptions however seems to be a severe measure; Freisen says these presumptions arose from a too

[167] c. 6, X, De Condit. Apposit., IV, 5; cfr. also c. 3, 5, ibid.; cfr. Lega, i, n. 539, 4.

[168] c. 4, X, Qui Mat. Accus. Possunt., IV, 18; cfr. also c. un., De Desponsatione Impuberum, IV, 2 in VI.; Gasparri, ii, n. 1411.

[169] In civil law, May, p. 291: "The marriage of a person under age may be ratified and made binding as from the beginning if the parties cohabit after attaining age of consent, or otherwise recognize the relation thereafter."

[170] c. 21, X, De Sponsal. et Mat., IV, 1.

[171] c. 7, X, De Desponsat. Impub., IV, 2.

strong inclination to establish presumptions in that age, from a too great preponderance of the legal side of marriage questions over the sacramental, and from the fact that the Church herself had not entirely disavowed all coercion in marriage contracts.[172]

432. The Tridentine decree ''Tametsi'' made the application of these presumptions impossible for all marriages whose invalidity was derived from a public impediment (cfr. c. 1037) in places where the decree was promulgated.[173] For wherever clandestine marriages were no longer valid, the clandestine renewal of consent could not validate a marriage that was invalid by a public impediment.[174]

433. For places not subject to the provisions of the ''Tametsi,'' these presumptions, with the full effects of their inevitability, have come down in the Canon law almost to the present time. The Instruction for Austria decreed that if a marriage were invalidly contracted because of duress, error, or abduction, the party who might contest the suit must do so at the first opportunity or consent to the marriage. If he did not contest the marriage during a period of six months or more, but rather waived the opportunity and lived in marital relations or at least in peaceful cohabitation, this fact constituted an inevitable presumption that the marriage had been validated by the party's consent.[175] The Instruction of the Propaganda repeated the same presumption, and confirmed its inevitability, for cases of marriage entered into under duress and afterward not promptly contested, but complemented by long cohabitation and willing coition.[176]

172 Freisen, pp. 209, 210, 274.

173 SCC., Mat., 17 mai. 1879, 3 feb. 1880 (ass., xii, pp. 421, 422).

174 R., Veszprimien., Null., 2 jun. 1911 (rd., iii, pp. 232, 233); Tarvisina, Null., 11 mart. 1912 (rd., iv, p. 138; aas., iv, p. 516); Vic. Ap. Nov. Pomeraniae, Null., 30 apr. 1913 (rd., v, p. 286; aas., v, p. 467); Null., 23 mart. 1914 (rd., vi, p. 151); Null., 21 mai. 1915 (rd., vii, p. 242; aas., viii, n. 51); Null., 9 aug. 1915 (rd., vii, p. 391); Parisien., Null., 11 dec. 1916 (rd., viii, p. 371; aas., ix, p. 470); Null., 5 jun. 1917 (rd., ix, p. 130; aas., x, p. 161); Bassibey, n. 179.

175 IA., §§ 116, 120. This provision of the Austrian Instruction presents a serious difficulty in as much as the form prescribed by the "Tametsi" was generally obligatory in Austria (Gasparri, ii, p. 534 ff.). Perhaps the answer to the difficulty is to be sought in the fact that the Austrian Instruction was bound up with the Concordat of 18 Aug. 1855, and implicitly effected a change in the substantive law, whereby, to the effect in question, marriages might be privately validated in Austria, even when the impediment could be publicly proved.

176 PF, 1883, § 36; similarly SO, 1883, Pars II, tit. vi, art. 3.

434. There has been a question whether the Constitution "Consensus Mutuus" annulled these presumptions of consent, as it did annul the presumption of consent derived from betrothals and coition (cfr. n. **428**). Gasparri states in one passage that they were probably annulled,[177] but in another place he says that more probably they were not annulled,[178] for the "Consensus Mutuus" in abrogating an inevitable presumption, was derogatory to the established law, and hence must be strictly interpreted, and cannot be extended to other cases than those expressly mentioned, without an authentic declaration of the competent ecclesiastical authority.[179] This opinion Chelodi calls the more common opinion.[180]

As a matter of fact the Rota has introduced the presumption into decisions dating from the period between the "Consensus Mutuus" and the Code, and has treated it as an inevitable presumption, when the trial arose from places where, and in times when the observance of neither the "Tametsi" nor the "Ne Temere" was required for validity. Thus in the C.-G. case it declared that since the "Tametsi" had never been promulgated in New York the coition willingly undertaken by the wife, after the faithlessness of Count C. was known to her, constituted an implicit renunciation of the stipulation she had made, and thus the marriage became valid in the external forum by reason of the presumed consent.[181] More often however, the Rota has found that the inevitable presumption could not be applied to a case, either because it was elided by indirect proof, for instance that the coition was not willingly conceded, and the cohabitation was not peaceful,[182] or because it was elided by the presumption of the continuance of the invalidating intimidation even during and after the coition and cohabitation (since the cause of the invalidating fear continued during that time),[183] or because the spouses themselves were admitted to testify against the presumption that the coition was undertaken with marital consent,[184] or because it seemed

[177] Gasparri, i, n. 43.

[178] Gasparri, ii, n. 990; cfr. W-Vidal, v, n. 516.

[179] Gasparri, ii, n. 990; Lega, i, n. 539, 4; Smith, n. 141.

[180] Chelodi, p. 137.

[181] R., Neo Eboracen., Null., 9 dec. 1911 (rd., iii, p. 518).

[182] R., Parisien., Null., 11 dec. 1916 (rd., viii, p. 371; aas., ix, p. 470).

[183] R., Null., 1 jul. 1912 (rd., iv, p. 322); Null., 9 aug. 1915 (rd., vii, p. 390); Null., 24 nov. 1917 (rd., ix, p. 295).

[184] R., Sueciae, Null., 19 aug. 1914 (rd., vi, p. 307; aas., vii, p. 51).

doubtful whether the "Consensus Mutuus" had abolished the presumption of revalidation and the judges preferred to adhere to the other presumption: "conditio semel posita virtualiter perseverare censetur" (cfr. nn. **474, 476**),[185] or finally because it asserted, as in a recent case from China, that it was not to be presumed that the coition was rendered with marital intent but that this must be proved.[186]

435. Meanwhile the almost universal application of the "Ne Temere" decree, requiring the marriages of Catholics to be performed with prescribed solemnities, made the presumption of renewed consent practically inoperative in the external forum for recent Catholic marriages. But marriages contracted in Germany and Hungary before the promulgation of the Code, 19 May 1918, under circumstances provided for in the decree "Provida" of 18 Jan. 1906, might be valid even though clandestine,[187] and hence the presumption of renewed consent could still be operative in such cases.

436. Now by its universal requirement of the essential form of marriage, the Code has made the presumption inoperative for the marriages of all Catholics of Latin rite, even those of Germany and Hungary entered into since 19 May 1918[188] with a public diriment impediment: for validation requires the repetition of the prescribed solemnities (c. 1135,§1). But in cases of non-Catholics or Catholics of Oriental rites not obligated by such solemnities as are required in the Code, the legal presumptions of consent and validation may be applied even when there is a public diriment impediment or when a stipulation has been publicly attached to the contract.

Even in the case of a Catholic of Latin rite who has contracted marriage with an occult impediment, validation may be effected without the solemnities of form (c. 1135,§§2,3), and in a wide or improper sense, the presumption of validation may apply in such cases to the internal forum.[189]

185 R., Null., 28 jan. 1914 (rd., vi, p. 32).

186 R., Vic. Ap. Taikon., Null., 16 jan. 1913 (rd., v, p. 61; aas., v, p. 261); cfr. Cosci, lib. I, cap. viii, n. 83: "libidinis tantum impetu propter occasionem proximam etc."; Gasparri, ii, n. 1398, and Gasparri, nov., ii, n. 1192 to the contrary: "praesumitur autem hanc haberi affectu maritali, nisi aliud probetur."

187 cfr. R., Vic. Ap. Nov. Pomeraniae, Null., 30 apr. 1913 (rd., v, p. 286; aas., v, p. 467).

188 cfr. W-Vidal, v, p. 649 (83).

189 Smith, n. 172; SCC., Mat., 17 mai. 1879, 3 feb. 1880 (ass., xii, p. 422).

437. Marital coition and cohabitation may even now beget a presumption of validation, or better said, of definite ratification, in the case of a marriage of a Catholic of Latin Rite, entered into with prescribed form, but suspended by a stipulation attached. Stipulations affixed to the marriage contract have respect either to a past or present fact, or to a future event (cfr. nn. **152, 153**). A marriage may be entered into with a stipulation respecting a past or present fact, as for instance, when a person marries under the stipulation that the other party has not had, or, be not suffering from a sexual disease. In that case the marriage is valid and effective from the beginning if the stipulation has been fulfilled, or respectively, is being fulfilled at the time of the marriage. If such a stipulation is not fulfilled at the time of the marriage, the marriage is simply invalid. And hence the subsequent renunciation of the stipulation, as indicated *e. g.* by the marital relations of the parties, has no effect upon the case,[190] even if the party who has stipulated, enters willingly upon marital relations, after learning that the stipulation was not fulfilled. Hence neither Canon law nor ecclesiastical jurisprudence has set up the presumption of validation for this case.

A marriage may be also contracted with a stipulation pending future event, and in that case, provided the stipulation is not contrary to the substance or essential properties of marriage, the marriage is contracted so as to be suspended and ineffective until the future event takes place or is renounced. When the parties have renounced a stipulation pending future event before the event, the marital consent is no longer suspended, and this sealing of the marital consent has the effect of definitely completing the marriage, just as the fulfillment of the stipulation would complete it.

In this case, though the pastor should be notified of the renunciation for purposes of record, no renewal of consent before pastor and witnesses is necessary to complete the marriage (supposing there was no diriment impediment), for the stipulation did not render the marriage invalid (cfr. c. 1136), but simply suspended the effects of contract (conditio nec vitiat m. nec. vitiatur).[191]

[190] R., Null., 18 dec. 1913 (rd., v, p. 639); Commissio Specialis Card., Versalien., 2 aug. 1918 (aas., x, p. 389).

[191] Chelodi, n. 126; De Smet, i, n. 153; Capello, iii, n. 640; W-Vidal, v, pp. 605, 606 (23); Gasparri, nov., ii, nn. 917, 919; Timlin, p. 203. Contrary: Rzewnicki, in jp., viii (1928), pp. 102, 104, wrongly arguing, as it seems, from c. 1136.

438. Proof that the marriage has been thus definitely ratified is necessary if the stipulation was affixed previous to the marriage, in such a way that it could be later proved in the external forum, and much more so, if it was affixed before pastor and witnesses in the act of entering upon the marriage. Documentary proof of this will be derived from the pastor's signed annotation in the marriage record, that the stipulation which had been attached was later renounced; and to this end the parties should notify the pastor that they have renounced the stipulation publicly affixed to the contract.

439. Proof by presumption may be derived from the words and conduct of the parties concerned, and notably from marital cohabitation and coition. Some authors hold that the Code by its silence, has withdrawn all juridical significance from the fact of coition pending event of the stipulation, and that this matter must henceforth be considered as a mere fact, upon which the judge may build his personal presumption.[192] Others are more mindful of the past jurisprudence,[193] and mention the presumption as a legal presumption.[194] More accurately it should be stated that in the stricter sense there is no legal presumption, since the Code does not mention it; but there is a legal presumption in the wider sense of the word (cfr. n. **392**).[195] The question of presumptive renunciation of a stipulation was brought up in a case arising in Paris in 1921, and the Rota there considered the application of the presumption but made no mention of its abolition through the silence of the Code.[196] Thus when it is shown that a Catholic of Latin rite, who had previously married under stipulation pending future event, has thereafter knowingly and willingly engaged in marital coition with the other party without awaiting the fulfillment of the stipulation, there is a presumption derivable from this, that he renounced the stipulation and its fulfillment and gave absolute, definite consent, whereby the marriage was completed.[197] But to this end the party must have known that the marriage was heretofore incomplete (cfr. n. **441**).[198]

192 W-Vidal, v, n. 516; Chelodi, n. 126; Haring, Grundzuege, p. 450 (2).

193 cfr. *e. g.* IA, § 54.

194 Linneborn, p. 300; aer., lxi, (1919), p. 203.

195 Capello, iii, n. 640.

196 R., Parisien., Null., 11 aug. 1921 (aas., xiv, p. 519; rd., xiii, p. 210 fol.). cfr. also Null., 18 mai. 1922 (rd., xiv, p. 160).

197 Timlin, pp. 203, 213.

198 De Smet, i, n. 156: "Quando coram tribunalibus ecclesiasticis deferuntur causae in nullitatem matrimonii, initi sub conditione, frequenter abstinet

440. It is certain that there is no longer an inevitable presumption: that the inevitability of this presumption is abolished. In the Rotal case from Paris above referred to, witnesses were admitted to prove that the wife's marital relations with her husband, could not be construed as a renunciation of the stipulation that had been attached to the marital consent.[199] Even before the Code it would be difficult to find any case tried before the reëstablished Rota, in which the presumption was so insisted on, that proof to the contrary was absolutely excluded.[200]

441. In every case where an act or succession of acts of the parties, or of one of them, is presumed to be an expression of consent given or renewed, the person who performed such act must have known that the marriage was until then invalid, or the presumption does not hold (cfr. c. 586,§1).[201] This requirement holds whether the presumption apply to the marriage of Catholics or non-Catholics.[202] Such knowledge is not generally presumable but must be proved.[203] The requirement of knowledge of invalidity does not derive from the nature of the case, for marital consent can be given or renewed even without the person's knowing that the marriage has been heretofore invalid; but rather from the positive will of the Canon law, which requires this knowledge for validation and does not establish the presumption of consent from cohabitation or coition unless the party concerned knew the marriage was theretofore invalid,[204] or suspended in its effect.

442. *Scholion:* Alexander III and Innocent III held that, when sexual coition had followed upon conditional betrothals for future

judex a nullitate declaranda, cum haud facile constet in foro externo de intentione contrahentium. Non desunt quidem sententiae nullitatem admittentes, sed saepius, si convincens habetur probatio inconsummationis matrimonii, consulitur supplicandum SSmo pro dispensatione super matrimonio rato non consummato."

[199] R., Parisien., Null., 11 aug. 1921 (aas., xiv, pp. 519, 520; rd., xiii, pp. 218, 219).

[200] cfr. DS, Ordin., nn. 65-67.

[201] R., Null., 21 dec. 1912 (rd., iv, p. 476); Vic. Ap. Nov. Pomeraniae, Null., 30 apr. 1913 (rd., v, p. 292; aas., v, p. 472); Gasparri, ii, n. 1398.

[202] R., Southwarkensis, Null., 29 jul. 1926 (aas., xviii, p. 505); cfr. Gasparri, ii, n. 1398.

[203] R., Southwarkensis, Null., 29 jul. 1926 (aas., xviii, p. 505); (cfr. n. **434**).

[204] De Smet, ii, n. 728.

marriage, it was presumptive evidence of the waiving of the stipulation to the betrothals.[205] The presumption is repeated by Haring as applicable under the Code,[206] but it can hardly have any practical application in the external forum, except in a suit for damages according to Canon 1017,§3.

443. *Scholion:* In cases of separation because of adultery, a party loses his right to disrupt the married life, if he has meanwhile condoned the adultery of the spouse (c. 1129,§1). There is a tacit condonation if the innocent party has willingly continued the married life with marital intent, after learning of the crime of adultery; and such tacit condonation is presumed, unless he has expelled, or left, or brought suit against the adulterous party within six months after learning of the adultery (c. 1129,§2).

When it is shown that the innocent party knew of the crime, during a period of six months, the presumption holds against his affirmation that he did not continue marital relations, or that it was only by reason of duress, fear, or ignorance of his right to sue for separation.[207] The presumption is however merely legal and admits proof to the contrary.[208]

444. IV. In cases of public concubinage in which the parties appear to the public as a married couple: As marriage is naturally a public relationship between the parties, the laws of cultured countries have regularly preferred to have the relationship publicly acknowledged and publicly entered upon. Nevertheless Freisen points out that Roman law not only admitted marriage without the customary exchange of dowry, but held a continued relationship with a woman "ingenua et honestae vitae" as a presumptive marriage. This presumption could however be elided by a solemn contestation declaring the woman to be only a concubine. If the relationship existed with a " liberta " or with an "ingenua" of such low standing that the man in the case could not lawfully take her to wife, the presumption stood for a mere concubinage (cfr. n. **410**).[209] In 458 A. D. however, the Emperor Majorian decreed that in order to safeguard the interests

[205] c. 3, 6, X, De Conditionibus Appositis, etc., IV, 5. The same had been stated by Tancred: cfr. Freisen, p. 237.

[206] Haring, Grundzuege, p. 429.

[207] Chelodi, n. 161.

[208] Chelodi, n. 161; W-Vidal, v, n. 639.

[209] Freisen, p. 49.

of brides, persons entering upon marriage without the customary exchange of dowry would incur the marks of infamy and that neither the union would be adjudged a marriage nor the issue legitimate.[210]

445. Thus the question of whether or not the presumption of validity, involving a presumption of consent, extends to clandestine marriages, was not entirely new to jurisprudence when it was discussed in the marriage tangle of Lothar. Pope Nicholas instructs the legates whom he sends to Lorraine as judges of the King's marriage affair, to inquire whether Lothar's pretended marriage with Waldrada had been celebrated "praemissis dotibus coram testibus secundum legem et ritum," and "per benedictionem scilicet sacerdotis." On this principle the Pope meant to come to the bottom of the evasions of Lothar; for if the marriage was celebrated in form, there was presumption of true marriage, but if the form was not observed, the presumption was rather against the marriage.[211] Similarly Pseudo-Isidor;[212] and Gratian commenting on directions given by Popes Sixtus and Victor, calls attention that such clandestine marriages are not in themselves invalid, but must be judged invalid until their validity is proved by confession, testimony, *etc.*[213] Freisen draws attention to another view of this withholding of the presumption of validity from clandestine marriages: he quotes Robert of St. Victor, writing in 1207 on the effects of public and clandestine marriages. Robert says that the children of clandestine marriages must be considered legitimate in respect to inheritance, tutelage and right of action in secular courts, but illegitimate in respect to their rights before the Church courts. For, " in clandestinis matrimoniis non est interpretandum in melius . . . ne sub tali pratextu adulterium et fornicatio commitantur."[214]

446. After the fourth Lateran Council in 1215, the publicity of marriage depended upon the publishing of the banns, and even those

[210] Nov., Maj., tit. vi, *de sancttm.*, §9 (apud Freisen, p. 50).

[211] c. 4, C. XXXI, q. 2; cfr. Freisen, pp. 136, 142.

[212] c. 1, C. XXX, q. 5: "Aliter legitimum non fit coniugium, nisi ab his, qui super . . . , et suo tempore sacerdotaliter, ut mos est, cum precibus et oblationibus a sacerdote benedicatur, . . . Ita peracta legitima scitote esse connubia; aliter vero praesumpta non coniugia, sed adulteria, vel contubernia, vel stupra, aut fornicationes potius, quam legitima coniugia esse non dubitate, nisi voluntas propria suffragaverit, et vota succurrerint legitima."

[213] c. 9, C. XXX, q. 5.

[214] Freisen, pp. 81, 147.

marriages which were performed in the presence of, and with the blessing of the priest, but were not published, were called clandestine, and there was a presumption of invalidity for marriages thus clandestinely entered upon. After the Council of Trent, which prescribed anew the publishing of the banns, but attached the character of publicity to the form of celebrating the marriage, the presumption held against validity whenever the marriage had not been entered upon in accordance with the "Tametsi."[215] Yet even in the case of the so-called surprise marriage, when the parties pronounced their consent in the presence of a surprised, unprepared and even unwilling pastor, and without the banns having been published, the influence of the presumption against marriages contracted without banns made itself felt, and such surprise marriages, when a doubt of their validity was raised, bore the presumption of invalidity.[216]

447. The basis of all this lay in the presumption that clandestine assent was directed rather to a concubinage than to a Christian marriage.[217] Sometimes this presumption of non-consent was maintained against strong evidence that the consent was genuinely marital, but we are told by Haring, that this so-called intentionalistic standpoint, whereby true consent was not at all presumable in civil marriages of Catholics, was discontinued in the Instruction of Cardinal Rampolla of 30 Aug. 1897 (akk., lxxxiv (1904), p. 160 fol.), at least with respect to mixed marriages in Hungary.[218] Since then the Roman Curia has followed the new spirit of this Instruction and we find the Rota deciding such cases of civil marriage in Germany and Hungary with less stress upon the older legal presumption of non-consent and with more effort to establish newer presumptions that arise from an intimate examination into the true state of the matter, viewed in the changed conditions of the times.[219]

448. Accordingly the authors who wrote on matrimony and procedure have regularly laid down the presumption against validity of clandestine marriages as fundamental,[220] but they inclined lately to

[215] Pallotini, xiii, p. 153, nn. 55, 56, 57.

[216] R., Ausculana in Picino, Null., 28 mai. 1909 (aas., i, p. 532; rd., i, p. 58).

[217] R., Argentinen., Null., 23 feb. 1912 (rd., iv, p. 95; aas., iv, p. 377); Null., 18 nov. 1918 (rd., x, p. 130 sq.).

[218] Haring; Grundzuege, p. 423 (3).

[219] These are considered in detail under the presumptions on consent in nn. **460, 461**.

[220] Smith, n. 461; Chelodi, nn. 7, 114; Schaefer, p. 17; V-Creusen, ii, n. 277.

an exception in favor of marriages of Catholics among themselves or with non-Catholics, entered into before a non-Catholic minister or civil officer, in a place and time, before the Code, when the observance of the form was not required for validity, if the marriage was in possession, *i. e.* if the parties were in good faith and were looked upon by all acquaintances as really married, in which case there was public repute of marital consent having been expressed by the public conduct of the parties.[221]

449. The Code has now made the adherence to the ceremony or form of contract universally necessary for validity of marriages to which at least one of the parties is a Catholic of Latin rite (c. 1099,§1), unless, in danger of death, the bishop or pastor *etc.*, shall have dispensed (cc. 1043; 1044). Even in the circumstances described in Canon 1098 it is required that the marriage be formally contracted, although the form required is less solemn than the usual form. Thus, except where there is record of dispensation having been granted in danger of death, there is now no presumption of validity for marriages of Latin Catholics that are totally informal or clandestine (cfr. n. **426**).[222]

The union of two non-Catholics clandestinely entered upon, must generally be considered a true marriage if marital intent is demonstrated; but there is no legal presumption of intent, in ecclesiastical procedure, when the marriage is entirely clandestine. If no one's rights are prejudiced the marital intent may be proved by the sworn assertions of the parties (cfr. n. **567**). But if there is question of another's rights, *e. g.* if the validity of a later contracted marriage is questioned, the marital intent must be demonstrated by public repute, *etc.* (cfr. n. **485**).

When marital intent is proved but validity is contested because the civil law has invalidated common-law marriages, the invalidating law must be proved, and it must be shown that the civil law is competent in the case by reason of the non-baptism of the parties.[223]

221 Gasparri, i, n. 18; J. Selinger in aer., lxix (Oct. 1913), p. 485; Schaefer, pp. 17 (54), 273; Chelodi, nn. 7, 114.

222 cfr. PC., 16 oct. 1919 (aas., xi, p. 479); cfr. also Chelodi, n. 7, p. 6 (7); n. 128; what seems to be contrary in Chelodi, n. 7, b), does not refer to clandestine marriage of Catholics, but rather of infidels.

223 In some states the civil law holds common-law marriages to be entirely invalid: thus in Illinois. In others, *e. g.* New Jersey, it holds them valid. In New York they were held invalid from 1 Jan. 1902 to 1 Jan. 1908, but those

If in respect to a prior clandestine marriage the marital intent is doubtful, and the subsequent marriage has not yet been contracted, the doubtful marriage is sufficient to hinder the proposed marriage only until further inquiry can be made; but if the former marriage remain doubtful, the subsequent marriage must be allowed.[224]

450. V. There is the question whether clandestine marriages, which have certainly been contracted with marital consent and are not voided by the want of form, bear the presumption for validity in respect to any other impediment which makes the marriage doubtful. If two Protestants, Schismatics or Catholics of Oriental rite who are not bound to contract in form, enter upon a clandestine marriage and this marriage is later contested because of the impediment of impotence or consanguinity or affinity, *etc.*, but it is certain that the marriage is not invalid for want of form or for any defect of consent, does the marriage bear a presumption of validity against the doubtful impediment? No case has come to my notice where the Roman Curia denied the presumption of validity after it was shown that the contract was valid as far as the expression of consent was concerned. The general presumption for validity must therefore be followed whenever the marriage cannot be contested for defect of form or defect of consent. If anyone claim that an impediment invalidates the marriage he has the burden of proving the impediment.[225]

§ 5. Presumption of Consent

451. Conformable to the presumption on the validity of legal acts, the Roman law held likewise to the validity of consent ostensibly given,[226] and the Church has held the same presumption. Thus when a marriage has been contracted in form there is a presumption that the ostensibly given consent is genuine, earnest, and conformable to

entered upon during that time were later validated by statute: N. Y. State Codified Laws: Supplement 1924, § 11 (McKinney); cfr. Tiffany, pp. 35, 37, 44. On 2 May 1933 statute provided that thenceforth common-law marriages are invalid.

[224] Gasparri, nov., i, n. 221 quotes c. 12, X, De Sponsalibus et Mat., IV, 1, but it seems that Alexander III is here writing of pre-Code affinity rather than of previous marriage bond.

[225] Gasparri, nov., i, p. 27 (1).

[226] L. 7 ff. De Supell. Legat. (Dig., 33, 10).

the external words or signs used in the marriage ceremony (c. 1086, §1). But the presumption of consent is not inevitable and must give way before a proved contrary truth (cfr. c. 1086,§2).[227] [228]

Non-consent is proved by showing that there was a cause for simulating the consent, and then by establishing a proper and logical presumption of simulation (cfr. n. **151**).[229]

If witnesses testify that a party said openly, before the marriage was contracted, that, no matter what he was about to say or do during the ceremony, he would not say or do it with the intention of contracting marriage, the gloss to the Chapter "Tua Nos"[230] denied that this constitutes sufficient proof to overcome the presumption of true consent, and held that the judge must pronounce for validity.[231] The Congregation of the Council decided accordingly in a case,[232] and the Rota took note of the principle in a recent case from Oregon.[233] But Gasparri says this is too severe a rule for universal application, and that the reasoning of Sanchez, allowing the protestation in advance of the marriage as proof of non-consent, at least in cases where the other party was made aware of the protestation and consented to it, is better.[234] And in fact the Congregation of the Council goes further and says that non-consent is effectively proved when the party protests, even immediately after the ceremony, that he has feigned consent, and carries out his protest by deeds that are incompatible

[227] Gasparri, ii, n. 915; Linneborn, p. 283.

[228] Our civil law inclines to an inevitable presumption of consent, and to make a person "chargeable with the natural consequences of his acts, whether he intended them or not"; cfr. McKelvey, p. 106.

[229] Cosci, lib. I, cap. viii, nn. 99, 100: "coniecturae et praesumptiones . . . simulationem concludentes, leviores et duae tantum sufficiunt."

[230] c. 26, X, De Sponsalibus et Matrimonio, IV, 1.

[231] "Talia enim verba non possunt servire suae intentioni: praeterea si probet, quod illa verba protestatus fuit primo, potuit postea recedere ab illa voluntate, et consentire in illam, et hoc videtur per illud quod postea publice fecit: et si dicat quod adhuc tempore contractus erat in eadem voluntate non creditur ei, quia contra eum fieri debet interpretatio, qui dolum adhibet . . . "

[232] SCC., 17 aug. 1606 (pall., xii, p. 453, § II, n. 32).

[233] R., Oregonopol., Null., 6 jul. 1914 (rd., vi, pp. 245, 246; aas., vi, p. 517): "Etsi non nimis rigorose applicanda sit haec glossae regula, ut videantur excludi etiam probationes moralem certitudinem gignentes, tamen praesumptiones iuris et favor quo gaudet matrimonium dictant consensum matrimonialem, semel rite expressum, esse verum non simulatum."; (cfr. n. **423**).

[234] Gasparri, ii, n. 915..

with the having given true marital consent, such as the leaving the pretended spouse and contracting a new marriage.[235] And the decisions of the Rota have constantly taken the circumstances surrounding the marriage ceremony into consideration when the presumption of consent is contested. Among such circumstances immediate flight of one of the parties gives ground for a strong presumption of non-consent; but when the flight is not immediate after the ceremony, but is rather delayed for a longer time, the presumption of non-consent is not established.[236] [236a]

When it is shown that a party to the marriage viewed the forthcoming ceremony with contempt, horror, aversion and unwillingness, this is a strong foundation for the presumption that the same sentiments actuated the party during the ceremony and that the consent apparently given was but feigned.[237]

452. When there is question of marriage contracted in a jest, the jest is not to be presumed; but when it is shown that the ceremony of marriage was entered upon by parties who by every external appearance were but perpetrating a jest, the presumption of true consent is overcome.[238] The now universally required form of marriage almost entirely precludes such jest marriages among Catholics, and the ecclesiastical judge rarely encounters them. Nevertheless the Curia of X. recently tried such a case.

[235] SCC., Chien., Mat., 12 mart. 1729 (capello, iii, n. 594; pall., xii, p. 493, n. 90): "Ista enim consensus ficti citissima manifestatio, . . . demonstrare dicetur suum fictum consensum, cum praesumendum non sit, si vere consensisset, tam cito se poenitere, . . . " (not in cicf., v, n. 3344).

[236] R., Null., 29 feb. 1916 (rd., viii, p. 58); Colonien., Null., 1 jul. 1912 (rd., iv, p. 333; aas., iv, p. 674).

[236a] In civil law likewise, cohabitation and reputation as husband and wife beget the presumption of marital consent and common law marriage: Abbott, p. 101; May, p. 297.

[237] R., Vic. Ap. Ce-Li Centr., Null., 10 feb. 1917 (rd., ix, p. 29; aas., ix, p. 508): "Haec mutatio voluntatis esset probanda: neque praesumi potest ex eo, quod puella ecclesiam ingressa confessarium libere adiverit; nam haec duo, voluntaria peccatorum confessio et subsequens matrimonii celebratio non sunt adeo inter se connexa, ut si primum ponatur cum plena voluntate, alterum etiam dici debeat libere positum."; cfr. SCC., Mutinen., 19 aug. 1724; 9 jun. 1725 (cicf., v, nn. 3282; 3299).

[238] Pallotini, xii, p. 472, n. 20: ". . . ut enim admittatur fictio, necesse est revera, ut argumenta indubitata et clarissima adsint indicia, sed non item pro ioco, sicut lucide probat Reiffenstuellius in lib. 4 Decret. tom 5 de spons . . ."

453. In questions pertaining to betrothal the same presumption holds: the betrothed are presumed to have truly consented to the betrothal whenever they have become parties to the written promise of marriage delineated in Canon 1017.[239] And thus too, when information is brought to a pastor concerning the lack of consent on the part of a person about to contract marriage, if after serious investigation a doubt remains whether the party in question is prepared to give genuine consent to the forthcoming marriage, the presumption stands for the genuineness of the forthcoming consent and marriage.[240]

454. Similarly if a promise is made before marriage in fulfillment of a stipulation to the marriage, it is presumed that the promise is seriously made. A Catholic lady of Paris was asked to marry a man who had been baptized Catholic, but who had become a bitter Atheist. She consented only on condition that he would promise to allow her the freedom of her religion and the Catholic baptism and education of her children. He appeared to promise, but it was soon plain that he did not intend to carry out the promise. When the lady contended that the promise was feigned the Rota held that the presumption lay in favor of the sincerity of the promise given, but that such presumption was superseded in the case, by the proofs taken from his conduct before, during, and after the marriage.[241]

The same presumption for the genuineness of a promise holds in the case of a non-Catholic who promises freedom to the Catholic party and Catholic education of the children,[242] as a condition to obtaining a dispensation from disparity of cult; and the same proofs are admissible to destroy the presumption.

455. The presumption of marital consent conformable to the words used in celebrating the marriage (c. 1086,§1), holds also when the party knows or believes that the marriage is invalid because of a diriment impediment of ecclesiastical law.[243] Thus marital consent is *per se* presumable even when Catholic persons attempt marriage before a judge or minister (cfr. nn. **447, 460, 461**). This presumption, of course, admits proof to the contrary; and among the proofs

[239] Cerato, p. 25.

[240] R., Impedimenti ad Mat., 22 jan. 1911 (rd., iii, p. 35).

[241] R., Parisien., Null., 11 aug. 1921 (aas., xiv, p. 520; rd., xiii, p. 219).

[242] On the excommunication that awaits a Catholic who marries with stipulation to bring up progeny outside the Church, cfr. c. 2319, § 1, n. 2.

[243] Gasparri, ii, n. 906.

to the contrary personal presumptions or conjectures may be numbered. For when it is proved that a party had the knowledge or opinion of the nullity of a marriage he was contracting, there may arise a suspicion that he did not intend a true marriage, even though true marital consent be compatible with the knowledge of the existence of an impediment (c. 1085), and this suspicion or conjecture increases or diminishes in value according to the circumstances of the case.[244]

The same presumption applies to a case where a party is of the opinion that he is impotent. If it appears after his marriage that he is not really impotent, the opinion of impotence and invalidity does not hinder the presumption that true marital consent was given (c. 1085).[245] [246]

456. If a party has not really given genuine consent, no presumption of consent in the external forum can affect the forum of his conscience. But if the party is in doubt whether his consent was genuine or not, it is presumably a true consent. The conscience of the husband or wife of the doubtfully consenting party, must generally follow the presumption established in the external forum, until there is moral certainty to the contrary.[247] Gasparri, quoting St. Alphonse, gives the rule that one spouse is not obliged to believe the other asserting even under oath, that he did not consent to the marriage, unless the circumstances make the assertion morally certain.[248]

457. The internal consent is presumably conformable to the words used in the marriage ceremony (c. 1086,§1), but if no words are used, and the party thus remaining silent can speak, there is no presumption of consent. Under the Decretals the silence of a party might be viewed as an indication of consent,[249] although even then, there was no presumption of consent unless positive signs of consent were given.[250] But the use of words, though they are the most com-

[244] Gasparri, ii, n. 906.

[245] cfr. Lehmkuhl, ii, n. 972.

[246] In civil law, Abbott, p. 106: "Marriage may be presumed, where cohabitation under circumstances that would have been matrimonial but for the impediment of an existing marriage of one of the parties, is continued after that impediment is removed and known to the parties to be so removed."

[247] Cerato, p. 146.

[248] Gasparri, ii, n. 1300.

[249] Reg. Iur. xliii in VI.

[250] Gasparri, ii, n. 964.

mon means of expressing consent, was not required.[251] The Code now requires that the consent be expressed in words, nor may those who can speak use other equivalent signs (c. 1088,§2). And thus when a party keeps silence during the marriage ceremony there is, in case of true doubt, presumptive dissent rather than a presumption of consent,[252] and the marriage is presumably invalid.

But this applies only to those who are bound by the Code to express their consent in words. Non-Catholics may express consent by the signs or acts customary to them, and their consent so expressed, is presumed to be genuine as long as there are no sufficient positive reasons for concluding the contrary.[253]

458. The legal favor accorded the Faith is one of the sufficient reasons for concluding that there was no marital consent, whenever the intention of the infidel parties otherwise remains doubtful. In two instructions the Holy Office directed that the oath of an infidel affirming that he had no marital intent when he took his infidel consort was to be decisive to the court, although such oath cannot constitute full proof of non-intent when the parties are Christians. (cfr. nn. **561, 562**). The presumption that he speaks the truth when he asserts his non-consent, is here accorded the infidel party as a means of promoting his conversion to the Faith (cfr. n. **418**).

459. *Scholion:* Boniface VIII states the presumption that, when parents contract betrothals for their children not yet attained to puberty, and the children, knowing this, do not contradict, the silence indicates consent.[254] Canonists have generally repeated the presumption up to the time of the "Ne Temere." But the provisions of that Decree and of the Code, requiring that engagements to marry be entered upon in form in order to have juridical effect, cause this presumption to vanish.[255]

460. The earlier jurisprudence denied the presumption of marital consent in the case of a Catholic entering upon a so-called civil marriage; more recently however, the presumption of non-con-

[251] Schaefer, p. 232.

[252] Chelodi, n. 121; Cerato, p. 152.

[253] In civil law, Abbott, pp. 102, 103: "From the fact of solemnization assent is presumed even though it was not expressed."

[254] c. un., De Desponsatione Impuberum, IV, 2, in VI.

[255] Schaefer, pp. 35, 36; De Smet, i, n. 13.

sent has been less rigorously applied (cfr. nn. **447-449**). The matter is especially pertinent to some mixed marriages contracted in Germany and Hungary before 19 May 1918,[256] or in other parts not subject to the "Tametsi," before the "Ne Temere" went into effect on 19 April 1908, and the Rota has recently adjudged a number of such cases in which the decision hangs upon the presumption that is to be given to the consent of a Catholic party to a mixed marriage performed before a civil magistrate. Is it to be presumed that the consent thus given was real marital consent? The Rota establishes the presumption that, because of the pastoral letters of the German bishops and the catechetical instruction everywhere given, teaching that civil marriage is but a mere ceremony, well instructed, practical Catholics of Germany are not presumed to have given genuine marital consent when they contract before a civil magistrate, but are rather presumed to intend a mere civil ceremony, until positive evidence or the stress of circumstances causes the presumption to be superseded.[257] Some difficulty is caused to this principle by the letter of the Congregation of the Inquisition written to the Archbishop of Cologne, 2 July 1892, but the Rotal decision in the case of Strassburg solves the difficulty.[258]

If however the marriage was contracted by Catholics who were not practical in their religious duties, who were addicted to forbidden societies, or who were ignorant of the requirement of the Church that they be married before a priest, the presumption favors the sincerity of their consent to true marriage (cfr. n. **447**).[259]

461. The presumption that genuine marital consent is not given by practical Catholics who enter upon a merely civil ceremony holds for marriages thus entered upon in Germany, because of the circumstance that well instructed, practicing Catholics of that country have generally looked upon civil marriage as a mere civil ceremony, rather

[256] cfr. Prov, 1906.

[257] R., Argentinen., Null., 23 feb. 1912 (rd., iv, pp. 105, 106; aas., iv, p. 387); Argentinen., Null., 22 jul. 1912 (rd., iv, pp. 377, 380); Null., 19 mai. 1910 (rd., ii, p. 159); Argentinen., Null., 18 nov. 1918 (rd., x, p. 131; aas., xi, p. 359); Linneborn, p. 37.

[258] R., Argentinen., Null., 18 nov. 1918 (rd., x, pp. 131, 132; aas., xi, p. 361); cfr. however, Null., 19 mai. 1910 (rd., ii, pp. 160, 162).

[259] R., Null., 19 mai. 1910 (rd., ii, p. 159); Colonien., Null., 10 jun. 1912 (rd., iv, p. 293; aas., iv, pp. 632, 633); Argentinen., Null., 22 jul. 1912 (rd., iv, p. 377).

than as a true marriage. Hence the presumption against such consent does not hold if the civil marriage was contracted in a country where Catholics looked upon civil marriage as a true, even though illicit marriage. Thus in a case from Hungary the Rota adhered to the presumption of validity of a mixed marriage performed before a minister of the Reformed Church.[260] And of course, there can be question of a presumption against marital consent for those marriages which took place in America before the "Ne Temere" came into force, only in an exceptional case,[261] or in those dioceses where the "Tametsi" had held sway.[262]

Non-Catholics who contract marriage are presumed, on their part, to have genuine marital consent whenever they contract marriage according to the civil laws, among themselves,[263] or with Catholics.

462. When it is shown that marital consent was given, such consent is presumed to be enduring, unless the contrary is proved (c. 1093).

This matter is pertinent to a marriage contracted by proxy, in a case where it is afterward claimed that the consent to marry was withdrawn by the principal before his proxy had effected the exchange of agreement to the marriage contract (cfr. c. 1089,§3). It has been the constant practice of the Congregation of the Council in such cases to pronounce the marriage valid, unless the party can prove, apart from his own assertion, that he had revoked his consent before the marriage was contracted by his proxy.[264]

Similarly when a marriage is entered upon invalidly because of a diriment impediment, the endurance of marital consent once given, is presumed until it is plain that the consent has been revoked (c.

[260] R., Null., 22 jan. 1914 (rd., vi, p. 9).

[261] R., Philadelphien., Null., 9 feb. 1920; 16 jul. 1921 (rd., xii, p. 30; xiii, pp. 175, 176).

[262] R., Null., 2 mart. 1914 (rd., vi, p. 91).

[263] Linneborn, p. 37; J. Elliot Ross, in hpr., xxxi, (Nov. 1930), p. 128, makes a plea for the establishment of a presumption against consent to indissoluble marriage on the part of non-Catholics who contract civil marriage. There is no likelihood of a legal presumption of this kind being established (cfr. nn. **415, 472**). But if the circumstances and indications point sufficiently to lack of consent, the judge may draw his own inference.

[264] SCC., Florentina, Mat., 29 jul. 1854 (pall., xiii, p. 428); In Eugubina, seu Perusina, Mat., 5 jul. 1727 (gasp., ii, n. 973); Oveten., Mat., 22 jun. 1894 (ass., xxviii, p. 338).

1093). When the diriment impediment ceases to exist, under circumstances that may permit the validation of the marriage without a renewal of consent in the public form (cfr. nn. **431-436**), the existence or rather continuance of marital consent is thus presumed,[265] with regard to the validation of the marriage. So too when there is question of correction at the root.[266] [267]

In Canon law the consent is not so rigidly presumed to endure, when there has been no formal marriage ceremony. Thus if there is brought to court a case wherein two non-Catholics, to whom valid clandestine marriage is possible, have lived in concubinage, and one of them proposed marital consent to the other, but was not then accepted nor for a long time afterward, and it is claimed that after such a long interval the other party did finally give consent, the judge will not decide that a marriage has been established, even though the concubinage was continued, if the first party assert that he had meanwhile revoked his consent. For if one party tender his consent to the marriage and the other does not accept it and give reciprocal consent at once or within a short time, the presumption stands for the revoking of consent on the part of the first party. But if the first party had given the other a term for consideration, or if other facts point to the continuance of his marital consent, the presumption of revocation of consent is overcome.[268]

463. Marriage is effected by the expression of consent of parties who are capable of giving consent (c. 1081,§1). This capability springs from nature and law, and consists in the first place in the

[265] Schaefer, p. 230 (27).

[266] Schaefer, p. 230 (27); Capello, iii, n. 853; Chelodi, n. 168: "Imo non censetur revocatus etiamsi coniuges in *discordia* vivant et parati discedere si matrimonium irritum cognoscerent, aut licet *separationem* instituerint a toro et mensa, aut declarationem nullitatis postulaverint adhuc lite pendente.";—It should be noted however, that the suit for separation or declaration of nullity may be the basis of a violent personal presumption that marital consent no longer exists. For this reason the Holy See does not grant correction at root in such cases.

[267] Similarly in civil law, N. Y. S. Codified Laws (McKinney), Supplement, 1924: "Where in an action to annul a marriage on the ground that at the time it was entered into defendant was married to another man, it appears that plaintiff had lived with and acknowledged the defendant as his wife for 14 years after the death of her first husband . . . it will not be held that plaintiff was never in fact defendant's husband . . . they were husband and wife by reason of a common law marriage."

[268] Gasparri, ii, n. 876; Chelodi, n. 108.

use of reason. The child who has not attained to puberty nor reached the age of seven, is presumed not yet to have the use of reason; but when the seventh year is passed the use of reason is presumed (c. 88,§3). Hence adolescents and adults are generally presumed to have the use of reason and the claim of insanity must be strictly proved.[269] [270] Hence if there be a doubt of the sanity of a person about to contract marriage, the marriage will be impeded for a time in order to settle the doubt, but if the doubt remain, the presumption will favor the parties and the licitness of the marriage.[271] In proving insanity not only natural, but artificial proofs are admissible, and in a recent case that arose in China, the Rota derived a personal presumption of insanity from the fact that five of the relatives of the party's mother were known to have been insane.[272]

464. If after natural and artificial proofs on the question of sanity have been considered, it be still doubtful whether the now insane party was sane at the time of the marriage, the presumption stands in favor of sanity as long as it is not proved that he had been at some time insane before the marriage was contracted,[273] or was insane immediately after it.[274] [274a]

465. If the person is shown to have been insane at some time before the marriage was contracted, but it has not been shown that he thereafter enjoyed lucid intervals, it is presumed that the insanity endured.[275] If he had been insane at some time before the marriage,

[269] R., Matrimonii, 13 feb. 1913 (rd., v, pp. 144, 145).

[270] N. Y. S. Codified Laws, Art. 2, § 7, III: "In accordance with the general rule that every man is presumed sane until the contrary is proved, where a marriage is sought to be annulled on the ground of the mental incapacity of a party thereto, such party is presumed to have been of sufficient understanding, and the decree of annulment will not be granted until that presumption has been overthrown by proof clear and satisfactory."; cfr. McKelvey, p. 101 fol.

[271] cfr. Bouix, i, n. 331, Reg. 4.

[272] R., Ton-Kin Central., Null., 27 jun. 1916 (rd., viii, p. 209; aas., ix, p. 248).

[273] R., Mat., 13 feb. 1913 (rd., v, pp. 144, 145); Null., 11 aug. 1913 (rd., v, p. 570).

[274] Linneborn, p. 270.

[274a] In civil law, May, p. 294: "Findings of an inquisition in lunacy are only presumptive evidence of previous incapacity."

[275] R., Mat., 13 feb. 1913 (rd., v, p. 144): "Quando autem constat dementia aliquem fuisse affectum, nec constat consuevisse habere dilucida intervalla, praesumitur adhuc demens. Quod tamen procedit si probatum fuerit furorem durasse quodam continuo tempore, ut anno vel mense; secus si probatur in aliquibus actibus furiosum fuisse, non enim praesumitur permanere furorem."

but the insanity has afterward permanently left him, and it is doubted whether he was sane or insane at the time the marriage was contracted, the presumption holds for sanity if the marriage was contracted a long while after the known spell of insanity; but militates against sanity if the marriage was entered upon shortly after the time when the party was known to be insane.[276] If he is shown to have been insane at some time before marriage and again after marriage, there may be question whether the marriage was performed during one of those periods that are commonly called "lucid intervals." Now this term is used to denote either the complete, even though but temporary, cure of insanity, or it denotes the mere lessening of insanity to such a degree that the disease, though still present, is outwardly quite imperceptible. If it is doubted whether at the time of the marriage, the person in question was really cured temporarily, so that he could validly marry, or rather labored under a hidden spell of insanity, the presumption holds the lucid interval to have been a mere lessening, rather than a cure, for the disease is of its nature enduring,[277] and this is all the more to be maintained since modern medical opinion tends to view all such lucid intervals as the mere screening of a latent insanity, and modern civil laws do not generally hold contracts valid, when entered upon during such intervals.[278]

466. It is required for marital consent that the contracting parties be at least not ignorant that marriage is a permanent union of a man and woman for the purpose of begetting children (c. 1082, §1). Knowledge of this is generally given by nature at about the age of puberty. Taking this fact as the presumptive basis of law, the Romans required the age of fourteen or twelve years respectively for the valid marriage of a young man or woman, and did not allow argument to prove that anyone had reached the proper fitness before the required age.[279] The early Canon law adopted the same age limit and established an impediment, based on the presumption that before

[276] R., Mat., 13 feb. 1913 (rd., v, pp. 144, 145).

[277] SCC., Argentinen., 23 nov. 1907 (cicf., vi, n. 4343); R., Null., 10 jul. 1909 (rd., i, p. 92); Null., 23 dec. 1909 (rd., i, p. 168); Mat., 13 feb. 1913 (rd., v, pp. 144, 145); Null., 11 aug. 1913 (rd., v, p. 565); Buscoducen., Null., 15 mai. 1915 (rd., vii, p. 218; aas., vii, p. 575); Ton-Kin Central., Null., 27 jun. 1916 (rd., viii, p. 209; aas., ix, p. 248); Quebecen., Null., 23 dec. 1918 (rd., x, p. 143; aas., xii, p. 339).

[278] Gasparri, nov., ii, n. 785.

[279] Freisen, p. 328; Gasparri, nov., i, n. 489.

these ages, the qualities of puberty, actual potency, necessary knowledge, and, above all, maturer discretion would be absent, and Canon 1082,§2 evidently implies this presumption that the necessary knowledge is wanting to those who have not reached puberty.[280] However, the Canon law did not follow the Roman law in the inevitability of this presumption, as is shown from the constant earlier practice of the Church in considering those as validly married, in whom precocity supplied for age (malitia supplebat aetatem).[281]

Under the pretension of supplementary precocity no one was allowed to contract marriage before the required age, without a previous declaration of the bishop that the parties had attained to the required qualities. But there are only a few instances on record of such declaration having been made in advance of the marriage. More frequently the marriage was illicitely contracted, and the proof that precocity supplied for age, came afterward. Formerly only natural proofs were admitted, and no presumption of fitness for marriage was allowed to have weight.[282] But lately the Holy Office held for the validity of the marriage until both the non-age and the lack of precocity should be proved.[283]

467. Now the Code, in seeking to have marriage contracted only with maturer discretion (cfr. c. 1067,§2), has returned to an absolute minimum age-standard, and bases the impediment of non-age upon the simple fact of non-attainment of the required age of sixteen or fourteen years (c. 1067,§1). The impediment is no longer based on a presumption that before the required age is attained, the proper puberty, potency and knowledge are wanting. Hence in nullity suits on the impediment of non-age, the presumption will be in favor of validity, until it is proved that one of the baptized parties had not attained the canonical age at the time of the marriage.

468. For persons who have reached puberty, sufficient knowledge for valid marriage has always been presumed,[284] and the pre-

[280] Cfr., R., Null., vel Disp. Mat., 27 apr. 1915 (rd., vii, p. 210); Linneborn, p. 269; V-Creusen, ii, n. 369.

[281] c. 8, 9, X, De Desponsat. Impuberum, IV, 2; Freisen, p. 327; Chelodi, n. 68; Haring: Grundzuege, p. 477.

[282] SCC., In Theatina, Matrimonii, 16 mart. 1771, § Defuisse (pall., xii, p. 538); Smith, n. 213.

[283] SO., Africae, 18 mart. 1903 (cicf., iv, n. 1264; cpf., ii, n. 2165).

[284] R., Null., 17 mart. 1910 (rd., ii, p. 120); Null., 14 nov. 1919 (rd., xi, p. 173); Gasparri, ii, n. 901; Smith, n. 111.

sumption of ignorance where knowledge is not proved,[285] was never applied in this matter. The Code states: ignorance that marriage is a permanent union of a man and woman for the purpose of begetting children is not presumed after puberty is attained (c. 1082,§2).

This presumption however is merely legal, and proof may be brought to show that a party even of mature age, did not have the required knowledge.[286] It is however difficult conclusively to bring such proof, and cases of nullity hinging on this matter frequently meet with an adverse decision.

469. *Scholion:* Under the Decretals there was a presumption whereby children, not attained to puberty and in whom there was no supplementing precocity, having invalidly contracted marriage, were presumed by reason of this invalid contract, to have entered upon valid betrothals of future marriage.[287] This presumption is now devoid of any practical value.

470. In case it is claimed that the marriage was celebrated by virtue of an error regarding the identity of the spouse (cfr. cc. 47; 104; 1083; 1092, n. 4), the presumption generally stands against the error. Innocent III answering the Bishop of Gebenna nicely discerned between an error in the name of the person and an error in the person himself, and laid it down that even when an error in the name was proved, the presumption held for consent to marry that person,[288] especially if the marriage was arranged between the persons themselves rather than by proxy. This presumption however may be overcome by facts shown to be contrary, as in the case of a blind Chinese who arranged by proxy to marry a certain "Mary," unknown to him, but described by that name, and to whom another woman impersonating this Mary, was later brought for marriage.[289]

When the marriage is contested as having been contracted by virtue of an error regarding a quality that redounds to error in identity, this must be proved, and the presumption generally is that the

[285] Reg. iur., xlvii in VI.

[286] R., Vic. Ap. Chanci Merid., Null., 14 nov. 1919 (rd., xi, p. 173; aas., xiii, p. 56).

[287] cfr. c. 14, X, De Desponsat. Imp., IV, 2; c. un., De Desponsat. Imp., IV, 2 in VI.

[288] c. 26, X, De Spons. et Mat., IV, 1.

[289] R., Ce-Li Meridio-Occident., Null., 16 apr. 1913 (rd., v, p. 242 fol.); Gasparri, ii, nn. 889, 890; Smith, n. 126.

error respected merely a quality of the spouse, not his identity, even though perhaps, it offered the motive for the marriage.[290]

471. In suits for declaration of nullity by reason of an error regarding the servile condition of the spouse (c. 1083,§2,n.2), it must be shown that the plaintiff was free at the time of the marriage and the respondent was a slave properly so called. When these facts are proved, the existence of the error is presumed,[291] for the marriage of a freeman with a slave is so strained a condition of affairs, that it is easier to suppose that the party did not know of the other's slavery than to suppose that he knowingly married a slave. This holds only however, for the case where the slavery of the respondent was not commonly known, and as long as the contrary is not proved. But if the slavery of the respondent was generally known, the presumption stands against the existence of an error in this respect on the part of the plaintiff (c. 16,§2).[292]

472. The presumption favoring the validity of the consent given holds against the assertion of a party that the consent was invalid because of restrictions affecting the substance or essential properties of marriage. If it is claimed that there was an intent against or stipulation affixed contrary to unity, indissolubility, or issue, on the part of one or both of the parties, the presumption is against this claim, and the parties are presumed to have accepted the obligations with the marriage.[293] For an intent or stipulation of that kind is a positive act of the will, which is not to be presumed but must be proved like other facts. And generally it will be found that there was but a simple error in the mind of the party regarding these basic qualities of marriage, which even though it be the motivating cause of the contract, does not vitiate the matrimonial consent (c. 1084).[294] Thus the Church has constantly held for the validity of the marriages of infidels, Greek Orthodox schismatics, Calvinists and so on, in the

[290] Gasparri, ii, n. 893: ". . . si e contrario, Titius tractat de matrimonio ineundo cum filia regis ignota, et tandem Mariam ducit sive absentem, e. g. per procuratorem, sive praesentem, putans esse regis filiam, praesumitur error qualitatis redundans in errorem personae."

[291] Freisen, p. 295.

[292] Feije, n. 123 (4): The advice of Clericatus here given, to place the burden of proof upon both parties, may be allowable as a matter of procedure in taking the evidence, but is not enlightening as to its appraisal.

[293] R., Null., 7 feb. 1914 (rd., vi, p. 59); Gasparri, nn. 903, 920.

[294] cfr. R., Neo-Eboracen., Null., 8 feb. 1915 (rd., vii, pp. 23, 24, 28).

face of their error regarding the dissolubility of marriage, unless the contrary intent of the will is proved by a stipulation openly affixed,[295] or by the wording of the marriage rite, *etc.*

When it is shown that there was some irregularity to the consent of the party with respect to the basic obligations of unity and issue, but it remains doubtful whether this irregularity consisted in a positive intent of not obliging oneself to them, or whether it consisted in an intent of merely not fulfilling the obligation incurred, the presumption stands for the party's having taken the obligation with the intention of not fulfilling it.[296] This presumption is very difficult to overcome, but it is not inevitable and proof to the contrary is admissible, but must be strictly conclusive (cfr. n. **413**).[297]

Such conclusive proof is had if it is shown that a party to the marriage made the declining of one of these basic obligations a stipulation, either by formally appending it to the marriage contract,[298] or by agreement with the other spouse, in such terms that its import cannot be mistaken.[299] Such conclusive proof is also had if it is shown that one of the parties plainly asserted before the contract was entered upon, his intention not to take upon himself any one of the essential obligations of marriage.[300]

473. Such conclusive proof is had also by presumption in some cases. Thus when one or both parties are shown to have excluded all future progeny from their intent, the presumption is that their consent was so restricted as to exclude the basic obligation of a union whose purpose is progeny. But if a party limits in his intent the

295 Gasparri, ii, nn. 902, 903.

296 R., Null., 17 jan. 1912 (rd., iv, p. 50); Null., 10 dec. 1914 (rd., vi, p. 346); Null., 15 dec. 1915 (rd., vii, p. 461); Null., 31 oct. 1919 (rd., xi, p. 146).—The distinction between the obligation and its fulfillment is not admitted with regard to the indissolubility of the marriage: cfr. R., Neo-Eboracen., 8 feb. 1915 (rd., vii, p. 22); Null., 29 apr. 1922 (rd., xiv, p. 124).

297 R., Null., 17 jan. 1912 (rd., iv, p. 50): "Quapropter . . . invaluit in Ecclesia praxis habendi generatim matrimonia ut invalida, quando praefata conditio turpis in pactum deducta est; ut valida vero, quoties in pactum non fuerit deducta. Quae tamen praxis, cum nitatur sola praesumptione, non obstat quominus haberi possit matrimonium nullum ex intentione substantiae matrimonii contraria, etiam in pactum non deducta, quando concludentissime demonstretur."; Null., 10 dec. 1914 (rd., vi, p. 346).

298 V-Creusen, ii, n. 381.

299 R., Null., 29 apr. 1922 (rd., xiv, p. 123); Null., 5 jul. 1923 (rd., xv, p. 144).

300 R., Paderbornen., Null., 27 jul. 1917 (rd., ix, p. 163; aas., x, p. 217).

number of children he is going to have, or the period of time during which he is going to beget children, the presumption is that he intended to accept the marital obligation, but at the same time intended to violate it, at times.[301]

Similarly there is a presumption of marital consent being vitiated by a will to soluble marriage, if parties commit themselves, *e. g.* by notary's document, to an arrangement for division of goods or dowry in case of divorce; for they show their intent to contract a marriage that is dissoluble by divorce, and their reservation of a right to divorce their marriage.[302]

Furthermore the Holy Office in an Instruction to the Bishop of Nesqually (now Seattle) says a presumption that some heretical marriages are entered into with the intention of not obliging the parties to indissoluble marriage, may properly be derived from the examination of the rituals of the sects, some of which explictly protest in the marriage ceremony, that the bond is dissoluble in case of the adultery of one of the parties.[303]

474. When an intention or a stipulation contrary to the substance of marriage is shown to have been formulated, the presumption holds that such intention or stipulation was not withdrawn, unless its withdrawal be proved.[304] The withdrawal of such a stipulation against the substance of marriage is presumed whenever the stipulation has been proposed by one party but stoutly contradicted by the other, and the marriage was thus entered upon without more to do

[301] Rzewnicki in jp., viii (1928), p. 102.

[302] Pellegrini, in jp., x (1930), p. 58; cfr. ime., lxiii (1931), p. 75; V-Creusen, ii, n. 374 hold that even in this case nothing is proved beyond an intention to violate the moral duty assumed. However, the distinction between the obligation and its fulfillment is not possibly applied to indissolubility.

[303] SO, Nesquallien., § 3: "Similiter considerandae, et etiam examinandae erunt formulae, quibus in istis regionibus uti solent haeretici dum ritum nuptialem exercent. Etenim illae haereticorum formulae in quibus inserta inveniuntur ea SS. Scripturarum testimonia, quibus iidem haeretici abutuntur ad proprium errorem tuendum et propugnandum de dissolubilitate vinculi coniugalis: qualia sunt illud, quod habetur apud S. Matthaeum 19, 9 ...... interdum merito censentur conditionem irritantem continere."; cfr. SO., 20 mai. 1754; 22 jul. 1840 (cicf., iv, n. 883; cpf., i, n. 903); 6 apr. 1843 ad Vic. Ap. Oceaneae (cicf., iv, n. 894; cpf., i, n. 965).

[304] R., Paderbornen., Null., 27 jul. 1917 (rd., ix, p. 162; aas., x, p. 216); Westmonasterien., Null., 11 apr. 1927 (aas., xix, p. 224).

about it.[305] Some authors, according to Gasparri, contend that even the silence of the second party to the proposed stipulation constitutes a presumption of the stipulation having been withdrawn, a conclusion which however Chelodi rightly denies.[306]

475. A stipulation affixed to the marriage contract respecting a necessary, impossible, or shameful future event, but not directed against the substance of marriage, is held not to have been affixed (c. 1092,n.1). The Church supposes in favor of marriage, that no one means thus to condition so sacred a contract, and that if mention of such future shameful, impossible, or necessary event be made, it is jestingly, not seriously done,[307] or at least, that the qualifying of the consent is rather a representation than true stipulation.[308]

Gregory IX had established the same presumption with explicit mention of the impossible and shameful contingencies,[309] but the Code has found it equally pertinent to include the stipulation of necessary contingencies. There was some discussion among authors, whether the presumption held with respect to a stipulation regarding a past shameful event, as for instance, if a party gave his marital consent with the stipulation: "if you did commit murder, I marry you," and some authors maintained that since the Decretal of Gregory made no distinction between stipulations looking to the future and those looking to the present or past, the presumption pertained to all such stipulations. But it must be remembered that Gregory, without making a formal distinction, really instanced only future events, and De Becker called attention to the fact that this presumption of Gregory was quite extraordinary and was therefore to be restricted to those stipulations which alone could be called stipulations in a strict sense, namely those respecting the future.[310]

The Code has upheld this view and states the presumption only for stipulations respecting a future event (c. 1092,n.1). So if a party affix a stipulation respecting a shameful present or past event, the validity of the marriage depends upon whether, at the time of contract, the stipulation was fulfilled or not (c. 1092,n.4).

305 Gasparri, ii, n. 1003; Chelodi, n. 125.

306 Chelodi, n. 125.

307 Gasparri, ii, n. 986; De Becker, p. 77; Linneborn, p. 301.

308 Gasparri, ii, n. 997.

309 c. 7, X, De Conditione Apposita, IV, 5.

310 De Becker, p. 77.

The presumption against such stipulations respecting future events is not inevitable, but admits proof to the contrary. This has been the common opinion among authors, and hence the presumption, when viewed in conjunction with Canon 6, nn. 2, 4 must be looked upon as a simple, rebuttable presumption (cfr. n. **386**).[811]

476. A stipulation affixed to the marriage contract and not revoked, suspends the marital consent and validity of the marriage if it respect a future licit event (c. 1092,n.3); but if it respect a present or past event the marriage is valid or invalid from the beginning according to whether the stipulated fact exists or not (c. 1092,n.4; cfr. c. 104). Proof of such stipulation is at hand whenever the stipulation is affixed to the marriage contract, and signed by the parties or recorded in the marriage record. But when the stipulation was not brought into the formal contract of marriage, and it is claimed that the marriage was nevertheless entered upon under such a stipulation privately affixed (cfr. n. **153**), and that the marriage is consequently invalid, the presumption militates against the fact of such stipulation having been affixed, and in favor of unconditional marriage.[812] This presumption is not inevitable, but merely legal and rebuttable.[813] It is however generally difficult to bring proof to the contrary sufficient for the external forum, although the decisions of the Rota contain many instances of its having been successfully offered.

If it be shown that there was some qualifying of the marital consent, but it is still doubtful whether the intention of the party was to formulate a true stipulation, the presumption holds the party's restriction of consent to have constituted only an intention or proposal or representation, but not a stipulation.[814] However, the judge must sedulously inquire into the true nature of the affixed qualification. As an aid to discernment let the party or witness be asked whether he understood that the marriage was at once valid, or on the contrary, was to be valid only later when the condition was fulfilled. If he understood that the marriage was at once valid (and

[811] De Smet, i, p. 140 (1); V-Creusen, ii, n. 381; Gasparri, nov., ii, nn. 887, 888.

[812] De Smet, i, p. 141 (4).

[813] R., Null., 24 jul. 1909 (rd., i, pp. 106, 107); Cameracen., Null., 23 jun. 1911 (rd., iii, p. 305).

[814] IA., § 55; R., Null., 20 mai. 1912 (rd., iv, p. 240); Neo-Eboracen., Null., 9 dec. 1911 (rd., iii, p. 517); Null., 28 nov. 1914 (rd., vi, p. 327); Null., 6 aug. 1915 (rd., vii, p. 375); Null., 19 mai. 1920 (rd., xii, p. 116).

this may be more clearly discerned by inquiring whether and why the party entered upon coition with the other), but that the other party was expected to fulfil a condition later on, it is a sign that the contract was entered upon under representation only, but if the party understood that the marriage was not valid until the condition had been fulfilled, it is a sign of true stipulation suspending the validity of the marriage.[315]

Or again, if a marriage is said to have been contracted under a condition that the other party undertake to do something perpetually after marriage, *e. g.* care for a parent or child of the spouse, the continual future performance of the obligation cannot be a true stipulation suspending the marriage, and is to be held as a mere representation, however clearly the words "condition" or "stipulation" may have been affixed to the contract. For the words are in this case confounded by the innate contradiction which arises when one tries to conceive of a true, suspensive stipulation to marriage requiring continual fulfillment. But it may be found upon inquiry that a true stipulation was affixed, not to the future fulfillment of the obligation assumed, but rather to the present sincerity of the promise to fulfil the obligation later. Then if the stipulation is found not to have been fulfilled, *i. e.* if the promise was not sincerely given, the marriage is void for want of fulfillment of a stipulation hinging on a present fact.[316]

When the stipulation is shown to have been affixed to the marriage contract, the presumption stands for its endurance, and against its having been revoked.[317] Even when the party affixing the stipulation has thereafter acquired subjective certainty that the matter stipulated is as it should be, this does not militate against the presumed endurance of the stipulation, for the marital consent is still subordinated to the stipulation, in spite of the certainty.[318] Hence if anyone claim that a stipulation affixed has been revoked, he must prove this fact.[319]

315 R., Null., 13 feb. 1915 (rd., vii, p. 46); Null., 28 apr. 1922 (rd., xiv, p. 103).

316 R., Null., 13 feb. 1915 (rd., vii, p. 51); Null., 11 aug. 1921 (rd., xiii, p. 219); Null., 28 apr. 1922 (rd., xiv, pp. 104, 105); Null., 23 jul. 1923 (rd., xv, p. 176).

317 R., Parisien., Null., 11 aug. 1921 (rd., xiii, p. 218; aas., xiv, p. 519); Cameracen., Null., 23 jun. 1911 (rd., iii, p. 302); cfr. nn. **462, 474, 484**.

318 Commissio Specialis Card., Versalien., 2 aug. 1918 (aas., x, p. 390); R., Null., 28 apr. 1922 (rd., xiv, p. 106); Null., 23 dec. 1922 (rd., xiv, p. 355).

319 cfr. R., Null., 6 aug., 1915 (rd., vii, p. 383).

477. There is no legal presumption of the fulfillment of a stipulation: the nature and kind of stipulation together with the attendant facts must be carefully considered in examining the question of its fulfillment.

478. A marriage is invalid when entered upon under grave duress unjustly inflicted by another, under such circumstances that the person oppressed is obliged to choose marriage in order to free himself from the duress (c. 1087,§1). The duress is sometimes inflicted by persons unrelated to the parties, sometimes it is inflicted by one of the parties or his relatives upon the other party, and sometimes it is inflicted upon the bride by her own parents. In the last named case the oppression generally causes reverential fear and such cases are by far the most numerous of all those brought before the Rota. It is especially in the Latin and Slavic countries that such cases arise. In America and other countries where girls enjoy more freedom of action, are by character more independent, and can more easily provide for themselves without help from their parents, cases of duress occur less frequently, and consequently the presumptions established by Rotal jurisprudence do not frequently come into play.

If it has been reported to a pastor that one of the parties about to contract a marriage is acting under duress, it will be the pastor's duty to secretly examine that party, and perhaps other witnesses, postponing the marriage, for a time, if necessary. The matter should thus become clear, but if it still remains doubtful whether there be duress or not, the presumption stands for the freedom of the party from duress, and the marriage is not to be further impeded.

When a marriage is contested as having been entered upon under duress, the presumption is against the duress, and the plaintiff has the burden of a manifest, weighty and conclusive proof.[820]

This presumption is not however inevitable, but must cede to the proof of duress whenever such proof is properly adduced.[821]

479. Cases of duress are not restricted to natural proofs, but the judge may also regard pertinent and justifiable presumptions of duress.[822]

[820] R., Parisien., seu Nicien., Null., 30 dec. 1915 (rd., vii, p. 468; aas., viii, p. 327); Mediolanen., Null., 1 (17) aug. 1916 (rd., viii, p. 308; aas., ix, p. 459); Tarvisina, Null., 9 mart. 1917 (rd., ix, p. 40; aas., x, p. 110); Gasparri, ii, n. 62.

[821] R., Massilien., Null., 30 apr. 1917 (rd., ix, p. 109; aas., ix, p. 579).

[822] R., Null., 29 nov. 1913 (rd., v, p. 622); Parisien., Null., 11 dec. 1916 (rd., viii, p. 370; aas., ix, p. 469); Nicien., Null., 11 jun. 1920 (rd., xii, p. 132).

Thus if it be shown that persons have attempted a conspiracy to coerce others to marry, and the marriage follows upon this, it is presumed that the party or parties entered the marriage under duress.[323]

A similar presumption holds if it be shown that the party alleging duress, fled precipitately from the other party immediately after the marriage ceremony.[324]

480. If it is proved that one of the parties to the marriage was possessed of a great and continued aversion to the other party before marriage, there is a presumption that the marriage was entered upon under duress.[325] It must be shown however that the aversion was great and continuous. The Rota pronounced against the existence of such a presumption in a case where the plaintiff averred: "For my part I did not detest him but I did not have a true attraction to him."[326]

The Rota recently deduced such aversion and the presumption of duress from the conduct of the parties after the marriage was celebrated.[327] On the other hand, in a case where the duress was otherwise sufficiently well established, the court refused to accept the gay and joyful conduct of the bride at the wedding feast, as a presumption in favor of her freedom and against duress: the less so, says the decision, since nature's law impels young ladies dressed in their festal fineries to be moved with gayety.[328]

481. In cases of reverential force and fear the Rotal judges constantly form personal presumptions on the infliction of duress, from the known characters of the parents of the girl who is said to have married under duress. Thus *e. g.* they argued the existence of

[323] R., Null. vel Disp. Mat., 27 apr. 1915 (rd., vii, p. 209).

[324] R., Null. vel Disp. Mat., 27 apr. 1915 (rd., vii, p. 209).

[325] R., Null., 24 jan. 1912 (rd., iv, p. 304); Null., 22 jul. 1916 (rd., viii, p. 227); Lugdunen., Null., 2 apr. 1917 (rd., ix, p. 62; aas., x, p. 71); Massilien., Null., 30 apr. 1917 (rd., ix, p. 105; aas., ix, p. 575); Gravinen., Null., 2 jul. 1918 (rd., x, p. 64; aas., xi, p. 197); Tarraconen., Null., 15 feb. 1919 (rd., xi, p. 13; aas., xi, p. 431); Cosci, lib. I, cap. viii, n. 54.

[326] R., Lugdunen., Null., 28 jun. 1912 (rd., iv, p. 311; aas., iv, p. 650).

[327] R., Transylvanien., Null., 1 mai. 1912 (rd., iv, p. 223; aas., iv, p. 483); Null., 21 mai. 1915 (rd., vii, p. 242).

[328] R., Null., 2 jul. 1918 (rd., x, p. 70).

duress from the fierce and imperious character of the girl's mother,[329] and in one case discerned such imperious character from the mother's haughty and contemptuous letter received in answer to the summons.[330] On the other hand the gentle nature of the father of a girl was taken by the Rota as an indication that no threats had been made by him, or in any case, that they were not such as to cause grave reverential fear.[331]

In the forming of such personal presumptions the characters of the parents or those who are said to have inflicted duress, must be compared with the character of the person said to have been oppressed. In a case from Marseilles there was testimony that, on the wedding day, the groom inadvertently stepped upon the wedding dress of his bride, whereupon she actually threatened him with a knife taken from the table: a role, says the decision, which well displayed the vivacity of her character, and thus shows her aggressive disposition to be out of keeping with the idea of her having been oppressed by parental duress.[332]

Again the Rota deduced some personal presumption of duress, from the motive for inflicting duress which evidently actuated the mother of the bride. For it was shown that she hoped to retrieve her depleted fortune from the wealth of the proposed husband.[333]

In a case from Milan however, the Rota refused to admit the presumption of duress, given by Cosci and Menochius, from the private and almost secret wedding.[334]

482. Duress invalidates a marriage only when it constitutes a grave oppression (c. 1087,§1). When there is a doubt whether the duress inflicted was grave or light, it is to be measured by the gravity of the evil threatened or sustained. The plaintiff must show that

[329] R., Parisien., Null., 26 apr. 1916 (rd., viii, p. 134; aas., ix, p. 146); Pitilianen., Null., 20 oct. 1916 (rd., viii, p. 329; aas., ix, p. 359); Massilien., Null., 30 apr. 1917 (rd., ix, p. 109; aas., ix, p. 578); Tarraconen., Null., 15 feb. 1919 (rd., xi, pp. 12, 13; aas., xi, p. 431).

[330] R., Null., 21 dec. 1912 (rd., iv, p. 473).

[331] R., Montereyen. Angelorum, Null., 21 dec. 1917 (rd., ix, p. 323; aas., x, p. 427).

[332] R., Massilien., Null., 10 aug. 1912 (rd., iv, p. 403; aas., iv, p. 710); cfr. Pitilianen., Null., 20 oct. 1916 (rd., viii, p. 329; aas., ix, p. 359); Tarraconen., Null., 15 feb. 1919 (rd., xi, pp. 12, 13; aas., xi, p. 431).

[333] R., Pitilianen., Null., 20 oct. 1916 (rd., viii, p. 329; aas., ix, p. 359).

[334] R., Mediolanen., Null., 1 (17) aug. 1916 (rd., viii, p. 312; aas., ix, p. 462).

this evil was grave; otherwise it will be presumed to have been but light.[335] In proving that the fear was grave it is sufficient to show that it was based on grounds that appeared to the party constrained as a solid reason for fear:[336] it is not however required that the basis of the fear was by all means a grave cause of fear in itself. The Rota pronounced the invalidity of the marriage in a case wherein the plaintiff confessed that some of the threats inflicted were practically beyond the possibility of being carried out, but stated that she did not doubt their actuality at the time.[337]

On the other hand certain evils are presumed to be grave, and hence the fear derived from them is presumed to be grave fear. Among such evils Gasparri enumerates the loss of a great sum to which one has a right as *e. g.* paternal inheritance, threatened rape and abduction.[338] Similarly, there is a presumption of duress, if a girl is bought from her parents or others for the purpose of marriage, and without her consent to the purchase. This holds as well for places where it is the custom to buy and sell brides, as for places where there is no such custom.[339]

Some evils are generally presumed to be grave for one class of persons but not for another. Thus the threat of ejection from home is not considered a cause of grave fear to a man, as it is to a girl.[340] And the threat of a comparatively short imprisonment is not considered a grave evil for a man who has often and justly been im-

[335] R., Parisien., Null., 26 apr. 1916 (rd., viii, p. 136; aas., ix, p. 148): "Notandum insuper est hic non agi de metu proprie dicto et ordinario, sed de metu reverentiali; in metu quidem ordinario, gravitas vexationum aut minarum clare demonstrari debet; non ita in metu reverentiali, ad quem sufficiunt, praeter ipsum metum reverentialem, reprehensiones, vexationes, iurgia, minae, suasiones importunae et diuturnae, nec quidem copulative, sed etiam separatim."; Parisien., seu Nicien., Null., 30 dec. 1915 (rd., vii, p. 468; aas., viii, p. 327); Mediolanen., Null., 1 (17) aug. 1916 (rd., viii, p. 308; aas., ix, p. 459); Gasparri, ii, n. 944; Chelodi, n. 118; Shaefer, p. 17.

[336] cfr. De Smet, ii, n. 536 (1).

[337] R., Parisien., Null., 4 mart. 1916 (rd., viii, p. 62; aas., viii, p. 203).

[338] Gasparri, ii, n. 941.

[339] R., Vicariatus Apostolici Nov. Pomeraniae, Null., 30 apr. 1913 (rd., v, p. 287; aas., v, p. 468): ". . . omnino enim verisimile est, illos qui eam emerunt et vendiderunt sine eius consensu, omni modo institisse, etiam puella repugnante, ut scopus emptionis attingeretur."

[340] R., Parisien. seu Nicien., Null., 30 dec. 1915 (rd., vii, p. 479; aas., viii, p. 337).

prisoned for a longer term,[341] though it would be presumed a grave evil for a gentleman who had never been imprisoned.

The mere indignation of parents is not generally presumed to be a grave evil for a daughter, unless it be shown that the accompanying loss, or punishment, or confinement *etc.* was sufficient to impel her to give her consent under duress.[342] When serious threats of such loss, disinheritance *etc.*, quarrels, slaps in the face and the like are added to the indignation, there is a presumption that they were grave enough to constitute real duress.[343]

483. Duress conformable to the terms of Canon 1087,§1, invalidates marriage whether it is inflicted with intent to procure consent in marriage or not, whether it is directly or only indirectly inflicted. This matter was formerly under controversy,[344] and the earlier legislation seemed to require that the duress be inflicted directly and with the purpose of procuring marital consent. But the courts and the authors presumed that the intent was there, and that the duress was directly inflicted, whenever the contrary was not proved.[345]

484. In order to invalidate the marriage, the invalidating force and fear must have held sway at the time the marriage was celebrated. If there is no reason to believe that it was then operative, the marriage is presumed to be valid.[346] However, it may be shown that the duress held sway at the time of the marriage, either by natural proofs or by presumption. For he who was under the spell of duress before the marriage, is presumed to have continued in the state of fear until and during the wedding, if the same cause for

[341] Gasparri, ii, n. 941.

[342] R., Transylvanien., Null., 1 mai. 1912 (rd., iv, p. 217; aas., iv, p. 477); cfr. Parisien. seu Nicien., Null., 30 dec. 1915 (rd., vii, p. 479; aas., viii, p. 337).

[343] Gasparri, ii, n. 942.

[344] On the evolution of c. 1087, § 1, cfr. Gasparri, ed. nov. ii, n. 856.

[345] R., Gravinen., Null., 2 jul. 1918 (rd., x, p. 67; aas., xi, p. 201); Gasparri, ii, n. 951; cfr. R., Null., 26 jul. 1919 (rd., xi, pp. 134, 135).

[346] R., Parisien. seu Nicien., Null., 30 dec. 1915 (rd., vii, p. 468; aas., viii, p. 327): "Saepissime evenit, ut quod prius non placuit, re melius perpensa, postea acceptetur; et ideo potest contingere, ut qui antea matrimonium noluit, et nonnisi coactus in illud convenit, postea, mutato consilio, sponte ac libere illud admittat. Hoc sufficit, ut matrimonium, quod iuris gaudet favore, libere contractum praesumatur, si metus existentia tempore celebrati matrimonii non probetur."

fear existed,[347] especially if the threats *etc.* had been of recent occurrence, and most especially if it is shown that the party in question was under such fear both before and after the wedding ceremony.[348]

§ 6. Presumption of Validity in Dual Marriage

485. It becomes increasingly difficult to apply the presumption in favor of validity when a person has contracted two marriages. For it is naturally asked whether the first or second of these marriages is to have the presumption in its favor. To meet this question properly it is necessary to discriminate between various possible cases: I. When it is known that all parties to both marriages are still alive and the question hinges on validity alone.

The case wherein a Catholic has successively contracted two marriages with two Catholic spouses is complicated and has a long history coming down from the period of the glossaries. In some instances the case concerned one marriage merely contracted, *i. e.* ratified but not consummated, and another subsequent marriage ratified and consummated. That the practice of the Roman Church in its decisions up to the time of Alexander III frequently or usually favored the succeeding consummated marriage, against the merely ratified union, is not to be doubted.[349] But Alexander III, following the contention of the School of Paris, directed that a merely ratified marriage was not to be overcome by a subsequent marriage even though the latter were contracted in form and consummated.[350]

In other instances the case concerned one marriage contracted clandestinely and another contracted in form. The question at issue is generally a question of fact: whether namely, the clandestine marriage was really contracted. Under the Decretals there was, after

[347] SCC., Cameracen., Null., 27 aug. 1859 (pall., xiii, p. 361, n. 180); R., Null., 21 dec. 1912 (rd., iv, p. 475): "Porro, absque dubio admittenda est regula desumpta etiam ex iurisprudentia H. S. O., nempe metum illatum praesumi perdurare usque dum non removeatur causa metum inducens."; Pitilianen., Null., 20 oct. 1916 (rd., viii, p. 330; aas., ix, p. 360).

[348] R., Varsavien. seu Lublinen., Null., 21 jul. 1910 (rd., ii, p. 290); Null., 1 mai. 1912 (rd., iv, p. 216); Parisien., Null., 26 apr. 1916 (rd., viii, p. 137; aas., ix, p. 149); Cosci, lib. I, cap. viii, n. 82.

[349] cfr. c. 3, X, de Sponsa Duorum, IV, 4 etc.; Freisen, §§ 18-22 (pp. 151-219); Chelodi, n. 77.

[350] c. 3, X, De Sponsa Duorum, IV, 4.

betrothal and coition, an inevitable presumption that it was contracted (cfr. n. **427**). In cases where there was no inevitable presumption of marriage the Church accepted the joint testimony of both parties as proof of their having clandestinely married (cfr. n. **567**), as long as such a clandestine marriage did not redound to the prejudice of another, *e. g.* as long as there was no formal marriage subsequent to the clandestine. For if another marriage was afterward contracted in form, the assertions of the parties which tend to establish a previous clandestine marriage cannot be taken in prejudice to the subsequent formal marriage. In order to overcome the formal marriage it must be completely proved either that the previous clandestine marriage was really contracted, or that the subsequent formal marriage was otherwise invalid.[351] And if the formal marriage preceded the clandestine, the case is all the stronger for the formal marriage. And just so today in the case of those, *e. g.* non-Catholics whose marriage may be valid though clandestine: when a couple have lived together in what was certainly a life of concubinage at the beginning, and it is doubted whether this concubinage has been changed into marriage by the marital consent of the parties, this consent is not to be presumed to the prejudice of a subsequent marriage which one of the parties to the union may have formally contracted with a third person (cfr. nn. **444-448**). An interested party may however prove that there was marital consent in the first union, by proving that the parties spoke of one another as husband and wife or registered themselves as husband and wife, *e. g.* at the time of a birth or baptism of child. When it is proved that the previous clandestine marriage was in fact contracted by the parties, and that the clandestinity does not invalidate the consent, this is sufficient to establish the presumption of validity in favor of the marriage (cfr. n. **450**). So when the fact is proved, the subsequent formal marriage is overcome by this *prima facie* evidence, and must give way before the presumption of validity in favor of the first clandestine marriage. Then the party who would uphold the validity of the subsequent formal marriage must prove the invalidity of the first.

486. When there have been two marriages duly contracted in form, each is, by reason of the general principle, entitled to the presumption of validity. Thus, *e. g.* when there is a question of a present marriage being invalid by reason of the certain existence of

[351] Feije, n. 200; De Smet, i, n. 149.

a former marriage bond (ligamen), both marriages, on general principle, bear the presumption of validity before the court. But the presumption of validity in favor of the second marriage is at once overcome by the impediment which the first marriage establishes *prima facie* against the second. Hence it has been the frequent practice and style of the Congregation of the Council to solve cases of dual marriage by simply formulating the judicial doubt: "Is it certain that the first marriage is null?" In a complicated case that arose from Palermo, one Catherine Bonfilio was married under duress to Francis Alvarez. After four months of unhappy life Francis left her and went away to join the navy, whence the rumor of his death returned to his former place of residence, and then, fifteen years after the desertion, Catherine seized the opportunity of marrying Ignatius Colli, from whom four children were born. But then, alas, Francis returned, married to a second spouse Claudia. The Congregation ordered that both parties be separated from their second spouses, pending decision whether the first marriage was proved invalid.[352] And this order of things is preferred by some authors.[353] But the Congregation has also in several cases formulated the judicial doubt with regard to the second marriage: "Is it certain that the marriage is null?"; and the first marriage then automatically became an incidental and prejudicial question, of which the judicial doubt is formulated: "Is it certain that the first marriage is valid?"[354] This procedure seems to be the more logical in respect to its judicial form, because it takes cognizance that the latter marriage is in apparent possession, but it does not really affect the issue nor shift the burden of proof. For in order to prove the prejudicial question on the validity of the first marriage it is not necessary that the interested party establish the non-existence of every possible impediment, but it is sufficient to show that the first marriage was formally contracted and

352 SCC., Panormitana, 30 sept., 18 nov. 1719; 8 jun. 1720 (cicf., v, nn. 3192, 3210; pall., xiii, § xiv, nn. 17-19): "1. *An constet de nullitate primi matrimonii in casu?* Et quatenus affirmative: 2. *An secundum matrimonium contractum cum Ignatio Colli sit validum . . . in casu? . . . Sacra, etc. respondit ad 1. Constare. Ad 2. Satis provisum in 1.*"; cfr. also SCC., Eystadien., 17 nov. 1731, 9 feb., 8 mart., 21 jun. 1732 (cicf., v, nn. 3376, 3385, 3393).

353 Cfr. Smith, nn. 234, 460; Stanislaus in aer., xlviii (Feb. 1913), p. 186.

354 SCC., In Ratisbonen., Mat., 9 aug. 1704 (pall., xiii, § xiv, n. 11); In Dubium Mat., 14 nov. 1699; 7 mai., 30 jul. 1701, 3 sept. 1707 (pall., xiii, § xiv, n. 16); In Viennen., Mat., 22 sept. 1691 (pall., xiii, § xiv, n. 20): "An constet de validitate primi matrimonii?"

that the first spouse was still alive at the time of contracting the second marriage. When these two facts are established, the first marriage obtains the presumption of validity and overcomes the presumption of validity of the second marriage. He who would overcome the presumption of validity of the first marriage must prove that the marriage is invalid.

In the trials on nullity reported in the Decree and the Decretals,[355] as well as those that later came before the Congregation of the Council, it is never mentioned that the plaintiff in a nullity suit based on bigamy, had to prove that the former marriage was valid.[356] And the Congregation of Propaganda in its Instruction on marriage trials, treating specifically of cases where a former marriage is concerned, simply instructs that the existence of the former marriage be proved: no question about proving its validity.[357] Finally the Code, by placing the impediments of already existing bond and affinity among those impediments that are to be settled by the simpler procedure of Canon 1990, evidently understands that the present marriage is to be pronounced invalid, if it is shown by peremptory document, that there was a bond of marriage or affinity extant at the time when the present marriage was attempted; and it does not intend that the validity of that former bond be proved under every possible heading: its validity is presumed even to the effect of declaring the second marriage invalid.[358]

This seems to be beyond question in cases where the former marriage is thus presumably valid, and the former spouse is still alive. But even in case the former spouse is dead at the time when the latter marriage is brought to trial, the presumption of validity applies also to the former marriage, and not exclusively to the marriage which is in apparent possession and on trial. The Instruction of Propaganda explicitly directs, for cases of nullity by reason of already extant marriage bond, that proof of the existence of the former marriage be introduced by document, and in case of subsequent death of

[355] *e. g.* c. 1, 2, C. XXXIV q. 1, 2; c. 13, X, De Spons. et Mat., IV, 1.

[356] Cfr. *e. g.* SCC., Oveten., Mat., 22 jun. 1894 (ass., xxviii, p. 333) where the first marriage contracted by proxy, is presumed valid, to the prejudice of the second marriage contracted formally and in person.

[357] PF, 1883, § 42.

[358] Smith, nn. 460-463; contrary, Nau, Append. I, n. 12 (p. 225), who however, gives no ground for his contention, except the Canon 1014 that is to be interpreted.

the former spouse, that comparison be made between the date of death and the date of the later marriage,[359] in order to ascertain whether this later marriage was attempted while the former still existed. The validity of the former is presumed.

487. *Scholion.* When a competent ecclesiastical court has declared a marriage invalid, if necessary by two conformable sentences which have not been further appealed, such a decision participates in some of the effects of an unassailable judgment (res iudicata),[360] and one of these effects is the presumption that the decision is true and just (c. 1904,§1). And thus if one of the parties acting on this decision enters upon a second marriage with a third person, the second marriage has the presumption of validity. But if the first marriage is canonically reinstated to trial, either at the motion of a party or *ex officio,* the presumption arising from the adjudication is thereby superseded,[361] and, as it seems to me, the couple are to be separated pending the reinstated trial.[362]

488. When one or both of the marriages were contracted in infidelity, the favor accorded the Faith must be considered in connection with the presumption of validity (cfr. nn. **416-418**). If the first marriage was entered upon between two infidels, and then one of these contracted a new marriage before a Catholic priest, the favor to the Faith secures the presumption of validity to the second marriage. When both the first and second marriages were contracted in infidelity but one of the parties to the second marriage has since been admitted to Catholic baptism, there is the presumption that everything which the Canons order for such cases has been fulfilled before the infidel party was admitted to baptism; but if the second marriage is contested the judge will make opportune inquiry, and if the matter still remains doubtful, the judge must have recourse to the Holy See.[363] [364]

359 PF, 1883, § 42.

360 Chir.

361 cfr. Roberti, ii, n. 524; Feije, n. 546.

362 Smith, n. 867 contrary.

363 PF, 1883, § 45.

364 In civil law: Abbott, p. 107: ". . . the fact, if shown, that either or both of the parties have been previously married, and that such wife or husband of the first marriage is still living, does not destroy the *prima facie* legality of the last marriage. The presumption in such a case is that the former marriage has been legally dissolved and the burden that it has not rests upon the party seeking to impeach the last marriage."

Acting on this principle of favor to the Faith the Holy See has gone further. It has allowed that a convert from paganism who has had several wives simultaneously and does not remember which of them he first took to wife, may, upon his conversion to the Faith, choose whom of them he pleases and live with her as his legitimate wife.[365] It has allowed that a convert from paganism who has had several simultaneous wives, may without regard to which was his first wife in infidelity, choose that one who will be converted to the Faith, and retain her as his legitimate, *i. e.* Christian wife.[366] Finally it has allowed that when a pagan has been taken captive to remote parts to which there is no access by which the interpellation may be made, this person or his spouse, when converted to the Faith, may, without making any interpellation, marry any eligible Catholic.[367] The Code has recently reasserted these applications of the favor to the Faith and extended them, for like circumstances, to the whole world.[368]

489. II. When there is question about the life or death of a first spouse, the second marriage is invalid or valid according to the true solution of the question of life or death. If it is certain that the first spouse died before the second marriage was contracted, this second marriage is certainly valid (at least with respect to previous marriage bond) even though the remaining spouse was in bad faith about the death, at the time of the second marriage. But frequently there is no certainty whether the first spouse is dead. In that case the validity of a second marriage already contracted will likewise depend in reality upon whether the first spouse is dead and when he died. The judge may make use of personal presumptions to aid in the settlement of these questions, but must be especially careful lest he admit a fiction in place of a justifiable presumption.

When there is no moral certainty, but there is such grounded conjecture of the death that it is really probable, the judge may be faced on the one hand with the presumption of the continuance of life (cfr. nn. **491**, **494**) weakened by the probability of death, and on the other, with the presumption of validity of a second marriage contracted. If such a second marriage has, with this probability of

[365] Const. Pauli III, "Altitudo", 1 jun. 1537 (cicd. vi).

[366] Const. S. Pii V, "Romani Pontificis", 2 aug. 1571 (cicd. vii).

[367] Const. Greg. XIII, "Populis", 25 jan. 1585 (cicd. viii); cfr. SO., 8 jun. 1836 (cicf., iv, n. 874; cpf., i, n. 848); SO, Alberti, § 13; Gasparri, i, n. 21.

[368] Cfr. V-Creusen, ii, n. 436.

death of the first spouse, been contracted in form, it enjoys the presumption of validity even though the proper canonical procedure was not observed before the second marriage was contracted. The Congregation has settled numerous cases on this presumption,[369] and the Instruction of 1883 says that when a probability has been established that the first spouse was dead at the time of the second marriage, the latter must not be declared invalid,[370] before certain proof is offered that the former spouse was living at the time of the second marriage.[371] [372] And in a case from China the Holy Office declared that when the second marriage thus enjoying the presumption of validity, was entered upon in good faith, the parties are to be left in good faith regarding their marriage and its use.[373] When there is a merely negative doubt devoid of all grounded conjecture or probability of death, *i. e.* when there is no reason to think that the first spouse is dead and likewise no certainty that he is alive, as for instance, when absence alone has been taken as an excuse for a new marriage, the presumption of life's continuation attaches (cfr. n. **491**), and overcomes the presumption of validity of the second mar-

369 Cfr. Pallotini, xiii, § xiv, nn. 45-56.

370 PF, 1883, § 43: "non enim constaret de eius nullitate."

371 Schlenz, Wiederverehelichung (akk., 1924, p. 210; cfr. akk., 1918, p. 221); Haring in lqs., 1933, p. 376.

372 In civil law, May, p. 303: "There is a presumption in favor of the validity of a later marriage, the more so if the marriage was ceremonial, which puts on the opponent thereof the burden of proving its invalidity. The presumption does not arise if a party to the later marriage knows his prior spouse to be alive."; Tiffany, pp. 44, 45: Greensboro v. Underhill, 12 Vt., 604: "Is the intermarriage of Burdick with the pauper in 1836 rendered illegal and void from the fact of her intermarriage with Hyland in 1834, who, after a short cohabitation with her absconded and has not since been heard of? To render the second marriage illegal and void, we must presume the continuance of life of Hyland down to the time of the second marriage; and though, as a general principle, we are to presume the continuance of life . . . , still, when the presumption is brought into conflict with other presumptions in law, it may be made to yield to them."; similarly, Abbott, pp. 106, 107.

373 SO., Nankin, 22 mart. 1865 (cicf., iv, n. 982; cpf., i, n. 1272): "Q. 2. Caecilia, marito a rebellibus capto, nec post tres annos amplius comparente, eum habuit pro mortuo, et, absente proprio sacerdote, nupsit Petro rei conscio, sed similiter de morte prioris viri persuaso. Missionarius, cum impossibilis sit scire vel inquirere utrum Paulus vir prior vivat, censet eos non esse inquietandos, et relinquendos esse in matrimonio donec non habeatur certus nuntius de vita Pauli. An bene?—R. ad 2. Relinquendos esse in bona fide."

riage. The Holy Office declared a couple that had not contracted in good faith must be separated without however allowing even the hitherto unmarried party to contract a new marriage until the doubt was dispelled.[374] But bad faith on the validity of the marriage is not necessarily denoted by the parties' having contracted the second marriage without first satisfying the requirements of canonical procedure.[375]

490. *Scholion:* A. For the forum of conscience note: if the second marriage was contracted in bad faith because both parties or either of them knew the first spouse to be alive, the use of marriage is certainly illicit. 1) If the marriage was contracted in bad faith because both parties doubted the death of the first spouse, most authors hold the use of marriage is illicit for both, as long as the doubt remains.[376] Others hold that, after serious investigation, both parties may both exact and render marital coition even if the doubt still remains, because of the presumption for validity.[377] In this question of moral theology let the judge of conscience follow the opinion that seems true. 2) If one party was in bad faith and the other in good faith, the latter may ask and render marital coition, but the former, in logical accordance with the first opinion given above, may not ask: he may render only at the other's request.[378] According to the second opinion both parties are allowed to ask and render; but it seems the

[374] SO., Nankin, 22 mart. 1865 (cicf., iv, n. 982; cpf., i, n. 1272): "Q. 1. Titio capto a rebellibus, eoque frustra per duos aut tres annos desiderato, Martha eius uxor sine assistentia proprii sacerdotis, quae ad valorem ibi necessaria non est, et contra monitum missionariorum, contraxit cum Marco. Marcus autem graviter reprehensus a missionariis, vult quidem dimittere Martham, sed petit ad alias transire nuptias. Quid agendum? R. ad 1. Separandos esse coniuges, et virum non posse secundas inire nuptias, usque dum moraliter sit certum, quo tempore ipse matrimonium iniit cum muliere de qua agitur, primum virum eiusdem mulieris non obiisse."

[375] Lehmkuhl, ii, n. 1077.

[376] De Becker, p. 288; De Smet, i, n. 238; Chelodi, p. 75 (3); their position seems to be supported by PF., 1792, Tunkin. Occid. (cpf., i, n. 606); SO., 22 mart. 1865, Nankin (cicf., iv, n. 982; cpf., i, n. 1272); 28 jun. 1865, Pondichery (cicf., iv, n. 984; cpf., i, n. 1273). These decisions however, given for the external forum, do not, as it seems to me, definitely settle the question for the internal forum.

[377] Ballerini, vi, p. 321 ex cit. De Becker, p. 288; Vermeersch, De Castitate, n. 235, ex cit. De Smet, i, p. 224 (1).

[378] c. 2, X, De Secundis Nuptiis, IV, 21.

innocent party may rightly refuse the other, as long as the doubt remains, because of the injury done by contracting in bad faith. 3) If both parties were in good faith, they may both ask and render as long as the good faith remains, even after a slight doubt arises,[379] but a grave doubt gives rise to the duty of inquiring, and during the inquiry, the party who doubts may, according to most authors render but not ask the marital coition; but according to the logical conclusion from the second opinion given above, both parties may both ask and render.[380] If the doubt remains after diligent inquiry, the use of marriage is not forbidden.[381] For in this case, not only the presumption of validity, but the rights of possession acquired in good faith, seem to supersede the obligation deriving from the now doubtful bond of the former marriage.

B. The more liberal principles that derive from the second opinion given above, hold usually (cfr. c. 1076,§3) for the internal forum, when a marriage has been duly contracted with a doubtful impediment other than former marriage bond. But in most such cases, a precautionary dispensation (c. 15) and validation will make the doubtful marriage certainly valid.

491. III. The matter is quite different before the second marriage has been contracted in form. For probability of death then gives no presumption in favor of the desired marriage. If a party who has been married desires to marry again on the claim that his former spouse is dead, the claim of death must be established by proofs that beget at least moral certainty. The judge starts from the principle that everyone is presumed to be among the living until his death is proved.[382] [383] And this presumption deters one from contracting a

[379] c. 44, X, De Sententia Excommunicationis, V, 39.

[380] Schlenz in akk., 1924, p. 213 seems to agree; but later states that the doubting party may render but not ask the marriage right.

[381] PF., 1792, Tunkin Occident. (cpf., i, n. 606): this decision is somewhat opposed to that of Innocent III in c. 44, X, De Sent. Excom., V, 39, and now has general adherence among authors, *e. g.* Lehmkuhl, ii, n. 1077; Chelodi, p. 75 (3).

[382] Synod. Prag., an. 1605 (akk., 1918, p. 55; Synod. Mechlin., an. 1609 (akk., 1918, p. 56); Gasparri, i, n. 723; Feije, n. 441.

[383] In civil law, Abbott, p. 92: ". . . the presumption of law is that a person of whom nothing is known but that he was living at a certain time, continues to live, at least until he would reach the age of one hundred, after which he may be presumed to be dead . . ."

new marriage, not only because of presumed extant marriage bond, but also because of presumed impediment of crime. Thus when a party, after long absence of the spouse, has had sexual coition with another and exchanged the promise of future marriage, or entered upon a civil marriage, the former spouse is not presumed to have been dead at the time of the crime, but rather to have been alive (even though he is now dead), and the party is thus restrained by the presumed impediment, until it is proved the spouse was dead at the time of the crime.[384]

The legal presumption of the continuance of life is not superseded by the mere fact that there have been wars and wide disasters in the place of residence of the absconded spouse, for all these beget no legal presumption of death.[385]

492. There is no legal presumption of death derivable from the long absence of a spouse. From the words of Gratian,[386] we conclude that the courts of the Church in earlier centuries were required to wait three years after the disappearance of a spouse, before they might pronounce on the presumable death of that spouse, but his words give no indication that a legal presumption of death was established by the absence of three years. And Clement III answered the inquiry of the Bishop of Caeserea Augusta with the sharp cut statement that no elapse of time since the captivity or absconding of a husband was sufficient to permit the remarriage of the wife, until there was certain knowledge of the former's death.[387] This principle has been frequently reasserted, particularly with regard to long absence combined with war-captivity,[388] and is maintained even when the desired party has been summoned by court edict or by newspaper advertisements.[389]

In opposing the establishment of a legal presumption of death derivable from a determinate time of absence, the Church has all along had to contend with the opposite tendency of civil governments.[390] The early Roman law had already established the principle

[384] Cerato, p. 118.

[385] DS., Massinensis, Praesumptio de Morte, mart. 1910 (aas., ii, p. 197).

[386] Gratian. in c. 2, C. XXXV, q. 9.

[387] c. 19, X, De Spons. et Mat., IV, 1.

[388] SO., 23 jun. 1671 (cicf., iv, n. 745; cpf., i, n. 196).

[389] SO, 1868; cfr. PF., 21 apr. 1788 (cpf., i, n. 595); SO., 12 jun. 1822 (akk., 1918, p. 56).

[390] cfr. Conc. Trid., sess. XXIV, de Mat., Canon V.

that a new marriage was to be permitted after one of the parties to a first marriage had absconded during a definite period of time, but this was corrected by Justinian under the influence of Christianity.[391] In England under James I, the statute of bigamy of 1604 (ch. II,§2) declared for presumption of death after seven years absence, and this presumption was soon adopted by the common law courts.[392] The New York State statute has amended this to a rebuttable legal presumption of death at the end of five years absence.[393] But the ecclesiastical judge is not allowed to make use of the legal presumption established by the state in this matter.[394] And the ordinaries of Germany and Austria have lately resisted the recent war-decrees of the German and Austrian governments of 1916 and 1918 respectively, wherein the legal presumption of death was established after war-absences of one and two years respectively.[395]

493. When a person has absconded from his family, or left his fatherland and has not been heard of for a long time by those who would naturally have heard of him if he were alive, the court may pronounce upon the presumable death of such spouse if a personal presumption of death is warranted by an examination of the circumstances, causes and conditions of the case (cfr. c. 1053).[396] [397]

391 Gasparri, i, n. 723; Feije, n. 442.

392 Abbott, p. 107.

393 N. Y. State, Art. 2, § 6, 3: . . . unless; Such former husband or wife has absented himself or herself for five successive years then last past without being know to such person to be living during that time."; cfr. McKelvey, p. 86.

394 SO., 28 jun. 1865, Pondichery (cicf., iv, n. 984; cpf., i, n. 1273).

395 cfr. Erlass des Fuerstbischofs von Breslau . . . 26 apr. 1917 (akk., 1917, p. 441); Schlenz, Nachtrag (akk., 1924, p. 218).

396 c. 5, X, Ut Lite non Contestata, II, 6; SO, 1868, § 6: "Hoc in casu probatio obitus ex coniecturis, praesumptionibus, indiciis et adiunctis quibuscumque, sedula certe et admodum cauta investigatione curanda erit, ita nimirum ut pluribus hinc inde collectis, eorumque natura perpensa, prout scilicet urgentiora vel leviora sunt, seu propiore vel remotiore nexu cum veritate mortis coniunguntur, inde prudentis viri iudicium ad eamdem mortem affirmandam probabilitate maxima, seu morali certitudine promoveri possit. Quapropter quandonam in singulis casibus habeatur ex huiusmodi coniecturis simul coniunctis iusta probatio, id prudenti relinquendum est iudicis arbitrio."; cfr. PF, 1883, § 43.

397 In civil law, Abbott, p. 93: "Death within a very recent time may be inferred from the circumstances of absence or disappearance. Sudden dis-

In all this the judge may take into consideration the love that existed between the absconded person and the remaining spouse, the onetime constancy, in sending letters *etc.,*[398] and the great length of time since the departure of that spouse from his family. Thus in 1914 the Congregation drew the presumption from the forty-eight years since the husband's departure, the more than seventy years he would have attained and the waywardness of his life that pointed to an early death.[399] But such great length of time is not always required for justifiable presumption of death: in a case from Livonia the Congregation permitted the remarriage of the remaining party after only six years,[400] and in another case after only two years.[401]

The Church more readily accepts the proof or presumption of deaths as conclusive nowadays[402] because of the greater ease of communication and investigation.[403]

494. When the death of a former spouse is properly established, but it is not known just when he died, there is no legal presumption as to the time of the death. If then, the validity of a second marriage now contracted, depends upon the time when the first spouse

appearance is not alone enough, in the case of a man without social or pecuniary ties, or fixed abode, though it may be in that of one endeared to his home and fixed in his habits, or having strong pecuniary motive to appear, according to his habit, if alive, or in case of one who was last seen in proximity to danger, and left his effects in a situation suggestive of accident or suicide. Where the presumption of death turns upon unexplained absence, all the circumstances surrounding the absentee within a reasonable time before his departure, or at any time afterward, which, in their nature, have reasonable bearing on the probabilities, are relevant—such as the state of his domestic and business relations, his habits, his health of body and mind, previous threats of suicide, the immediate and ultimate purposes of his departure, the circumstances of his correspondence and its cessation, etc. The presumption of death from absence rests on the fact that it is strange that a man should absent himself, without communicating with his friends if living; hence it is aided by whatever in his situation and habits makes it the more strange, and is impaired by whatever makes it easily credible."

[398] PF, 1883, § 43.

[399] DS., Praes. Mort. Conj., 28 nov., 18 dec. 1914 (aas., vii, pp. 40, 41).

[400] DS., Mohilovien., Praes. Mort. Conj., 16 dec. 1910 (aas., iii, p. 26).

[401] Schlenz, in akk., 1924, p. 220, n. 3.

[402] cfr. Schlenz, in akk., 1918, pp. 52, 215, 381, 549; 1924, p. 206.

[403] cfr. DS., Praes. Mort. Conj., 29 apr. 1915 (aas., vii, p. 235); 25 jun. 1915 (aas., vii, p. 476); 25 feb. 1916 (aas., viii, p. 151); 19 jan. 1917 (aas., ix, p. 120); 18 nov. 1920 (aas., xiv, p. 96).

died, as in the impediments of existing marriage bond and of crime, only natural proofs and justified personal presumptions derived from proved facts will be admitted to prove that the former spouse died at any specified time. And a subsequent marriage that has been contracted in form will be presumed valid, even when this presumption entails the inference that the former spouse, whose death is now legitimately established, died shortly after his disappearance. For the presumption of validity of a second marriage contracted in form prevails over the presumption of continuance of life of the first spouse (cfr. n. **489**).

§ 7. Presumption of Baptism

495. A marriage is null if contracted by a non-baptized person with a person baptized in the Catholic Church or converted to it from heresy or schism (c. 1070,§1). When there is no question either of the fact of baptism or of its validity, but there is doubt precisely whether a party was baptized in the Catholic Church and thus aggregated to it, the judge will discern whether the person was baptized in the Catholic Church by considering: 1) the intention of the person baptized or 2) of those in whose care he was at the time of baptism, and 3) the intention of the minister of the sacrament.

1) If the person baptized had the use of reason, his expressed or implied intention to be aggregated to the Catholic Church or another determines whether he is baptized Catholic or not. Hence if he asked for or consented to Catholic baptism he is considered baptized in the Catholic Church. If he asked for baptism or consented to baptism with expressed or implied intent of being aggregated to another Church, he is considered baptized in another than the Catholic Church. When there is doubt of his intention, the presumption is that he intended to be baptized in that Church of whose minister he asked or knowingly received the baptism.

2) If the person baptized had not the use of reason, the expressed or implied intention of his parents or others in whose permanent charge he is, determines whether he is baptized Catholic or not. Thus if Catholic parents or one parent, or, in the permanent loss of parents, if Catholic guardians brought the child to the Catholic priest for baptism, the child is considered baptized in the Catholic Church. On the other hand if non-Catholic parents or one parent, or if the child's guardians brought the child to their minister for baptism, the child is

considered baptized outside the Catholic Church. If non-Catholic parents or one of them, or the guardians, brought the child to be baptized by the Catholic priest, and guaranteed the Catholic education of the child (cfr. c. 750,§2,n.1), the child is considered baptized in the Catholic Church. If such guarantees were not given and the child has been raised outside the Catholic Church, there is doubt of the original intention of the parents or guardians, and in doubt of their intention the presumption is that they intended the child to be aggregated to their own Church. Thus too if a Catholic parent requested a non-Catholic nurse or doctor, or even in urgent emergency, a non-Catholic minister to baptize his child, the child will be considered baptized in the Catholic Church. But this presumption of intent may be overcome by the careless and wavering Catholicity of a parent, especially if the baptism was done without urgency.

3) When the intention of the person baptized, or the intention of his parents is discernible, the contrary intention of the person who baptizes has no bearing on the matter. If the parents have no definite intention, because *e. g.* they themselves have no religion, but leave the matter to the will of the person who baptizes, his intention will govern the matter. If there are no parents, grandparents, or guardians, or if they have lost their right to custody, or if they cannot exercise their right, and their intention cannot be conjectured, the intention of the person baptizing governs the matter (cfr. c. 750,§2, n. 2). If the child of infidel parents is baptized when it is prudently foreseen that death is about to overtake him (cfr. c. 750,§1), the intention of the person baptizing governs the matter, and in this case the intention of the person who baptizes prevails against the unreasonable contrary intention of the infidel parents, who would ignorantly hinder the eternal salvation of the child (cfr. also c. 751).[404] In doubt about the intention of the person who baptizes, it will be presumed that he intended to aggregate the child to his own Church.[405]

496. Under pre-Code law the impediment of disparity of cult affected all marriages to which one party was an infidel and the other baptized, regardless of whether the latter was a Catholic or apostate, schismatic or heretic. And many marriages contracted in non-Cath-

[404] V-Creusen, ii, n. 344 contrary: erroneously, as it seems.

[405] Gasparri, nov., i, nn. 569-573; Woywod, i, n. 1053; Davis in hpr., xxxii (1932), p. 854, quoting prm., apr. 1931, gives concrete cases, of which (h) and (i) seem to be erroneous; cfr. also Ayrinhac, n. 133; Hilling in akk., 1927, p. 180.

olic form were thus made doubtful, for it was doubted whether one or perhaps both parties had been baptized. This doubt of baptism was not infrequent even among Catholics, especially when, previous to the Council of Trent, parish records were not universally kept (cfr. n. **334**).

The question of whether baptism has been received is a question of fact, and facts must be proved (cfr. nn. **147, 398, 407**). Therefore the Church does not presume that a person has been baptized,[406] except when the presumption deriving from the solid Catholicity of the parents amounts to a true proof. A practical case of this kind was brought before Innocent III by a young man in orders of whom it was doubted whether he had ever been baptized. Innocent directed the Bishop of Ferrara to ordain him priest without further ado, on the presumption that, as the child of Christian parents, he must have been baptized.[407] This presumption found its way into the marriage courts, when there was a merely negative doubt of the baptism of a person born of and reared by Catholic parents, and is still retained in practice as a legal presumption.[408] If therefore a Catholic reared by practical Catholic parents wishes to marry but cannot produce a baptismal certificate, either because he does not know where he was baptized, or because there is no record of his baptism to be found among the registers of the place where it is asserted he was baptized, it is more natural to conclude that a pastor once neglected to make the proper baptismal entry on the occasion of the baptism, or that people have forgotten where the person in question was baptized, than that the Catholic parents of the person in question persistently neglected a duty so urgent and so universally observed in the Church. The proper procedure in such cases is to call for witnesses (c. 1031, §1, n. 1), who can testify to the baptism; the testimony of parents, sponsors, and relatives, and even of the party himself (c. 779) will be of the highest order. But when no testimony on the baptism can be obtained, there is a presumption that the person was baptized, pro-

[406] cfr. c. 110-113, Dist. IV, De Consecratione.

[407] c. 3, X, De Presbytero non Baptizato, III, 43: "Et certe de illo, qui natus de Christianis parentibus, et inter Christianos est fideliter conversatus, tam violenter praesumitur, quod fuerit baptizatus, ut haec praesumptio pro certitudine sit habenda, donec evidentissimis forsitan argumentis contrarium probaretur."

[408] SO., Albanen. in America, 10 jun. 1896 (cicf., iv, n. 1180); Linneborn, p. 201; Schaefer, p. 145.

vided there be testimony that the parents were good, religious, practical Catholics at the time of the birth and during the education of the person in question. In witness of this fact the person in question may well testify to the religious practices of his parents (cfr. c. 1031,§1, n. 1). When the presumption in favor of baptism has been thus established, the proposed marriage is not to be impeded.

This presumption has found application when the person in question came of non-Catholic parents who certainly belonged to a sect that faithfully adhered to the necessity of baptizing children,[409] but it does not always amount to a true proof in such cases today, and the judge must beware of rashly applying the presumption nowadays when irreligion is rampant.[410]

497. If there persist, even after investigation, a positive and solid doubt of the baptism of a person who has been reared in the Catholic Church and is now about to marry, such Catholic person must be first rebaptized conditionally and in some cases secretly,[411] and then the marriage is allowable.[412] If the person whose baptism is under positive and solid doubt is neither a Catholic nor willing to be converted, the baptism cannot be conditionally bestowed, and the ordinary must be consulted for dispensation from mixed religion and for precautionary dispensation from disparity of cult (c. 1031,§1, n. 3; cfr. c. 15).[413] If the person in question was born of and reared by parents who belonged to a sect that rejects baptism entirely, or leaves it to the discretion of children after they grow up, or if the parents openly professed atheism or agnosticism, the presumption is that the person was not baptized.[414]

[409] R., Parisien., Null., 13 jun. 1911 (rd., iii, p. 261); Linneborn, p. 201; Schaefer, p. 145; cfr. n. **499**.

[410] SO, Savannah, II, n. 6: "Casu quo nulla pro baptismo militat praesumptio, applicanda est regula: factum non praesumitur, sed probandùm est. Huius regulae applicatio in his Foederatis Statibus ubi inter acatholicos plurimi sunt, qui de baptismo infantibus suis conferendo nihil aut parum curant, potiori forte iure locum habere debet, quam in multis aliis regionibus."; Lehmkuhl, i, p. 125 (1).

[411] cfr. Capello, ii, p. 447 (12).

[412] SCC., In Neapolitana, Mat., 1 sept. 1714 (pall., xii, p. 605, n. 4); Gasparri, i, n. 687; Schaefer, p. 181; Cerato, p. 110; cfr. also De Smet, ii, nn. 587, 588.

[413] cfr. W-Vidal, v, p. 308 (31).

[414] SO, Savannah, II.

498. When a baptized heretic or schismatic is newly converted to the Church and it is doubted by solid and positive doubt, whether the baptism is valid, the matter is not dismissed with a presumption of validity, but as is well known, the baptism is repeated conditionally. When a baptized non-Catholic who is not converted to the Faith is about to contract marriage with a Catholic, and there is positive and solid doubt whether the non-Catholic's baptism is valid, the presumption in favor of validity (cfr. n. **500**) still holds,[415] but because of the necessity of securing the certain validity of the sacrament (cfr. c. 1019,§1), this presumption can no longer be urged as supplying the want of a dispensation from disparity of cult.

The older practice of the Holy Office was to grant only dispensation from mixed religion in doubtful cases,[416] and some dioceses of America have until lately retained the practice of petitioning only dispensation from mixed religion, when it was certain that a non-Catholic had been baptized but there was positive doubt whether the baptism was valid.[417] Such practice was undoubtedly founded on the one-time principle of the Holy Office which had in practice acknowledged the validity, for the external forum, of marriages contracted by Catholics, even when it was afterward discovered that one of them had not been baptized.[418] But the Holy Office has changed this practice and has been granting precautionary dispensation from disparity for such cases, these many years.[419] Hence in many dioceses notice has long since been taken of the changed policy, and the better practice of applying for precautionary dispensation from disparity has been customary. This practice must now be followed to secure the certain validity of such marriages, since the marriage is not really

[415] cfr. Instr. Ep. Osnabruck, 26 mai. 1920 (akk., 1920, pp. 66, 67); Haring, Grundzuege, p. 503.

[416] Gasparri, nov., i, n. 579.

[417] aer., lxiv (1921), p. 413.

[418] cfr. Gasparri, nov., i, nn. 578, 579; De Becker, p. 237 fol.

[419] Gasparri, nov., i, n. 580; Woywod, i, n. 1054 wisely says: "The faculties given to the bishops of America seem to suggest that the dispensation from disparity of cult ad cautelam should be given in case of doubtful baptism for Faculty No. I of the faculties of the Holy Office reads: 'Dispensandi . . . super impedimento mixtae religionis, et si casus ferat, etiam super disparitate cultus, ad cautelam.'" For nothing in this faculty makes it imperative to apply for precautionary dispensation from disparity, in cases of doubtful validity as well as in doubt of the fact of baptism.

valid unless the non-Catholic party is validly baptized or unless a dispensation from disparity of cult has been obtained.[420]

The presumption stands in favor of the validity of a non-Catholic's baptism in another respect; it makes the baptized non-Catholic who is about to contract marriage, presumably a subject of the Church, and obligated by impediments of ecclesiastical origin.[421] But as long as the baptism is doubtful as to fact or validity, the impediment is doubtful by factual doubt, and the ordinary is delegated to dispense, provided it is a matter in which the Roman Pontiff is used to dispense (c. 15), and provided the proposed marriage is to be contracted with a Catholic.

499. If the marriage has already been contracted, and is now under doubt because the baptism of one or both parties is doubtful, the same presumption of baptism favors the person born of and brought up by Catholic parents. If serious doubt of the baptism persists after investigation, the person upon whom the doubt centers is to be rebaptized conditionally and in some cases secretly,[422] provided he wishes to live as a Catholic,[423] but without prejudice to the validity of the marriage (cfr. nn. **502-506**).[424]

If the party was born and reared outside the Church, the Holy Office, acting at the instigation of the Bishop of Savannah, has drawn a distinction between those whose parents, or who themselves belonged to a sect that habitually confers baptism also on children, and those whose parents or who themselves have had no such affiliation; and has established the following presumptions: Baptism is presumed in persons whose parents pertained to and were zealous members of a sect which holds baptism as necessary, or in which it is at least commonly administered, or if at least one of the parents of the party pertained to and was thus zealous in such a sect, and this parent undoubtedly was foremost in the rearing of the child and if the other parent is not known to have been positively adverse to the conferring of baptism.[425] And in a recent marriage case the Rota applied this

[420] cfr. Gasparri, nov., i, n. 582; Somewhat otherwise: Capello, iii, n. 418.

[421] SO., ad Vic. Ap. Japon. Merid., 4 feb. 1891 (cicf., iv, n. 1130; cpf., ii, n. 1746); V-Creusen, ii, nn. 298, 345; Noldin-Schmitt, iii, n. 575.

[422] cfr. Capello, iii, p. 447 (12).

[423] V-Creusen, ii, n. 345.

[424] Gasparri, i, nn. 687, 688.

[425] SO, Savannah, II.

presumption of baptism to a woman brought up in the Anglican sect.[426]

On the other hand if the non-Catholic party or parties to the marriage had parents who pertained to a sect that rejects baptism as the Socinians and Quakers, or considers it unnecessary as the Congregationalists, Unitarians, Universalists,[427] or does not admit infant baptism, or at least does not, in fact, confer baptism except upon adults, as the Baptists, or if the parents professed during their lives that they adhered to no sect, or were atheists or agnostics, the baptism is not to be presumed,[428] but must be proved.[429]

500. Similarly when the fact of baptism has been established, but the validity remains doubtful, there is a general presumption in favor of validity. This is especially true of Catholic baptism, and the presumption is elided only by strict proof to the contrary.

In order to take account of conditions that are strictly proper to modern times and to just such lands as our own however, the Holy See has laid down more pertinent presumptions on the validity of heretical baptisms: 1) The baptisms of those heretics who according to the ritual of their sect baptize validly, are to be considered valid, even if some doubt remains after investigation in an individual case.[430] Thus the Rota quoting a decree of the Holy Office of 5 Feb. 1851, declared that persons baptized in the national Church of Holland are presumed to be validly baptized.[431]

2) As to heretics belonging to sects whose rituals prescribe the conferring of baptism without the necessary use of the essential matter and form, each particular case must be examined, and if after examination there is still doubt regarding the baptism of such heretic, the baptism is to be presumed valid in respect to the validity of marriage.

3) Where a sect is certainly known from actual customary practice to confer baptism invalidly, a person baptized in such sect is presumed to be invalidly baptized.[432]

426 R., Parisien., Null., 13 jun. 1911 (rd., iii, p. 261).

427 Smith, n. 29.

428 SO, Savannah, II.

429 cfr. Chelodi, p. 81.

430 SO., 17 nov. 1830 (cpf., i, n. 821).

431 R., Parisien., Null., 13 jun. 1911 (rd., iii, pp. 260, 261); Linneborn, p. 201; Chelodi, p. 82.

432 SO., 17 nov. 1830 (cpf., i, n. 821; cicf., iv, n. 869); SO., 18 sept. 1890 (ass., xxiv, p. 574; akk., 1920, p. 66); DS., Validitatis Baptismi, 17 nov. 1916

501. When it is presumed that baptism has been conferred and is valid, the presumption is merely legal and not inevitable. At one time the Holy Office and the Congregation of the Council seem to have followed an inevitable principle in favor of baptism, the effect of which was that a marriage, to which one party was certainly baptized and the other party but doubtfully baptized, would be considered valid by a rule of law having the effect of an implicit dispensation, whether the doubtful baptism was really valid or not. The Congregation decided the case of one Laura Delphini, born, apparently, "in partibus infidelium," who had later been placed by her supposed grandmother in an orphan asylum, no one doubting her baptism. Later she was confirmed and finally married to a friend and benefactor. Then there arose a serious and probable doubt whether she had been baptized, and quarrels, and separation from her husband. To the proposed question whether Laura must be baptized conditionally, the Congregation answered: "In the affirmative, and secretly, and without prejudice to the validity of the marriage." [433] This, says Gasparri,[434] shows that the marriage was valid not only by presumption in the external forum, but also in the internal forum, *i. e.* the marriage was considered simply valid, whether the baptism had been previously conferred or not. Otherwise, he says, the response could not have been that the conditional baptism must be without prejudice to the marriage, but rather the Congregation must have added that consent was to be renewed precautionally, or at least, that correction at the root was precautionally granted. On the ground of this and similar documents, as well as because the practice of the Roman Curia had not always required a precautionary dispensation from disparity

(aas., viii, p. 478); Smith, n. 29: "Presbyterian and Methodist ministers confer baptism by dipping their fingers or the sprinkle in water, and sprinkling with it those who are to be baptized, often in such a manner that the water scarcely touches them." This statement is however too categorical; for some Methodist rituals certainly prescribe a normal and valid form of baptism: cfr. The Baptismal Font, A Manual by Rev. Frank Albert Domer, Ph.D., Buffalo, N. Y., 1903.

Donovan in aer., lxxiv (1926), p. 158 and lxxxiv (1931), p. 124 pleads for a wide presumption of invalidity of Protestant, especially Baptist baptisms, because of lack of intention, on the part of the ministers, to effect spiritual regeneration by the baptism. That this contention is erroneous see in SO, 1872, § Denique; Schaaf in aer., lxxv (1926), pp. 136, 358.

[433] SCC., Tarvisina, 26 apr. 1736; 4 mai. 1737 (cicf., v, nn. 3458; 3475).

[434] Gasparri, nov., i, n. 578.

of cult in doubtful cases before marriage (cfr. n. **498**), Gasparri sought in his earlier edition to maintain that even in recent pre-Code law, the inevitable principle in favor of marriage had the effect of an implicit dispensation, and made the marriage valid, whether the baptism presumably conferred and presumably valid, had been validly bestowed or not.[435] Most authors however, notably among them Wernz,[436] denied that the presumption was, in recent times, inevitable, or constituted a principle having the effect of objective validity of the marriage by reason of an implied dispensation from the impediment.[437] In his new edition Gasparri says the Holy Office later changed its practice and began to settle cases on the simple legal presumption of validity of baptism, which presumption must thenceforward cede to the truth. The changed practice is shown in the fact that precautionary dispensations from disparity were granted by the Holy Office in cases of doubtful baptism, and the parties could also seek to have the marriage declared invalid.[438] And he cautions readers to have this change before their minds, in order to avoid confused notions deriving from the apparently conflicting decisions of the Curia and the conflict of opinion among authors.[439]

502. With respect to the impediment of disparity of cult, and in some cases with respect also to other impediments (cfr. n. **508**), this more recent pre-Code policy determined that the objective validity of the marriage depended entirely upon the objective validity of the baptism. This has been retained in the Code: a marriage is null if contracted by a non-baptized person with a person baptized in the Catholic Church or converted to it from heresy or schism (c. 1070, §1).[440] Hence if it is proved that baptism has not been conferred or

[435] Gasparri, i, nn. 686-689; somewhat similarly Lehmkuhl, ii, n. 985.

[436] Wernz, iv, n. 507, and p. 380 (28); cfr. also De Becker, p. 237 fol.

[437] cfr. SO., 29 apr. 1842 (cicf., iv, n. 888; cpf., i, n. 948); Chelodi, n. 80: "Cum impedimentum sit iuris canonici, theoretice nulla est difficultas, quia Ecclesia potest libere de eo statuere, vel potius, uti dicit Gasparri . . . quia consuetudo, quae illud induxit, hos casus non respexit, ideoque impedimentum in eis non existit. At num quod fieri potuit factum sit est quaestio; rationes quae afferuntur non sunt cogentes ad statuendam exceptionem a *regula generali*, . . ."

[438] Gasparri, nov., i, n. 580.

[439] Gasparri, nov., i, n. 585.

[440] G. Arendt in jp., v (1925), p. 136 following Lehmkuhl, ii, n. 985, holds that the mind of the Church is to consider one as an actual subject of the Church and of ecclesiastical laws when he has outwardly been baptized or

is not valid, even though the contrary presumption had been established, the subsequent marriage will be valid or invalid according to the proper legal effects of the absence or invalidity of baptism.

503. In recent pre-Code jurisprudence the presumption of validity of baptism took precedence over the presumption of validity of marriage. The presumption in favor of baptism has generally coincided with and supported the presumption in favor of the validity of marriage. Thus if two Catholics were married but a doubt has arisen regarding the baptism of one of them, the presumption favored the baptism and the marriage. Similarly if a Catholic had married a heretic or schismatic whose baptism is doubtful, or if heretics or schismatics were married among themselves and the baptism of one or both was doubtful, the presumption has always been in favor of the baptism and in favor of the validity of the marriage.[441]

In cases where the presumption in favor of baptism places the parties to a marriage in such a position that their marriage appears to be thereby invalid, there is an evident conflict between the presumption favoring baptism and the presumption favoring the validity of the marriage. This conflict between the two presumptions has found its natural solution in the principle that the more particular and direct presumption must elide the more general and remote (cfr. n. 397). Thus in cases where the presumption in favor of baptism created a situation whereby the marriage seemed invalid because of the impediment of disparity of cult, as *e. g.* when a certainly unbaptized person was married without dispensation to a doubtfully baptized person, the Holy See gave precedence to the presumption of valid baptism over the other presumption for the validity of the marriage, and pronounced such marriages invalid, because of the impediment of disparity of cult.[442]

504. Now the Code has clothed the rule for judging marriage cases, in the doubt that arises from doubtful baptism, in new form. If a party was commonly looked upon as baptized at the time of contracting marriage, or if his baptism was doubtful, one must hold for the validity of the marriage according to the norm of Canon 1014,

is generally held to have been baptized, even though this baptism was not conferred or is actually invalid. But cfr. SO., 29 apr. 1842 (cicf., iv, n. 888; cpf., i, n. 948) contrary.

[441] SO., 9 sept. 1868, Japoniae (cicf., iv, n. 1007; cpf., ii, n. 1334).

[442] SO, 1872; SO., 14 jul. 1880, Japoniae (cpf., ii, n. 1536; cicf., iv, 1065).

until it is certainly proved that one party was baptized and the other was not baptized (c. 1070,§2). For the interpretation of this be it said: First, that the entire question deals with judgment of marriages already entered upon and in no way with marriages about to be contracted (cfr. nn. **496-498**). Second, it seems certain that Paragraph 2 of Canon 1070 does not, at least directly, give a general norm that is to apply throughout the realm of marriage and impediments, as some have thought,[443] but rather a limited norm applicable to the case of disparity of cult specifically mentioned with it in Paragraph 1. This is clear from the position, context, and wording of Paragraph 2 itself: it is placed immediately beneath and subordinated to the paragraph that explains wherein the impediment of disparity consists, and speaks of a presumption on disparity of cult. Hence all interpretation of Paragraph 2 must refer to the case where at least one party is *prima facie* a baptized Catholic.[444] Third, it must be interpreted, as far as the text and context do not contradict, to agree with the pre-Code legislation and practice of the Roman Curia (cc. 6, nn. 3, 4; 22).

Evidently Paragraph 2 does not apply to the case of a doubtfully baptized heretic or schismatic not aggregated to the Church, who has married an infidel or another heretic or schismatic not aggregated to the Church (as the above quoted decisions of SO. formerly applied). For the doubt touching the baptism of either does not now affect the marriage, however the doubt may be solved. All authors agree that Canon 1070,§1 has explicitly changed that.

The word "party" (pars) in Canon 1070,§2 certainly refers to the non-Catholic party whose baptism is doubtful and who is married to a Catholic. Thus there is perfect accord between this Paragraph and pre-Code jurisprudence, for both presume the bestowal and validity of a doubtful baptism and the consequent validity of the ensuing marriage (cfr. n. **503**). Hence this case is certainly a true application and interpretation of Paragraph 2 as all authors agree. The word "party" also refers to a Catholic whose baptism is now doubted, who has married another Catholic. The doubtful baptism of the first Catholic is presumed to have been validly bestowed and the ensuing marriage is presumed valid. Similarly too, if there is doubt regarding the baptism of both parties, whether both are Catholics or only one, the word "party" certainly refers to both, and Canon 1070,§2 thus excludes, by presumption, the impediment of disparity of cult.

[443] W-Vidal, v, n. 268.

[444] G. Arendt, in jp., v (1925), pp. 134, 135.

505. If Paragraph 2 is to be interpreted so as to agree perfectly with pre-Code practice and legislation, the word "party" cannot refer to the Catholic party who is married to an infidel. For the pre-Code presumption is that the baptism is valid in reference to the marriage, even when that validity results in the invalidity of the marriage (cfr. n. 503). And when the Catholic's baptism is doubtful his marriage with an infidel is held to be invalid. Some writers hold that the same principle must now apply, even under Canon 1070,§2,[445] and this interpretation is certainly not devoid of merit.

506. Most authors hold however, that Paragraph 2 introduces a change from recent pre-Code jurisprudence and acknowledges the precedence of the presumption in favor of validity of marriage over the presumption in favor of baptism.[446] Hence they view the word "party" as applicable to the Catholic of doubtful baptism who is married to an infidel. Then the Canon reads that the doubtful baptism of the Catholic is considered invalid,[447] in order that the marriage may be considered valid as between two unbaptized persons. For if the baptism of the Catholic were presumed valid in respect to the marriage, the marriage would be pronounced invalid by Canon 1070, §1. In behalf of such a change there is the wording of Canon 1070,§2. For this Paragraph seems to be so formed as to claim a wider ambit for the presumption of validity of marriage. For if the Code meant merely to repeat the old presumption of baptism in its respect to marriage, it is hard to understand why Paragraph 2 should have sought a new wording so much less clear than that expressing the old presumption in favor of baptism.[448]

[445] G. Arendt, in jp., v (1925), p. 138; Simon in aer., lxxvi (1927), pp. 44, 50, 51; cfr. also Capello, iii, n. 419 who however does not clearly disentangle the difficulty.

[446] De Smet, ii, n. 587; V-Creusen, ii, n. 345; Chelodi, n. 80; Blat, n. 467; Schaefer, p. 181; Cerato, n. 65; Farrugia, n. 170; De Becker, nov. p. 49; Gasparri, nov., i, n. 584; Ayrinhac, n. 135.

[447] De Smet, ii, n. 587.

[448] Canon 763, § 2 seems also at first sight to offer a parallel text, for it states that spiritual relationship and an impediment to marriage are not produced if a baptism is repeated conditionally, unless the same sponsor was taken at both baptisms. But on consideration, one sees that Canon 763 does not express any precedence of presumptions but rather makes a regulation touching the substantive law on marriage, in order to avoid double impediment.

Certainly the Code has not reverted to any inevitability of the presumption in favor of the marriage; it has rather retained the recent pre-Code principle that the marriage is objectively invalid if there is objective disparity of cult within the terms defined by Canon 1070, §1, and it allows suit to prove nullity of marriage on this ground of disparity of cult (cc. 247,§3; 1990).

507. If a marriage has been contracted before the promulgation of the Code between a doubtfully baptized person and an infidel, and is now brought before the ecclesiastical court on the ground of disparity of cult, shall the court now give the precedence to the presumption favoring baptism, or (supposing that a change has been introduced by Canon 1070,§2), to the presumption favoring valid marriage? Marriages by whatever impediment invalidly contracted before the promulgation of the Code remain invalid even after the Code has abolished the impediment, for the laws of the Code are not retroactive.[449] Hence the ecclesiastical court may not apply any change in the substantive law to the marriage contracted before the Code. Hence too, some authors would hold to the pre-Code presumption in such cases.[450] But in so far as the Code states a precedence of the presumption of valid marriage over the presumption of baptism, this constitutes a rule of present procedure for the court, whether a marriage now under consideration was contracted before or after the Code was promulgated.[451]

508. The question of doubtful baptism may affect other impediments than disparity of cult: if two persons doubtfully baptized and connected by the bond of blood or affinity have been married, there is a question whether the presumption of valid baptism should have precedence with the consequent incurring of the impediment and the invalidity of the marriage, or whether the presumption of valid marriage should prevail and the question of valid baptism be neglected in this connection. Previous to the Code this conflict between the two presumptions was settled as in the case of doubtful disparity of cult. The question was brought to Rome for decision, and the Holy Office did not hesitate to grant precedence to the presumption in favor of baptism. Upon being asked whether the marriage of two doubtfully baptized persons is valid even if they are related by blood

[449] PC., 2-3 jun. 1918, nn. 6, 7 (aas., x, p. 346).

[450] *e. g.* W-Vidal, v, n. 270; Chelodi, n. 80.

[451] V-Creusen, ii, n. 345; For an authentic decision in a similar question respecting applicaton of c. 1017, § 3, cfr. PC., 2-3 jun. 1918, n. 6 (aas., x, p. 346).

or affinity, the Holy Office answered that the marriage is to be considered invalid by reason of the impediment of blood relationship or affinity.[452] Similarly, the Rota declared a marriage invalid because of spiritual relationship, in a case where the solemn baptism from which the spiritual relationship derived was open to doubt. For there was some incomplete proof that a private baptism had been bestowed, which would have invalidated the solemn baptism. The Rota held to the presumption of validity of the solemn baptism, to the effect of invalidating the marriage.[453] Whether this principle is now to be retained, whereby valid baptism is presumed in such cases, to the effect of pronouncing the later contracted marriage invalid, does not appear certain from the Code, for no mention of it is made there. Generally we must not recede from former jurisprudence unless a change is evidently ordered (cc. 20; 23), and it seems to me that the judge must adhere to the traditional presumption of baptism now, even to the effect of creating a presumptive invalidity of the marriage.[454] It is however true that Canon 18 directs us in doubt to parallel passages of the Code, and Canon 1070,§2 just now discussed, seems to offer some parallel, so that if it shall later appear certain that Canon 1070,§2 is to be interpreted to contain a precedence of the presumption of marriage over that of baptism, this would be an argument for the similar solution of the present problem. Besides, there is an argument deriving from Canon 15 stating that diriment and inhabilitating laws (impediments) do not hold in doubt of law, by which one might conclude that since the whole question of presumption of baptism and marriage is not now clear, no impediment accrues, now since the Code, by reason of the presumption of baptism. These considerations cannot be spurned, and hence for definite certainty in this question we must await a greater concordance among authors or an authoritative decision from the Pontifical Commission on Interpretation, or perhaps from the Holy Office. Meanwhile diocesan Curiae must refrain from declaring marriages invalid on the ground of the precedence of the presumption for validity of baptism as formerly stated by the Holy Office, and any case of this kind now arising in the interim, must be referred to Rome.

[452] SO., Iaponiae, 14 jul. 1880 (cicf., iv, n. 1065; cpf., ii, n. 1536); Ep. S. Galli, 3 apr. 1893 (apud Blat, iii, pars I, n. 467); Slater in aer., lxi, (1919), p. 22.

[453] R., Null., 25 feb. 1911 (rd., iii, p. 93).

[454] Thus too Capello, iii, pp. 447, 448 (14); Chelodi, n. 80; Farrugia, n. 170; V-Creusen, ii, n. 345.

509. Baptism conferred in the Catholic Church obliges the baptized person who is about to marry to contract in the Catholic form of marriage described in Canons 1094-1099 (cfr. n. **150**), even if a doubt arise respecting the validity of the baptism.[455] And if the doubt center on the fact of baptism, the person in question is likewise bound to contract in Catholic form, providing he is commonly supposed to have been baptized.[456] However, some authors of the highest rank hold that a Catholic's informal marriage is to be presumed valid, until the fact and validity of Catholic baptism are proved, if the doubtfully baptized Catholic has already contracted with an infidel or other non-Catholic, or with an Oriental Catholic, or with another doubtfully baptized Catholic of Latin rite.[457] But this contention seems to be based on an exaggerated understanding of the ambit of Canon 1014. For only those marriages of Catholics are valid (c. 1094), or carry the canonical presumption of validity (c. 1014), which are contracted in Catholic form, and the natural presumption for the validity of acts done (cfr. n. **408**) does not apply when the person in question is restricted to a definite form of contract, and the precise question at issue is whether or not the necessary form has been observed (cfr. nn. **415**, **425**).[458] If it is proved that the person in question was not bound to contract in Catholic form, either because he was the child of a non-Catholic and was brought up from infancy outside the Church (cfr. c. 1099,§2), or because the baptism was conferred outside the Church and there was no subsequent conversion, or was invalid, or was not conferred at all, the presumption gives way to fact, and the marriage contracted bears the natural presumption of validity (cfr. n. **412**).[459]

510. The change introduced into the Code with reference to the impediment of disparity of cult (c. 1070,§1) now prevents the curia from pronouncing invalid the marriage of an infidel with a doubtfully baptized person, *v. g.* heretic or schismatic. But there is a question whether the Pauline privilege or a pontifical dispensation can dissolve the marriage that is valid and has been consummated in in-

[455] V-Creusen, ii, n. 407.

[456] Lehmkuhl, ii, n. 426; V-Creusen, i, n. 106; G. Arendt in jp., v (1925), pp. 136, 137.

[457] Capello, iii, n. 700; De Smet, i, n. 140; W-Vidal, v, n. 553.

[458] cfr. Gasparri, nov., i, nn. 568, 574; with ii, n. 1020.

[459] Contrary, G. Arendt, in jp., v (1925), pp. 136, 137.

fidelity but has not been consummated since being ratified by the baptism of the parties. Before the Code the Holy Office was asked whether, when a doubtfully baptized person had married a non-baptized person, either one could use the Pauline privilege after renewed or conferred baptism, provided the other party refused to be converted or live in peaceful cohabitation. And the answer was that provision was made for this case by the fact that such a marriage was void because of disparity of cult.[460] Thus there was no necessity of answering directly, whether the Pauline privilege could be applied to such a case; but now, since the Code, there is no impediment of disparity in the case, at least when the doubtfully baptized party is a non-Catholic. Yet if either party desires to be converted, the law's favor rests with the privileged Faith (c. 1127), to the effect that the Pauline privilege be used or a pontifical dispensation be obtained, whenever the divine or ecclesiastical law or practice does not clearly contradict. To determine this in detail, four cases are considered:

I. When there is a marriage between a certainly baptized non-Catholic and an infidel, there is the question whether the Pauline privilege is applicable. Most authors answer in the negative on the ground that the Pauline privilege requires the non-Baptism of both parties, and this view is considered certain for present-day, practical jurisprudence.[461] But even if the Pauline privilege cannot be applied, the Supreme Pontiff can and has dispensed such marriages to favor the conversion of one party. In some cases the dispensation has been granted to favor the conversion of the infidel party. Thus in a case from Helena, Mont.,[462] and again in a case apparently from

[460] SO., 7 jul. 1880 (gasp., i, n. 691).

[461] V-Creusen, ii, n. 428.

[462] SO., 4 nov. 1924 (akk., cv, (1925), p. 574): "*Beatissime Pater.*—Episcopus Helenensis, ad pedes S. V. humillime provolutus, exponit: Die 30 septembris 1919, apud . . . G.G.M. acatholicus non baptizatus, matrimonium iniit cum F. E. G. acatholica baptizata in secta anglicana, coram praecone haeretico, sectae anglicanae, proindeque absque ulla dispensatione obtenta. Die 4 novembris 1920, G. G. M. divortium civile a F. E. G. obtinuit. Nunc desiderat G. G. M. catholicam fidem amplecti et matrimonium inire cum puella catholica. F. E. G. novas nuptias iam iniit. Quapropter supplicat S. V. ut dispensatio concedatur super vinculo naturali primi matrimonii.

"*Feria IV, die 5 novembris 1924.*—In Congregatione generali S. R. et U. Inquisitionis, proposito suprascripto supplici libello, attentis expositis, praehabitoque RR. DD. Consultorum voto, E.mi ac Rev.mi DD. Cardinales in rebus Fidei et morum Generales Inquisitores decreverunt: 'Consulendum SS.mo, pro

Holland.[463] But such a marriage has also been dissolved by papal dispensation to favor the conversion of the already baptized party.[464]

gratia dissolutionis vinculi naturalis primi matrimonii contracti a G.G.M. cum F. E. G. in favorem fidei.'

"Insequenti vero feria V. eiusdem mensis et anni, SS.D.N.D. Pius, divina Providentia Papa XI, in audientia R.P.D.Assessori S. Officii impertita, habita de hac re relatione, resolutionem EE.Patrum adprobavit et petitam gratiam concedere dignatus est.

"Contrariis quibuscumque non obstantibus.

"Aloysius Castellano, *Supremae S. C. S. Officii Notarius.*"; cfr. also Donovan in aer., lxxii (1925), pp. 191, 624.

[463] SO., 16 apr. 1926 (akk., cvii (1927), p. 183; ex Neederlandsche Katolieke Stemmen, Oct., 1926, p. 310 ff.) : "B. P. Ordinarius N. ad pedes S. V. provolutus exponit: Die . . . 1919 M. acatholicus non baptizatus matrimonium iniit cum N. acatholica baptizata in secta haeretica, coram magistratu civili proindeque absque ulla dispensatione obtenta. Die . . . 1922 M. divortium civile a N. obtinuit. Nunc desiderat M. Catholicam fidem amplecti et matrimonium inire cum puella catholica. Quapropter supplicat S.V. ut dispensatio concedatur super vinculo naturali matrimonii.

"Resp. . . . Ille et Revme Dne. De casu matrimoniali M. N. haec suprema Congregatio Sancti Officii, omnibus mature perpensis decrevit: Attentis expositis nihil obstare quominus M. iam ad Fidem Catholicam conversus et rite baptizatus admittatur ad matrimonium cum muliere catholica, ut in precibus, contrahendum: facto verbo cum Sanctissimo. Et. SSmus D. N. Pius divina providentia Papa XI, de omnibus audita relatione, resolutionem adprobavit." This text seems to leave some reason to think that such a marriage may be dissolved in favor of the infidel party, even by the Pauline privilege, for according to it the Supreme Pontiff has done nothing more than approve the decision of SO. that the converted infidel is not impeded from marrying anew. Cpre. also c. 1120, § 2.

[464] SO., 10 jul. 1924 (akk., cvii (1927), pp. 181, 182) : "Georges, baptizé par les hérétiques, s'est marié legitimement avec une infidèle. Mais peu après, celle-ci abondonne son mari, retourne dans sa famille et se marie avec un infidèle. Georges, lui, embrasse la religion catholique et, comme il est trop dur de garder la continence, il interpelle régulièrement sa première femme et contracte ensuite mariage devant le missionaire avec une personne catholique. Le missionaire, en effet, se basant sur le sentiment de certains auteurs, a jugé le mariage de George hérétique avec une infidèle équivalent au mariage conclu dans infidélité.

"On demande en conséquence: Le second mariage de Georges est-il valide, soit que le baptême qu'il a reçu du ministre hérétique fût douteux soit qu'il fût valide?

"Resp. Notre Très Saint Père le Pape Pie XI, dans l'audience qu'il a accordée au Rév. Assesseur du S. Office, après avoir entendu la relation de la supplique ci-dessus, a daigné accorder la faveur de la dispense du mariage contracté avec l'infidèle afin que, en renouvelant le consentiment ad cautelam,

511. II. In the case of marriage between a doubtfully baptized non-Catholic and an infidel, most authors have thought that bishops may even of their own accord allow the use of the Pauline privilege, and to this end the doubtful baptism is dealt with as non-existent or invalid. But these authors explain that, if the marriage cannot be dissolved by that means, there is an implicit dispensation of the Supreme Pontiff which automatically applies in case one party is actually baptized.[465] This view seems to have considerable merit from the wording of Canon 1120,§2 taken into consideration with Canon 1127, but has not been canonically established as certain. But whether or not the Pauline privilege can be simply applied, it is certain that the Supreme Pontiff can and does dispense in these cases, just as when the non-Catholic's baptism is certain.[466]

512. III. When there is a marriage between two doubtfully baptized non-Catholics some few authors hold that the presumption may be applied in favor of the Faith, so that after conversion of a party to the Church, a new marriage may be permitted, either by the usual application of the Pauline privilege,[467] or at least by special dispensation of the Supreme Pontiff.[468] But most authors, with better reason, it seems, deny that either Pauline privilege or papal dispensation is in place as long as there is probable and positive reason for holding both baptisms as valid.[469] For, besides the theological reasons advanced, there is a pre-Code instruction of the Holy Office denying that the Pauline privilege may be applied in a case of conversion to the Catholic Faith after a doubtful baptism in heresy.[470] Although

le mari puisse contracter validement un nouveau mariage avec la personne catholique avec laquelle il vit. Contrariis non obstantibus quibuscunque."; cfr. also Ayrinhac, n. 300, B.

465 W-Vidal, v, n. 631 (p. 757); Farrugia, n. 326; Donovan in aer., lxxii (1925), p. 628; cfr. Hilling in akk., cvii (1927), pp. 185, 186; contrary Ayrinhac, nn. 300, 301; Arendt in jp., v (1925), pp. 140, 141; de quibus cfr. Gregory, pp. 120-123.

466 In the cases of SO., 10 jul. 1924 and SO., Helena, 4 nov. 1925 just above cited, it seems that the validity of the baptism was doubtful, though the fact of baptism was certain.

467 Hilling in akk., cvii (1927), p. 186.

468 Cerato, p. 224; Schaepmann (cit. in Ned. Kath. Stemmen, 1925, p. 58); aer., lxi (1919), p. 202 fol.

469 V-Creusen, ii, n. 437; De Becker, nov., p. 262; Ayrinhac, n. 301; Gregory, pp. 127, 128.

470 SO, 1872.

this response must be accorded great value for the interpretation of Canon 1127, it is not entirely decisive in the solution of our present problem:[471] first, because it contemplates a marriage case which is complicated with the double question of doubtful validity of baptism and doubtful consent to the marriage; secondly, because it is not impossible that the Church may now, because of a change of circumstances in heretical sects, disregard the doubtful baptisms of non-Catholics in order to favor the Faith and use of the Pauline privilege, even though in the past, the precedence was given to the presumption of baptism.[472] However, a similar decision seems to have been lately given in a case, where, apparently, only doubtful baptisms come into question.[473] Hence in practice, bishops may certainly not permit the use of the Pauline privilege in these cases, and as to the possibility of papal dissolution to favor the Faith, it is certainly the present norm of the Holy See to require full proof of the infidel condition, *i. e.* the non-baptism of one party during the entire time of conjugal life, and the non-use of the marriage after the baptism of the party who had been hitherto unbaptized.

IV. And this holds good *a fortiori* when the case entails the marriage of a certainly baptized non-Catholic and a doubtfully baptized non-Catholic.

§ 8. Presumption of Order and Vow

513. Marriages attempted by clerics ordained in holy (major) orders are invalid (c. 1072). The invalidity of a subsequent marriage depends upon the validity of the ordination. When the ordination is shown to have been undertaken in the proper canonical form and the ordaining prelate is a Catholic, there is a presumption of law for its validity, unless the contrary is proved.[474] If the ordination of a schismatic or heretic ordained by a schismatic or heretic bishop is doubtful, the obligation of celibacy and the impediment against marriage do not hold, because the natural right to marry takes precedence

[471] Hilling, in akk., cvii (1927), p. 185.

[472] Hilling in akk., cvii (1927), p. 185; Donovan in aer., lxxii (1925), p. 625 fol.

[473] Schaepmann in Ned. Kath. Stemmen, 1925, p. 53 fol. ex cit. akk., cvii (1927), p. 184; cfr. also SO., Bulgariae, 5 jul. 1853 (cicf., iv, n. 925; cpf., i, n. 1096).

[474] DS, Ordin., n. 62, § 1.

over whatever presumption there may be for validity of ordination until the contrary is proved, and in the case stated the contrary is not provable.[475]

514. The invalidity of a subsequent marriage depends also upon the ordained man's knowing that he assumes the obligation of celibacy. Schismatics and heretics are not bound by the impediment of order unless they know of the obligation of celibacy attaching.[476] If a Catholic in major orders claims that he did not know of the obligation of celibacy, and is therefore not bound by it, this ignorance is not presumed and must be proved (c. 16,§2).[477] In the case of schismatics or heretics ordained by schismatic or heretic bishops, there is no presumption that they knew of the obligation of celibacy. On the contrary, this matter is surely for them a "factum alienum non notorium" of which ignorance is presumed (c. 16,§2). There is furthermore the presumption that these schismatics or heretics did not intend or accept the obligation of celibacy, and this lack of intention, in their cases, redounds to ignorance of the obligation as applicable to themselves. Hence Gasparri's statement, that valid ordination of heretic or schismatic priests begets obligation to observe clerical chastity,[478] must be construed in concurrence with the principle that the impediment against marriage is not incurred, unless the obligation of celibacy was knowingly intended and taken.[479]

In the case of apostates ordained by schismatic or heretic bishops, the Church, by a fiction of law, considers them as not ordained, and

[475] Gasparri, nov., i, n. 616 seeks also to solve the difficulty arising from the contrary conclusion of SO., 23 mai. 1892.

[476] That this ignorance excuses, in spite of c. 16, § 1, is due to the fact that there is no question here of ignorance of the invalidating law (impediment), but of ignorance of the obligation, knowledge of which is the prerequisite of the impediment.

[477] cfr. DS, Ordin., n. 62, § 2; V-Creusen, ii, n. 347; De Smet, ii, n. 571; Gasparri, nov., i, n. 611.

[478] Gasparri, nov., i, n. 616: "Quod si haereticus aut schismaticus ordinatus fuerit ab Episcopo haeretico aut schismatico, et assumptis omnibus necessariis et opportunis informationibus, per iudicium a S. Sede ferendum in singulis casibus, constiterit ordinationem fuisse certe validam, quia nil defuit ad validitatem sive in consecratione ipsius Episcopi ordinantis, sive in ordinatione ab eodem peracta, ordinatum teneri obligationibus clericalibus, palam est."

[479] Gasparri, nov., i, n. 611.

hence they are bound by no obligation of celibacy and by no impediment against marriage.[480]

515. The subsequent marriage of a cleric in holy orders is not invalid if there was grave duress imposed to force the ordination, and if the cleric has not thereafter ratified the ordination and the clerical obligations (c. 214,§1). The duress is not presumed but must be proved according to the norm of Canons 1993-1998 and the Instruction of the Congregation of the Sacraments of 9 June 1931. It is the duty of the judge and of the defender of the ordination (c. 1586) to pertinently question the witnesses as to the person to whose charge the duress must be laid, and besides, as to the facts and circumstances that indicate and qualify the duress. If it is seen that the mode and circumstances of the cleric's life beget argument for defect of intention or free will, such proof by indication and presumption is allowable.[481] And with due allowances, the same presumptions will hold with regard to duress in these cases, as with regard to duress imposed to effect marriage itself (cfr. nn. **479-482, 484**).

516. Canon 214,§1 says it must be proved that the ordination and obligations have not been ratified by the coerced cleric. Nevertheless when grave duress has been proved, the later ratification with the consequential impediment to marriage is not presumed by law, even when the cleric has exercised the orders received under duress. But the judge may come to a justified personal presumption of ratification if the proved facts give sufficient basis for it: it must appear that the cleric in question ratified the ordination and accepted the obligations at least tacitly by exercising his orders, after the duress or other defect of consent had ceased, and after perceiving, at least indistinctly, that the obligation was not as yet assumed.[482]

Ratification is not presumable while the case is pending; but when sentence has been judicially rendered against the nullity of orders or of the obligations deriving, the presumption of ratification arises both from failure to appeal and from the appeal having been adversely decided, together with the cleric's willingly and freely resuming exer-

[480] SO., 18 nov. 1931 ad Ap. Delegatum in Indiis (apud Gasp., nov., i, n. 615): "Ecclesiam non habere nec unquam habituram esse oratorem tamquam ordinatum, eumque propterea nullis teneri obligationibus statui clericali adnexis."

[481] DS, Ordin., nn. 62, 63.

[482] DS, Ordin., n. 65.

cise of his orders, or his having continued to duly exercise them, especially if he failed to take the necessary means to acquire freedom from the obligations under circumstances in which the absence of all inconvenience and difficulty made it easy to take them.[483] But even this presumption is merely legal and may be destroyed by contrary indications or proofs clearly showing that the will to ratify was by no means present, in spite of the external appearances of circumstantial evidence.[484]

517. Religious who have professed solemn vows invalidly attempt marriage (c. 1073). As with ordination so with solemn vows the invalidity of a subsequent marriage depends entirely upon the validity of the solemn profession. When the profession of solemn vows is shown to have been undertaken in the proper canonical form, there is a presumption of law for its validity. Thus if a person who has professed solemn vows maintains that he but fictitiously took the vows and that these were therefore invalid by reason of want of consent, he is considered bound by the vows and by the impediment to marriage, until he shall have proved that his consent was not given.[485] But if this is proved, there is no presumption of law that he afterward ratified the profession by his consent (cfr. c. 586) (cfr. n. **516**).

§ 9. Presumption of Abduction and Crime

518. There can be no marriage between an abductor and the woman he has abducted with a view to marriage, as long as she remains in the power of the abductor (c. 1074,§1). And if, with a view to marrying her, a man detains a woman by force in the place where she resides or in a place to which she has freely come, this forceable detention is on a par with abduction in nullifying the marriage (c. 1074,§3). But crimes are not to be presumed, and abduction in a given case is not presumable but must be proved by arguments that are above suspicion.[486] The Church is however intent upon preserving the freedom of marriage and thus in doubtful issues, she grants some favor of law to the party who claims her liberty has been violated.[487] Thus when there is complete *prima facie* evidence of the

[483] DS, Ordin., n. 66.

[484] DS, Ordin., n. 67.

[485] Cerato, p. 115.

[486] Pallotini, xiii, p. 294, n. 35.

[487] Gasparri, i, n. 622; Feije, n. 151; Schaefer, p. 194.

impediment, that is, when the fact of carrying off or detaining a woman together with the fact of subsequent marriage contracted with her during the flight or detention are proved, those elements of the impediment which lie hidden in the will of the parties are presumed by rebuttable presumption (cfr. c. 2200,§2).

Chief among these hidden elements is the intent to marry. The abduction constitutes a diriment impediment only when it is perpetrated with intent to marry (c. 1074,§1). If a woman is abducted and married to a man while in his power it is presumed that he carried her off for the purpose of marrying her,[488] even if no engagement or proposal to marry had preceded.[489] This presumption however is not inevitable: proof that the abductor had at the time of the abduction another intent than marriage with the woman, as *e. g.* receiving a ransom or mere sexual rape, may be offered.[490]

If it be shown that the abduction was not perpetrated with a view to marriage, the subsequent marriage is not invalid because of the impediment of abduction, but there remains nevertheless the legal presumption that any person stolen away for whatever purpose, and married to the abductor while in his power, feigned consent to the marriage under force or fear, or at least gave a consent that was vitiated by the duress inflicted.[491] This presumption too is merely legal and admits proof to the contrary.

This same presumption of non-consent to the marriage or at least of consent forced by duress, holds when the qualities of the persons concerned are such, that the abduction does not itself constitute a diriment impediment to their marriage. This is the case when an unbaptized woman is abducted by an unbaptized man, for abduction is not an impediment invalidating the marriages of in-

488 IA., § 173; De Becker, p. 72; Smith, n. 379; Feije, n. 151: ". . . . sed Boeckhn hoc facile quidem admittit pro eo qui nescit raptum dirimere matrimonium; difficultatem vero sentit quod spectat ad eum qui id novit, quum in eo gravius et geminatum delictum ita praesumeretur; quare aliis rem judicandam relinquit. Favor libertatis matrimonii generaliter exigit illam praesumptionem; ac praeterea in foro externo argumentum duci practice nequit ex ignorantia vel scientia impedimenti, et juris ignorantia non admittitur."

489 Gasparri, i, n. 622; Schaefer, p. 194; W-Vidal, v, n. 314.

490 IA., § 173; Gasparri, i, n. 622; Feije, n. 151.

491 IA., § 173; R., Vic. Ap. Manchuriae Sept., Null., 6 jun. 1917 (rd., ix, p. 145; aas., x, p. 213); SO., ad Ep. Albaniae, 15 feb. 1901 (cicf., iv, n. 1250; cpf., ii, n. 2101) states that the Council of Trent established the impediment of abduction on the presumption of non-consent to marry in such cases.

fidels.[492] And the curiae, especially in missionary lands, when called upon to judge such marriage cases, will consider that lack of consent invalidates even the marriage of infidels, and that there is in these cases a presumption of lack of consent.[493]

This presumption is also pertinent to the rare case of a man whether baptized or infidel, being stolen away by a woman, even though she acts through agents, and married to her while in her power.[494]

519. If a woman freely consents to her being carried off, it is generally held that there is no impediment but merely an elopement.[495] But there is no legal presumption of the consent to elope.[496] On the contrary, it is to be presumed that she was abducted against her will, the more so if there was no previous agreement to marry.[497] And if it be a case of seduction of a minor girl, still under the care of parents or guardian, the presumption of non-consent to the abduction is the stronger.[498] If it is maintained that the girl or woman at first resisted but then consented to the abduction, the presumption will hold for the continuance of her original non-consent.

Although there have been canonists who in recent times maintained the inevitability of the presumption of non-consent, this presumption is nevertheless rebuttable, and proof may be offered to show that the woman willingly accompanied her abductor.[499] Such proof is the more easily acceptable in America and other lands where elopements are of frequent occurrence, especially if the woman abducted is of age and of loose character.[500] The detention of a woman, when proved, bears a much stronger presumption that it took place against her will.[501]

[492] Gasparri, i, 650: ". . . nisi hoc impedimentum a civili auctoritate latum fuerit."

[493] R., Vic. Ap. Nyanzae Sept., 10 mai. 1918, 13 mai. 1919 (rd., x, p. 36; xi, p. 87; aas., xi, p. 89); Gasparri, i, n. 641.

[494] Gasparri, i, n. 621.

[495] De Becker, pp. 70, 71; Feije, n. 160; Schaefer, p. 196.

[496] Gasparri, i, n. 631.

[497] Gasparri, i, n. 618; Feije, n. 160; Smith, n. 371; W-Vidal, v, n. 314.

[498] SCC., In Olomucen., Matrimonii, 14 mart. 1772 (pall., xiii, p. 285, n. 6); Feije, n. 161; De Smet, ii, n. 648; Chelodi, n. 90.

[499] Gasparri, i, n. 618; De Smet, ii, pp. 47 (4), 146 (1); Schaefer, p. 196; Chelodi, n. 90; W-Vidal, v, n. 314.

[500] Gasparri, nov., i, n. 643.

[501] cfr. Gasparri, nov., i, n. 649.

Even when the consent to the abduction has been proved however, some authors insist that the impediment is not overcome unless the woman knew that the elopement was meant to end in marriage.[502] In any case, she must later consent to the marriage or it is invalid. This consent to the marriage, and much more so, her consent to an elopement precisely meant to terminate in marriage is not presumable nor inferable from the consent to the abduction but must be proved.[503] Such proof, says Feije, can hardly be forthcoming, unless it be shown that, previous to the abduction, the parties were betrothed or had planned to be married.[504] On the other hand if it is shown that such steps had been taken toward being married, this constitutes strong circumstantial evidence of the woman's consent in the abduction and marriage.[505]

520. Those who, while a legitimate *i. e.* canonically valid marriage of either still subsisted, have committed adultery together, and have given each other a promise of future marriage, or have attempted marriage even by a merely civil ceremony, cannot validly contract matrimony together (c. 1075, n. 1). It is however difficult to establish the invalidity of a marriage contracted under this impediment of crime, "neutro patrante," for most frequently the parties to the marriage have no other proof of the adultery and promise of marriage than their own assertions, and this does not establish the case.

The fact of adultery is not simply to be presumed. But if there be proof of other facts upon which adultery almost invariably follows, there may be a presumption of the adultery, admissible as part proof of the case. This was established by Alexander III with respect to the adultery committed by a married woman and a relative of her husband. A husband had brought suit for separation from his wife on the grounds of adultery, but he had no witnesses who had actually seen her in the very act of adultery. The witnesses testified however that they had found the persons "solum cum sola, nudum cum nuda, in eodem lecto iacentem, ea, ut credebant, intentione, ut eam cognosceret carnaliter." Alexander decreed that both from the confession of the parties, and from the violent and sure presumption of forni-

[502] De Becker, p. 71; Feije, n. 160; De Smet, ii, n. 648.

[503] Pallotini, xiii, p. 286, n. 9; Feije, n. 160; De Becker, p. 71; Gasparri, i, n. 631; Cerato, p. 117.

[504] Feiji, nn. 160, 161, 171, 185.

[505] Smith, n. 373; De Becker, p. 71; Chelodi, n. 90.

cation, the sentence of divorce was to be pronounced.[506] The case had nothing to do with the nullity of the marriage but merely with a separation from bed and board; nevertheless the presumption of fornication derived from proof that a man and woman have been alone, devoid of clothing, in the same room, has been considered so strong that it has been adopted by practically all writers since that time, and has been regularly applied, even in cases where the fornication or adultery thus presumed affects the validity of the marriage. And this doctrine has been universally followed by the Rota, even in recent trials.[507]

In the establishment of these crimes it is likewise in accord with the practice of the courts to make use of the proper personal presumptions derivable from the known propensities and characters of the persons concerned, and by these presumptions to assist the other arguments in the case. Thus Celestine III states that the reputations of the parties may be powerful factors in the establishment of the fact of coition in cases where the natural proofs are not otherwise entirely conclusive.[508] And the Rota established the same personal presumption in a recent case of nullity that arose in Bologna.[509] But merely frequenting a woman's abode does not beget legal presumption of adultery in respect to suits on nullity or suits on separation, as it does with respect to contumacious clerics (cfr. c. 133,§4).

521. When it is established either by natural proofs or by the proper presumptions (cfr. n. **393**), that the coition has been effected between the parties in question, there is a further presumption that

[506] c. 12, X, De Praesumptionibus, II, 23.

[507] R., Null., 31 mart. 1909 (rd., i, pp. 25, 26); Null., 11 apr. 1911 (rd., iii, p. 167); Null., 10 feb. 1912 (rd., iv, p. 87): "Non ideo ad violentam praesumptionem iudicandam sufficeret, si solus cum sola esset inventus (Sanchez, lib. II, disp. 12, n. 45): neque oscula et amplexus, 'quia licet coniecturis probatur adulterium, et illae debent esse res a natura vel a lege receptae et probatae: oscula autem et amplexus a natura neque a lege (cap. Litteris) pro urgenti coniectura admittuntur, nec etiam ab homine recipi debent, cum nulla urgens ratio id suadeat' (Sanchez, 1. c., n. 47). 'Idem dicatur (ait Gonzales, lib. II, tit. 23, cap. 12) si vir cum alterius uxore per nemora et vias occultas simul confabulantes reperiuntur . . . His indiciis verosimilibus et probabilibus adulterium certo non probatur."; Null., 4 jul. 1913 (rd., v, pp. 426, 427); Null., 23 mart. 1915 (rd., vii, p. 124).

[508] c. 27, X, De Test. et Attest., II, 20.

[509] R., Imolen., Null., 2 aug. 1913 (rd., v, p. 503): "Mores enim tum Paschalis tum Adelindis a testibus tales describuntur, ut commercium carnale inter ipsos locum habuisse sat probabile videatur."

such coition was natural and complete. This presumption has derived from pre-Code teaching and jurisprudence.[510] Since the Code it has been repeated by the Rota and the authors;[511] and, generally speaking, it is very difficult to establish conclusive proof that the coition was not natural or complete. Nevertheless, a recent decision of the Rota has warned, that it is no longer a legal presumption in the strict sense, and hence gives way before a violent personal presumption to the contrary.[512]

In any case, none of the presumptions just above mentioned is inevitable and proof to the contrary is admitted.

What is here written is also applicable in cases of pre-Code affinity, or of the impediment of public decency as described in Canon 1078.[513]

522. In establishing the impediment of crime "neutro patrante" as described in Canon 1075, n. 1, the promise of marriage must be proved: it is not to be presumed from the fact that the persons concerned have been guilty of adultery prior to the death of the spouse of one of them. Innocent III in responding to the Bishop of Spoleto on how to conduct a case in which a citizen of that city, having left his wife, lived with another woman in concubinage until the death of his wife, when he married the concubine, directed him to adjudge the marriage valid unless, during the life of the first wife, the man had given the concubine a promise of future marriage.[514] Evidently the promise was not to be presumed by reason of the adultery. And Cosci

[510] R., Null., 31 mart. 1909 (rd., i, p. 26); Null., 29 jul. 1909 (rd., i, p. 124); Null., 10 feb. 1912 (rd., iv, p. 85); Gasparri, i, n. 736; Feije, nn. 370, 450.

[511] R., Null., 3 aug. 1922 (rd., xiv, p. 243); Null., 10 aug. 1923 (rd., xv, p. 232); Gasparri, nov., i, n. 673; V-Creusen, ii, n. 440.

[512] R., Null., 10 aug. 1923 (rd., xv, p. 232): ". . . contraria et fortiori praesumptione elidi facilius potest. Et ad rem iudex omnia causae adiuncta prae oculis habere debet, locorum et personarum circumstantiis ac conditione pensatis, ita ut si agatur de muliere corrupta vel coniugata, praesumptioni illi facile locum dabit, at si de honesta ac innupta res sit, cuius maxime interest publicam infamiam vitare, caute in ea applicanda procedere debet. Hominum enim malitia, hac praesertim tempestate, plura excogitavit media ad copulae effectus in ipsa copulatione frustrandos, quae antenatos auctores ut plurimum latebant."

[513] R., Null., 3 aug. 1922 (rd., xiv, p. 243).

[514] c. 6, X, De Eo Qui Duxit in Matrimonium Quam Polluit per Adulterium, IV, 7.

quotes decisions of the early Rota to the effect that there is no such presumption.[515]

If it is shown that the promise of marriage was given by one party to the adultery, it will be presumed in the external forum that it was seriously given, and, if accepted, the acceptance of the promise will be presumed to have been serious.[516] If it is shown that the promise of marriage was given by one party, and that the other received this promise in silence, Feije says the silence will be considered a sign of acceptance in the external forum and it must be presumed that the promise was accepted.[517] Whatever the theory about silence being presumptive consent, there are a number of solid authors who hold that no impediment arises from this species of crime (cfr. n. **523**) unless there is positive acceptance of the promise or even a repromising on the part of the second party, and hence Gasparri derived the practical conclusion from reflex principles, that the marriage must not be adjudged invalid where the proposal of marriage has been received in silence.[518]

Authors have written much about ignorance that the party is already married, excusing one from incurring the impediment (cfr. n. **423**). But whatever may be maintained with respect to the internal forum, such ignorance is not presumable in the external forum,[519] and is very difficult to prove.

523. To incur the impediment of crime, "uno patrante" or "utroque patrante" as described in Canon 1075, nn. 2, 3, it was always necessary that the murder shall have been perpetrated with a view to future marriage with the accomplice. Hence Gasparri remarks that some authors have formulated presumptions upon this intention, but he does not seem to commit himself with respect to these presumptions.[520] Feije is more pronounced in his adherence

[515] Cosci, lib. I, cap. vi, nn. 33, 34. It seems therefore, that Smith, n. 365 has erred when he states: "whenever the crime of adultery, as set forth above, is proved, then the law presumes that either a promise of marriage intervened or that an attempted marriage occurred." Nor has any other author, as far as my observation goes, espoused this presumption of Smith.

[516] Feije, n. 451.

[517] Feije, n. 451.

[518] Gasparri, i, n. 737; cfr. c. 1075,n.1: "Qui . . . fidem sibi mutuo dederunt . . . "

[519] Gasparri, i, n. 746.

[520] Gasparri, i, nn. 733, 739.

to the presumption of intent: and states that when the murder was committed by the conspiracy of the two who afterward attempt marriage, the presumption holds in the external forum that the crime was done with a view to marriage, and thus the impediment is established above doubt.[521] Since the issuance of the Code this presumption has been repeatedly restated with respect to the intent in the crime "utroque patrante."[522] Similarly with respect to the manifesting of the intent to marry the adulterous party in cases of crime "uno patrante," the authors state that the intention and its manifestation are to be presumed in the external forum.[523]

A decision of the Congregation of the Council shows that the presumption of intent has not been considered inevitable. A certain John F. S. committed adultery with Mary C. although he had a wife living in another city. When he learned that his own wife had meanwhile also committed adultery, he killed her and was freed by civil court, according to the law of the land, upon proving that his wife had committed adultery. Then he wished to marry the adulterous Mary, but was restrained by injunction of the ecclesiastical court, until it should be decided whether he was bound by the impediment of crime, and particularly whether he had killed his wife with a view to marrying the other woman. It was declared that he had proved in civil court that his motive in killing his wife was vengeance of her adultery rather than intent to marry his own accomplice in adultery.[524] Some authors have recently reasserted that proof against the presumption of intent must be received.[525]

524. In order that the impediment be incurred it is necessary that the marriage against which the crime is committed be objectively valid, and that it shall not have been dissolved at the time of the crime.[526] When the fact of the marriage is established its validity is presumed (cfr. nn. **411, 412, 486**), and he who would establish the impediment of crime against a subsequent marriage, either contracted

[521] Feije, n. 453.

[522] De Smet, ii, n. 663; Linneborn, p. 224; Schaefer, p. 201; Chelodi, n. 93; Cerato, p. 119; V-Creusen, ii, n. 351; W-Vidal, v, n. 332; cfr. c. 2220, § 2.

[523] Schaefer, p. 201 (202); Chelodi, n. 93; W-Vidal, v, n. 332; Donohue, pp. 71, 72.

[524] SCC., In Ulixbonen., 28 sept. 1726 (pall., xii, p. 600, n. 7; gasp., i, n. 739).

[525] Chelodi, n. 93; Cerato, p. 119; Donohue, p. 72.

[526] Gasparri, nov., i, nn. 672, 679.

or about to be contracted, need not prove the validity of the former against all conceivable impediments.

If a second marriage has been contracted in form, and there is merely negative doubt whether the first spouse was alive or dead at the time when the crime of adultery and the promise of marriage was committed, the presumption is that life continues until death is proved,[527] and the impediment is presumably incurred (cfr. c. 1053). If there is positive probability that the first spouse was dead at the time of the crime, the second marriage must not be pronounced invalid (cfr. n. **489**). Before the second marriage has been contracted in form, probability of death of the first spouse is not sufficient proof of freedom to marry (cfr. n. **491**).

§ 10. Presumption of Potency

525. Impotence that is perpetual and antecedent to the marriage nullifies marriage by the law of nature itself (c. 1068,§1). No one is presumed to be impotent. On the contrary there is a general presumption favoring the potency of every man and woman, for everyone is presumed to have been born endowed with those faculties which are commonly bequeathed by nature (cfr. n. **142**).[528] This presumption is not limited with respect to the age of the person, but applies to persons however old, who have a desire to marry.[529]

Hence in cases of doubtful potency the presumption holds for validity of the marriage contracted,[530] and for the licitness of contracting a proposed marriage.

526. The presumption of potency applies to doubts of law as well as to doubts of fact. There are pathological conditions in which persons are canonically impotent for marriage, even though they are capable of sexual coition. If a woman is dispossessed of certain post-vaginal members it has been doubted and long disputed,[531]

[527] Gasparri, nov., i, n. 673.

[528] SCC., In Romana seu Tiburtina, Null., 12 mart. 1853 (pall., xiii, p. 69, n. 162); R., Null., 16 jul. 1910 (rd., ii, p. 280); Null., 17 feb. 1917 (rd., ix, p. 32); Bouix, i, 331, Reg. 4; Antonelli, ii, n. 581; De Smet, ii, n. 558; Schaefer, p. 170 (27).

[529] Gasparri, i, n. 566.

[530] Gasparri, i, n. 600.

[531] cfr. Antonelli, ii, nn. 476 fol.

whether this condition is one that makes her canonically impotent for marriage. And this theoretical question has not been settled by the Code or by any other decree of the Holy See.[532]

In fact the Congregation of the Council gave judicial decisions for nullity in particular cases between the years 1863 and 1899.[533] But the Holy Office then took up the question and gave practical decisions based on the reflex presumptive principle, and declared the parties were not to be disquieted or, in the case of marriage about to be contracted, that the marriage was not to be hindered.[534] Lately the Congregation of the Sacraments has given the same decision,[535] or has stated that approved authors were to be consulted.[536]

Such authors have long since given the practical solution of the doubt on the presumptive principle. Thus Gasparri says the dispossession of post-vaginal genital members leaves the potency doubtful: sometimes by doubt of fact, namely when it is doubted whether there is a defect or whether the defect is sufficient to make it entirely impossible for the woman to enter upon proper conjugal relations or conceive, and sometimes by doubt of law, namely when it is known that she has a defect that certainly prevents conception, but it is doubted whether this defect renders her canonically unfitted for marriage; and he adds that whether the doubt be doubt of law only, or doubt of fact only, or, *a fortiori,* doubt of fact and law, the marriage is subject to application of the reflex principle and is not to be impeded, and the parties already married are not to be disquieted.[537] Linneborn calls attention that the solution given by Gasparri is now incorporated in the Code, and in fact, Canon 1068,§2, without touching upon the theoretical question of what constitutes impotence, repeats, almost in the very words of Gasparri, that if the impediment of impotence is doubtful, whether by doubt of law or by doubt of

532 cfr. Toso, in jp., vii (1927), pp. 97 fol.

533 cfr. cases apud Chelodi, n. 71.

534 SO., Quebec., 23 jul. 1890 (cpf., ii, n. 1733; cicf., iv, n. 1124); In Rhegien., 30 jul. 1890 (ass., xxvii, p. 128); Westmonasterien., 31 jul. 1895 (cicf., iv, n. 1174; cpf., ii, n. 1907).

535 DS., 2 apr. 1908 (chelodi, n. 71); DS., 2 apr. 1909 (vermeersch, de castitate, n. 58 fol.).

536 Chelodi, n. 71.

537 Gasparri, i, n. 578; De Becker, p. 269; De Smet, ii, n. 718; Linneborn, p. 187; Cerato, p. 106.

fact, the marriage is not to be impeded.[538] Much less is a contracted marriage to be dissolved for such doubtful impotence.

Antonelli disallows that Canon 1068,§2 may be applied to the case where there is a doubt of law with respect to post-vaginal defects,[539] but his undoubtedly learned and weighty arguments tend rather to disprove the theoretical proposition that such marriages are valid (though his proofs do not attain to certainty), than to disprove the practical proposition that the Canon may be applied to favor the licitness of marriages where there are such defects.[540]

Several decisions of the Rota have lately applied the presumption of Canon 1068,§2 to this case, and have explicitly stated that it does cover the case.[541] And even more lately the Apostolic Signature has confirmed the same principle, and applied it to a doubt where, not post-vaginal defects, but a defect of the vagina itself, according to the view of the Rota in the matter,[542] gave rise to a question of impotence. The case was this: the vagina of the respondent wife was of normal condition except that it was occluded or turned away from the uterus, in such a way that the penetration of the vagina by the virga and the emission of semen into the vagina were possible, but the progress of the semen from the vagina into the uterus was impossible. The Signatura reversed the two favorable decisions of the Rota, and decided against both nullity and non-consummation.[543] These decisions show that Antonelli has erred in this canonical respect,

[538] W-Vidal, v, p. 254 (49) applies this even to probable relative impotence; V-Creusen, ii, n. 341 (ed. 1925) stated: "Qui relativa tantum impotentia probabiliter laborat, certum matrimonium eligere debet," but this statement is omitted from the late edition.

[539] Antonelli, ii, n. 549.

[540] cfr. Toso, in jp., vii (1927), pp. 97 fol.; Pruemmer in jp., ix (1929), p. 241 fol.

[541] R., Null., 17 apr. 1916 (rd., viii, pp. 105, 111, 112); Null., 14 jul. 1917 (rd., ix, p. 150); Null., 28 mai. 1921 (rd., xiii, p. 116); Null., 29 apr. 1922 (rd., xiv, p. 111).

[542] cfr. R., Null., 28 mai. 1921 (rd., xiii, p. 121 fol.); 29 apr. 1922 (rd., xiv, p. 112 fol.).

[543] SA., 27 jun. 1931 (gasp., nov., i, n. 534): "1. An constet de nullitate matrimonii in casu. Et quatenus negative: 2. An saltem constet de inconsummatione ita ut consilium praeberi possit SSmo pro dispensatione a matrimonio rato et non consummato in casu":—R.: Negative ad utrumque, seu nec de nullitate nec de inconsummatione matrimonii constare in casu."

and there has come to my notice no author since the Code who adheres to him in this question.[544]

527. The presumption in favor of potency is similarly applied in the case of vasectomy. At the present stage of canonical and theological opinion on the question, it is not certain that the vasectomy of a man constitutes a diriment impediment against valid marriage.[545] Hence in this doubt of law the presumption stands for validity of the marriage, and if a man who has undergone this operation seeks to marry he is not to be impeded; if he is already married he is not to be disquieted, and if the case is brought to trial, the presumption will stand for validity until an authentic decision of the Apostolic See directs otherwise, or at least until the Rota or Apostolic Signatura shall have shown by an adverse decision that the presumption cannot be safely applied in the case.

528. The question presents itself whether the presumption in favor of potency may be applied for the practical solution of a case in which the sex of an hermaphroditic person is in doubt. Antonelli denies the licitness of a marriage in cases where the external appearance of one sex is not plainly preponderant, and alleges the principle that marriage is radically impossible unless the persons are of certainly opposite sexes.[546] And the Congregation of the Council declared a marriage invalid, in which the wife was found upon examination, to pertain most probably to the male sex.[547] Hence it does not appear certain that Canon 1068,§2 covers the case where the probable impotence is occasioned by a doubtful sex. Nevertheless as long as it is truly probable that a person is potent according to a determined sex, his marriage according to that sex is not to be impeded.

[544] cfr. however on the theoretical question jp., vii (1927), p. 90 fol. Nor does R., Null., 3 feb. 1916 (rd., viii, p. 19) favor Antonelli's opinion, in stating that this case does not constitute a "dubium iuris proprie dictum," for 1) it uses the word "dubium iuris" here, in a sense different from that understood by Canon 1068, § 2, and 2) the appellate Turn of the Rota, in confirming the decision for nullity, states precisely that Canon 1068, § 2 does cover this case: Null., 14 jul. 1917 (rd., ix, p. 150).

[545] Capello, iii, nn. 377-379; Cerato, p. 106; Gasparri, nov., i, Appendix de Vasec.; V-Creusen, ii, n. 339; Chelodi, p. 68 (2) however says: "Conveniunt canonistae fere omnes talem hominem esse *impotentem*"; Ayrinhac, n. 121 refers to two decisions of R. and states that these hold for impotence. But in fact no mention is made in them, of impotence derivable from vasectomy.

[546] Antonelli, ii, n. 691.

[547] SCC., 8 aug. 1888 (Matharan, n. 203).

529. Impotence invalidates a marriage only when it is antecedent to it (c. 1068,§1). Whether in particular cases the impotence is antecedent or subsequent has been a hard question to answer, ever since these cases have begun to be judicially settled, and thus from the age of the glossaries onward, attempts have been made to lay out proper presumptions for the guidance of the judge. The efforts of the glossarians to solve these questions led to a distinction between impotence as a result of bad magic (maleficium) and impotence as a result of nature (frigiditas). What we now know as relative impotence was frequently looked upon as an artifice of bad magic whereas absolute impotence was considered to be of natural origin. The presumptions built up by the glossarians with respect to the time when the impotence came about, were not always of one accord. Thus Bernhard says that upon a woman's complaining that her husband cannot effect the coition, natural impotence will be presumed and the husband will be forbidden any further marriage, unless the husband retorts that he can effect the coition with another woman, and in that case the presumption holds for impotence effected by bad magic, and the man may enter upon another marriage. And when the bad magic impotence is alleged, the Church always presumes that it preceded the marriage.[548] Robert of St. Victor on the other hand says that in favor of the marriage, such impotence must always be presumed to be subsequent to the marriage.[549] The jurisprudence of the Church has retained neither of these views, and has rejected several other similarly futile presumptions set up by earlier authors. The presumption of antecedent or subsequent impotence based upon the time when the complaint of impotence was raised, has met with better favor.

In conformity with c. 1. X, De Frig. et Mal. et Impotentia Coeundi, IV, 15, Gasparri and other authors distinguish between the case where the doubt as to the party's impotence arises immediately after the marriage is contracted or the first attempt at coition is made, and the case where the doubt arises or is brought to court only after a considerable time has elapsed since the marriage was entered upon. In the first case the presumption holds the impotence to have anteceded the marriage.[550] This presumption is the stronger if the impotence

[548] Freisen, p. 353: "Diese angefuehrte Praesumption ist sonderbar; den waehrend sonst die Kirche stets fuer die Giltigkeit der Ehe praesumiert, thut sie hier gerade das Gegenteil; jedoch ist Gegenbeweis zulaessig."

[549] Freisen, p. 357.

[550] Gasparri, i, n. 590; Chelodi, n. 74; W-Vidal, v, p. 245 (12).

is shown to be of natural derivation rather than the result of violence.[551] And in doubt whether the impotence be natural or accidental, it is more reasonable to presume it to be natural, because of the favor accorded to marriage contracted primarily to beget offspring.[552] If on the other hand the doubt arises only after a considerable period has elapsed since the marriage was contracted, the presumption stands for the impotence being subsequent to the marriage.[553] [554]

But even when neither party has contested the marriage for a considerable time, and the impotence has evidently resulted from violence, the presumption that it came subsequently to the marriage, must cede to proof that the impotence was actually antecedent.[555]

530. Only perpetual impotence invalidates a marriage (c. 1068, §1). The question whether in a specific case the impotence is perpetual or merely temporary has always been difficult for the courts to answer, and Robert of St. Victor tells us, that it is because of this difficulty that the Roman Church followed the practice of having the parties live together as brother and sister.[556] Early attempts were made however, to lay out proper presumptions for the more accurate guidance of the judge. According to Robert and Tancred, the impotence which resulted from bad magic was presumed to be but temporary, until the three-year experiment had unsuccessfully elapsed, after which the presumption held for permanent impotence.[557] This presumption has been taken into the jurisprudence of the courts and applied to cases of impotence without regard to the source of the infirmity. The older Rota, in Ianuen, Mat., 20 July 1793 stated that impotence proved to have existed before the marriage, is by a compelling presumption, presumed to have existed at the time of the marriage and to become greater with age.[558] And again it is stated

[551] R., Null., 15 nov. 1909 (rd., i, p. 139); Menochius, lib. I, praes. 14, n. 3: "... Quod enim a natura inest, semper inesse videtur"; Gasparri, i, n. 590.

[552] Gasparri, i, n. 590; nov., i, n. 540.

[553] Cosci, lib. I, cap. xiii, nn. 28-32; Gasparri, i, n. 590; Chelodi, n. 74.

[554] In civil law, Abbott, p. 946: "The burden of proving impotence as a ground of action is on plaintiff, and increases with the lapse of time from the date of marriage to the bringing of the action."

[555] SCC., In Romana, Mat., 22 aug. 1840, § Eodem (pall., xiii, 45, § XIII).

[556] Freisen, p. 357.

[557] Freisen, pp. 357-359.

[558] Pallotini, xiii, p. 61, n. 122.

in Causa Mandalen, Null., 23 Feb. 1850, that in doubt whether the impotence is perpetual or whether it can be cured by medical means, we must hold that it is perpetual and incurable, especially if it has been tried out during the three-year period.[559]

The three-year experiment is no longer in force (cfr. n. **127**), but the ecclesiastical judge is permitted to draw a personal presumption of permanent impotence from the fact that the parties to a suit have tried unsuccessfully during a notable period of time to consummate the marriage contracted.[560]

531. When it has been established that a person is impotent, the burden of proof lies upon him to show that his potency has been regained. Thus, if and when it becomes certain that vasectomy constitutes the diriment impediment of impotence (cfr. n. **527**), and it is likewise certain that the generative potency can be restored after vasectomy, as some part of medical opinion seems to hold, the man who has undergone vasectomy will have the burden of proving that his generative potency has been regained, before he may contract marriage.[561]

§ 11. Presumption of Consummation

532. A valid marriage between baptized persons is said to be ratified if it is not yet completed by consummation; ratified and consummated if that conjugal act, to which the marital contract tends by its nature, and whereby the spouses become one flesh (coition), has taken place between them (c. 1015,§1), subsequently to their marriage. If the spouses have shared the same dwelling since the marriage was entered upon, the consummation of the marriage is presumed (c. 1015,§2). For nature itself provides the motivating instinct to the accomplishment of this marital act. The non-consummation is a

[559] Pallotini, xiii, p. 102, n. 281; cfr. also SCC., Leopolien., 15 dec. 1877; 23 mart. 1878 (cicf., vi, n. 4239).

[560] R., Null., 15 nov. 1909 (rd., i, p. 139 fol.).

[561] W-Vidal, v, n. 233: ". . . quomodo autem *per media licita* cognosci possit factum restitutae communicationis, non liquet."; Capello, iii, n. 378: "Quae probatio nullam difficultatem praesefert; sicuti enim de operatione vasectomiae constat ex attestatione medici, illius qui eam passus est, et aliorum, ita de redintegratione constat ex testimonio earundem personarum."; cfr. De Smet, ii, p. 69 (2).

great exception, is not presumed,[562] and must be proved.[563] The same presumption holds if the parties have entered upon a merely civil marriage,[564] unless the church wedding was arranged for one or two days later, in those countries where the civil marriage must, by law, precede.

But proof of non-consummation is admitted (c. 1015,§2), and thus the presumption is not inevitable.[565]

533. It is likewise presumed that complete and perfect coition has taken place whenever "vir coivit et modo dubitat num seminaverit vel num seminaverit intra vas" (cfr. nn. **393, 521**).[566] And although fecundation without coition is possible, the consummation of the marriage by complete and perfect coition is always presumed when pregnancy has taken place. Even this presumption however may be elided by proof to the contrary.[567]

534. The proof whereby the presumption of consummation is rebutted, consists generally in the physical inspection of the wife. The fact of integrity of the hymen constitutes a rebuttable presumption that coition has not taken place, and this presumption elides the other derived from sharing the same dwelling, that the marriage has been consummated (cfr. nn. **320-325**). This presumption of non-consummation is again overcome by direct proof of coition, such as is afforded by reliable expert testimony,[568] the admission of both parties that they have consummated the marriage, *etc.*

Other presumptions and indications of non-consummation are derived from external facts and circumstances pertaining to the wedded life of the parties. Thus non-consummation is indicated when it is shown that there was a defect of marital consent, force and fear, an aversion and hate on the part of at least one party from the very beginning of the wedded life, impotence either absolute or relative.[569] In order that the judge avail himself of these indications of non-consummation, it is not required that the defect of consent, the duress

[562] DS, Reg., n. 79, § 1.

[563] cfr. SCC., Neapolitana, 31 mart., 28 apr. 1770; 28 sept. 1771; 18 jul., 29 aug., 19 sept. 1772 (cicf., vi, nn. 3772, 3780, 3783).

[564] Chelodi, n. 104; cfr. also Schaefer, p. 217.

[565] DS, Reg., n. 79, § 2.

[566] Gasparri, ii, n. 1304; W-Vidal, v, n. 218.

[567] cfr. R., Null., 29 mai. 1916 (rd., viii, p. 147); Null., 19 nov. 1917 (rd., ix, p. 274).

[568] De Smet, i, p. 144 (1).

[569] DS, Reg., nn. 80, 81, 82.

and fear, or the impotence be so complete that they themselves invalidate the marriage. It happens not infrequently that marriage cases are brought to court with a view to proving lack of consent, or duress, or impotence as a diriment impediment, but although something is shown to be irregular in the matter, the proofs of a diriment impediment are not conclusive, but are sufficient to beget an admissible presumption of non-consummation.

Proof that the parties sought to avoid progeny is not, of itself, full proof that their coition was never perfect.[570]

§12. Presumption of Paternity and Legitimacy

535. Though the ecclesiastical court but rarely nowadays has to do directly with questions of paternity and legitimacy, the Canon law clings to the presumption established by the Roman jurist Paulus, and handed down in the fifth century Digests: "Pater is est quem nuptiae demonstrant".[571] By this presumption of paternity the peace of families and the good of society is secured, for it is better that some illegitimates should be considered as born of wedlock than that any legitimates should be considered merely natural or spurious.

The Code has adopted the very words of the Roman law (c. 1115, §1), qualifying the noun "nuptiae" with the adjective "justae"[572] to indicate that the presumption pertains to a union that has the *prima facie* status of a marriage even though the marriage be not really valid but only putative (cfr. c. 1015,§4). Hence if a marriage is contracted in form there is a presumption of legitimacy of the children as long as it is not proved both that the marriage is invalid and that both spouses were culpable causes of the invalid marriage, at least by their previous knowledge of the impediment. Thus the presumption is based upon and is a favor to the good faith of the parties. But if a union has not the *prima facie* status of a marriage, good faith is not presumed and the presumption of legitimacy does not hold. Hence it is generally held that there is no presumption of legitimacy of children begotten from Catholics who are united only by an attempted informal marriage (cfr. n. **449**).[573]

[570] R., Null., 3 jul. 1923 (rd., xv, p. 141).

[571] L. 5, De in Ius Vocatione, D. II, 4.

[572] As Gaius (D, I, 6, 3 Inst.) and Paulus (D, I, 5, 12 Resp. xix) had done.

[573] cfr. Benedictus XIV, epist. "Redditae sunt" 17 sept. 1746, § 3 (cicf., ii, n. 372); Ayrinhac, n. 278; Linneborn, p. 361; Blat, De Sacramentis, n. 522; slightly otherwise: Chelodi, n. 150; De Smet, i, p. 267 (3); W-Vidal, v, n. 610;

Thus when a marriage has been contracted, of which there is a doubt whether the parties are cousins by reason of the adultery of a parent, the presumption of legitimacy prevails over the doubtful impediment, and the court must not pronounce the marriage invalid without conclusive proof of the consanguinity. And, in question of legitimacy, the same holds, most probably, in case there is a similar doubt whether the parties are half-brother and half-sister (cfr. nn. **401, 415, 422**).[574] But as long as the marriage has not been duly contracted, the prohibition of Canon 1076,§3 must be observed.

The presumption is not inevitable, but may be overcome by evident arguments to the contrary (c. 1115,§1).[575] This proof to the contrary is not obtained by a confession of the wife or other proof that she had been guilty of adultery during the time when the child might have been conceived,[576] but it must be shown that the husband has not had marital coition with the wife at any time during the possible period of conception.[577] [578]

536. Almost as a corollary to the presumption of paternity by reason of marriage, the Code states the presumption of paternity and legitimacy by reason of the date of birth and its relation to the marriage. Children are presumed to be legitimate who are born at least six months after the day marriage was celebrated (counting the day of marriage), or within ten months from the day the marriage was dissolved (c. 1115,§2), by death or otherwise. The canonists, follow-

The omission of banns has now no bearing on the presumption of legitimacy: Capello, iii, n. 746 contra Linneborn, p. 361.

[574] Pruemmer, in lqs., lxxx (1927), p. 544 fol.; cfr. R., Impedimenti ad Contrahendum, 11 mart. 1910 (rd., ii, pp. 99, 100); cfr. V-Creusen ii, n. 420.

[575] R., Impedimenti ad Contrahendum, 11 mart. 1910 (rd., ii, p. 100) relying on Roman law and classical canonists, to the contrary. But these are now obsolete in this.

[576] Gasparri, ii, n. 1307.

[577] Chelodi, n. 150 (p. 164).

[578] In civil law, Abbott, p. 113: "The burden of proof is on the party denying the legitimacy of one shown to have been born from a wife, and his evidence must show illegitimacy beyond a reasonable doubt. . . . A child born during the mother's coverture (even so soon after marriage that conception must have preceded marriage), is presumed legitimate in the absence of competent evidence to the contrary, and this is a strong legal presumption, and can only be rebutted by proof that no sexual intercourse occurred at any time (whether before or after marriage), when the child could have been begotten . . . "

ing Roman law, have generally calculated the six-month period as one of 180 days, and the ten-month period as one of 300 days.[579] The Code now seems to require that the periods be calculated according to the calendar (c. 34,§3, n. 1).[580] This would bring the actual number of days somewhat higher, and the number would vary according to the period of the year from which the term is calculated. Hence this change in method of calculation is not without its difficulties, and most authors hold that the calculation of Canon 34 is not meant to apply to this case, and that the terms of six and ten months must be calculated as formerly.[581]

If the child was born within a shorter period than six months from marriage or after a longer period than ten months from the dissolution of the marriage, the Roman law no longer extended to the case the presumption of legitimacy, and there is certainly no legal presumption in Canon law for this case.[582]

The presumption of legitimacy, derived from the term within which the child is born, is not inevitable but admits proof to the contrary. If therefore, it is shown that a child was born seven months after the death of the husband, and that the husband could not have had marital coition with his wife at any time during the last three months of his life, this evidence will overcome the presumption that the child is legitimate.

537. *Scholion:* In the case of foundlings who wish to be promoted to tonsure and orders, the presumption of legitimacy holds as long as the contrary is not proved, and no precautionary dispensation need be sought.[583]

579 De Becker, p. 397; cfr. however, Linneborn, p. 361; who, following Ulpianus, gives 181 and 302 days.

580 Linneborn, p. 362.

581 Thus: De Becker, nov., p. 206; Gasparri, nov., ii, n. 1113; Chelodi, n. 150; Ayrinhac, n. 279; cfr. also V-Creusen, ii, n. 420.

582 De Becker, p. 397: "Attamen si speciales adsint circumstantiae, et praesertim si terminus ad paucos tantum dies protraheretur, posset adhuc in curia ecclesiastica sustineri legitimitas, ideoque, non debet dici *necessario* naturalis seu spuria proles nata post decem a morte mariti menses."; idem in De Becker, nov., pp. 206, 207; Chelodi, n. 150.

583 V-Creusen, ii, n. 420; Gasparri, nov., ii, n. 1114; Benedictus XIV, in ep. "Redditae Nobis," 5 dec. 1744, §4 (cicf., i, n. 350): "Cum. . . . incertum sit . . . iudex in dubio debeat in bonum et commoda prolis propensus esse."; contrary, Scherer, ii, p. 519 (19) ex cit. Linneborn, p. 362 (4).

CHAPTER XIII

Oaths of the Parties

"Homines enim per maiorem sui jurant, et omnis controversiae eorum finis, ad confirmationem, est juramentum."—Heb., vi, 16.

538. The proofs of a marriage case should generally accrue from the witnesses, experts, and documents taken in conjunction with the proper presumptions. Nevertheless the Code foresees that there will be cases where sufficient evidence does not derive from all these, and provides a means of further proof by the oaths of the parties (iusiurandum, juramentum, sacramentum).

Public society has from the beginning been prone to call upon litigants for their oath, and to place trust in it, basing the trust on a presumption that the litigant would be impelled by virtue of religion to tell the truth under oath. Although in private matters the early Church abhorred the calling upon God's name, and was content with the "est, est; non, non" of interested persons, she followed in public matters, the customs of the Roman and German laws, as Saint Paul testifies in the Epistle to the Hebrews. The later Roman law expressly mentioned the oath as a means of proof,[1] and the Church has continued its use, though, for a time during the middle ages, the oath fell into almost complete desuetude.[2] The Code makes liberal use of the oath without neglecting to take precaution against abuse and desecration. With this precaution in mind, the Code places the oaths of the parties as the last form of proof, and means it to be generally subsidiary to other proofs.

§ 1. Definition and Kinds of Oath

539. The oath is an act of religion whereby one calls upon the name of God in witness of the truth. This witnessing may refer to the truthfulness of purpose wherewith a person swears that he will

[1] Gaius, L. 2, ff. De Iureiurando: "Maximum remedium expediendarum litium in usum venit iurisiurandi religio."

[2] cfr. C. XXII, q. 1; Noval, n. 447, Roberti, ii, n. 379.

do or omit some future thing, and then it is called a promissory oath, or it may confirm a statement of fact and then it is a confirmatory oath. The promissory oath is considered in Book III, Part III, Title xix, Chapter 2 of the Code (cc. 1316-1321), and is employed when the officers of the court (cc. 1621; 1941,§2), and the experts (c. 1797,§1) take oath to faithfully perform their duties, as well as when persons at court swear to keep secret what is said or done there (cc. 1623,§3; 1625,§§2,3; 1769; 1944,§1; cfr. c. 364,§2,n.3). Besides these, the oath that is taken before giving testimony is also a promissory oath to speak the truth. We are not here concerned with any other promissory oath than this last mentioned, for we have to do only with the oaths which the parties take in the course of trial as a help to or a means of proof (iusiurandum iudiciale) (cfr. nn. **104-109, 221-226**).

540. I. According to the diversity of formal purpose, judicial oaths are ranged into: Those that are intended to go hand in hand with and are subsidiary to and corroborative of testimony (iusiurandum de veritate dicenda, de veritate dictorum), and those that are conceived as a means of proof in themselves (iusiurandum suppletorium, aestimatorium, decisorium).[3]

541. II. According to the solemnity with which the oath is taken, it is known as the solemn oath (sacramentum) or simple oath (juramentum). The simple oath is enhanced by the formality of placing the hand upon the breast or scriptures (cfr. n. **223**), and this is the form followed in tendering the oath to witnesses. The solemn oath is still more enhanced by such practices as the placing a special crucifix before the parties,[4] the lighting of two candles, the causing the parties to kneel, the using more formal expressions to clothe the oath, *etc.* This more solemn oath is sometimes tendered when the parties take supplementary, estimatory or decisive oath.

There is however no difference between these various forms of oath, in respect of the obligation by which the oath binds the party who takes it. Under any oath, solemn or simple, supplementary, de-

[3] Under the Decretals, X, De Iuramento Calumniae II, 7, another oath (iuramentum calumniae) was largely in use: by this the parties established their good faith in the suit and avoided the implication of fraud or calumny. This form of oath, differed but little, in its object, from the oath to speak the truth, but has long since been almost entirely abandoned in ecclesiastical procedure (cfr. Bassibey, p. 225 (3)), although the Code still retains the name in c. 2037, § 4; cfr. W-Vidal, vi, n. 407.

[4] The diocesan court-room always has a crucifix (c. 1636).

cisive, estimatory, or the plain oath taken by the party when he begins his testimony, the party is bound by the virtue of religion in strictest conscience to abide by the truth (cfr. c. 1743,§3) (cfr. n. **107**). And hence there is no essential difference in the intrinsic value of the oath as means of begetting proof.

§ 2. Supplementary Oath

542. In marriage trials, especially those that affect the marriage bond, the parties are always heard under oath (c. 1744), and thus their depositions have from the beginning much the same effect as the special supplementary oath taken in ordinary contentious cases.[5] And in fact, it appears from the Rotal decisions that the deposition of a party given under oath to speak the truth is frequently accepted as tantamount to a supplementary oath; no case has come under my observation where it is clear that the Rota required that the party be especially called upon to take a new supplementary oath, after the other proofs, including the party's sworn deposition had been exhausted.[6] And the Instruction of the Congregation of the Sacraments supplementing the Code, speaks only of the oath to speak the truth.[7]

Nevertheless the Code provides for taking a special supplementary oath. If the case is partly but not sufficiently proved, and there are at hand no further props to the incomplete proofs, the judge may order or admit a sworn statement to supplement the case (c. 1829).

It is for the judge to determine at what period of trial this oath may be taken (c. 1830,§5). By way of exception he may even permit the supplementary oath before the proofs are advanced; but then this will be for the sake of foresight, and provisionally, *i. e.* dependent upon the future proofs promised by the interested party.[8] Generally this oath is not tendered until all other proofs have been gathered; *i. e.* just before the conclusion of the trial, or even after it.[9] The

[5] On the derivation of the supplementary oath from Roman law, cfr. W-Vidal, vi, n. 527.

[6] cfr. however, SCC., Neapolitana, 11 apr. 1761 (cicf., vi, n. 3707); R., Argentinen, 23 feb. 1912 (rd., iv, p. 108; aas., iv, p. 389).

[7] DS. Reg., Appendix, xviii.

[8] W-Vidal, vi, n. 532.

[9] W-Vidal, vi, p. 481 (28): "Debet deferri, *causa cognita*, ut dicebant Commentatores iuris Decret., atque eundem sensum habet clausula Codicis de *examinandis omnibus circumstantiis*, can. 1830, § 5."

judge will formulate the oath according to his own discretion, and the opposing party may be present.

543. The supplementary oath is especially in place in marriage cases. Canon 1830,§2 requires as a condition to the admission of supplementary oath, that the matter at hand shall not be of great price or moment; this refers to cases of purely civil character in which a large monetary burden or its equivalent is in question. Although marriage cases are of the greatest moment, the supplementary oath is not excluded from them. This is plain from Canon 1830,§§1,3, as well as from the traditional interpretation of writers. Lega expressly allows that the supplementary oath may be taken on the merits of the marriage case, though in the same paragraph he disallows it for cases "maxime arduis et magni praeiudicii ob periculum periurii."[10]

544. The supplementary oath is generally given only when some proof of the facts is already at hand (c. 1829). Nevertheless official decrees and authors have customarily spoken of the supplementary oath as applicable in some marriage cases, when no other proof is available. Thus the Holy Office speaks of the supplementary oath as proof of free status, when all other proofs are wanting.[11] Evidently in this case, the oath is identical with the decisive oath, at least with respect to its effects (cfr. n. **554**).

If the proofs already gathered fully settle the matter, there is no reason for a supplementary oath and it should not be tendered.[12]

545. Under the Decretals the respondent was regularly allowed to take the supplementary oath.[13] Under the Code this oath is generally to be administered to that party who has the weightier proofs for his contention (c. 1830,§4).[14] But the rule is not ironclad and

[10] Lega, i, n. 467, 2°; cfr. also V-Creusen, iii, n. 208; Hohenlohe, p. 62; Noval, n. 568; W-Vidal, vi, n. 529; Hence Eichmann, p. 160 seems not to have sufficient ground for saying: "Der Richter soll von seiner Befugnis keinen Gebrauch machen . . . so oft es sich . . . um Nichtigkeit von Weihen, Ehen . . . handelt"; IA., §§ 169, 175 allowed the supplementary oath in cases of nullity, only with considerable restrictions. Similarly, Roberti, ii, n. 381.

[11] SO., 13 jan. 1869 ad Deleg. Ap. Aegypt., (cicf., iv, n. 1008; cpf., ii, n. 1342); cfr. also PC., 2-3 jun. 1912, IV, 4 (aas., x, p. 345).

[12] c. 2, X, De Prob., II, 19; Feije, n. 543; V-Creusen, iii, n. 208.

[13] c. 36, X, De Iureiurando, II, 24.

[14] Noval, n. 568: "Pleniores; id est, potiores seu meliores probationibus alterius partis, non autem pleniores in se, prout probatio plenior opponitur plenae. Et hoc est indubium . . . "

the judge is sometimes free to allow that party to take oath who has the lesser proofs for his contention, especially when that party is evidently the more conscientious or supports a suit that is favored by law.[15] Evidently the supplementary oath must never be allowed the party who contests a marriage, when the direct proofs for validity are overwhelmingly strong.

546. The judge will not administer the supplementary oath if the matter at hand (ius, res, factum) does not intimately pertain to the person who is to take the oath (c. 1830,§2). The defender may not take supplementary oath on the merits of a case, for although he is officially concerned with the marriage trial, the matter in hand is not his own.

547. The oath may be given a party *ex officio* or at the instance of the opposing litigant, or of the defender of the bond (c. 1830,§3).

It is the judge's part to consider carefully whether and when a supplementary oath shall be administered; if a party or the defender call for the oath, the judge will settle the matter by his decree (c. 1830,§5). But in cases to be decided by a court of three judges, the question of whether and to whom the formal supplementary oath shall be tendered is to be decided by the entire court, and if the trial judge deem it advisable to tender such oath, he will refer the matter to the court.[16]

548. In ordinary contentious cases the party invited to take the supplementary oath may decline it, or reverse it upon the adversary (c. 1831,§1).[17] In cases affecting the marriage bond the party called upon cannot decline to swear to the truth.

In any case of refusal to swear it is the part of the judge to decide what shall be made of the refusal, and whether it is equivalent to a confession (c. 1831,§2).

When taken, the supplementary oath is not incontestible, but may be impugned by the opposing party as false or erroneous (c. 1831,§3). In that case it is for the judge to decide where the truth is to be found.

15 Lega, i, n. 468, 2°; Noval, n. 568; V-Creusen, iii, n. 208.

16 R. Norm., art. 103.

17 c. 36, X, De Iureiurando, II, 24 allowed this only when the adversary proposed the oath.

§ 3. Estimatory Oath

549. If a party is plainly entitled to reimbursement for loss inflicted, but the amount of loss cannot be surely estimated, the judge may administer a special oath to the claimant, who then states under oath what was the extent of the loss (c. 1832; cfr. c. 1833). This estimatory oath can have no place in cases where the marriage is at issue, and will hardly be administered even in the rare suit for damages because of broken betrothals (cfr. c. 1017,§3).[18]

§ 4. Decisive Oath

550. In matters that admit of cession and transaction, the parties may agree before trial to settle their controversy by an oath to be taken by one or the other party, and after the trial is begun and at any moment and stage of it, one party can, with the approval of the judge, tender the other party an oath, with the understanding that the question, whether principal or incidental, be considered settled according to the oath sworn, and apart from any other proof and without appeal (c. 1880, n. 5). Such an oath is called decisive (c. 1834).

The decisive oath can only be tendered on a matter that admits of cession and transaction or compromise (c. 1835,§1). Hence cases of separation may be settled by decisive oath, for the injured party can waive his suit or compromise it.[19] In some parts of Europe, there is long-standing custom of clearing up suspicion of marital infidelity, by demanding that the suspected party take oath that he or she is innocent.

When there is question of the dissolution of betrothals the decisive oath is likewise applicable.[20]

551. In cases that affect the marriage bond, the decisive oath is not admissible with respect to the merits of the principal question, *i. e.* the status of the marriage (c. 1835, n. 1).[21] It may be admitted

[18] On the history and development of the estimatory oath cfr. W-Vidal, vi, nn. 535, 536 fol.

[19] IA., § 233.

[20] Bassibey, n. 326.

[21] In civil law, Abbott, p. 952: "A confession, not connected with other proof, is not competent. However explicit, it will not alone justify a decree; (3) but may, in the discretion of the court, be sufficient when clearly proved,

to decide questions that are incidental and not prejudicial to the question of the marriage. Thus if it seem that a party, by the provision of Canon 1971,§1,n.1 has no right to contest his marriage, the decisive oath may be administered to clear up the doubtful point.[22] The decisive oath is likewise admitted to disprove intentional contempt of court, or neglect in availing oneself of the peremptory periods for taking exceptions, *etc.*[23] The decisive oath may also be administered to a woman who would avoid the necessity of undergoing physical inspection in non-consummation cases; to this end her oath will be decisive if she acknowledge that her body is no longer intact, and swear that the violation has occurred by another cause than the consummation of her present marriage, *e. g.* by a former marriage, by extramarital coition, by a surgical operation (cfr. also cc. 1628,§1; 1764,§4; 1824,§3).

552. The decisive oath can be tendered only when the one who tenders it has the right to cede or compromise, and when the party who is to take the oath can cede or compromise the matter at hand, and when full proof has not been established in his favor (c. 1835, nn. 2, 3).

553. The oath may be formulated only upon a matter that pertains to the party as his own, or upon the testimony of a fact noticed by the party himself. Thus in separation cases, the respondent may be called upon to swear that he did not commit the suspected adultery; the plaintiff may be called upon to swear that he witnessed the acts as claimed, which begot the suspicion or knowledge of perfidy.

554. The demand for decisive oath can be recalled at any time by the party who tenders it, as long as the oath has not actually been taken; the other party can accept the demand and take the oath, or he can decline, or he can turn it back upon the adversary (c. 1836,§1), by demanding that he take oath.

if accompanied with evidence effectually repelling all suspicion of collusion, or corroborated by other evidence of guilt, and free from any appearance of collusion . . .

"(3) . . . By the N. Y. Statute 'no sentence of nullity of marriage shall be pronounced solely on the declarations or confessions of the parties; but the court shall in all cases require other satisfactory evidence of the existence of the facts on which the allegation of nullity is founded.'"

[22] cfr. IA., § 170; Bassibey, n. 184.

[23] R., Biturgen., Locationis, 27 apr. 1917 (rd., ix, p. 91; aas., ix, p. 545).

When the oath is taken the question at issue is decided according to the oath, just as if a cession or judicial compromise had taken place (c. 1836,§2).

If the oath is declined but is not reversed upon the adversary, it is for the judge to estimate what shall be made of the refusal to swear: whether it rests on just grounds, or should rather be held tantamount to a confession (c. 1836,§3).

If the oath is reversed upon the adversary, he must take it or the case collapses (c. 1836,§4).

In order that the oath may be reversed upon the adversary, there must be at hand those same conditions which are required for tendering the oath (cfr. c. 1835), and the judge must take part in the matter (c. 1836,§5; cfr. c. 1834,§1).

The formula for decisive oath and the question of who shall take it, as well as the decision as to what shall be made of its refusal is reserved to the entire court as in the case of supplementary oath (cfr. n. **547**).[24]

§ 5. Appraisal of Sworn Depositions

555. The most natural and direct means whereby a judge may learn the truth in a controversy is from the statement of the parties, and no doubt the supreme pontiffs and bishops of the early Church gave their decisions on questions of marriage according to the depositions of the parties concerned.[25] And even at a much later period Pope Urban II in the provincial council of Apulia of 1091 expressly stated that marriages were to be dissolved as invalid, when the parties acknowledged an existing consanguinity.[26] And Roland glosses c. 29, C. XXVII, q. 2, by saying that the assertion of both spouses that the marriage cannot be consummated is sufficient to consider it invalid and permit new nuptials.[27] Again Celestine III laid

[24] R. Norm., art. 105.

[25] Synodus Liftinae (Freisen, p. 335) (an. 743 or 745): "...si...debitum conjugale non potuerit reddere et hoc aut amborum confessione aut certa qualibet adprobatione fuerit manifestum, ut separentur et mulier, si se continere nequiverit, alteri viro legaliter nubat."

[26] c. 4, C. XXXV, q. 6: "Si duo vel tres viri consanguinitatem iureiurando firmaverint, vel ipsimet forte confessi fuerint, coniugia dissolvantur . . . Si negaverint, sibi ipsis relinquendi sunt . . . "

[27] (Freisen, p. 342); "Si quis acceperit uxorem, cui carnaliter concordari non possit, si uterque eorum idem asseverat, divertere ab invicem atque aliis copulari licebit, . . . "

it down that a new marriage might be entered upon if, after a three year attempt, it should appear from the testimony of the parties, supported by the character witnesses, that they could not consummate the marriage.[28]

Nevertheless with the recession from primitive severity of life on the one hand and the development of Canon law on the other, the curiae became gradually aware of the danger lest interested persons assert falsehoods in order to be freed from marriage bonds that no longer had any charm for them, or at least be subjectively influenced by their desires. Hence there grew up a principle of jurisprudence that marriage cases must be evidenced by other proofs than the testimony, confession, or oath of the parties concerned, for the word of the parties was looked upon with suspicion.[29] This attitude of suspicion was brought to its highest point in the well known Instruction of Cardinal Rauscher for Austria, where it was directed that neither the testimony of the parties, nor a confession of one even against his case, nor an oath taken by either party could have any value as proof in cases affecting the marriage bond.[30] In this as in some other matters the Austrian Instruction held to a degree of severity that went beyond that of the jurisprudence of Rome. The Rota has indeed held that the testimony and confession of the parties is generally suspected proof;[31] but there has also been some tendency away from the more severe carrying out of this principle. The Propaganda Congregation explicitly stated that the sworn deposition of trustworthy parties acknowledging they had contracted implicating espousals before marriage, was sufficient to prove the impediment then known as "public decency."[32] The Rota has declared in a recent case that the principle against admitting the confessions of parties in favor of nullity, cannot be absolutely followed.[33] And De Becker, commenting on the same

[28] c. 5, X, De Frig. et Mal. et Impot. Coeundi, IV, 15.

[29] c. 5, X, De Eo Qui Cognovit, IV, 13; Cosci, lib. I, cap. vi, nn. 37-43; Pallotini, xi, p. 562, n. 73.

[30] IA., §§ 148, 169, 172, 174.

[31] R., Null., 16 mai. 1914 (rd., vi, p. 210); Parisien., seu Nicien., Null., 30 dec. 1915 (rd., vii, p. 469; aas., viii, p. 327); Montereyen Angelorum, Null., 21 dec. 1917 (rd., ix, p. 319; aas., x, p. 423).

[32] PF, 1883, § 34.

[33] R., Null., 27 aug. 1912 (rd., iv, p. 441): "Quamvis haec regula vera sit non *absolute* sumpta, sed attentis peculiaribus rerum adiunctis . . ."; Colonien., Null., 1 jul. 1912 (rd., iv, p. 330; aas., iv, p. 671).

principle, remarks that it must be taken with a grain of salt.[34] And if, in spite of the general danger, canonical practice nevertheless values the sworn depositions of the parties, this is because the judge is expected to reach his conviction by considering all the circumstances of the case.[35] [36]

556. The deposition of a party who contests the marriage has always been accepted as valid proof in cases where the defender and the respondent have the burden of proof, *e. g.* when these contend that the originally invalid marriage has been validated by correction at root (cfr. n. **407**),[37] or by subsequent consent at least implicitly given through rendering the marital coition (copula affectu maritali). The Holy Office has declared in several cases that sufficient proof of nullity is at hand to allow a new marriage, when the plaintiff asserts under oath that the clandestine marriage, invalid for being contracted without the solemnities of the "Tametsi," was never validated by a renewed exchange of consent in a place where the "Tametsi" had not been promulgated.[38] The Congregation of the Council decided similarly regarding a marriage contracted under duress, when the plaintiff swore that he had never, with marital intent, rendered the sexual obligation, and declared the marriage invalid in the forum of conscience.[39]

In a case where the parties had originally given a defective consent which left the marriage contract invalid, it was argued that the

[34] De Becker, pp. 489 (5), 500 (1); cfr. Mansella, 187.

[35] W-Vidal, vi, n. 534.

[36] In civil law on divorce, Abbott, p. 951: "The competency of the parties has been stated. Plaintiff's testimony alone may, in the discretion of the court, in a perfectly clear case, be sufficient if other evidence does not exist or cannot be obtained."

[37] cfr. Nau, p. 221, n. 7.

[38] SO., 29 jul. 1896 (bass., n. 213 (3), n. 326): ". . . 1. Utrum matrimonium Titiae cum Sempronio . . . constet firmum, an possit ex capite clandestinitatis irritum declarari a judice ecclesiastico?—Res delata est ad Emos DD. Cardinales una mecum Inquisitores generales, qui in Congregatione generali habita in fer. IV die 29 Julii . . . respondendum decreverunt: Ad 1. Matrimonium in casu omnibus consideratis, esse nullum; modo constet per juramentum a muliere praestandum, consensum (scientibus sponsis nullitatem prioris consensus) non fuisse renovatum in loco ubi Tridentinum non viget."; SO., 31 aug. 1887 (bass., n. 213 (5), n. 326); SO., 8 mart. 1899 (cpf., ii, n. 2041; cicf., iv, n. 1217).

[39] SCC., Mat., 30 mai. 1699 (pall., xii, p. 626, nn. 86, 87).

subsequent cohabitation of the parties, during a period of six years, constituted an implicit renewal of consent. But the depositions of the parties were accepted by the Rota as conclusive, to the effect that the valid consent had never been, even implicitly, given.[40] In a case where the parties had contracted marriage with a stipulation pending future event, and had afterward consummated the marriage without awaiting the outcome of the stipulated event, it was argued that this act was presumably an implicit renewal of unconditional consent, and that hence the marriage was definitely validated. But the Rota accepted the deposition of the parties that the coition was not done with marital intent, and declared the parties free to enter upon new nuptials.[41]

But the party's deposition may be rejected even in cases of presumed validation if there is evidence of its falsity. In a case of that kind the Rota in first instance fully admitted the depositions of the parties that the marriage was not rightly consummated through natural coition, argued hence that the presumption of validation was not tenable, and declared for nullity; but in second instance the court found that the depositions of the parties were actually unreliable, because the case presented conclusive internal evidence contradictory of their pretensions.[42]

557. Similarly it has been the accepted rule that the oath of a party constitutes sufficient proof of nullity, if after having married a slave, properly so called (cfr. c. 1083,§2, n. 2), he swear that he did not know of the other's servile condition at the time of the marriage. For the Church presumes against a freeman's desire to marry a slave, unless the latter's condition of servitude is generally known (cfr. n. **471**).[43]

558. And in cases of marriage supposedly contracted by proxy, the courts have been accustomed to receive the oath of a party as

[40] R., Vicariatus Apost. Sueciae, Null., 19 aug. 1914 (rd., vi, p. 311; aas., vii, p. 55).

[41] R., Null., 28 jan. 1914 (rd., vi, p. 32): "Hanc copulam non fuisse perfectam ipse etiam Hyginus fatetur implicite, . . . Neque obiiciatur in casu coniugum confessionem utpote pugnantem contra matrimonium contractum esse respuendam, nam id verum est, quando agitur de illo dissolvendo ob impedimentum dirimens, aliud autem in matrimoniis praesumptis obtinet, ut est in praesenti casu in quo ex posita copula vellet praesumi recessus a posita conditione."; cfr. V-Creusen, iii, n. 205.

[42] R., Null., 28 jan. 1914; 28 nov. 1914 (rd., vi, p. 32; p. 328).

[43] W-Vidal, v, n. 481; Freisen, p. 295.

proof, when he protests that he did not consent to or sign the mandate of proxy to contract marriage.[44] The provisions of the Code have now made it impossible to marry by proxy unless the mandate be given in a signed and authenticated document (c. 1089,§§1,2), and thus the question of valid mandate will hardly ever be devoid of all other proofs than the oath of the party. But the question of revoking the mandated consent may be thus devoid of other proofs, and in case a party swear that he did thus revoke his consent (cfr. c. 1089,§3), it is for the judge to appraise the oath in view of the presumption of continued consent according to Canon 1093 (cfr. n. **462**).

559. But even when the plaintiff has the full burden of proof, his deposition and that of the respondent may form part proof of nullity. In a case which arose in China, a decision of nullity was given chiefly on the testimony of the party, even though there were two witnesses who upheld the validity of the marriage.[45] So likewise in another case from Sweden.[46]

560. It is abundantly plain that in cases of impotence and non-consummation, the Congregations and the Rota have steadily attributed great worth to the depositions of the parties asserting the impotence and non-consummation. After sixteen years of wedded life, a couple contested their marriage on the ground of impotence and non-consummation, the only proofs being the depositions of the parties supported by the character witnesses. The Rota gave a favorable decision and counselled the Supreme Pontiff to grant dispensation from non-consummated marriage.[47]

[44] SCC., In Casertina, 27 feb. 1717 (pall., xiii, § xxiv, n. 22).

[45] R., Vic. Apost., Ce-Li Central., Null., 10 feb. 1917 (rd., ix, p. 27; aas., ix, p. 506).

[46] R., Vic. Apost. Sueciae, Null., 19 aug. 1914 (rd., vi, p. 310; aas., vii, p. 54); cfr. also Null., 11 aug. 1910 (rd., ii, p. 303): "magnae tamen est auctoritatis"; Cameracen., Null., 23 jun. 1911 (rd., iii, p. 298); Null., 16 aug. 1913 (rd., v, p. 574); Null., 28 jan. 1914 (rd., vi, p. 28).

[47] R., Null., et Dispensationis, 18 aug. 1917 (rd., ix, p. 221); cfr. also IA., § 175: ". . . His peractis coniugibus permitti potest, ut impotentiam adesse jurejurando attestentur, et istud plenam probationem efficit."; Cosci, lib. I, cap. xvi, quoting Rot. dec. 101, n. 5 sq.: "Secundo non obstat quod stante dormitione Julii cum Olympia in eodem lecto per tres noctes praesumitur consummatio Matrimonii iuxta text., etc. Quia haec praesumptio tollitur per probationem contrariam resultantem ex confessione Julii facta coram SSmo . . . "; SCC., Bononien., Mat., 23 mai. 1857 (pall., xiii, n. 142); In Varsavien., Disp. Mat., 14 mai. 1887, et in Parisien., 3 aug. 1889 (bass., p. 247 (3)); R., Null., 15 nov. 1909 (rd., i, p. 138); Null., 16 mai. 1914 (rd., vi, p. 210); Null., 25 mart. 1920 (rd., xii, p. 76); Null., 17 aug. 1920 (rd., xii, p. 242).

An even more remarkable case of impotence was decided in 1916. A child had been born to the couple; yet the wife deposed under oath that this child had been begotten from "semen ad orificium vaginae emissum" and that the marriage had not been and could not be consummated, because of the debility and hyperesthesia of the husband, who contumaciously refused to depose or submit to physical inspection. There were indeed the testimonies of a physician and an obstetrician who had privately tended the parties, but neither these testimonies nor the hearsay testimonies of those to whom the wife had related her difficulty were sufficient of themselves to pronounce the marriage invalid. The Rota declared the marriage invalid because of the impotence of the husband, and when the case was appealed, the succeeding Rotal Turn confirmed the decision.[48]

Canon 1975,§2 speaks of the character witnesses as adding value to the depositions of the parties; hence it is plain that the Code presupposes that the parties' sworn depositions shall already have had some value of themselves.[49]

561. The sworn testimony of the party concerned is likewise of great value in those many various cases where the validity of the marriage depends on whether a true and complete consent was given. When a specific cause for dissimulating consent has been established by proof, the confession of a party that the consent was actually dissimulated may be received as part proof. In fact, the confession of the simulating party is generally necessary before the marriage can be declared void,[50] although cases have been favorably settled without such confession.[51]

The pivotal point of a recent case from Germany rested upon the wife's view of her civil marriage, for by virtue of the decree "Provida" the observance of the "Ne Temere" was not essentially necessary for the validity of her marriage. Did she then view her civil union as a true marriage, or only as a civil ceremony? She swore that she had always looked upon her civil marriage as invalid before the Church, *etc.*, and had had the intention of later validating the marriage before a priest. Her oath was accepted as part proof and

[48] R., Null., 29 mai. 1916 (rd., viii, p. 147); 19 nov. 1917 (rd., ix, p. 275).

[49] Noval, n. 856; Bassibey, n. 328; De Smet, i, n. 331.

[50] R., Massillien., Null., 10 aug. 1912 (rd., iv, p. 406; aas., iv, p. 712).

[51] R., Parisien., Null., 11 aug. 1921 (rd., xiii, p. 216; aas., xiv, p. 517).

nullity was declared.[52] Similarly in a case where the plaintiff sought to establish a case of nullity, because of a stipulation imposed by herself.[53] But without supporting evidence, the sworn testimony of the party alone is not sufficient to prove simulated consent.

562. When there is question of conversion to the true Faith, the Church seems to set even more value upon the party's oath. The Holy Office answered the Bishop of Sioux Falls that if a neo-convert swear that, according to Indian custom, he had intended his previous infidel marriage not to be permanent or indissoluble, his oath might be taken as final (cfr. nn. **120, 418**).[54]

563. In cases of reverential fear and intimidation the Rota is likewise accustomed to accept the sworn depositions of the parties as part proof of the invalid marriage.[55]

In a case from Africa the Rota decided for invalidity because of absolute duress, upon the deposition of the party alone, supported however, by the *prima facie* indications in the case.[56]

564. In regard to the Decretal impediment of affinity from illicit coition, Celestine III set it down that the sworn confession of the culpable persons, even when joined to a rumour in some part of the neighborhood, was not of itself to be considered sufficient proof.[57] This policy has been followed by the Congregation of the Council and the Rota;[58] nevertheless, the sworn confessions of the culpable

[52] R., Argentinen., 23 feb. 1912 (rd., iv, p. 108; aas., iv, p. 389); cfr. Argentinen., 22 jul. 1912 (rd., iv, p. 380); Null., 22 feb. 1919 (rd., xi, pp. 44, 45).

[53] R., Parisien., Null., 19 jun. 1920 (rd., xii, pp. 172, 173); Gasparri, ii, n. 1019.

[54] SO., 18, 19 mai. 1892, Siouxormen; 18 mai. 1898 (cicf., iv, n. 1155; cpf., ii, nn. 1796; 1999).

[55] R., Tarvisina, Null., 11 mart. 1912 (rd., iv, p. 139; aas., iv, p. 517); Null., 9 aug. 1915 (rd., vii, pp. 389, 390): ". . . porro in causis de nullitate matrimonii ex capite metus, magni faciendam esse attestationem iuratam coniugis metum passi, concedunt communiter doctores."; Gravinen., Null., 2 jul. 1918 (aas., xi, p. 195; rd., x, p. 61); Terraconen., Null., 15 feb. 1919 (rd., xi, p. 10; aas., xi, p. 429); Southwarkensis, Null., 29 jul. 1926 (aas., xviii, p. 503).

[56] R., Vic. Nyanz. Sept., Null., 10 mai. 1918 (rd., x, p. 38; aas., xi, p. 91); Similarly R., Null., 8 mart. 1919 (rd., xi, p. 71); Null., 10 jul. 1923 (rd., xv, p. 153).

[57] c. 5, X, De Eo Qui Cognovit, IV, 13.

[58] cfr. Pallotini, xii, p. 553, n. 49; R., Null., 10 feb. 1912 (rd., iv, p. 86); Imolen., Null., 2 aug. 1913 (rd., v, p. 500); Cosci, lib. I, cap. vi, nn. 33, 34 says the same regarding confession of a promise to marry as a part proof of the impediment of crime. Cfr., however, PF, 1883, § 34.

persons have been accredited with great weight in such cases, provided there was other competent supporting evidence.[59]

565. In cases of the presumable death of a spouse, it is the custom of the Congregation of the Sacraments to accept the deposition of the surviving spouse as valid proof of death, and indeed, such deposition is sometimes the chief proof. A recent case was favorably decided almost entirely upon the sworn deposition of the surviving wife: no other testimony was offered, save that of the parish priest who stated that it was the current repute of the neighborhood that the husband was dead.[60] In another case the surviving wife, as the only witness, supported her deposition by exhibiting some letters sent her by her husband before his presumable death. The decision was favorable and she was allowed to marry anew.[61] But if there is no other proof whatever, than the testimony of the surviving spouse, the ordinary must submit each separate case to the Congregation.[62]

566. When a person about to marry is unable to provide the proper documents or witnesses as proof of his free status, he may be required to swear that no impediment prevents him, and on this supplementary oath, the marriage may be permitted (cpre. cc. 779; 800; 1019,§2; 1031,§1, n. 1).[63]

567. Marriages clandestinely contracted were valid under the law of the Decretals, but proof that they had been so contracted was not always available; so the Church had to determine whether any and what value should be given to the acknowledgment of the parties.

[59] R., Null., 29 jul. 1909 (rd., i, pp. 123, 124); Null., 20 mai. 1910 (rd., ii, p. 164); Null., 11 apr. 1911 (rd., iii, p. 167).

[60] DS., Praes. Mort. Conj., 25 jun. 1915 (aas., vii, p. 476).

[61] DS., Praes. Mort. Conj., 19 jan. 1917 (aas., ix, p. 120); Hence Schlenz, Wiederverehelichung, (akk., 1918, p. 382) seems to understate the matter when he says valid proof may accrue from "im allgemeinen alle im Rechte anerkannten Beweismittel . . . , ausgenommen der Eid des Ehewerbers."; cfr. likewise W-Vidal, v, pp. 294, 295 (53).

[62] De Becker, nov. p. 43 et ibi cit. SCC., 3 mai. 1893.

[63] SO., 1 feb. 1865 (cicf., iv, n. 980; cpf., i, n. 1267); SO., 13 jan. 1869 ad Del. Ap. Aegypt. (cicf., iv, n. 1008; cpf., ii, n. 1342); R., Impedimenti ad Contrahendum, 11 mart. 1910 (rd., ii, p. 105); PC., 2-3 jun. 1912 IV, 4 (aas., x, p. 345); De Smet, ii, n. 687: "Quod spectat *juramentum suppletorium* attento tenore can. 1019,§2, 1020,§3, 1023,§2, ac citati decr. Pont. Commiss. Cod. ad 4 um, jam non requiritur peculiare indultum ad hoc ut Ordinarius possit deferre illud juramentum, sicuti olim indulto habebat opus."

It came to be generally admitted by the Canons and the authors that the denial of both parties was proof of no marriage having been contracted, unless there was public repute of valid marriage, or public cohabitation; [64] and the acknowledgment of both parties that they had contracted constituted full proof of clandestine marriage, when other proofs were wanting. But an exception was made to this principle, not at first without some divergence of opinion,[65] when the acknowledgment of a clandestine marriage would have prejudiced another marriage publicly contracted.[66] The principle and the exception have now been canonized by a response of the Congregation of the Sacraments.[67]

When one party affirmed the marriage and the other denied it, the canonical jurisprudence established the principle that the burden of further proof lay with the one who affirmed the marriage,[68] and the latter's oath alone was not sufficient in this case.[69]

The almost universal requirement of the formal contract now required as a condition for validity, makes these norms generally impractical in the case of Catholics today; nevertheless, among non-Catholics common law marriage may be valid, and even the Code provides for the possibility of valid marriage of Catholics, somewhat informally contracted (cfr. cc. 1043, 1044); and if a case occur where no one could give testimony but the parties, the same principle must be applied.[70]

Likewise, if a marriage has been duly contracted in form, but the records are lost or cannot be obtained, or the marriage was not recorded, and no witnesses are available, the joint deposition of the parties is sufficient evidence whereon the proper pastor may make

[64] c. 2, X, De Clandestina Desponsatione, IV, 3.

[65] Freisen, p. 146: "Gratian laesst generell die *confessio* beider Teile als Beweis zu, Bernardus dagegen vertritt ohne Ausnahme den Satz: *semper manifesta desponsatio debet praejudicare, sive praecessisse sive successisse dicatur.*"

[66] Gasparri, ii, n. 1036; De Smet, i, n. 149; De Becker, p. 136; Bassibey, n. 326.

[67] DS., Venetiarum, Probationis Mat., 6 mart. 1911 (aas., iii, p. 103).

[68] c. 2, X, De Clandestina Desponsat., IV, 3; cfr. however e contra, c. 1, X, De Clandestina Desponsat., IV, 3 of which Gasparri, ii, n. 1038 says: "Difficilis est hic canon; nec plausibilem explicationem alicubi legimus."

[69] W-Vidal, v, n. 580.

[70] Chelodi, n. 128; De Smet, i, n. 149; cfr. R., Null., 29 feb. 1916 (rd., viii, pp. 50, 51).

an entry of marriage in the register, noting of course, that the entry is made on the sole acknowledgment of the parties.[71]

568. The sworn depositions of the parties can be accepted as proof, only when there attaches a strong personal presumption of veracity which warrants the inference that they would not collude or depose falsely even in their own behalf.[72] The judge must therefore look into the reputation and character of the persons. To this end character witnesses are introduced in some cases (cfr. nn. **189**, **263**); in others, testimonials of character.[73]

Sometimes the party is already known to the judge, or becomes known in the course of trial as a person to be implicitly relied upon. In a well known case from New York the Rota gathered a strong presumption for the truthfulness of the respondent, from the fact that she wrote to correct statements made in court, when after reviewing letters written on the matter, she found herself in error.[74] In another case the judges derived a presumption in favor of the truthfulness of a husband who upheld the marriage, from the artless and disinterested manner of his deposition.[75]

So too the Congregation of the Council decided that the oaths of the parties alone were sufficient to prove impotence or non-consummation in order that the parties might enter religion and take solemn vows.[76]

569. In case a party is known to be of bad character, unworthy of belief, his depositions do not constitute even a prop to other

[71] SCC., In Dubium Mat., 19 sept. 1684 (pall., xii, p. 503, n. 127); DS., Venetiarum, Probationis Mat., 6 mai. 1911 (aas., iii, p. 103); De Smet, i, n. 149.

[72] Mansella, 187: "Ceterum coniugum confessio, seu factorum et rerum ennaratio post initum matrimonium contra eiusdem valorem elicita, non **statim** probandi vim habet, imo ipsa sola et per se omni vi caret. Expendenda enim sedulo est et conferenda nedum **cum sanae criticis regulis** sed etiam cum ceteris recensendis probationum generibus, ut clare pateat an pro veritate, an vero in proprium commodum, aut ex collusione in sacramentalis vinculi iniuriam, rerum circumstantias exponant, factaque enarrent."

[73] R., Null., 11 apr. 1911 (rd., iii, p. 166).

[74] R., Neo Eboracen., Null., 8 feb. 1915 (aas., vii, p. 301; rd., vii, p. 30).

[75] R., Paderbornen., Null., 27 jul. 1917 (aas., x, p. 219; rd., ix, p. 165).

[76] SCC., In Neapolitana, Mat., 11 apr. 1761 (pall., xii, § iv, n. 13): "quia ingressus in religionem respicit perfectiorem statum, in cuius assumptione suspicari nequit de fraudibus et collusione."

proofs.[77] The question of a party's bad character may be introduced not only *ex officio* by the judge, but likewise by any of the interested litigants.[78] And by the test of character, the judge will know how to decide and whom to believe, when the parties contradict one another in a statement of fact. In a case where one party is of unprincipled life and morals, devoid of religious convictions, while the other party is religious and marked by a life of upright conduct, the sworn assertions of the latter must naturally and properly beget more confidence and better proof than the depositions of the former.

570. The outstanding contradiction that has beset the sworn depositions of parties throughout the history of Canon law is that respecting the consummation of a marriage. This occurs most frequently through the **denial of the wife** and the **assertion of the husband** that the coition has taken place. The ecclesiastical courts have not always been of one mind as to the norm by which the judge should decide. Synodal statutes (Vermeren., an. 753; Salisburgen., an. 799) called for the cross-ordeal or endurance test in the form of a cross as a means of settling the contradiction between husband and wife, when their oaths were at variance.[79] In the Council of Compendium (an. 756) it was declared that this contradiction be settled by crediting the assertion of the husband that the marriage had been consummated.[80] But Bernhard and Tancred were both quick to apply another norm in cases where the **wife asserted** the consummation and the **husband denied** it. In these cases the wife was to be believed, notwithstanding the text "quia vir caput est mulieris." And they state principles of Roman law as reason for the change in rule: the man, as plaintiff, cannot testify in his own behalf, and there is danger of perjury.[81]

But Gregory IX following Burchhard indicates that a distinction is in place: if the plaintiff whether man or woman makes plaint

[77] R., Null., 10 dec. 1914 (rd., vi, p. 342).

[78] In N. Y. State law the respondent only may initiate the question of the other's bad character; the plaintiff cannot do so unless character is directly the issue or equivalent to an issue in the case. The plaintiff may however rebut the respondent's charge against his character by proving that the respondent is of bad character himself. McKelvey, pp. 193-204.

[79] Freisen, p. 334.

[80] c. 3, C. XXXIII, q. 1: "in veritate viri consistit, quia vir caput est mulieris"; similarly, c. 6, X, De Desponsat. Imp., IV, 2.

[81] Freisen, pp. 255, 360.

of impotence shortly after the marriage is contracted, within *v. g.* two months, he may properly be believed; if the accusation is delayed for a longer period, the word of the plaintiff does not hold.[82] It has been the practice of the Roman Curia to hold this distinction in esteem and apply it in marriage trials.[83]

But these presumptions of truthfulness accorded one party or the other do not preclude rebuttal by other proofs, *v. g.* physical inspection.[84] Nor must they be applied without regard for the presumption that accrues to one party rather than to another because of character and reputation of truthfulness. And finally, the court may well consider the possibility of an illusory idea that coition has been perfected, or that a pregnancy and abortion have occurred.[85]

[82] c. 1, X, De Frigid. et Malef. et Impot. Coeundi, IV, 15: "quia si proclamare voluit, cur tamdiu tacuit?"

[83] SCC., S. Donati (S. Severini), Mat., 14 dec. 1737 (cicf., v, n. 3479; pall., xiii, p. 36, nn. 6, 7); R., Null., 8 jan. 1913 (rd., v, pp. 36, 37); Feije, n. 545.

[84] R., Null., 5 jun. 1913 (rd., v, p. 357 fol.).

[85] cfr. ime., xliii (1931), pp. 273, 274.

PART THREE

CHAPTER XIV

Publication of the Proceedings and Conclusion and Discussion of the Case

"Quid adhuc desideramus testimonium?"—Lc., xxii, 71.

I. PUBLICATION OF THE PROCEEDINGS

571. Contrary to the custom in modern civil procedure, ecclesiastical trials generally, and the marriage trial in particular, are not public in the sense that they are open to outsiders: but they are public in so far as the interested persons are given freedom of access to, and complete knowledge of what the court has decreed by way of procedure (acta processus), and of what the parties have brought forth by way of proof (acta causae). This is effected by the publication of the proceedings. Much of the proceedings and proof are regularly made known to both parties at the time they take place. The introductory plaint or petition is revealed to the respondent (cc. 1712,§1; 1715,§1), and all further petitions of either party are made known to the other (cfr. c. 1724). Both parties are summoned for the joinder and concordance of issue (cc. 1712,§3; 1727). Documents are at once opened to the inspection of the adversary (c. 1820), and in cases provided for in Canon 1990 the documents are published when the parties are summoned (cfr. n. **47**). Except in cases of impotence and non-consummation the parties may be present at the expert inspection or examination (1797,§2). They may be present at the taking of judicial notice (c. 1809), at the swearing in of witnesses (c. 1767,§2), and even at the hearing of testimonies (cfr. c. 1771), or, if they are not present, the testimonies may be at once published to them (c. 1782,§1).[1]

If however any of the proceedings was neither done in the presence of the parties, nor made known to an absent party, the Code provides for the complete publication of the proceedings that have remained heretofore secret, when all the proofs have been completed and before the discussion of the case, and the sentence (c. 1858). The

[1] PF, 1883, § 21 had directed that all proofs be kept secret until all were concluded and the acts were all published together.

Code speaks both of publishing the proceedings (de processus publicatione, Tit. XII, and XX, cap. v; cc. 1859; 1983,§1; 1985) and of publishing the proofs (c. 1858). The parties are, as a rule, interested only in the proofs. They have hardly any interest in the acts of procedure, *e. g.* the decrees nominating members of the court, summoning witnesses or appointing experts, and it is not necessary that the record of these acts be brought to the parties' attention.[2] But Bassibey recalls that the Congregation of Bishops and Regulars directed the diocesan curia to publish all the acts in a case in which an interested party demanded it.[3]

In the middle ages when the parties in contentious cases were always permitted to be present at the hearing of witnesses (cfr. n. 231), there was no publication of the acts. This was introduced after the proceedings began to be secretly held, and the necessity of publication is a corrollary of the secrecy of trial.

§ 1. Necessity of Publication

572. The publication of the acts is in justice due to the parties, but it does not clearly appear whether its omission vitiates the proceedings and the sentence. In a case appealed to the Rota, it was contended that the sentence of validity of marriage given by the Curia of Florence was nugatory because that Court had omitted to publish the acts. But the Rota, quoting Reiffenstuel in lib. II, tit. xx, nn. 523, 524, declared the procedure of the Florentine Court valid.[4] And pre-Code writers followed the same jurisprudence.[5]

But in an earlier case the Congregation had delayed its decision ("dilata") in a marriage case appealed to it from the Curia of Bordeaux, until that Curia had, according to the direction of the Congregation, acquainted the respondent with the proofs.[6] The Code seems to indicate that the making an adversary acquainted with the other's

[2] Bassibey, n. 479.

[3] S. C. EE. RR., 15 mart. 1817 (bass., n. 481).

[4] R., Florentina, Null., 28 jan. 1918 (rd., x, p. 14; aas., xi, p. 24): Note that this decision was given after promulgation of the Code, but before the date set for its validity.

[5] Gasparri, ii, n. 1502; Eichmann, p. 169 has the same since the Code, relying on the Florentine decision just given.

[6] SCC., 14 jun. 1890 (bass., n. 477).

proofs is so necessary that its omission vitiates the proceedings. For it says with particular reference to testimonies received after the conclusion of the case, that sufficient time must be given the adversary to become acquainted with the new proofs and defend himself; otherwise the trial is of no moment (c. 1861,§2). Hence with stronger reason, there appears to be an absolute necessity of publishing the earlier proofs as well, at least in ordinary trials.[7] And in fact, the knowing an adversary's proofs is so closely bound up with the preparation of a valid pleading that this is hardly possible without the proofs being made known.[8] In any event the omission of publishing the proofs certainly affords sufficient ground for reinstatement of the trial (c. 1905,§2, n. 4).

573. In cases of dispensation from non-consummated marriage however, the delegated judge does not proceed to the publication of the acts, but encloses the entire portfolio of acts with the animadversions of the defender and of the ordinary, in a sealed package, and sends them all to the Cardinal Prefect of the Congregation of the Sacraments (c. 1985).[9] Nevertheless all the acts are to be disclosed to the defender,[10] and if one or both of the parties ask to see the names of the witnesses, or their responses, or some document, and the petition is based on a grave reason, the judge may allow it in as far as it is shown to be helpful, but must preclude all danger of collusion and corruption of witnesses (cfr. n. **217**). Such publication of the acts or of part of them must be mentioned in the acts, and the defender together with the other party concerned, if there be occasion for it, must be heard beforehand on the matter.[11] Similar discipline should be observed when a trial judge is hearing a case whose decision is reserved to the Holy Office, *e. g.*, the dissolution of the merely legitimate marriage bond in favor of the Faith (cfr. c. 247,§3) (cfr. n. **156**).

[7] Roberti, ii, nn. 350, 435, 493; W-Vidal, vi, n. 476 is not so clear.

[8] It is significant that c. 1861, § 2 has added the words "probationes cognoscere" to the otherwise merely repeated text of Lex R., SA., can. 27, § 3: "debet congruum tempus alteri parti concedere ut super iisdem (probationes) respondere possit. Aliter nullum erit judicium." cfr. also R., Bonaeren., Remotionis, 5 apr. 1916 (rd., viii, p. 93; aas., ix, p. 92); Null., 8 jul. 1919 (rd., xi, pp. 120, 121).

[9] DS, Reg., n. 97, § 1; n. 98, § 2.

[10] DS, Reg., n. 98, § 1; cfr. cc. 1587,§2; 1969, nn. 1, 2.

[11] DS, Reg., n. 97, § 2.

§ 2. Procedure in Publishing

574. The acts may be published by reading aloud the proofs as they are contained in the record,[12] but this is not necessary. For there is sufficient publication if the judge grant the parties and their advocates permission to inspect the acts and obtain exemplars (c. 1859), and notify them to this effect. If original documents are to be examined, it must be under supervision of the notary, or archivist, to provide against mishap to the documents. Copies of the originals, printed, typewritten, or handwritten may be published and distributed (c. 1859), if the parties are prepared to bear the expense.

575. It seems to be sufficient if the acts are published to the advocates (c. 1859), or proctors of the parties. The Congregation of Bishops and Regulars did not allow proctors to undertake the inspection of the acts in place of the parties, except where the parties were physically unable to assist, because the proctors were not supposed to know the witnesses, and could not be pertinently and sufficiently instructed in advance.[13] And in fact, Canon 1859 omits mention of proctors. But Canon 1623,§3 presupposes that the proofs have all been made known to the proctors, and Haring invokes the principle that one can do by proxy what one can do oneself.[14]

576. Although the Code does not mention it, the testimonies and other proofs which have been brought forth by the promoter or defender are also published.[15] And publication includes the names of the witnesses as well as their testimonies.[16] The Regulations of the Rota allowed the withholding of names and provided otherwise for security against fraud in cases where the witness would testify only under condition that his name be withheld from the respondent.[17] These directions are not in conformity with the Code, and have no value now. But because the defender is in nullity cases a co-respondent and *ex officio* proctor (cfr. n. **41**), it seems to me that the name of a witness whom the plaintiff has produced, may, in an urgent case, be withheld from the respondent.

[12] IA., § 230; Bassibey, n. 479.

[13] S. C. EE. RR., 26 mart. 1823 (bass., n. 479).

[14] Haring, Eheprozess, p. 29 (1).

[15] Haring, Eheprozess, p. 18.

[16] c. 24, X, De Accusationibus etc., V, 1.

[17] R, Reg., § 116, n. 3.

577. The notary must remark in the minutes upon the acts having been published,[18] but no written decree of the judge is necessary.[19]

§ 3. Purpose and Effects of Publication

578. The publication of the acts has as its purpose and effect that each party is made aware of the complete state of the case and may compare the adversary's proofs with his own, so as to refute them, if necessary by calling new witnesses.

New witnesses may be heard or the same witnesses heard anew in marriage cases, after the publication of the proceedings (c. 1983) (cfr. nn. **252, 264**), but in these cases the new testimonies must likewise be published (c. 1861,§2).

Thus the publication of acts provides opportunity of defence, and enables both parties to draw up comprehensive and effective pleadings.

579. After the publication of testimonies, the right to take exception against the person of a witness ceases, except in the case provided in Canon 1764,§4, although the testimonies or the manner of questioning may still be contested (c. 1783) (cfr. nn. **217, 218**).

II. CONCLUSION OF TRIAL

580. When all has been done that pertains to the proofs, *i. e.* when all proofs have been duly brought forth, filed or recorded, and published, the trial comes to the formal conclusion or closing of the evidence (conclusio in causa: c. 1860,§1). Similarly to this provision of the Code, late pre-Code decrees on marriage cases had required the conclusion in trial just when the proofs were published,[20] but the Law and Regulations of the Rota and Signatura, following ancient canonists,[21] had postponed it until after the pleadings and rebuttals.[22] The Code now corrects this and directs the conclusion after the proofs have been published.

18 DS, Reg., n. 97, § 2.

19 PF, 1883, § 22 contrary.

20 SCC, 1840, § Quatenus; PF, 1883, § 22.

21 W-Vidal, vi, p. 528 (5).

22 Lex R., SA., can. 27, § 1; R, Reg., § 51; SA, Reg., art. 49.

§ 4. Procedure in Concluding

581. The conclusion may be brought about in any of three ways: 1) By the parties' declaring they have nothing further to adduce, after having been asked about this by the judge. In nullity and non-consummation cases the defender must likewise be asked (c. 1984,§2).[23]

2) By the elapse of the term provided and decreed for producing proof. In cases of separation the law makes no provision for the extension of the time, if the term elapse without the proofs having been brought forth. In nullity cases the law presumes that the defender has nothing further to adduce if he produce no further proof by the appointed time (c. 1984,§2).[24] But the presumption is rebuttable, and if the defender or a party reasonably request an extension of time, the judge will grant it (c. 1969, n. 1).

3) By the declaration of the judge that he is sufficiently provided with proof (c. 1860,§2). In cases requiring a tribunal of three, it may be sometimes advisable to consult the entire tribunal,[25] but the trial judge or auditor may declare the case concluded on his own responsibility. But if the defender make demand for further proofs, the sources of which he suggests, only the unanimous vote of the tribunal can override this demand (c. 1969, n. 4).

582. The judge must carefully consider the acts, compare the testimonies of the parties and witnesses, and see whether some points are incomplete, contradictory or ambiguous. If such be found, he shall summon the parties and witnesses anew, if it be helpful, and propose questions to them that may supply or clarify the matter, or even call new witnesses *ex officio* to the same purpose. In all this the defender's opinion must be heard (c. 1969, n. 3).[26] The defender must likewise examine the acts and consider whether anything further is to be adduced.[27] This last means of effecting a conclusion is not validly employed when it precludes opportunity for the defender to be heard last of all (c. 1984,§2).

The judge must be careful lest he be too easily satisfied with the proofs at hand. In a case at X. the trial judge ordered the conclusion of trial without hearing the respondent, because the latter had con-

[23] DS, Reg., n. 96, § 1.

[24] cfr. R., Vilnen., Null., 30 jan. 1930 (aas., xxii, p. 191).

[25] Roberti, ii, n. 437.

[26] DS, Reg., n. 96, § 2.

[27] DS, Reg., n. 96, § 3.

temned repeated summonses. When the proofs of non-consummation were sent to the Congregation, the case was delayed and the judge directed to make renewed efforts to question the respondent.[28]

583. Under the Decretals, the conclusion of trial was rather the act of the parties renouncing further proof and resting their case.[29] Hence it was not usually announced by judicial decree,[30] and was not necessary in summary cases.[31] Under the Code, it is the act of either the parties or the judge, but in both cases it is made known by the decree of the judge (c. 1860,§3).[32] In the same decree the judge may state a term for preparing the pleadings (c. 1862,§1).

§ 5. Effects of Conclusion

584. The effects of the conclusion of trial are: 1) The time for adducing proofs is brought to an end. Further questioning of the parties (c. 1742,§3) and new proofs are thereafter precluded in civil contentious cases, unless there be documents just now discovered, or witnesses who were legitimately impeded from appearing during the proper time (c. 1861,§1) (cfr. nn. **252**, **362**). Cases that affect the marriage bond are not thus restricted, and new inquiries may be undertaken at any time before the definite sentence is rendered; and,

28 Haring, Eheprozess, p. 29, however seems to err in stating that in these cases of non-consummation "findet . . . auch keine conclusio in causa statt."

29 Schmalzgrueber, Pars IV, tit. xxvii, n. 1.

30 Noval, n. 607.

31 c. 2, De Verborum Significatione, V, 11 in Clem.

32 DS, Reg., Appendix XXXIII: gives formula: "In the case between N. and N. on their marriage claimed to be non-consummated:

"The parties having been asked and having answered they have nothing further to adduce, and the defender having declared he has nothing further to inquire;

"All the acts, depositions of parties, witnesses and experts, reports and annexed documents having been considered;

"Now the trial is sufficiently drawn up, in view of the circumstances of persons and things, and the judge declares the proceedings closed and directs all the acts to be sent in authentic exemplar to the S. Congregation of the Sacraments, together with the written behest of the Most Rev. Bishop and of the defender of the bond.

"Given at ...., this .... day of .... A. D. ......

N. Judge,
N. Notary."

as is well known, they do not become unassailably adjudged (res iudicata) and may be reheard in higher instance at any time (cc. 1903; 1989).[33]

Even in cases that do not become unassailably adjudged however, some term must be placed upon the desires of parties to indefinitely protract the case by constant new hearings after the trial is concluded. Hence the Code prescribes that even in marriage cases, new hearings of witnesses are held only for a grave reason and cautiously and after having seen to it that all occasion of fraud and subornation shall have been obviated (c. 1786). Thus the judge is free to refuse such further hearings after the conclusion of trial, if he think that the true merits of the case would be rather impeded than aided (cfr. nn. **252, 264**); and in fact, the Rota has repeatedly refused to rehear cases when no new and grave arguments (proofs) or documents were forthcoming (c. 1903; cfr. however: cc. 1969, n. 4; 1987).[34] Even when further hearings are held the new testimony does not escape all suspicion (cfr. n. **264**).

585. The peremptory proofs afforded by confession of a party, and by decisive oath are admitted even after the conclusion (c. 1834, §1),[35] in civil contentious cases and in cases of separation from bed and board. In cases touching the marriage bond, the proper oath and confession may be likewise admitted after the conclusion of trial, but their proof value is limited (cfr. nn. **550-570**, cfr. also n. **167**).

586. If the judge so decide, he decrees the admission of new proofs, but must hear the defender and the other party, to whom he will concede sufficient time to become acquainted with the new proofs and defend himself; otherwise the trial is of no moment (c. 1861,§2).

587. 2) Similarly, any regress, on the part of the plaintiff, from petitory trial to one for acquiring or regaining possession, should take place before the conclusion of the trial, but the judge may allow

[33] Dei Mis., § 11; PF, 1883, § 26; cfr. *e. g.* R., Null., 16 mai. 1912 (rd., iv, p. 271); Wratislavien., seu Varsavien., Null., 7 dec. 1912 (rd., iv, p. 445 fol.); Massilien., Null., 30 apr. 1917 (rd., ix, p 109; aas., ix, p. 579).

[34] R., Treviren., Null., 19 mai. 1924 (aas., xvii, p. 84); Parisien., Null., 23 jun. 1926 (aas., xix, p. 74); Wratislavien., Reiectionis Libelli, 29 oct 1928 (aas., xxi, p. 92); Moguntina, Null., 11 feb. 1930 (aas., xxiii, p. 105); Parisien., Null., (sine dato), (aas., xxiv, p. 97); Antioquien et Iericoen., Null., 7 dec. 1931 (aas., xxiv, p. 100).

[35] Roberti, ii, nn. 329, 393, 438.

it afterward, but before the definite decision, for a good reason (c. 1671,§§1, 2).

3) The period of discussion and pleading is opened.

III. DISCUSSION OF THE EVIDENCE

588. Following the conclusion in trial, there ensues the discussion of the evidence, in which the parties or their advocates present their views on the law and the facts, so as to clearly inform the judges. This discussion has the nature of a pleading, brief, or defense, and is carried on between the court and the parties and defender: it has nothing to do with that later discussion which the judges engage in alone, even to the exclusion of the defender and notary (cfr. c. 1871).[36]

§ 6. Necessity of Discussion

589. It is necessary that the parties be given an opportunity to plead and defend their case; this necessity derives as well from the natural as from the positive law, and is so fundamental in canonical procedure, that, although the lack of opportunity for proper plea and defense is not expressly mentioned by Canons 1892, 1894, as one of the irritating deficiencies of a trial, the trial is nevertheless invalidated if no such opportunity be given.[37] But there is a difference between depriving one of all opportunity for plea and defence, and omitting opportunity to carry on that final discussion spoken of in Canons 1862-1867; for the essential right of plea and defense may be secured without a precise pleading at the conclusion of the trial in the accustomed forensic manner. Hence the omission of this does not invalidate procedure.[38] But in nullity and separation cases, and in cases of presumable death of a spouse, the parties or the supposed survivor should be admonished of their right to present a formal pleading and discussion of the case.[39] In cases provided for in Canon 1990, whatever pleadings are advantageous will be made when the parties are summoned. In non-consummation cases and cases of Pauline privilege there are no formal pleadings except that of the defender.[40]

[36] R, Norm., art. 137; Vinco Močnik in Iqs., lxxxv (1932), p. 362 fol.

[37] R., Biturgen., Locationis, 27 apr. 1917 (aas., ix, p. 543; rd., ix, p. 89); cfr. c. 1861, § 2.

[38] R., Null., 8 jul. 1919 (rd., xi, pp. 120, 121); Bassibey, p. 391 (3).

[39] PF, 1883, § 23.

[40] cfr. DS, Reg., nn. 97, 98; cpre. cc. 1555, § 1 with 1962.

590. In civil contentious cases the parties may renounce their right of pleading, either tacitly or expressly: tacitly if they neglect, during the useful term, to prepare a defence; expressly, if they declare they are prepared to abide by the findings and conscience of the judge (c. 1867). And the same may be done, it seems, in marriage cases, as far as the parties to the marriage are concerned. But in cases of nullity and non-consummation it is the duty of the defender to write and tender his pleading (animadversiones) against nullity or non-consummation and in proof of validity or consummation, and to do everything that shall seem to him useful in defence of the marriage (c. 1968, n. 3).

591. Both adversaries have equal rights in pleading, but it is the privilege of the defender to be last heard (c. 1984,§1).

592. If the parties neglect to prepare their defence within the appointed time, or if they leave the matter to the insight and conscience of the court, the definite sentence may be at once pronounced, according to the norms of Canons 1871-1877, provided the issue is clear from the evidence (c. 1867).

§ 7. Procedure in Discussion

593. The Code admits a twofold pleading: the principal and usual pleading is drawn up in writing (c. 1863,§1);[41] the secondary and exceptional pleading is oral.[42] In a written pleading words are chosen more carefully, texts more exactly, and arguments more concisely.

The pleadings before diocesan courts are generally written in the vernacular language,[43] but the use of Latin is advisable and causes less expense and difficulty if the documents are later brought to Rome.[44] However the Roman Curia is, of late, better prepared than formerly to consider documents written in English.[45]

[41] The Supreme Court of the U. S. and other higher courts of states adhere to similar practice.

[42] Roberti, ii, n. 439.

[43] Bassibey, n. 512.

[44] cfr. R, Norm., art. 123.

[45] cfr. Pii X, Ordo Servandus, 29 sept. 1908, Norm. peculiar., VI, 5 (aas., i, p. 73); Lex R., SA., can. 18, § 5.

594. The pleading may be written either by the party himself or by his advocate (c. 1862,§1), and the parties should be admonished of this fact.[46] But the Rotal law forbids that a party and his advocate each tender a separate pleading.[47] Nevertheless the party who upholds the marriage, or his advocate, may present his own pleading even when the defender presents the pleading or discussion that is required of him. But such double pleading occurs only rarely.

595. The chief qualities of a good pleading are brevity, clearness and correct canonical reasoning. The pleadings presented to the Rota must not exceed twenty printed pages, though the ponent may allow more for cases where the great mass of documents or other difficulties require it.[48] In diocesan courts where no statute controls the matter, it is for the judge, or in tribunals of three, the president, to prudently moderate the defence that gives promise of undue extension (c. 1864). But Roberti wisely remarks that it is far better if the advocates and defender are expert in the matter and then they will not be inclined to undue extension of the discussion.[49]

In clearness and canonical correctness the motivated decisions of the Rota give a pattern, by which advocates in diocesan courts may, with due allowances, shape their defence of a case. To write a good pleading it is necessary to carefully consider every word of the testimony and other evidence, not only for the value it may have of itself, but also for the importance that may derive by comparing it with the evidence as a whole and with the pleading that is made by the adversary. It seems almost needless to add that a thorough knowledge of the substantive law on marriage and of the law of evidence is presupposed.

596. The pleading is headed with the name of the diocese and the nature of the case and the names of the parties, thus: At X ...... on the Nullity of Marriage, Smith versus Jones: Plaintiff's Pleading.[50]

Then there are four parts: 1) The introduction is addressed: Reverend Judges. Then the history of the case is rehearsed: the names,

[46] PF, 1883, § 23.

[47] Lex R., SA., can. 18, § 6; R, Norm., art. 123.

[48] Lex R., SA., can. 29, §§ 1, 2; R, Reg., § 58, n. 1; R, Norm., art. 124, § 1.

[49] Roberti, ii, n. 440.

[50] Following heading in case before Rota: "Buffalensis, Nullitatis Matrimonii, pro Dna Margarita M., actrice, adversus Dnum Franciscum D. reum conventum.—Restrictus facti et iuris cum summario."

ages, and domiciles of the parties concerned, as well as the story of their courtship, marriage, disagreements, separation, *etc.* are recounted. The pleading then recalls the time and occasion whereat the party determined to bring suit, and mentions the cause, *v. g.* impediment, on which the suit is based.

2) The law on the matter (quoad ius, in iure, ius quod attinet). Here the pertinent Canons of the Code and other sources of present day Canon law and also decisions of the higher tribunals in like cases and the doctrine of approved authors are quoted.

3) The facts in the case (quoad factum, in facto, factum quod attinet). It is shown that the facts as proved by testimony, documents, reports of experts and other proofs correspond to the law requiring a favorable decision.

4) The conclusion draws attention to the fitness of a decision in favor of the party pleading, and in conformity with the issue as joined or subsequently corrected. The pleading is then signed by the party or advocate and is dated.[51]

597. After the conclusion of the trial the judge will appoint a proper term in which the parties and defender will draw up their pleadings and discussion (c. 1862,§1).[52] The term is measured according to the prudent behest of the judge, with due reference to the mass of proofs at hand and the intricacy of the case. The term can be prolonged at the motion of a party or the defender, after hearing the other party; or it can be shortened if both sides agree (c. 1862,§2).

598. The pleadings are drawn up in multiple copy, sufficient to provide each judge of the tribunal, the defender and promoter, if they participate, and the other party with a copy (c. 1863,§§1, 2). In the Rota the pleadings of the defender are also distributed to the parties or their proctors or advocates, and this should be done in diocesan courts.

599. To the pleading there may be added the summary (summarium) of documents. This consists in a portfolio containing copies of the plaint, articles or positions, testimonies of the parties or witnesses, documents, reports of experts, *etc.* As nothing can be gained by duplication of this summary it is generally provided only by the plaintiff, or at most, the respondent adds only a supplement. If the

[51] Lex R., SA., can. 18, § 4 requiring the party or procurator and the defender to sign all pleadings is obsolete.

[52] DS, Reg., n. 98, § 1.

president of the court deem it necessary and not too great a burden to the parties, he may order that the pleadings be printed together with such a summary of acts and documents bound in brochure (c. 1863,§3). Pleadings brought before the Rota must be printed with the summary, and must be committed only to approved printers.[53]

If the judge decree that the pleadings be printed he will at the same time admonish the parties not to have anything printed that is not first presented in manuscript and approved for printing (c. 1863, §4). In a recent contentious suit before the Rota, the plaintiff added to his defence a note not approved by the judge and distributed the printed copies to the persons concerned in the trial. The ponent decreed that no consideration should be given these pleadings because they were printed and distributed without the *Imprimatur* of the court.[54]

In diocesan courts however the pleadings are not usually printed,[55] and typewritten or manuscript pleadings are preferable in order to provide more securely for the required secrecy of the case (cfr. c. 1863,§3). Nor is it customary in diocesan courts to attach the summary or brochure of documents: the court has the originals in its possession.

600. The parties and defender having received copies of one another's pleadings may answer them within a short term appointed by the judge, by written rebuttals regulated like the pleadings (c. 1865,§1). Rebuttals are generally allowed but once, unless the judge decide for grave cause, to permit them again; but the double rebuttal permitted to one party or the defender is thereby permitted also to the other (c. 1865,§2). In the Rota the rebuttals are limited to half the length of the pleadings and must be made within twenty days.[56]

601. The secondary and exceptional pleading or discussion is oral. At the time when the orally conducted trials, inherited from the old Roman and German law, were discontinued, and the trial in which written acts predominated was instituted by Innocent III (an. 1215),[57] there continued the custom of conducting some part of the

[53] Lex R., SA., can. 26, §§ 1, 2; 29, § 4.

[54] R., Refectionis Damnorum, 5 aug. 1913 (rd., v, pp. 522, 523); cfr. SA, Reg., art. 41; 52.

[55] cfr. Bassibey, n. 510; Roberti, ii, p. 163 (4).

[56] Lex R., SA., can. 27, § 1; 29, § 1; R, Norm., art. 124, § 1.

[57] cfr. c. 11, X, De Probationibus, II, 19.

discussion by spoken word. Advocates were permitted to confer with the individual judges at their homes, with a view to enlightenting them on points of law and fact, and these private conversations were customary at Rome until Pope Pius X reëstablished the Rota.[58] Such private oral information (informationes orales) was then prohibited,[59] and the Code has renewed the prohibition (c. 1866,§1). It is easily understood that the reform was well grounded.[60]

602. In place of such private conversations a moderate discussion in court is now admitted (c. 1866,§2).[61] This oral discussion must be short and devoid of oratorical form;[62] it is intended to be a supplement to, not a substitute for the written pleadings, and is generally allowed in the Rota, only after the written pleadings and rebuttals have been distributed.[63] In diocesan courts the judge may permit the oral discussion when the case is sufficiently prepared by proofs,[64] even though no written pleadings have been tendered.

Likewise during the course of trial, the judge may admit, or even call for an oral discussion on such incidental matters as the precise concordance of issues, the appointment of judicial terms and delays, the choice of experts, *etc.*[65]

603. The Code does not expressly provide that the judge institute oral discussion of this kind *ex officio,* for he is always free to question the parties, and such questioning is not limited by the rules laid down for the oral discussion (cc. 1742,§2; 1861). The latter is instituted at the motion of one or both of the parties (c. 1866,§2), or their proctors or advocates, or of the defender.

604. A party petitions the oral discussion by a written bill containing, in a few words, the list of points to be discussed (c. 1866, §3).[66] The president will discern whether the discussion can be use-

[58] Lega, Praefatio, p. xx.

[59] Lex R., SA., can. 30; R, Reg., § 67, n. 1; SA, Reg., art. 53.

[60] cfr. Roberti, ii, n. 441.

[61] That the public oral discussion was not entirely new however, cfr. Bassibey, n. 511.

[62] Lex R., SA., can. 30, n. 4; R, Reg., § 67, n. 2.

[63] R, Reg., §§ 69; 71, nn. 3, 4.

[64] R, Reg., § 71, n. 4.

[65] R, Reg., § 94.

[66] R, Reg., § 74, n. 1 gives formula (trans.): "NN. party in the case moves that oral discussion be conceded, and a day appointed for it."

ful in the trial, and decide whether the petition is to be granted (c. 1866,§2). Not even in the privileged marriage case however, can there be any claim of the invalidity of the procedure because of the refusal to admit an oral discussion.[67]

605. If the judge decide to allow the oral discussion he will acquaint the other party and the defender with the points at issue, set a day and hour for the discussion, and be the moderator of the discussion when it takes place (c. 1866,§3).[68]

606. The oral discussion may take place before the entire court, or before the president or a judge delegated by him to hear it in the name of the court (c. 1866,§2). To provide against the discussion's becoming a personal and private conversation (cfr. n. 601), it is required that a notary be present. He will write in the record such discussed, confessed, or concluded matters as the judge orders, or consents to have written at the motion of one of the parties (c. 1866,§4); but no written record need be made of the oral discussion. In no case shall the oral discussion be written or printed for distribution.[69]

607. Although in most contentious cases the oral discussion is carried on by advocates,[70] the parties in marriage cases may themselves engage in oral discussion even though proctors and advocates have been appointed for the suit.[71] The judge may also call the experts who have examined a party and ask them to more clearly explain their views;[72] but witnesses and others who are not parties are not allowed to have an active part in the oral discussion.[73]

[67] R., Remotionis, 11 maii. 1909 (rd., i, p. 41): "Ast non requiri *ad validitatem,* oralem discussionem in processu *oeconomico* sequitur ex cit. Clem. *Dispendiosam,*—quae ordinat ut—procedi valeat *de cetero simpliciter et de plano, ac sine strepitu iudicii ac figura.*—Quodsi in Instr. S. Congr. EE. et RR. a. 1880, *ad art. 34* inter alias praescriptiones fit locus etiam discussioni orali, hoc statuitur non *praecceptive* et ad validitatem processus, sed tantum *directive* . . ."

[68] R, Reg., §74, n. 1: gives following formula (trans.): "Oral discussion is conceded this .... day .... and is appointed for .... day of .... A. D. .... Let the parties be notified."

[69] R, Reg., §71, n. 1.

[70] Lex R., SA., can. 30, n. 1; R, Reg., §73, n. 1; SA, Reg., art. 24.

[71] R, Reg., §73, n. 3.

[72] R, Reg., §73, n. 2.

[73] R, Reg., §73, n. 4.

608. If the discussion cannot be satisfactorily completed in one session, it may be adjourned to another.[74] If, by way of exception, it appear from the oral discussion that there are points in the case not as yet clear and matured, the judge may order that additional written pleadings be presented.[75] Regularly however, the oral discussion should be the last proceeding before the court adjourns to consider and issue its decision.[76]

609. *Scholion:* In cases of dispensation from non-consummated marriage or dissolution of the merely legitimate marriage bond in favor of the Faith, the ordinary does not pronounce sentence, but sends the acts to the Holy See together with information of his own. Thus if the petitioner for dispensation from non-consummated marriage is a non-Catholic the ordinary must state, through himself or through the trial judge, what special circumstances of fact or personality argue that the non-Catholic be heard.[77]

In cases of dissolution of marriage to favor the Faith, the ordinary is instructed to add information 1) Whether the petitioner has begotten progeny from the marriage or concubinage, and how he has provided for or intends to provide for its religious bringing up;

2) Whether and why there is hope or not, of restoring conjugal life, and whether the non-Catholic party has attempted a new marriage after divorce;

3) Whether there is danger of resultant scandal or amazement or calumnious interpretation among Catholics or non-Catholics (that, *v. g.*, the Church by her practice is favoring the impious usage of divorce), and what are the circumstances that exclude such danger or make it likely;

4) Whether the petitioner has attempted a new marriage or lives in concubinage, and what causes urge the granting of the favor.

[74] R, Reg., § 71, n. 1.

[75] R, Reg., § 71, n. 3 gives formula (trans.): "Let the litigants or their advocates or proctors write further on the controverted point."

[76] Roberti, ii, n. 441.

[77] DS, Reg., nn. 7; 9,§2; cfr. SO., 27 jan. 1928, n. 1 (aas., xx, p. 75).

INDEX OF SUBJECT MATTER

(Marginal numbers are given)

INDEX OF CANONS

www.ingramcontent.com/pod-product-compliance
Lightning Source LLC
LaVergne TN
LVHW050300080826

844660LV00012B/664

9780813222004